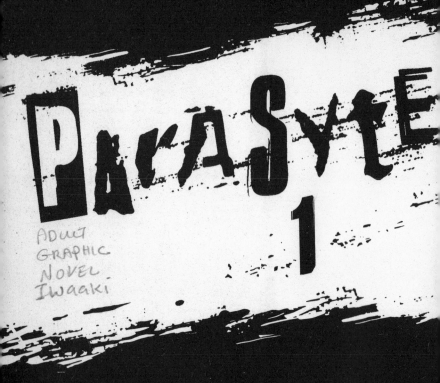

PARASYTE

1

ADULT
GRAPHIC
NOVEL
Iwaaki

HITOSHI IWAAKI

TRANSLATED AND ADAPTED BY ANDREW CUNNINGHAM
LETTERED BY FOLTZ DESIGN

DEL
REY

BALLANTINE BOOKS · NEW YORK

Parasyte volume 1 is a work of fiction. Names, characters, places, and incidents are the products of the author's imagination or are used fictitiously. Any resemblance to actual events, locales, or persons, living or dead, is entirely coincidental.

A Del Rey Trade Paperback Original

Published in the United States by Del Rey Books, an imprint of The Random House Publishing Group, a division of Random House, Inc., New York.

Del Rey is a registered trademark and the Del Rey colophon is a trademark of Random House, Inc.

Publication rights arranged through Kodansha Ltd.

First published in Japan in 1990 by Kodansha Ltd., Tokyo.

ISBN 978-0-345-49624-9

Printed in the United States of America

www.delreymanga.com

9 8 7 6 5 4 3 2 1

Translatorl/adapter: Andrew Cunningham
Lettering: Foltz Design

CONTENTS

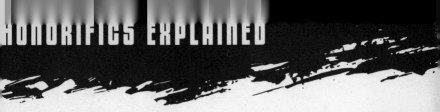

HONORIFICS EXPLAINED

Throughout the Del Rey Manga books, you will find Japanese honorifics left intact in the translations. For those not familiar with how the Japanese use honorifics and, more important, how they differ from American honorifics, we present this brief overview.

Politeness has always been a critical facet of Japanese culture. Ever since the feudal era, when Japan was a highly stratified society, use of honorifics—which can be defined as polite speech that indicates relationship or status—has played an essential role in the Japanese language. When addressing someone in Japanese, an honorific usually takes the form of a suffix attached to one's name (example: "Asuna-san"), is used as a title at the end of one's name, or appears in place of the name itself (example: "Negi-sensei" or simply "Sensei!").

Honorifics can be expressions of respect or endearment. In the context of manga and anime, honorifics give insight into the nature of the relationship between characters. Many English translations leave out these important honorifics and therefore distort the feel of the original Japanese. Because Japanese honorifics contain nuances that English honorifics lack, it is our policy at Del Rey not to translate them. Here, instead, is a guide to some of the honorifics you may encounter in Del Rey Manga.

-san: This is the most common honorific and is equivalent to Mr., Miss, Ms., or Mrs. It is the all-purpose honorific and can be used in any situation where politeness is required.

-sama: This is one level higher than "-san" and is used to confer great respect.

-dono: This comes from the word "tono," which means "lord." It is even a higher level than "-sama" and confers utmost respect.

-kun: This suffix is used at the end of boys' names to express familiarity or endearment. It is also sometimes used by men among friends, or when addressing someone younger or of a lower station.

-chan: This is used to express endearment, mostly toward girls. It is also used for little boys, pets, and even among lovers. It gives a sense of childish cuteness.

Bozu: This is an informal way to refer to a boy, similar to the English terms "kid" and "squirt."

Sempai/
Senpai: This title suggests that the addressee is one's senior in a group or organization. It is most often used in a school setting, where underclassmen refer to their upperclassmen as "sempai." It can also be used in the workplace, such as when a newer employee addresses an employee who has seniority in the company.

Kohai: This is the opposite of "sempai," and is used toward underclassmen in school or newcomers in the workplace. It connotes that the addressee is of a lower station.

Sensei: Literally meaning "one who has come before," this title is used for teachers, doctors, or masters of any profession or art.

-[blank]: This is usually forgotten in these lists, but it is perhaps the most significant difference between Japanese and English. The lack of honorific means that the speaker has permission to address the person in a very intimate way. Usually, only family, spouses, or very close friends have this kind of permission. Known as *yobisute*, it can be gratifying when someone who has earned the intimacy starts to call one by one's name without an honorific. But when that intimacy hasn't been earned, it can be very insulting.

PARASYTE 1

HITOSHI IWAAKI

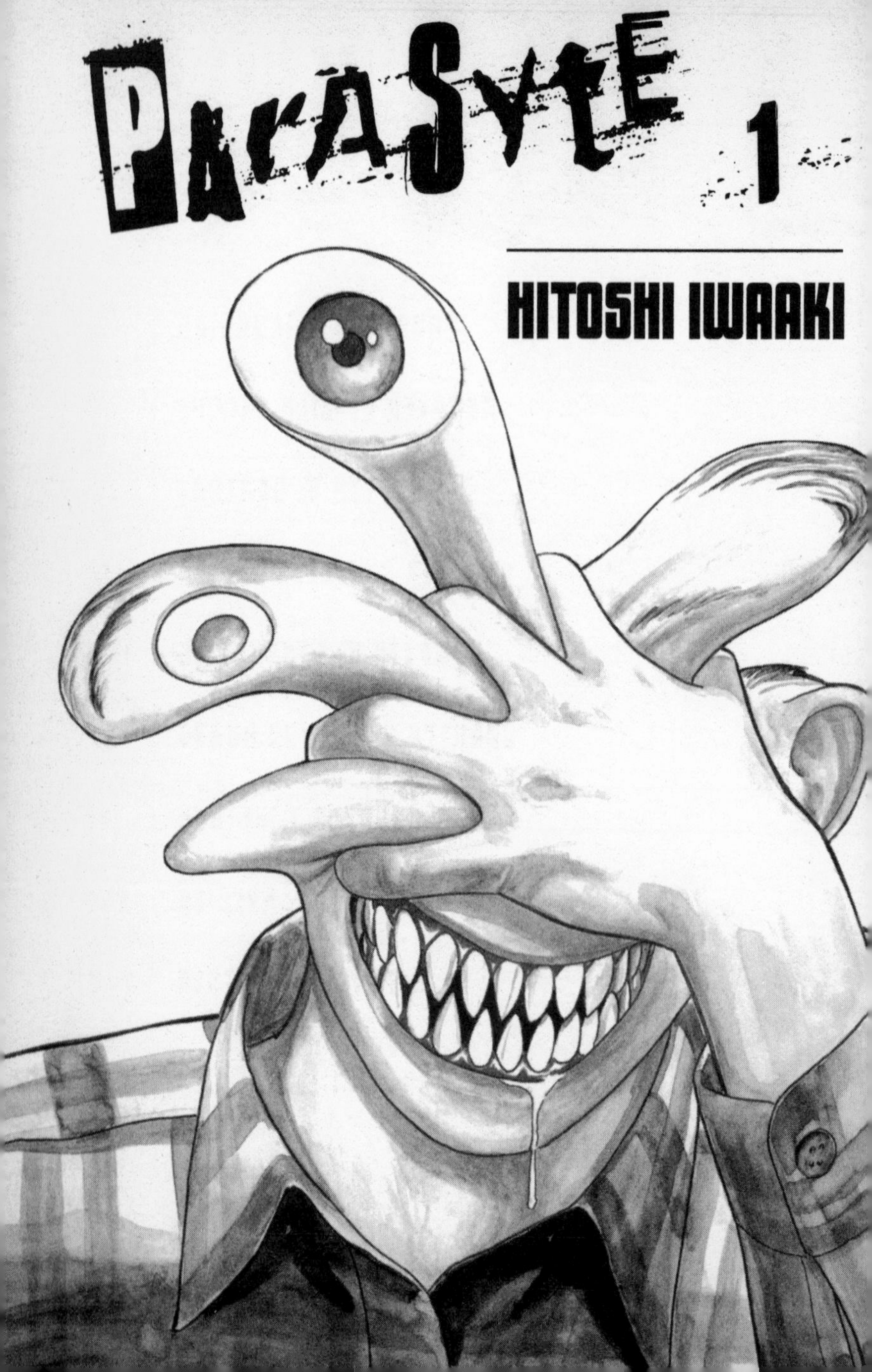

CONTENTS

CHAPTER 1: INVASION

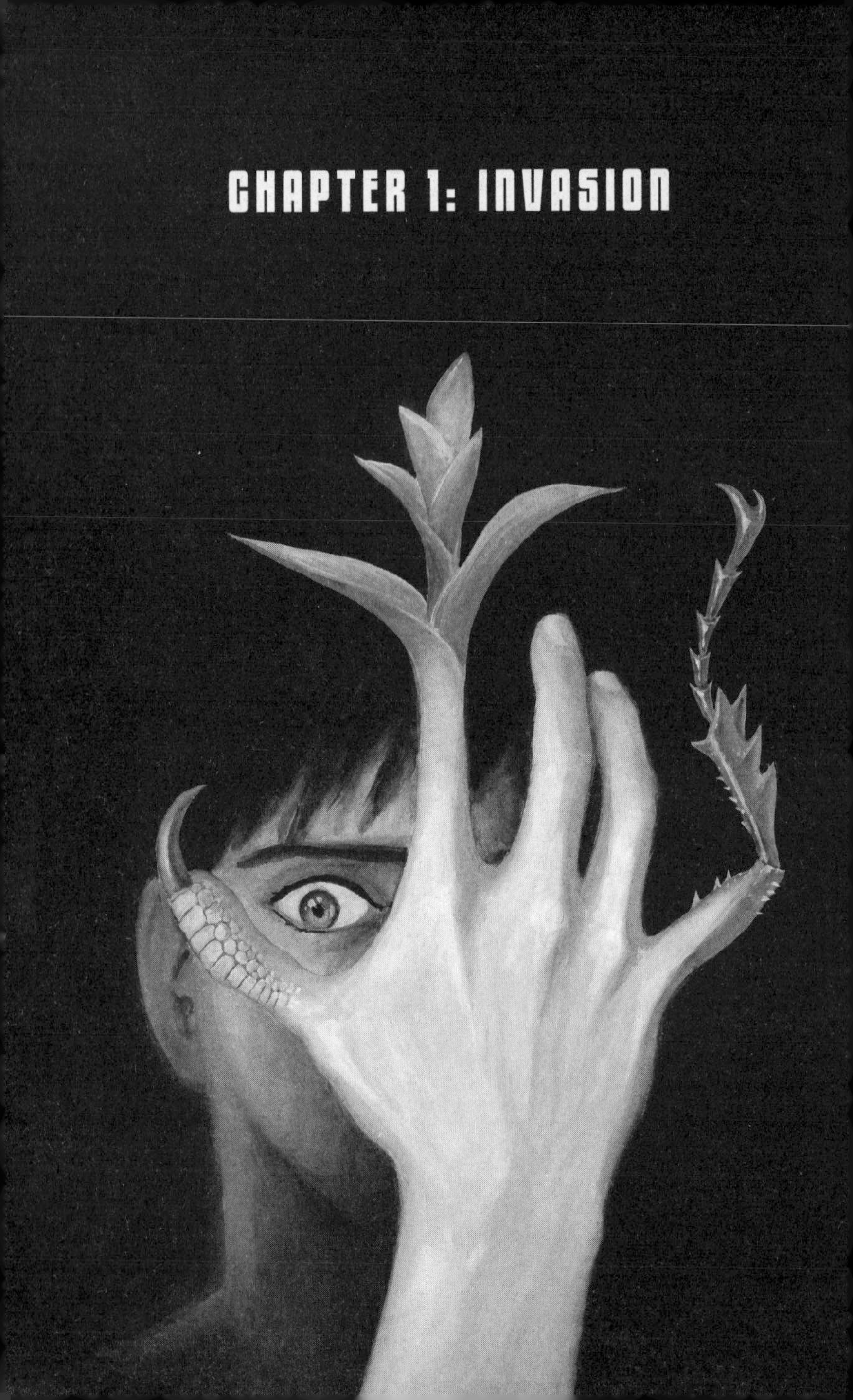

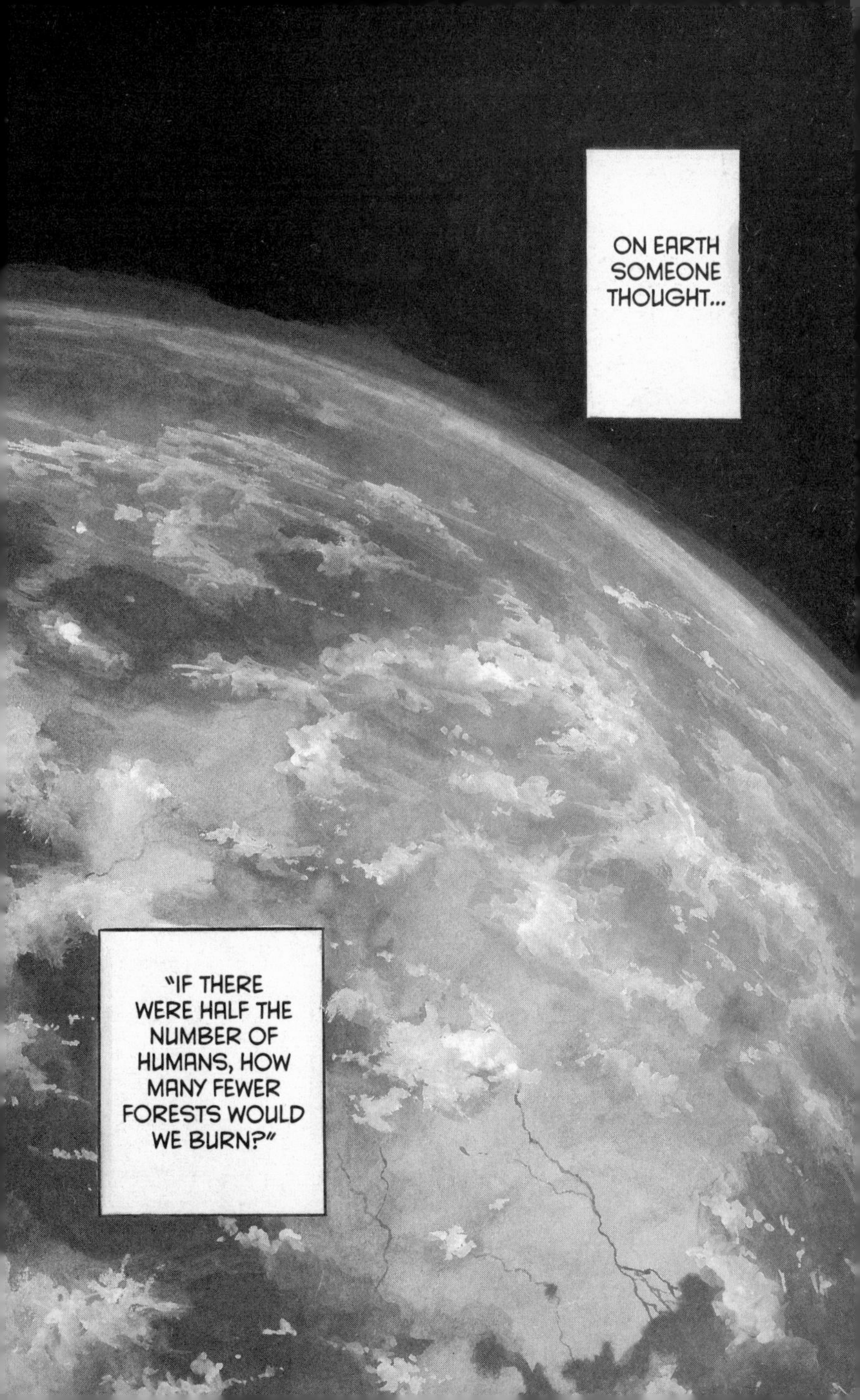
ON EARTH SOMEONE THOUGHT...
"IF THERE WERE HALF THE NUMBER OF HUMANS, HOW MANY FEWER FORESTS WOULD WE BURN?"

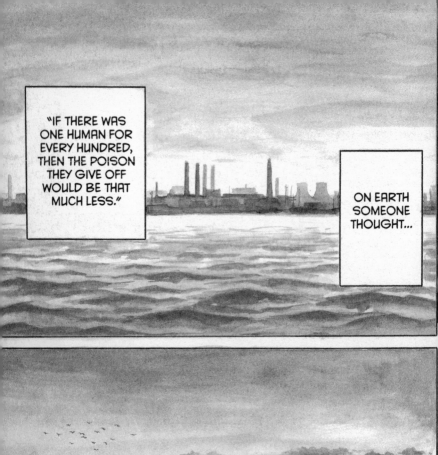

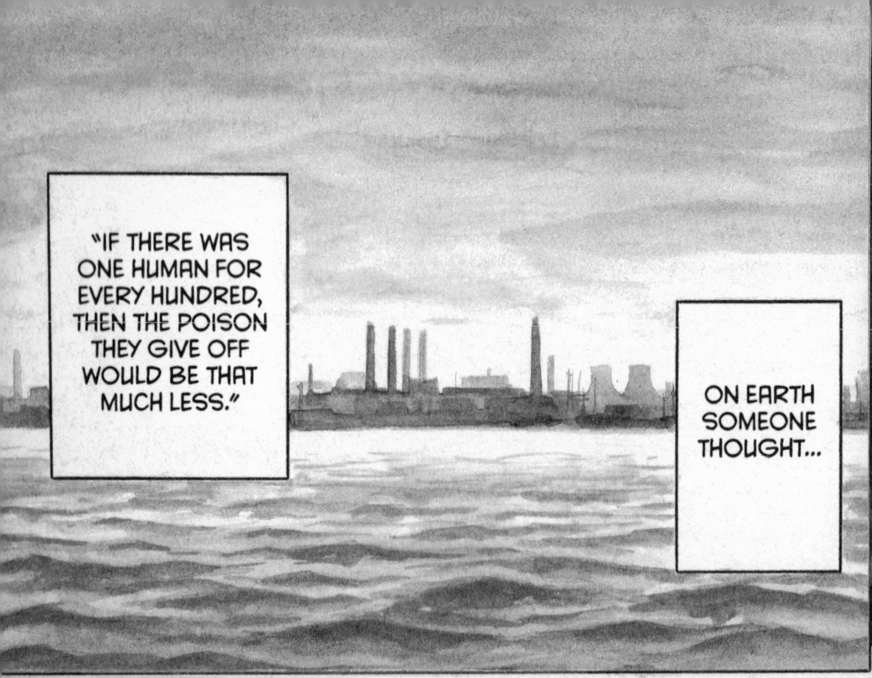
ON EARTH SOMEONE THOUGHT...
"IF THERE WAS ONE HUMAN FOR EVERY HUNDRED, THEN THE POISON THEY GIVE OFF WOULD BE THAT MUCH LESS."

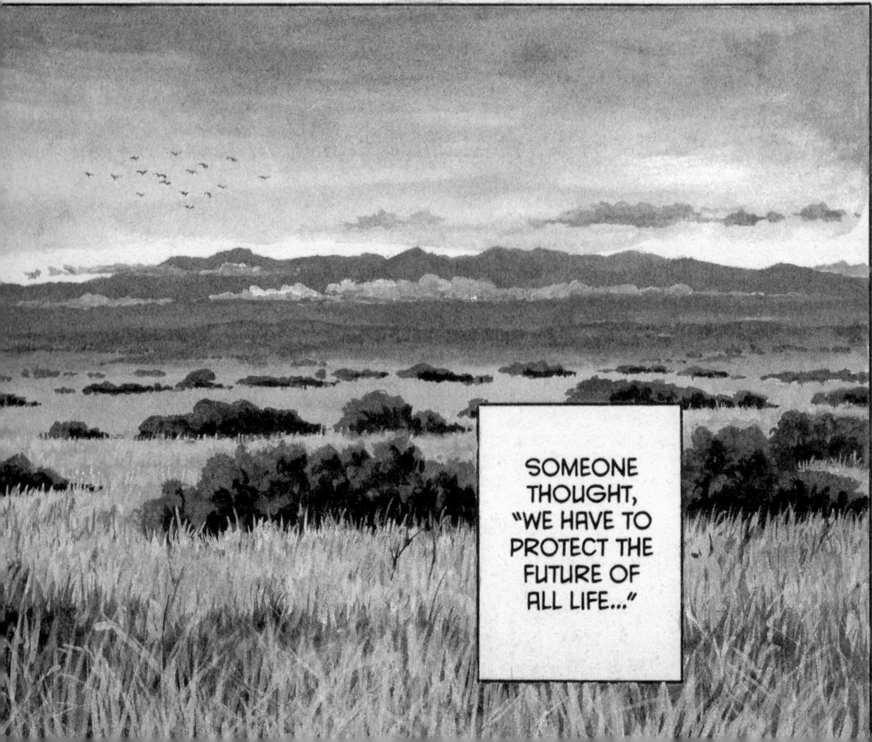
SOMEONE THOUGHT, "WE HAVE TO PROTECT THE FUTURE OF ALL LIFE..."

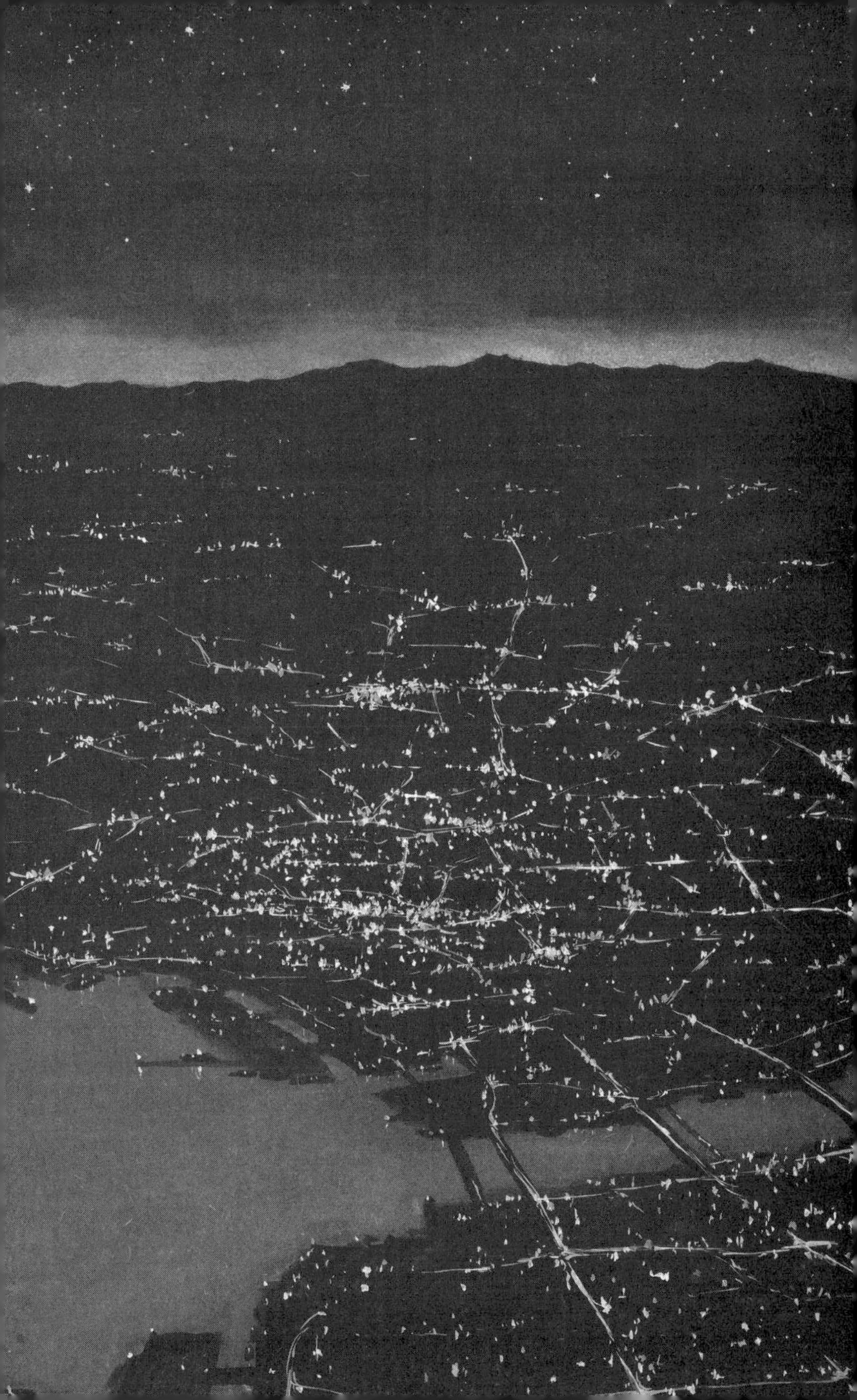

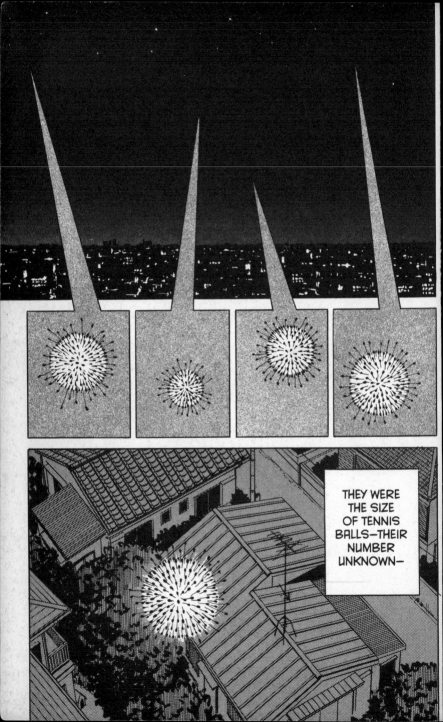

THEY WERE
THE SIZE
OF TENNIS
BALLS—THEIR
NUMBER
UNKNOWN—

ポヨン
BOING!
パン
POP
ニュル
SCHLUP

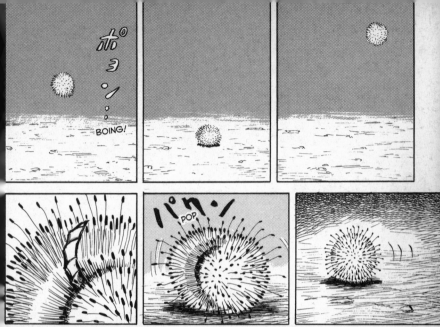

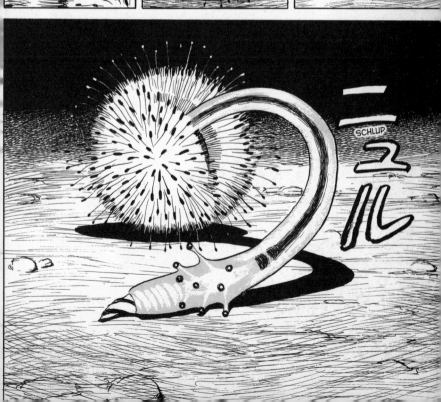

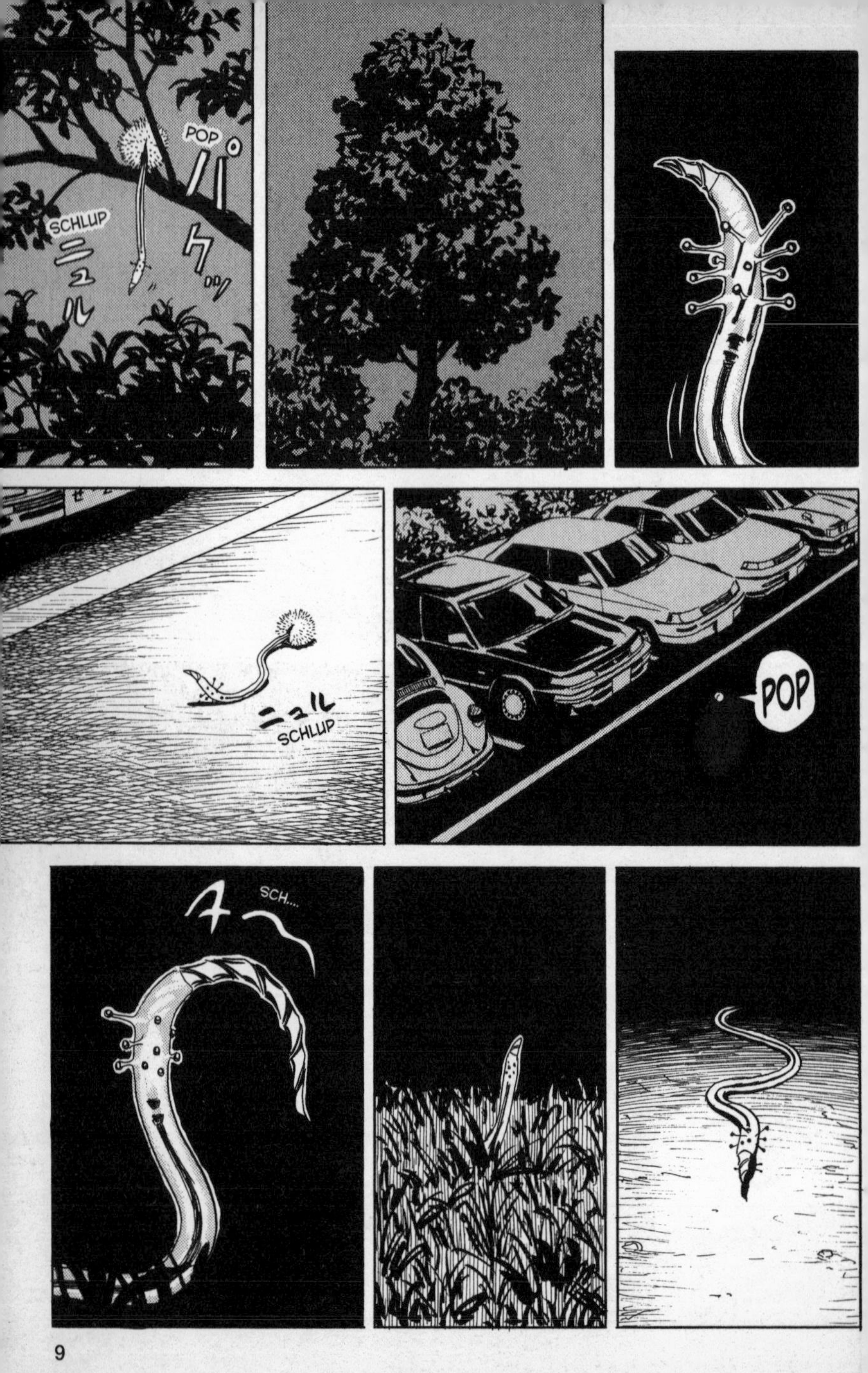
POP
パクッ
SCHLUP
ニュル
POP
ニュル
SCHLUP
ス
SCH...

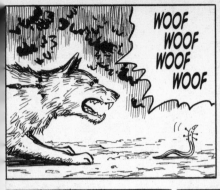WOOF
WOOF
WOOF
WOOF

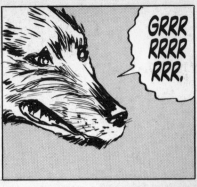GRRR
RRRR
RRR.

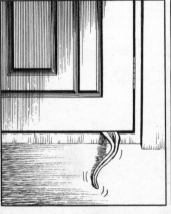

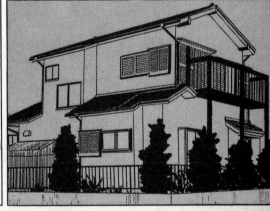

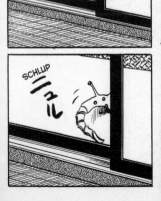SCHLUP

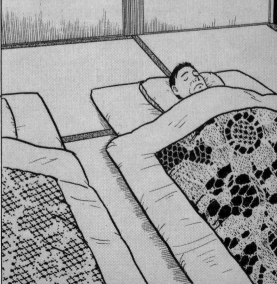

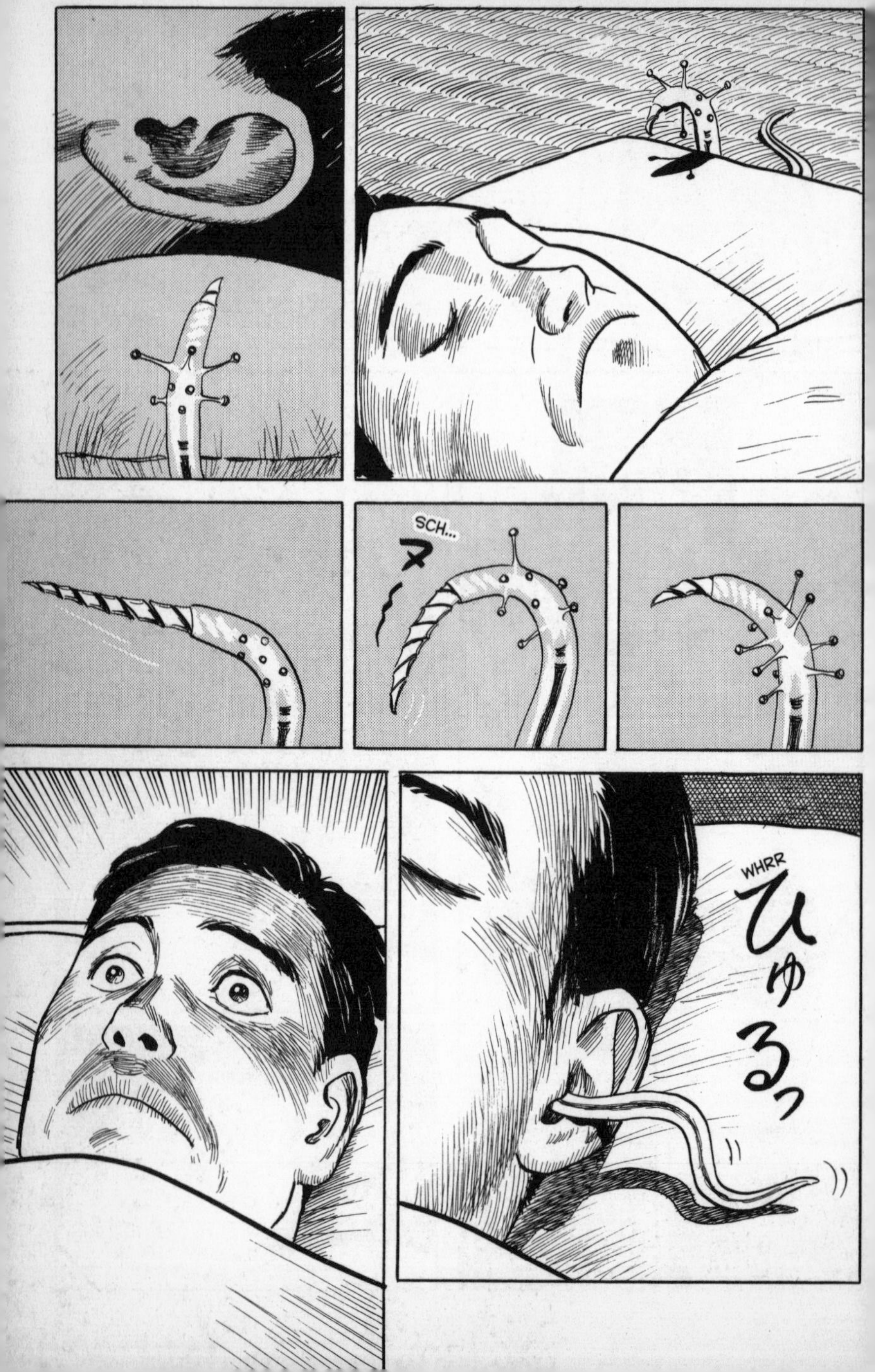
SCH...
ヌ
WHRR
ひゅるっ

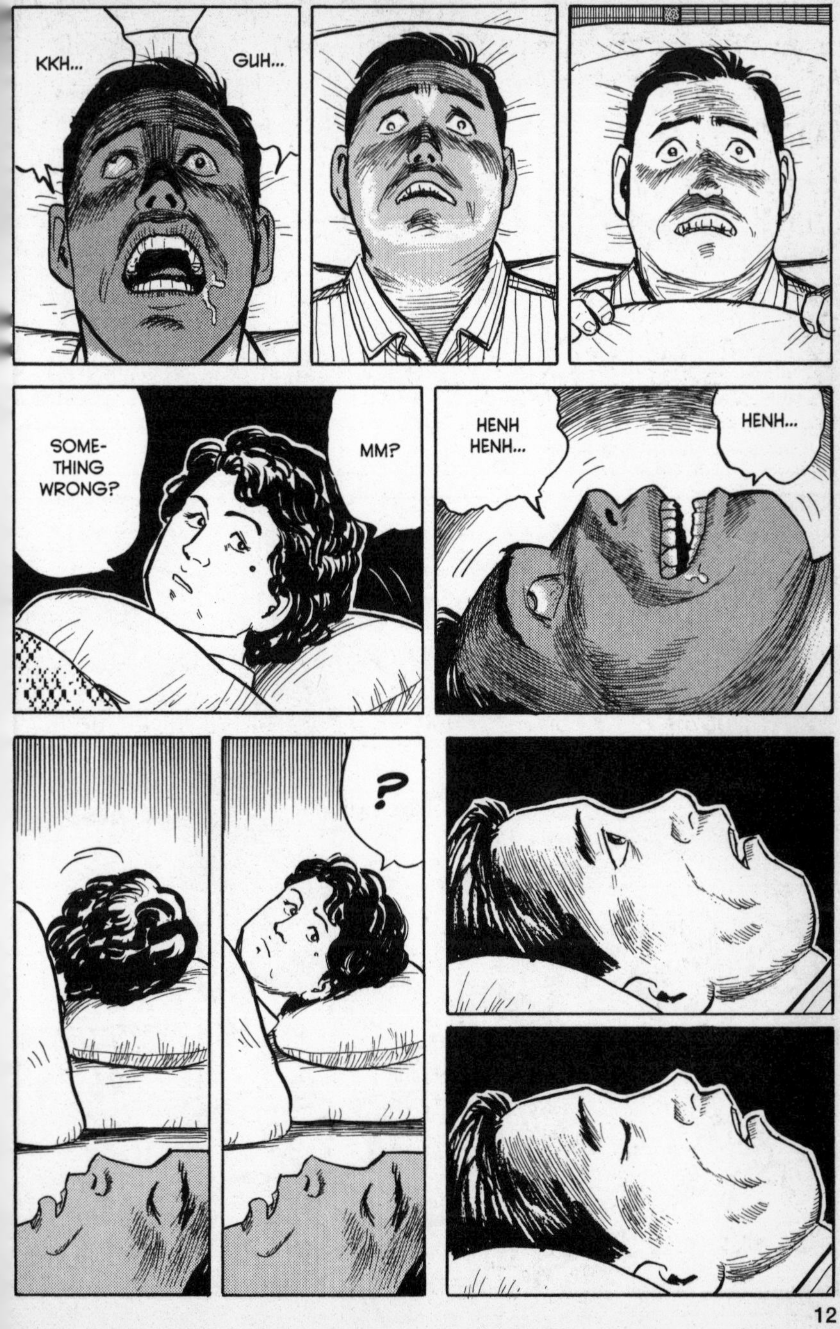
GUH...
KKH...
HENH...
HENH HENH...
MM?
SOME-THING WRONG?
?

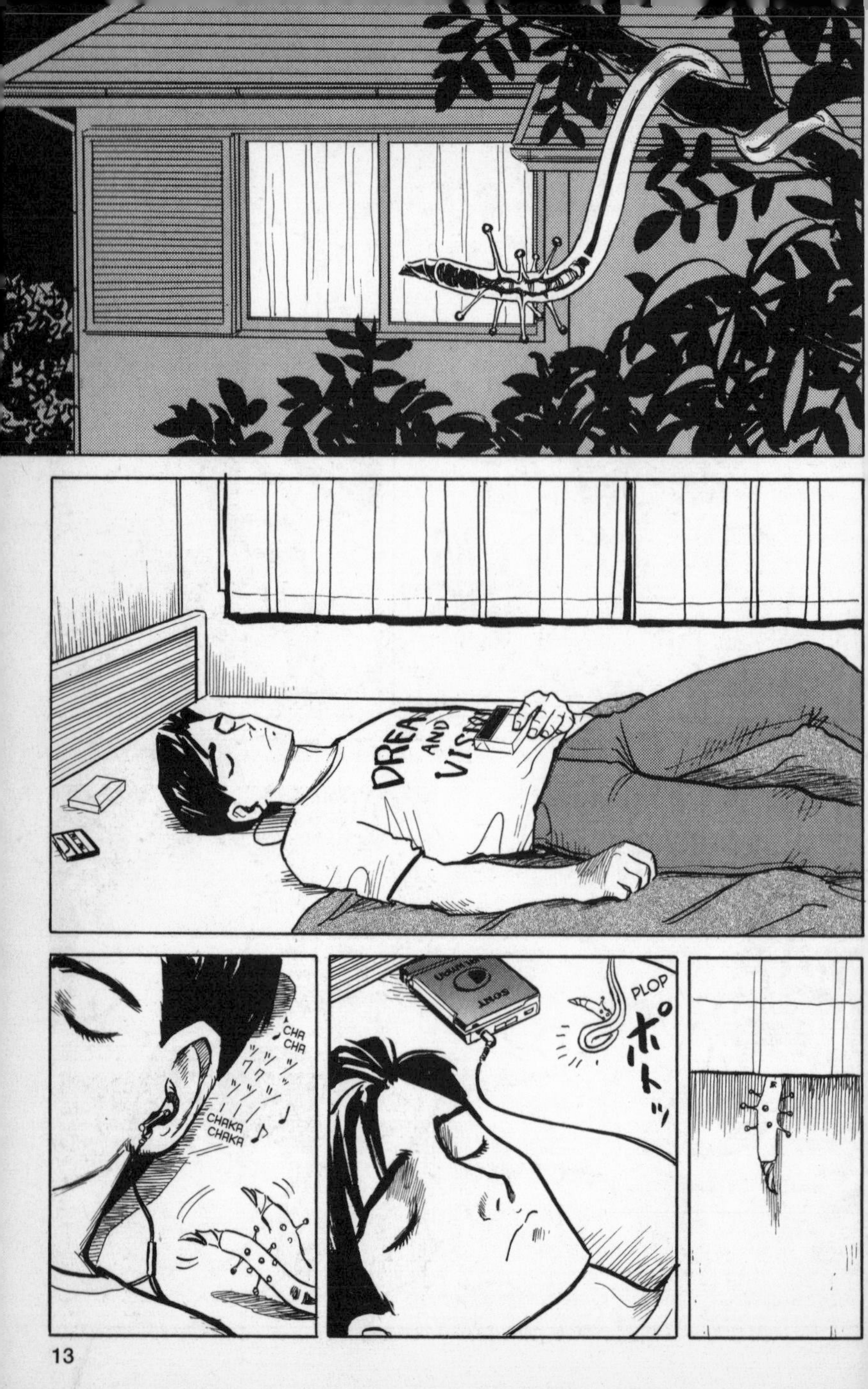
DREA
AND
VIS
PLOP
ポトッ
CHA
CHA
CHAKA
CHAKA

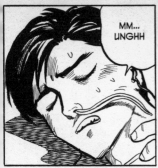

MM...
UNGHH

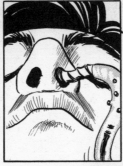

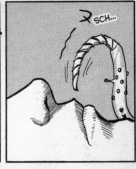

スッ SCH...

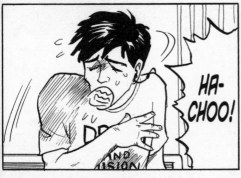

HA-
CHOO!

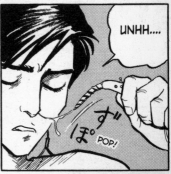

UNHH....

ぼっ POP!
ず"

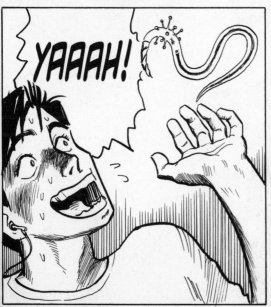

YAAAH!

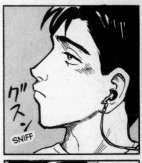

グスッ
SNIFF

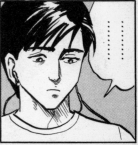

14

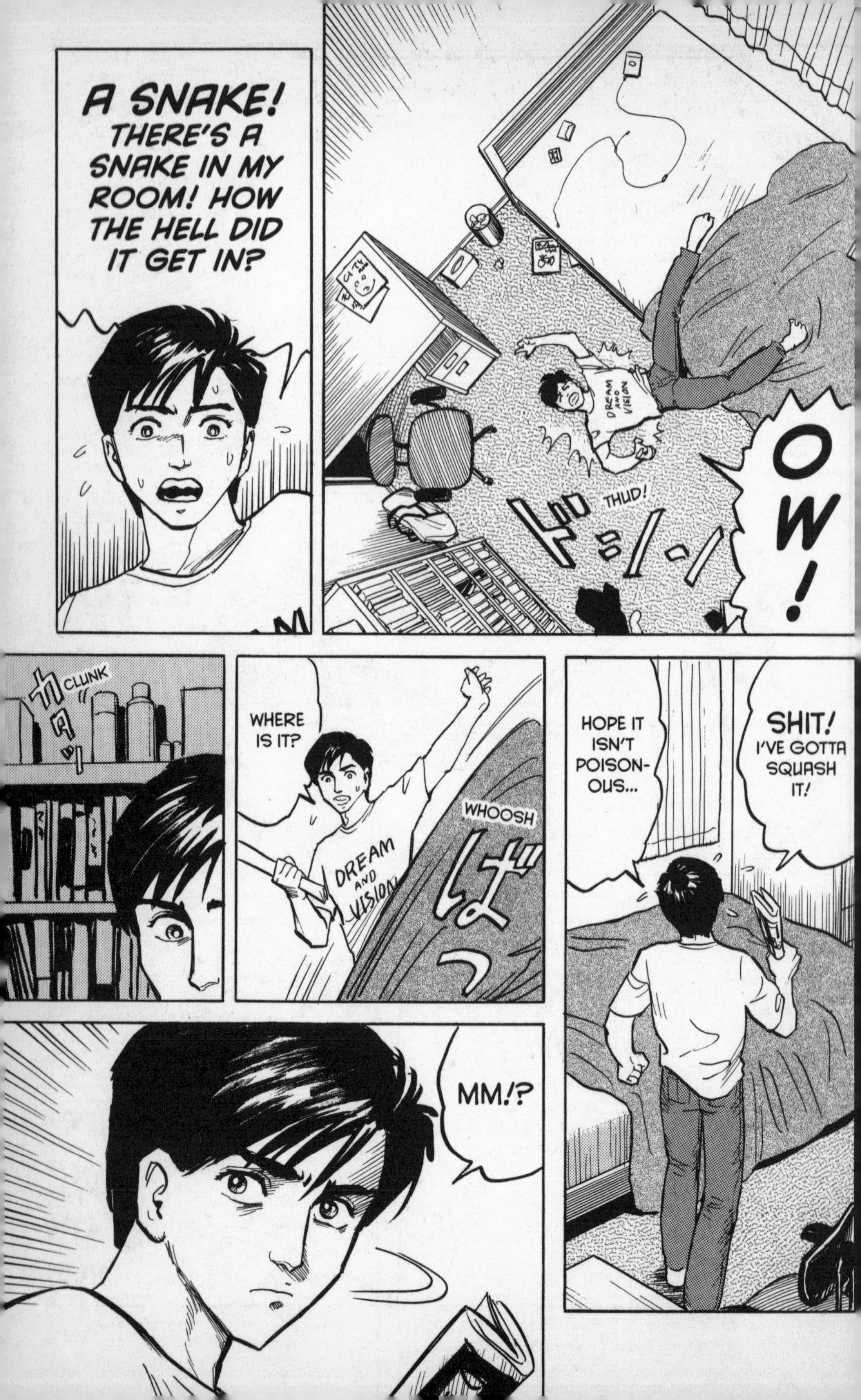
THUD!
OW!
A SNAKE! THERE'S A SNAKE IN MY ROOM! HOW THE HELL DID IT GET IN?
SHIT! I'VE GOTTA SQUASH IT!
HOPE IT ISN'T POISONOUS...
WHOOSH
ばっ
WHERE IS IT?
CLUNK
MM!?

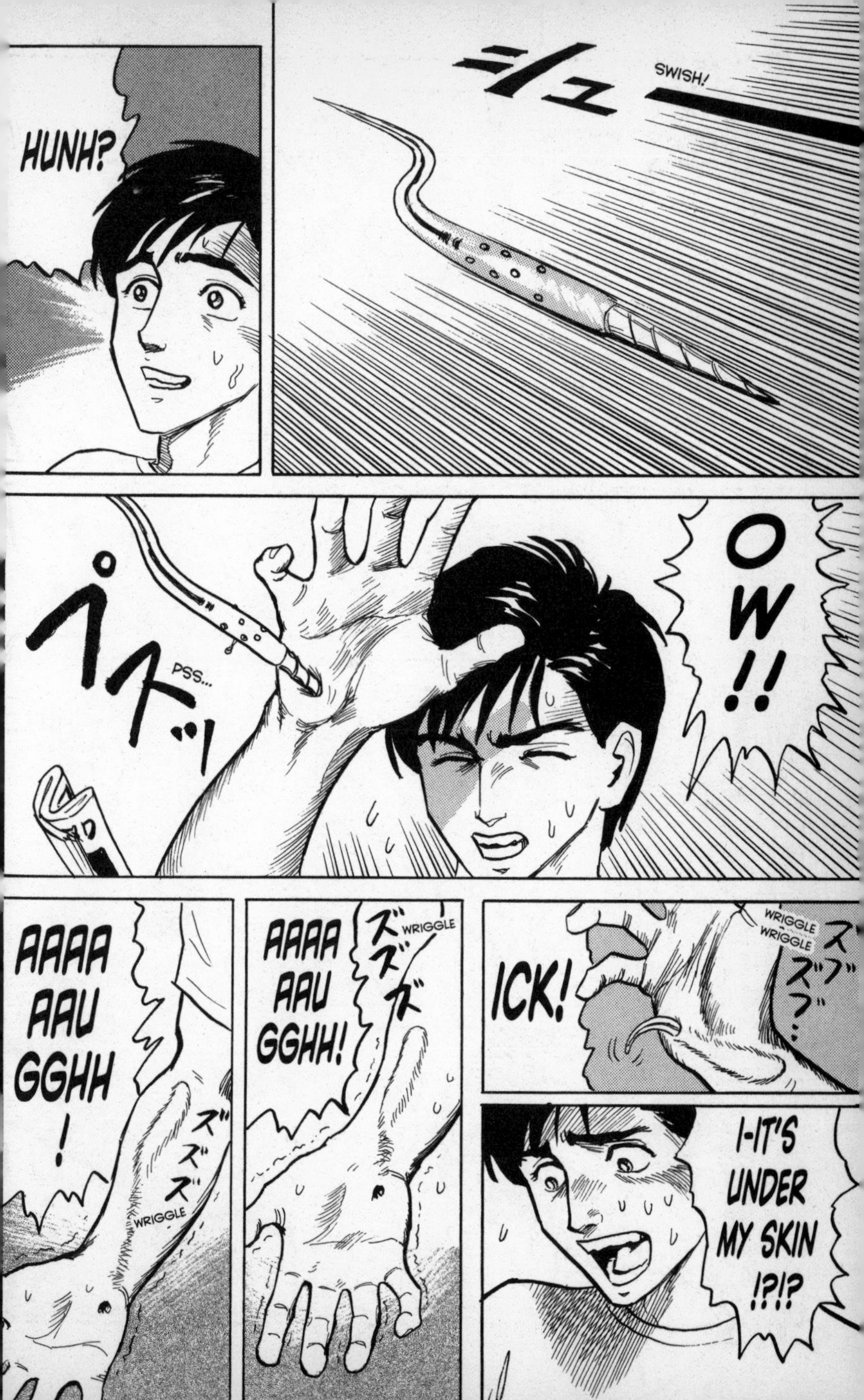

シュ
SWISH!
HUNH?
OW!!
ぷスッ
PSS...
ズブズブ…
WRIGGLE WRIGGLE
ICK!
I-IT'S UNDER MY SKIN !?!?
ズズズ
WRIGGLE
AAAA AAU GGHH!
AAAA AAU GGHH !
ズズズ
WRIGGLE

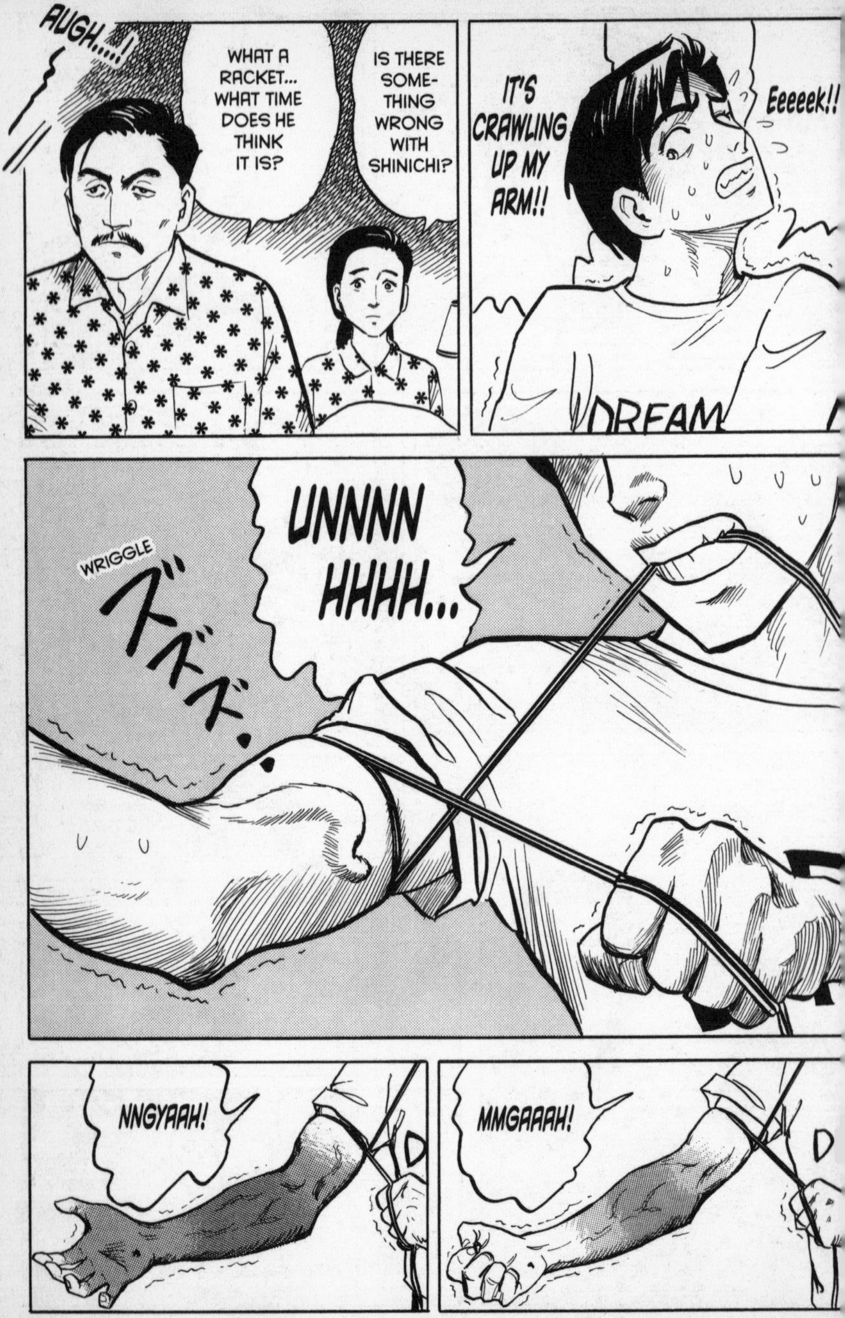
Eeeeek!!
IT'S CRAWLING UP MY ARM!!
DREAM
AUGH....!!
IS THERE SOMETHING WRONG WITH SHINICHI?
WHAT A RACKET... WHAT TIME DOES HE THINK IT IS?
UNNNN HHHH...
WRIGGLE
ズズズ.
MMGAAAH!
NNGYAAH!

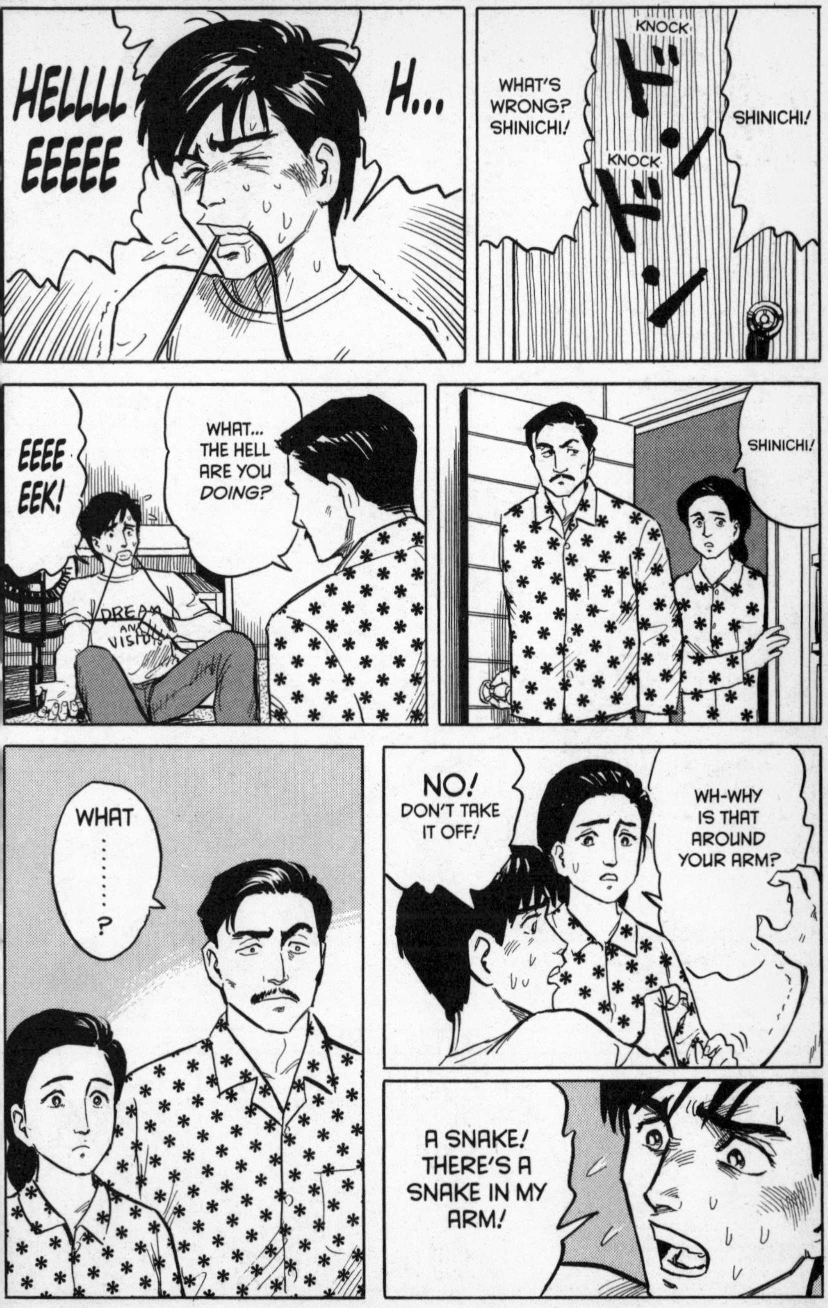
SHINICHI!
KNOCK
KNOCK
WHAT'S WRONG? SHINICHI!
HELLLL EEEEE H...
SHINICHI!
WHAT... THE HELL ARE YOU *DOING?*
EEEE EEK!
WH-WHY IS THAT AROUND YOUR ARM?
NO! DON'T TAKE IT OFF!
A SNAKE! THERE'S A SNAKE IN MY ARM!
WHAT ....?

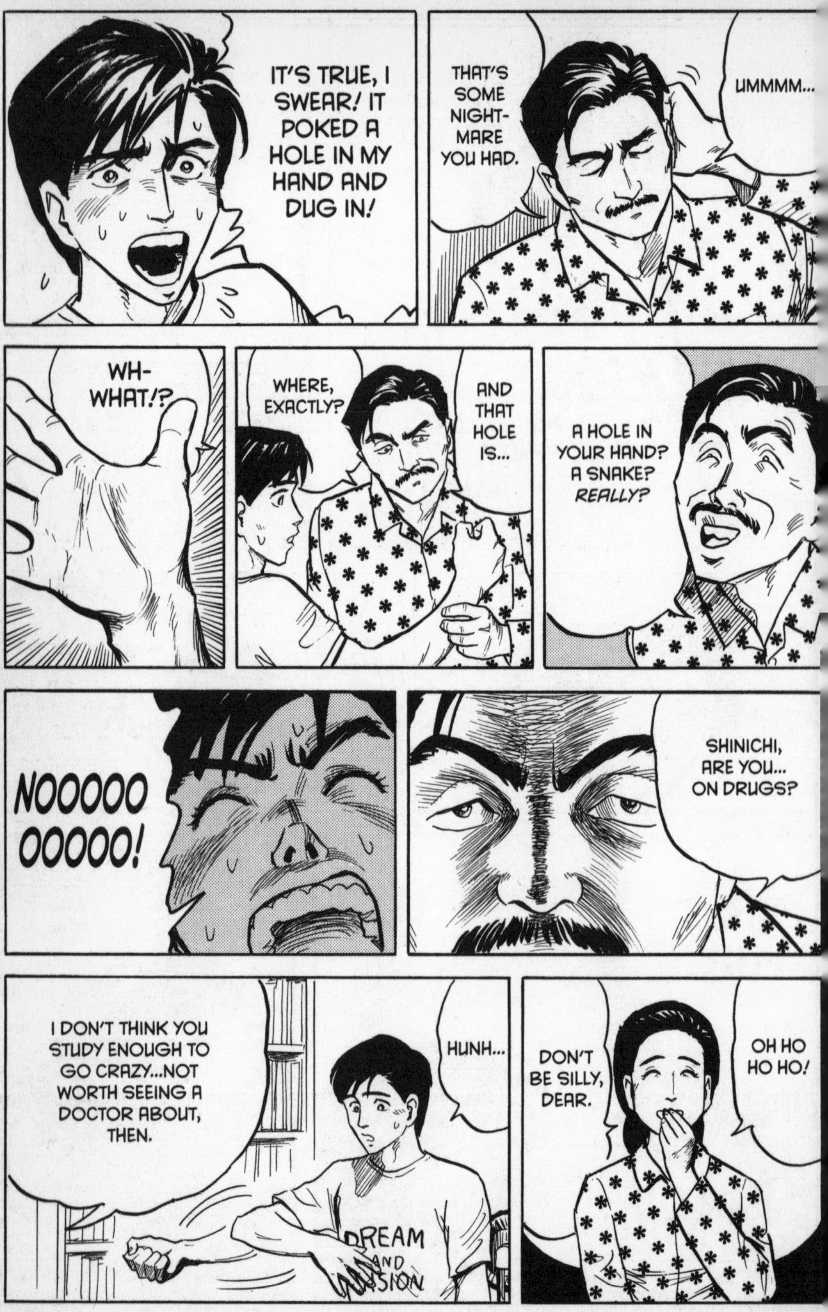

UMMMM...
THAT'S SOME NIGHT-MARE YOU HAD.
IT'S TRUE, I SWEAR! IT POKED A HOLE IN MY HAND AND DUG IN!
A HOLE IN YOUR HAND? A SNAKE? *REALLY?*
AND THAT HOLE IS...
WHERE, EXACTLY?
WH-WHAT!?
SHINICHI, ARE YOU... ON DRUGS?
NOOOOO OOOOO!
OH HO HO HO!
DON'T BE SILLY, DEAR.
HUNH...
I DON'T THINK YOU STUDY ENOUGH TO GO CRAZY...NOT WORTH SEEING A DOCTOR ABOUT, THEN.

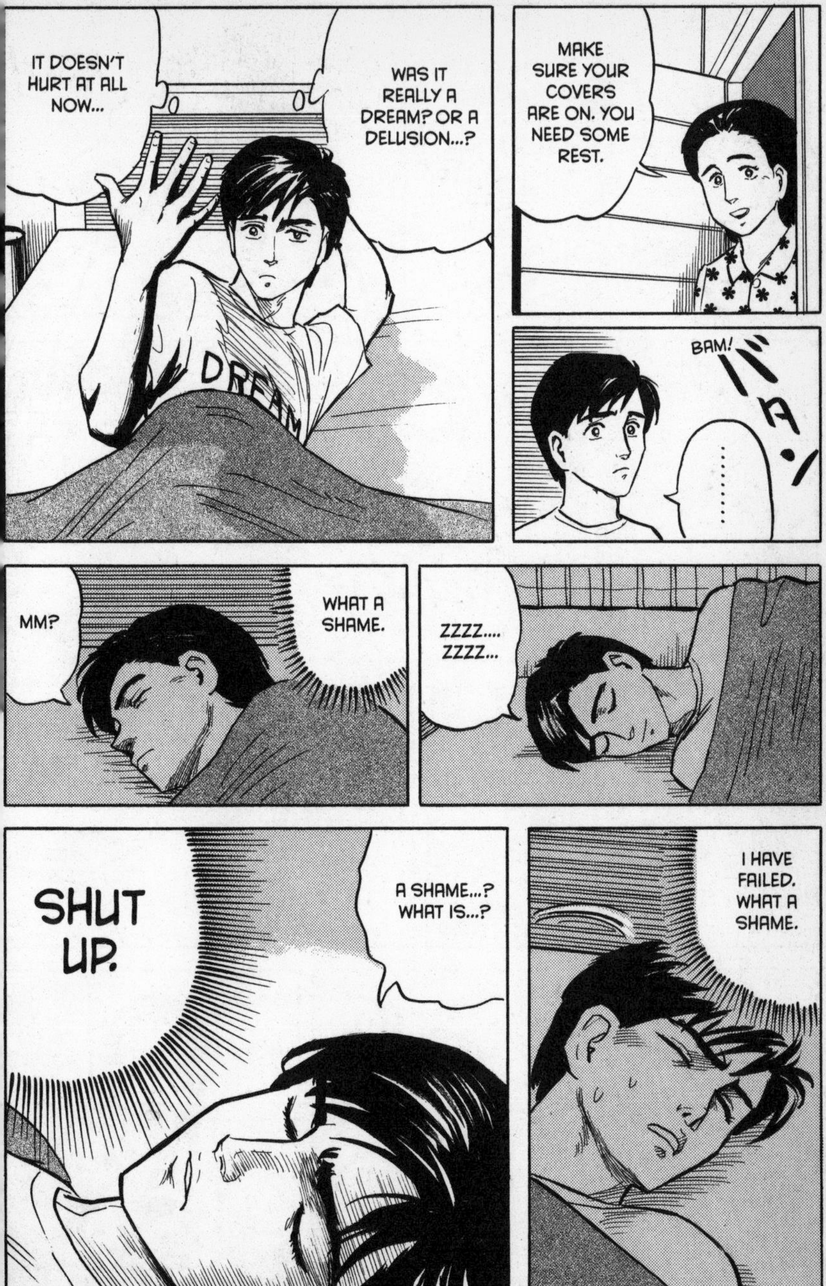
MAKE SURE YOUR COVERS ARE ON. YOU NEED SOME REST.
BAM!
......
WAS IT REALLY A DREAM? OR A DELUSION...?
IT DOESN'T HURT AT ALL NOW...
DREAM
ZZZZ.... ZZZZ...
WHAT A SHAME.
MM?
I HAVE FAILED. WHAT A SHAME.
A SHAME...? WHAT IS...?
SHUT UP.

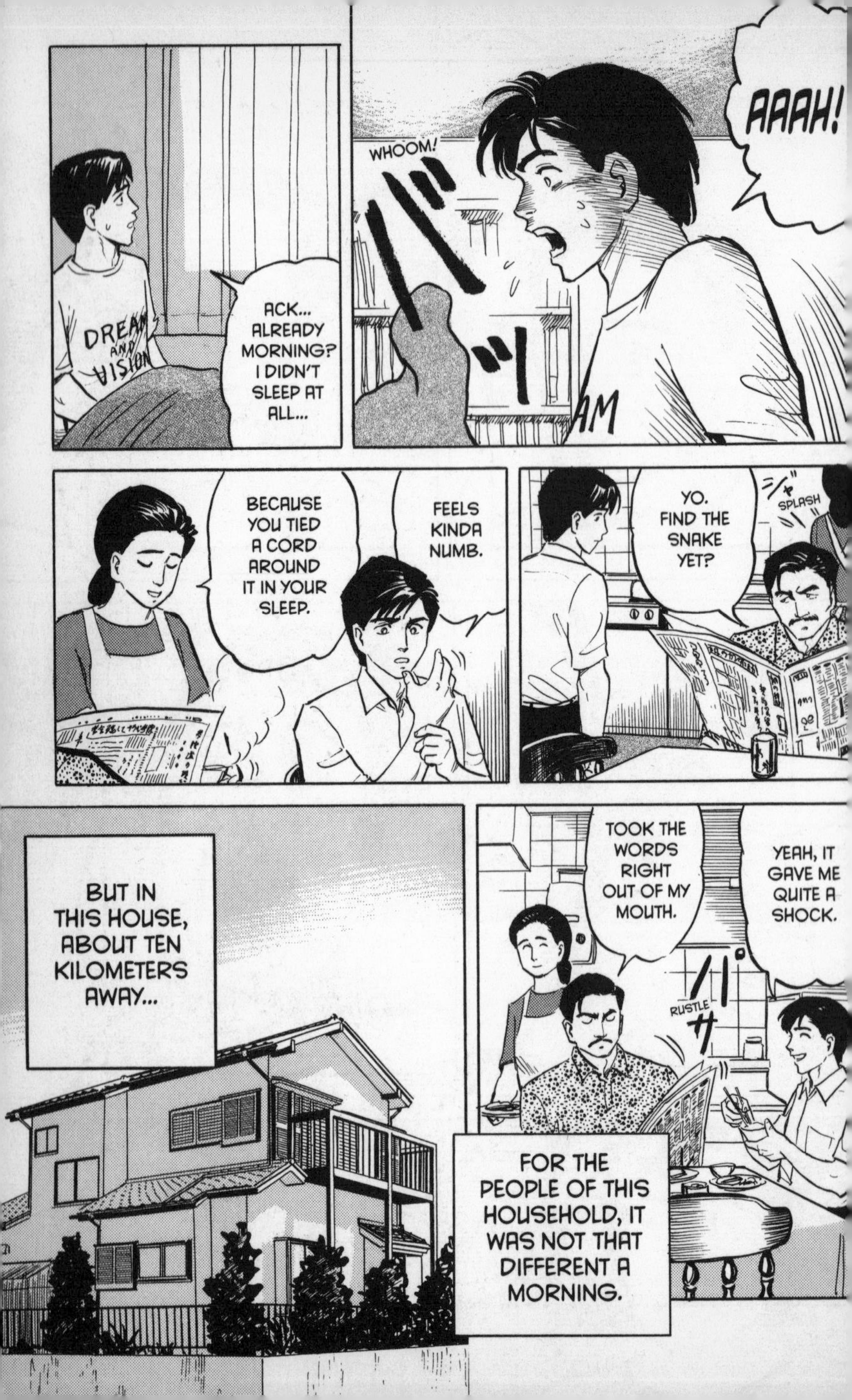
ACK... ALREADY MORNING? I DIDN'T SLEEP AT ALL...
WHOOM!
AAAH!
FEELS KINDA NUMB.
BECAUSE YOU TIED A CORD AROUND IT IN YOUR SLEEP.
YO. FIND THE SNAKE YET?
SPLASH
BUT IN THIS HOUSE, ABOUT TEN KILOMETERS AWAY...
YEAH, IT GAVE ME QUITE A SHOCK.
TOOK THE WORDS RIGHT OUT OF MY MOUTH.
RUSTLE
FOR THE PEOPLE OF THIS HOUSEHOLD, IT WAS NOT THAT DIFFERENT A MORNING.

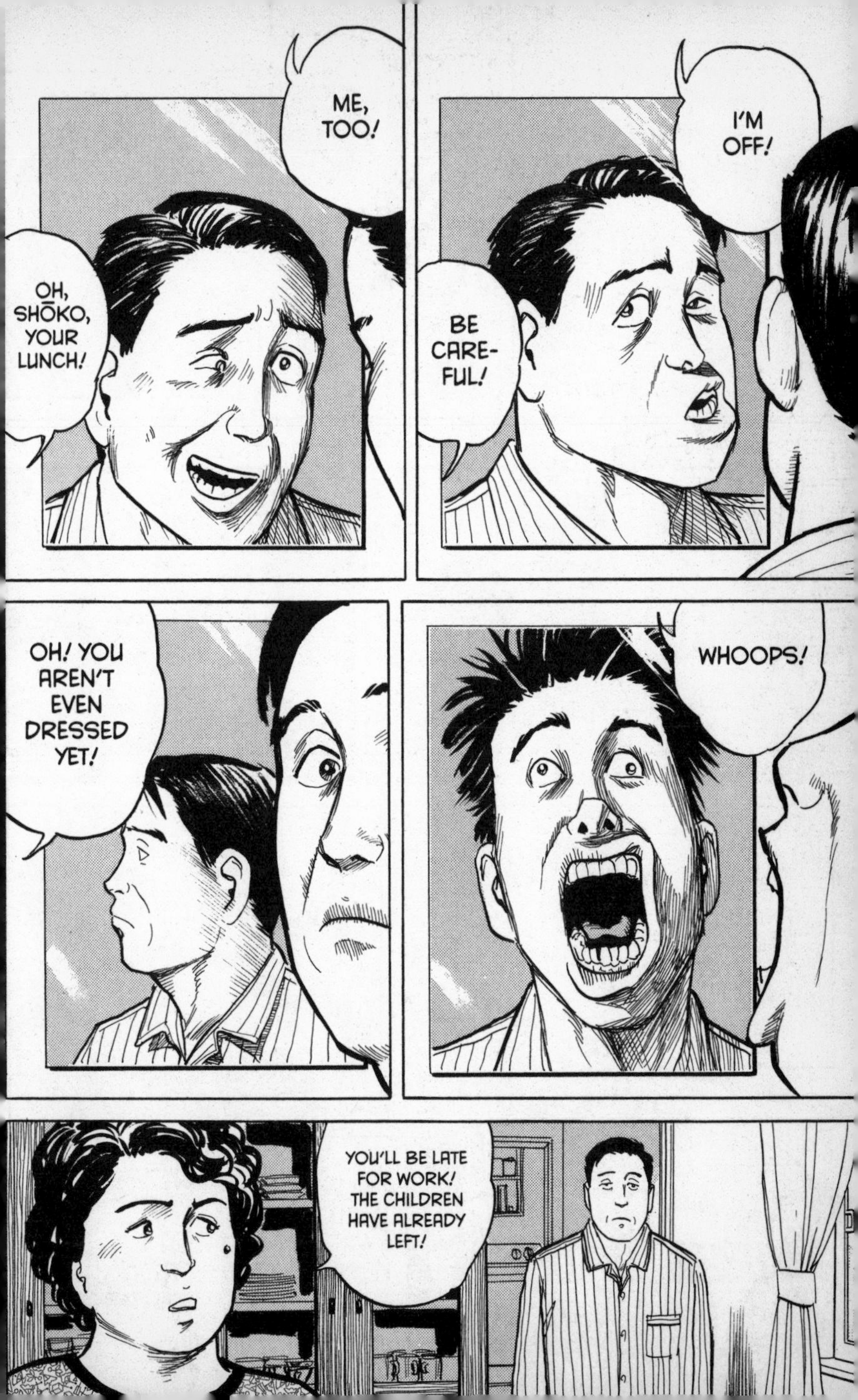
I'M OFF!
BE CARE-FUL!
ME, TOO!
OH, SHŌKO, YOUR LUNCH!
WHOOPS!
OH! YOU AREN'T EVEN DRESSED YET!
YOU'LL BE LATE FOR WORK! THE CHILDREN HAVE ALREADY LEFT!

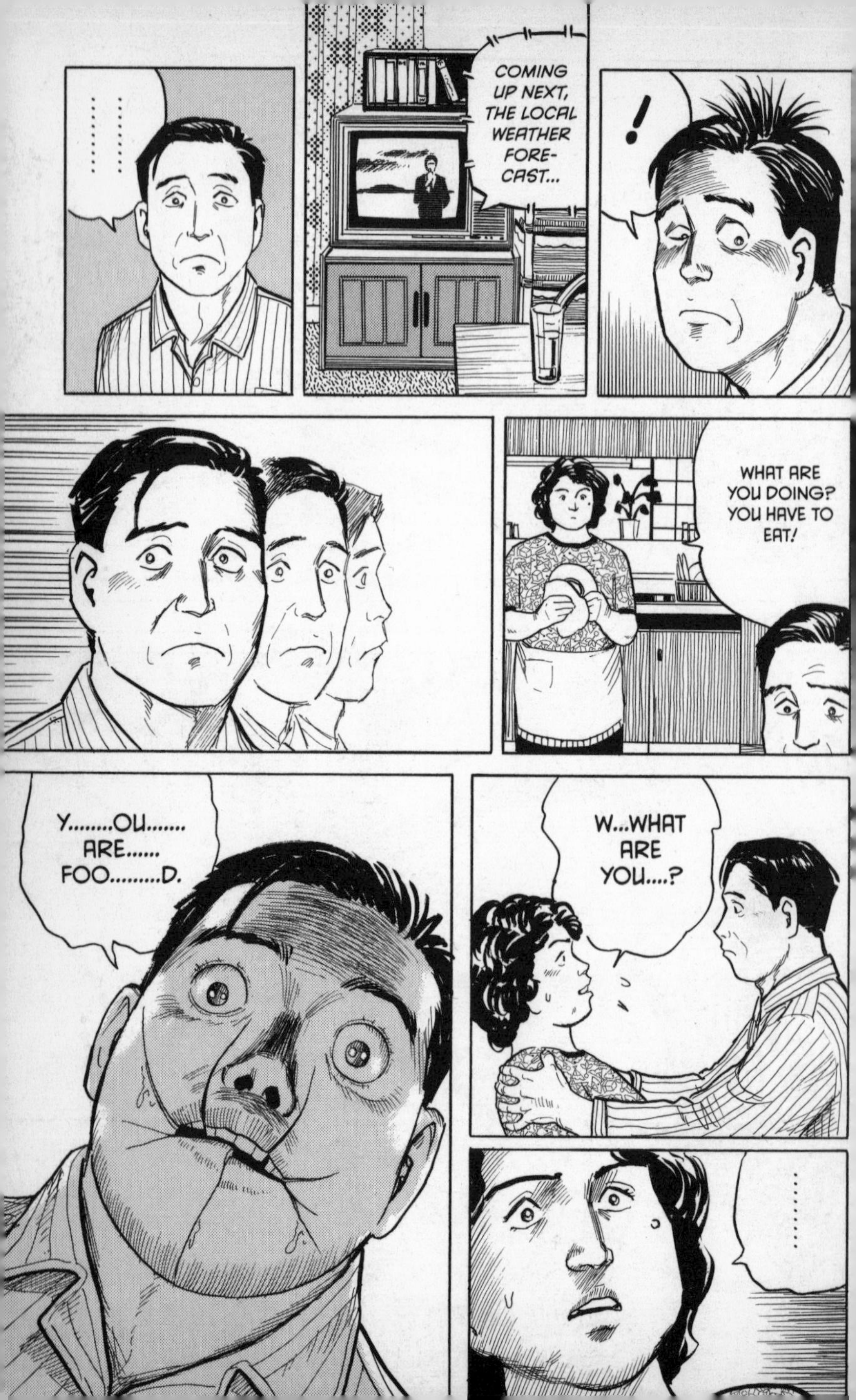
!
COMING UP NEXT, THE LOCAL WEATHER FORECAST...
......
WHAT ARE YOU DOING? YOU HAVE TO EAT!
W...WHAT ARE YOU....?
......
Y........OU....... ARE...... FOO.........D.

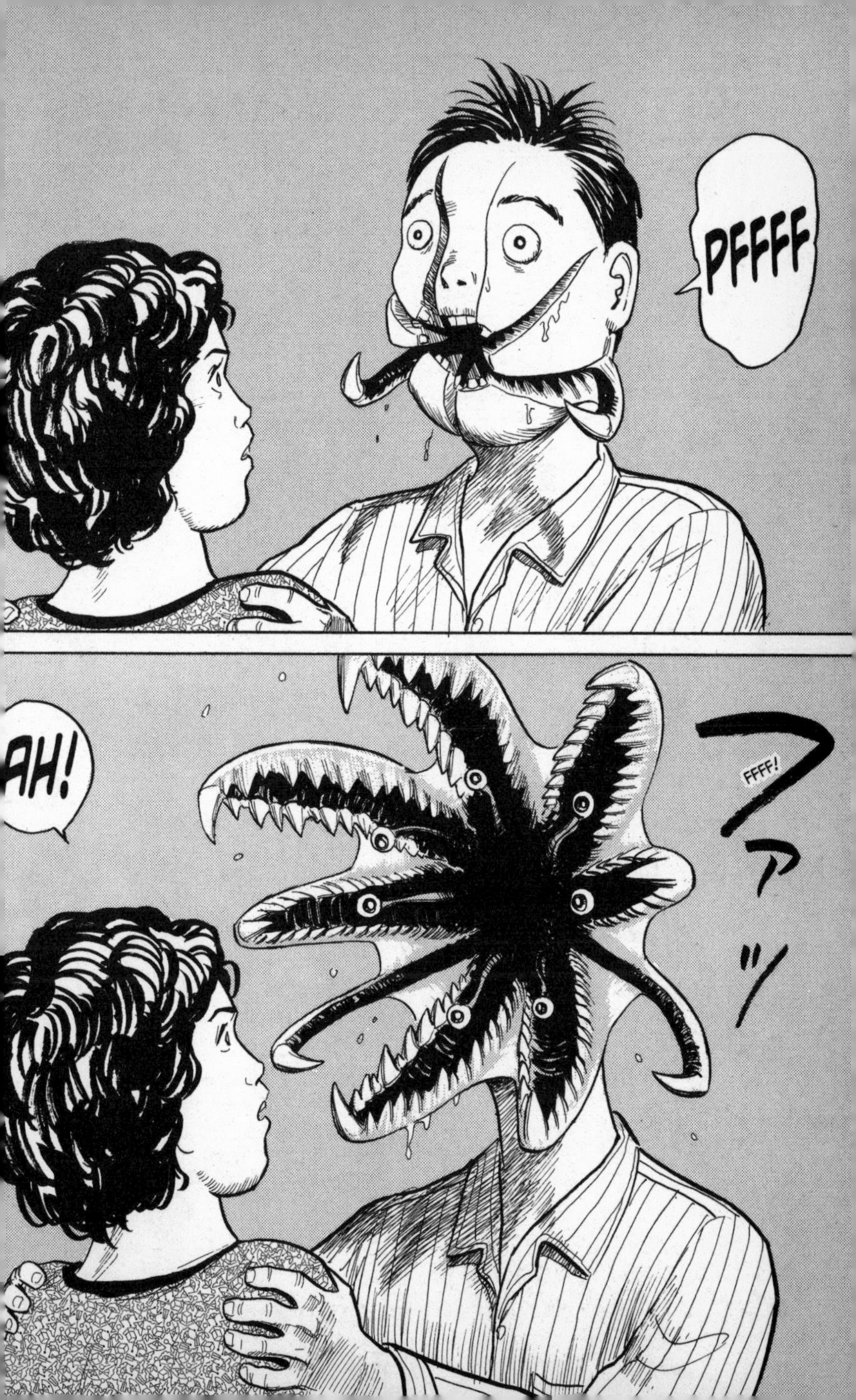
PFFFF
ファッ
FFFF!
AH!

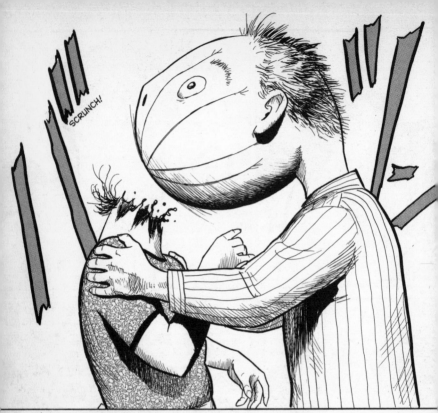

SCRUNCH!

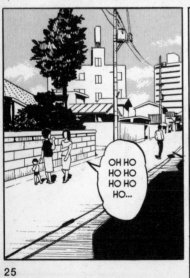

OH HO
HO HO
HO HO
HO...

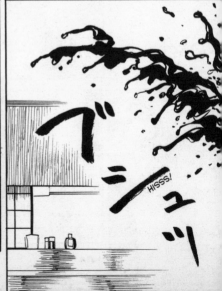

HISSS!

25

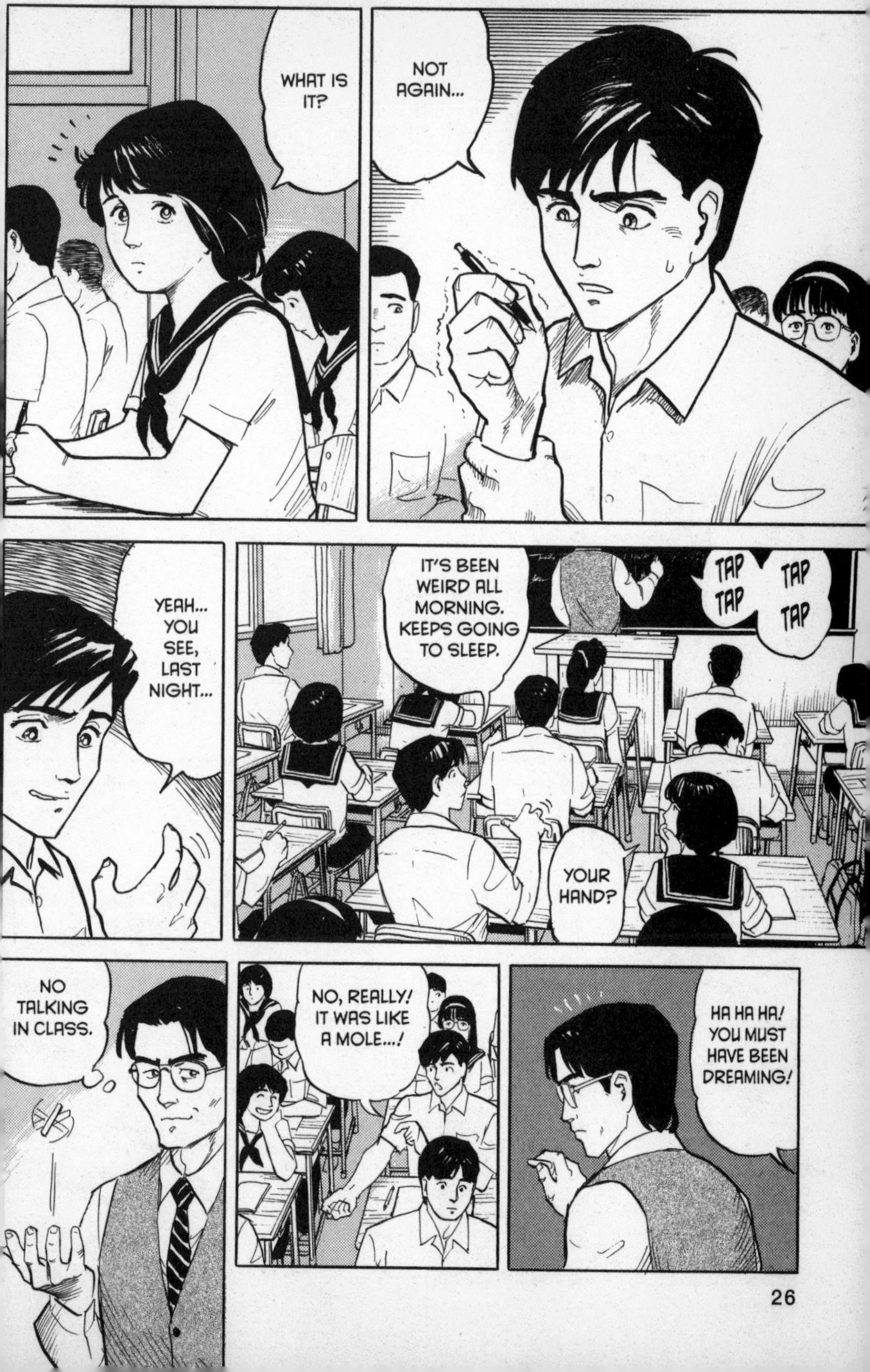
NOT AGAIN...
WHAT IS IT?
TAP TAP
TAP TAP
IT'S BEEN WEIRD ALL MORNING. KEEPS GOING TO SLEEP.
YOUR HAND?
YEAH... YOU SEE, LAST NIGHT...
HA HA HA! YOU MUST HAVE BEEN DREAMING!
NO, REALLY! IT WAS LIKE A MOLE...!
NO TALKING IN CLASS.

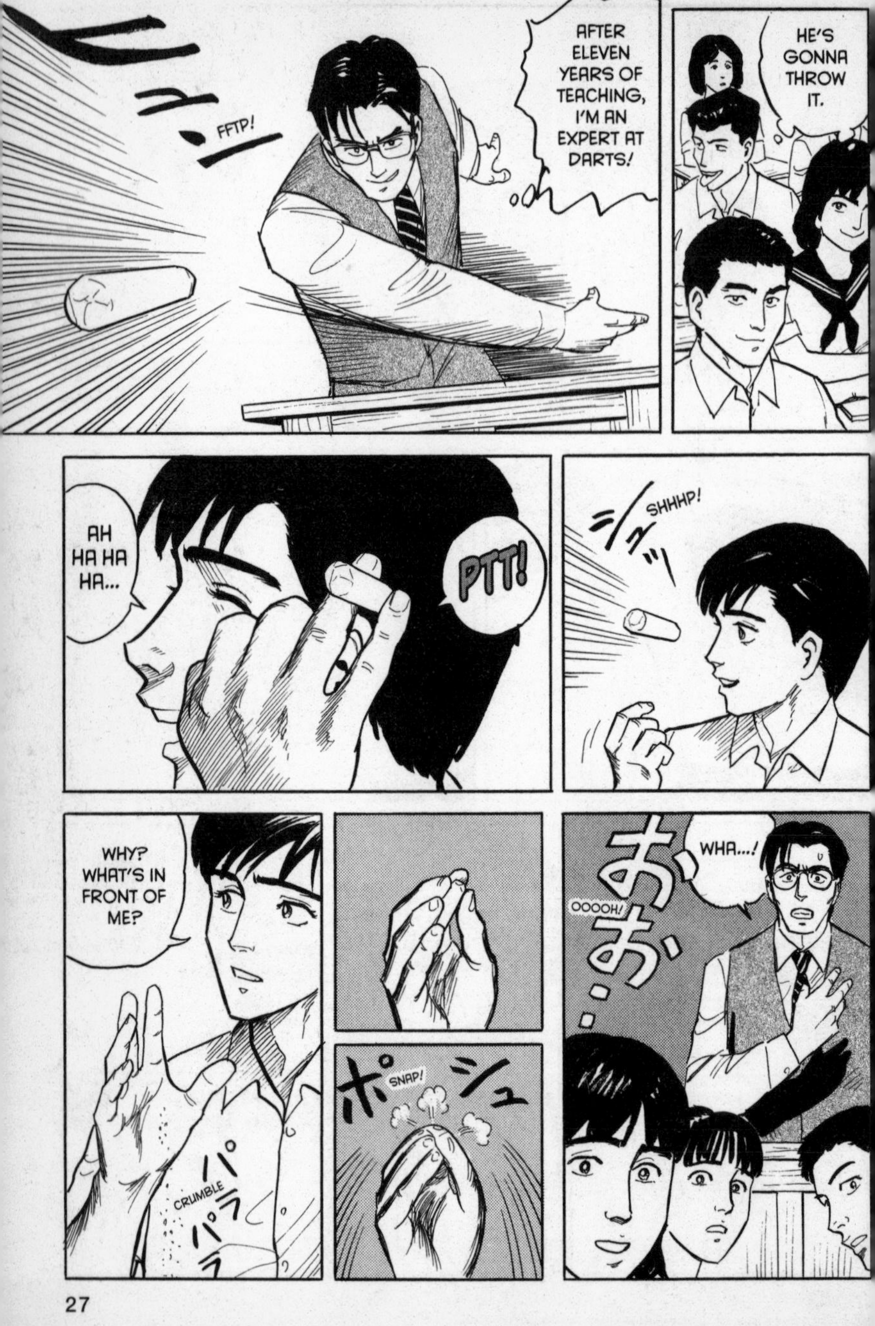
HE'S GONNA THROW IT.
AFTER ELEVEN YEARS OF TEACHING, I'M AN EXPERT AT DARTS!
FFTP!
SHHHP!
PTT!
AH HA HA HA...
WHA...!
OOOOH!
SNAP!
WHY? WHAT'S IN FRONT OF ME?
CRUMBLE

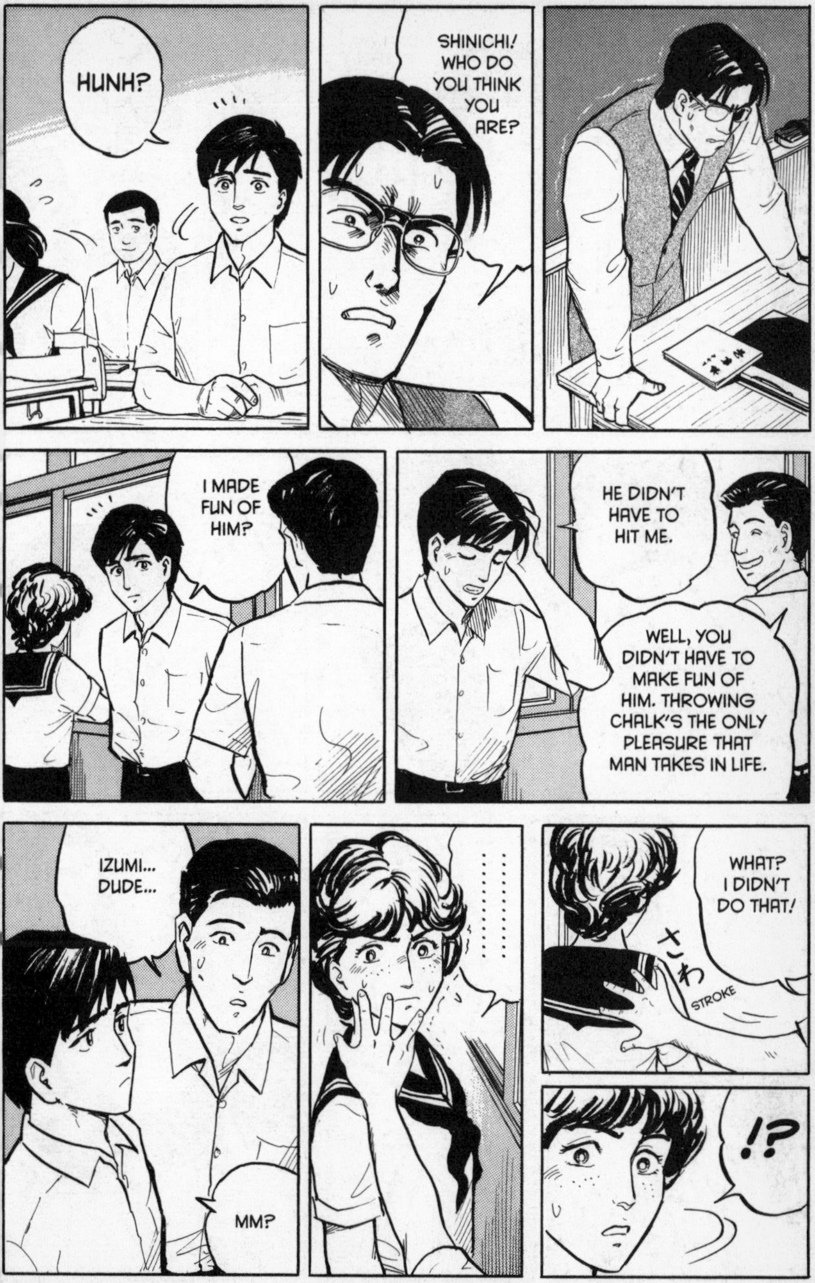
SHINICHI! WHO DO YOU THINK YOU ARE?
HUNH?
HE DIDN'T HAVE TO HIT ME.
WELL, YOU DIDN'T HAVE TO MAKE FUN OF HIM. THROWING CHALK'S THE ONLY PLEASURE THAT MAN TAKES IN LIFE.
I MADE FUN OF HIM?
WHAT? I DIDN'T DO THAT!
さわ
STROKE
!?
......
IZUMI... DUDE...
MM?

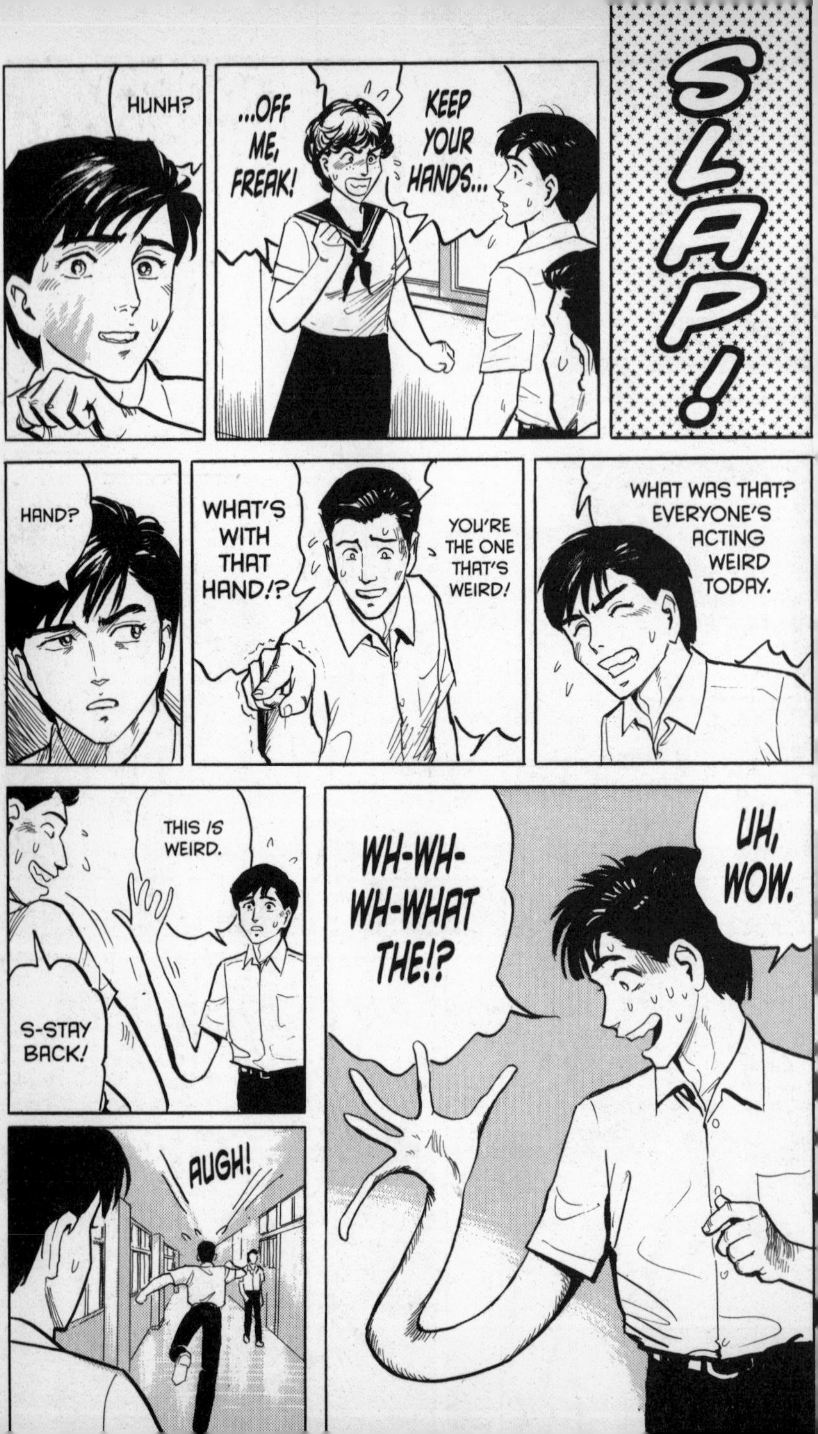
SLAP!
KEEP YOUR HANDS...
...OFF ME, FREAK!
HUNH?
WHAT WAS THAT? EVERYONE'S ACTING WEIRD TODAY.
YOU'RE THE ONE THAT'S WEIRD!
WHAT'S WITH THAT HAND!?
HAND?
UH, WOW.
WH-WH-WH-WHAT THE!?
THIS IS WEIRD.
S-STAY BACK!
AUGH!

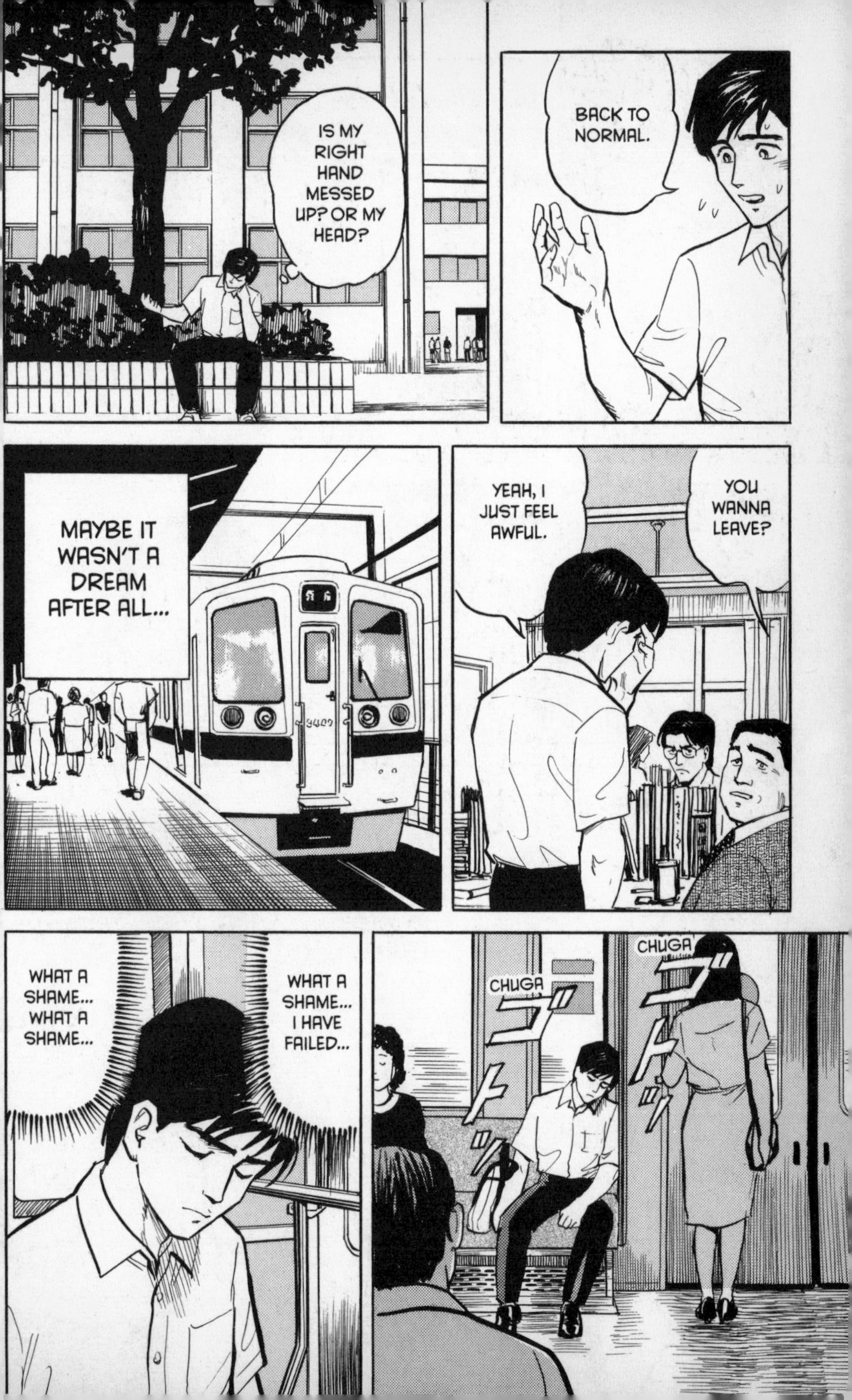
BACK TO NORMAL.
IS MY RIGHT HAND MESSED UP? OR MY HEAD?
YOU WANNA LEAVE?
YEAH, I JUST FEEL AWFUL.
MAYBE IT WASN'T A DREAM AFTER ALL...
CHUGA
CHUGA
WHAT A SHAME... I HAVE FAILED...
WHAT A SHAME... WHAT A SHAME...

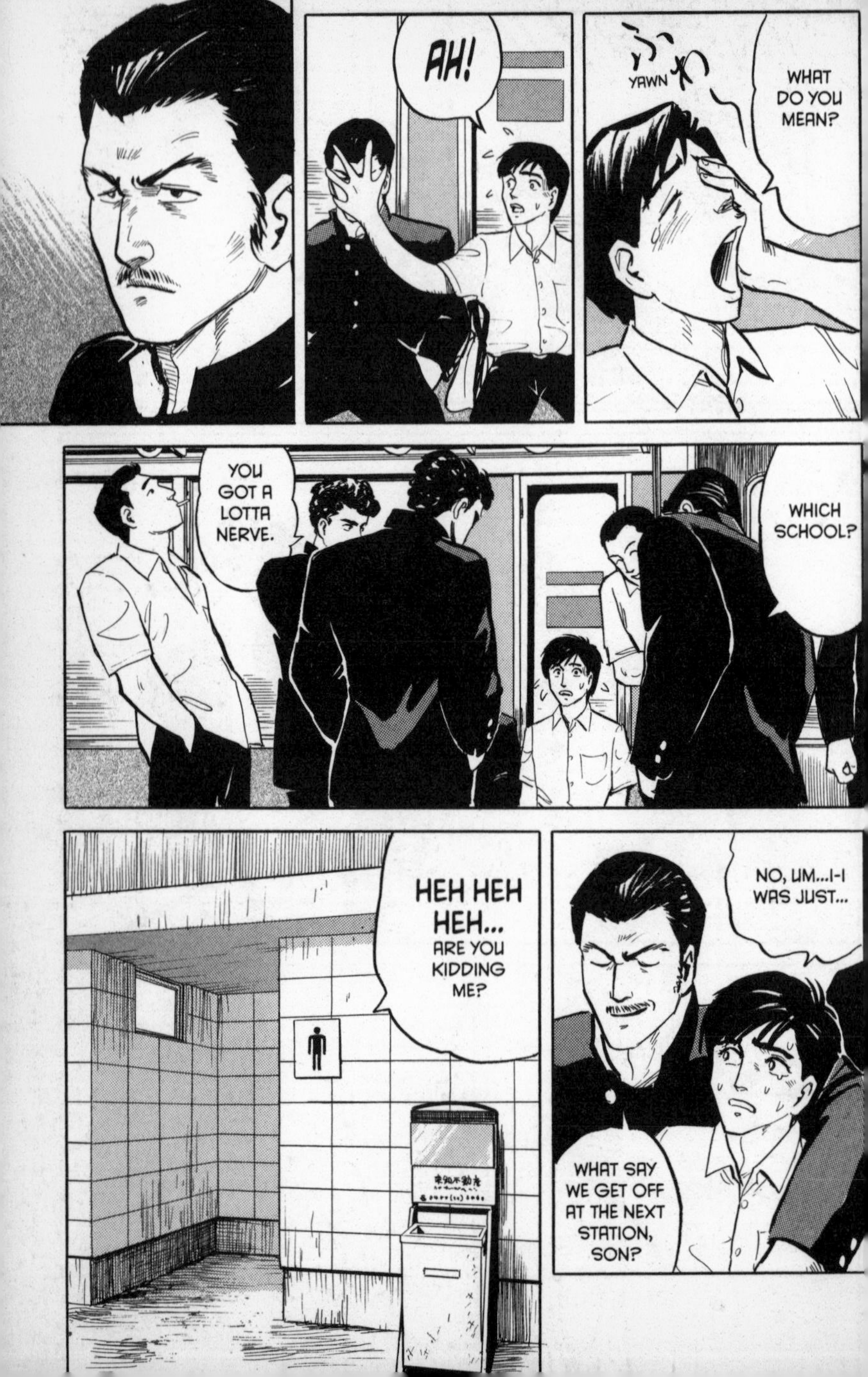
ふわ
YAWN
WHAT DO YOU MEAN?
AH!
WHICH SCHOOL?
YOU GOT A LOTTA NERVE.
NO, UM...I-I WAS JUST...
WHAT SAY WE GET OFF AT THE NEXT STATION, SON?
HEH HEH HEH... ARE YOU KIDDING ME?

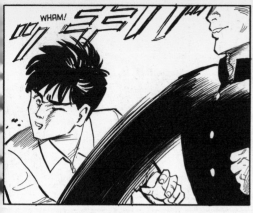

WHAM!

W-WAIT! THERE'S SOMETHING WRONG WITH THIS HAND!

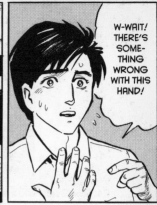

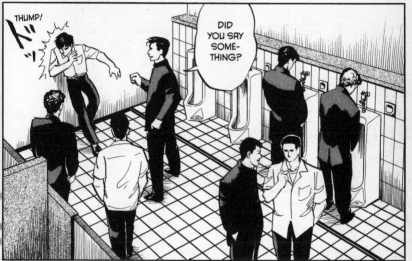

THUMP!

DID YOU SAY SOMETHING?

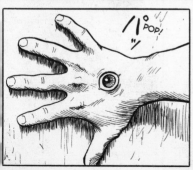

POP!

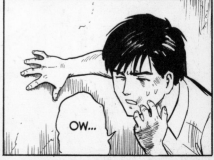

OW...

32

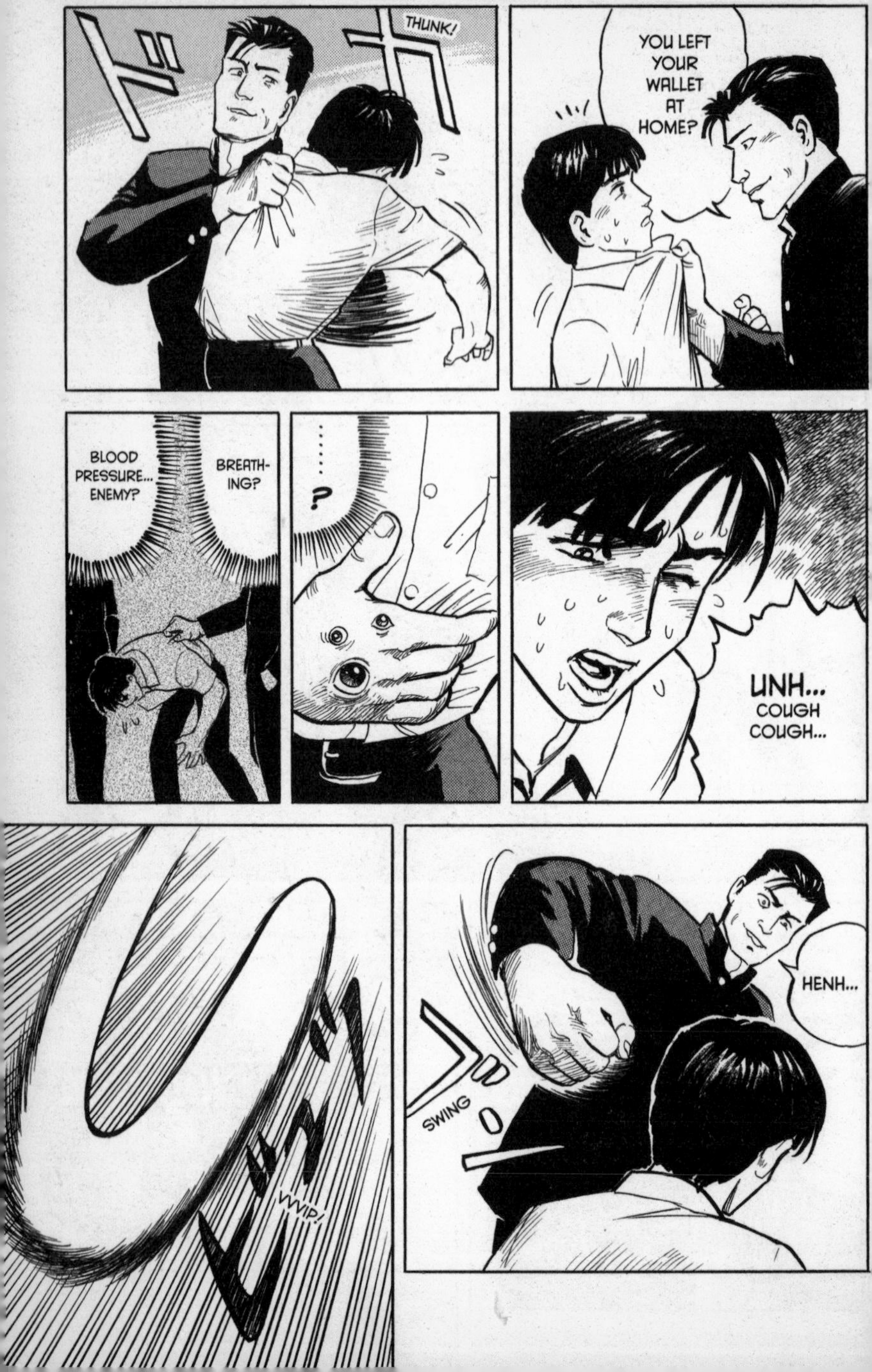
YOU LEFT YOUR WALLET AT HOME?
THUNK!
UNH... COUGH COUGH...
......
?
BREATH-ING?
BLOOD PRESSURE... ENEMY?
HENH...
SWING
VVIP!

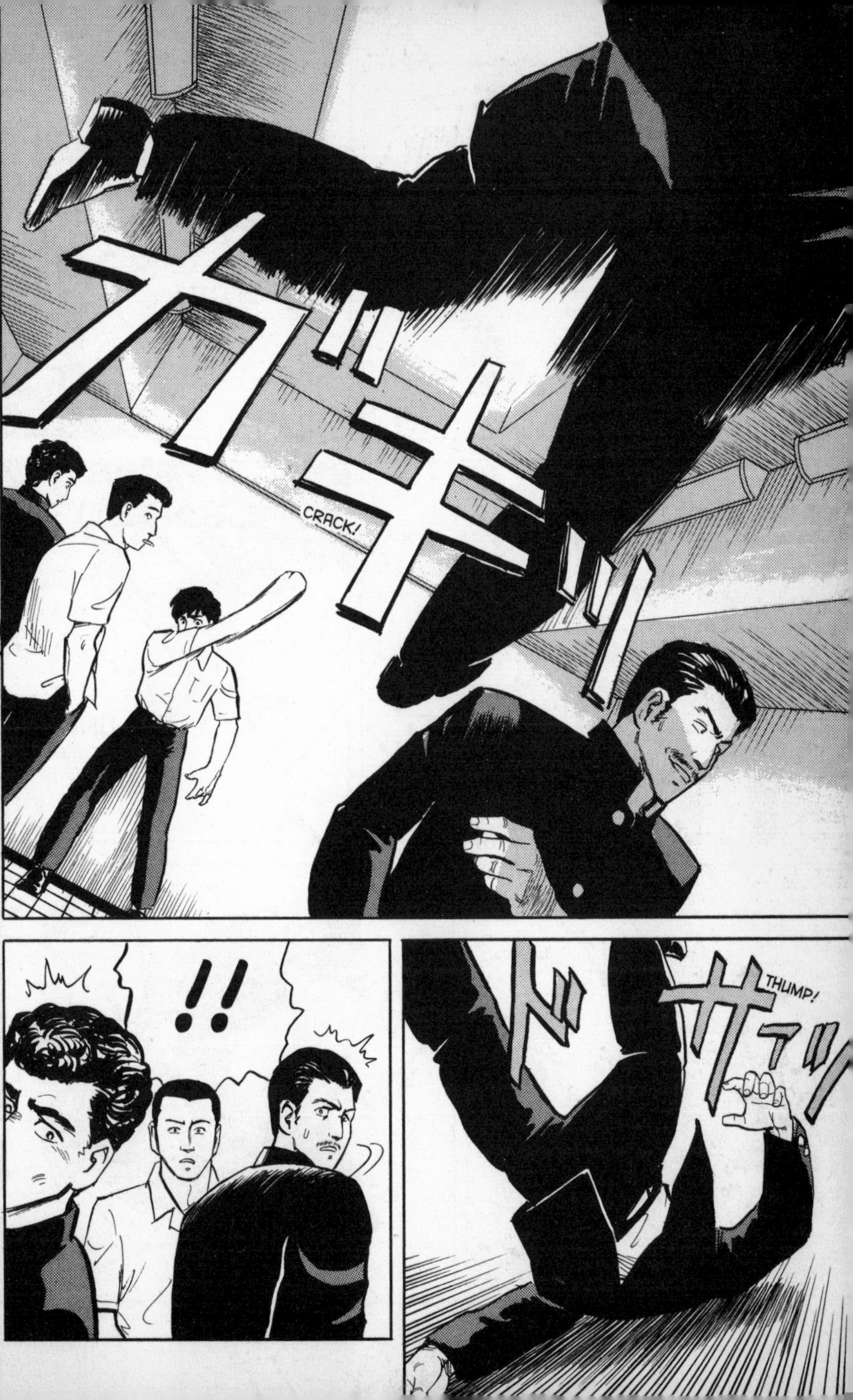
CRACK!
THUMP!
!!

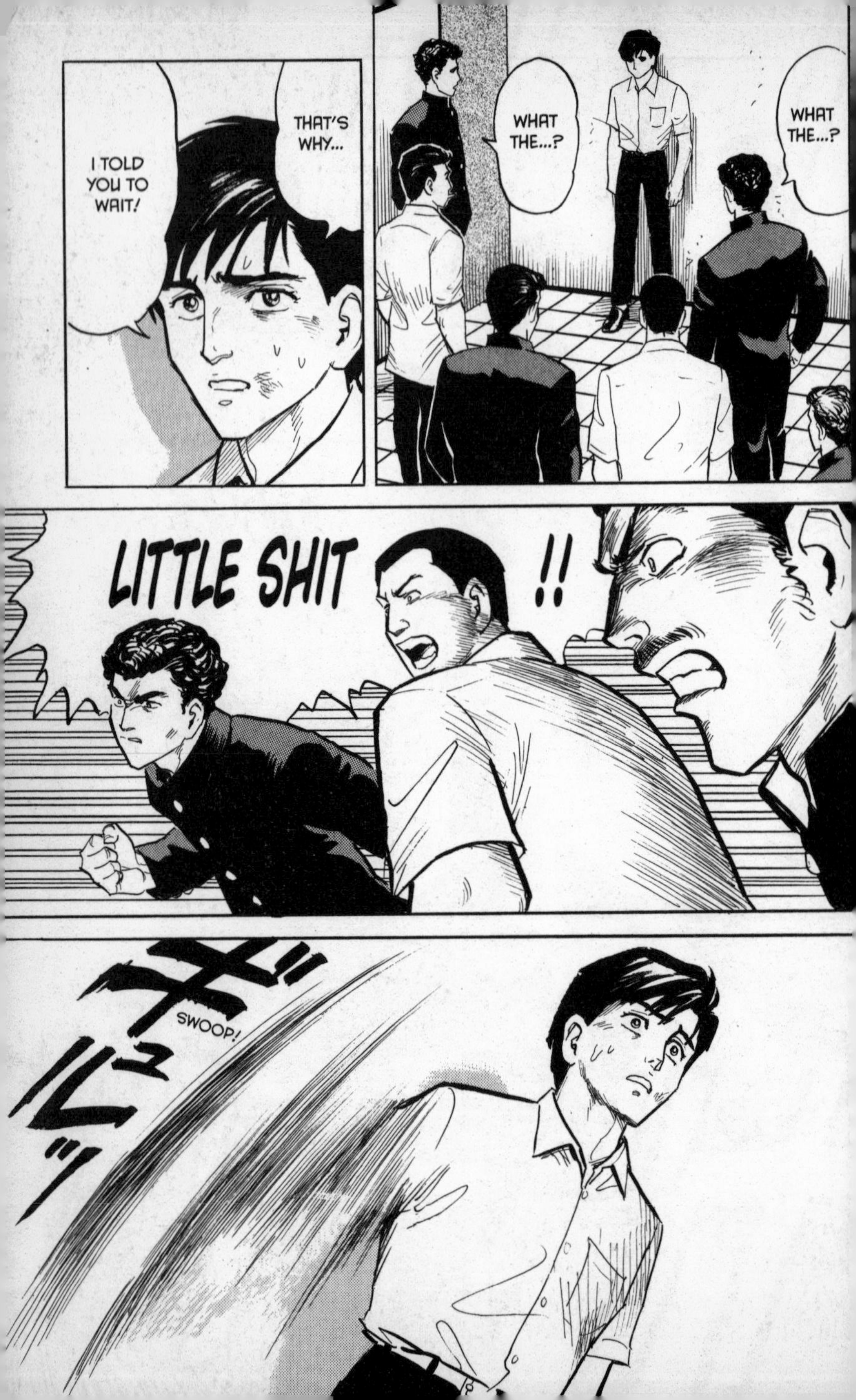
WHAT THE...?
WHAT THE...?
THAT'S WHY...
I TOLD YOU TO WAIT!
LITTLE SHIT !!
ギュルッ
SWOOP!

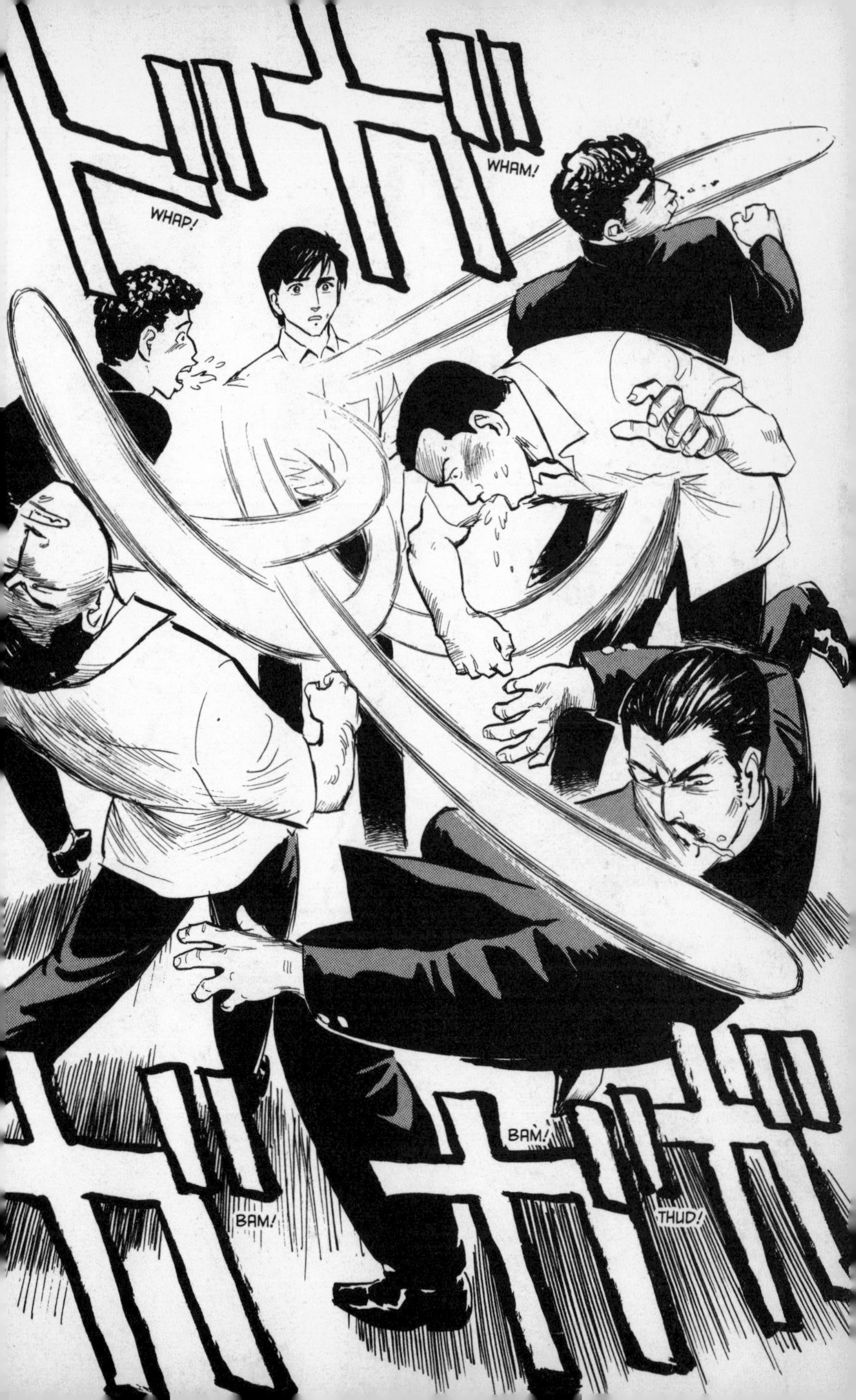
WHAM!
WHAP!
BAM!
THUD!
BAM!

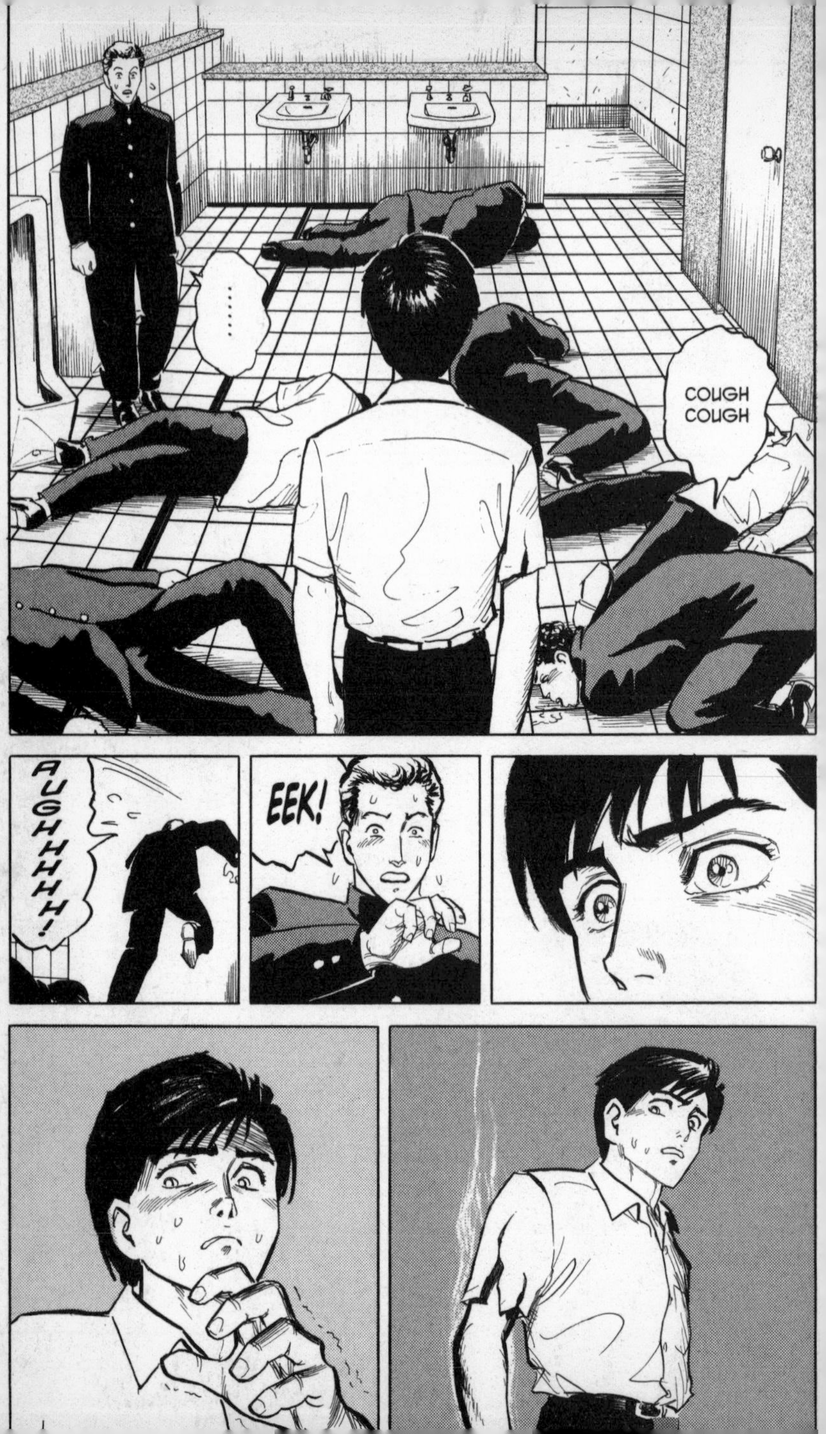
COUGH COUGH
......
EEK!
AUGHHHHHH!

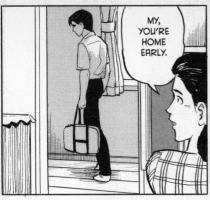

MY, YOU'RE HOME EARLY.

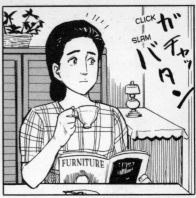

CLICK
SLAM
ガチャッ
バタン

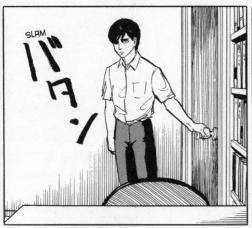

SLAM
バタン

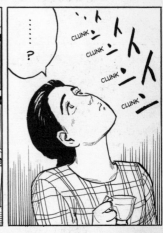

......
?

CLINK
CLINK
CLINK
CLINK

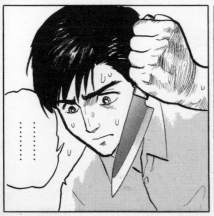

......

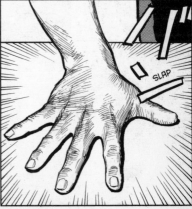

SLAP
バロ

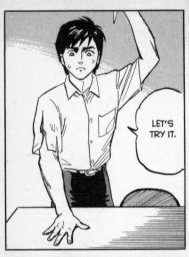

LET'S TRY IT.

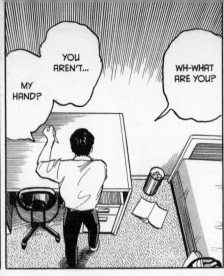

MY HAND?

YOU AREN'T...

WH-WHAT ARE YOU?

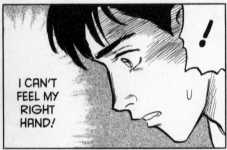

I CAN'T FEEL MY RIGHT HAND!

!

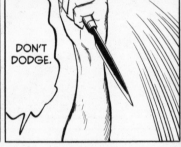

DON'T DODGE.

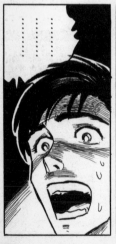

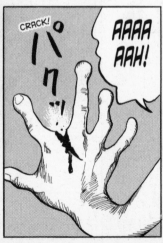

CRACK!

パン

AAAA AAH!

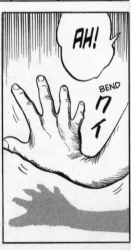

AH!

BEND

クイ

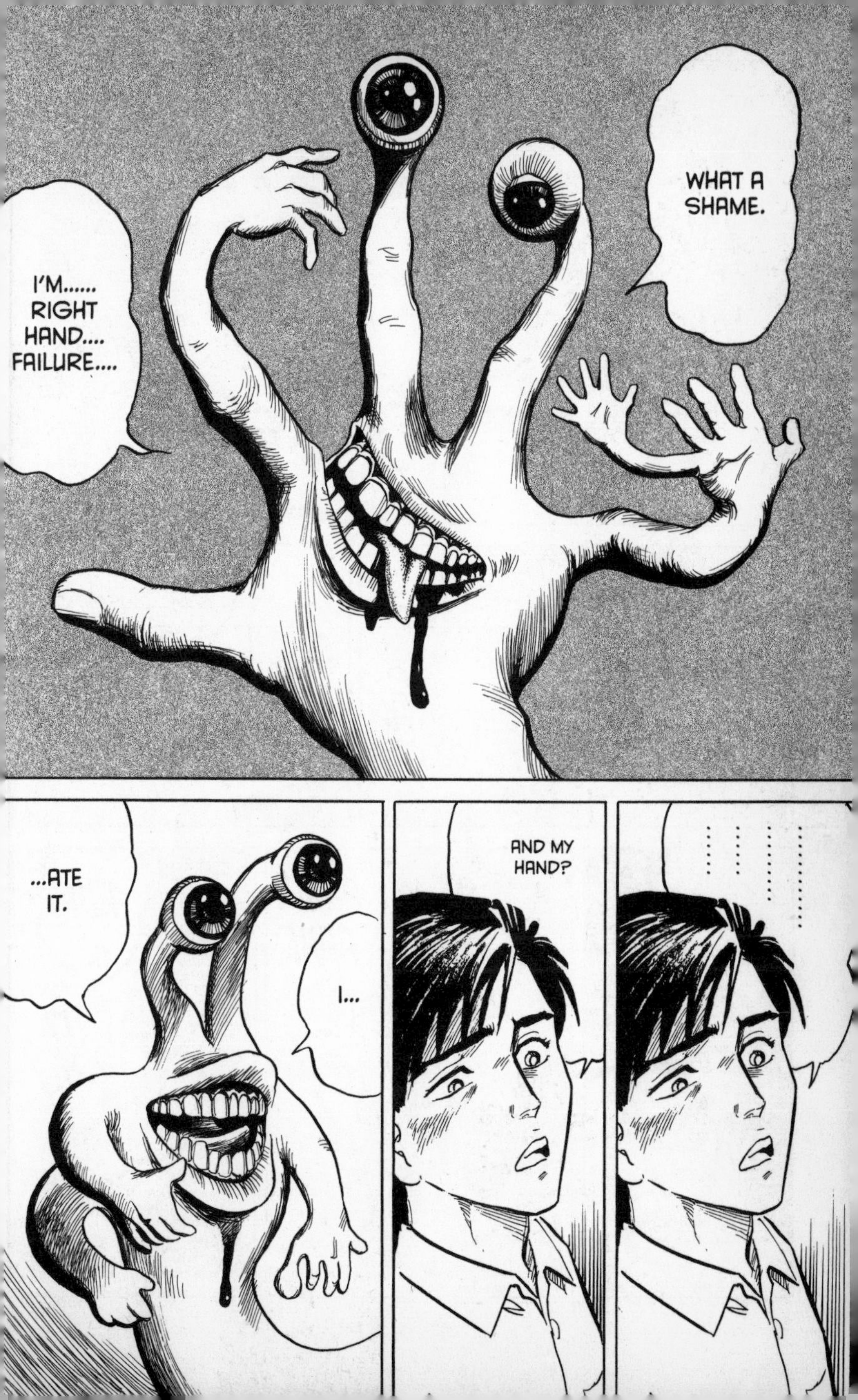

WHAT A SHAME.
I'M...... RIGHT HAND.... FAILURE....
......
AND MY HAND?
I...
...ATE IT.

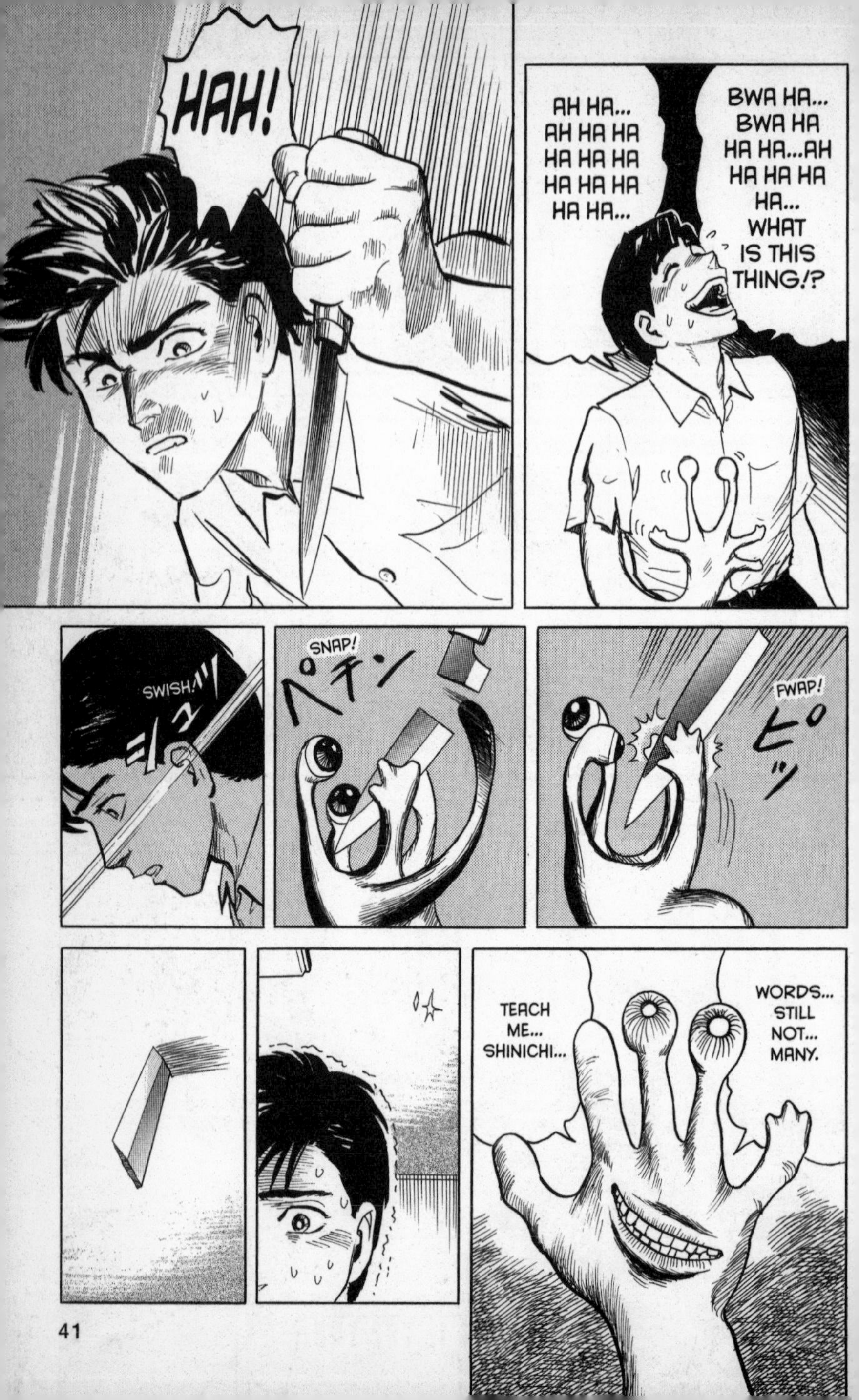

BWA HA... BWA HA HA HA...AH HA HA HA HA... WHAT IS THIS THING!?
AH HA... AH HA HA HA HA HA HA HA HA HA HA...
HAH!
FWAP!
ピッ
SNAP!
パチン
SWISH!
WORDS... STILL NOT... MANY.
TEACH ME... SHINICHI...

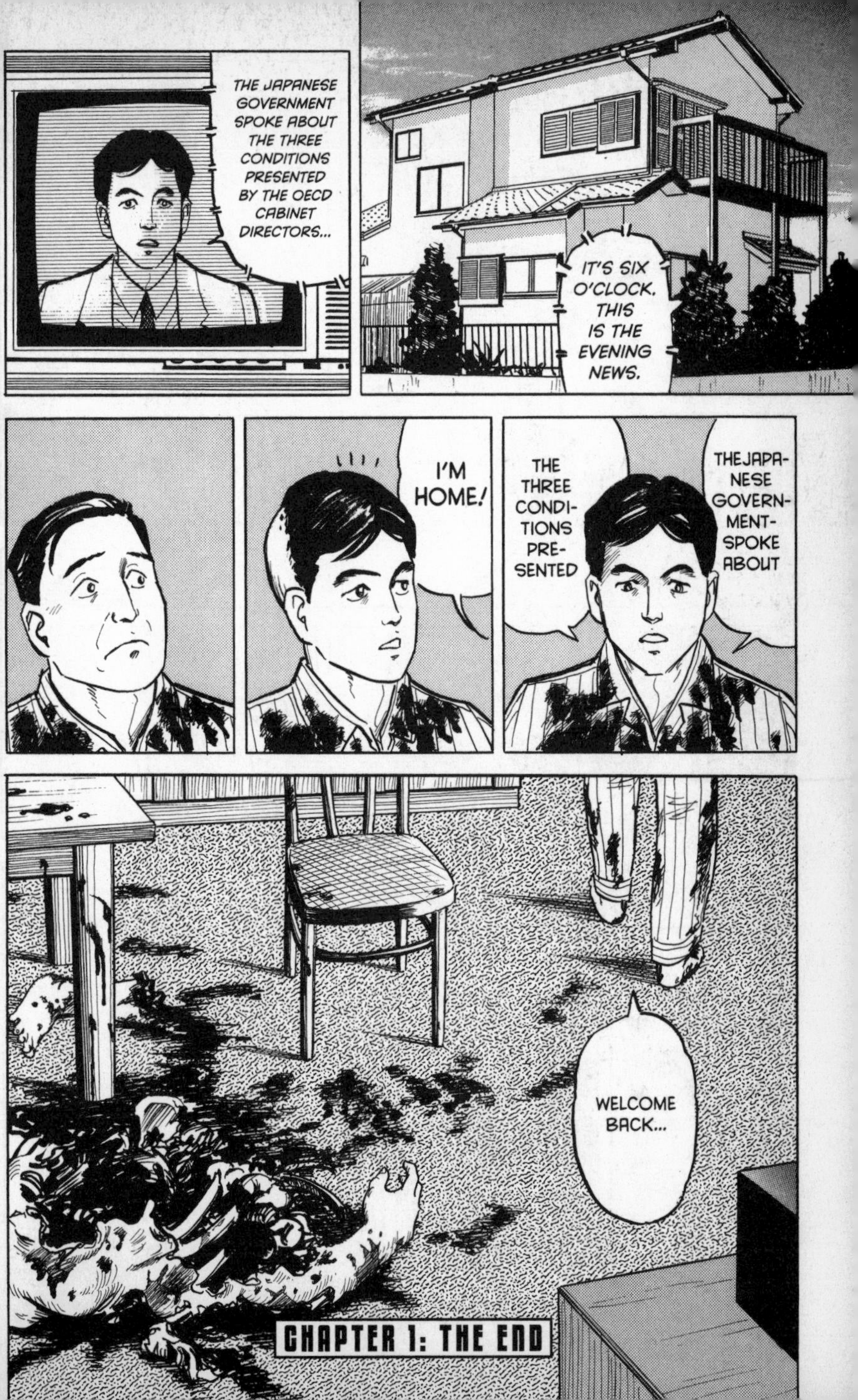
IT'S SIX O'CLOCK. THIS IS THE EVENING NEWS.
THE JAPANESE GOVERNMENT SPOKE ABOUT THE THREE CONDITIONS PRESENTED BY THE OECD CABINET DIRECTORS...
THEJAPANESE GOVERNMENT-SPOKE ABOUT
THE THREE CONDITIONS PRESENTED
I'M HOME!
WELCOME BACK...
CHAPTER 1: THE END

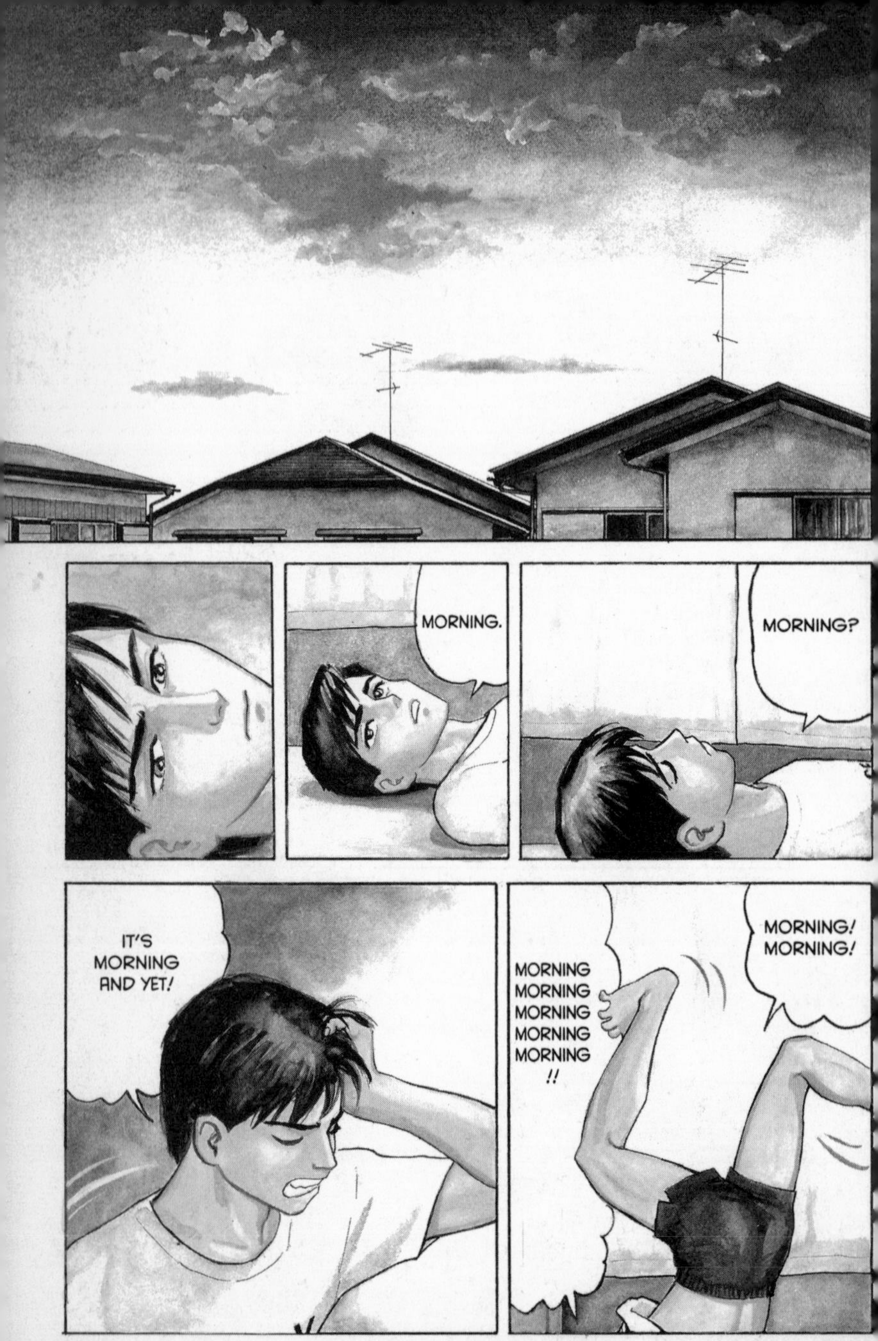
MORNING?
MORNING.
MORNING! MORNING!
MORNING MORNING MORNING MORNING MORNING !!
IT'S MORNING AND YET!

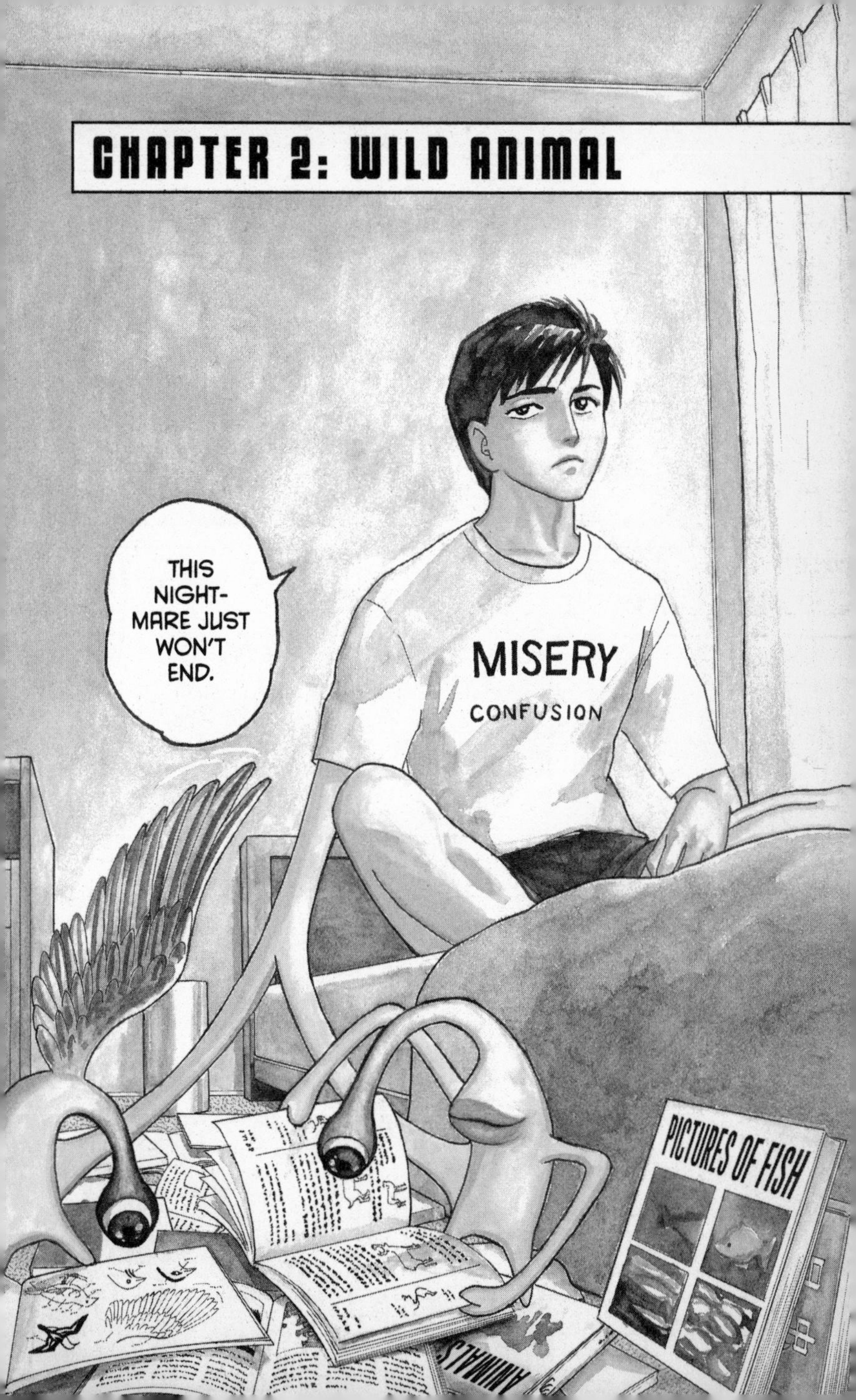
CHAPTER 2: WILD ANIMAL
THIS NIGHT-MARE JUST WON'T END.
MISERY
CONFUSION
PICTURES OF FISH
ANIMALS

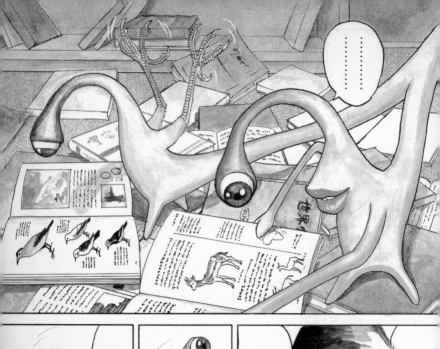

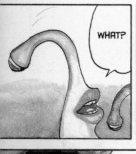

WHAT?

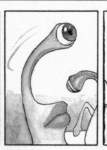

HEY!

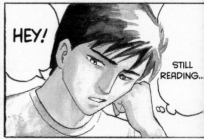

STILL READING...

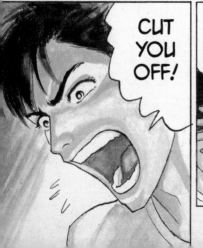

CUT YOU OFF!

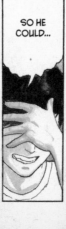

SO HE COULD...

I WAS THINKING ABOUT GOING TO THE DOCTOR.

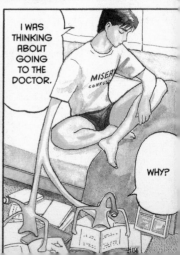

MISER
CONFUS

WHY?

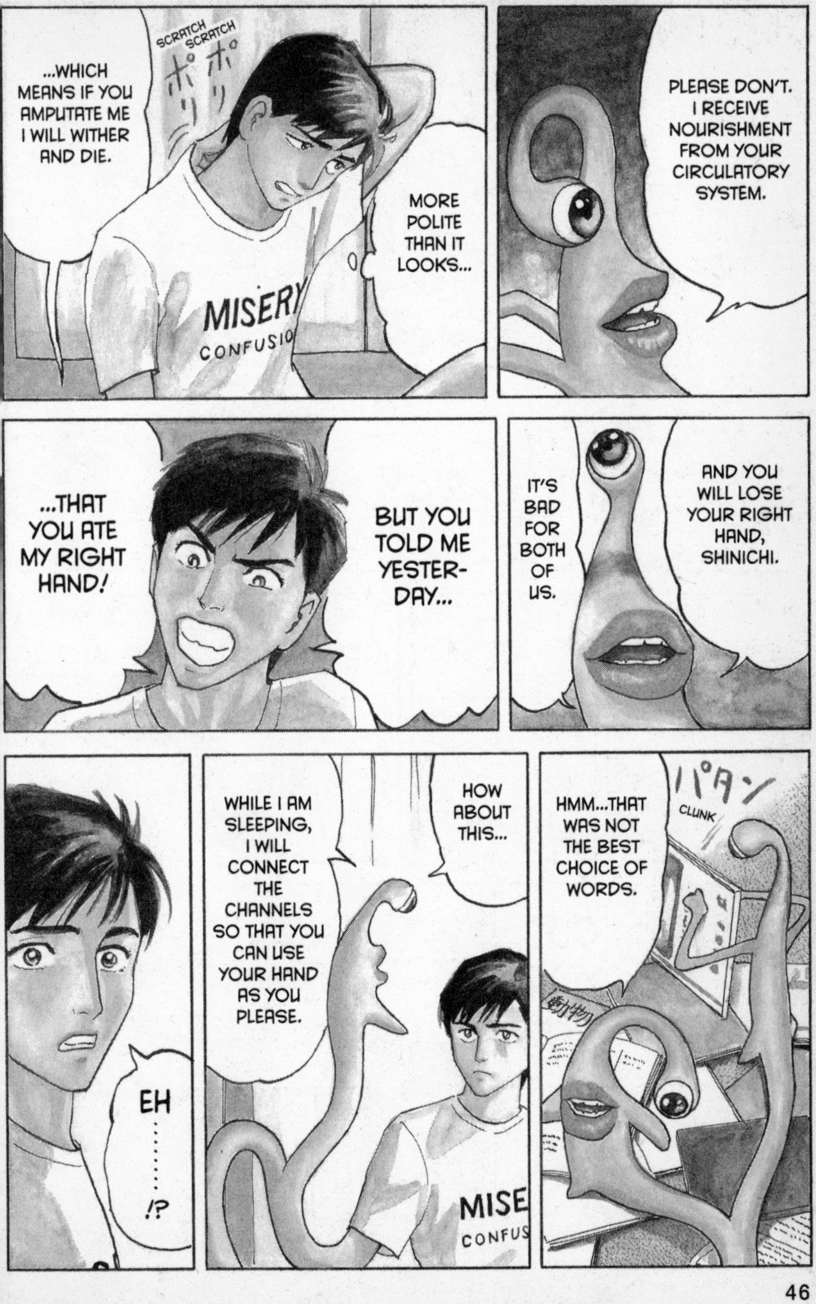
PLEASE DON'T. I RECEIVE NOURISHMENT FROM YOUR CIRCULATORY SYSTEM.
...WHICH MEANS IF YOU AMPUTATE ME I WILL WITHER AND DIE.
ポリポリ
SCRATCH SCRATCH
MORE POLITE THAN IT LOOKS...
AND YOU WILL LOSE YOUR RIGHT HAND, SHINICHI.
IT'S BAD FOR BOTH OF US.
BUT YOU TOLD ME YESTER-DAY...
...THAT YOU ATE MY RIGHT HAND!
パタン
CLUNK
HMM...THAT WAS NOT THE BEST CHOICE OF WORDS.
HOW ABOUT THIS...
WHILE I AM SLEEPING, I WILL CONNECT THE CHANNELS SO THAT YOU CAN USE YOUR HAND AS YOU PLEASE.
EH......!?

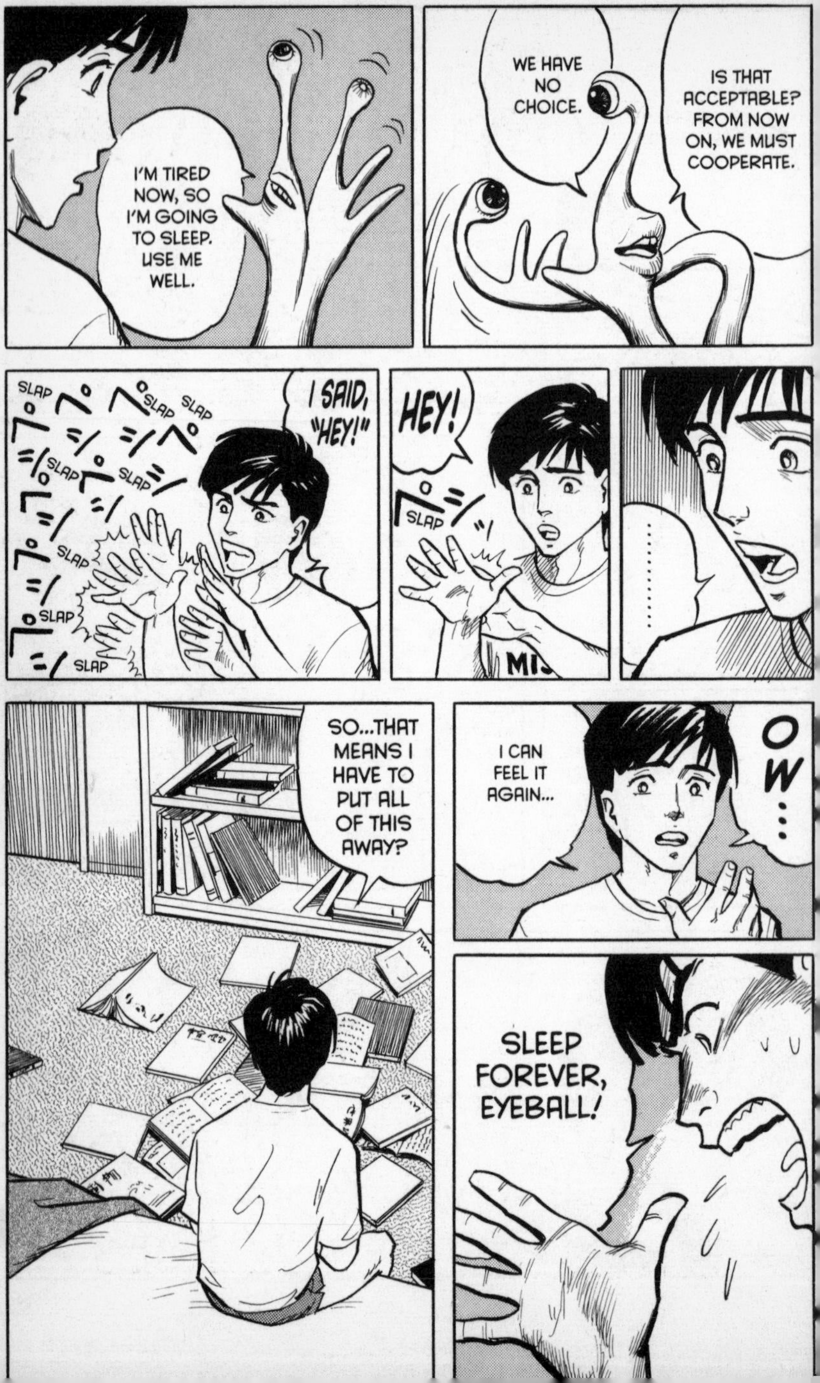
IS THAT ACCEPTABLE? FROM NOW ON, WE MUST COOPERATE.
WE HAVE NO CHOICE.
I'M TIRED NOW, SO I'M GOING TO SLEEP. USE ME WELL.
……
HEY!
SLAP
I SAID, "HEY!"
SLAP SLAP SLAP SLAP SLAP SLAP SLAP SLAP SLAP
OW...
I CAN FEEL IT AGAIN...
SLEEP FOREVER, EYEBALL!
SO...THAT MEANS I HAVE TO PUT ALL OF THIS AWAY?

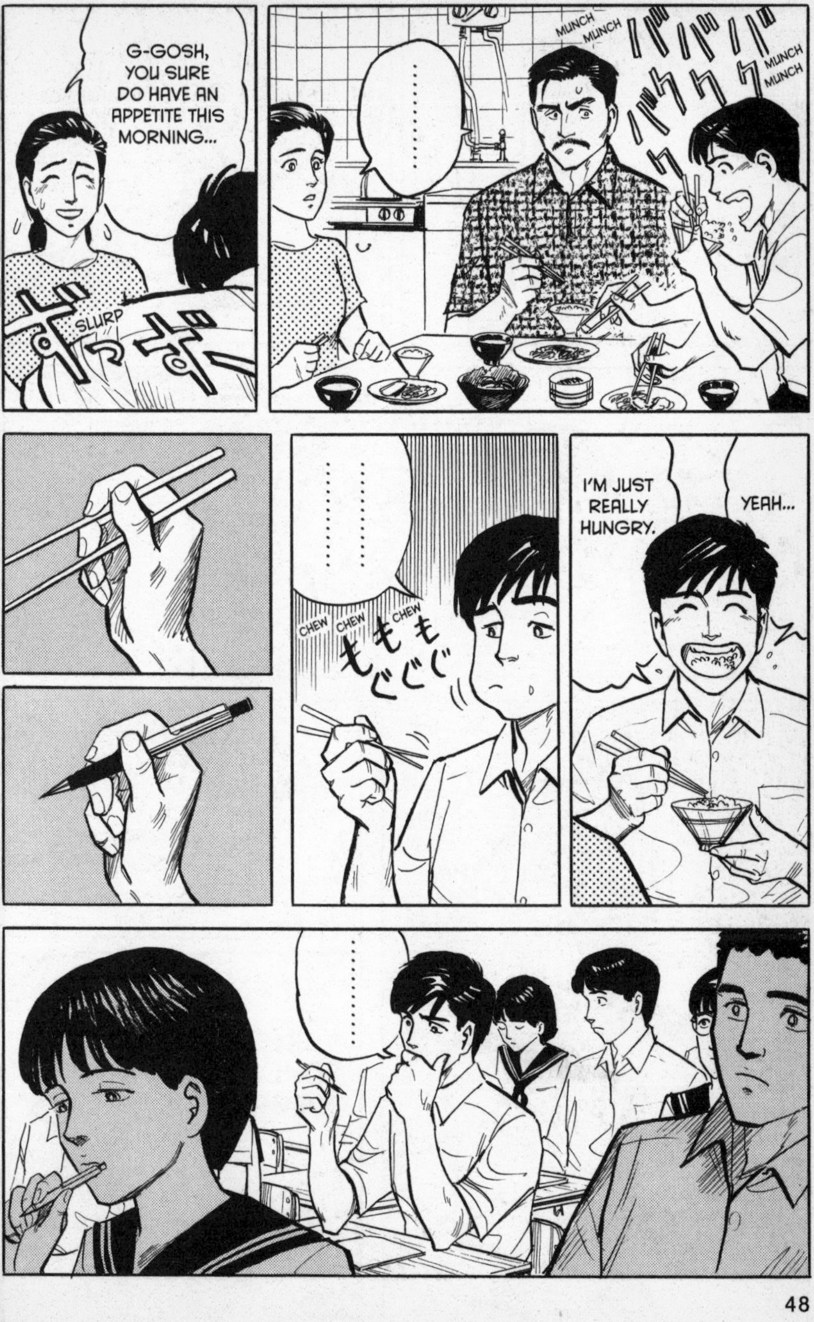
MUNCH MUNCH
MUNCH MUNCH
……
G-GOSH, YOU SURE DO HAVE AN APPETITE THIS MORNING...
SLURP
YEAH...
I'M JUST REALLY HUNGRY.
……
CHEW CHEW CHEW
……

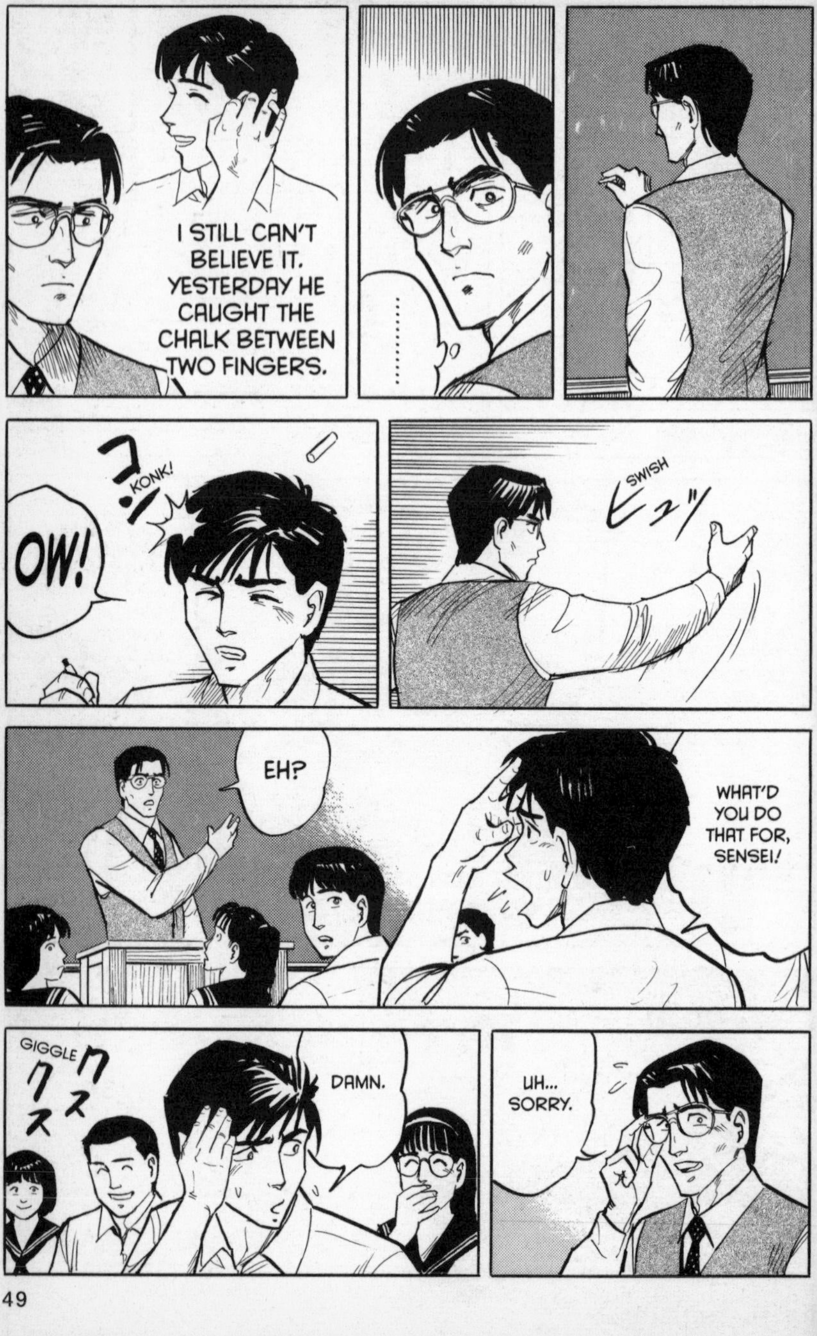
......
I STILL CAN'T BELIEVE IT. YESTERDAY HE CAUGHT THE CHALK BETWEEN TWO FINGERS.
SWISH
ヒュッ
KONK!
コツ
OW!
WHAT'D YOU DO THAT FOR, SENSEI!
EH?
UH... SORRY.
DAMN.
GIGGLE
クスクス

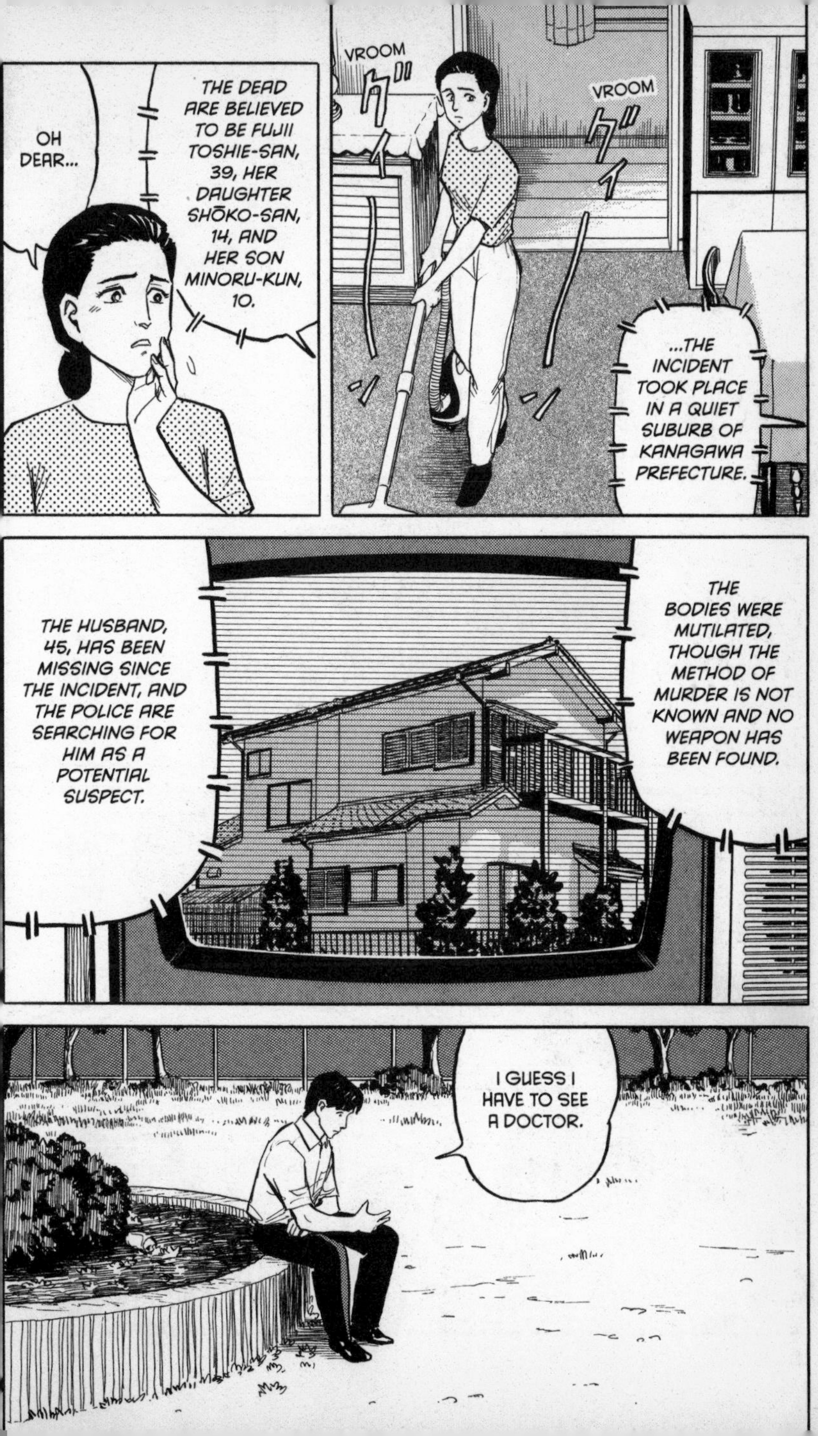
VROOM
VROOM
...THE INCIDENT TOOK PLACE IN A QUIET SUBURB OF KANAGAWA PREFECTURE.
THE DEAD ARE BELIEVED TO BE FUJII TOSHIE-SAN, 39, HER DAUGHTER SHŌKO-SAN, 14, AND HER SON MINORU-KUN, 10.
OH DEAR...
THE BODIES WERE MUTILATED, THOUGH THE METHOD OF MURDER IS NOT KNOWN AND NO WEAPON HAS BEEN FOUND.
THE HUSBAND, 45, HAS BEEN MISSING SINCE THE INCIDENT, AND THE POLICE ARE SEARCHING FOR HIM AS A POTENTIAL SUSPECT.
I GUESS I HAVE TO SEE A DOCTOR.

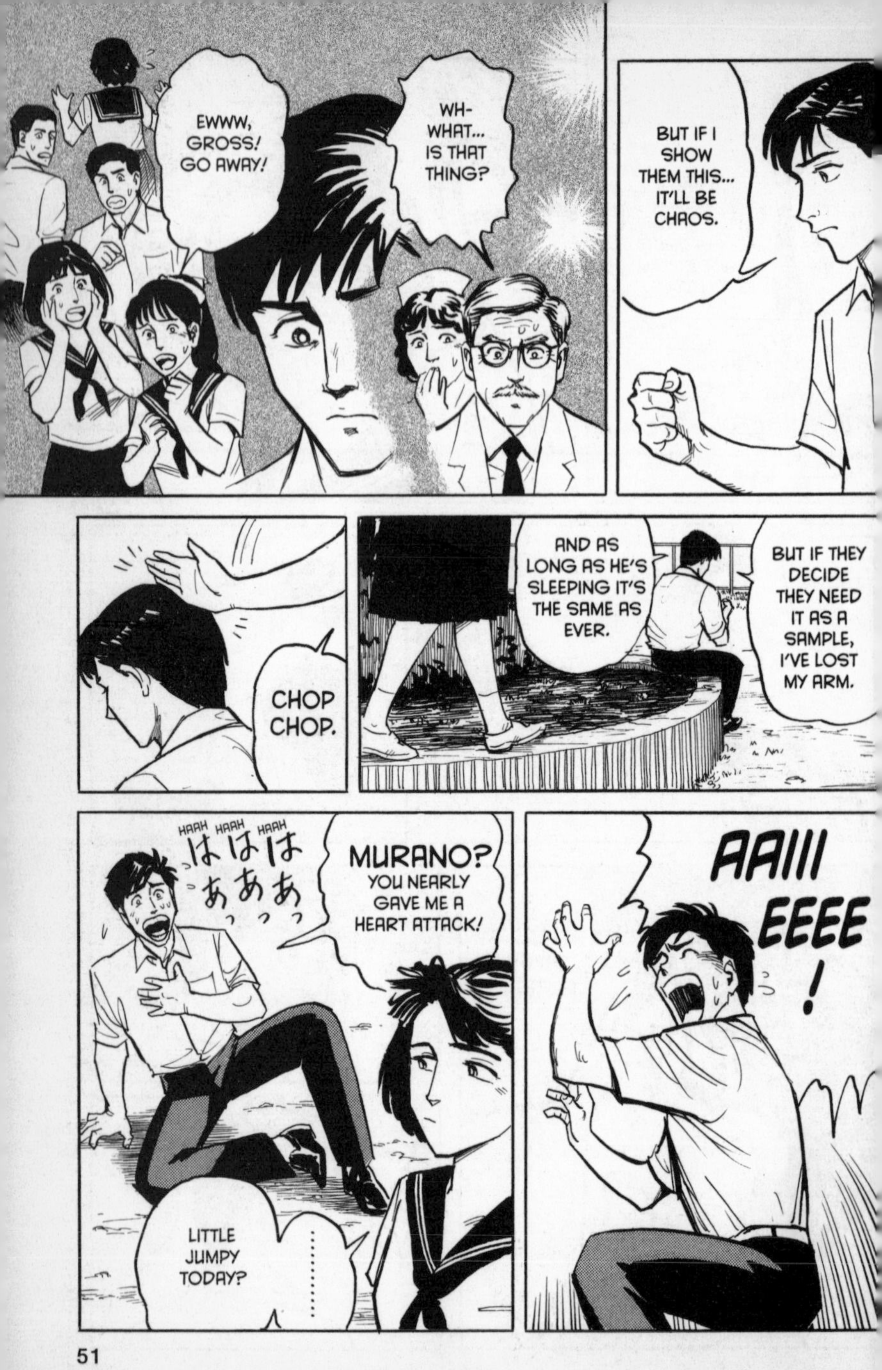
BUT IF I SHOW THEM THIS... IT'LL BE CHAOS.
WH- WHAT... IS THAT THING?
EWWW, GROSS! GO AWAY!
BUT IF THEY DECIDE THEY NEED IT AS A SAMPLE, I'VE LOST MY ARM.
AND AS LONG AS HE'S SLEEPING IT'S THE SAME AS EVER.
CHOP CHOP.
AAIII EEEE!
MURANO? YOU NEARLY GAVE ME A HEART ATTACK!
HAAH HAAH HAAH
はははあっあっあっ
......
LITTLE JUMPY TODAY?

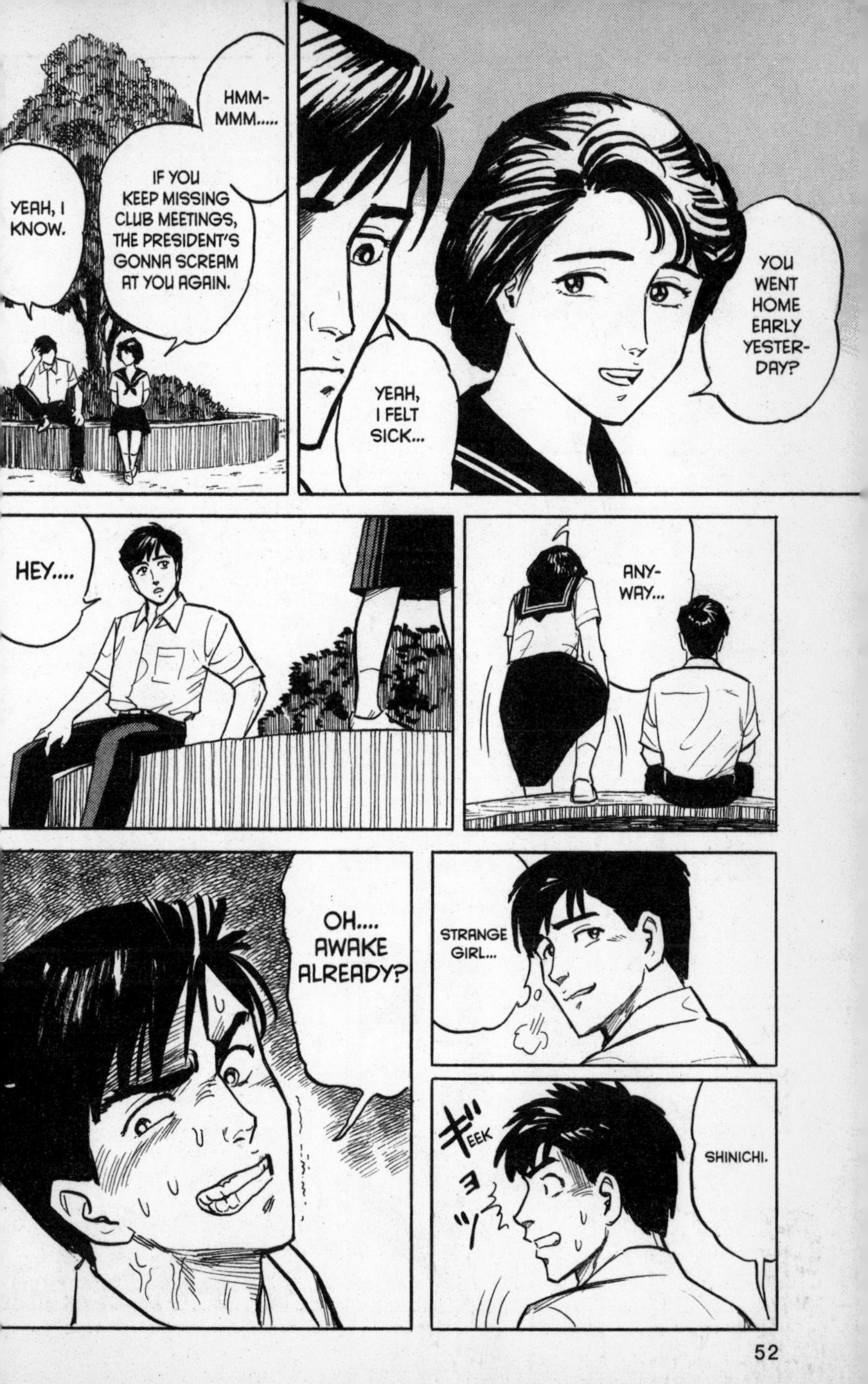
YOU WENT HOME EARLY YESTER-DAY?
YEAH, I FELT SICK...
HMM-MMM.....
IF YOU KEEP MISSING CLUB MEETINGS, THE PRESIDENT'S GONNA SCREAM AT YOU AGAIN.
YEAH, I KNOW.
ANY-WAY...
HEY....
STRANGE GIRL...
SHINICHI.
ギEEK
ヨッ
OH.... AWAKE ALREADY?

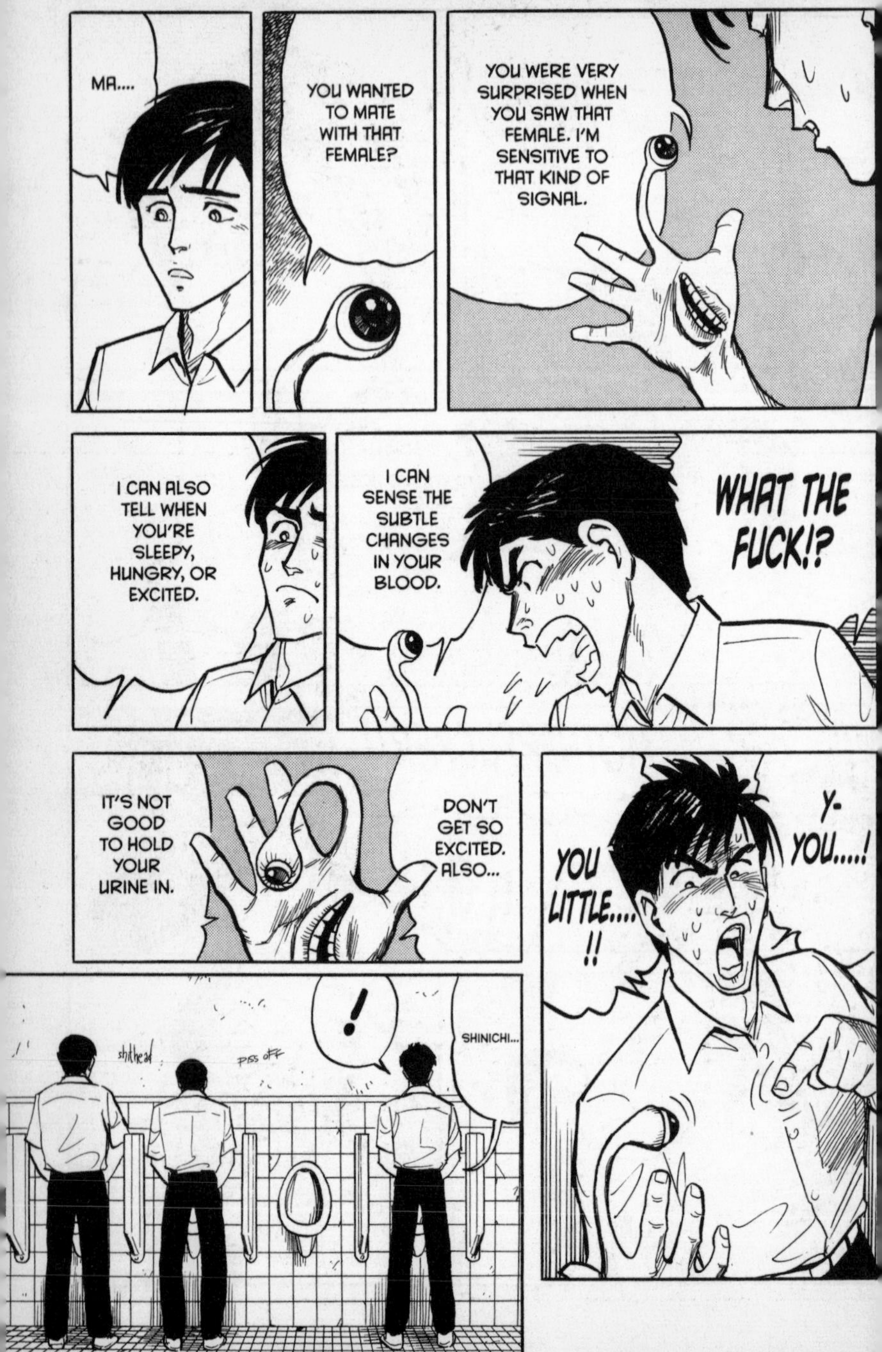
YOU WERE VERY SURPRISED WHEN YOU SAW THAT FEMALE. I'M SENSITIVE TO THAT KIND OF SIGNAL.
YOU WANTED TO MATE WITH THAT FEMALE?
MA....
WHAT THE FUCK!?
I CAN SENSE THE SUBTLE CHANGES IN YOUR BLOOD.
I CAN ALSO TELL WHEN YOU'RE SLEEPY, HUNGRY, OR EXCITED.
Y-YOU....!
YOU LITTLE....!!
DON'T GET SO EXCITED. ALSO...
IT'S NOT GOOD TO HOLD YOUR URINE IN.
SHINICHI...
!
piss off
shithead

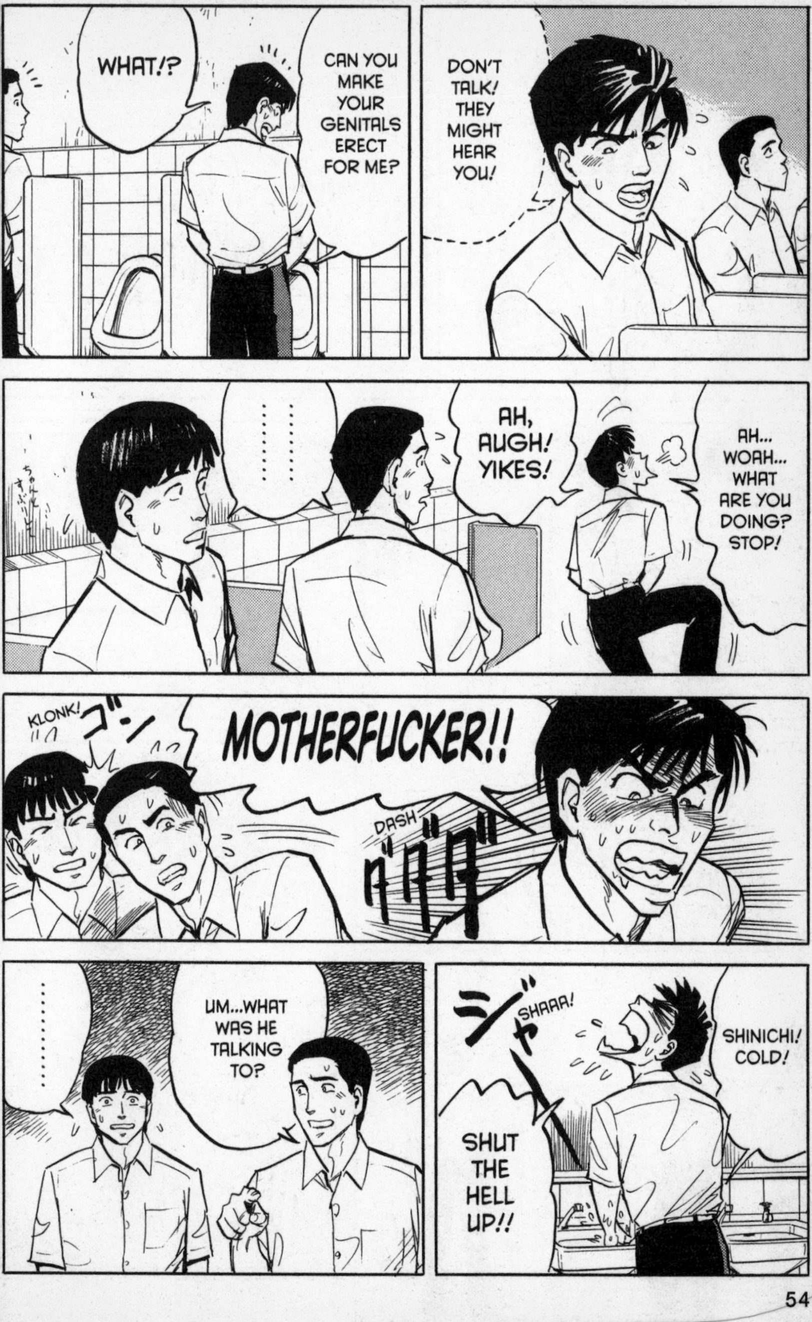
DON'T TALK! THEY MIGHT HEAR YOU!
CAN YOU MAKE YOUR GENITALS ERECT FOR ME?
WHAT!?
AH... WOAH... WHAT ARE YOU DOING? STOP!
AH, AUGH! YIKES!
......
MOTHERFUCKER!!
DASH
KLONK!
SHINICHI! COLD!
SHAAA!
SHUT THE HELL UP!!
UM...WHAT WAS HE TALKING TO?
......

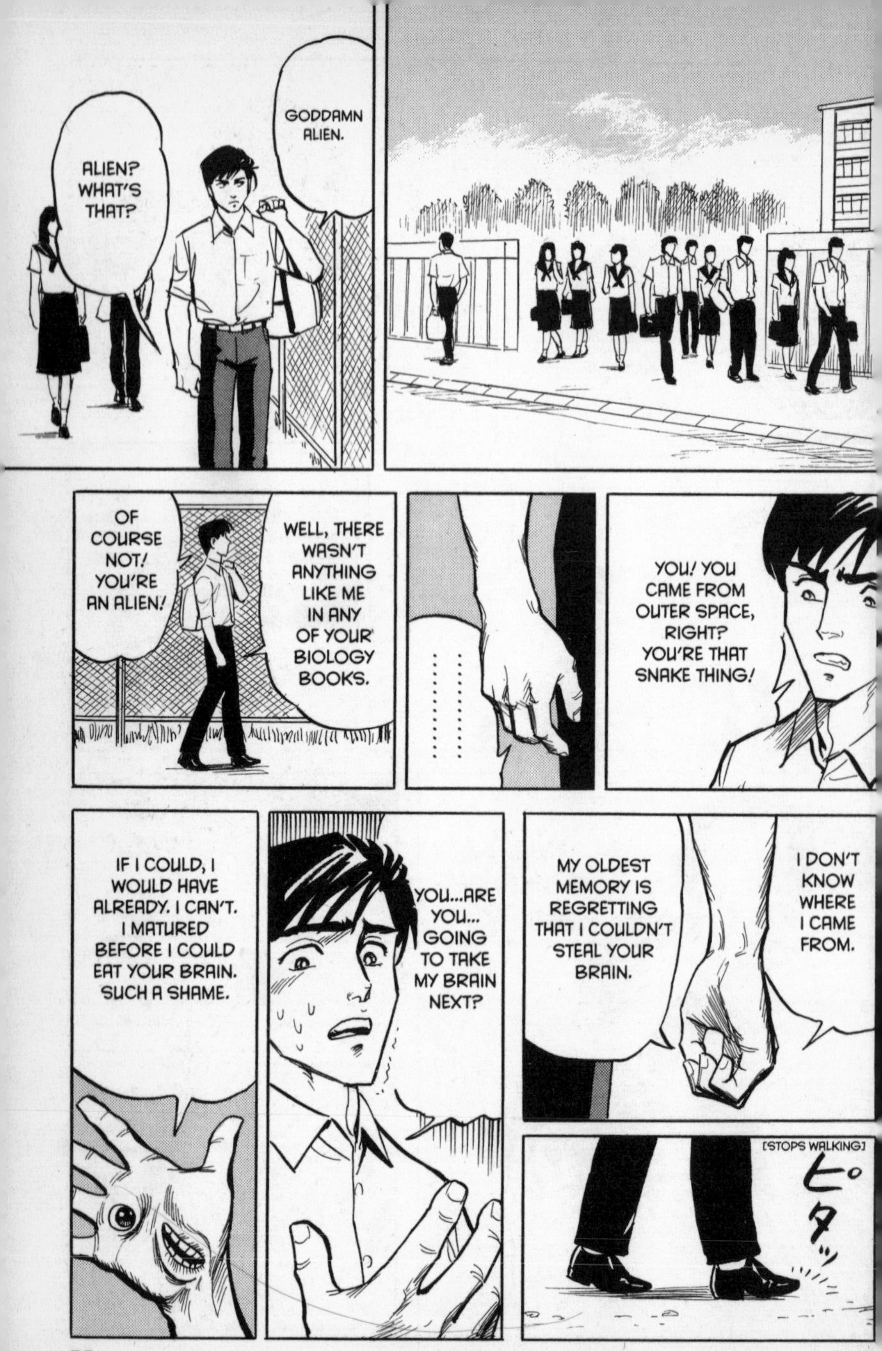
GODDAMN ALIEN.
ALIEN? WHAT'S THAT?
YOU! YOU CAME FROM OUTER SPACE, RIGHT? YOU'RE THAT SNAKE THING!
WELL, THERE WASN'T ANYTHING LIKE ME IN ANY OF YOUR BIOLOGY BOOKS.
OF COURSE NOT! YOU'RE AN ALIEN!
I DON'T KNOW WHERE I CAME FROM.
MY OLDEST MEMORY IS REGRETTING THAT I COULDN'T STEAL YOUR BRAIN.
[STOPS WALKING]
ピタッ
YOU...ARE YOU... GOING TO TAKE MY BRAIN NEXT?
IF I COULD, I WOULD HAVE ALREADY. I CAN'T. I MATURED BEFORE I COULD EAT YOUR BRAIN. SUCH A SHAME.

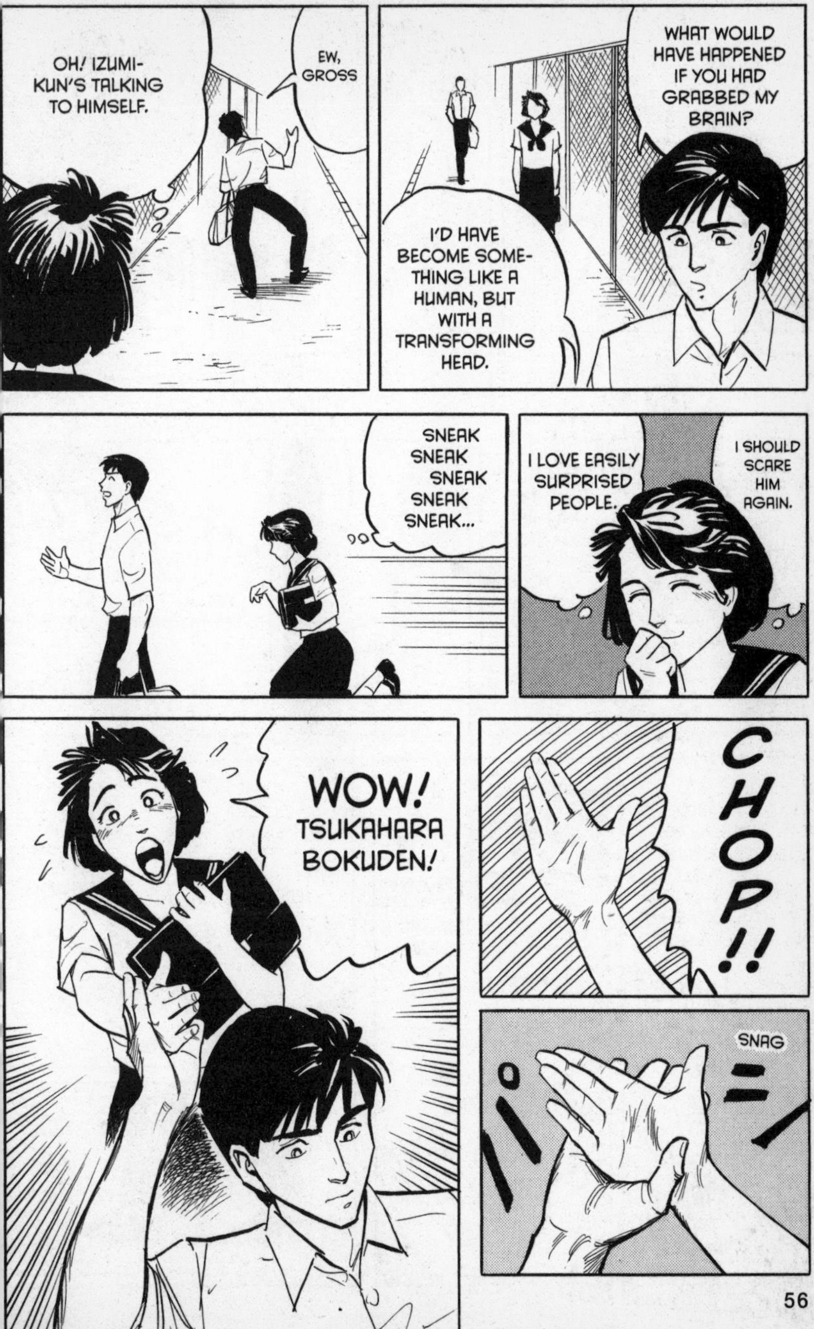
WHAT WOULD HAVE HAPPENED IF YOU HAD GRABBED MY BRAIN?
I'D HAVE BECOME SOME-THING LIKE A HUMAN, BUT WITH A TRANSFORMING HEAD.
EW, GROSS
OH! IZUMI-KUN'S TALKING TO HIMSELF.
I SHOULD SCARE HIM AGAIN.
I LOVE EASILY SURPRISED PEOPLE.
SNEAK SNEAK SNEAK SNEAK SNEAK...
CHOP!!
SNAG
WOW! TSUKAHARA BOKUDEN!

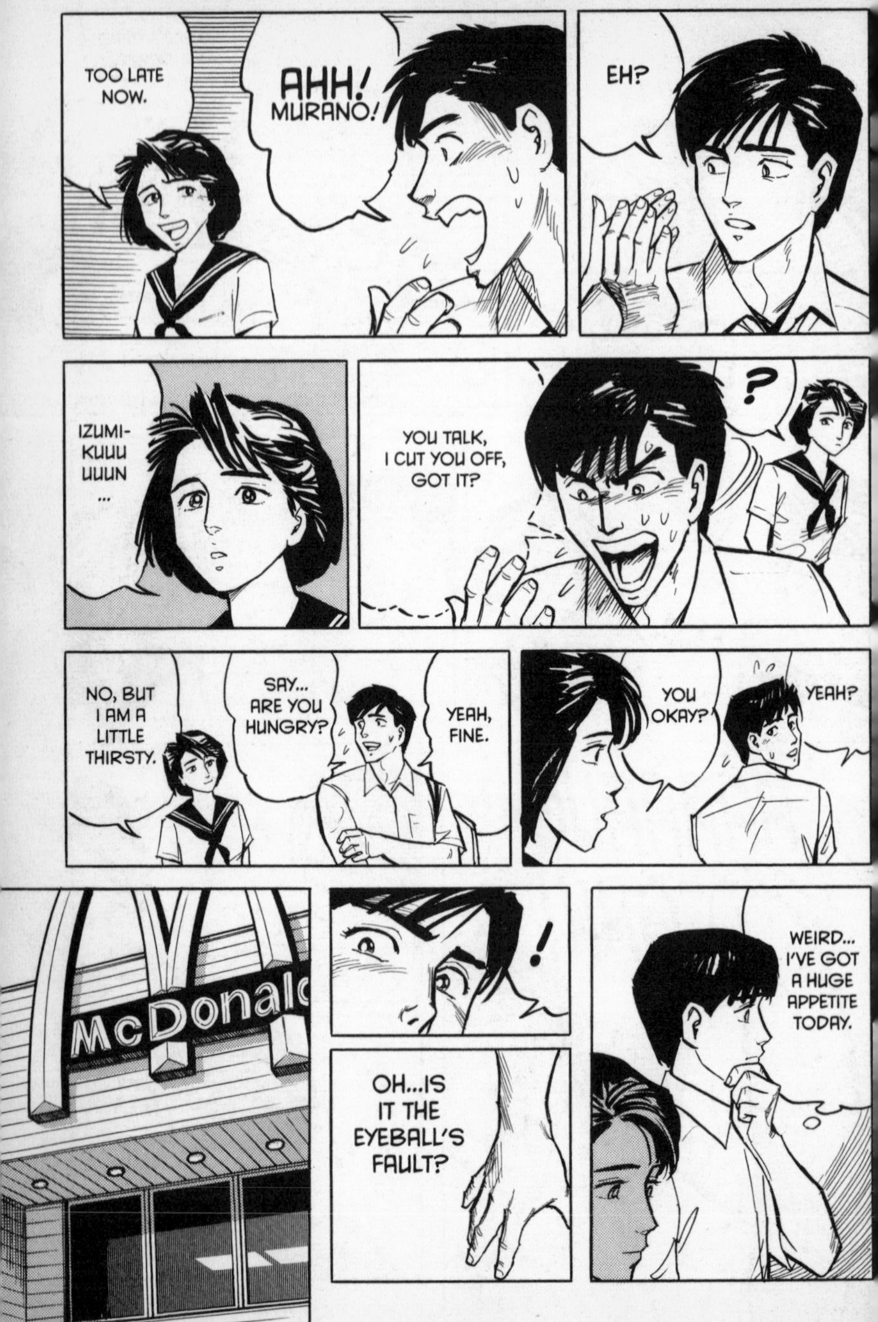
EH?
AHH! MURANO!
TOO LATE NOW.
?
YOU TALK, I CUT YOU OFF, GOT IT?
IZUMI-KUUUUUUN ...
YEAH?
YOU OKAY?
YEAH, FINE.
SAY... ARE YOU HUNGRY?
NO, BUT I AM A LITTLE THIRSTY.
WEIRD... I'VE GOT A HUGE APPETITE TODAY.
!
OH...IS IT THE EYEBALL'S FAULT?
McDonal

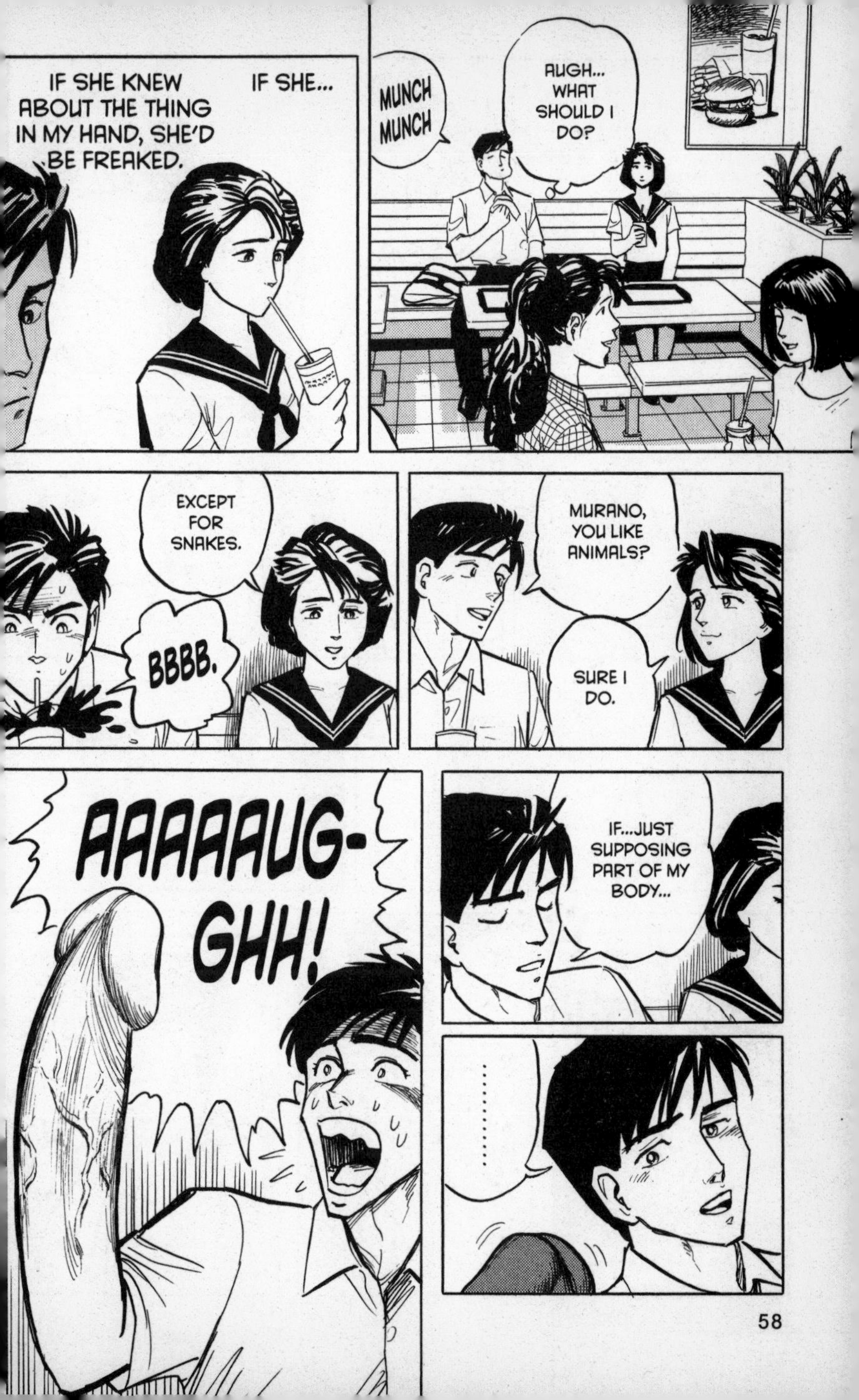
AUGH... WHAT SHOULD I DO?
MUNCH MUNCH
IF SHE...
IF SHE KNEW ABOUT THE THING IN MY HAND, SHE'D BE FREAKED.
MURANO, YOU LIKE ANIMALS?
SURE I DO.
EXCEPT FOR SNAKES.
BBBB.
IF...JUST SUPPOSING PART OF MY BODY...
......
AAAAAAUG-GHH!

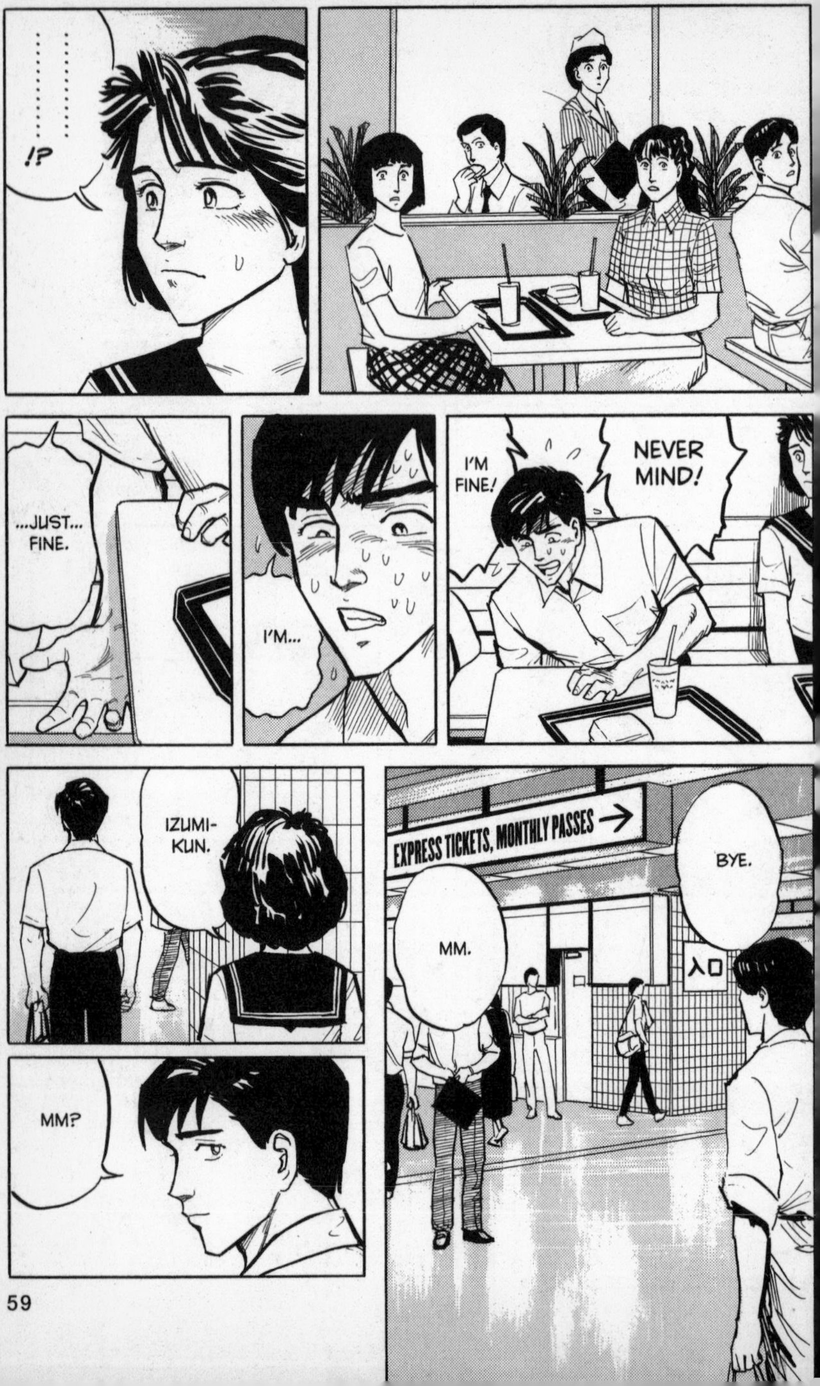
......
......!?
NEVER MIND!
I'M FINE!
I'M...
...JUST... FINE.
EXPRESS TICKETS, MONTHLY PASSES →
BYE.
MM.
入口
IZUMI-KUN.
MM?

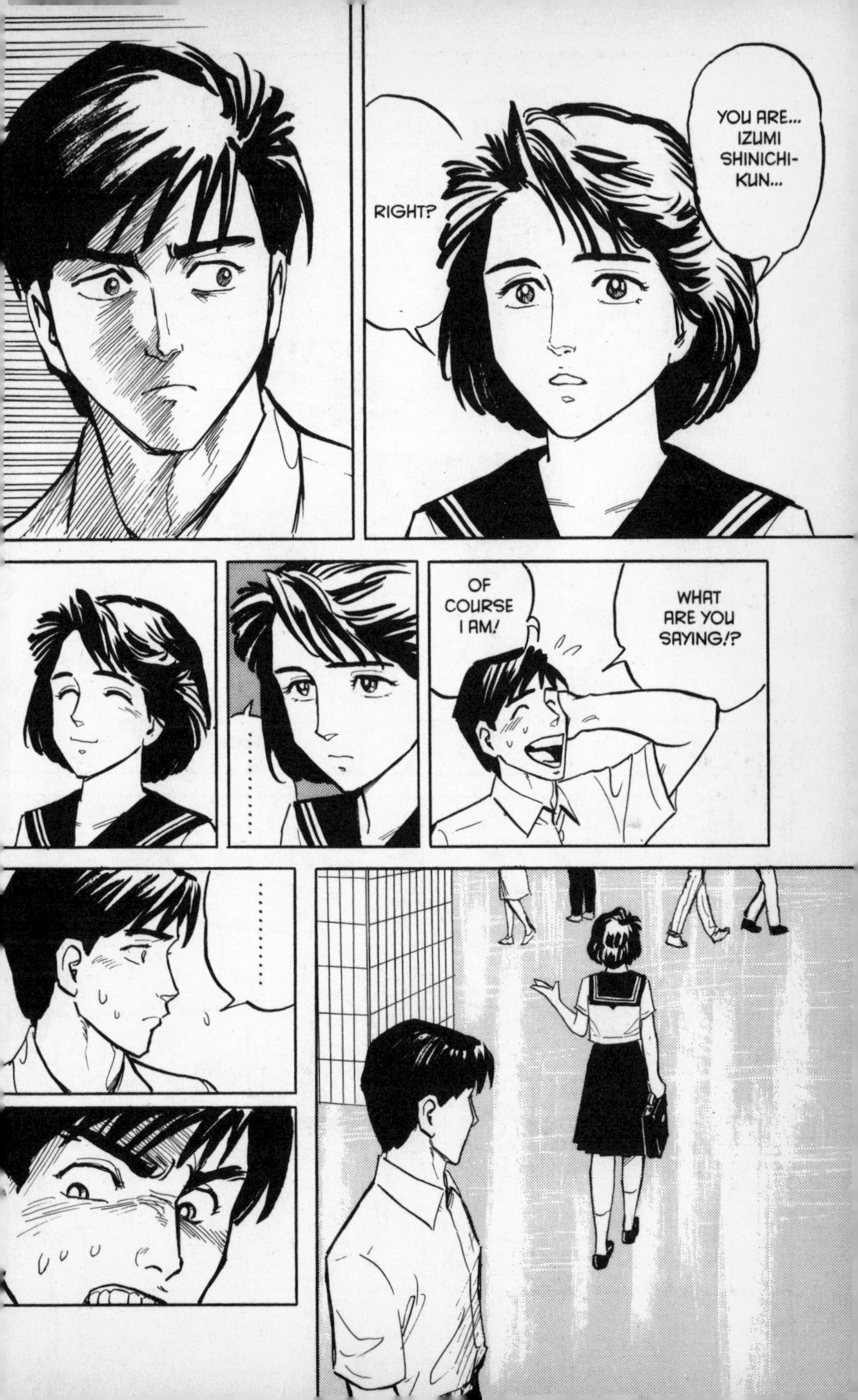
YOU ARE... IZUMI SHINICHI-KUN...
RIGHT?
WHAT ARE YOU SAYING!?
OF COURSE I AM!
......
......

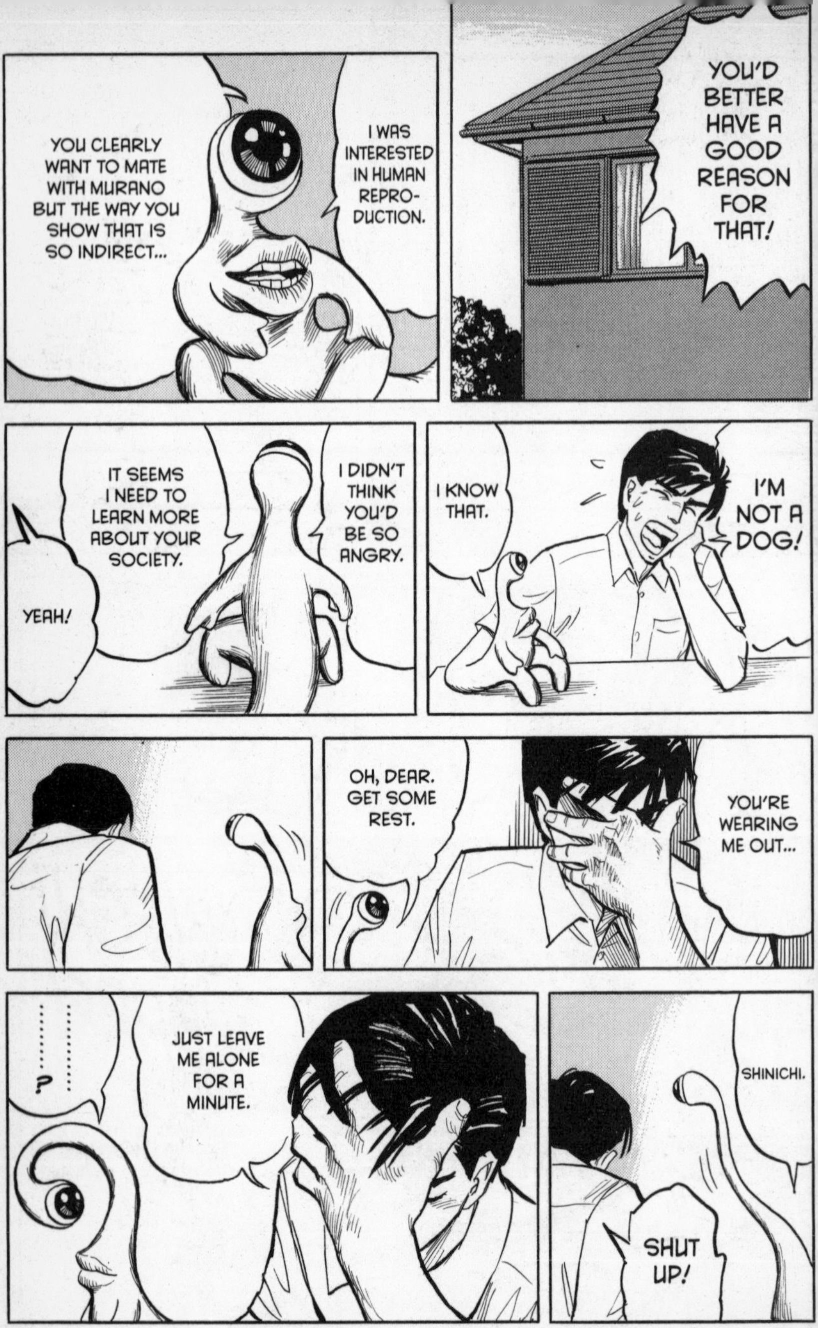
YOU'D BETTER HAVE A GOOD REASON FOR THAT!
I WAS INTERESTED IN HUMAN REPRODUCTION.
YOU CLEARLY WANT TO MATE WITH MURANO BUT THE WAY YOU SHOW THAT IS SO INDIRECT...
I'M NOT A DOG!
I KNOW THAT.
I DIDN'T THINK YOU'D BE SO ANGRY.
IT SEEMS I NEED TO LEARN MORE ABOUT YOUR SOCIETY.
YEAH!
YOU'RE WEARING ME OUT...
OH, DEAR. GET SOME REST.
SHINICHI.
SHUT UP!
JUST LEAVE ME ALONE FOR A MINUTE.
....?

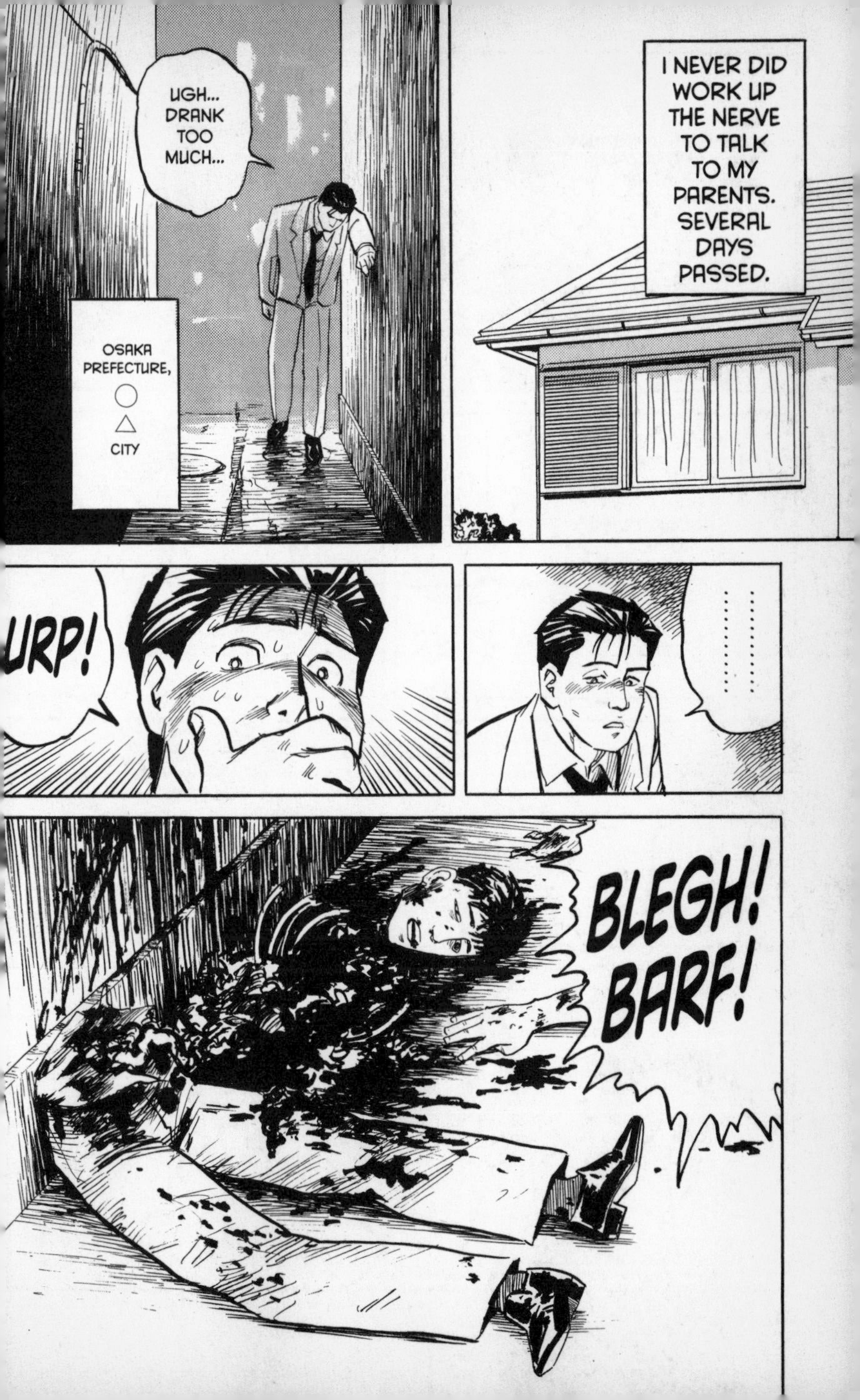
I NEVER DID WORK UP THE NERVE TO TALK TO MY PARENTS. SEVERAL DAYS PASSED.
UGH... DRANK TOO MUCH...
OSAKA PREFECTURE, ○ △ CITY
......
URP!
BLEGH! BARF!

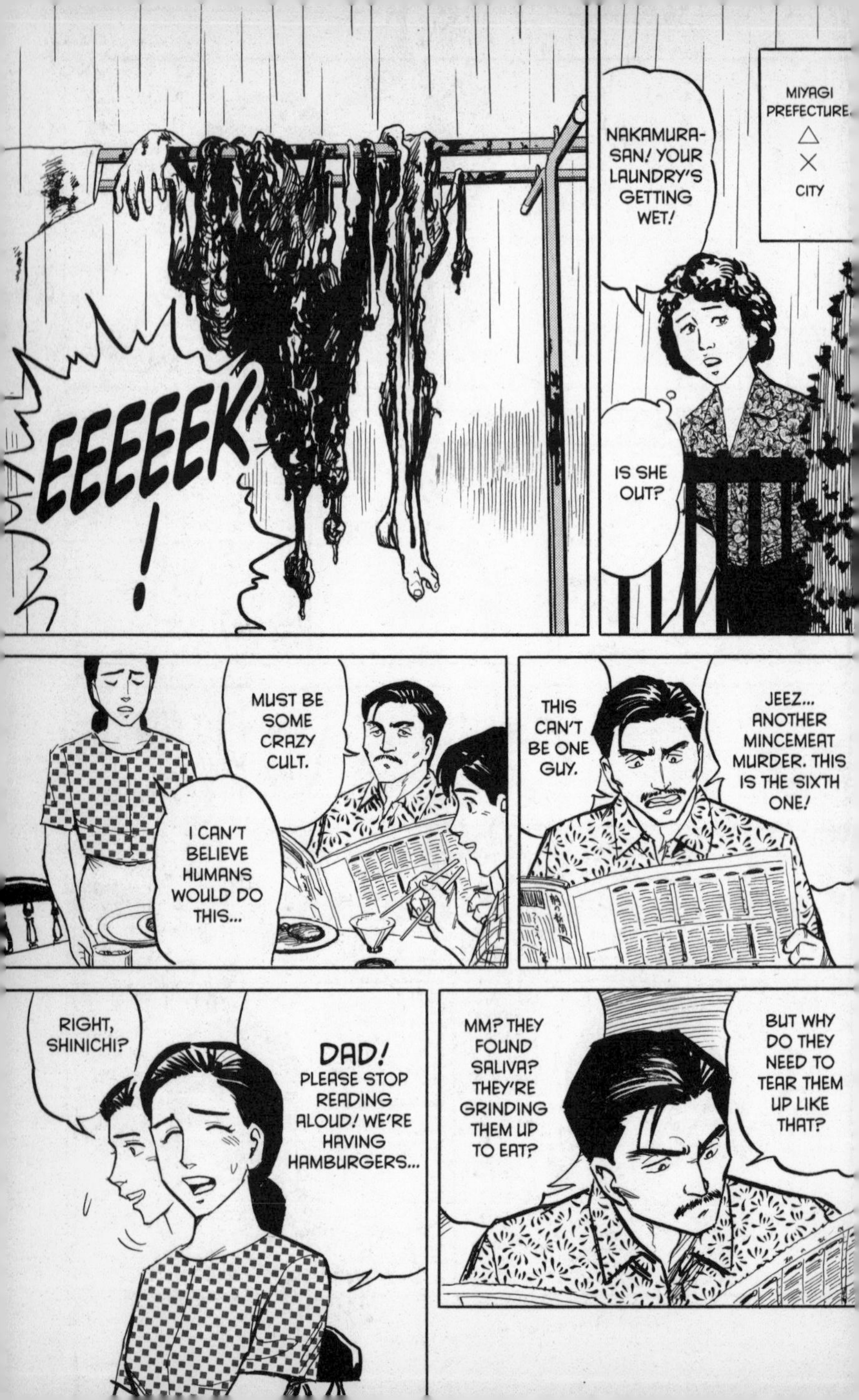
MIYAGI PREFECTURE. △ × CITY
NAKAMURA-SAN! YOUR LAUNDRY'S GETTING WET!
IS SHE OUT?
EEEEEK!
JEEZ... ANOTHER MINCEMEAT MURDER. THIS IS THE SIXTH ONE!
THIS CAN'T BE ONE GUY.
MUST BE SOME CRAZY CULT.
I CAN'T BELIEVE HUMANS WOULD DO THIS...
BUT WHY DO THEY NEED TO TEAR THEM UP LIKE THAT?
MM? THEY FOUND SALIVA? THEY'RE GRINDING THEM UP TO EAT?
DAD! PLEASE STOP READING ALOUD! WE'RE HAVING HAMBURGERS...
RIGHT, SHINICHI?

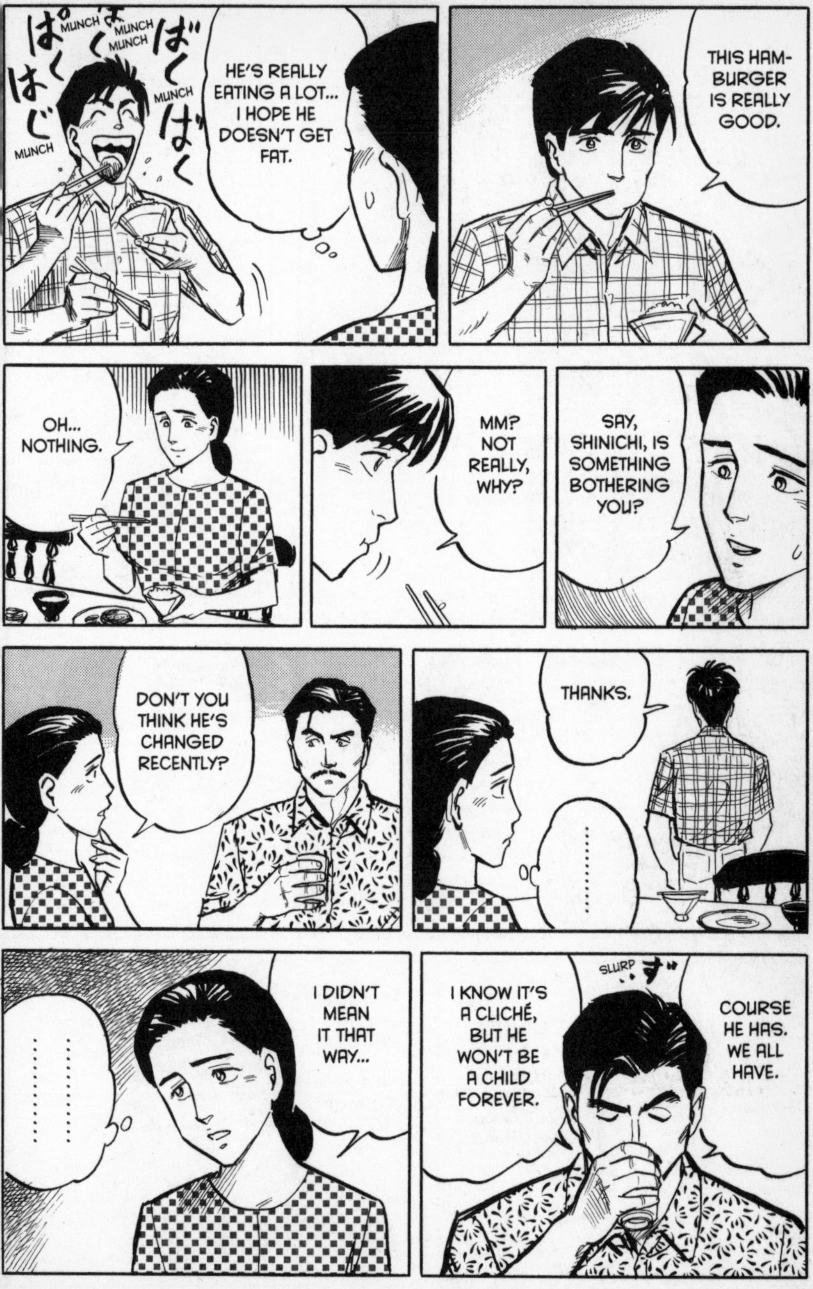
THIS HAMBURGER IS REALLY GOOD.
MUNCH MUNCH MUNCH
MUNCH
MUNCH
HE'S REALLY EATING A LOT... I HOPE HE DOESN'T GET FAT.
SAY, SHINICHI, IS SOMETHING BOTHERING YOU?
MM? NOT REALLY, WHY?
OH... NOTHING.
THANKS.
......
DON'T YOU THINK HE'S CHANGED RECENTLY?
SLURP
COURSE HE HAS. WE ALL HAVE.
I KNOW IT'S A CLICHÉ, BUT HE WON'T BE A CHILD FOREVER.
I DIDN'T MEAN IT THAT WAY...
....

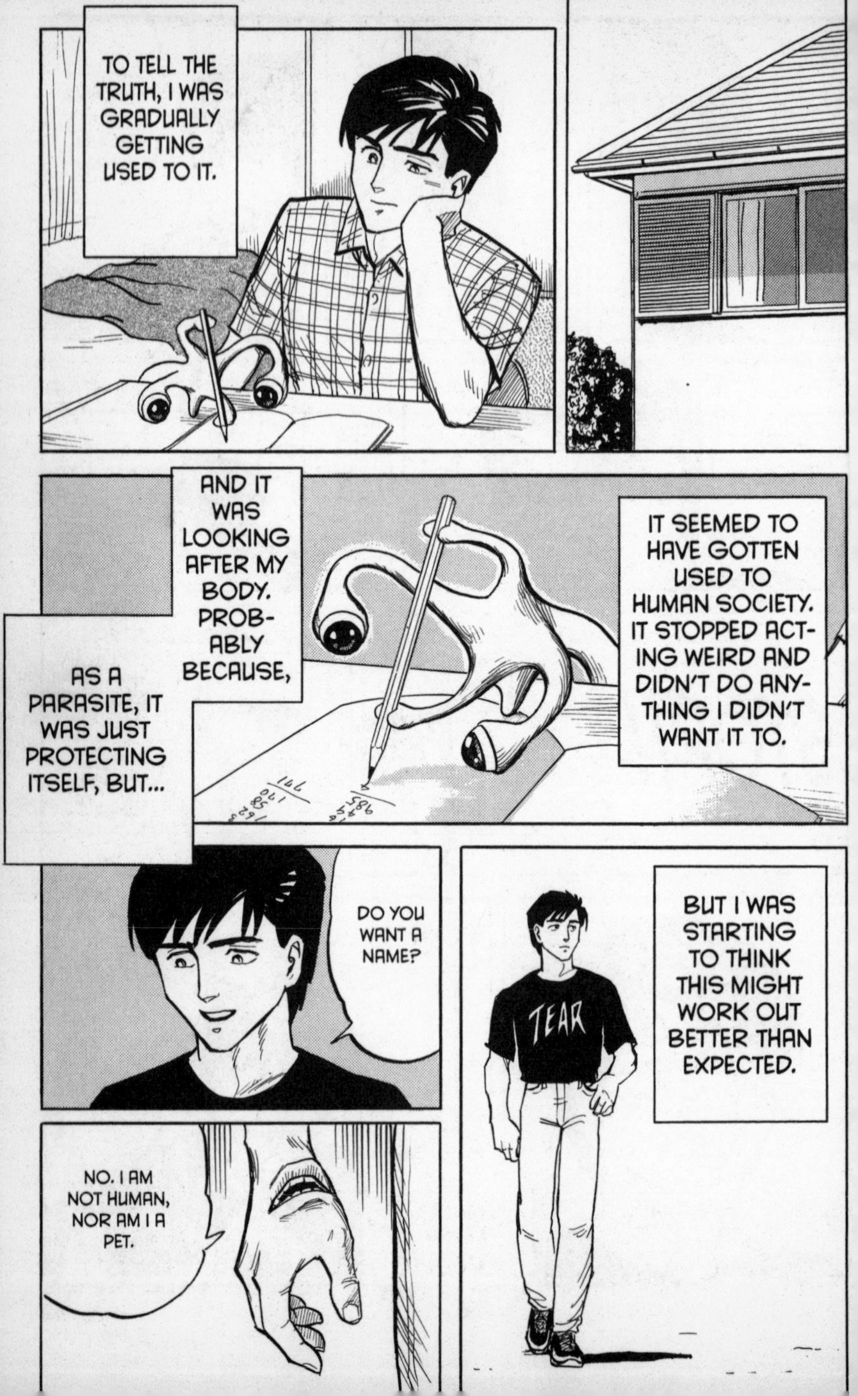
TO TELL THE TRUTH, I WAS GRADUALLY GETTING USED TO IT.
IT SEEMED TO HAVE GOTTEN USED TO HUMAN SOCIETY. IT STOPPED ACTING WEIRD AND DIDN'T DO ANYTHING I DIDN'T WANT IT TO.
AND IT WAS LOOKING AFTER MY BODY. PROBABLY BECAUSE,
AS A PARASITE, IT WAS JUST PROTECTING ITSELF, BUT...
BUT I WAS STARTING TO THINK THIS MIGHT WORK OUT BETTER THAN EXPECTED.
TEAR
DO YOU WANT A NAME?
NO. I AM NOT HUMAN, NOR AM I A PET.

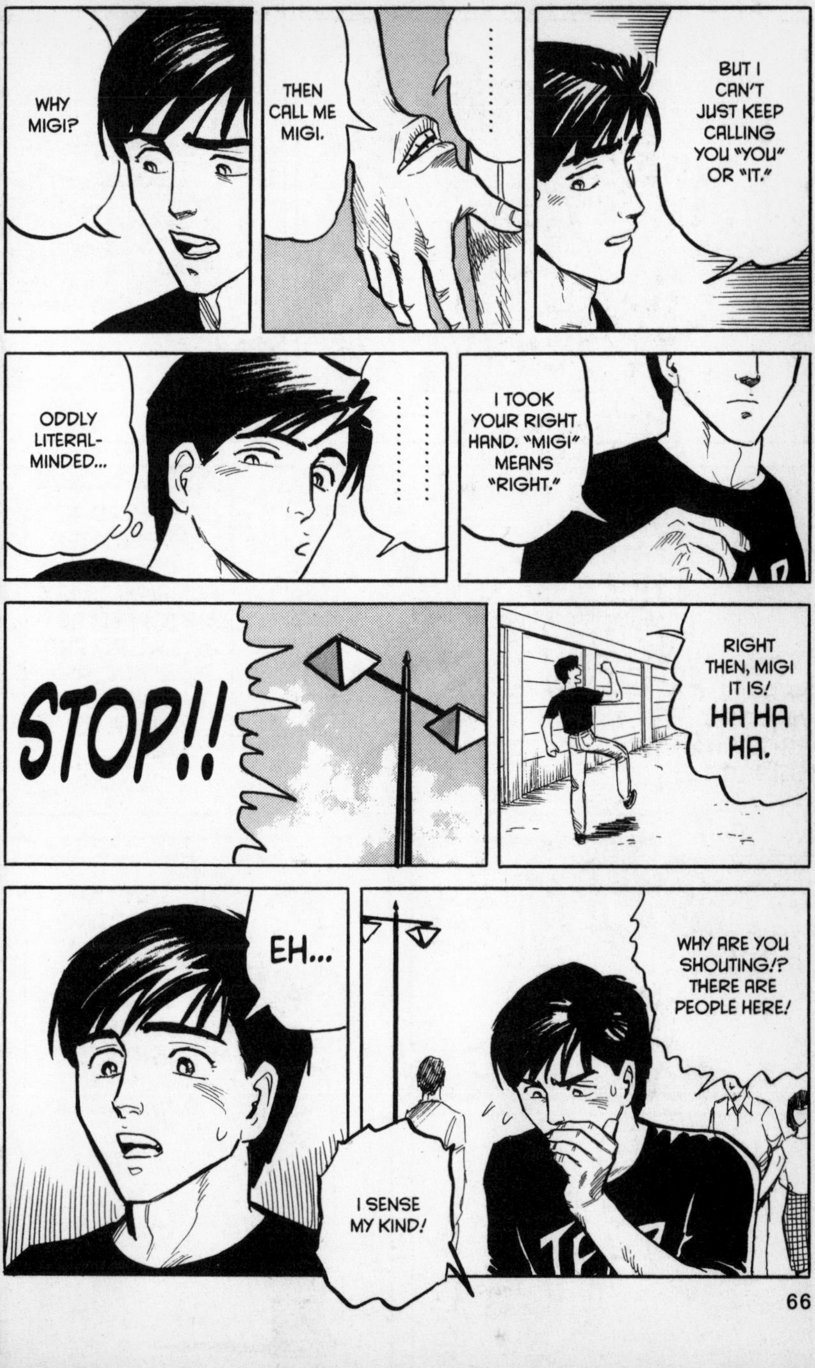
BUT I CAN'T JUST KEEP CALLING YOU "YOU" OR "IT."
THEN CALL ME MIGI.
WHY MIGI?
I TOOK YOUR RIGHT HAND. "MIGI" MEANS "RIGHT."
ODDLY LITERAL-MINDED...
RIGHT THEN, MIGI IT IS! HA HA HA.
STOP!!
WHY ARE YOU SHOUTING!? THERE ARE PEOPLE HERE!
I SENSE MY KIND!
EH...

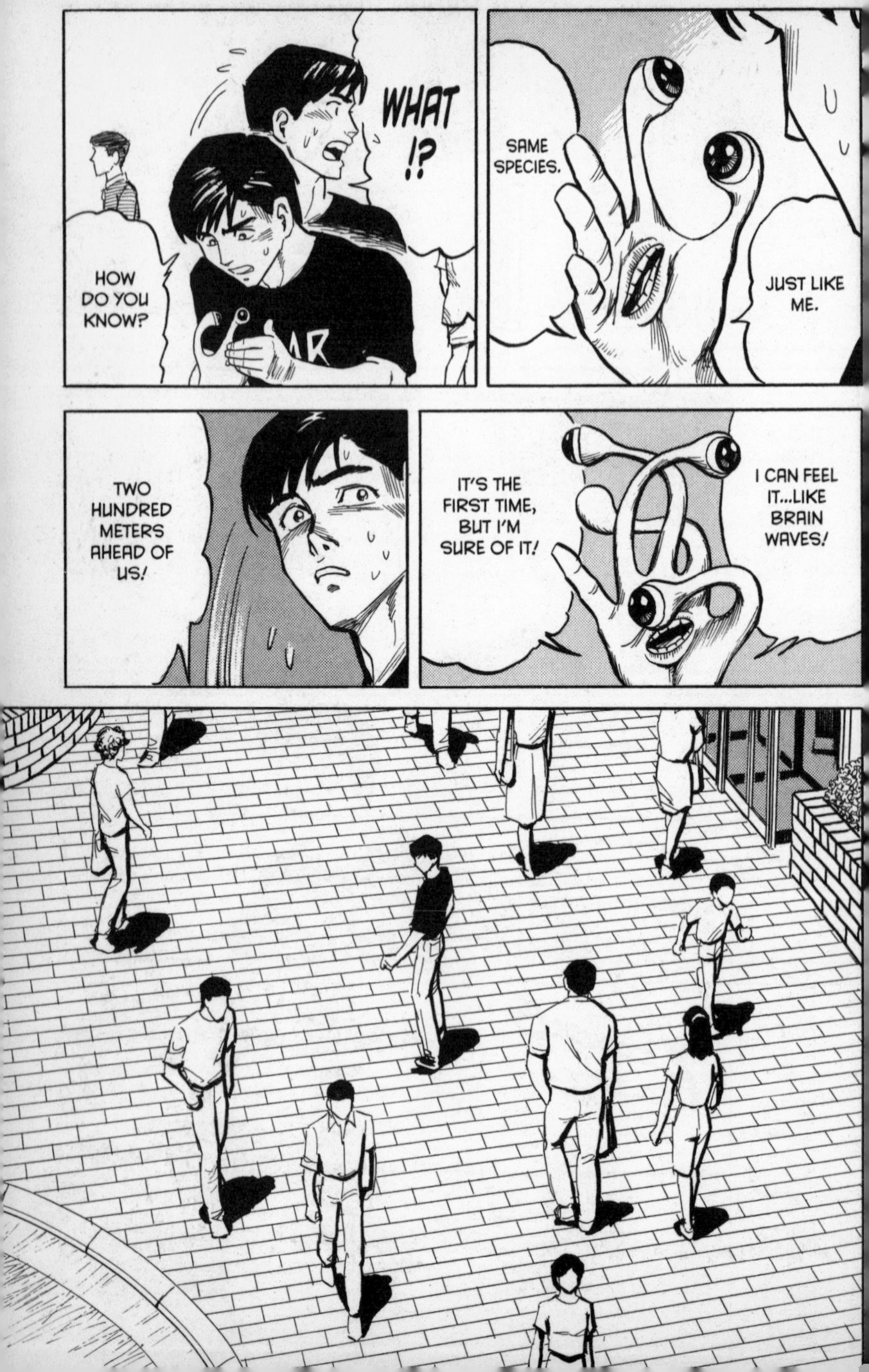
SAME SPECIES.
JUST LIKE ME.
WHAT !?
HOW DO YOU KNOW?
I CAN FEEL IT...LIKE BRAIN WAVES!
IT'S THE FIRST TIME, BUT I'M SURE OF IT!
TWO HUNDRED METERS AHEAD OF US!

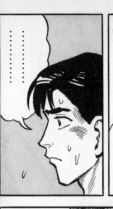

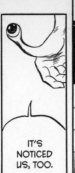

TAKE A LEFT UP HERE.
IT'S NOTICED US, TOO.
......
WHAT? GO ON.
BUT IF IT'S LIKE YOU...
THEN IT MIGHT HAVE EATEN A HUMAN'S BRAIN?
NO, THAT'S TOO CREEPY!
SWISH
M-MIGI!
SWACK!

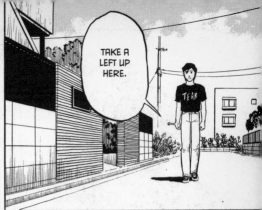

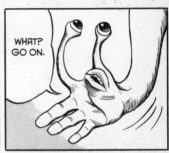

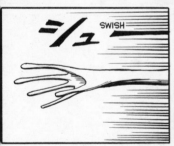

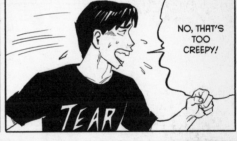

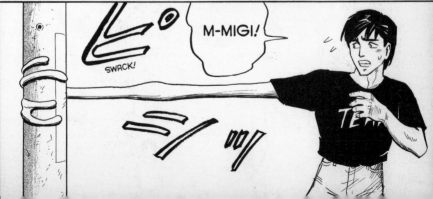

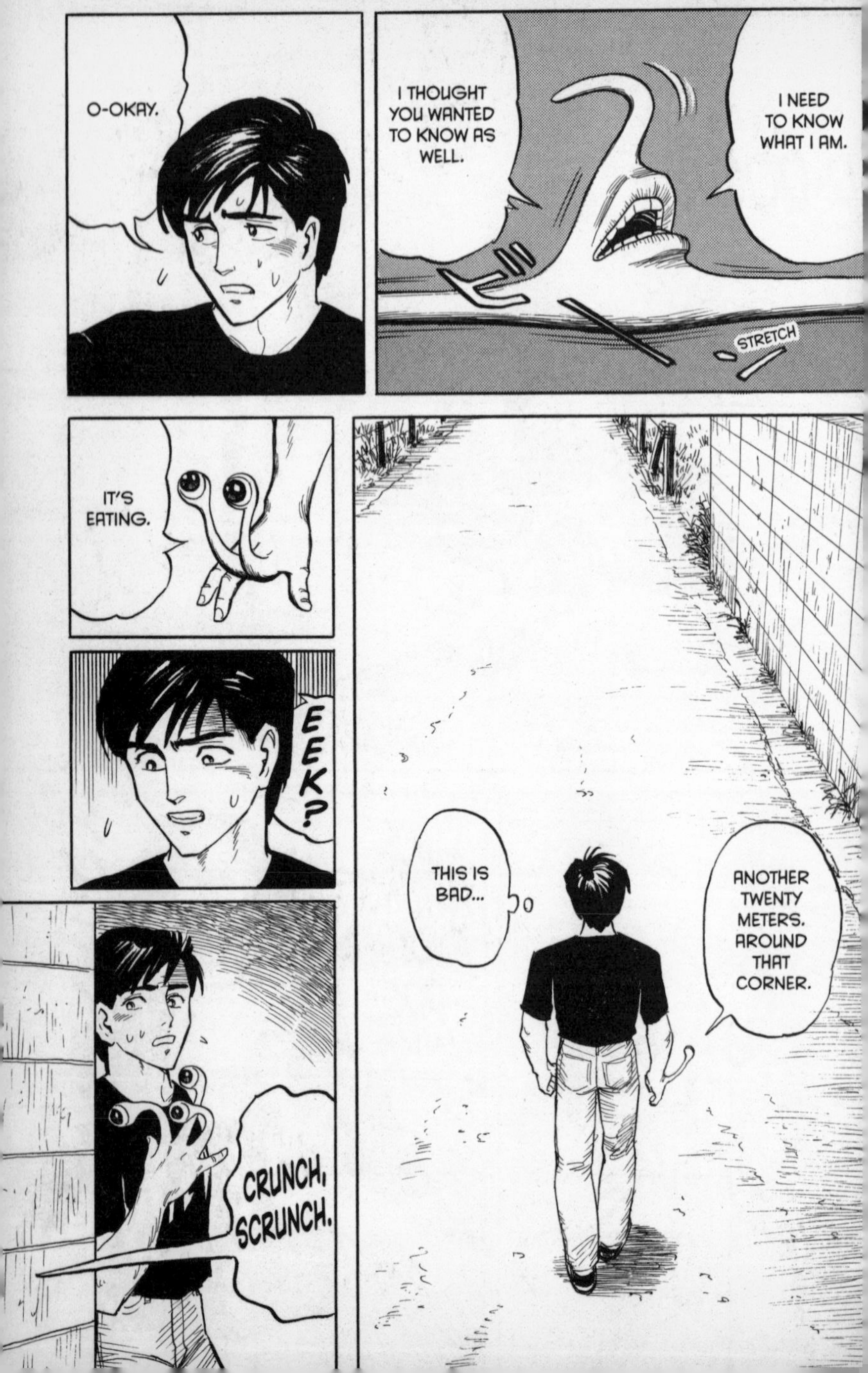
I NEED TO KNOW WHAT I AM.
I THOUGHT YOU WANTED TO KNOW AS WELL.
STRETCH
O-OKAY.
ANOTHER TWENTY METERS. AROUND THAT CORNER.
THIS IS BAD...
IT'S EATING.
EEK?
CRUNCH, SCRUNCH.

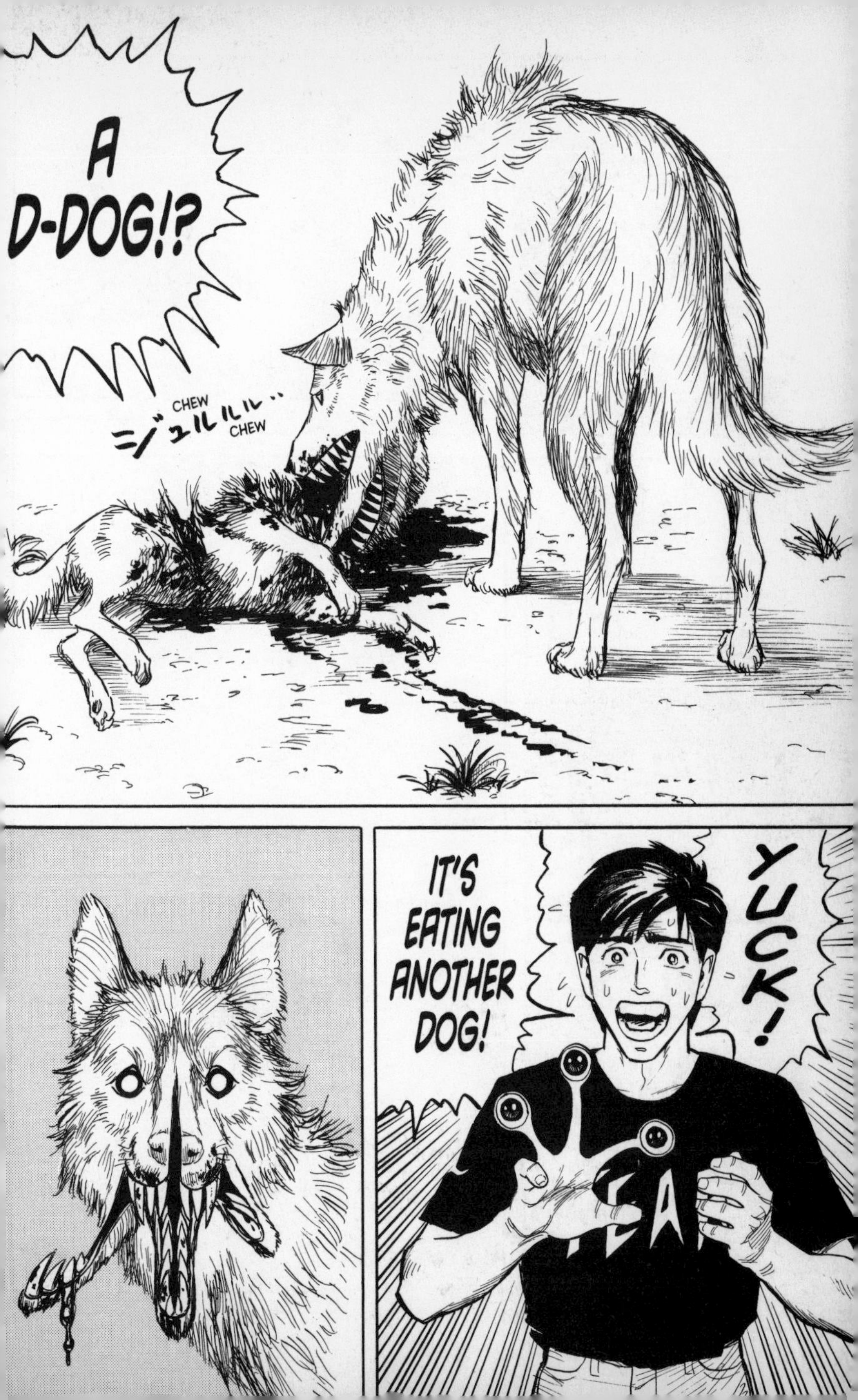
A D-DOG!?
ジュルルル‥
CHEW CHEW
YUCK!
IT'S EATING ANOTHER DOG!

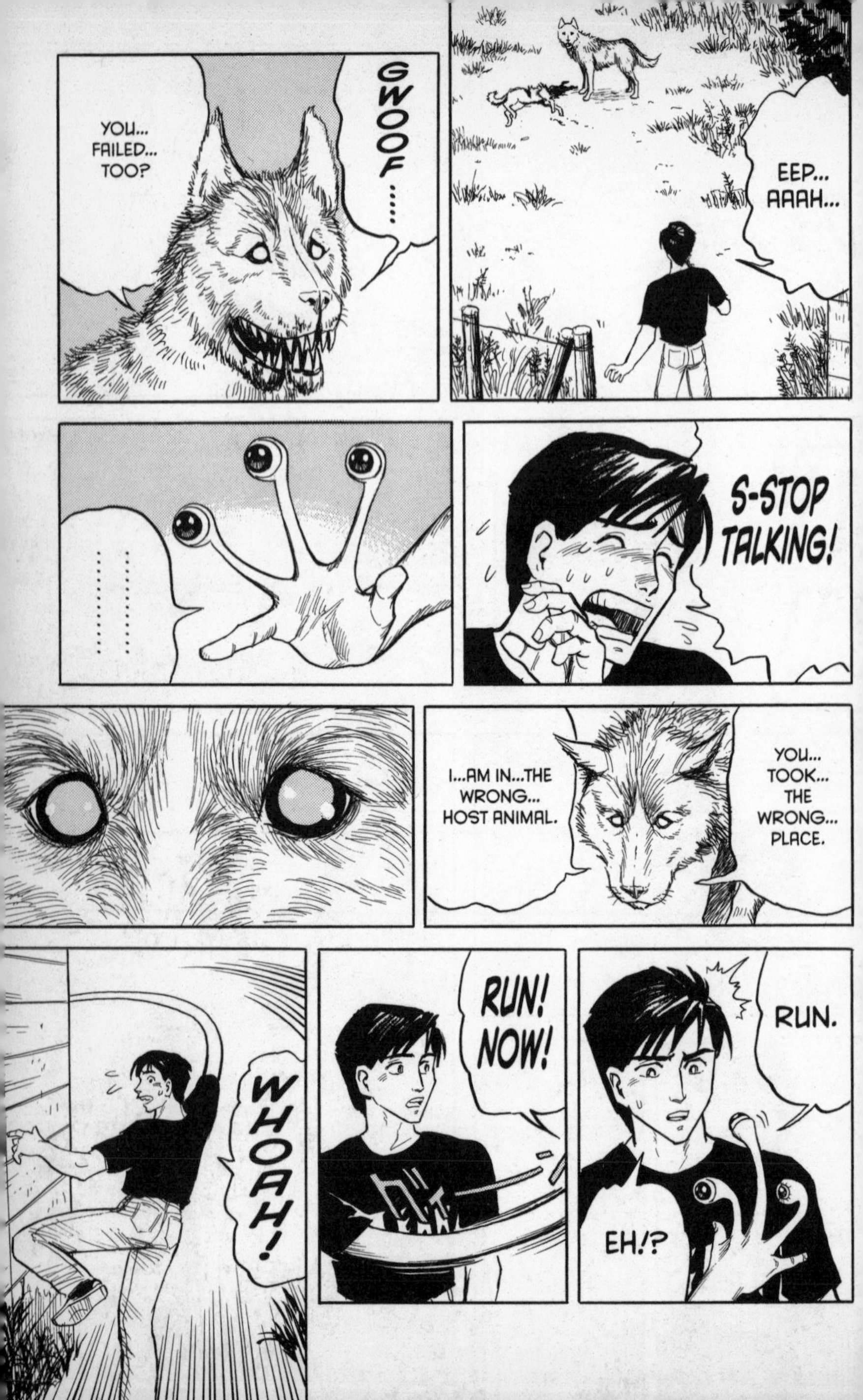

EEP... AAAH...
GWOOF....
YOU... FAILED... TOO?
S-STOP TALKING!
......
YOU... TOOK... THE WRONG... PLACE.
I...AM IN...THE WRONG... HOST ANIMAL.
RUN.
EH!?
RUN! NOW!
WHOAH!

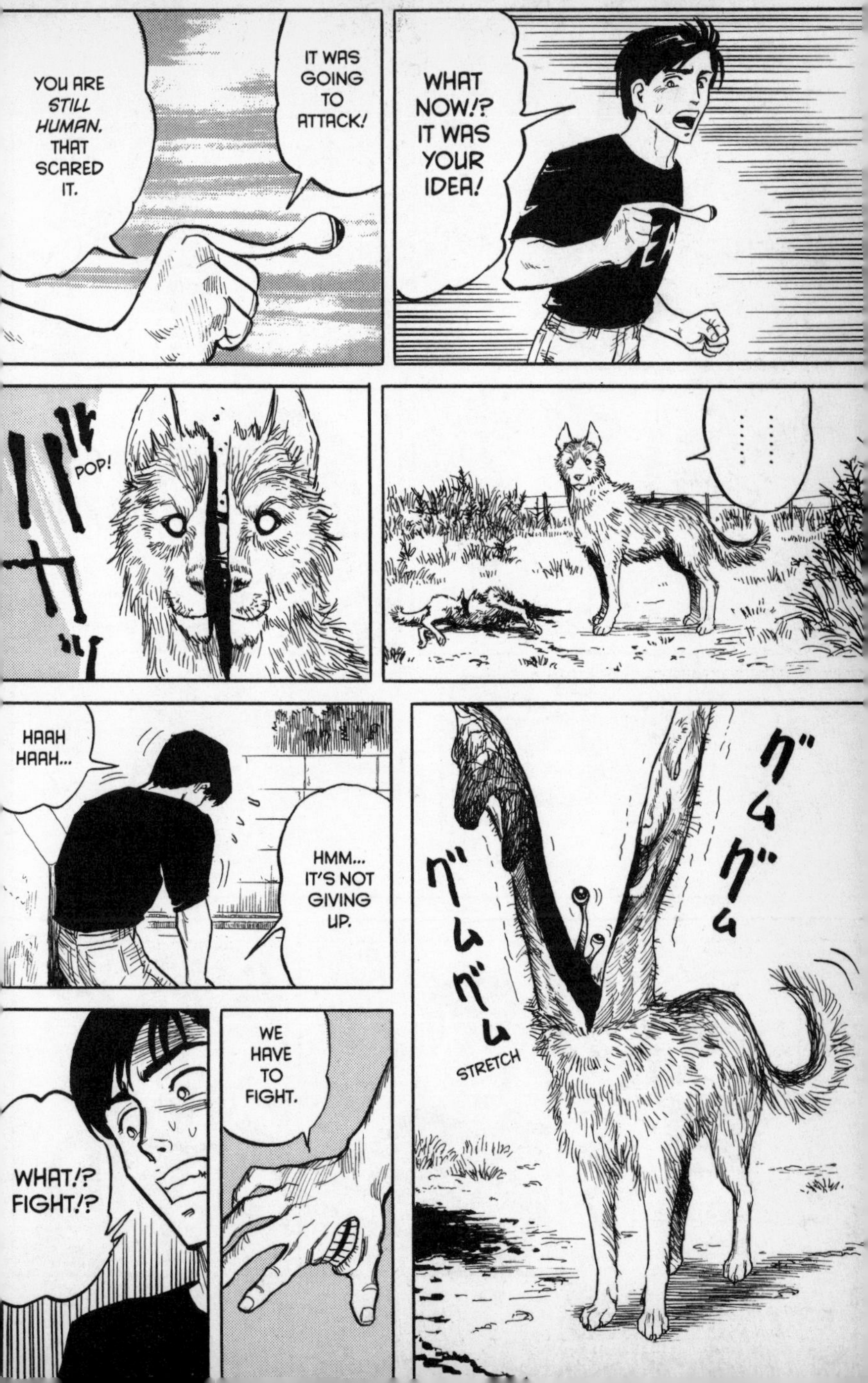
WHAT NOW!? IT WAS YOUR IDEA!
IT WAS GOING TO ATTACK!
YOU ARE STILL HUMAN. THAT SCARED IT.
......
POP!
グムグム
グムグム
STRETCH
HAAH HAAH...
HMM... IT'S NOT GIVING UP.
WE HAVE TO FIGHT.
WHAT!? FIGHT!?

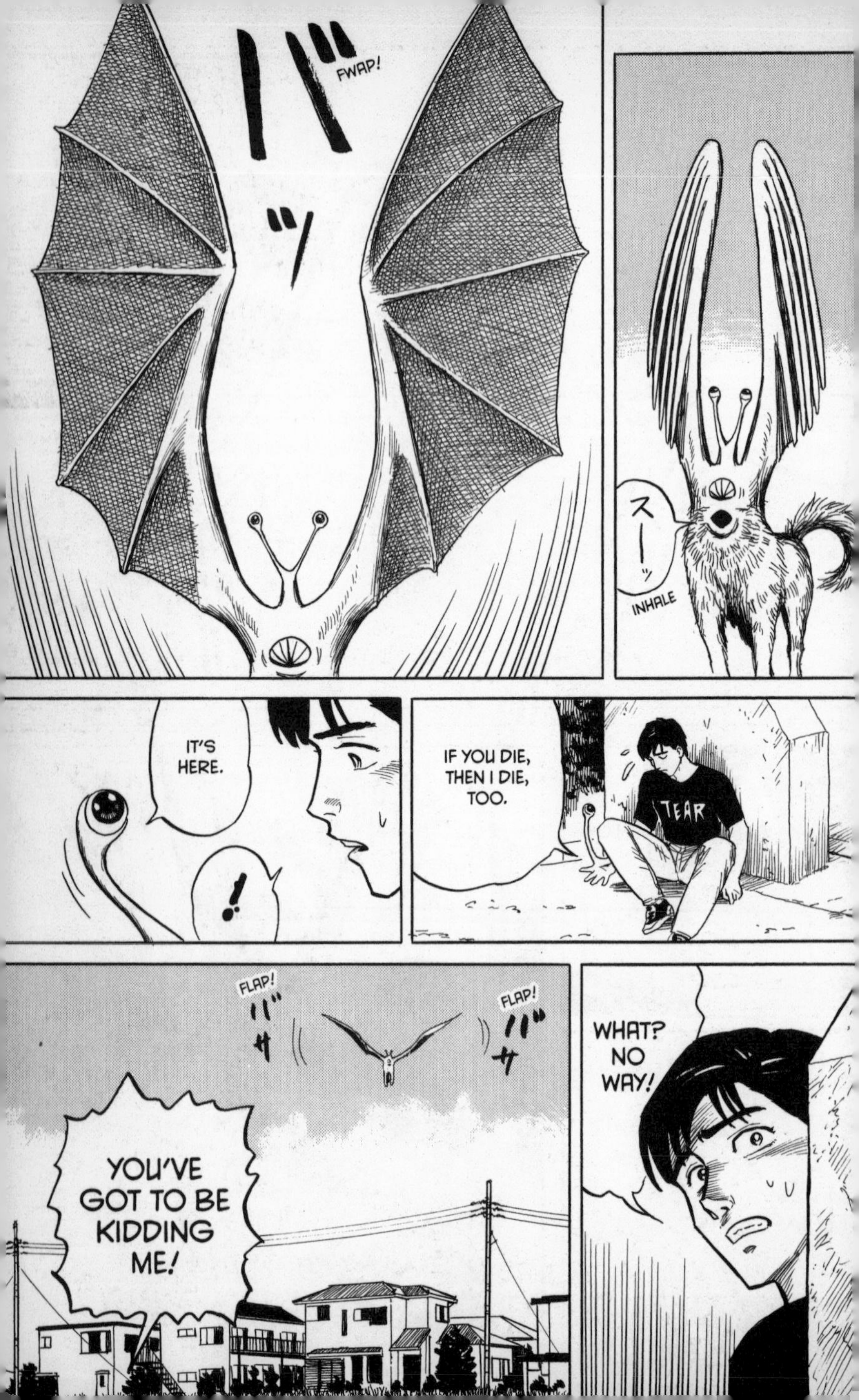
スーッ
INHALE
バッ
FWAP!
IF YOU DIE, THEN I DIE, TOO.
IT'S HERE.
!
WHAT? NO WAY!
バサ
FLAP!
バサ
FLAP!
YOU'VE GOT TO BE KIDDING ME!

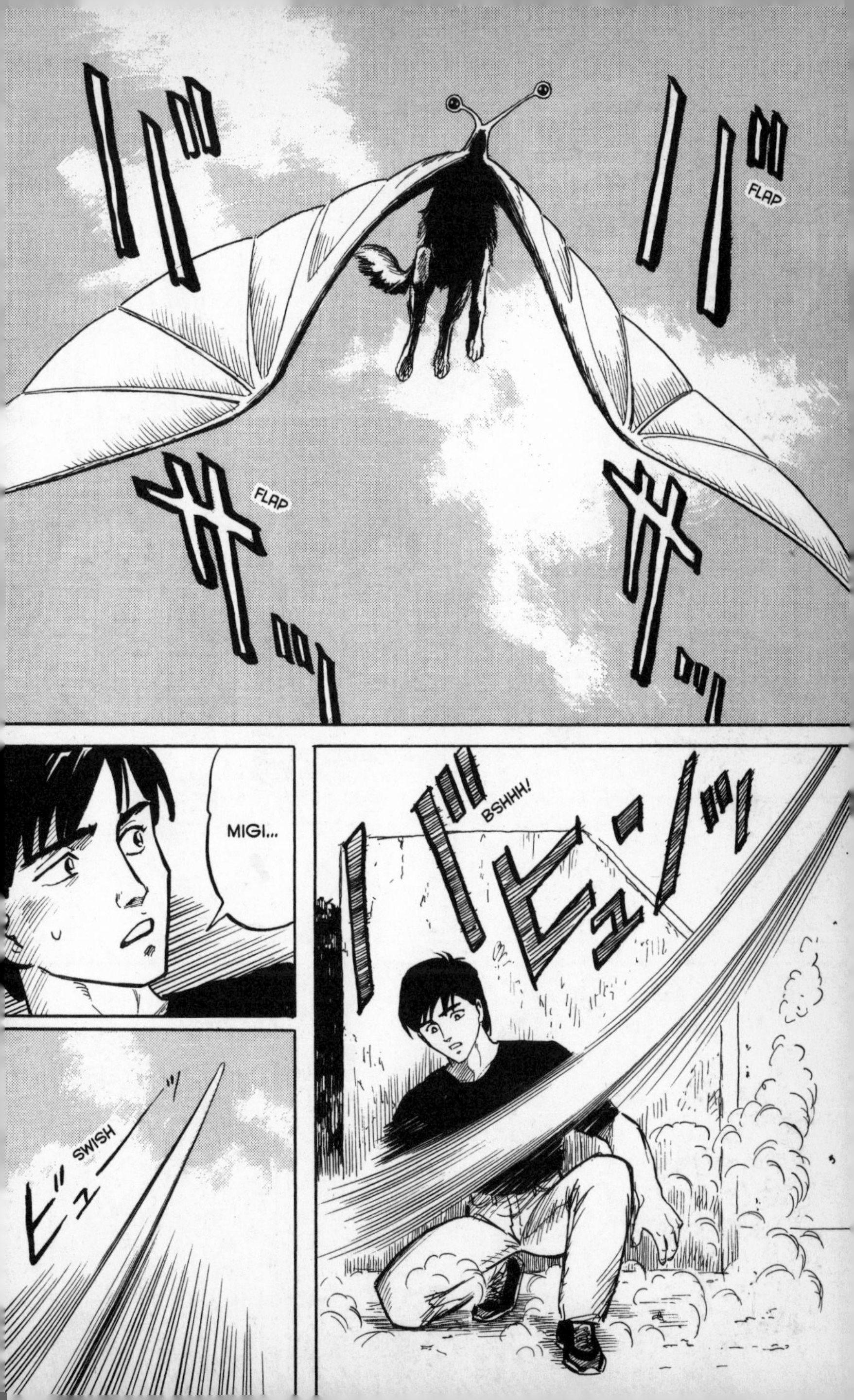
FLAP
FLAP
BSHHH!
MIGI...
SWISH

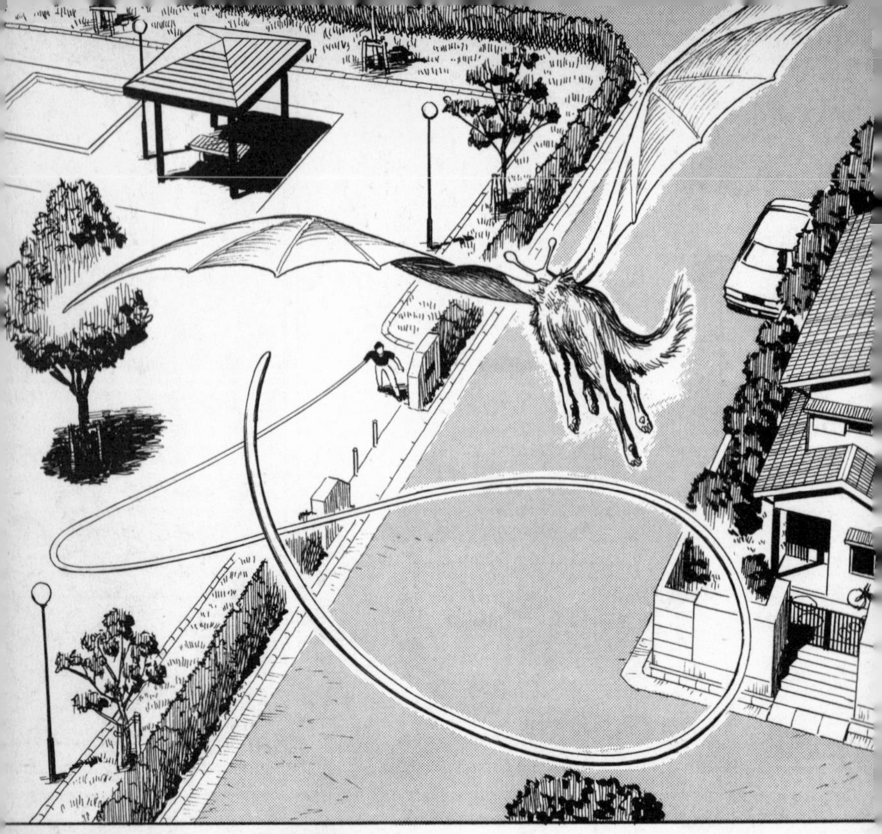

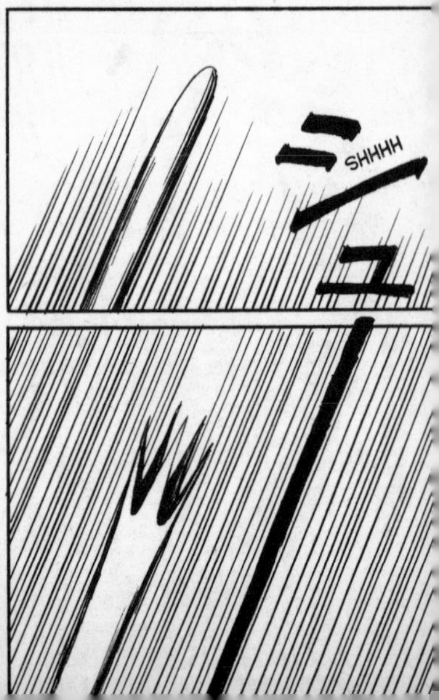
シュー
SHHHH

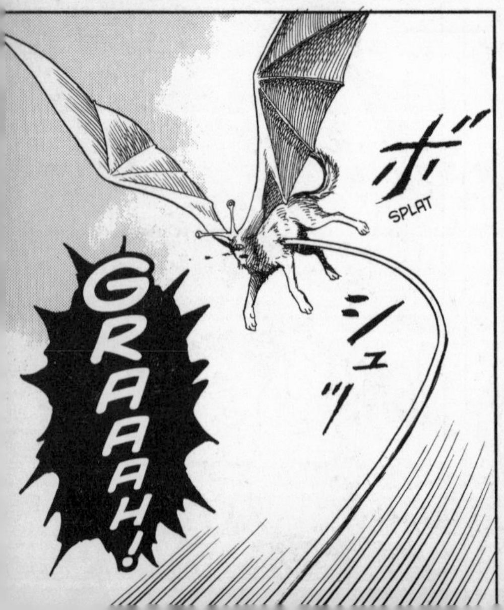
ボ
SPLAT
シュッ
GRAAAAH!

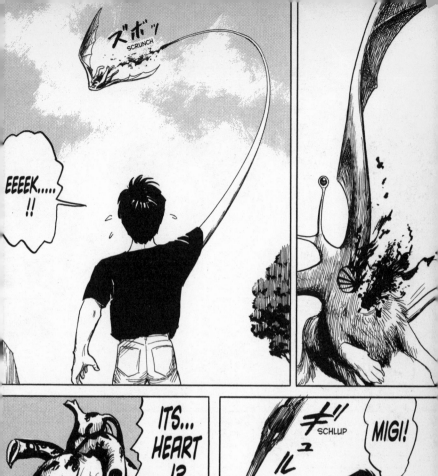

SCRUNCH

EEEEK.....
!!

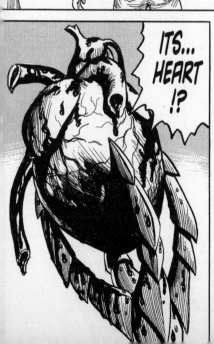

ITS...
HEART
!?

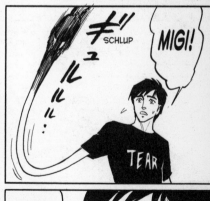

SCHLUP

MIGI!

TEAR

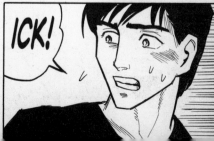

ICK!

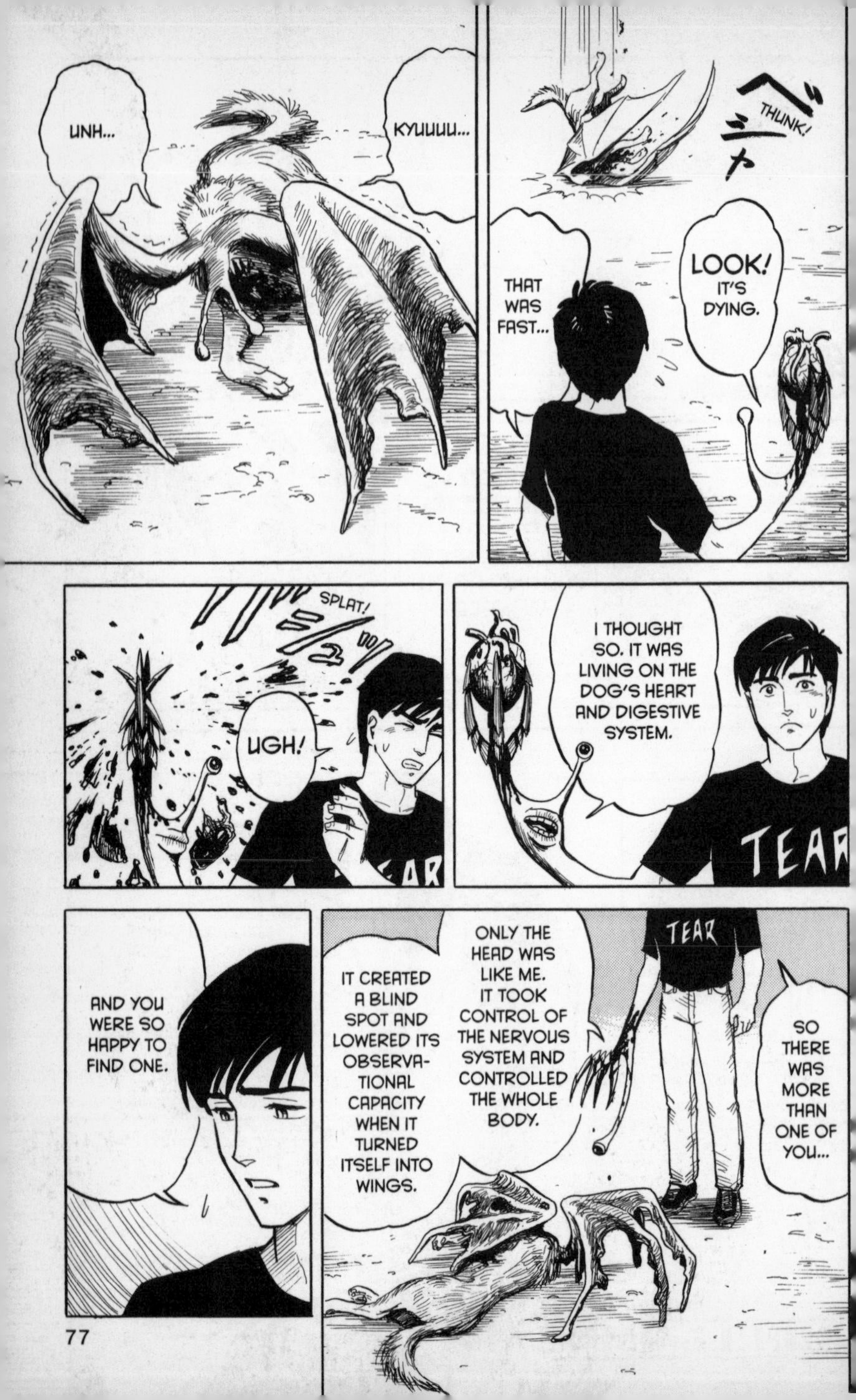
THUNK!
LOOK! IT'S DYING.
THAT WAS FAST...
KYUUUU...
UNH...
I THOUGHT SO. IT WAS LIVING ON THE DOG'S HEART AND DIGESTIVE SYSTEM.
SPLAT!
UGH!
SO THERE WAS MORE THAN ONE OF YOU...
ONLY THE HEAD WAS LIKE ME. IT TOOK CONTROL OF THE NERVOUS SYSTEM AND CONTROLLED THE WHOLE BODY.
IT CREATED A BLIND SPOT AND LOWERED ITS OBSERVATIONAL CAPACITY WHEN IT TURNED ITSELF INTO WINGS.
AND YOU WERE SO HAPPY TO FIND ONE.

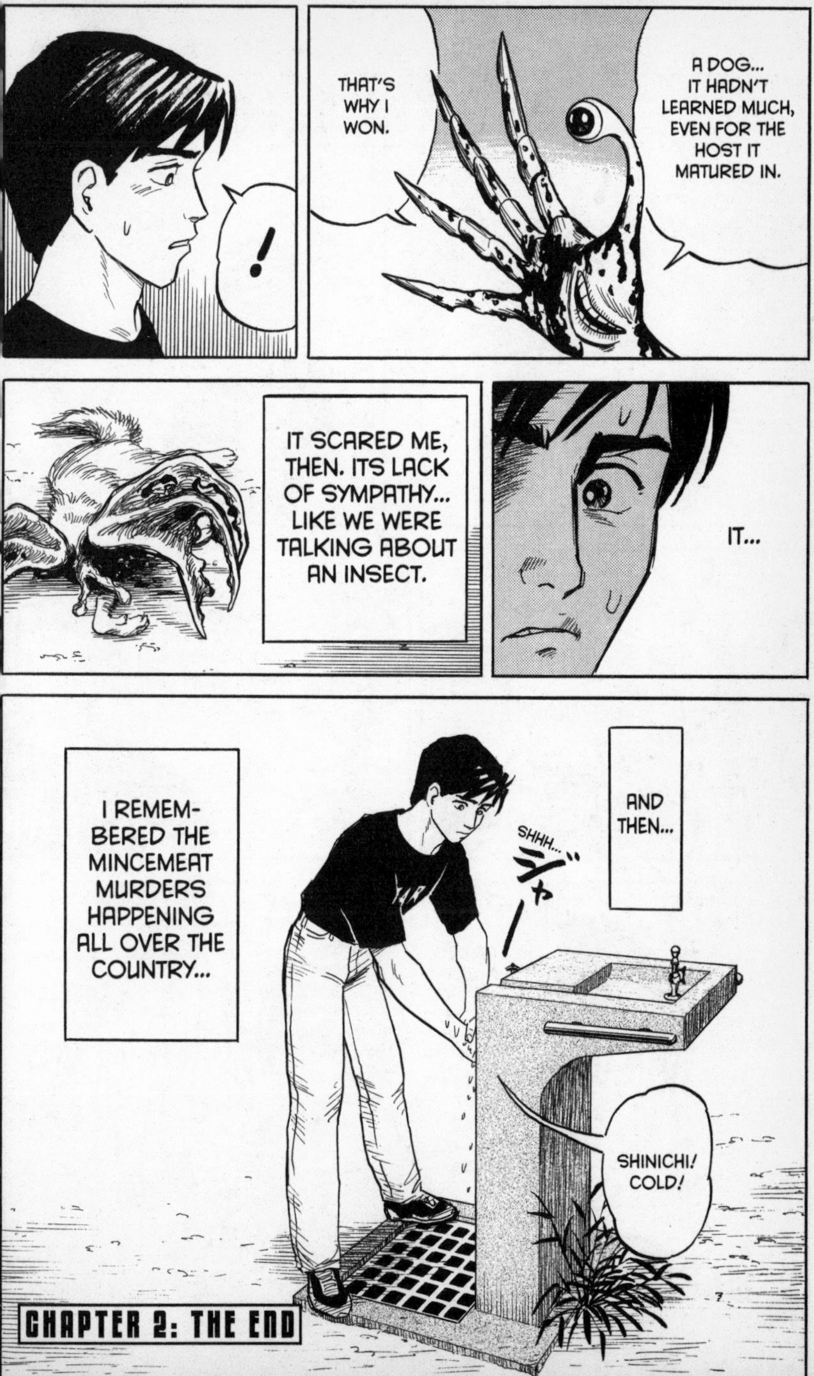
A DOG... IT HADN'T LEARNED MUCH, EVEN FOR THE HOST IT MATURED IN.
THAT'S WHY I WON.
!
IT...
IT SCARED ME, THEN. ITS LACK OF SYMPATHY... LIKE WE WERE TALKING ABOUT AN INSECT.
AND THEN...
SHHH...
ジャー
I REMEMBERED THE MINCEMEAT MURDERS HAPPENING ALL OVER THE COUNTRY...
SHINICHI! COLD!
CHAPTER 2: THE END

CHAPTER 3: CONTACT

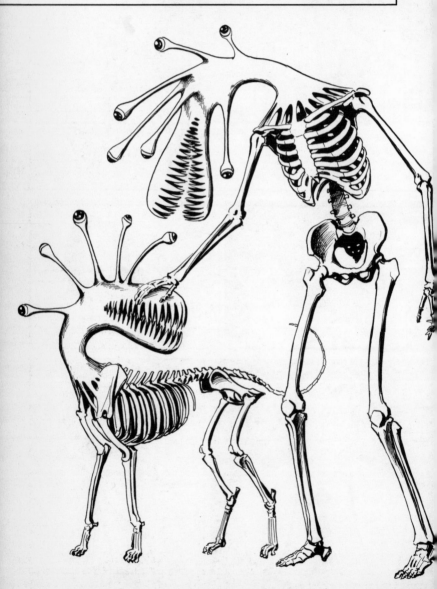

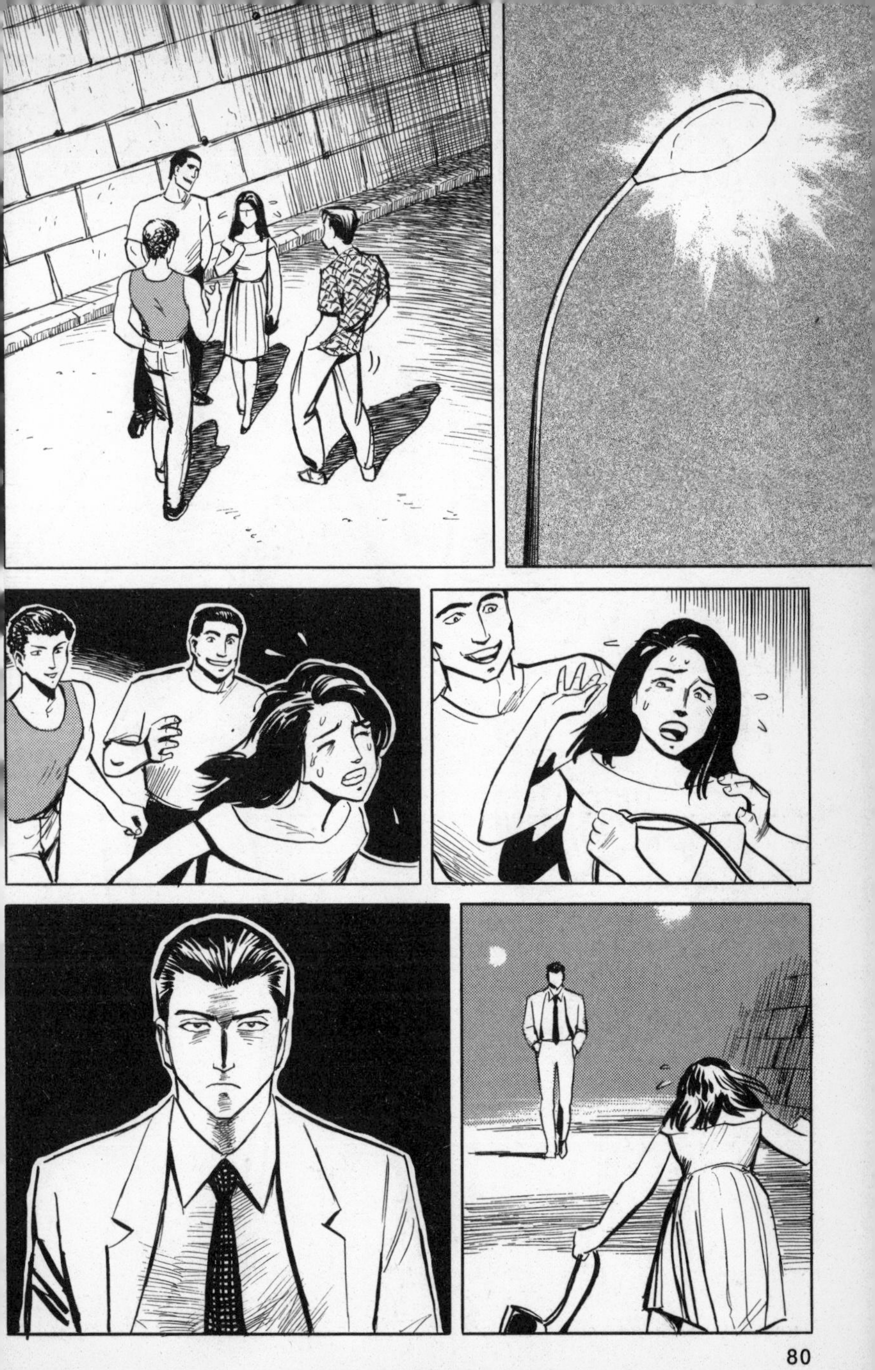

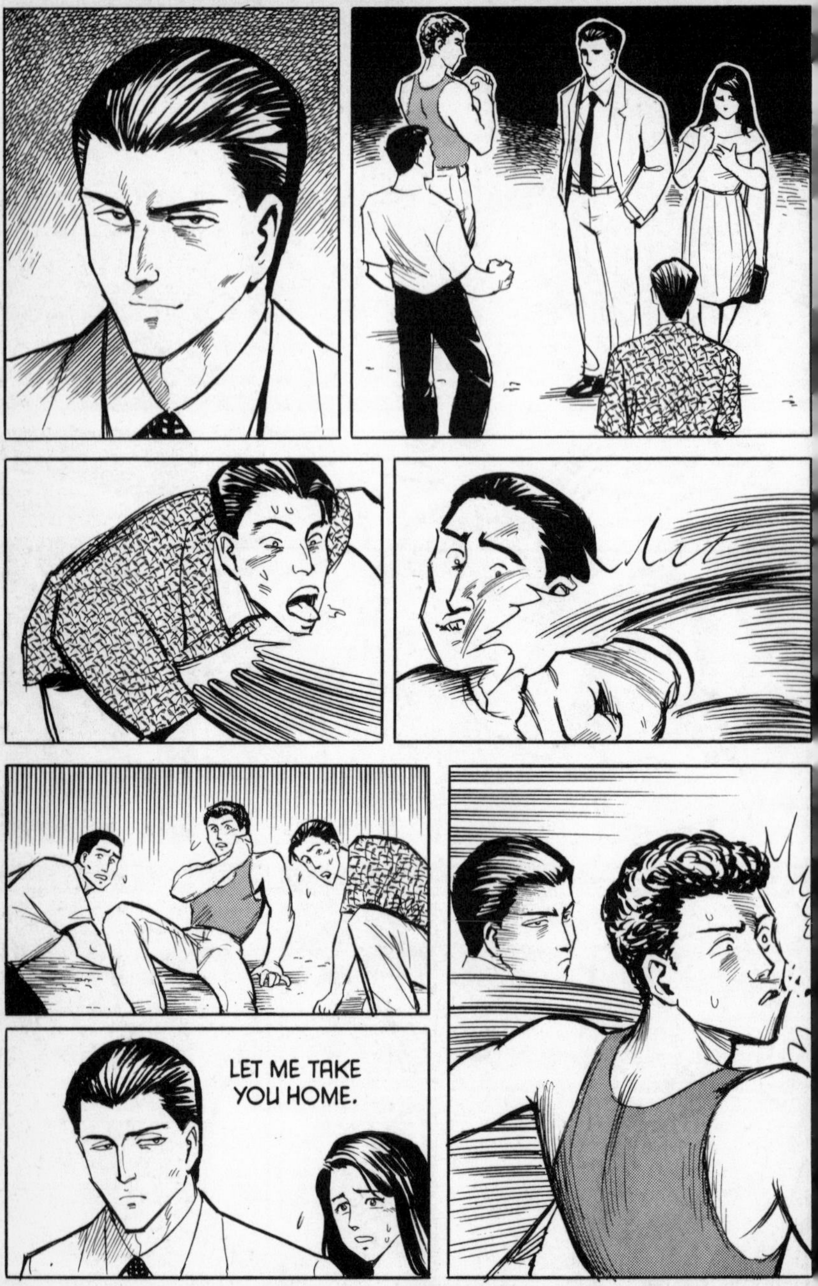
LET ME TAKE
YOU HOME.

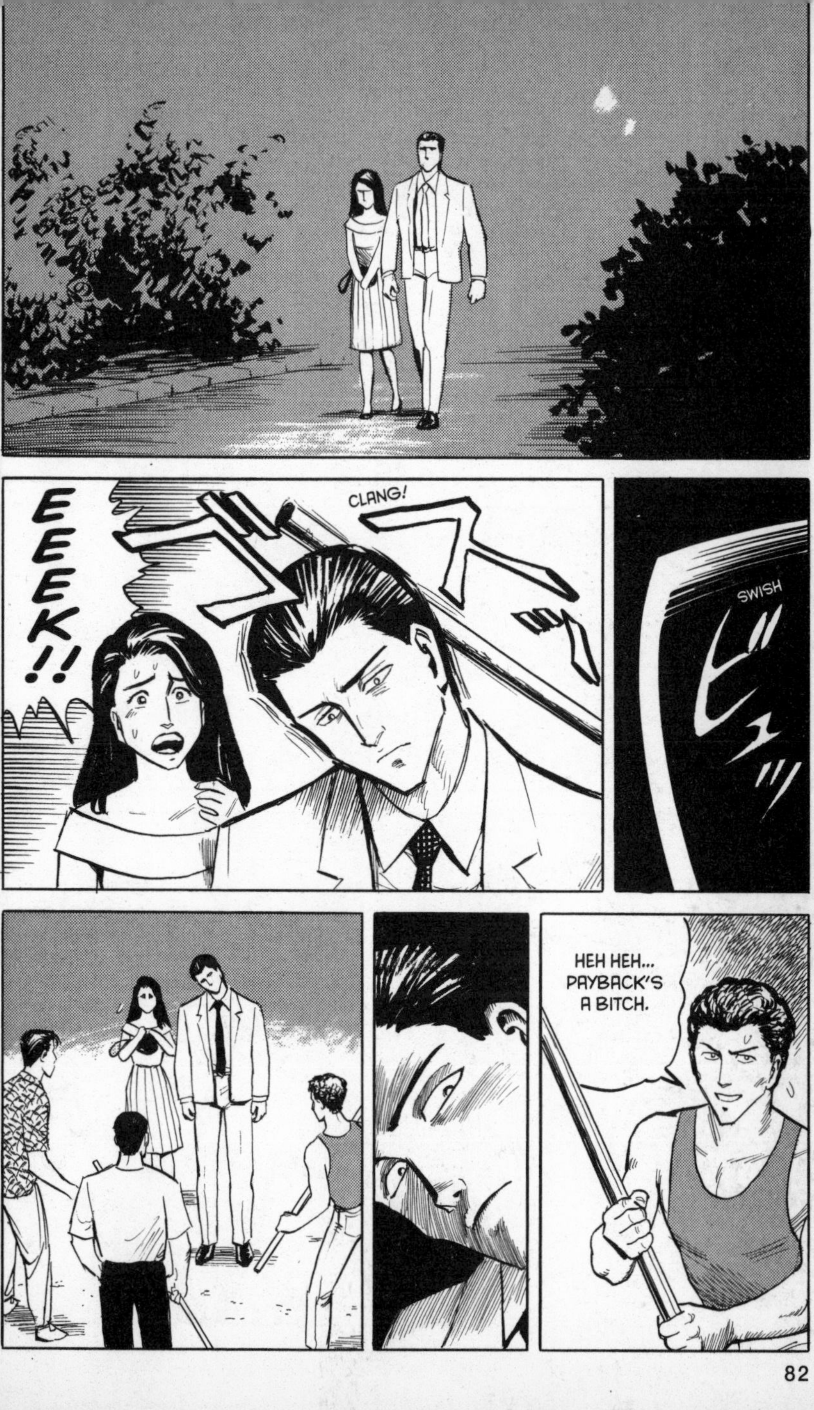
SWISH
CLANG!
EEEEK!!
HEH HEH... PAYBACK'S A BITCH.

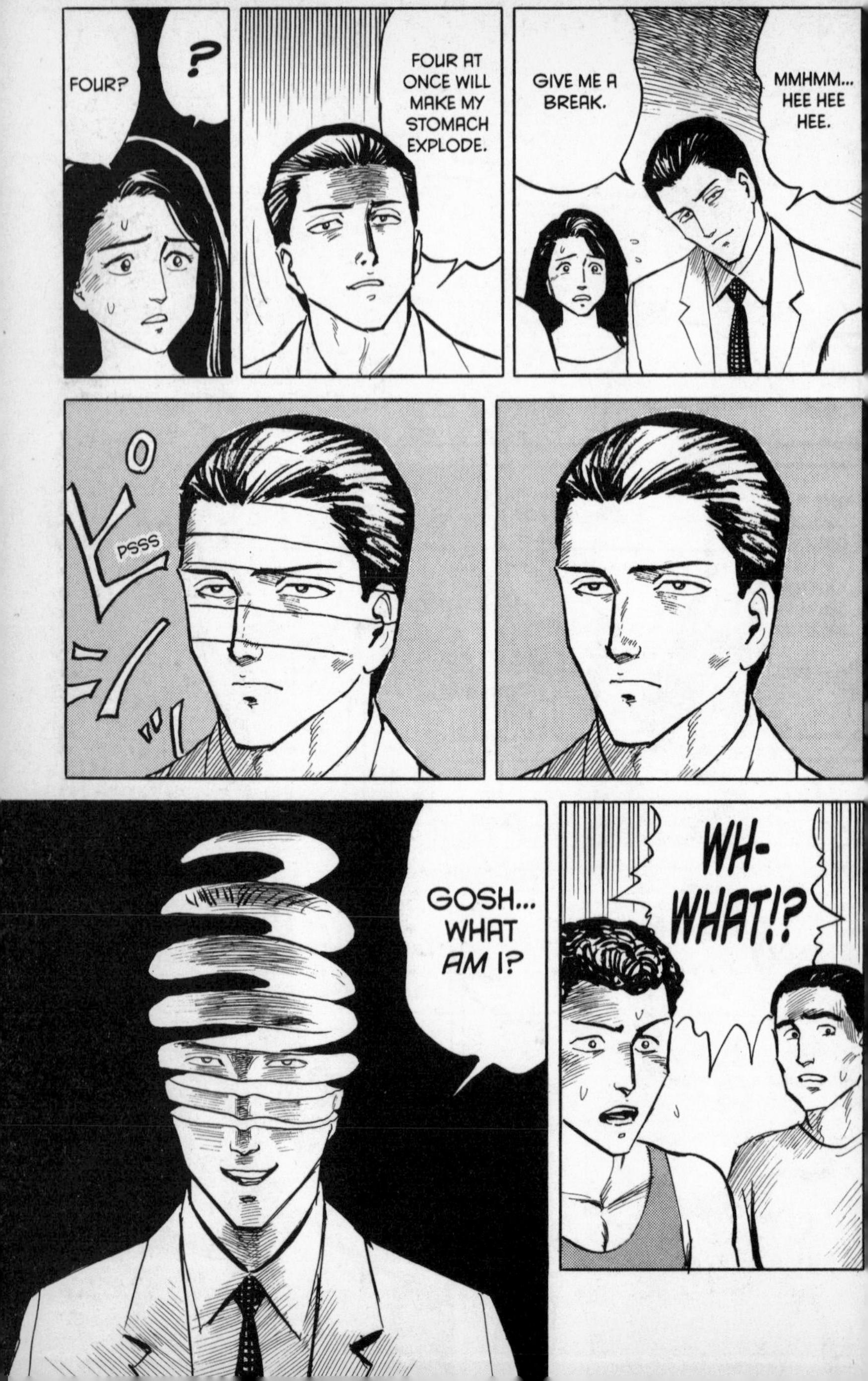
MMHMM... HEE HEE HEE.
GIVE ME A BREAK.
FOUR AT ONCE WILL MAKE MY STOMACH EXPLODE.
?
FOUR?
PSSS
WH-WHAT!?
GOSH... WHAT AM I?

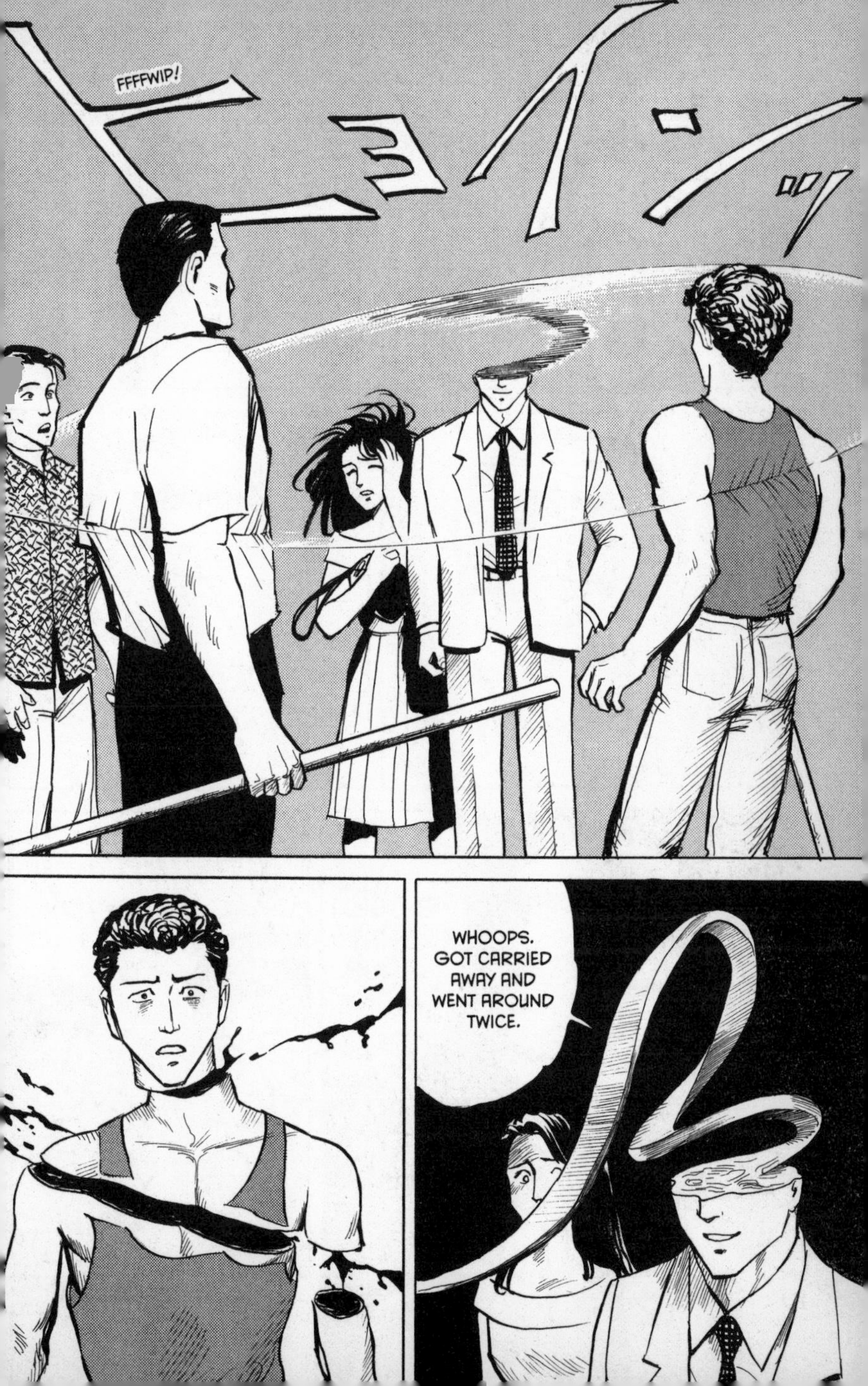
FFFFWIP!
WHOOPS. GOT CARRIED AWAY AND WENT AROUND TWICE.

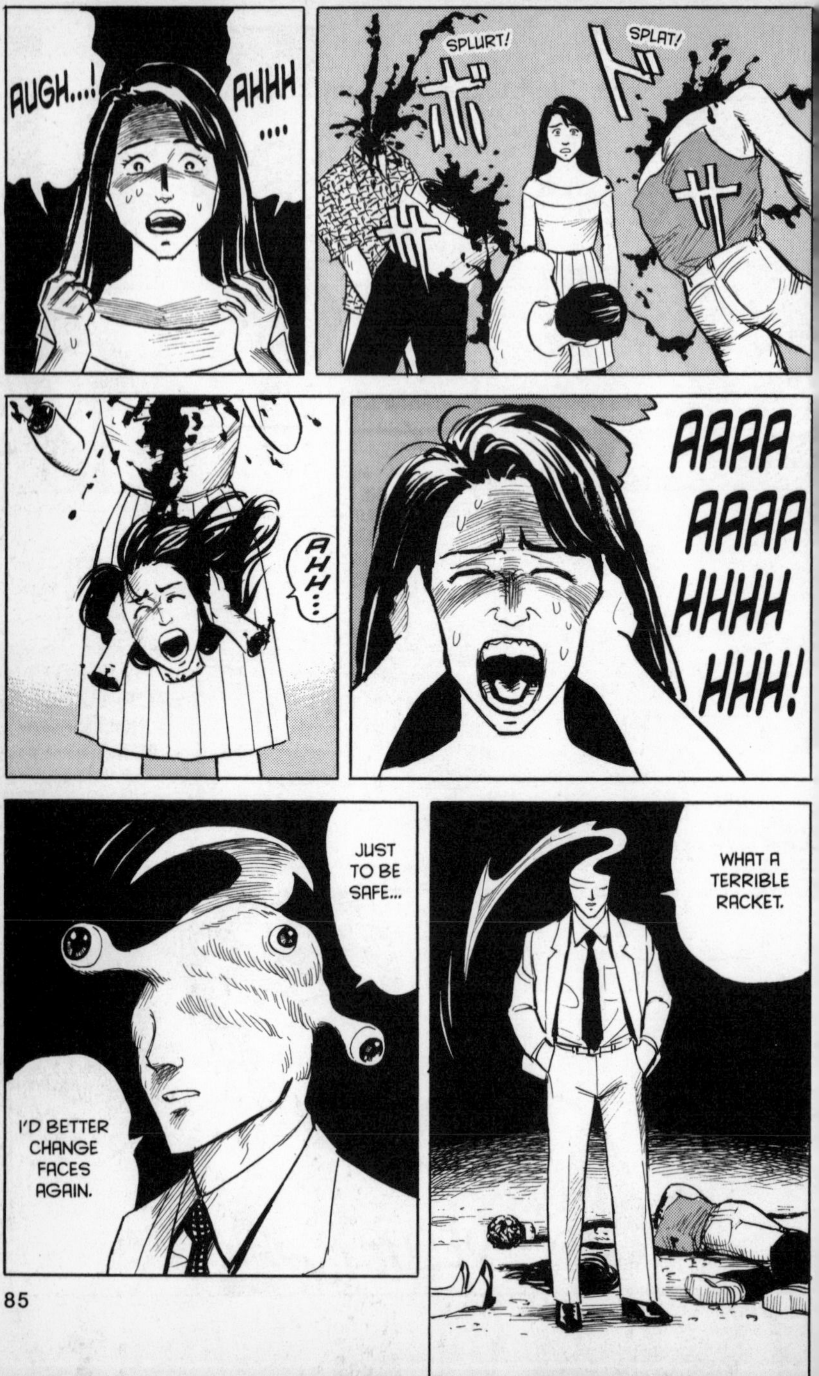
SPLAT!
SPLURT!
AHHH ....
AUGH...!
AAAA AAAA HHHH HHH!
AHH...
WHAT A TERRIBLE RACKET.
JUST TO BE SAFE...
I'D BETTER CHANGE FACES AGAIN.

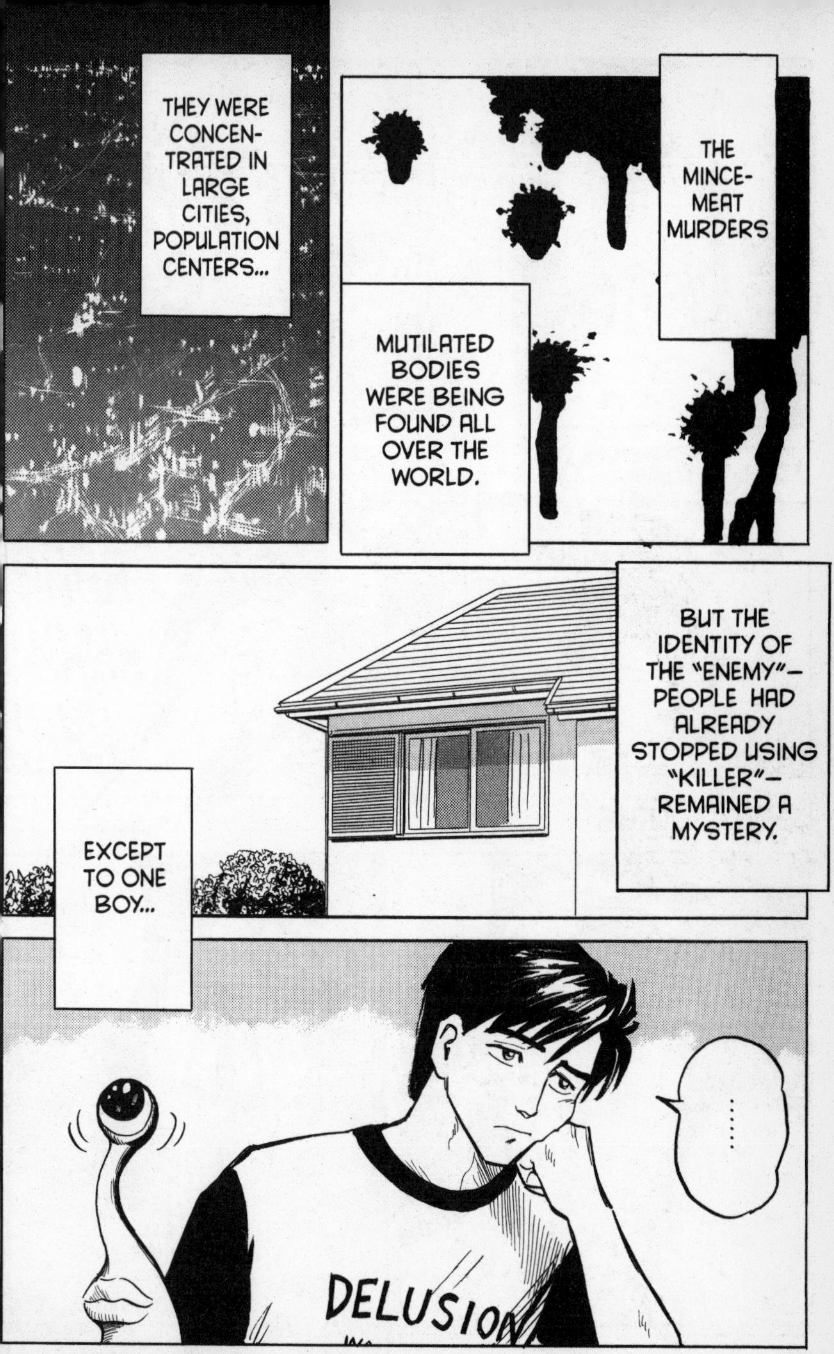
THE MINCE-MEAT MURDERS
MUTILATED BODIES WERE BEING FOUND ALL OVER THE WORLD.
THEY WERE CONCENTRATED IN LARGE CITIES, POPULATION CENTERS...
BUT THE IDENTITY OF THE "ENEMY"—PEOPLE HAD ALREADY STOPPED USING "KILLER"—REMAINED A MYSTERY.
EXCEPT TO ONE BOY...
......
DELUSION

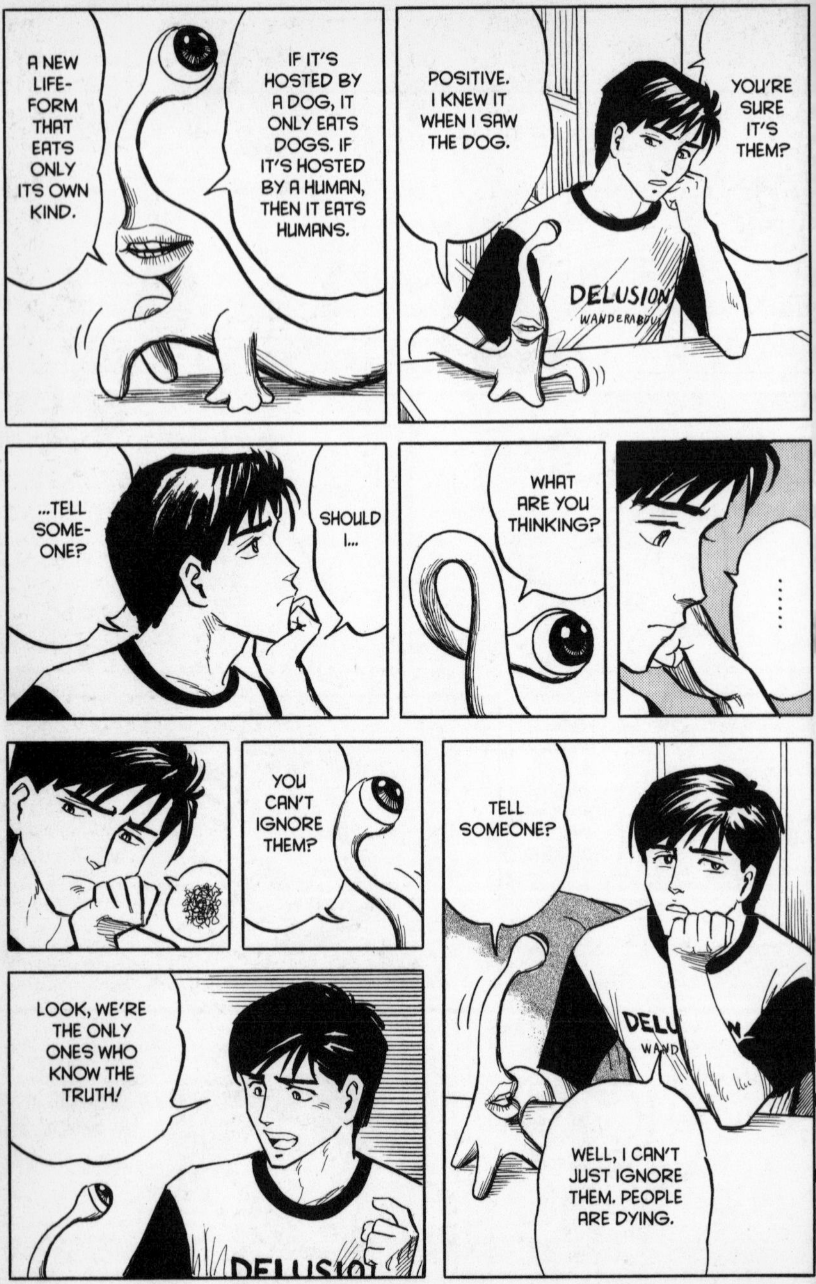
YOU'RE SURE IT'S THEM?
POSITIVE. I KNEW IT WHEN I SAW THE DOG.
DELUSION
WANDERABOUT
IF IT'S HOSTED BY A DOG, IT ONLY EATS DOGS. IF IT'S HOSTED BY A HUMAN, THEN IT EATS HUMANS.
A NEW LIFE-FORM THAT EATS ONLY ITS OWN KIND.
......
WHAT ARE YOU THINKING?
SHOULD I...
...TELL SOMEONE?
TELL SOMEONE?
WELL, I CAN'T JUST IGNORE THEM. PEOPLE ARE DYING.
YOU CAN'T IGNORE THEM?
LOOK, WE'RE THE ONLY ONES WHO KNOW THE TRUTH!

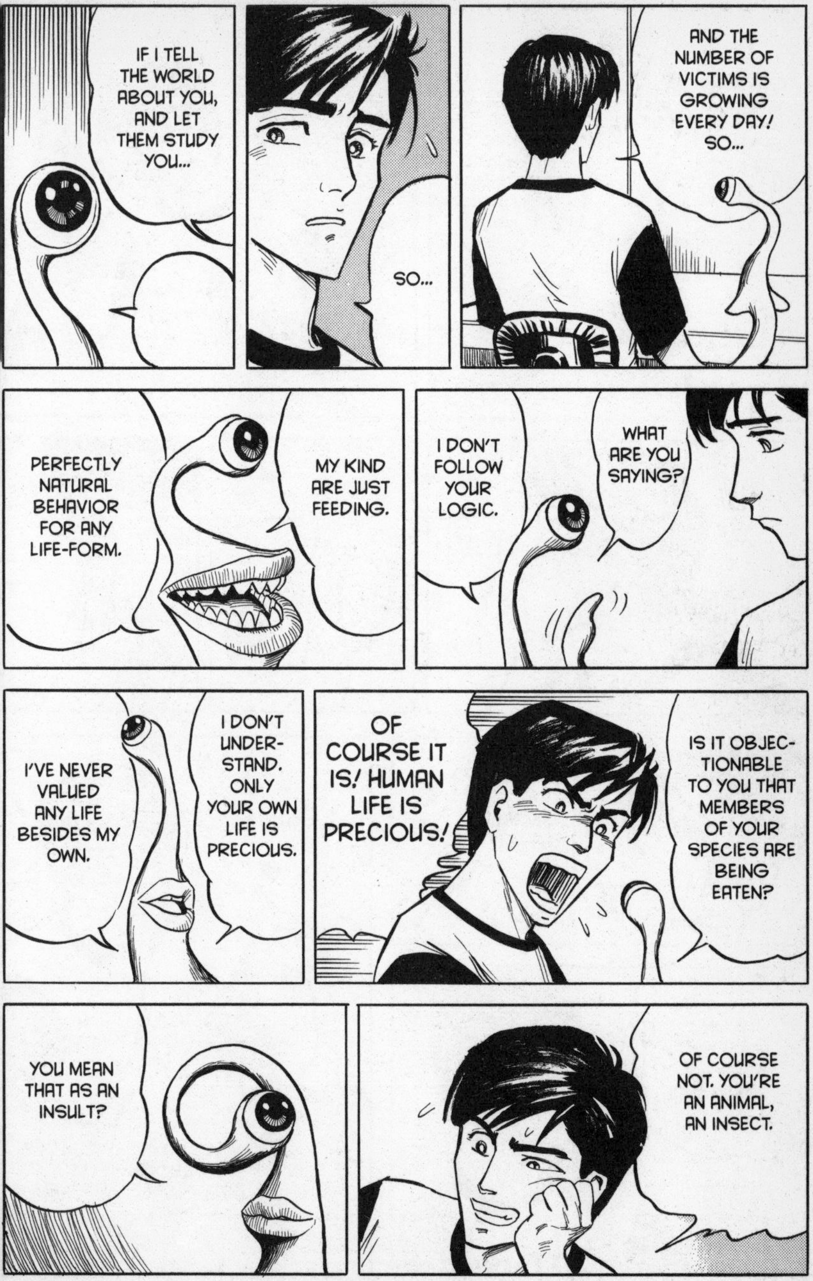
AND THE NUMBER OF VICTIMS IS GROWING EVERY DAY! SO...
SO...
IF I TELL THE WORLD ABOUT YOU, AND LET THEM STUDY YOU...
WHAT ARE YOU SAYING?
I DON'T FOLLOW YOUR LOGIC.
MY KIND ARE JUST FEEDING.
PERFECTLY NATURAL BEHAVIOR FOR ANY LIFE-FORM.
IS IT OBJECTIONABLE TO YOU THAT MEMBERS OF YOUR SPECIES ARE BEING EATEN?
OF COURSE IT IS! HUMAN LIFE IS PRECIOUS!
I DON'T UNDERSTAND. ONLY YOUR OWN LIFE IS PRECIOUS.
I'VE NEVER VALUED ANY LIFE BESIDES MY OWN.
OF COURSE NOT. YOU'RE AN ANIMAL, AN INSECT.
YOU MEAN THAT AS AN INSULT?

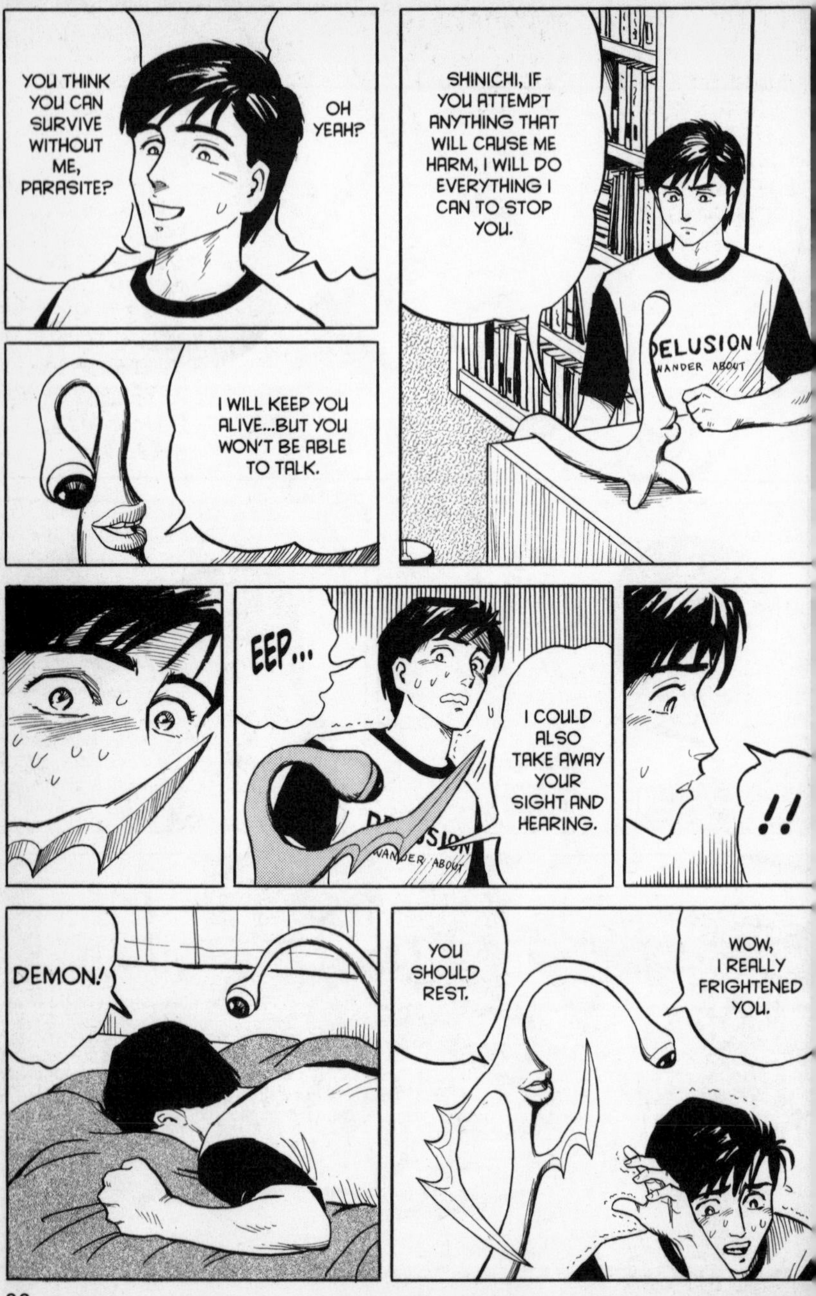
SHINICHI, IF YOU ATTEMPT ANYTHING THAT WILL CAUSE ME HARM, I WILL DO EVERYTHING I CAN TO STOP YOU.
DELUSION WANDER ABOUT
OH YEAH?
YOU THINK YOU CAN SURVIVE WITHOUT ME, PARASITE?
I WILL KEEP YOU ALIVE...BUT YOU WON'T BE ABLE TO TALK.
!!
EEP...
I COULD ALSO TAKE AWAY YOUR SIGHT AND HEARING.
WOW, I REALLY FRIGHTENED YOU.
YOU SHOULD REST.
DEMON!

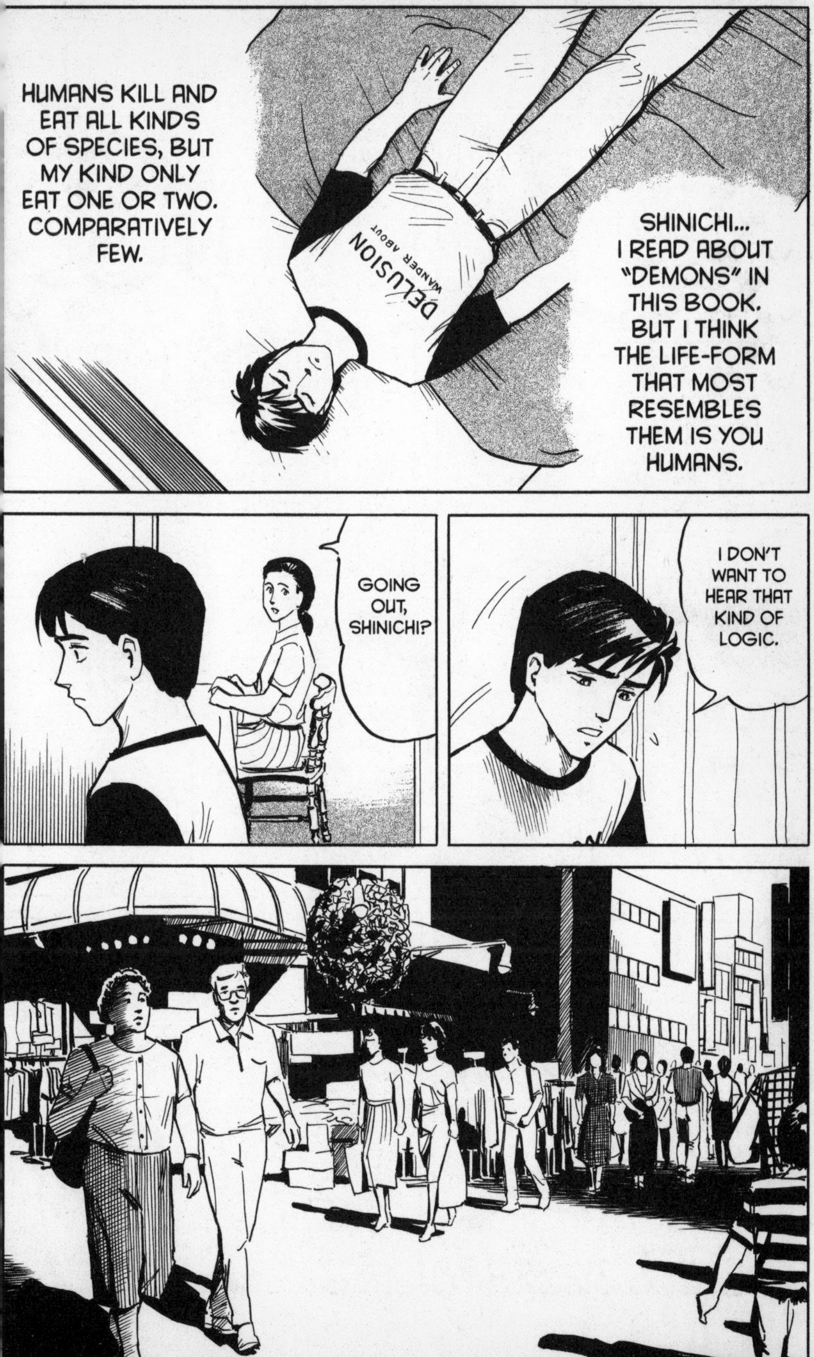
SHINICHI... I READ ABOUT "DEMONS" IN THIS BOOK. BUT I THINK THE LIFE-FORM THAT MOST RESEMBLES THEM IS YOU HUMANS.
DELUSION
WANDER ABOUT
HUMANS KILL AND EAT ALL KINDS OF SPECIES, BUT MY KIND ONLY EAT ONE OR TWO. COMPARATIVELY FEW.
I DON'T WANT TO HEAR THAT KIND OF LOGIC.
GOING OUT, SHINICHI?

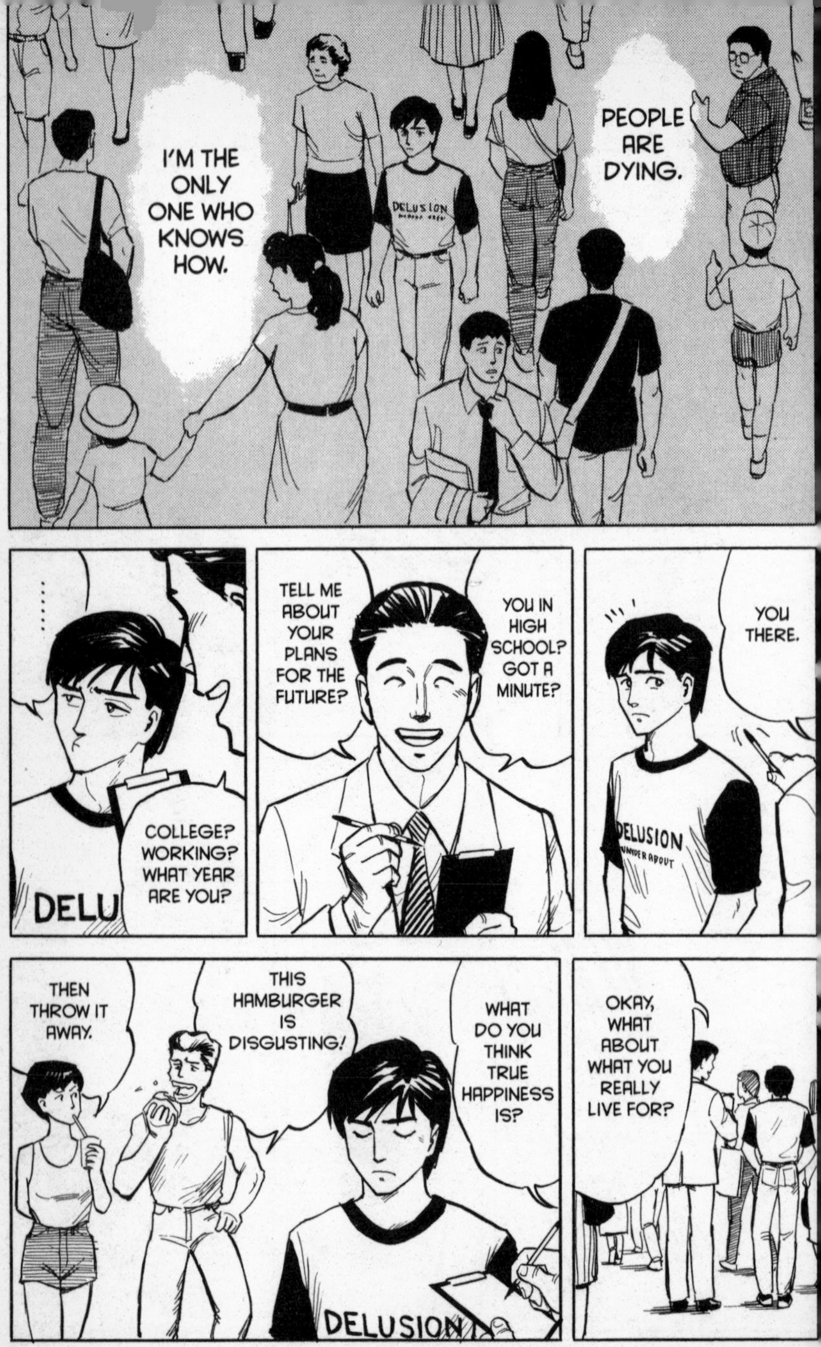
PEOPLE ARE DYING.
I'M THE ONLY ONE WHO KNOWS HOW.
DELUSION
YOU THERE.
DELUSION
YOU IN HIGH SCHOOL? GOT A MINUTE?
TELL ME ABOUT YOUR PLANS FOR THE FUTURE?
......
COLLEGE? WORKING? WHAT YEAR ARE YOU?
DELU
OKAY, WHAT ABOUT WHAT YOU REALLY LIVE FOR?
WHAT DO YOU THINK TRUE HAPPINESS IS?
DELUSION
THIS HAMBURGER IS DISGUSTING!
THEN THROW IT AWAY.

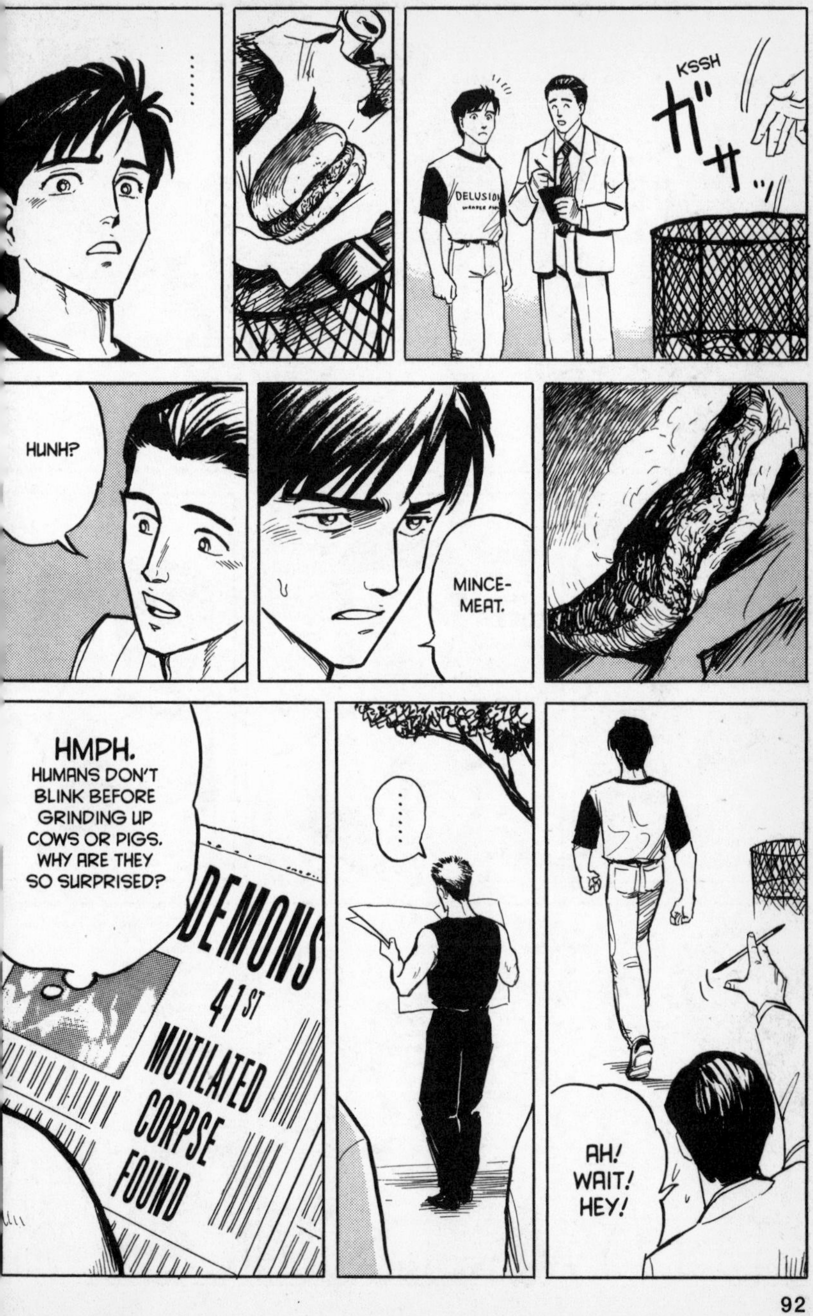
KSSH
ガサッ
DELUSION
......
MINCE-MEAT.
HUNH?
AH! WAIT! HEY!
......
HMPH. HUMANS DON'T BLINK BEFORE GRINDING UP COWS OR PIGS. WHY ARE THEY SO SURPRISED?
DEMONS
41ST
MUTILATED CORPSE FOUND

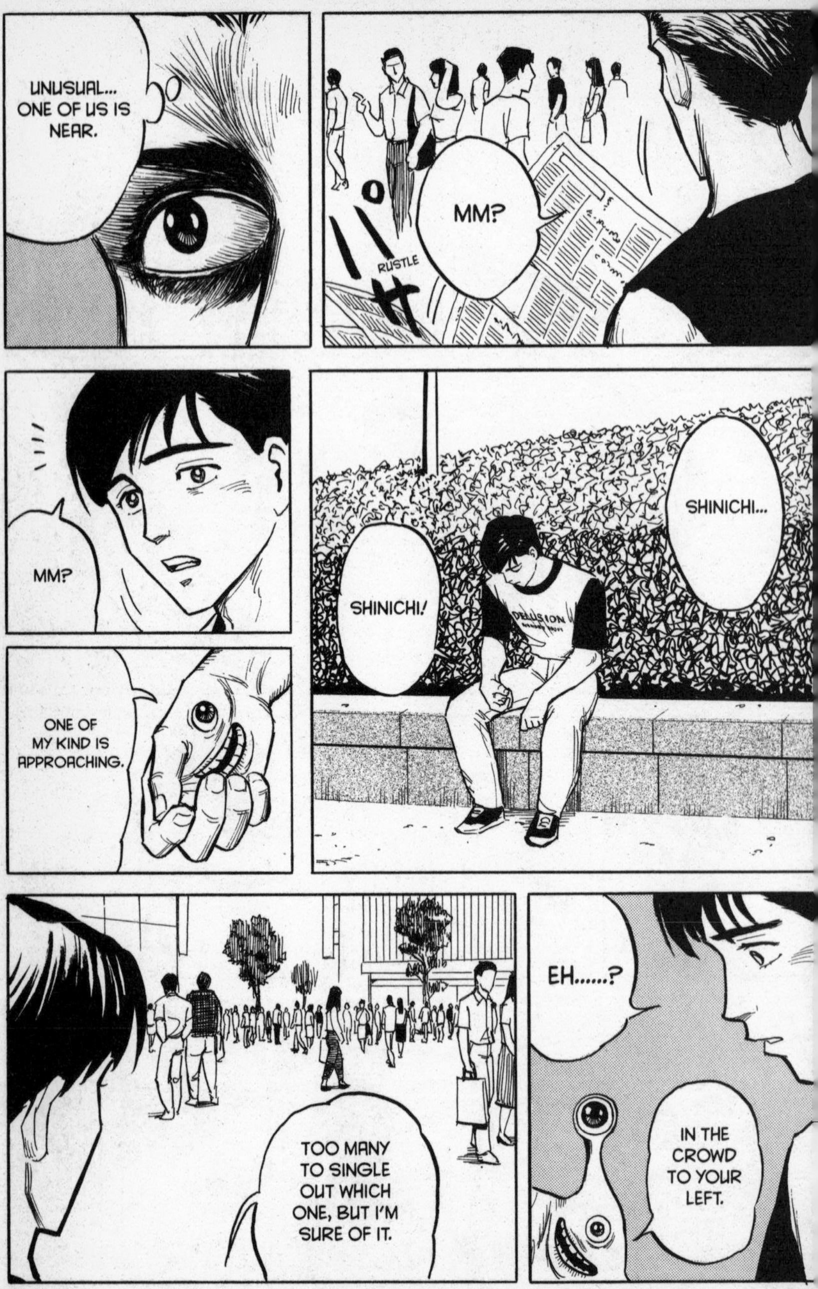

MM?
RUSTLE
UNUSUAL... ONE OF US IS NEAR.
SHINICHI...
SHINICHI!
DELUSION
MM?
ONE OF MY KIND IS APPROACHING.
EH......?
IN THE CROWD TO YOUR LEFT.
TOO MANY TO SINGLE OUT WHICH ONE, BUT I'M SURE OF IT.

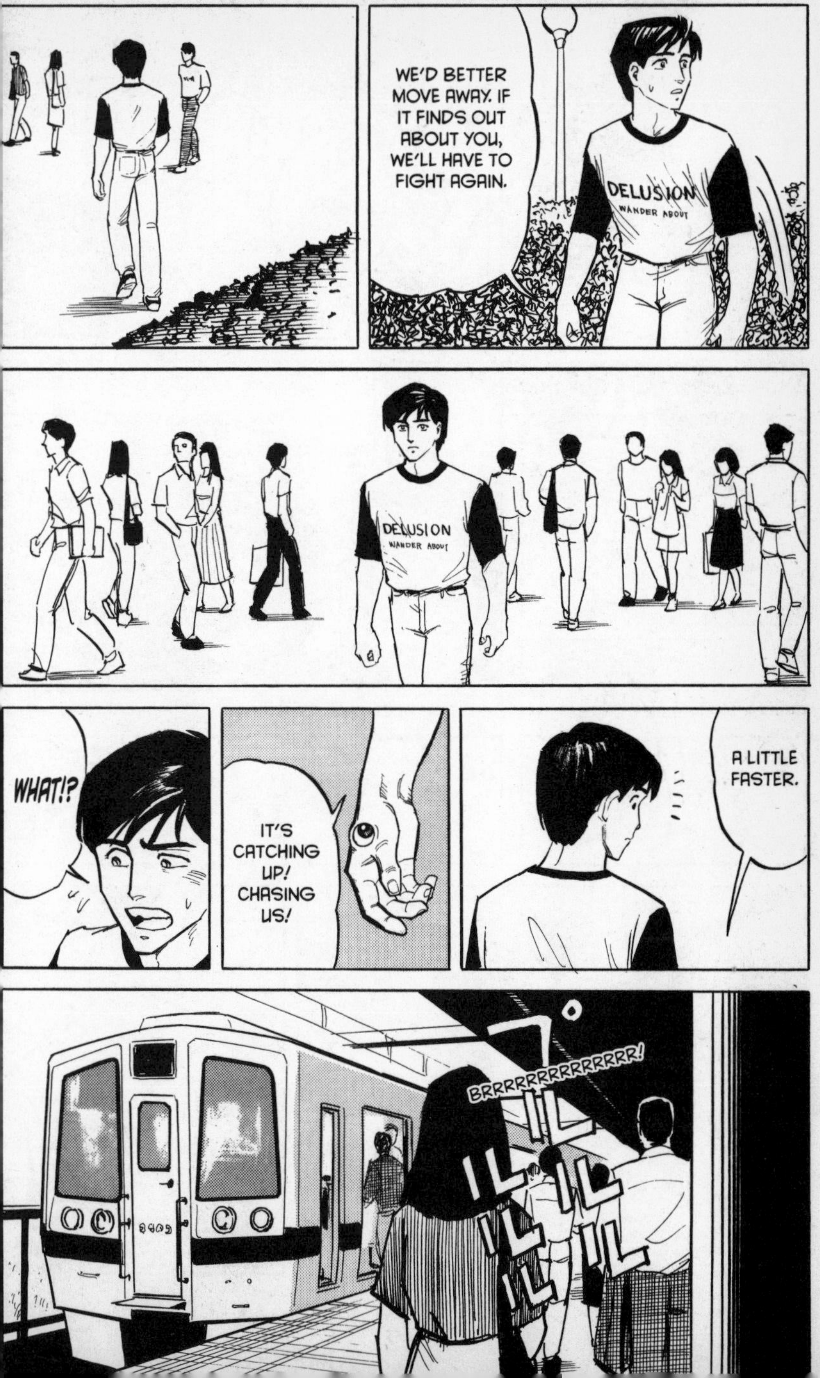
WE'D BETTER MOVE AWAY. IF IT FINDS OUT ABOUT YOU, WE'LL HAVE TO FIGHT AGAIN.
DELUSION
WANDER ABOUT
DELUSION
WANDER ABOUT
A LITTLE FASTER.
IT'S CATCHING UP! CHASING US!
WHAT!?
BRRRRRRRRRRRRRR!

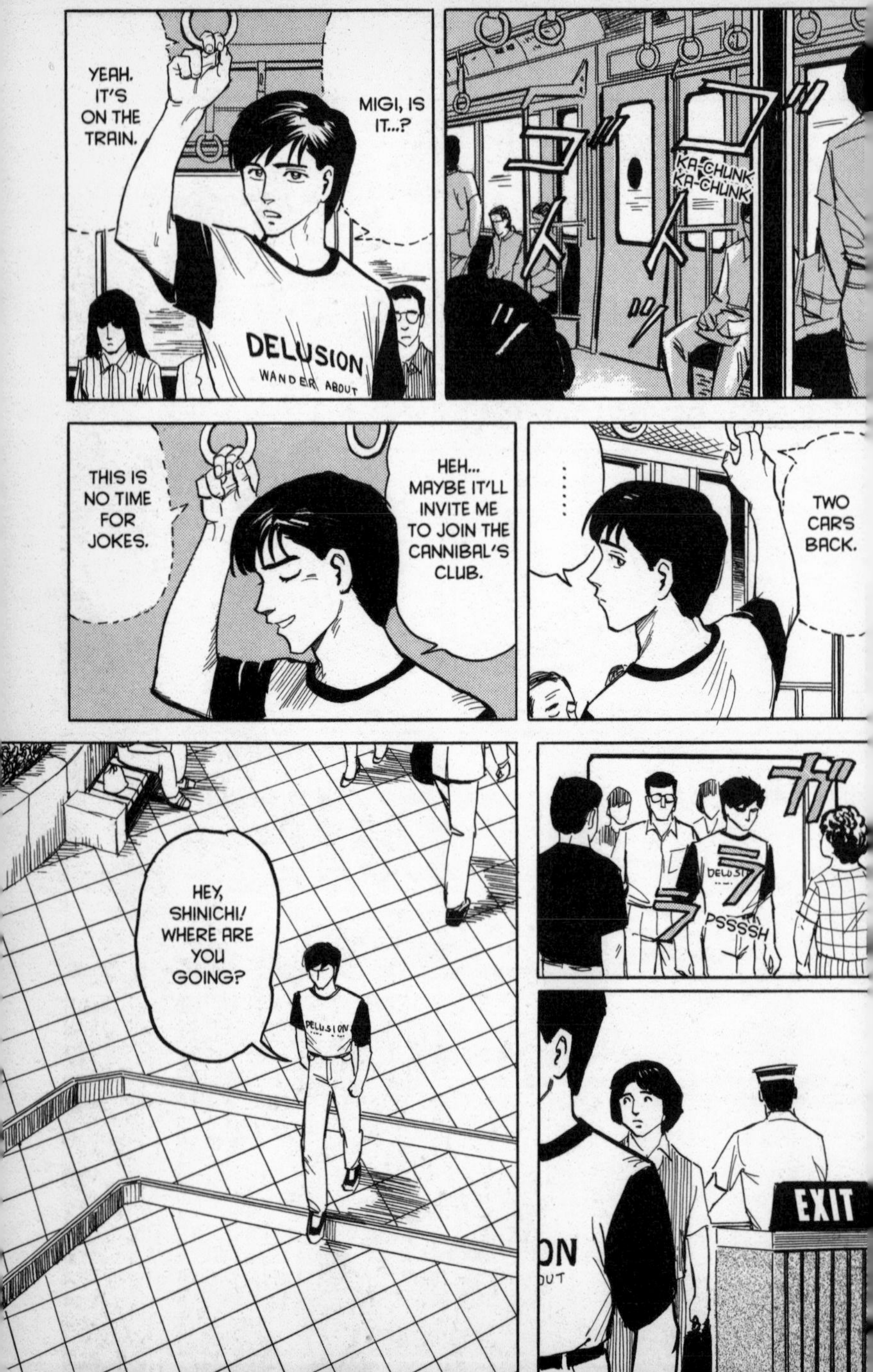
KA-CHUNK
KA-CHUNK
MIGI, IS IT...?
YEAH. IT'S ON THE TRAIN.
DELUSION
WANDER ABOUT
TWO CARS BACK.
......
HEH... MAYBE IT'LL INVITE ME TO JOIN THE CANNIBAL'S CLUB.
THIS IS NO TIME FOR JOKES.
PSSSSH
EXIT
HEY, SHINICHI! WHERE ARE YOU GOING?

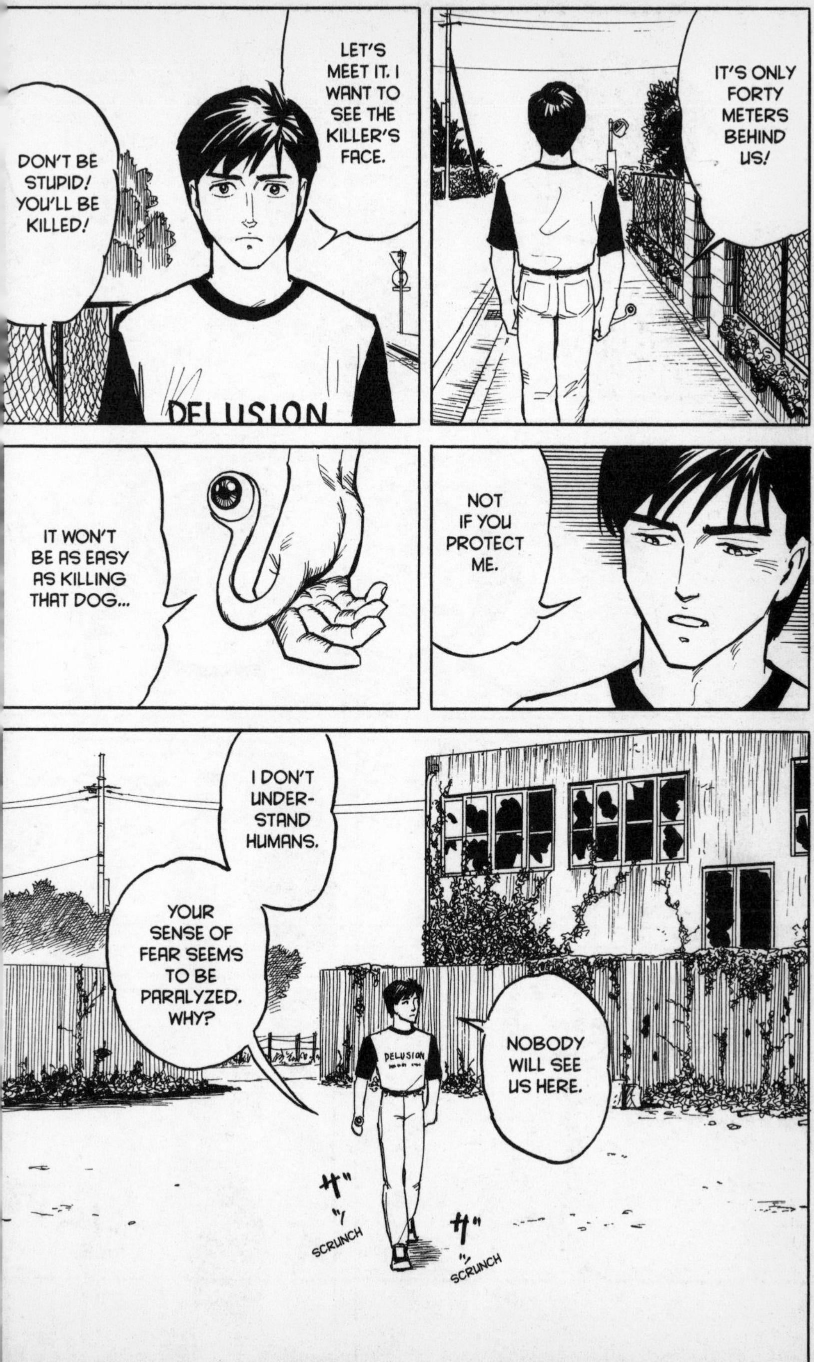
IT'S ONLY FORTY METERS BEHIND US!
LET'S MEET IT. I WANT TO SEE THE KILLER'S FACE.
DON'T BE STUPID! YOU'LL BE KILLED!
DELUSION
NOT IF YOU PROTECT ME.
IT WON'T BE AS EASY AS KILLING THAT DOG...
I DON'T UNDER-STAND HUMANS.
YOUR SENSE OF FEAR SEEMS TO BE PARALYZED. WHY?
NOBODY WILL SEE US HERE.
DELUSION
SCRUNCH
SCRUNCH

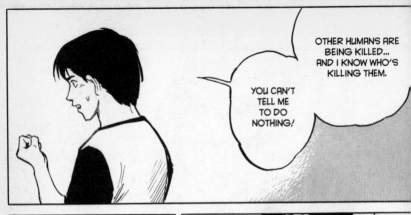

OTHER HUMANS ARE BEING KILLED... AND I KNOW WHO'S KILLING THEM.

YOU CAN'T TELL ME TO DO NOTHING!

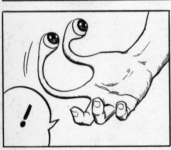

!

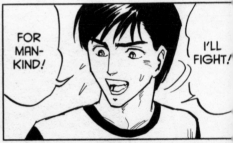

FOR MAN-KIND!

I'LL FIGHT!

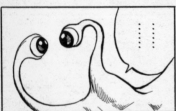

:::

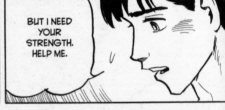

BUT I NEED YOUR STRENGTH. HELP ME.

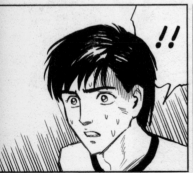

!!

FIVE METERS AWAY.

PLEASE, MIGI!

DELUSIC
WANDER ABOUT

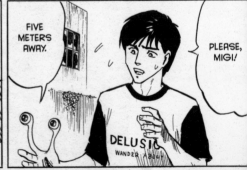

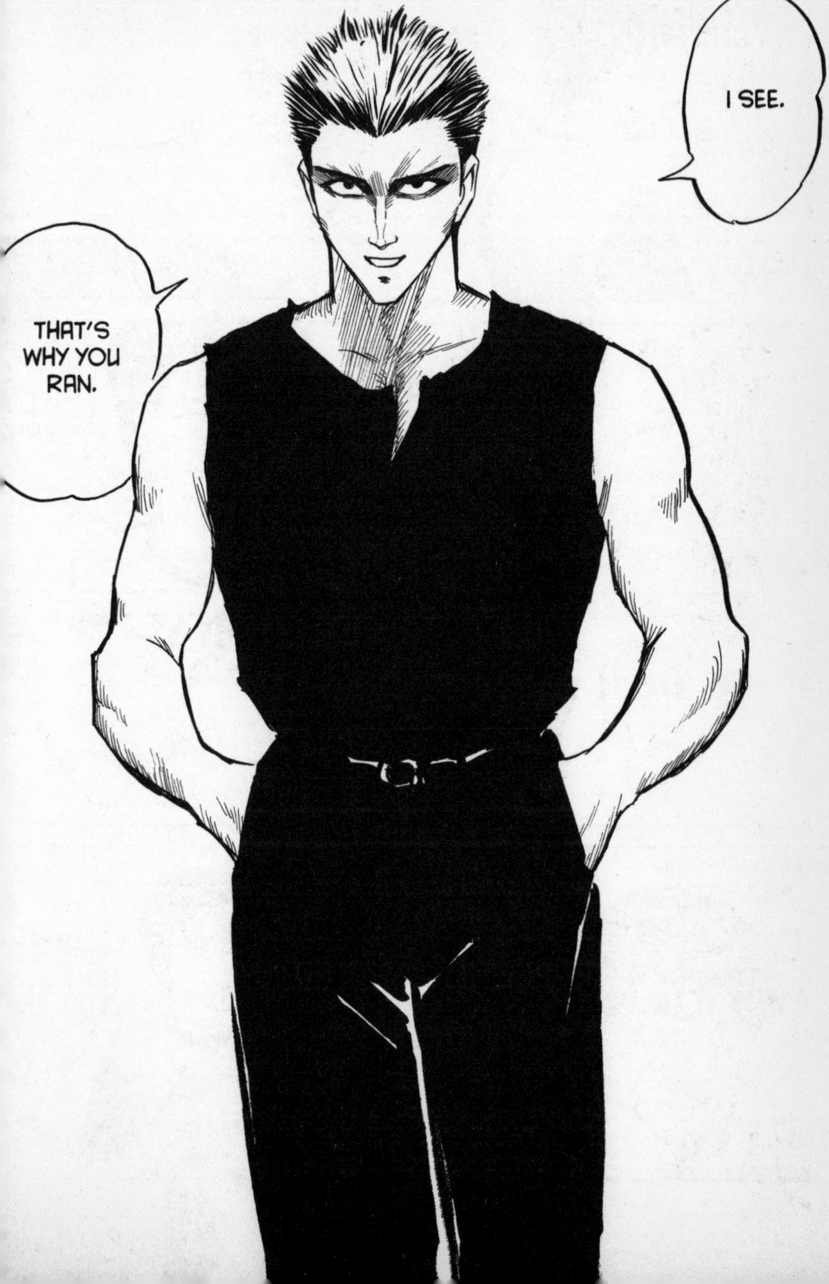
I SEE.
THAT'S WHY YOU RAN.

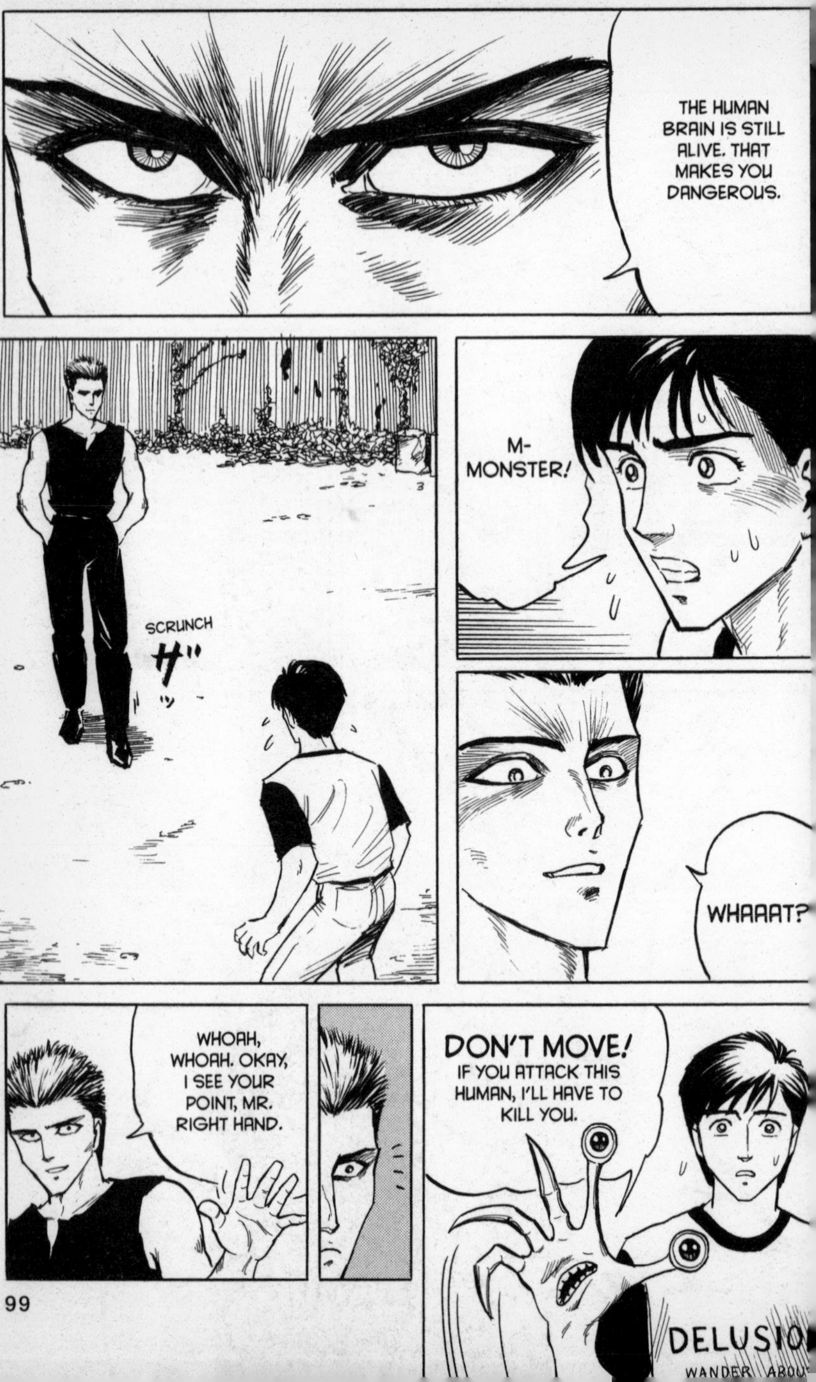
THE HUMAN BRAIN IS STILL ALIVE. THAT MAKES YOU DANGEROUS.
M-MONSTER!
WHAAAT?
SCRUNCH
ザッ
DON'T MOVE!
IF YOU ATTACK THIS HUMAN, I'LL HAVE TO KILL YOU.
DELUSIO
WANDER AROU
WHOAH, WHOAH. OKAY, I SEE YOUR POINT, MR. RIGHT HAND.

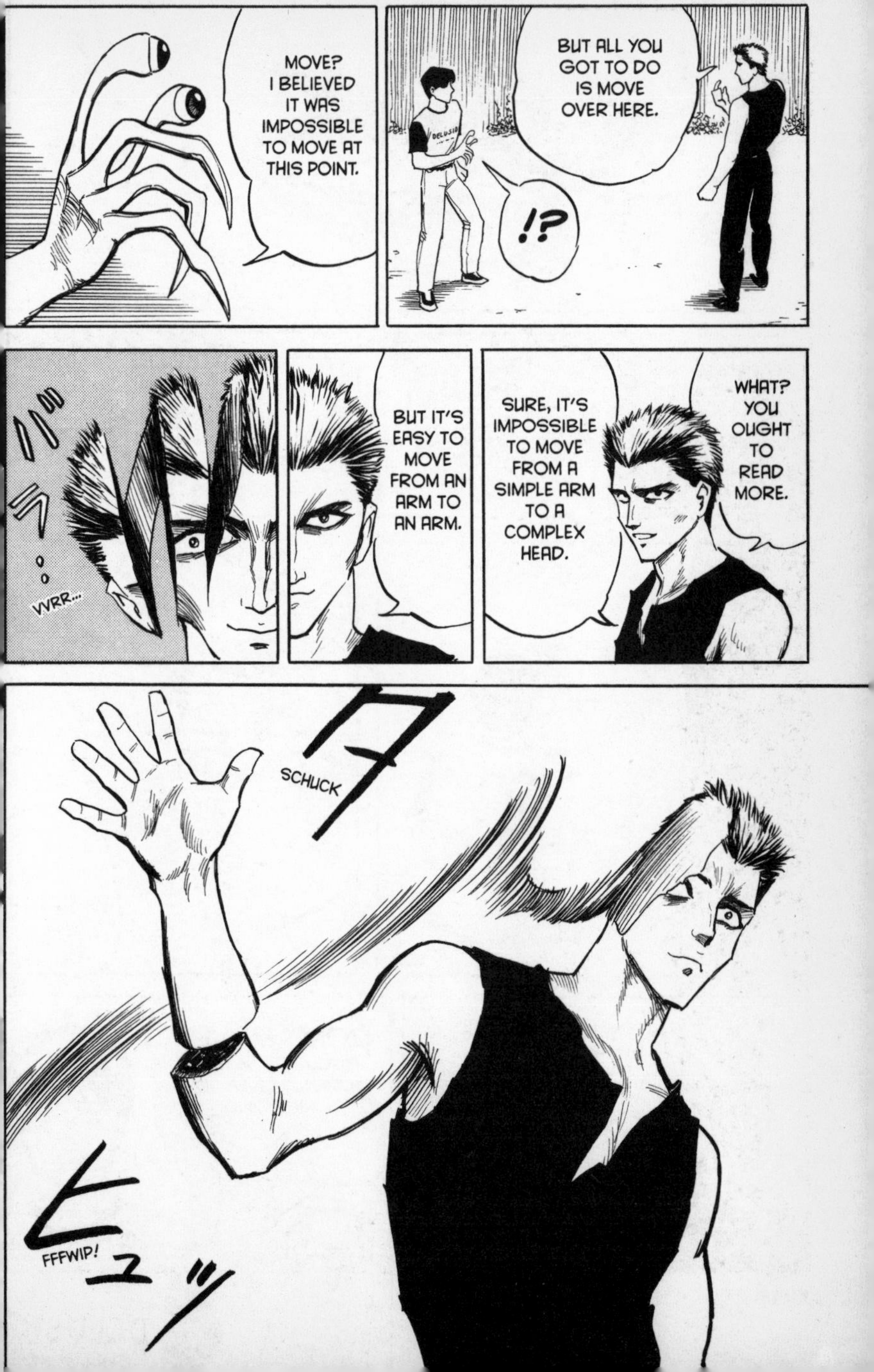
BUT ALL YOU GOT TO DO IS MOVE OVER HERE.
!?
MOVE? I BELIEVED IT WAS IMPOSSIBLE TO MOVE AT THIS POINT.
WHAT? YOU OUGHT TO READ MORE.
SURE, IT'S IMPOSSIBLE TO MOVE FROM A SIMPLE ARM TO A COMPLEX HEAD.
BUT IT'S EASY TO MOVE FROM AN ARM TO AN ARM.
VVRR...
SCHUCK
FFFWIP!

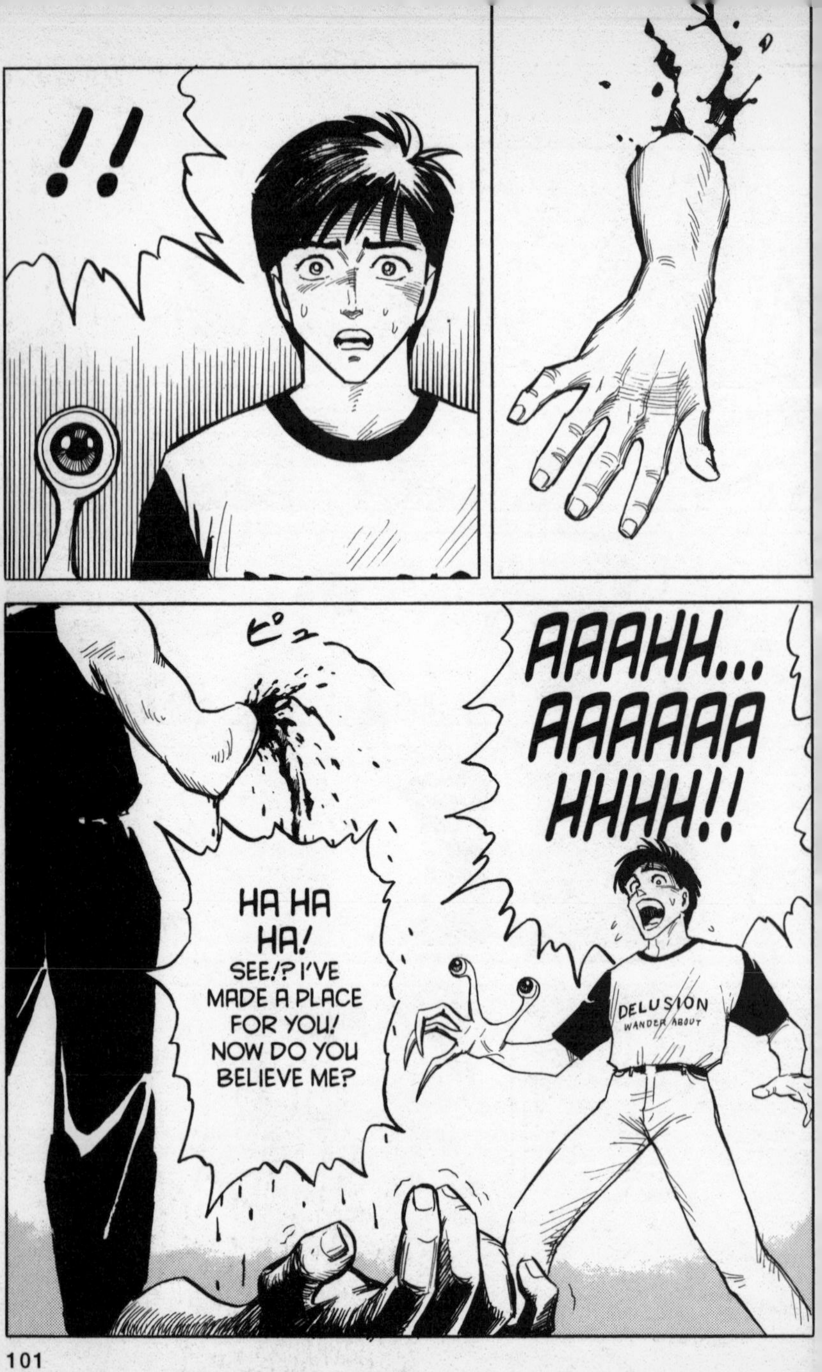
!!
AAAHH... AAAAAA HHHH!!
ピュ
HA HA HA! SEE!? I'VE MADE A PLACE FOR YOU! NOW DO YOU BELIEVE ME?
DELUSION WANDER ABOUT

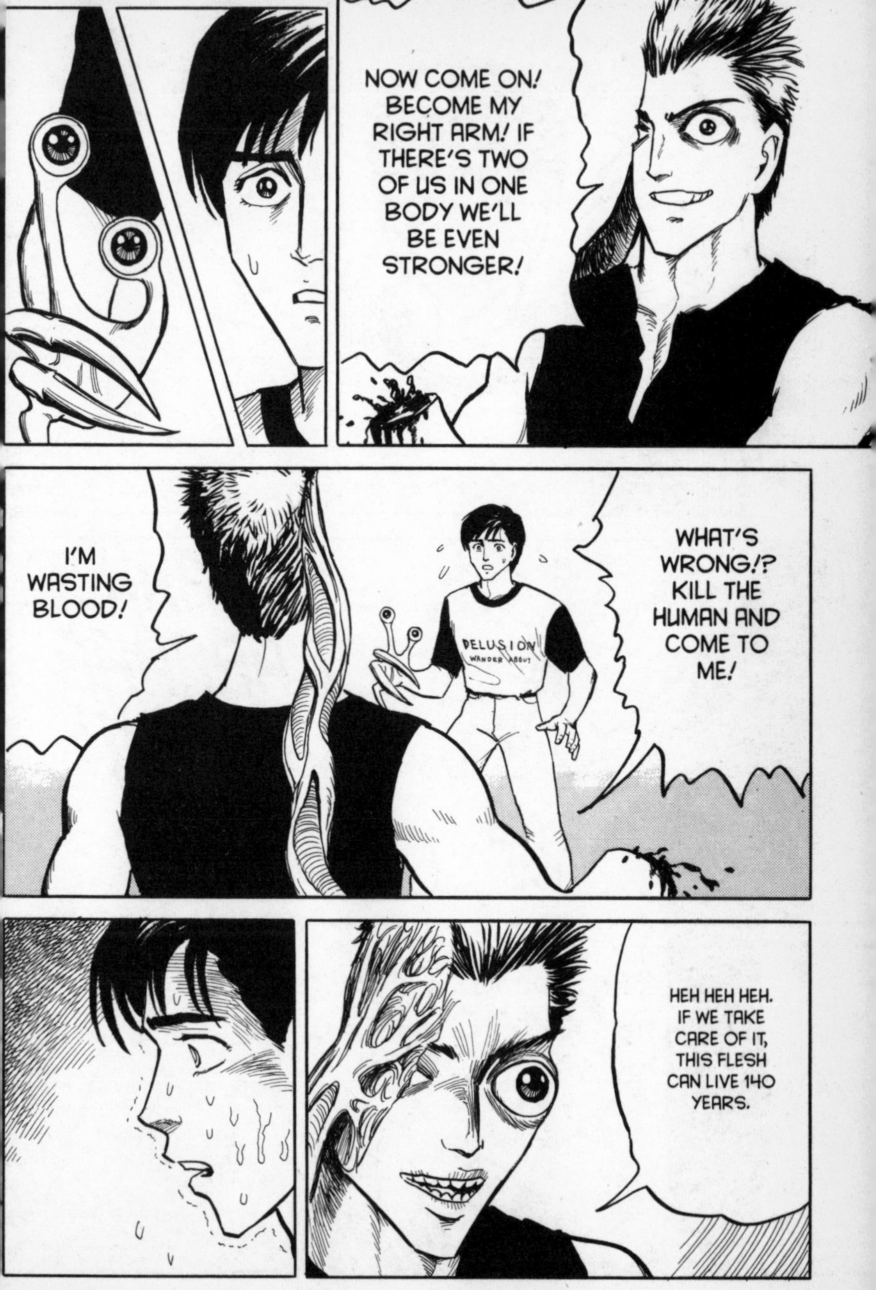
NOW COME ON! BECOME MY RIGHT ARM! IF THERE'S TWO OF US IN ONE BODY WE'LL BE EVEN STRONGER!
WHAT'S WRONG!? KILL THE HUMAN AND COME TO ME!
I'M WASTING BLOOD!
DELUSION
WANDER ABOUT
HEH HEH HEH. IF WE TAKE CARE OF IT, THIS FLESH CAN LIVE 140 YEARS.

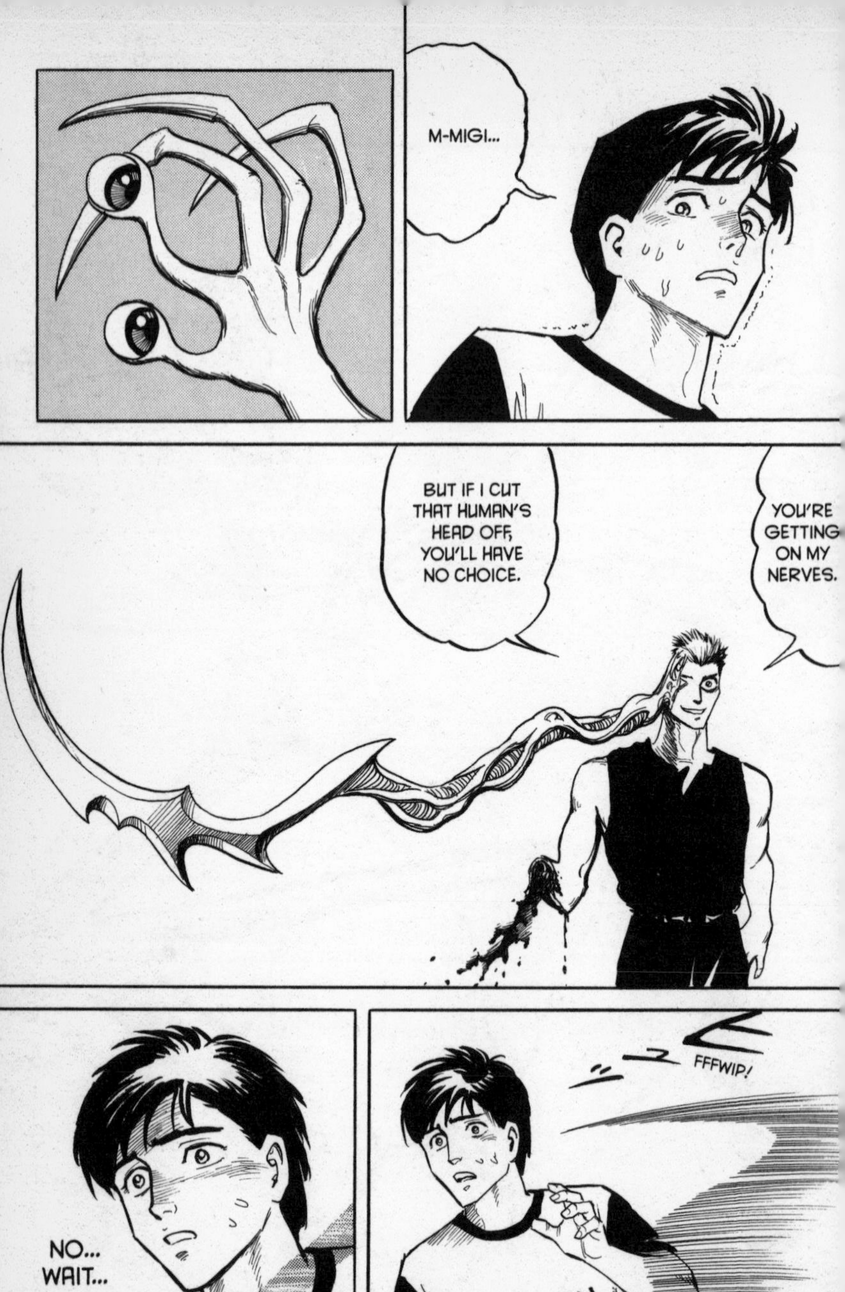
M-MIGI...
YOU'RE GETTING ON MY NERVES.
BUT IF I CUT THAT HUMAN'S HEAD OFF, YOU'LL HAVE NO CHOICE.
FFFWIP!
DELUSION
ABOUT
NO... WAIT...

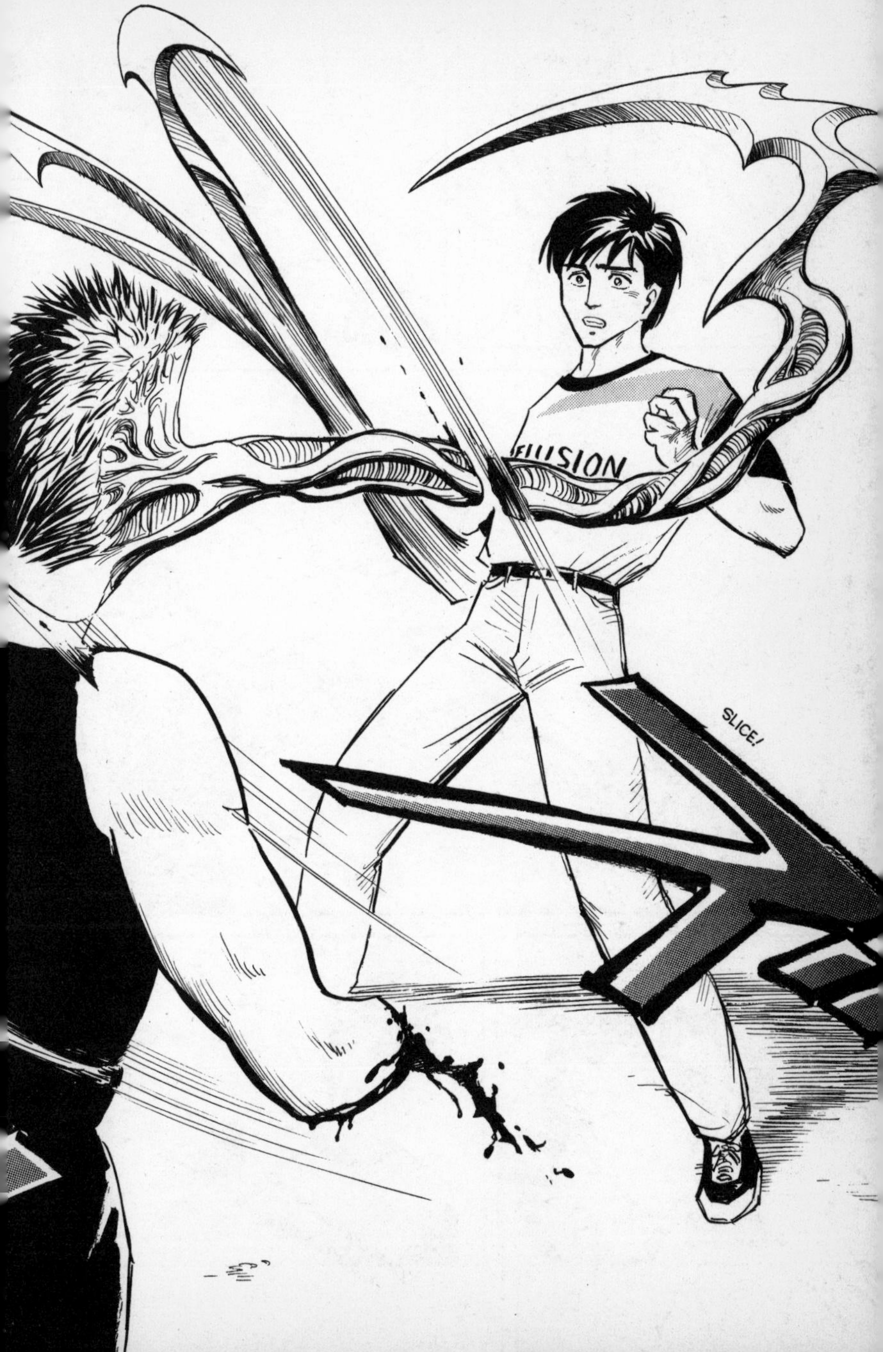
SLICE!

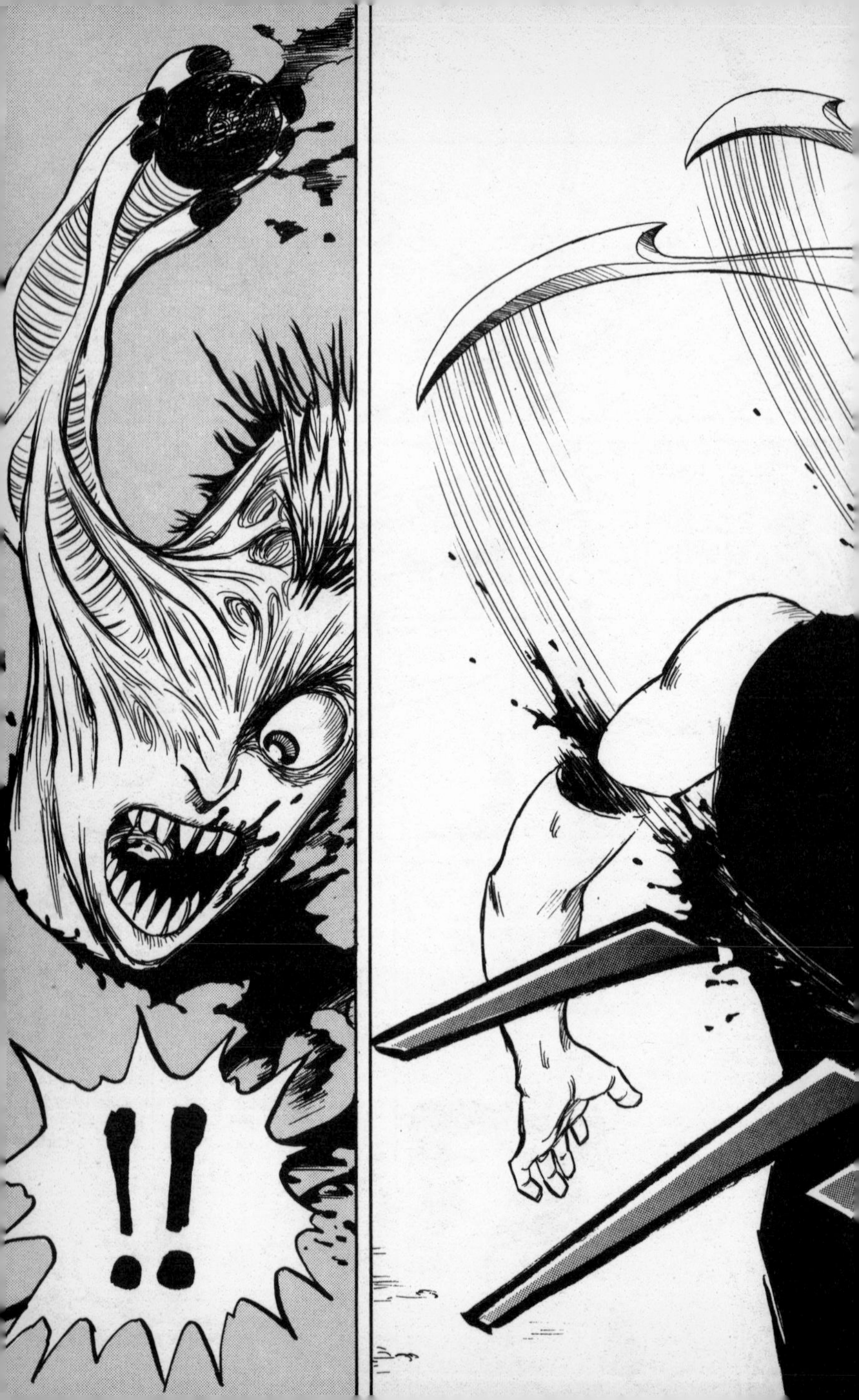
!!

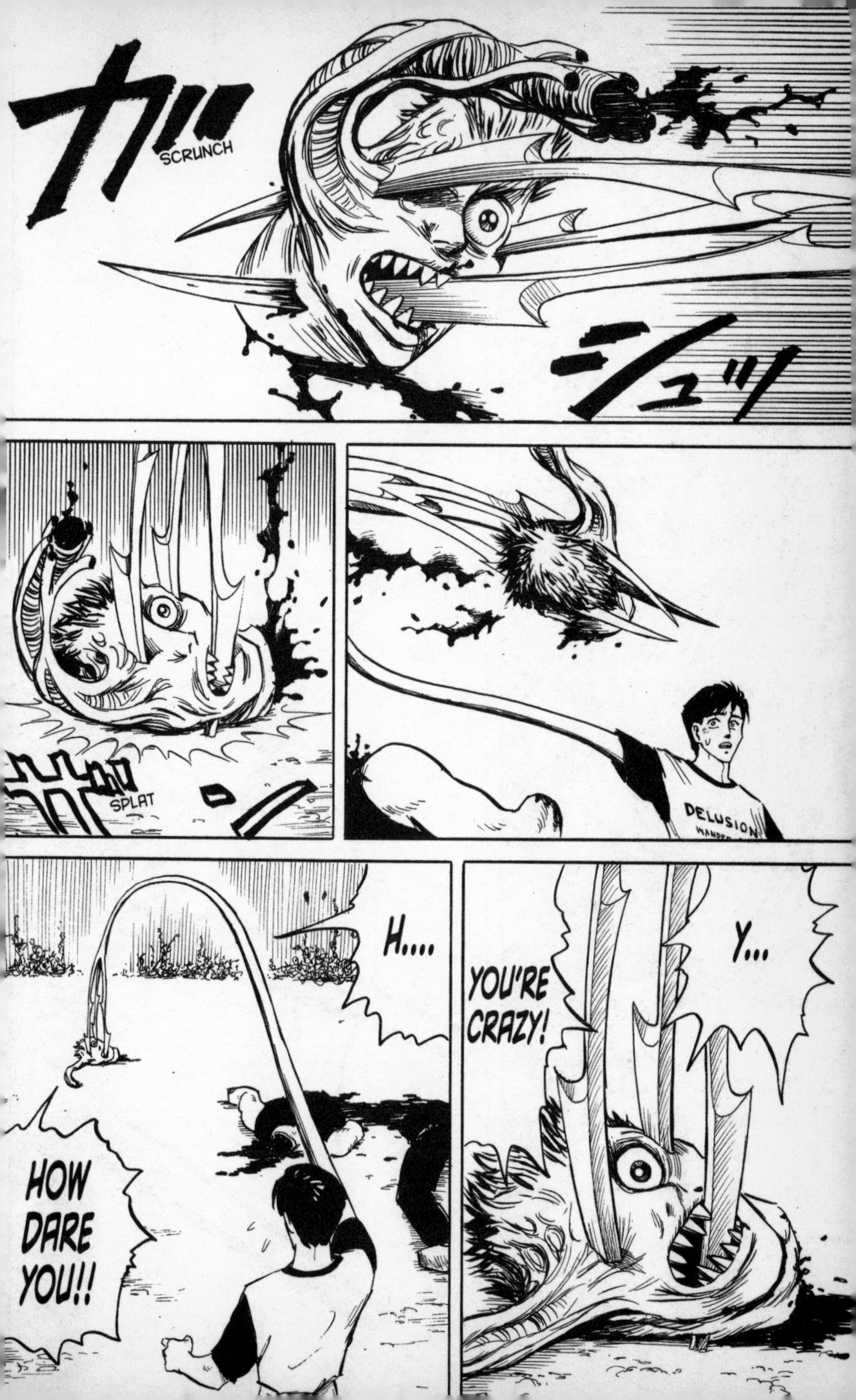
SCRUNCH
シュッ
DELUSION
SPLAT
Y...
YOU'RE CRAZY!
H....
HOW DARE YOU!!

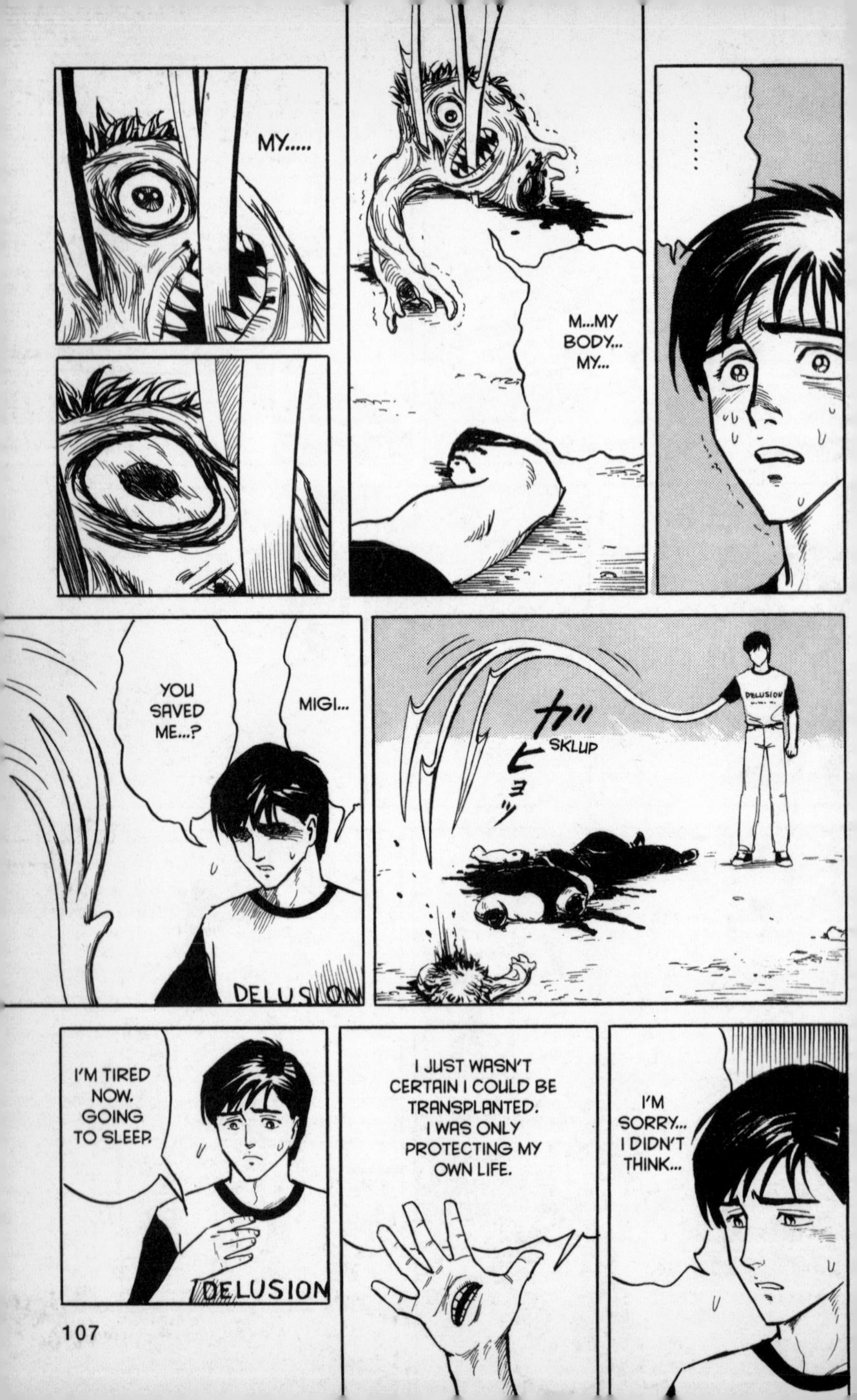

......
M...MY BODY... MY...
MY.....
ガ
ヒョッ
SKLUP
DELUSION
MIGI...
YOU SAVED ME...?
DELUSION
I'M SORRY... I DIDN'T THINK...
I JUST WASN'T CERTAIN I COULD BE TRANSPLANTED. I WAS ONLY PROTECTING MY OWN LIFE.
I'M TIRED NOW. GOING TO SLEEP.
DELUSION

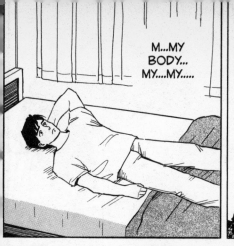

M...MY BODY... MY....MY.....

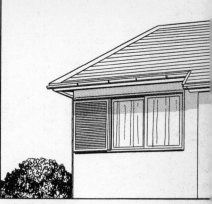

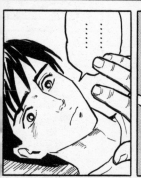

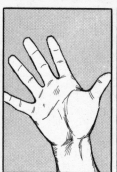

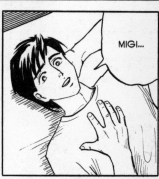

MIGI...

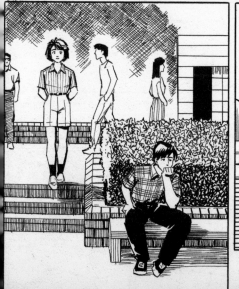

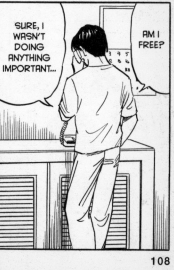

SURE, I WASN'T DOING ANYTHING IMPORTANT...

AM I FREE?

108

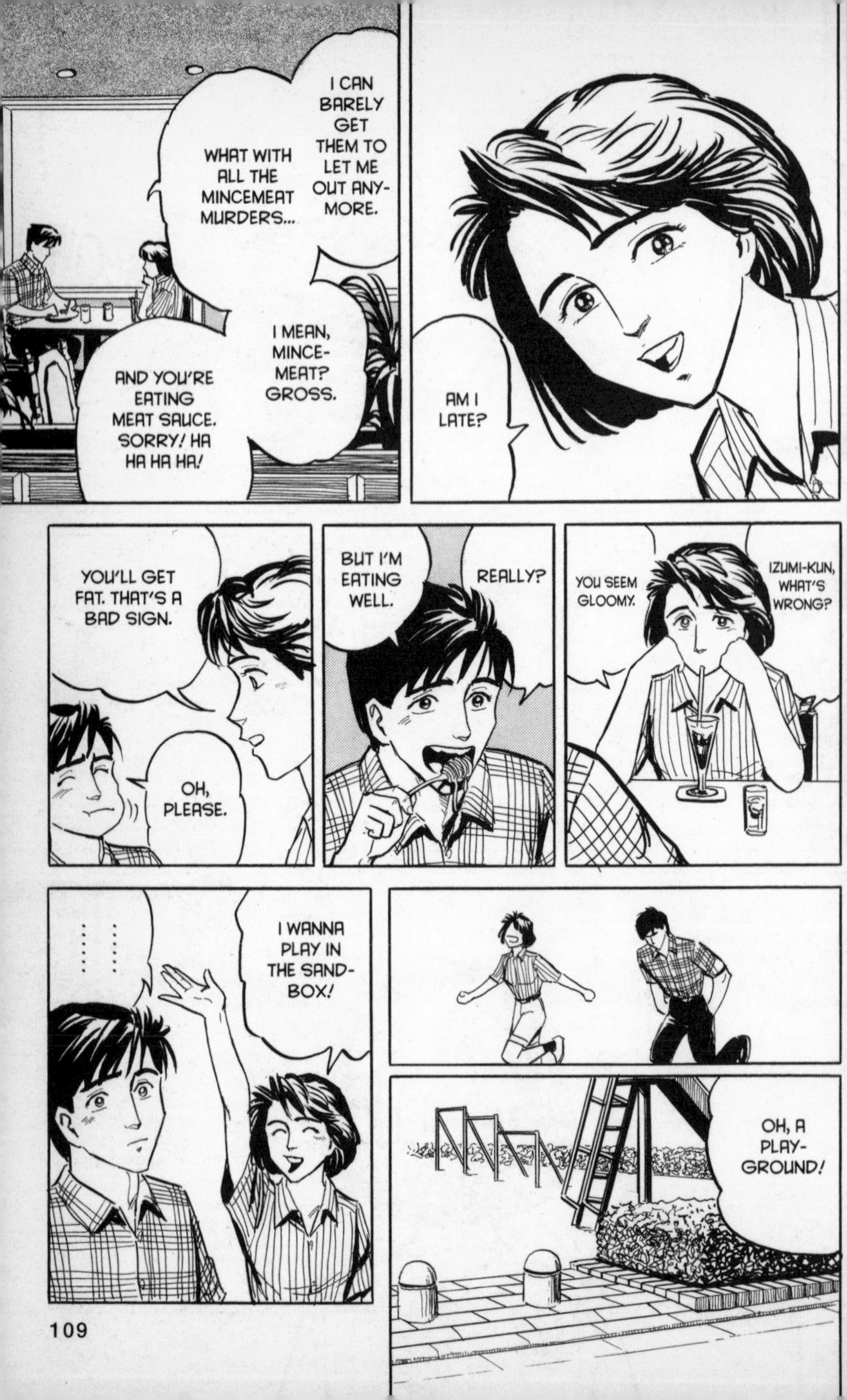
AM I LATE?
I CAN BARELY GET THEM TO LET ME OUT ANY-MORE.
WHAT WITH ALL THE MINCEMEAT MURDERS...
I MEAN, MINCE-MEAT? GROSS.
AND YOU'RE EATING MEAT SAUCE. SORRY! HA HA HA HA!
IZUMI-KUN, WHAT'S WRONG?
YOU SEEM GLOOMY.
REALLY?
BUT I'M EATING WELL.
YOU'LL GET FAT. THAT'S A BAD SIGN.
OH, PLEASE.
OH, A PLAY-GROUND!
I WANNA PLAY IN THE SAND-BOX!
......

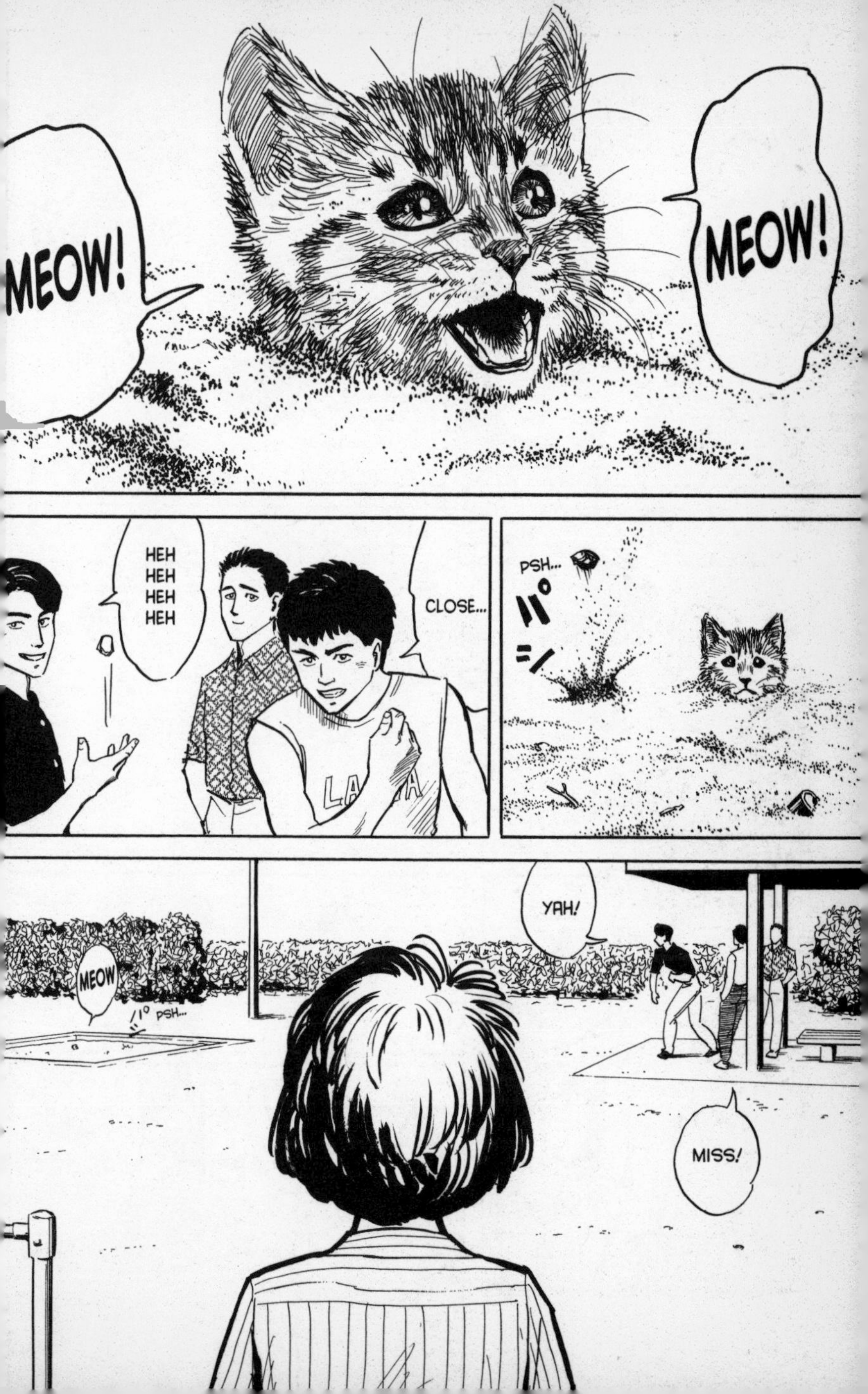
MEOW!
MEOW!
PSH...
CLOSE...
HEH HEH HEH HEH
YAH!
MISS!
MEOW
PSH...

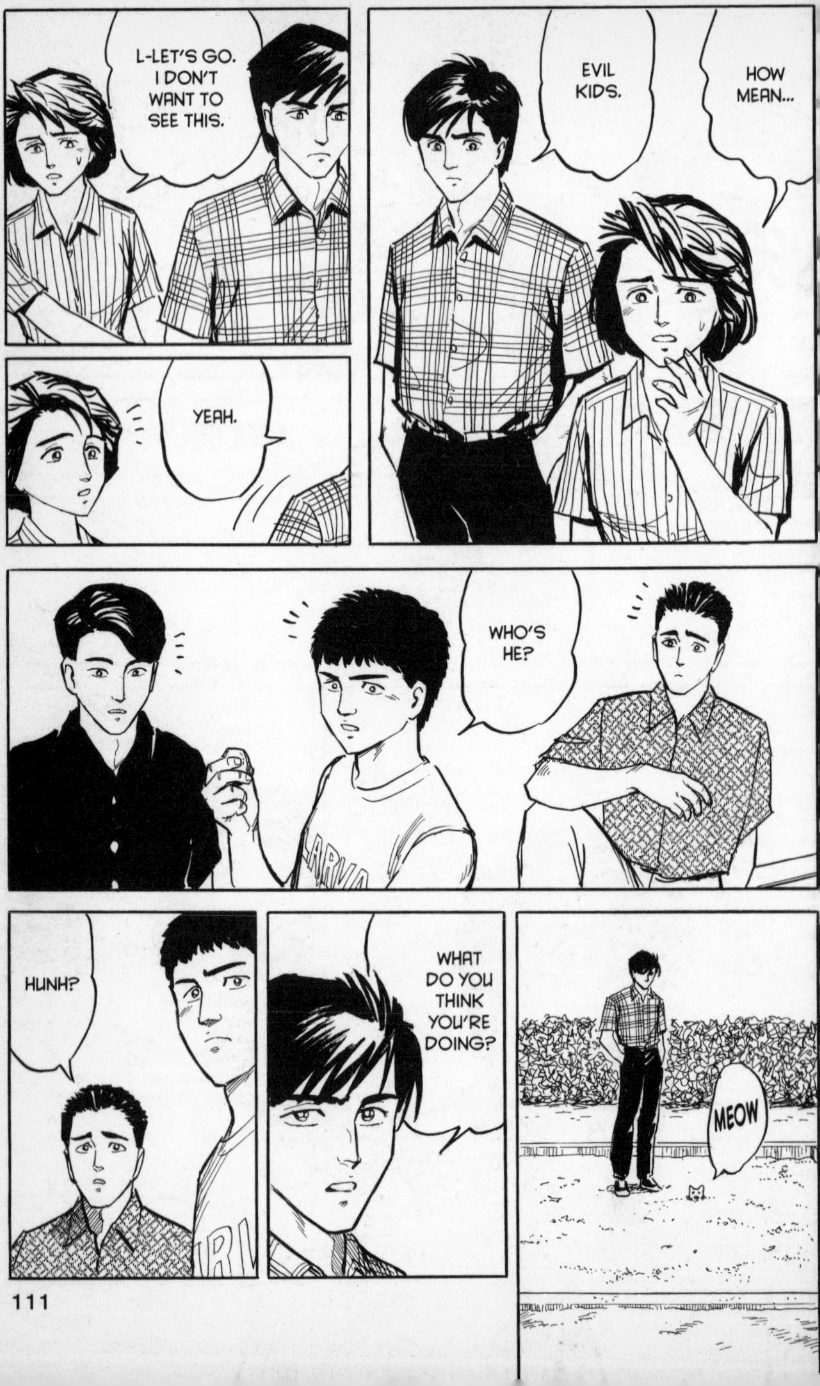
HOW MEAN...
EVIL KIDS.
L-LET'S GO. I DON'T WANT TO SEE THIS.
YEAH.
WHO'S HE?
MEOW
WHAT DO YOU THINK YOU'RE DOING?
HUNH?

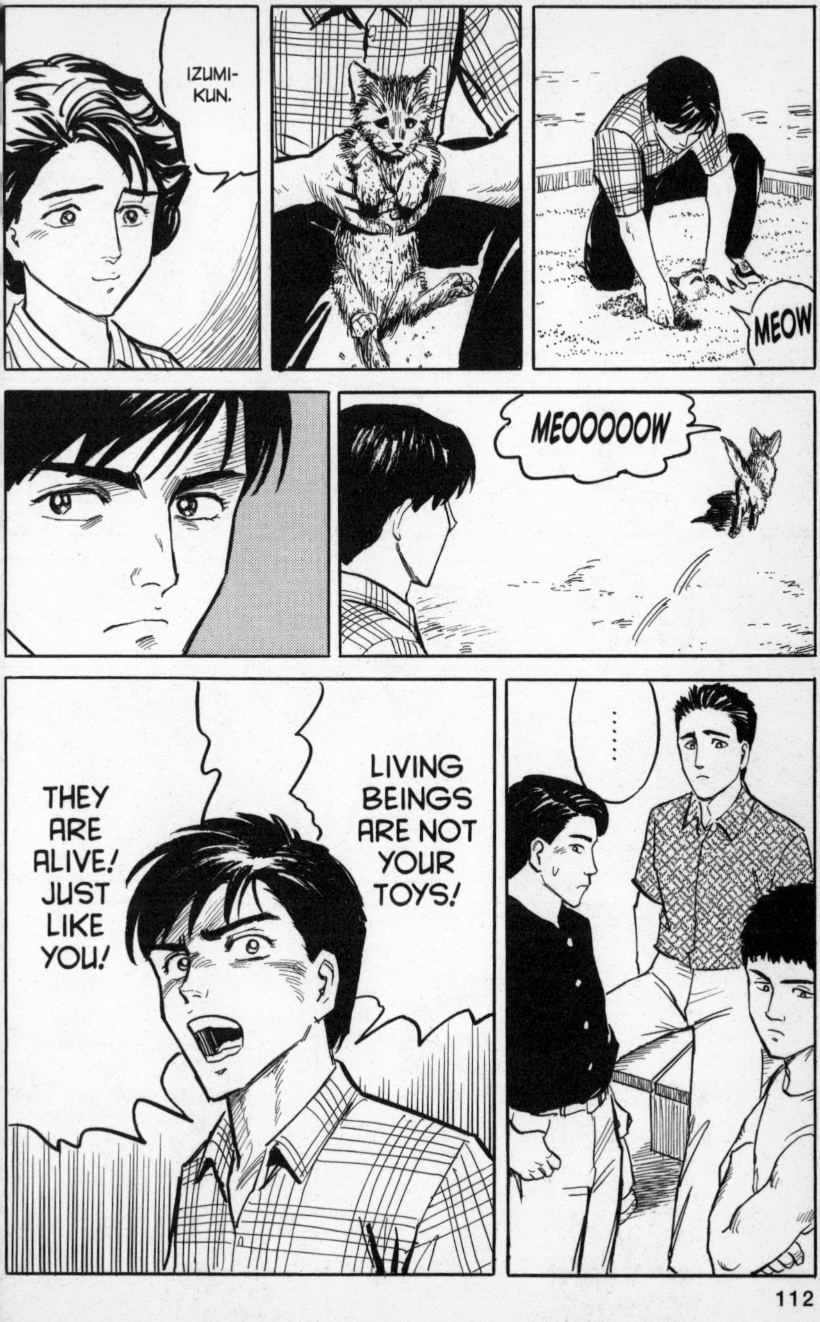
MEOW
IZUMI-KUN.
MEOOOOOW
......
LIVING BEINGS ARE NOT YOUR TOYS!
THEY ARE ALIVE! JUST LIKE YOU!

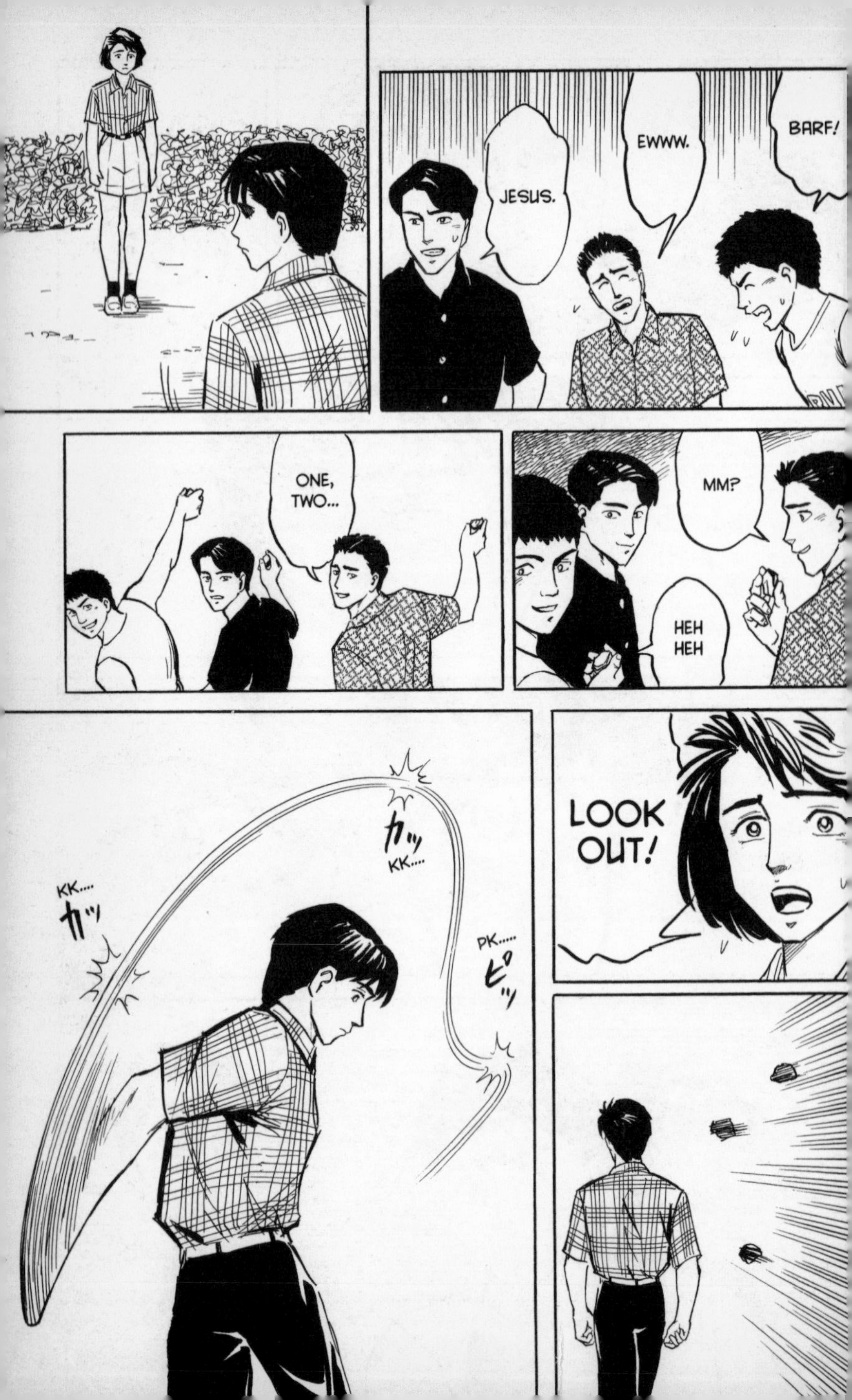
BARF!
EWWW.
JESUS.
MM?
HEH HEH
ONE, TWO...
LOOK OUT!
カッ KK....
PK..... ピッ
KK.... カッ

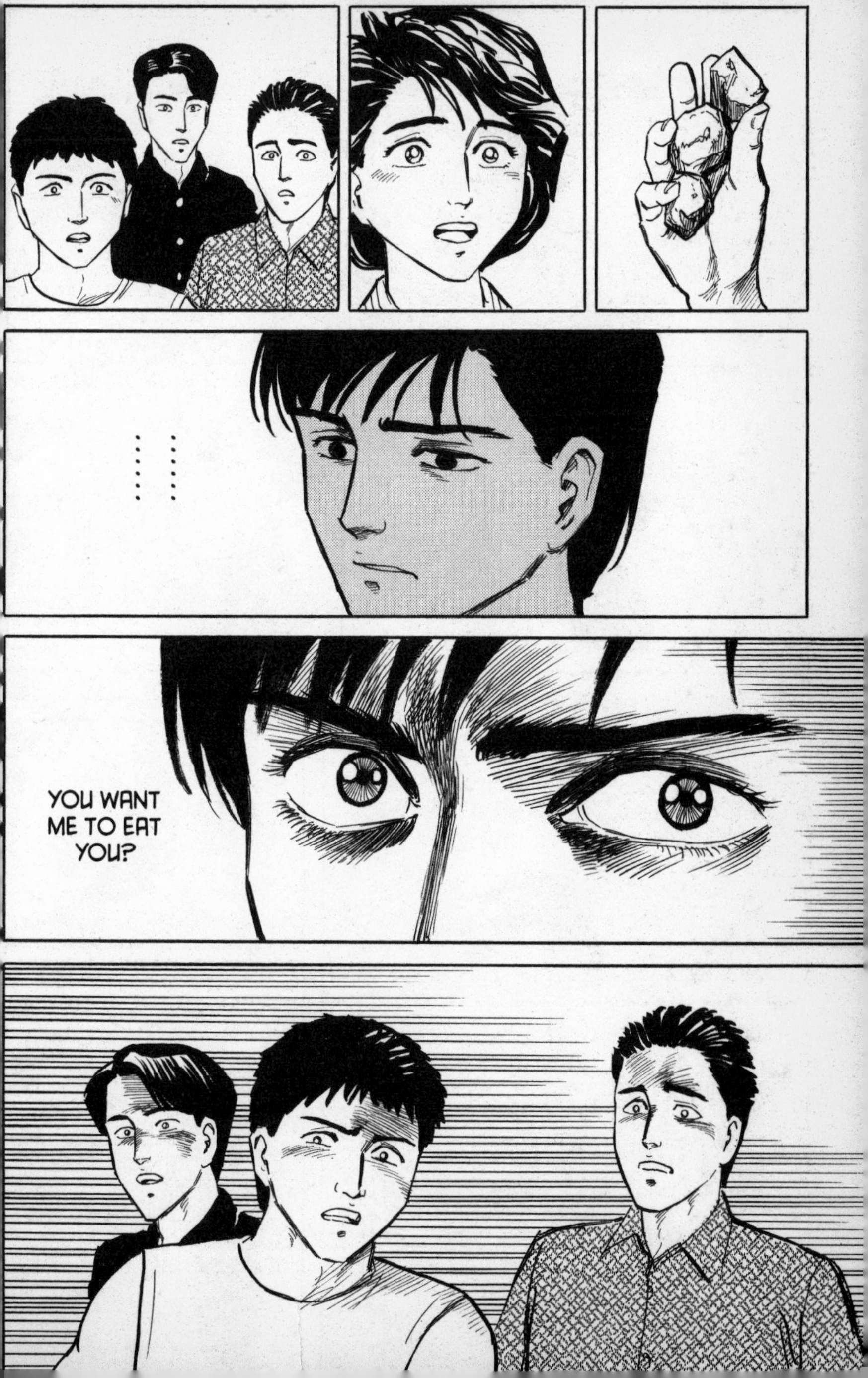
......
YOU WANT ME TO EAT YOU?

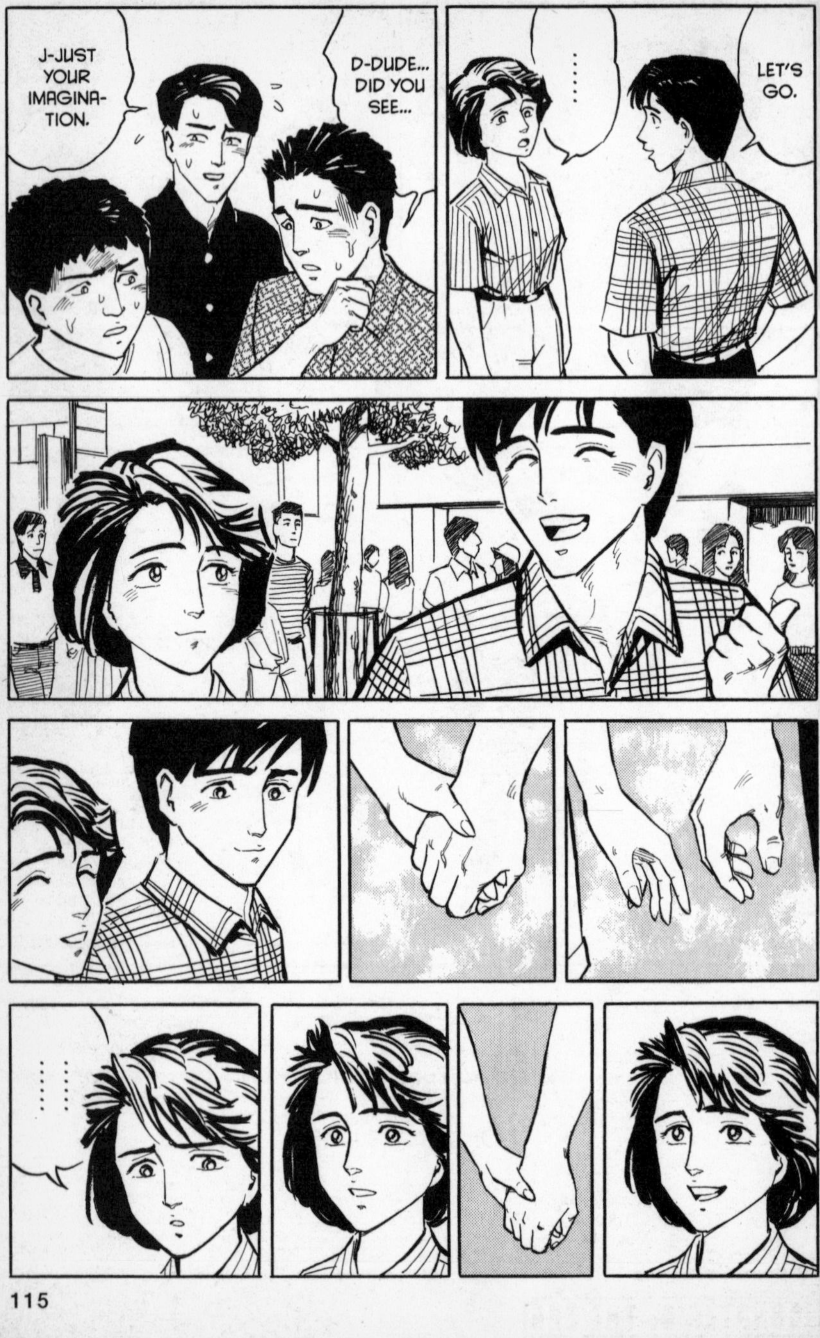
LET'S GO.
......
D-DUDE... DID YOU SEE...
J-JUST YOUR IMAGINA-TION.
......

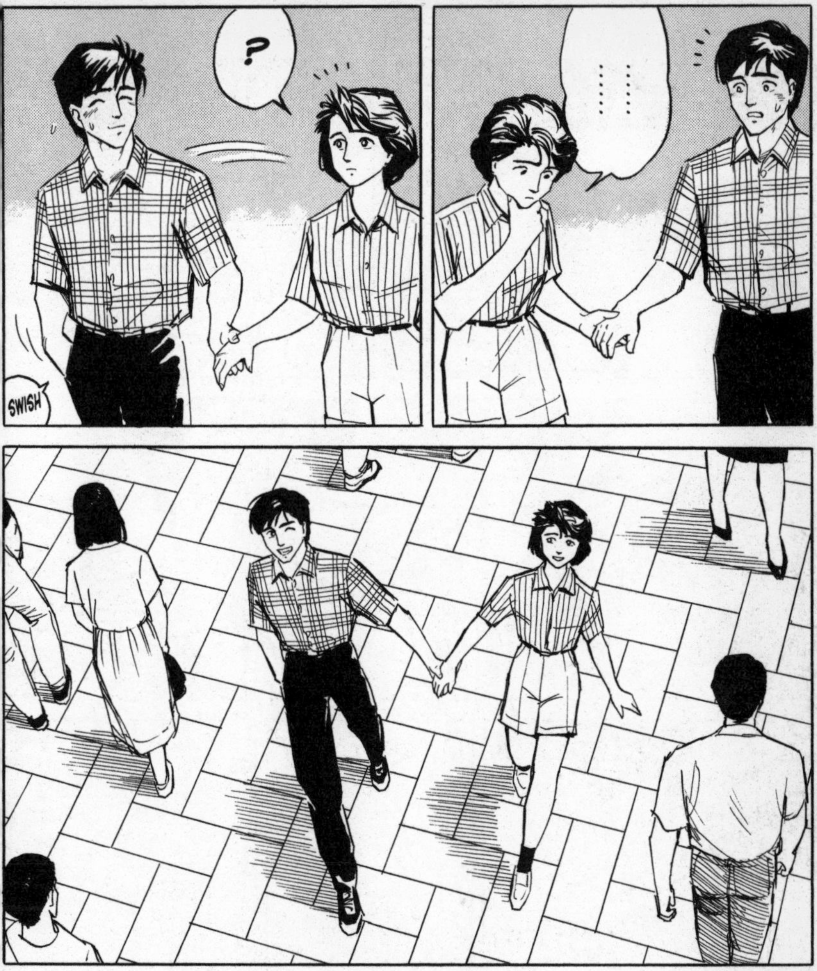

......
?
SWISH

"IZUMI-KUN."
"MM?"
"YOU ARE...IZUMI SHINICHI-KUN... RIGHT?"
"OF COURSE I AM!"

CHAPTER 3: THE END

CHAPTER 4: KILLER'S AURA

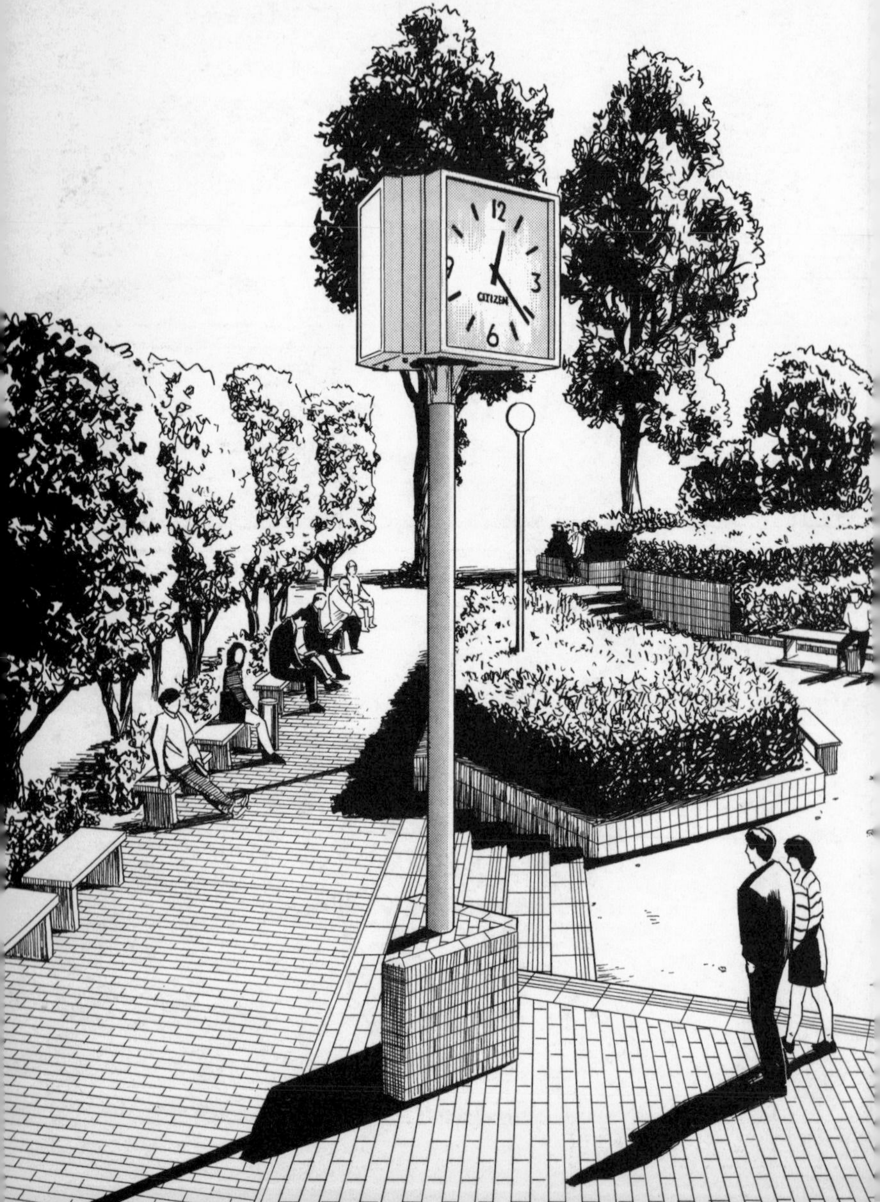
CITIZEN

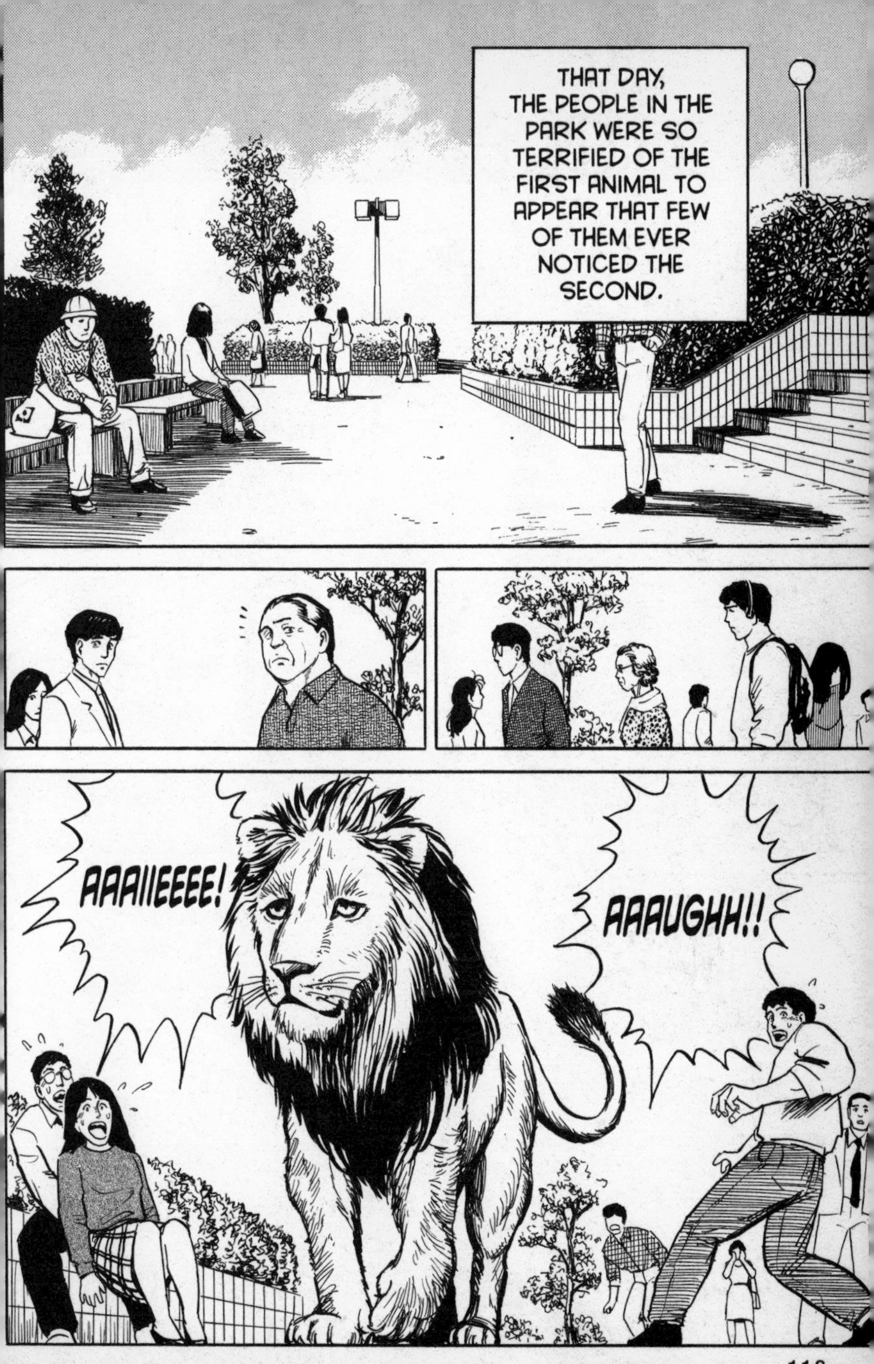
THAT DAY, THE PEOPLE IN THE PARK WERE SO TERRIFIED OF THE FIRST ANIMAL TO APPEAR THAT FEW OF THEM EVER NOTICED THE SECOND.
AAAUGHH!!
AAAIIEEEE!

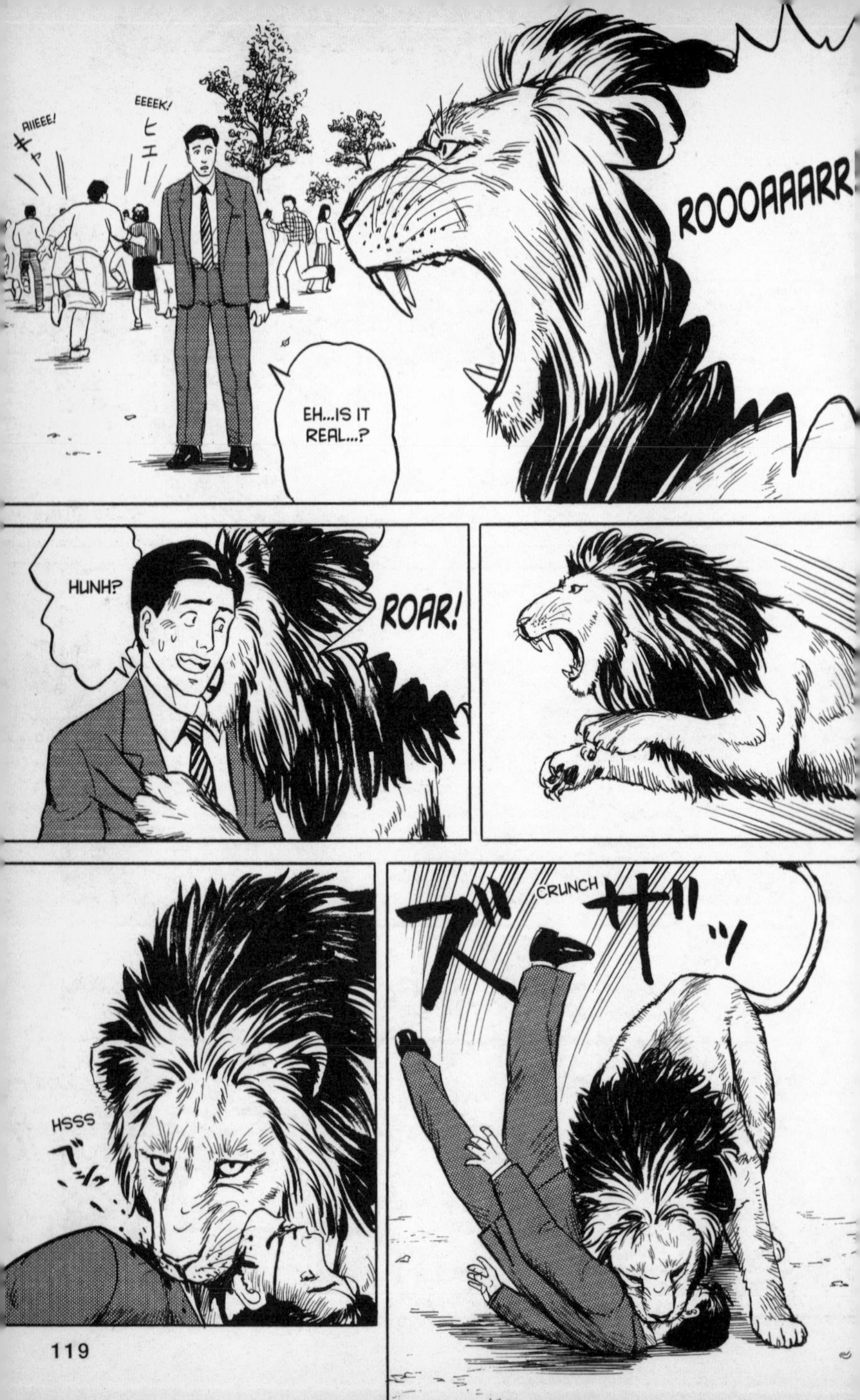
ROOOAAARR!
EH...IS IT REAL...?
EEEEK!
ヒエー
AIIEEE!
キャ
ROAR!
HUNH?
CRUNCH
ズーザッ
HSSS
ブシュ

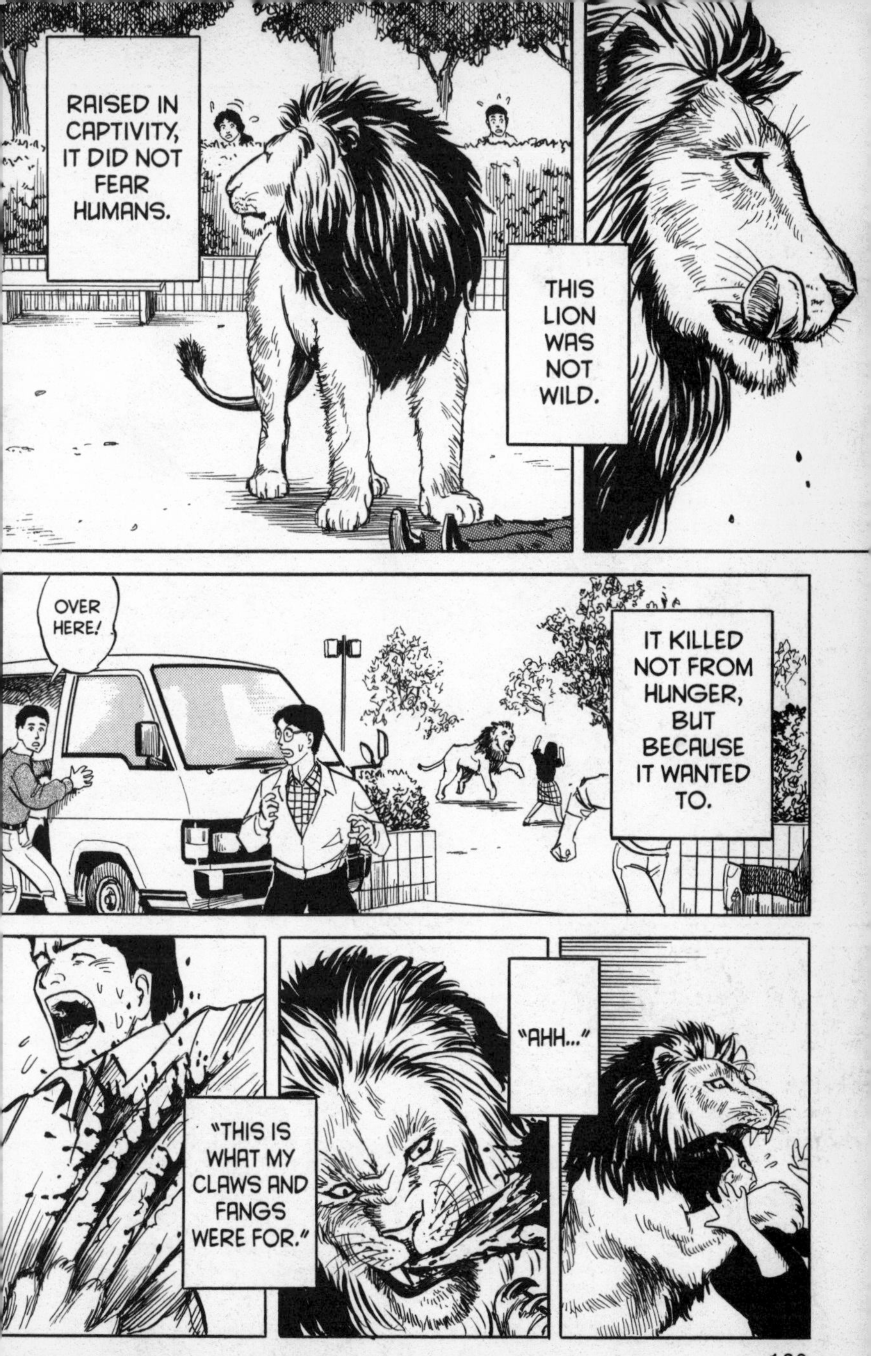
THIS LION WAS NOT WILD.
RAISED IN CAPTIVITY, IT DID NOT FEAR HUMANS.
IT KILLED NOT FROM HUNGER, BUT BECAUSE IT WANTED TO.
OVER HERE!
"AHH..."
"THIS IS WHAT MY CLAWS AND FANGS WERE FOR."

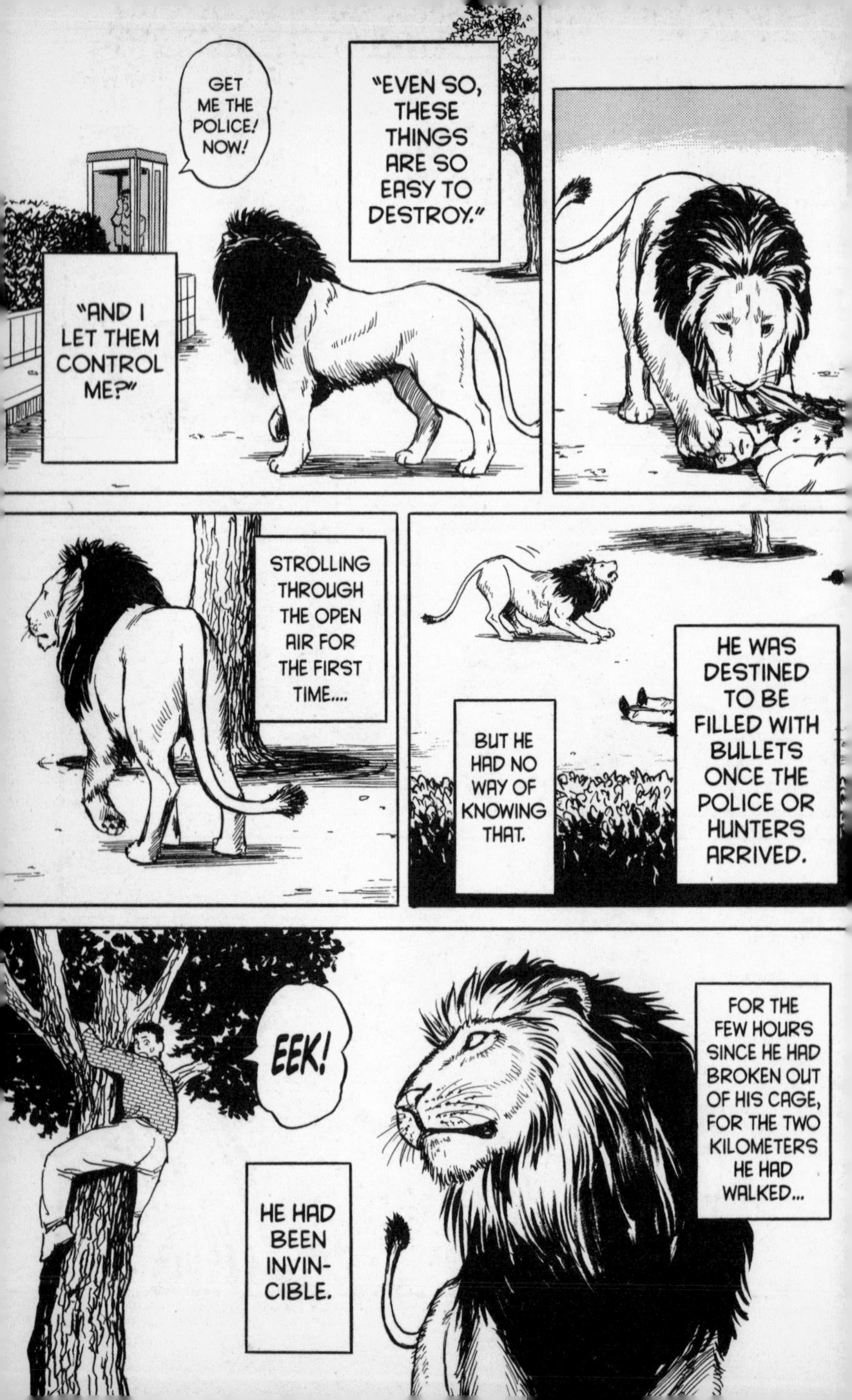
"EVEN SO, THESE THINGS ARE SO EASY TO DESTROY."
GET ME THE POLICE! NOW!
"AND I LET THEM CONTROL ME?"
HE WAS DESTINED TO BE FILLED WITH BULLETS ONCE THE POLICE OR HUNTERS ARRIVED.
BUT HE HAD NO WAY OF KNOWING THAT.
STROLLING THROUGH THE OPEN AIR FOR THE FIRST TIME....
FOR THE FEW HOURS SINCE HE HAD BROKEN OUT OF HIS CAGE, FOR THE TWO KILOMETERS HE HAD WALKED...
EEK!
HE HAD BEEN INVINCIBLE.

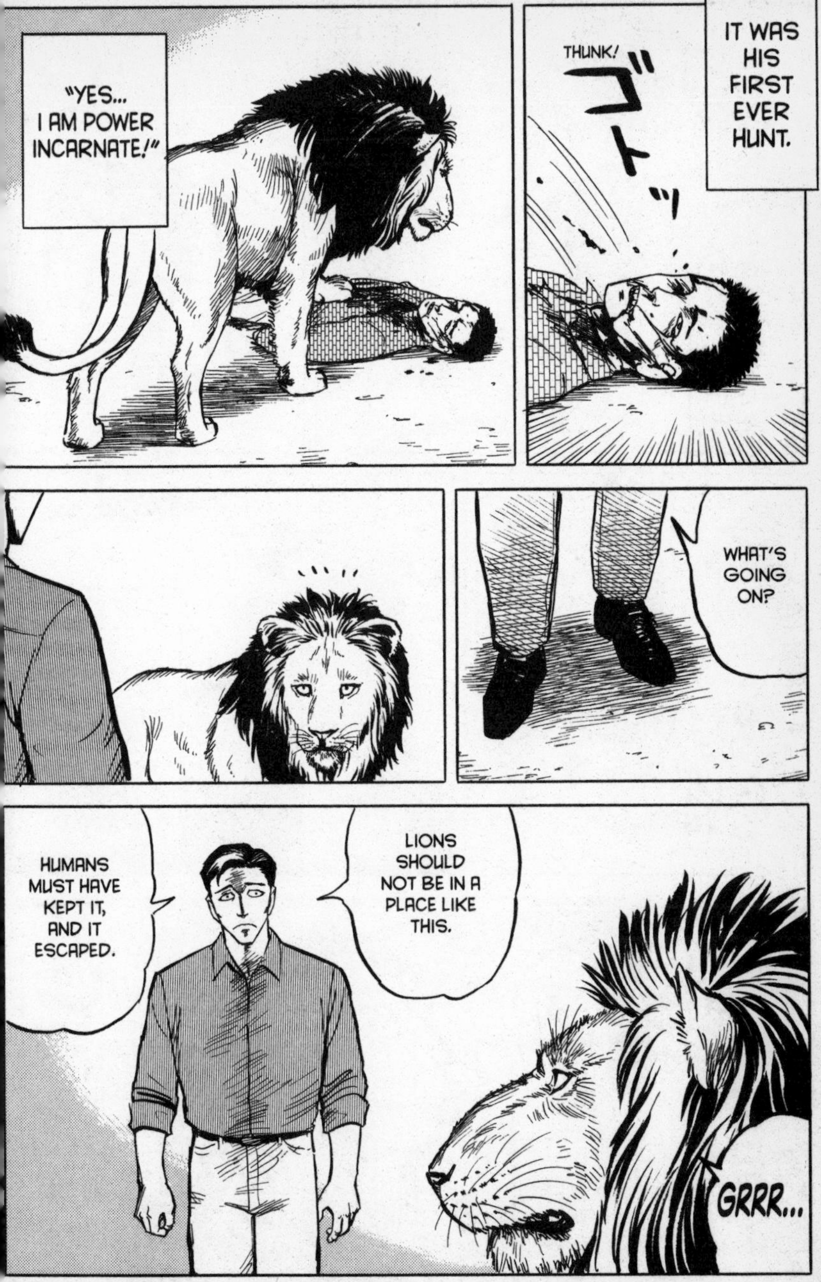
IT WAS HIS FIRST EVER HUNT.
THUNK!
ゴトッ
"YES... I AM POWER INCARNATE!"
WHAT'S GOING ON?
LIONS SHOULD NOT BE IN A PLACE LIKE THIS.
HUMANS MUST HAVE KEPT IT, AND IT ESCAPED.
GRRR...

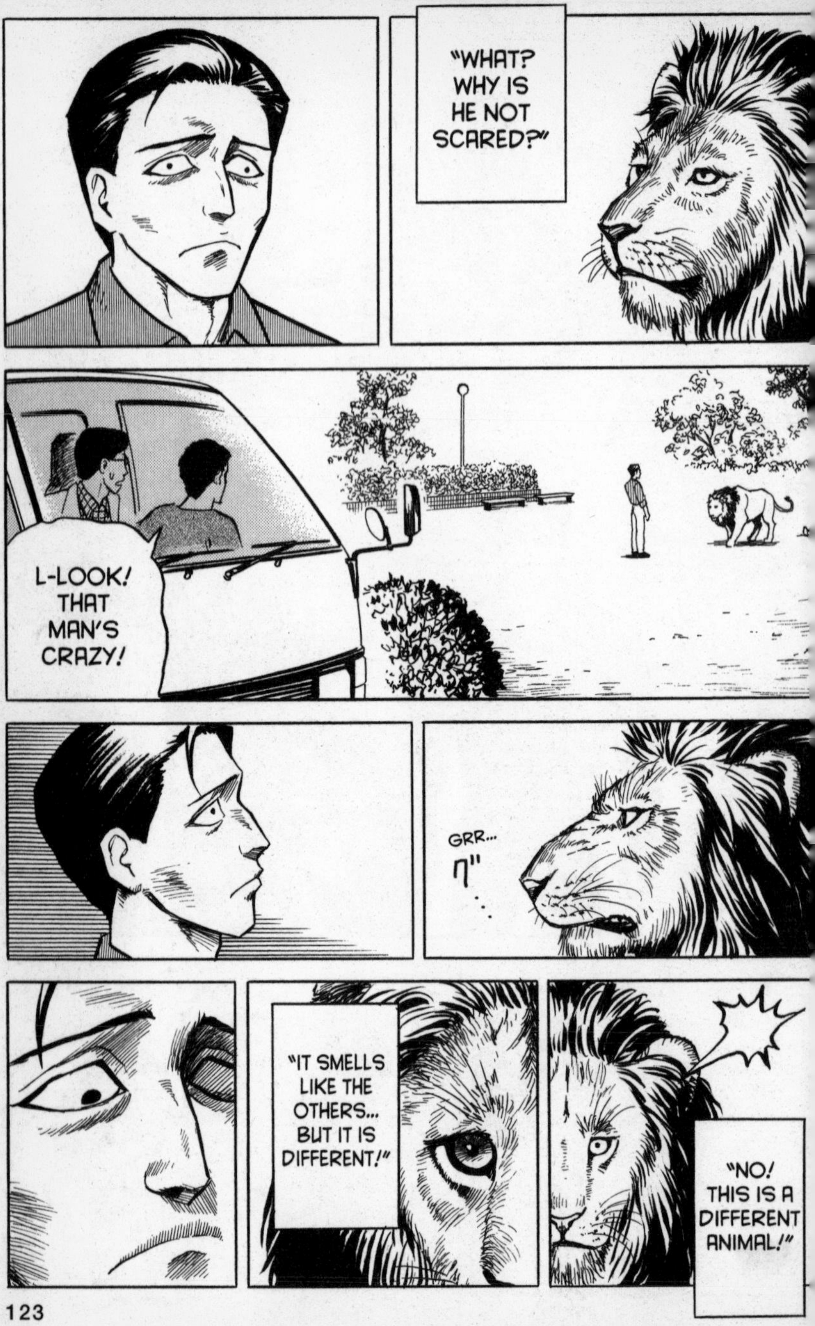
"WHAT? WHY IS HE NOT SCARED?"
L-LOOK! THAT MAN'S CRAZY!
GRR...
"NO! THIS IS A DIFFERENT ANIMAL!"
"IT SMELLS LIKE THE OTHERS... BUT IT IS DIFFERENT!"

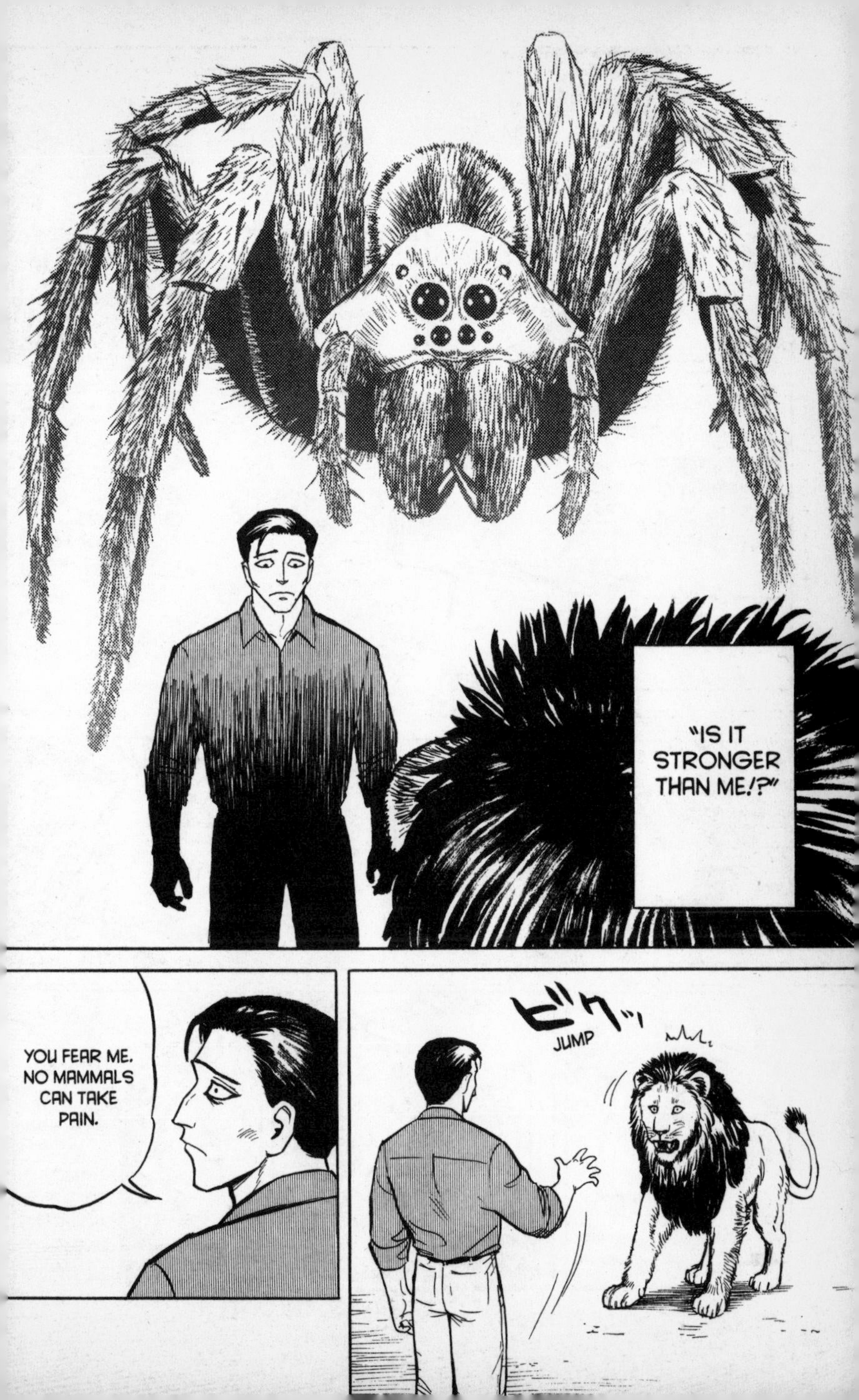
"IS IT STRONGER THAN ME!?"
ビクッ
JUMP
YOU FEAR ME. NO MAMMALS CAN TAKE PAIN.

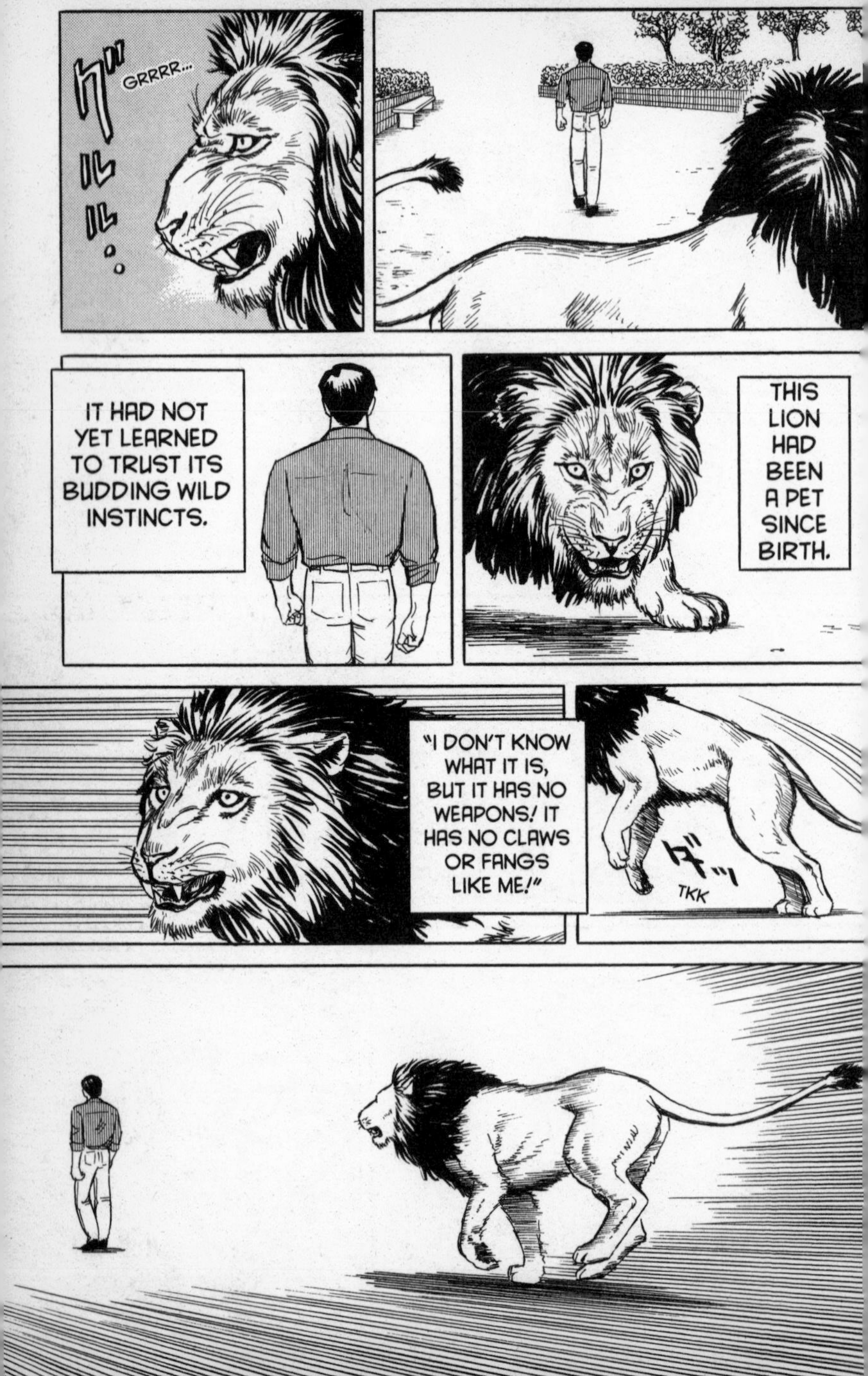

グルルル
GRRRR...
THIS LION HAD BEEN A PET SINCE BIRTH.
IT HAD NOT YET LEARNED TO TRUST ITS BUDDING WILD INSTINCTS.
ダッ
TKK
"I DON'T KNOW WHAT IT IS, BUT IT HAS NO WEAPONS! IT HAS NO CLAWS OR FANGS LIKE ME!"

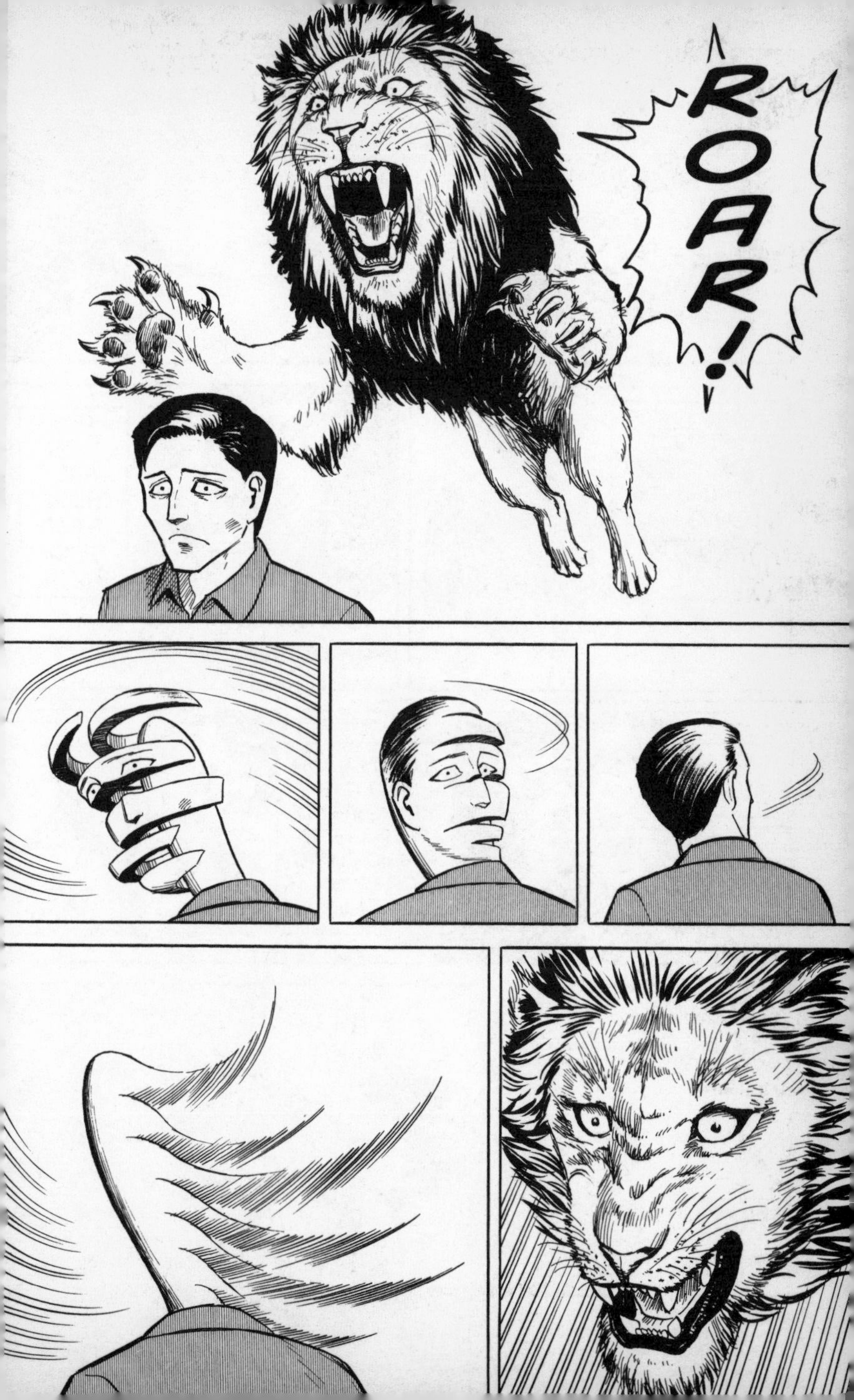
ROAR!

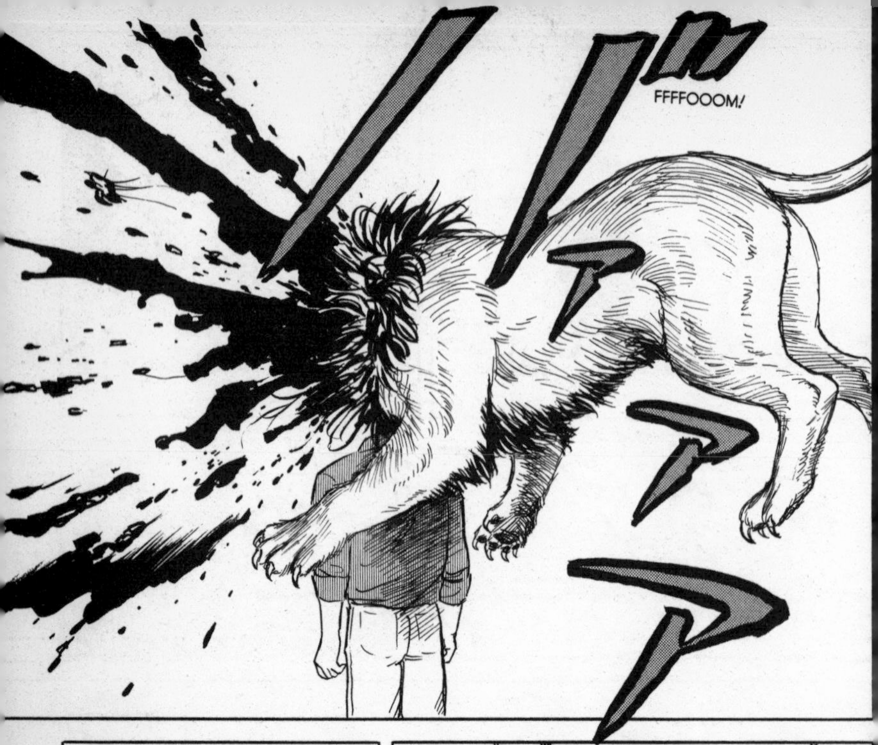
FFFFOOOM!

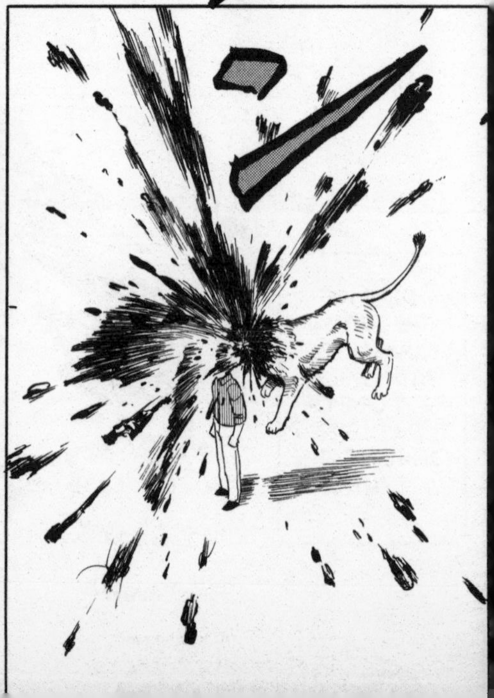

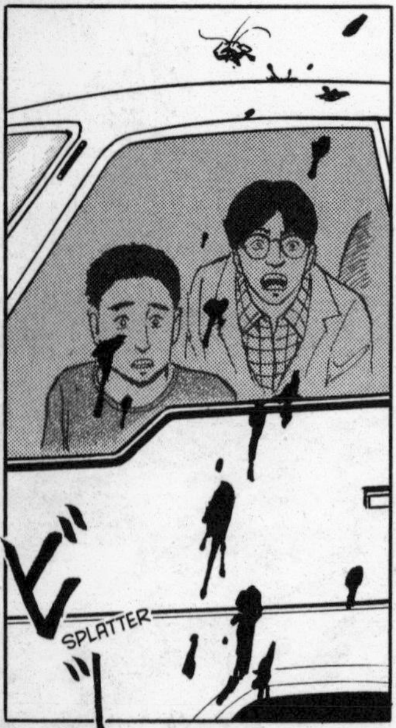
SPLATTER

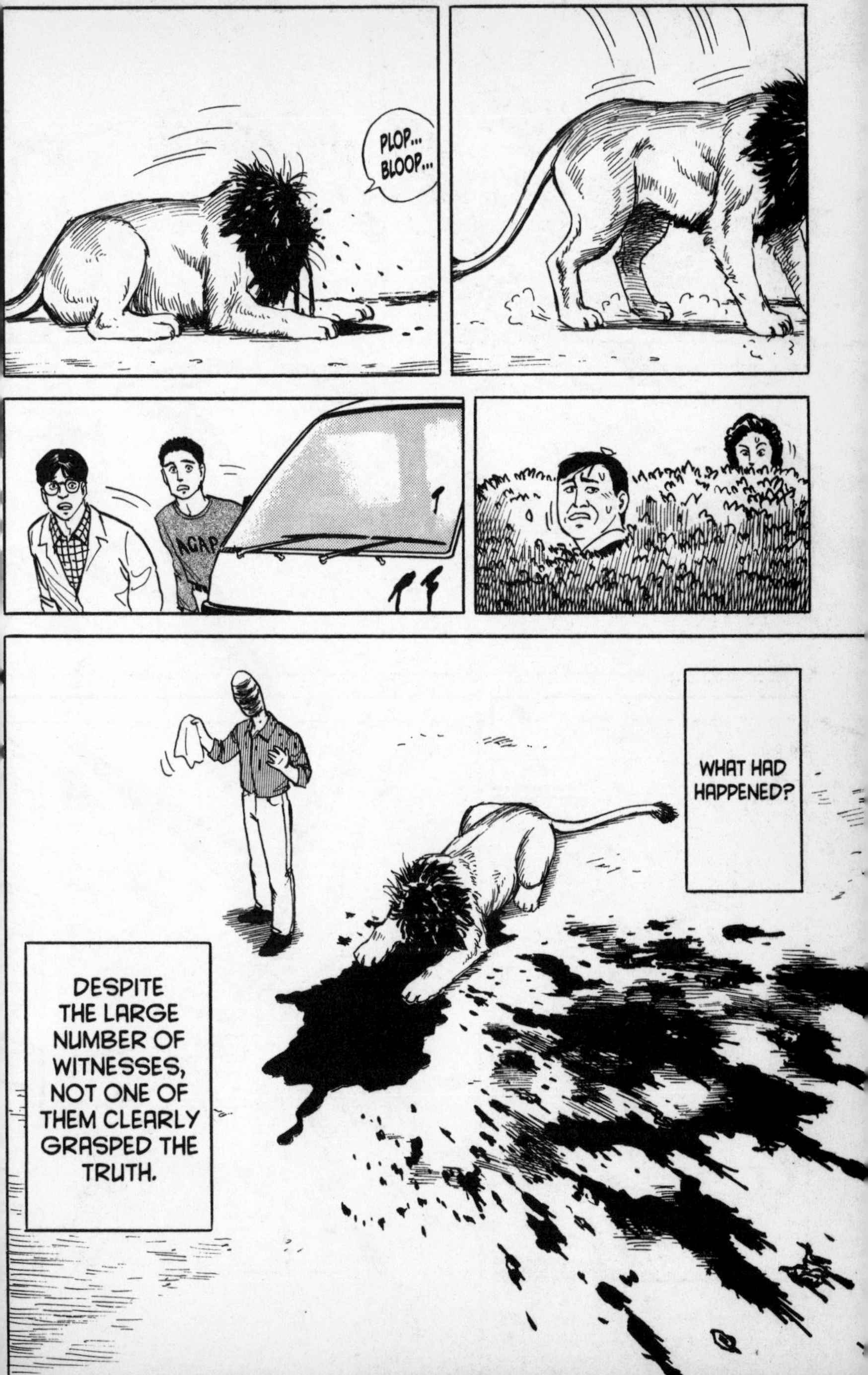
PLOP... BLOOP...
WHAT HAD HAPPENED?
DESPITE THE LARGE NUMBER OF WITNESSES, NOT ONE OF THEM CLEARLY GRASPED THE TRUTH.

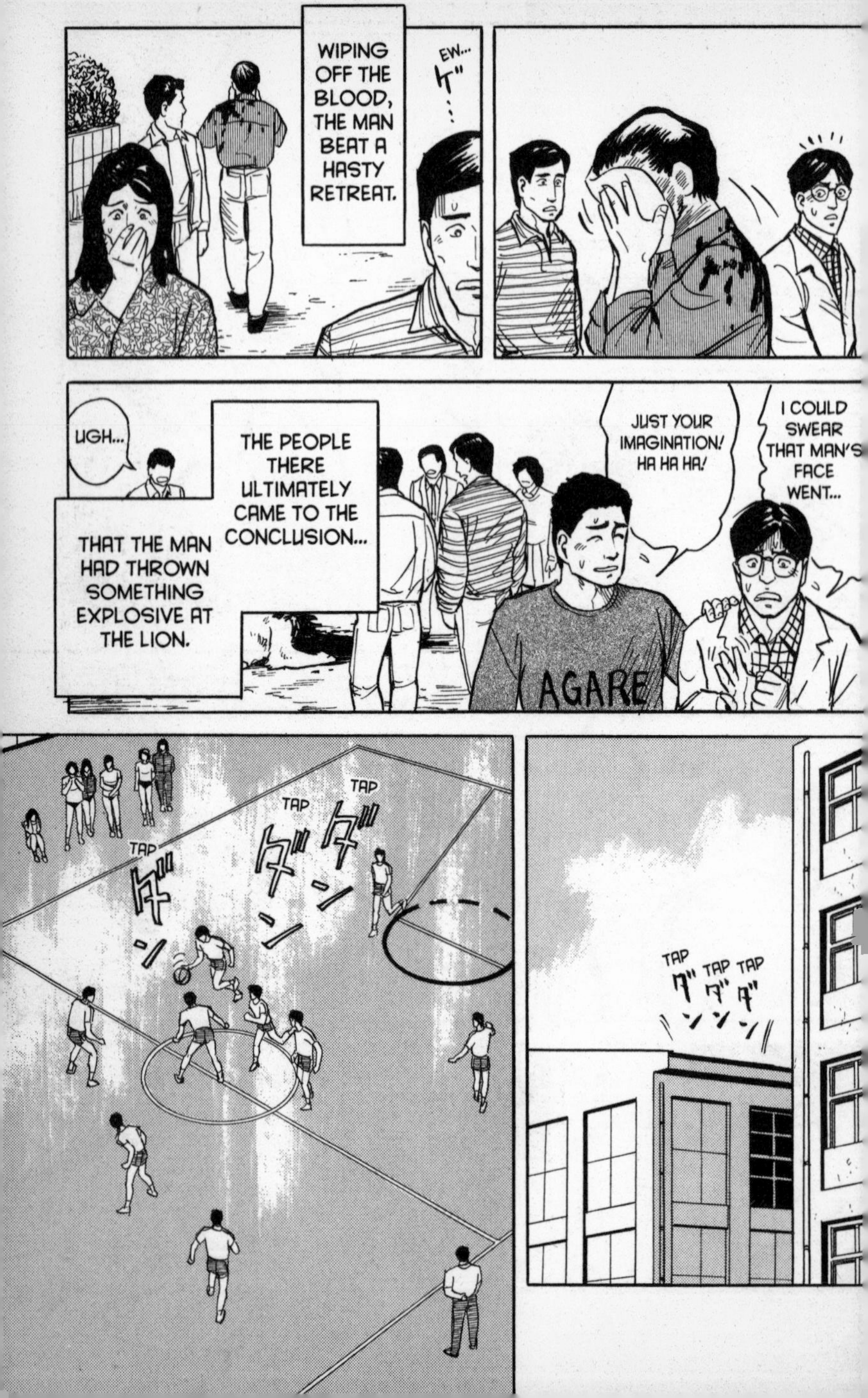

EW... ゲ"
WIPING OFF THE BLOOD, THE MAN BEAT A HASTY RETREAT.
I COULD SWEAR THAT MAN'S FACE WENT...
JUST YOUR IMAGINATION! HA HA HA!
AGARE
THE PEOPLE THERE ULTIMATELY CAME TO THE CONCLUSION...
UGH...
THAT THE MAN HAD THROWN SOMETHING EXPLOSIVE AT THE LION.
TAP TAP TAP
TAP TAP TAP

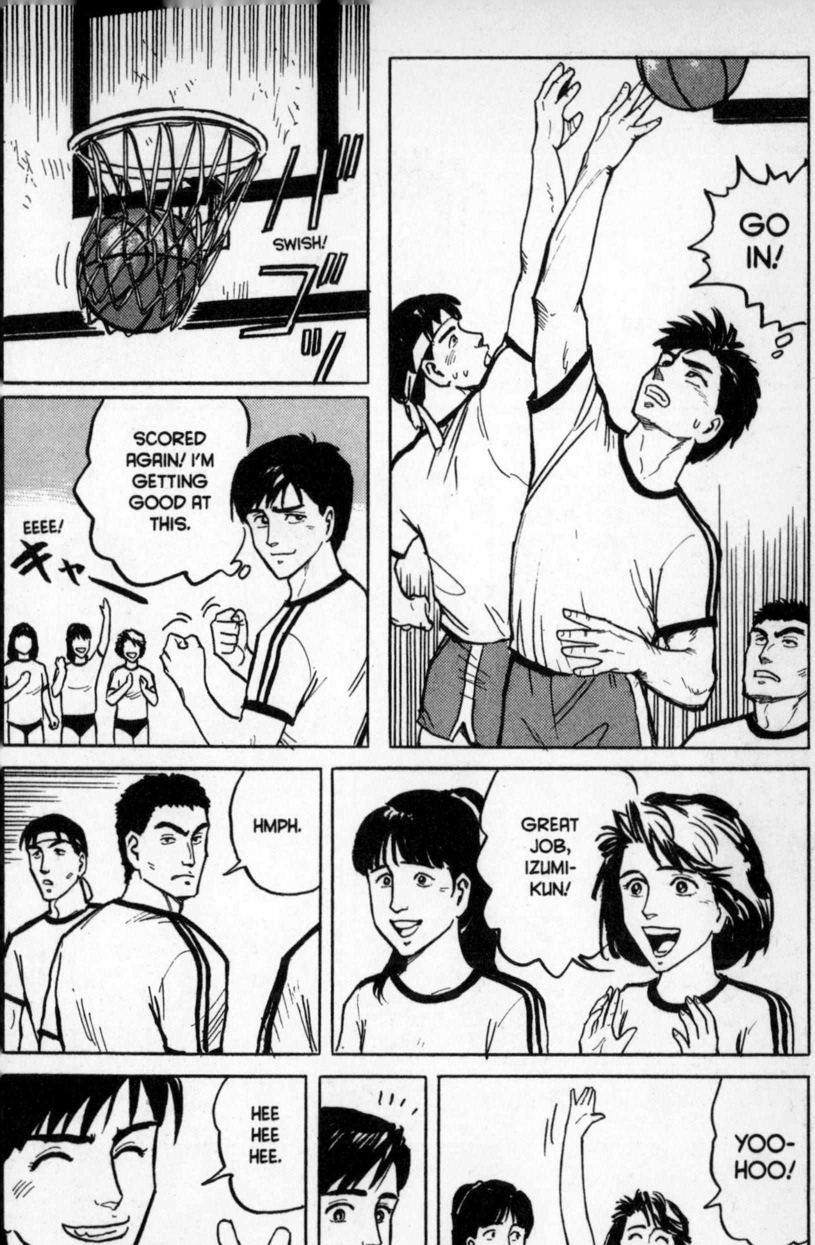
GO IN!
SWISH!
SCORED AGAIN! I'M GETTING GOOD AT THIS.
EEEE!
キャー
GREAT JOB, IZUMI-KUN!
HMPH.
YOO-HOO!
HEE HEE HEE.

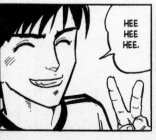

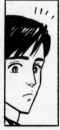

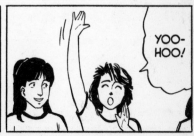

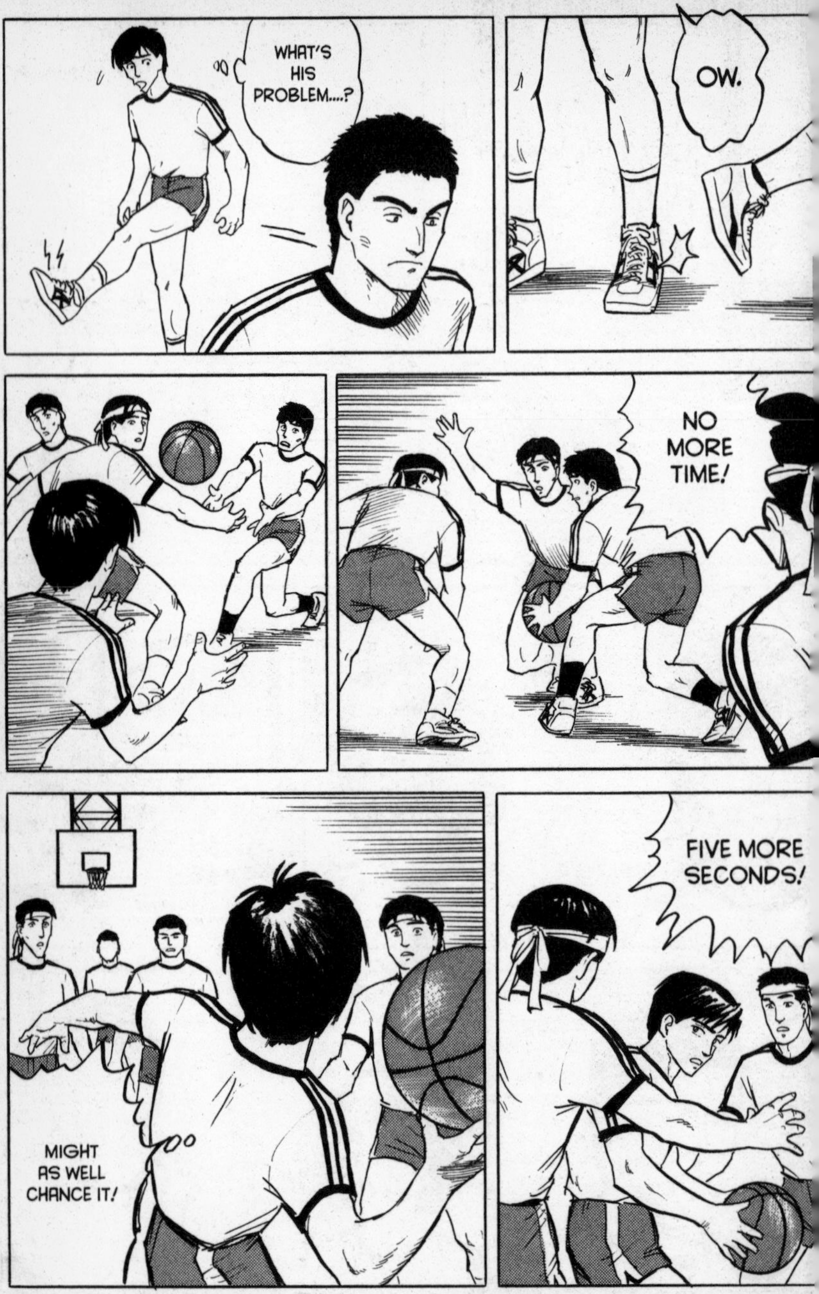
OW.
WHAT'S HIS PROBLEM....?
NO MORE TIME!
FIVE MORE SECONDS!
MIGHT AS WELL CHANCE IT!

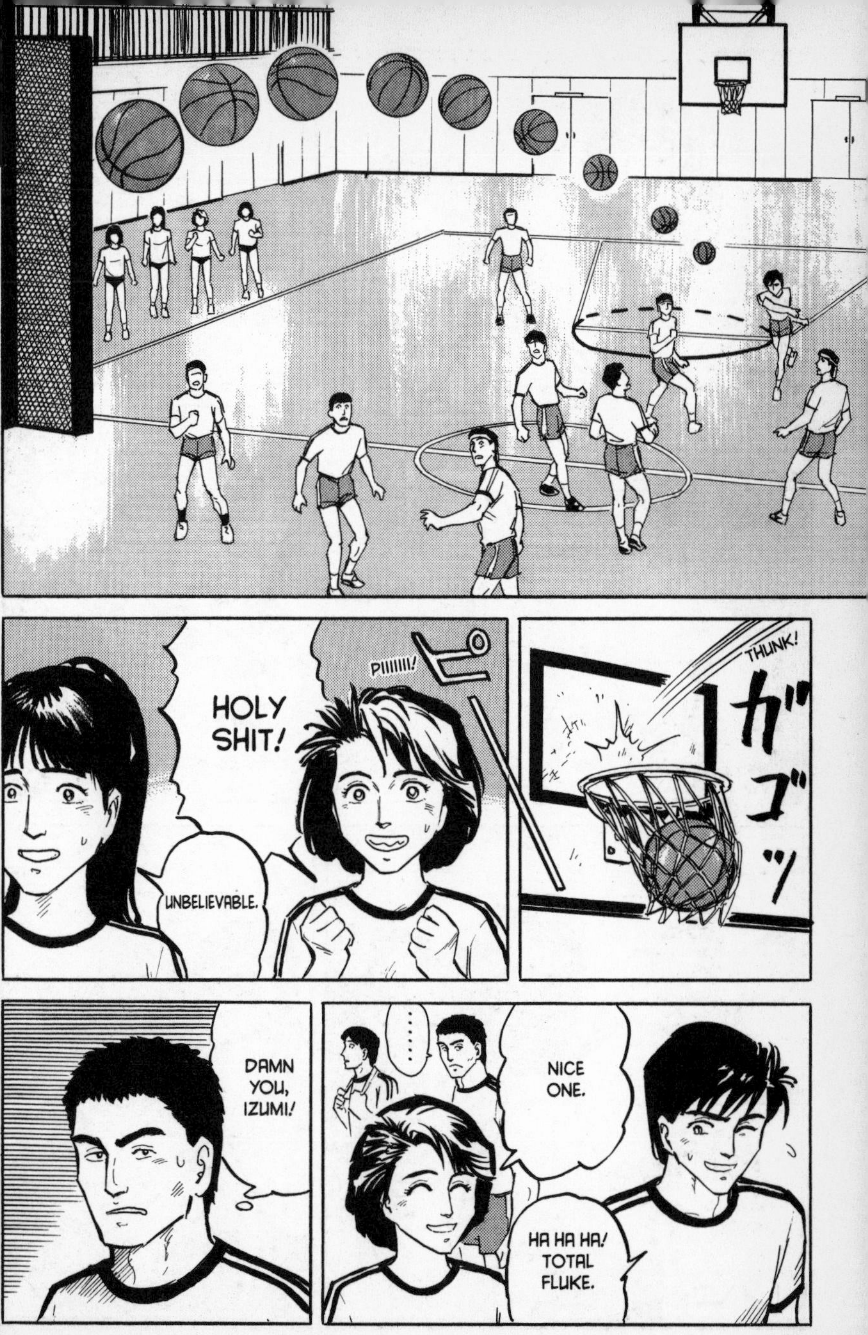
THUNK!
ガゴッ
PIIIIII!
ピ
HOLY SHIT!
UNBELIEVABLE.
NICE ONE.
......
HA HA HA! TOTAL FLUKE.
DAMN YOU, IZUMI!

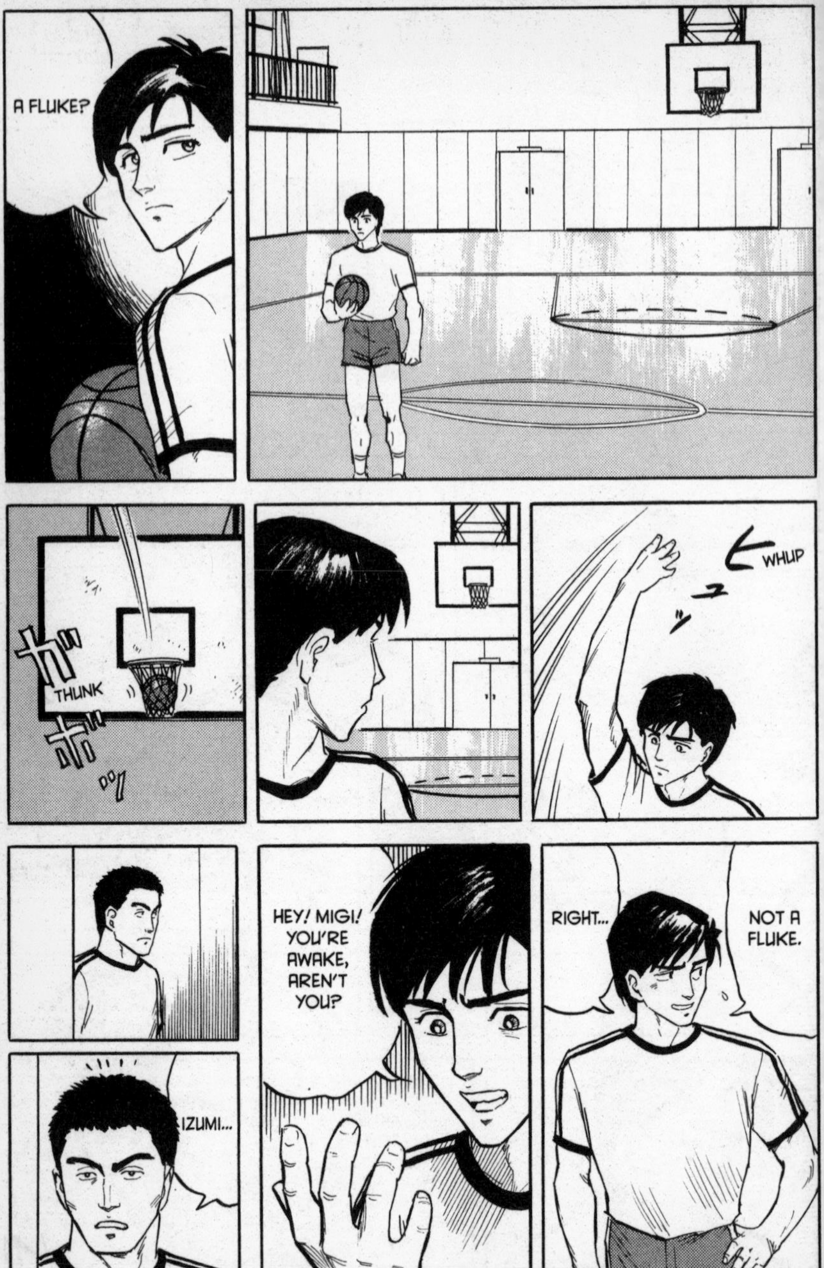
A FLUKE?
WHUP
THUNK
NOT A FLUKE.
RIGHT...
HEY! MIGI! YOU'RE AWAKE, AREN'T YOU?
IZUMI...

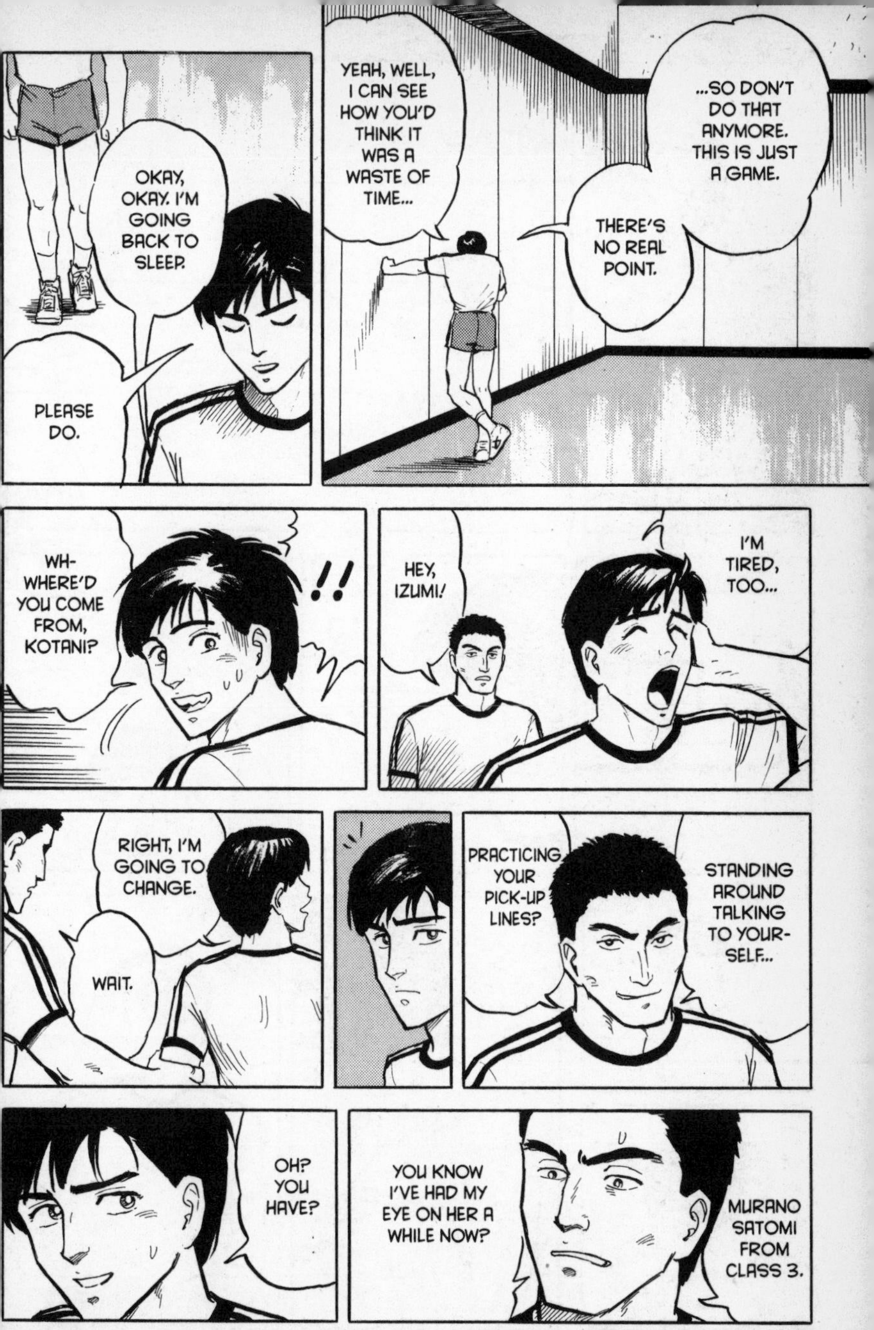
...SO DON'T DO THAT ANYMORE. THIS IS JUST A GAME.
YEAH, WELL, I CAN SEE HOW YOU'D THINK IT WAS A WASTE OF TIME...
THERE'S NO REAL POINT.
OKAY, OKAY. I'M GOING BACK TO SLEEP.
PLEASE DO.
I'M TIRED, TOO...
HEY, IZUMI!
!!
WH- WHERE'D YOU COME FROM, KOTANI?
STANDING AROUND TALKING TO YOURSELF...
PRACTICING YOUR PICK-UP LINES?
RIGHT, I'M GOING TO CHANGE.
WAIT.
MURANO SATOMI FROM CLASS 3.
YOU KNOW I'VE HAD MY EYE ON HER A WHILE NOW?
OH? YOU HAVE?

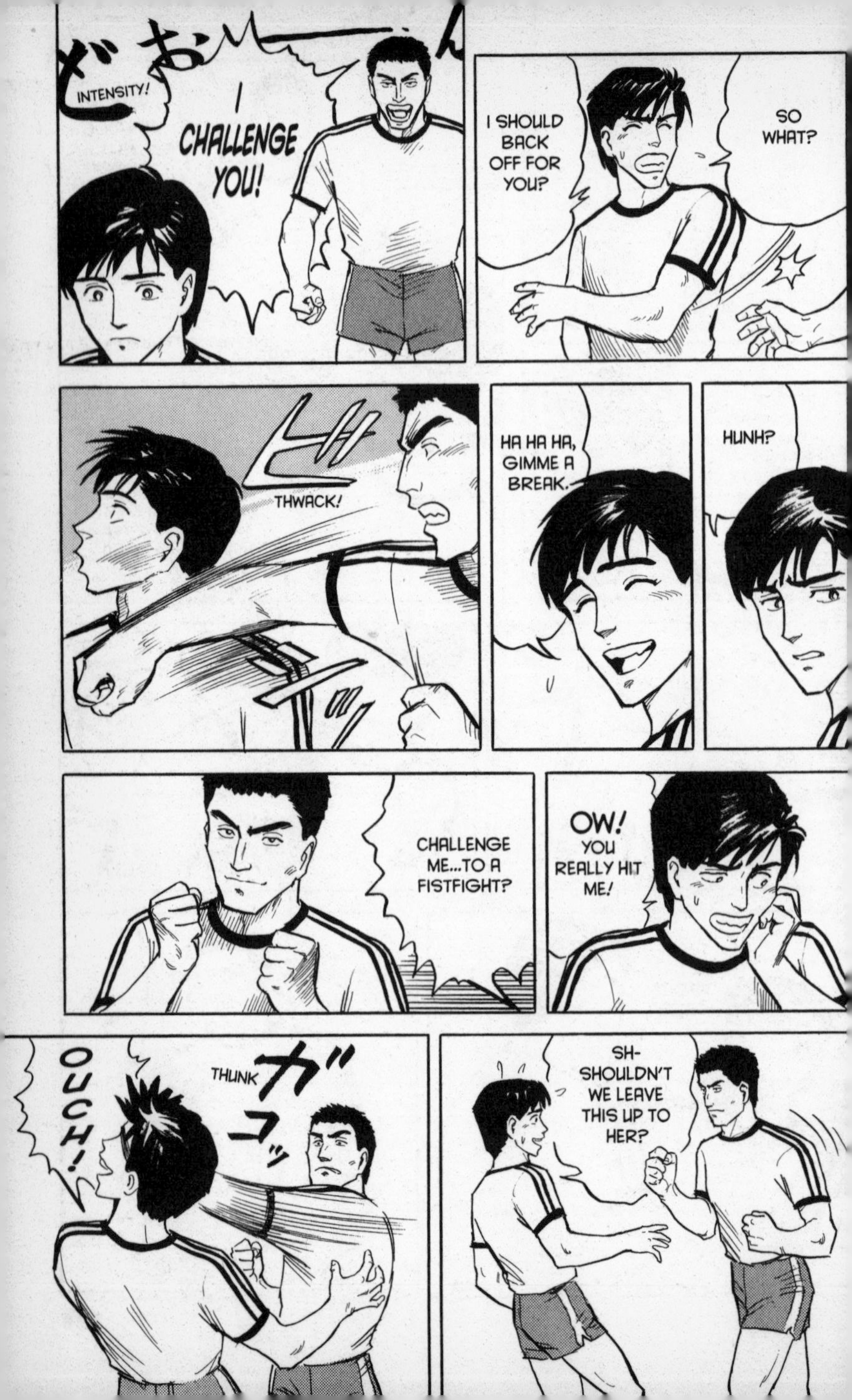
SO WHAT?
I SHOULD BACK OFF FOR YOU?
どおーーん
INTENSITY!
I CHALLENGE YOU!
HUNH?
HA HA HA, GIMME A BREAK.
THWACK!
OW! YOU REALLY HIT ME!
CHALLENGE ME...TO A FISTFIGHT?
SH- SHOULDN'T WE LEAVE THIS UP TO HER?
THUNK
ガコッ
OUCH!

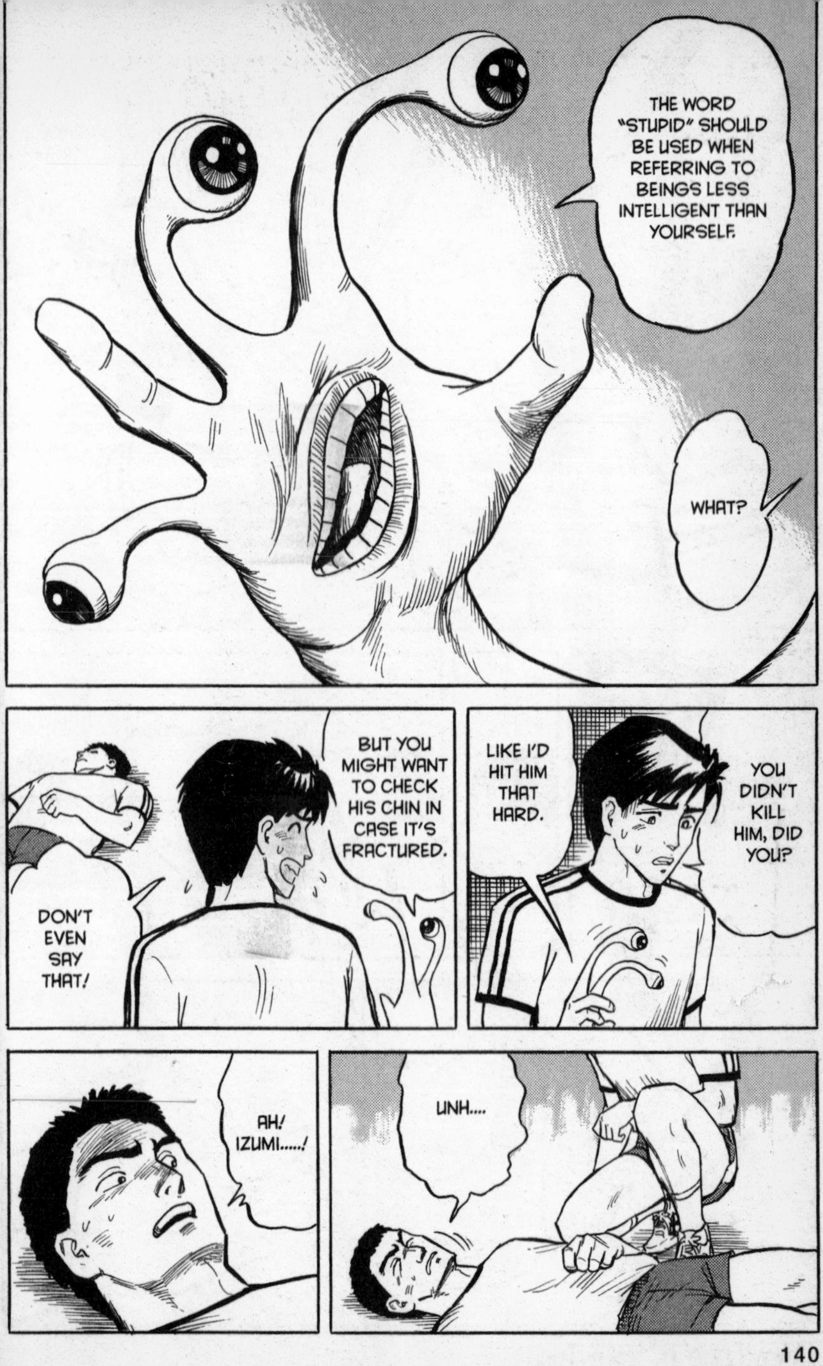
THE WORD "STUPID" SHOULD BE USED WHEN REFERRING TO BEINGS LESS INTELLIGENT THAN YOURSELF.
WHAT?
YOU DIDN'T KILL HIM, DID YOU?
LIKE I'D HIT HIM THAT HARD.
BUT YOU MIGHT WANT TO CHECK HIS CHIN IN CASE IT'S FRACTURED.
DON'T EVEN SAY THAT!
UNH....
AH! IZUMI.....!

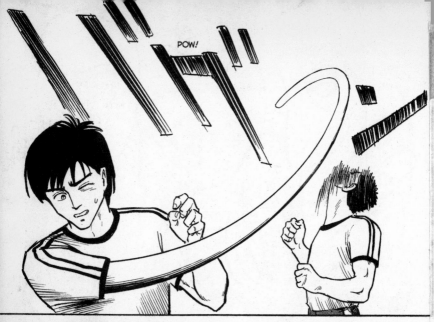

POW!

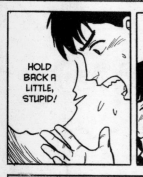

HOLD BACK A LITTLE, STUPID!

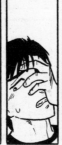

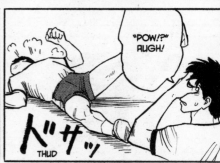

"POW!?" AUGH!

ド サッ
THUD

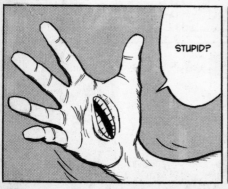

STUPID?

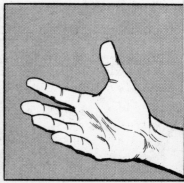

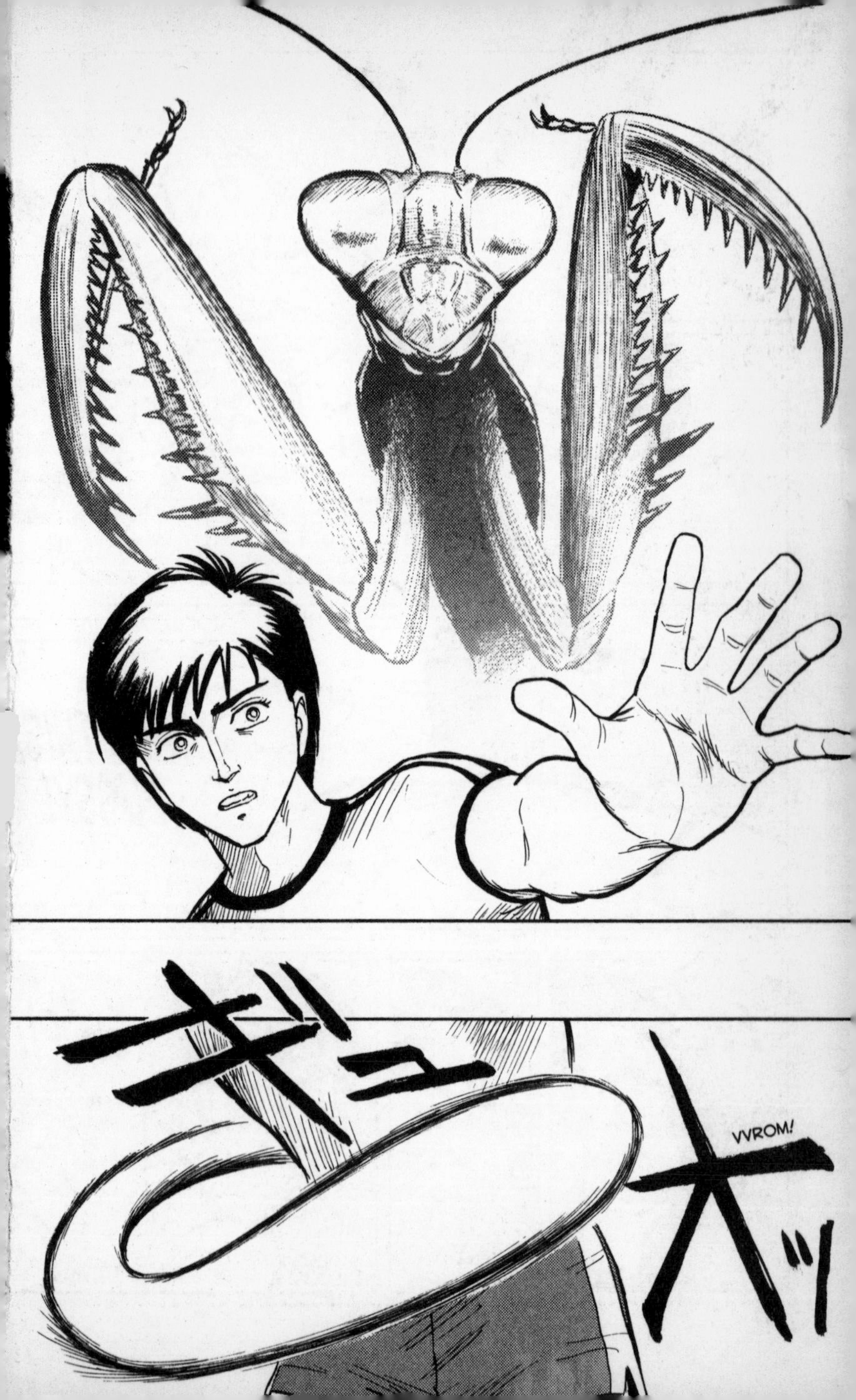
ギュオッ
VVROM!

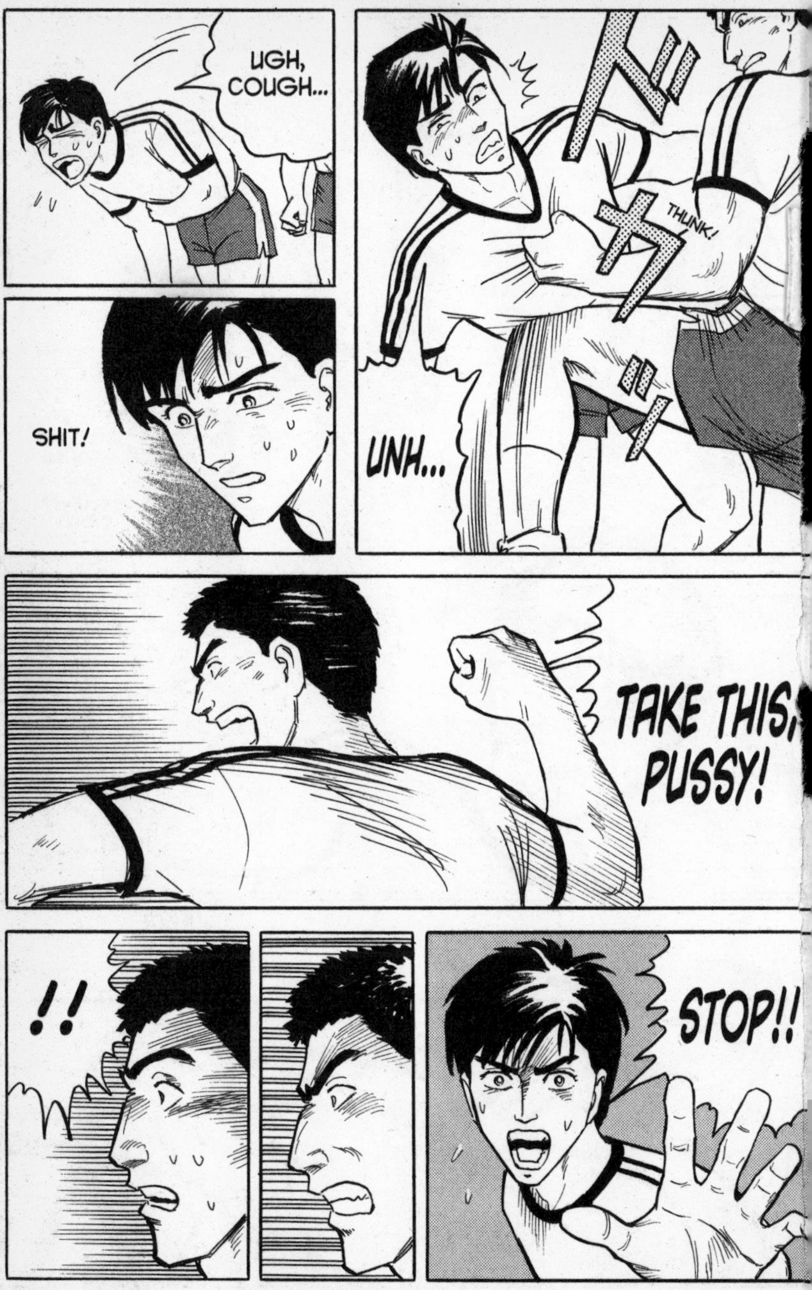
THUNK!
UNH...
UGH, COUGH...
SHIT!
TAKE THIS, PUSSY!
STOP!!
!!

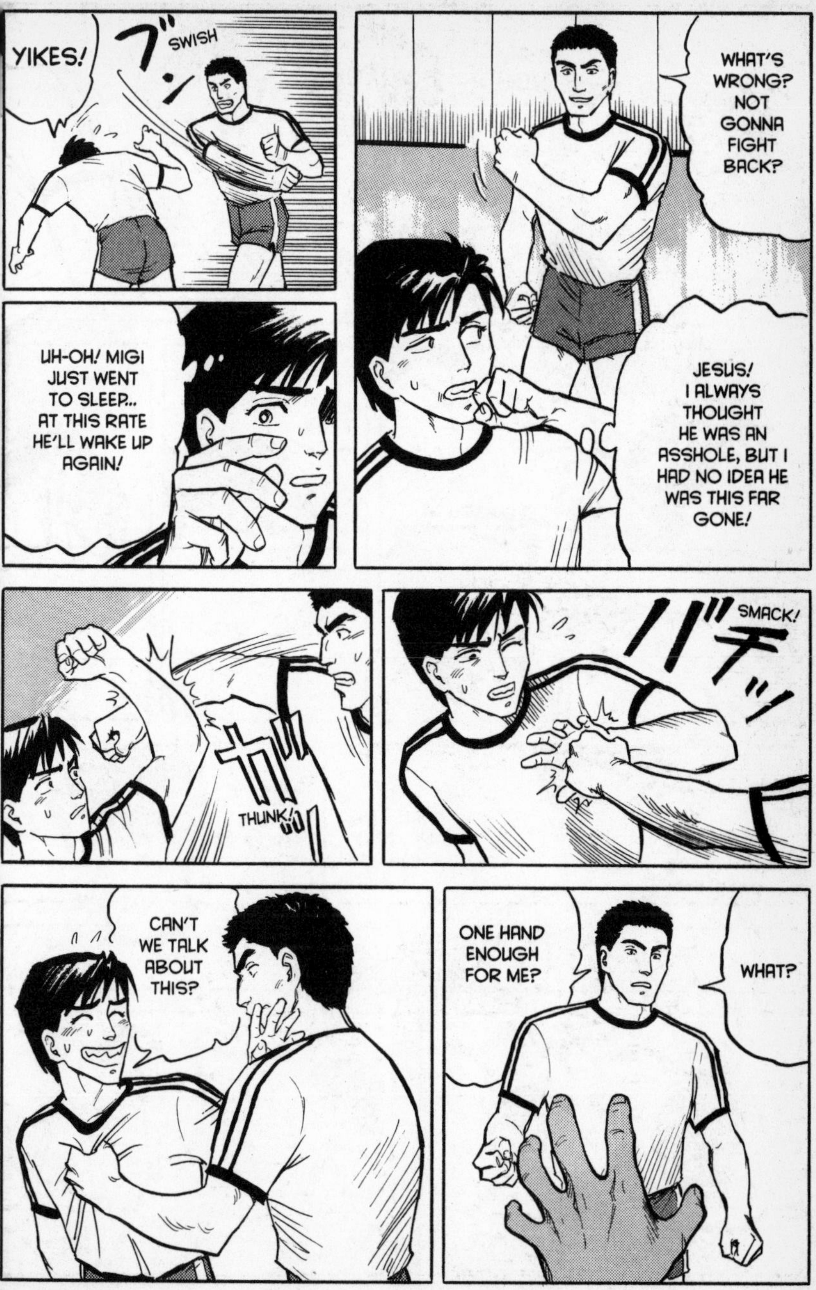
SWISH
YIKES!
WHAT'S WRONG? NOT GONNA FIGHT BACK?
UH-OH! MIGI JUST WENT TO SLEEP... AT THIS RATE HE'LL WAKE UP AGAIN!
JESUS! I ALWAYS THOUGHT HE WAS AN ASSHOLE, BUT I HAD NO IDEA HE WAS THIS FAR GONE!
THUNK!
SMACK!
CAN'T WE TALK ABOUT THIS?
ONE HAND ENOUGH FOR ME?
WHAT?

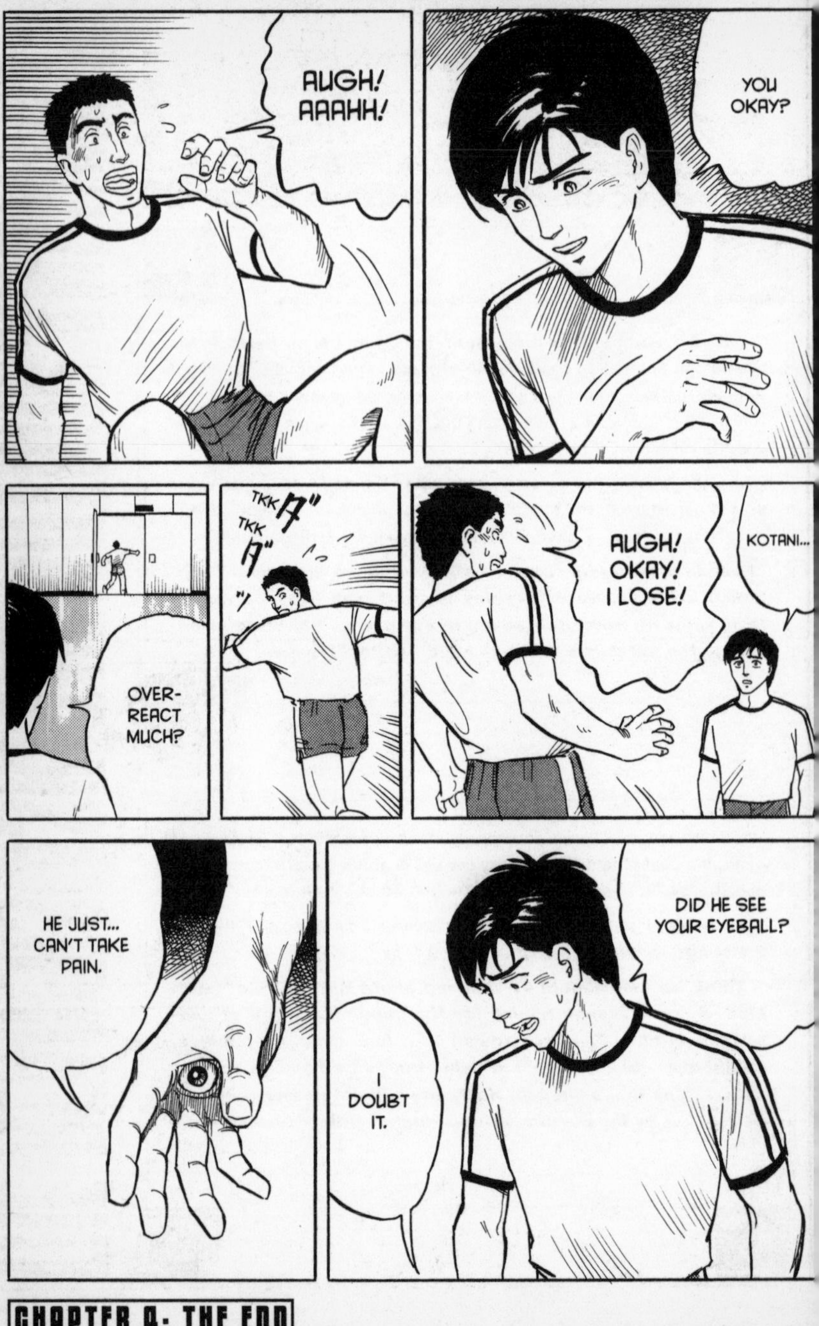
YOU OKAY?
AUGH! AAAHH!
KOTANI...
AUGH! OKAY! I LOSE!
TKK ダ
TKK ダ
ッ
OVER-REACT MUCH?
DID HE SEE YOUR EYEBALL?
I DOUBT IT.
HE JUST... CAN'T TAKE PAIN.

CHAPTER 4: THE END

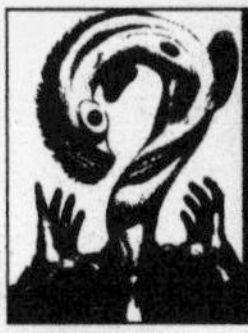

From the Monthly Afternoon Readers' page...

PARASYTE [PERFECT EDITION] 1

vol. 1

THE READERS ASK, THE AUTHOR ANSWERS

"I hate the horror and splatter genres, but oddly, I enjoy *Parasyte*. As the human population continues to expand, something like this might actually happen. It isn't just scary; it also makes us think. And it's also funny, which makes it a book I can't put down." (Kanagawa Prefecture, Kuroda Hisa, 30, Office Worker)

"*Parasyte* is really fun! I was amazed when the dog turned into some sort of bat! Shinichi and Migi's strange relationship is also neat. All hail Iwaaki-shi's ideas!" (Tokyo, Shiyotsuru Maiwa, 26, Office Worker)

"I began drawing this book when I wondered what would happen if living creatures besides humans, the lives we put so little value in, were granted enormous power. Pay close attention to the parasite's uncanny logic." (Hitoshi Iwaaki)

(From *Morning Open Extra H*, October 3, 1989)

"Will humans eventually consume the Earth? With that thought in mind, the belief that the parasites are evil is nothing more than human selfishness." (Saitama Prefecture, Tachi Chitchi, 22, Student)

"The future of mankind, unable to feel even a little pain, is..." (Ibaraki Prefecture, Nakai Yuusuke, 26, Student)

"I think we also should be thinking about the future of mankind. But one human hoping for the happiness of all accomplishes nothing. The best we can do is look after our families, neighbors, and any people or living things we come in contact with. I think that's enough. Humanity will not be saved by statistics, but by the warmth of individuals." (Hitoshi Iwaaki)

(From *Afternoon*, July 1991)

CHAPTER 5: STUDYHOLIC

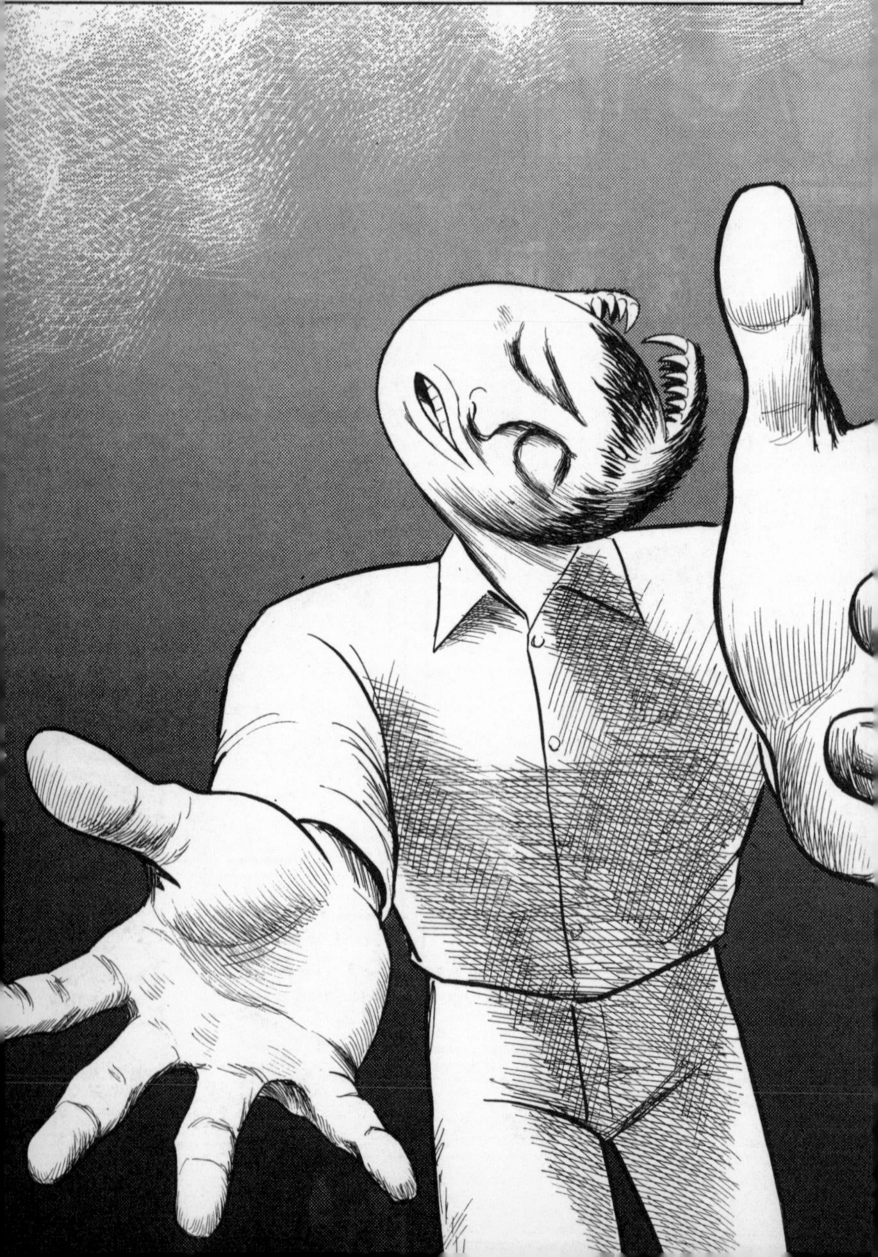

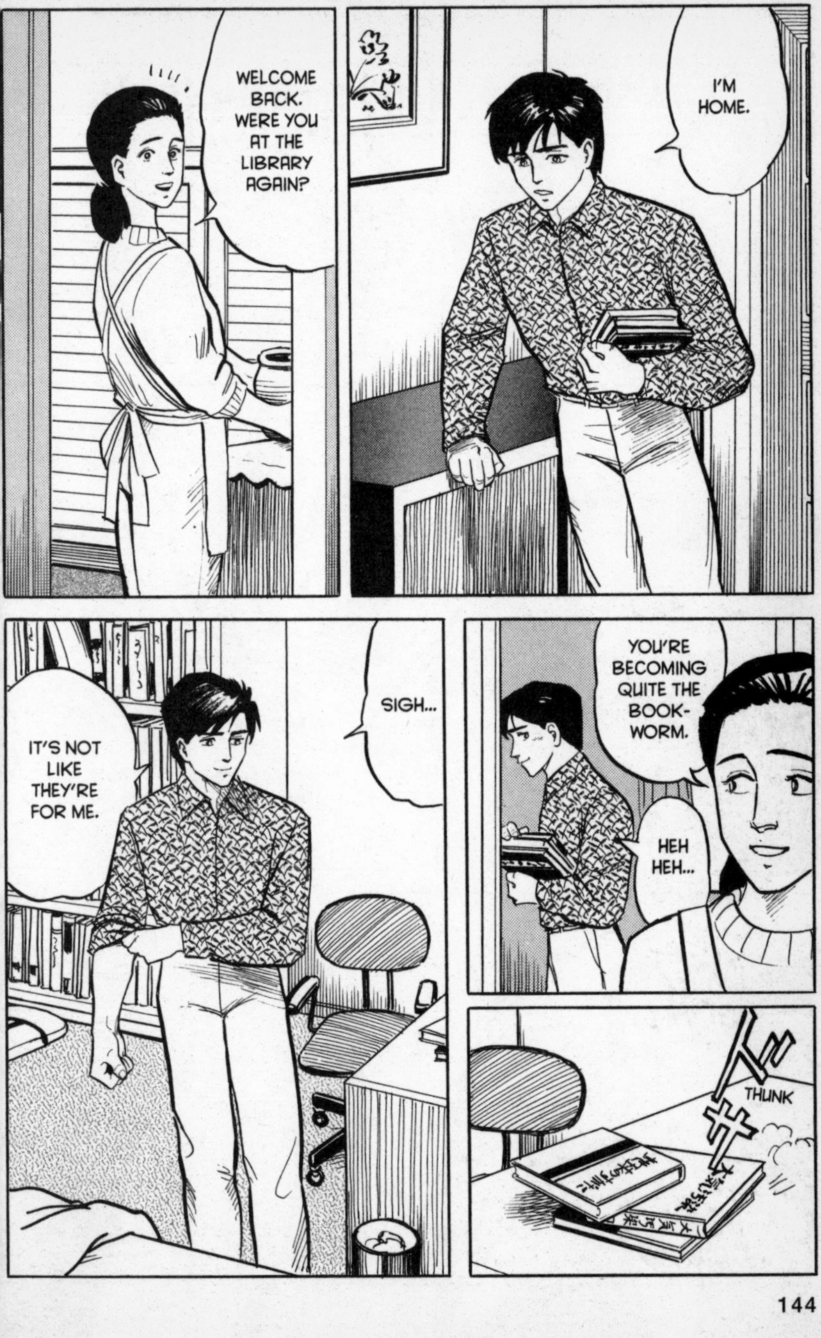
I'M HOME.
WELCOME BACK. WERE YOU AT THE LIBRARY AGAIN?
YOU'RE BECOMING QUITE THE BOOK-WORM.
HEH HEH...
THUNK
SIGH...
IT'S NOT LIKE THEY'RE FOR ME.

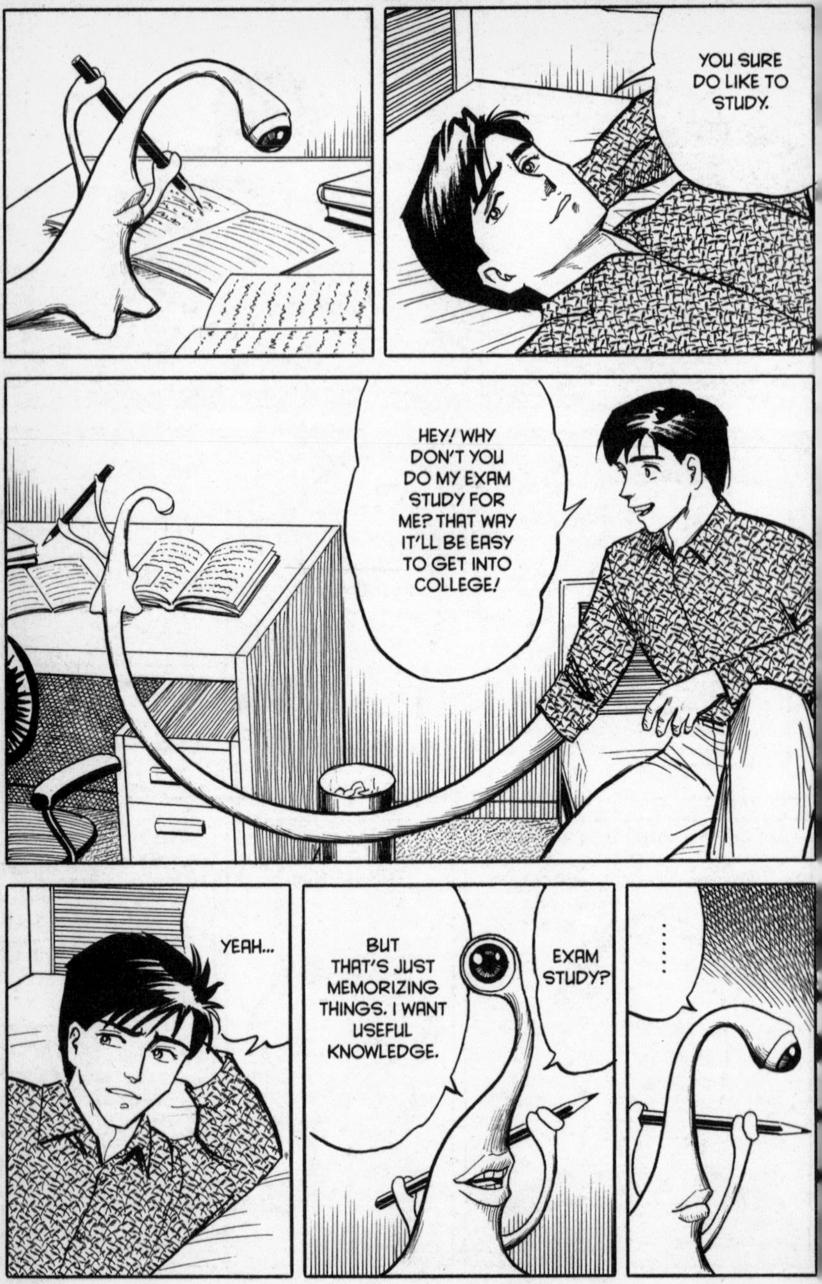
YOU SURE DO LIKE TO STUDY.
HEY! WHY DON'T YOU DO MY EXAM STUDY FOR ME? THAT WAY IT'LL BE EASY TO GET INTO COLLEGE!
......
EXAM STUDY?
BUT THAT'S JUST MEMORIZING THINGS. I WANT USEFUL KNOWLEDGE.
YEAH...

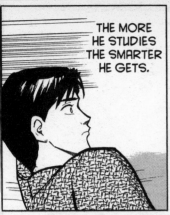

AW, MAN. AT THIS RATE MY RIGHT HAND'S GONNA BE SMARTER THAN ME...
THAT WOULD SUCK.
THE MORE HE STUDIES THE SMARTER HE GETS.
THE PARASITE THAT TOOK OVER MY RIGHT HAND...THERE ARE CREATURES LIKE IT ALL OVER THE WORLD.
I DON'T KNOW HOW MANY...BUT THEY MOSTLY APPEARED OVER THE LAST FIVE MONTHS.
WHAT ARE THEY LIKE?
THEY START OUT LIKE THIS, THEN ENTER THE BODY...
TAKE OVER THE BRAIN...
THEY THEN FUSE WITH EVERYTHING OVER THE NECK, CONTROLLING THE ENTIRE BODY.
IN OTHER WORDS, THEY BECOME THE HEAD.

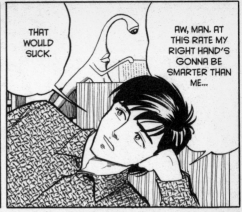

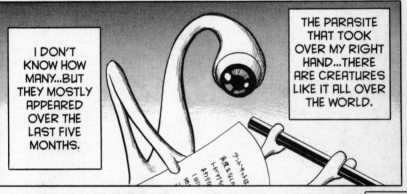

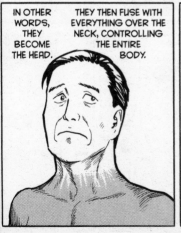

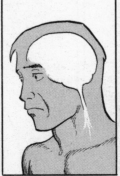

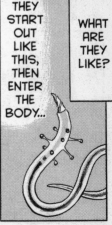

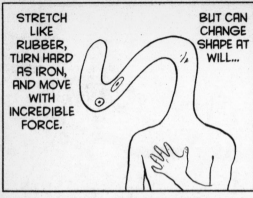

THEY LOOK LIKE HUMANS...
BUT CAN CHANGE SHAPE AT WILL...
STRETCH LIKE RUBBER, TURN HARD AS IRON, AND MOVE WITH INCREDIBLE FORCE.
THE ENTIRE PARASITE PORTION IS THE BRAIN.
AND THE EYES. AND TENTACLES.
BUT DESPITE THEIR INCREDIBLE POWER, THEY CAN'T LIVE WITHOUT BORROWING HUMAN ORGANS, THE HUMAN DIGESTIVE SYSTEM.
ULTIMATELY, THEY ARE NOTHING MORE THAN A PARASITE, AND WILL DIE IF YOU CUT THE HEAD OFF.
BUT WHAT PUZZLES ME IS THEIR FOOD.
WHY DO THEY EAT HUMANS?

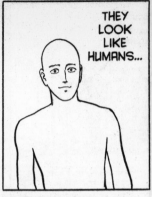

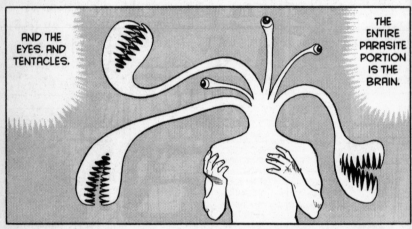

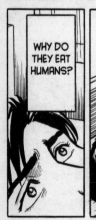

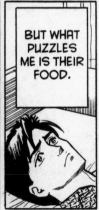

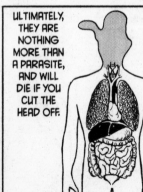

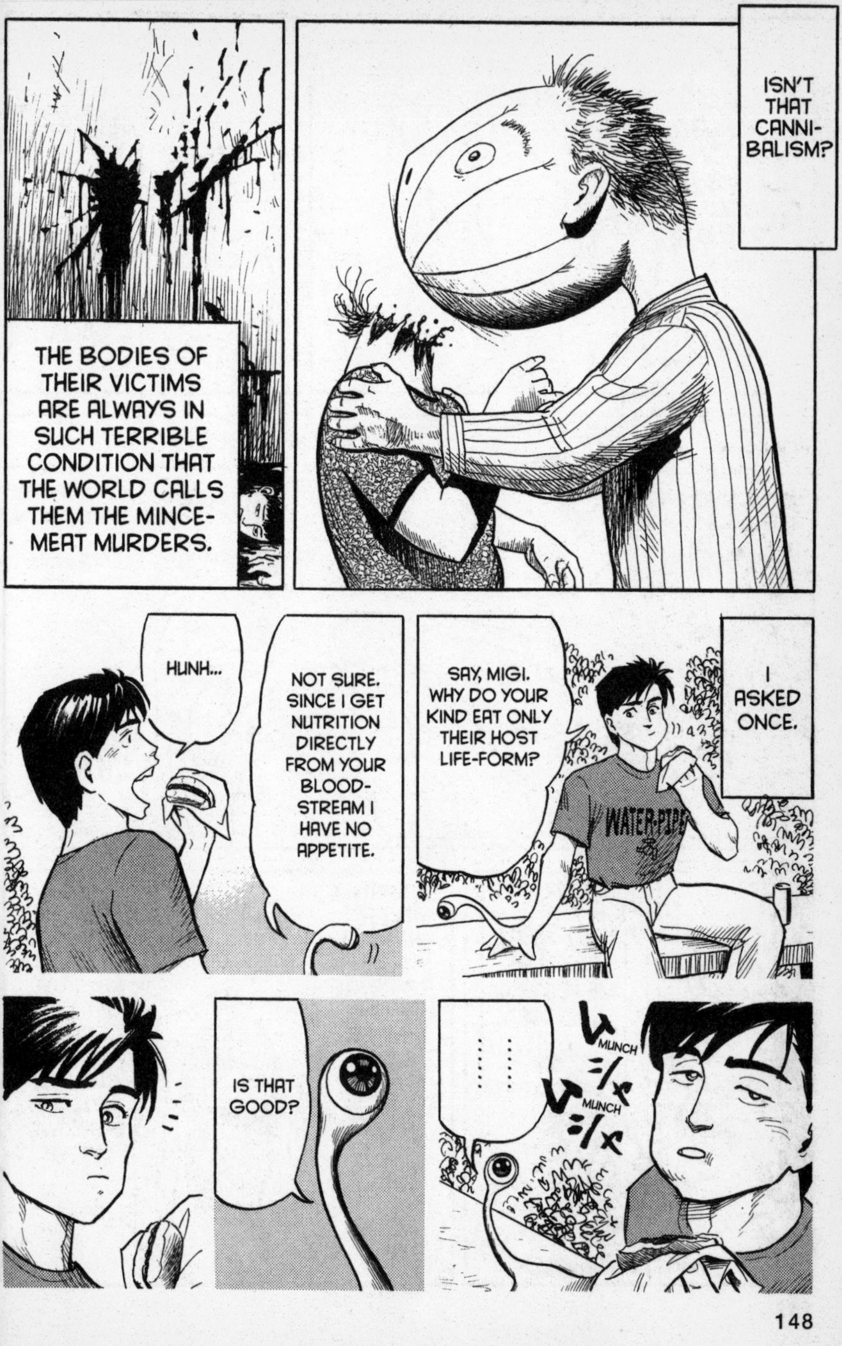
ISN'T THAT CANNIBALISM?
THE BODIES OF THEIR VICTIMS ARE ALWAYS IN SUCH TERRIBLE CONDITION THAT THE WORLD CALLS THEM THE MINCE-MEAT MURDERS.
I ASKED ONCE.
SAY, MIGI. WHY DO YOUR KIND EAT ONLY THEIR HOST LIFE-FORM?
WATER-PIPE
NOT SURE. SINCE I GET NUTRITION DIRECTLY FROM YOUR BLOOD-STREAM I HAVE NO APPETITE.
HUNH...
......
MUNCH
MUNCH
IS THAT GOOD?

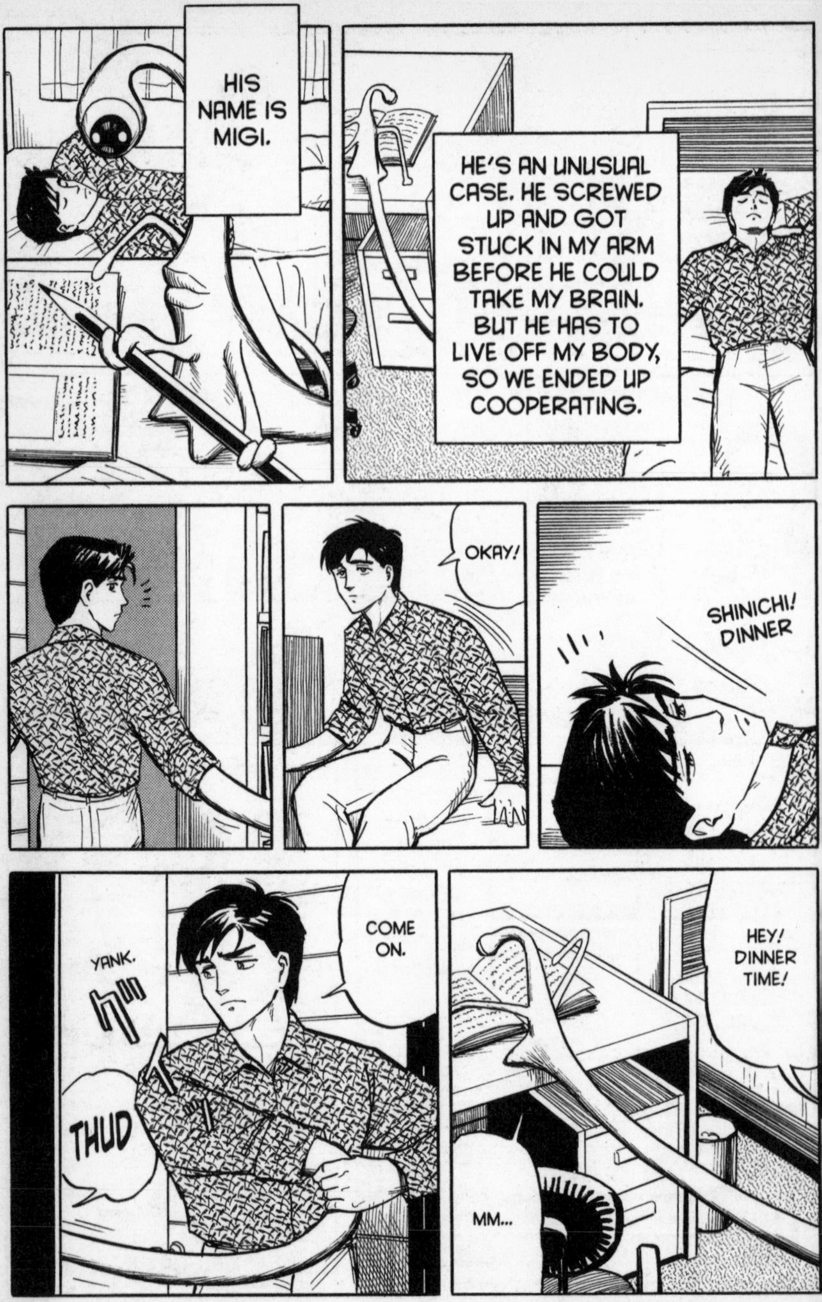
HE'S AN UNUSUAL CASE. HE SCREWED UP AND GOT STUCK IN MY ARM BEFORE HE COULD TAKE MY BRAIN. BUT HE HAS TO LIVE OFF MY BODY, SO WE ENDED UP COOPERATING.
HIS NAME IS MIGI.
SHINICHI! DINNER
OKAY!
HEY! DINNER TIME!
MM...
COME ON.
YANK.
THUD

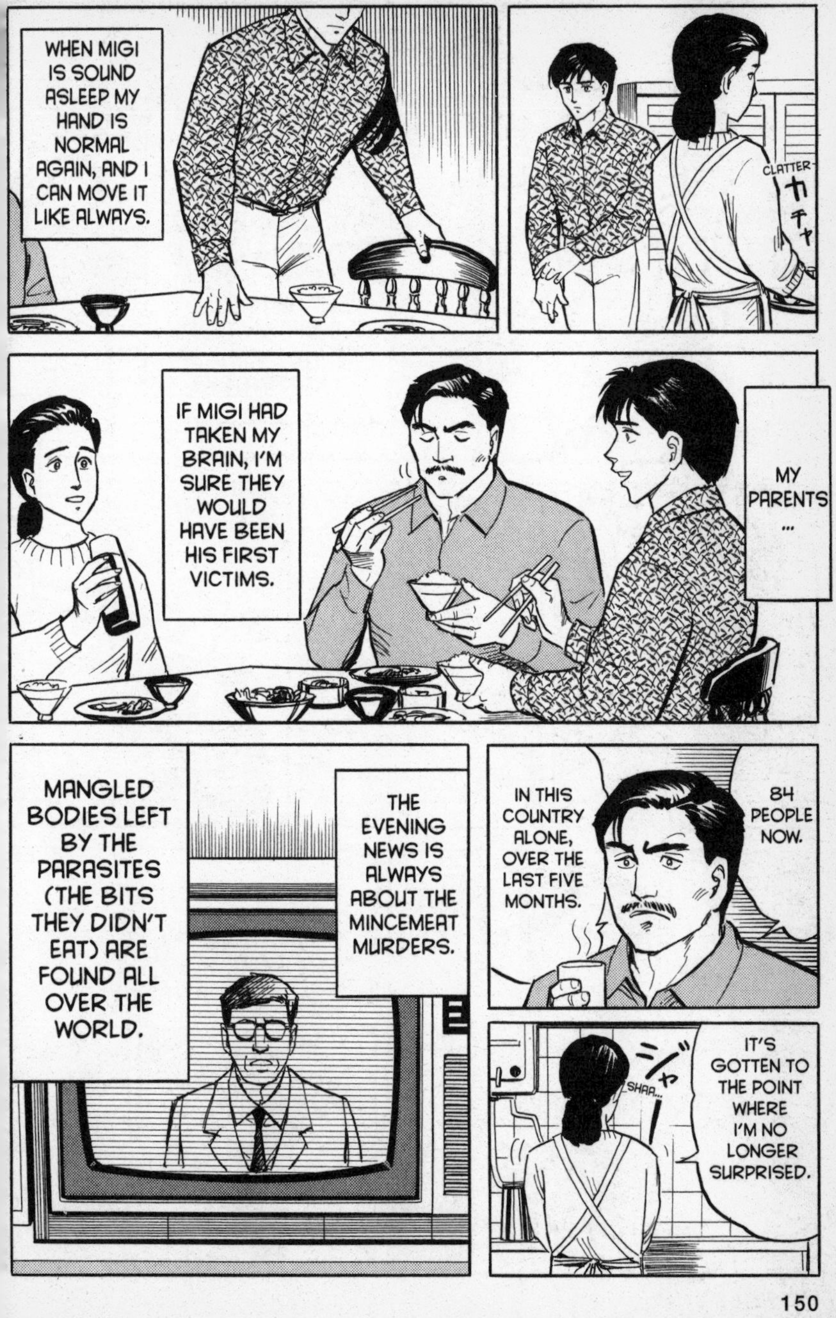

CLATTER
カチャ
WHEN MIGI IS SOUND ASLEEP MY HAND IS NORMAL AGAIN, AND I CAN MOVE IT LIKE ALWAYS.
MY PARENTS...
IF MIGI HAD TAKEN MY BRAIN, I'M SURE THEY WOULD HAVE BEEN HIS FIRST VICTIMS.
84 PEOPLE NOW.
IN THIS COUNTRY ALONE, OVER THE LAST FIVE MONTHS.
ジャー
SHAA...
IT'S GOTTEN TO THE POINT WHERE I'M NO LONGER SURPRISED.
THE EVENING NEWS IS ALWAYS ABOUT THE MINCEMEAT MURDERS.
MANGLED BODIES LEFT BY THE PARASITES (THE BITS THEY DIDN'T EAT) ARE FOUND ALL OVER THE WORLD.

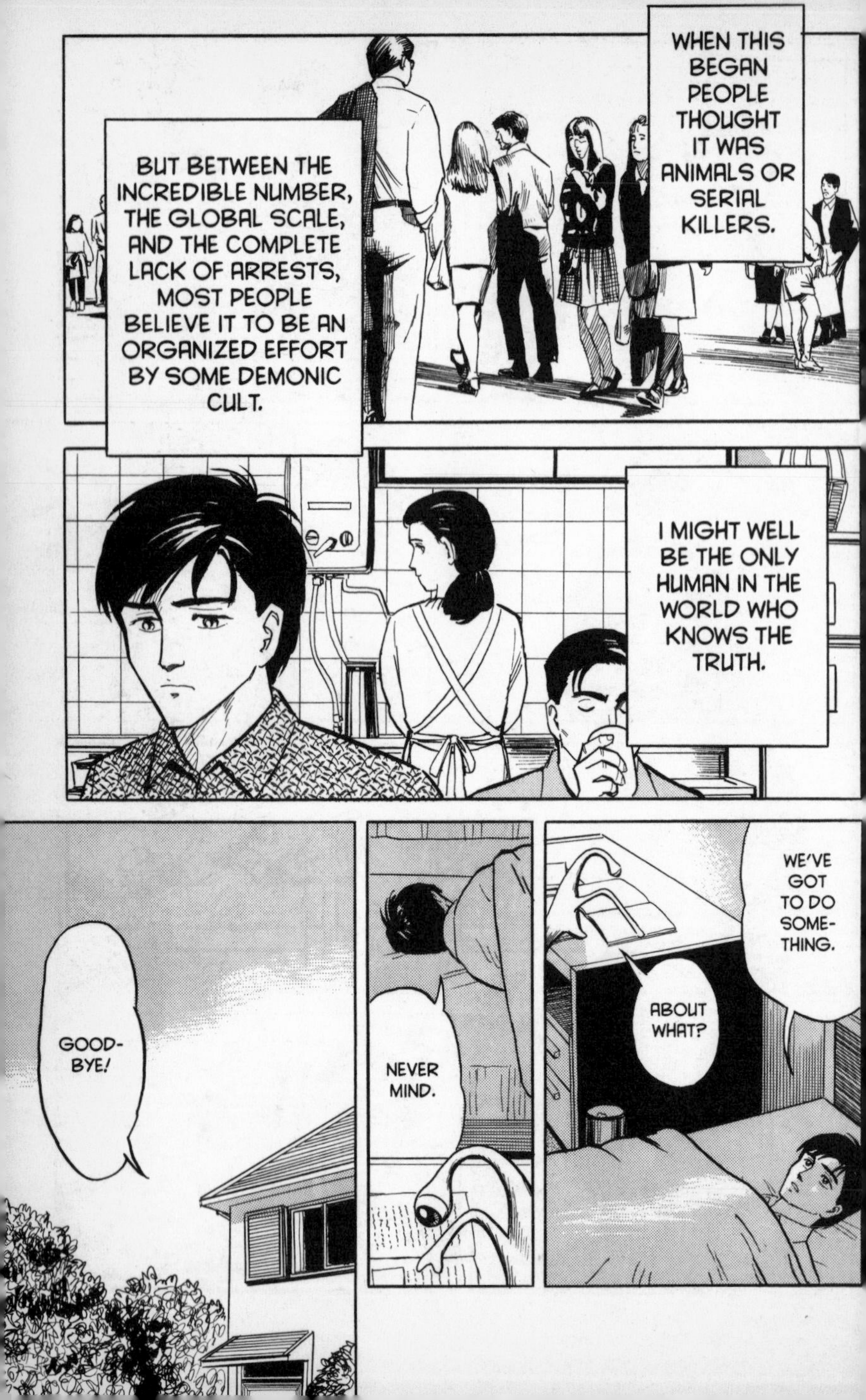
WHEN THIS BEGAN PEOPLE THOUGHT IT WAS ANIMALS OR SERIAL KILLERS.
BUT BETWEEN THE INCREDIBLE NUMBER, THE GLOBAL SCALE, AND THE COMPLETE LACK OF ARRESTS, MOST PEOPLE BELIEVE IT TO BE AN ORGANIZED EFFORT BY SOME DEMONIC CULT.
I MIGHT WELL BE THE ONLY HUMAN IN THE WORLD WHO KNOWS THE TRUTH.
WE'VE GOT TO DO SOME-THING.
ABOUT WHAT?
NEVER MIND.
GOOD-BYE!

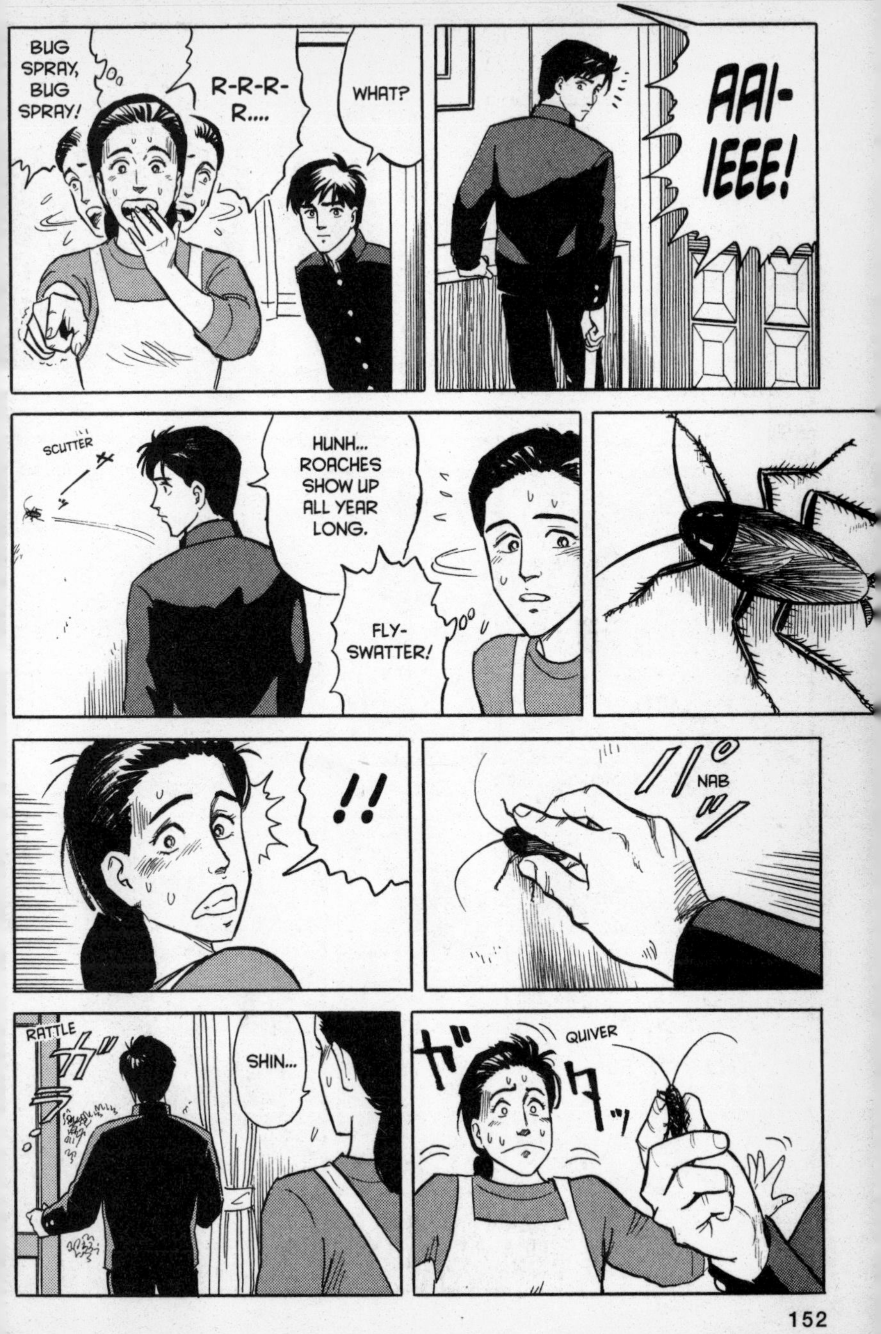
AAI-IEEE!
WHAT?
R-R-R-R....
BUG SPRAY, BUG SPRAY!
HUNH... ROACHES SHOW UP ALL YEAR LONG.
FLY-SWATTER!
SCUTTER
NAB
!!
QUIVER
SHIN...
RATTLE

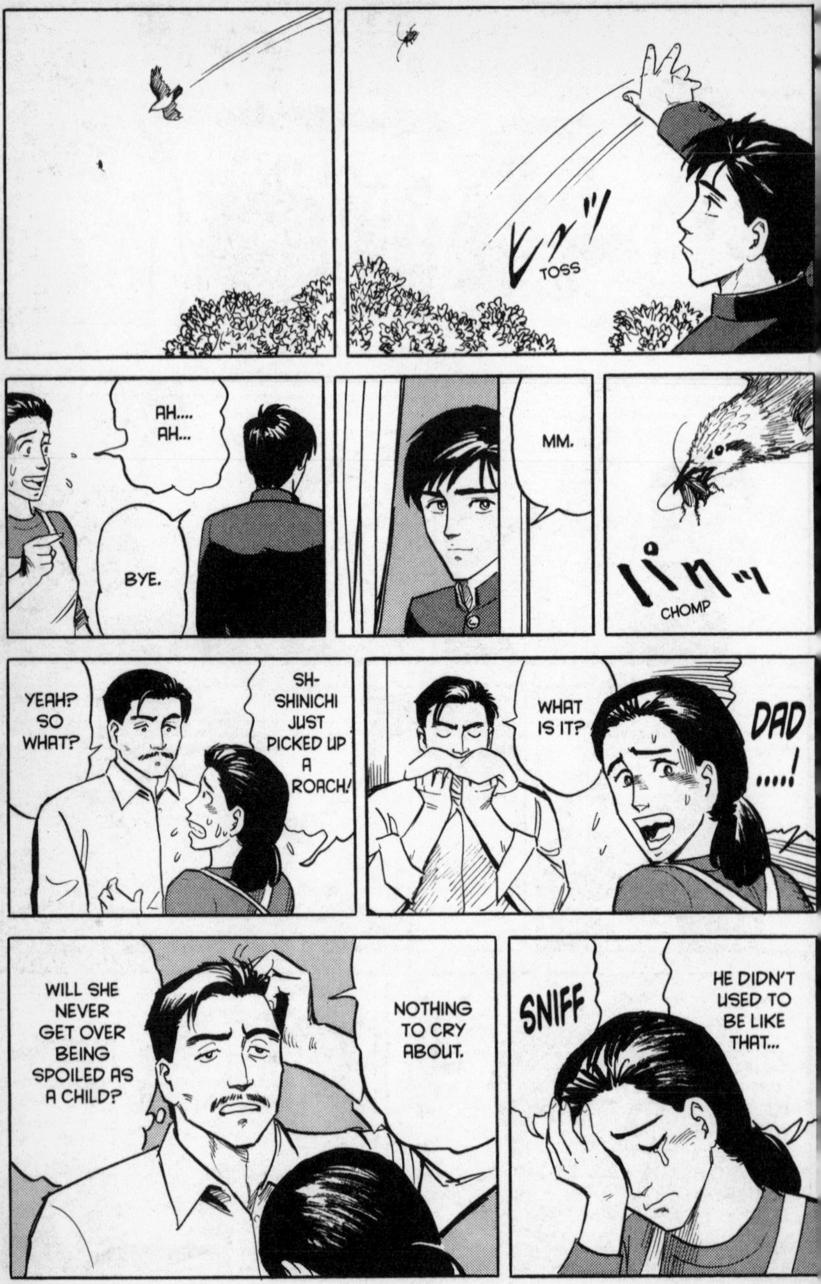
ヒュッ
TOSS
パクッ
CHOMP
MM.
AH.... AH...
BYE.
DAD .....!
WHAT IS IT?
SH-SHINICHI JUST PICKED UP A ROACH!
YEAH? SO WHAT?
HE DIDN'T USED TO BE LIKE THAT...
SNIFF
NOTHING TO CRY ABOUT.
WILL SHE NEVER GET OVER BEING SPOILED AS A CHILD?

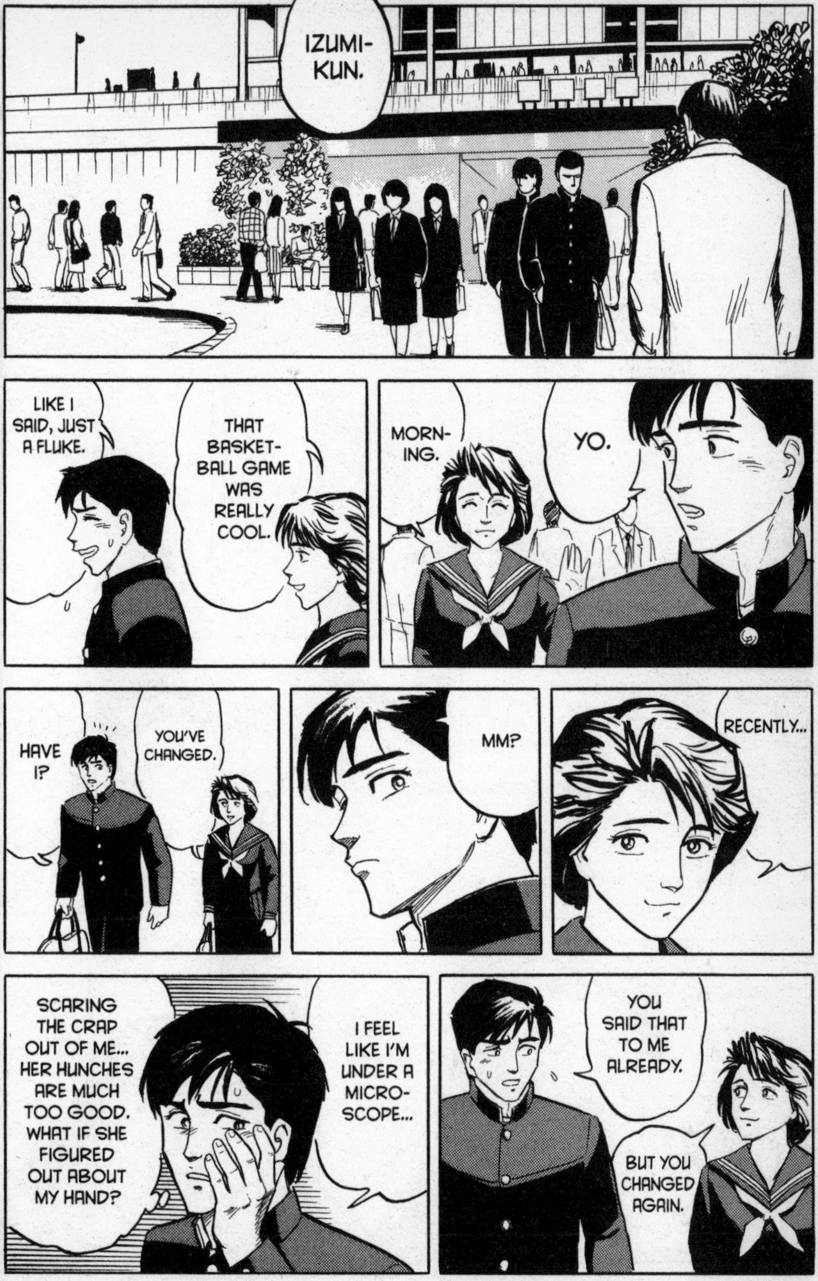
IZUMI-KUN.
YO.
MORN-ING.
THAT BASKET-BALL GAME WAS REALLY COOL.
LIKE I SAID, JUST A FLUKE.
RECENTLY...
MM?
YOU'VE CHANGED.
HAVE I?
YOU SAID THAT TO ME ALREADY.
BUT YOU CHANGED AGAIN.
I FEEL LIKE I'M UNDER A MICRO-SCOPE...
SCARING THE CRAP OUT OF ME... HER HUNCHES ARE MUCH TOO GOOD. WHAT IF SHE FIGURED OUT ABOUT MY HAND?

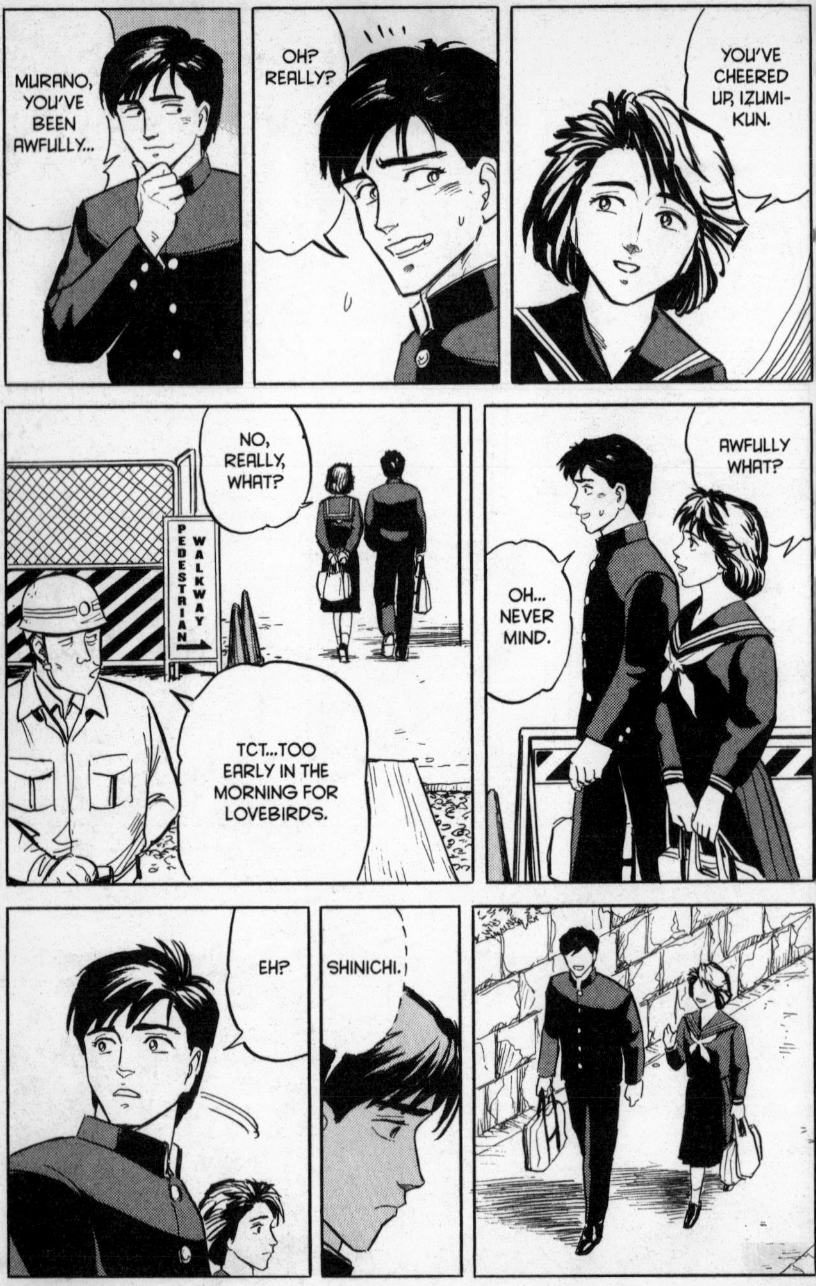
YOU'VE CHEERED UP, IZUMI-KUN.
OH? REALLY?
MURANO, YOU'VE BEEN AWFULLY...
AWFULLY WHAT?
OH... NEVER MIND.
NO, REALLY, WHAT?
PEDESTRIAN
WALKWAY
TCT...TOO EARLY IN THE MORNING FOR LOVEBIRDS.
SHINICHI.
EH?

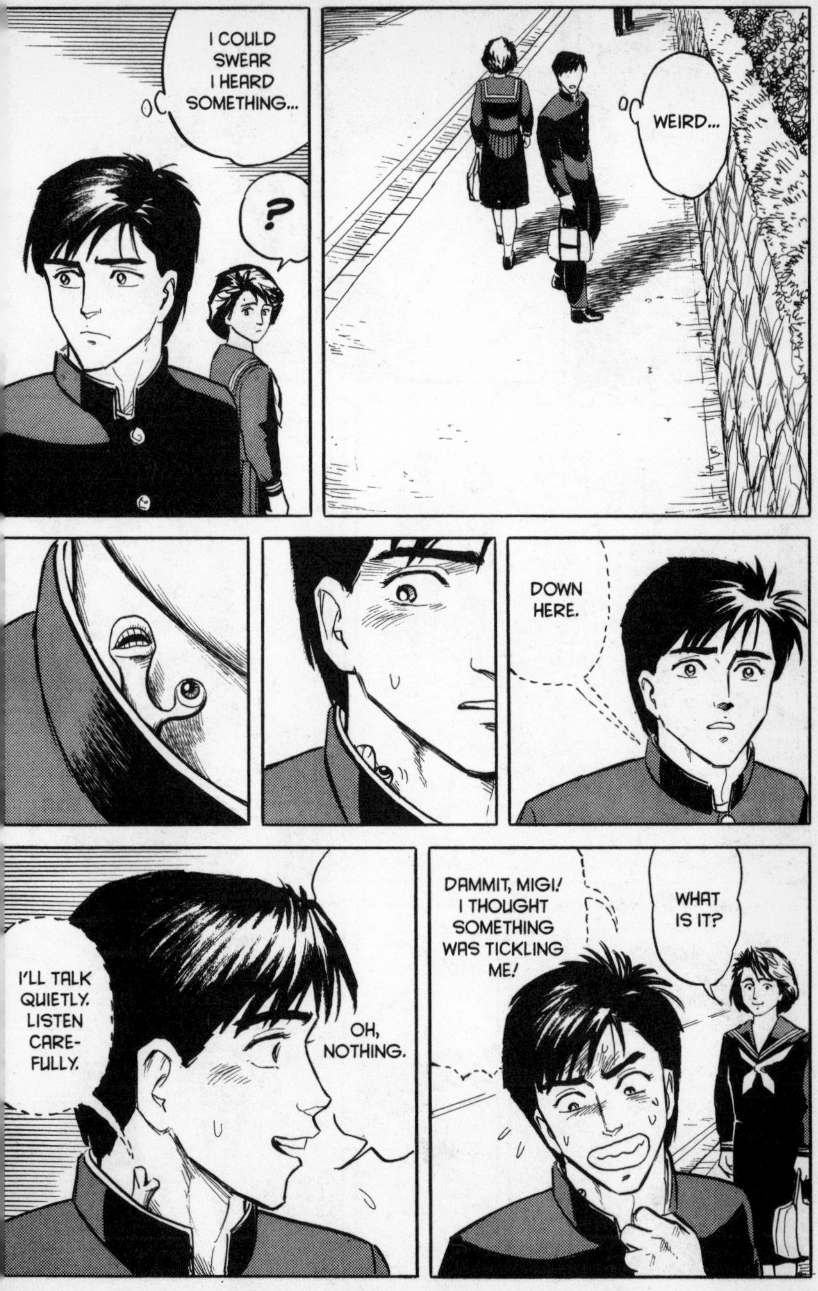
WEIRD...
I COULD SWEAR I HEARD SOMETHING...
?
DOWN HERE.
WHAT IS IT?
DAMMIT, MIGI! I THOUGHT SOMETHING WAS TICKLING ME!
OH, NOTHING.
I'LL TALK QUIETLY. LISTEN CARE-FULLY.

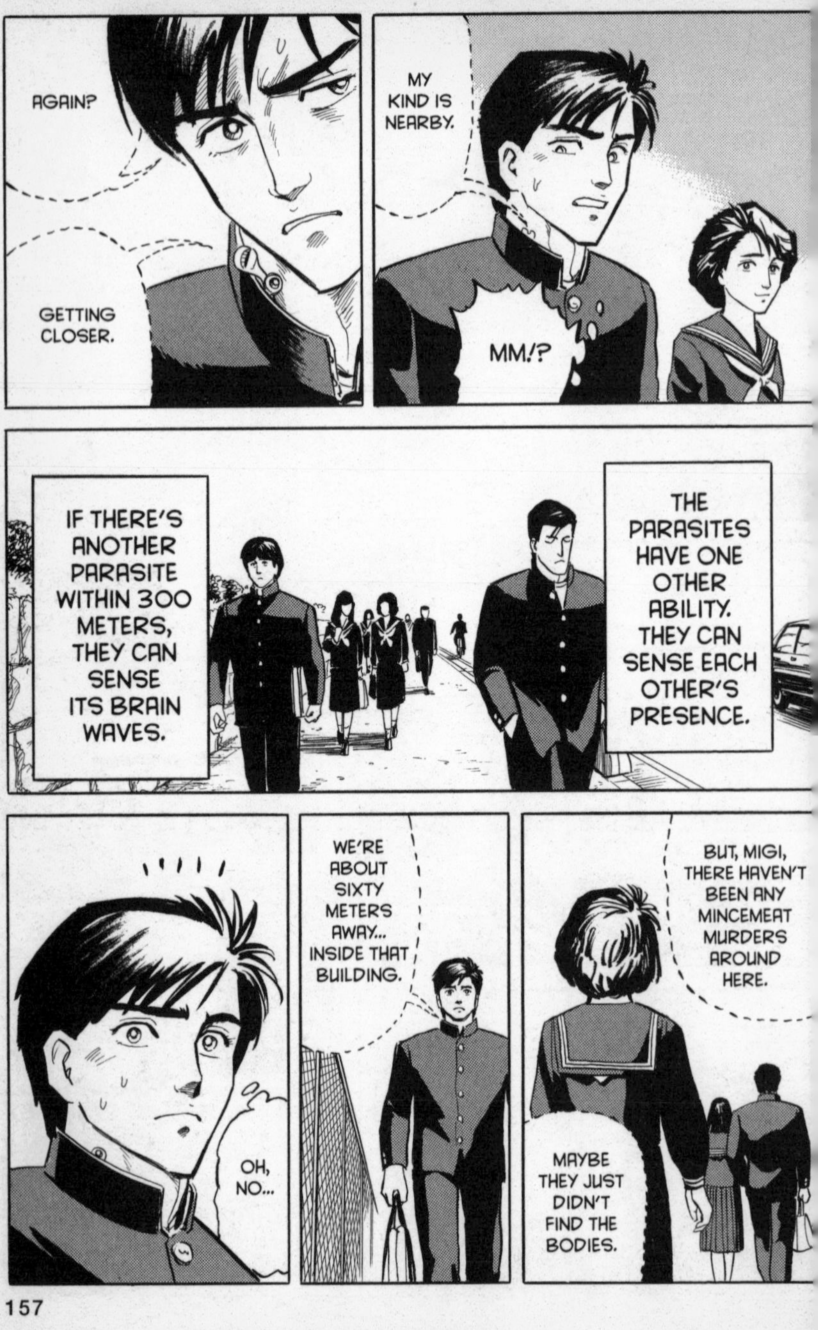
MY KIND IS NEARBY.
MM!?
AGAIN?
GETTING CLOSER.
THE PARASITES HAVE ONE OTHER ABILITY. THEY CAN SENSE EACH OTHER'S PRESENCE.
IF THERE'S ANOTHER PARASITE WITHIN 300 METERS, THEY CAN SENSE ITS BRAIN WAVES.
BUT, MIGI, THERE HAVEN'T BEEN ANY MINCEMEAT MURDERS AROUND HERE.
MAYBE THEY JUST DIDN'T FIND THE BODIES.
WE'RE ABOUT SIXTY METERS AWAY... INSIDE THAT BUILDING.
OH, NO...

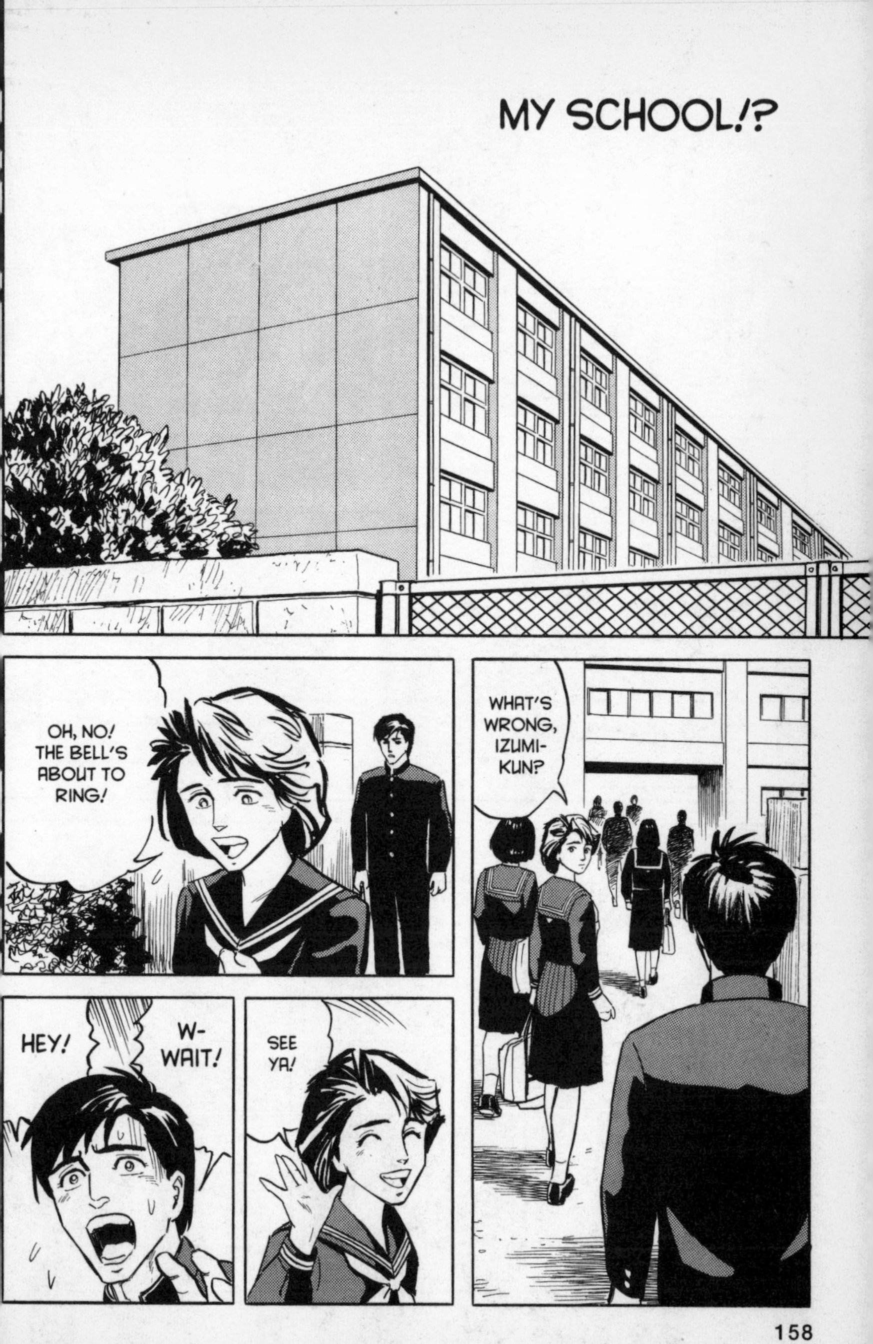
MY SCHOOL!?
WHAT'S WRONG, IZUMI-KUN?
OH, NO! THE BELL'S ABOUT TO RING!
SEE YA!
W-WAIT!
HEY!

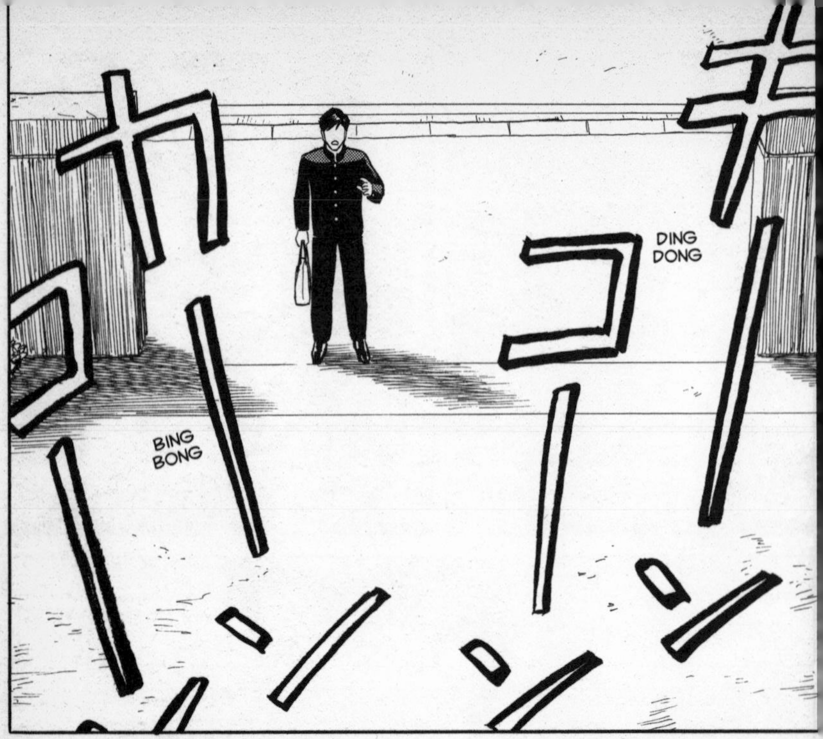
DING
DONG
BING
BONG
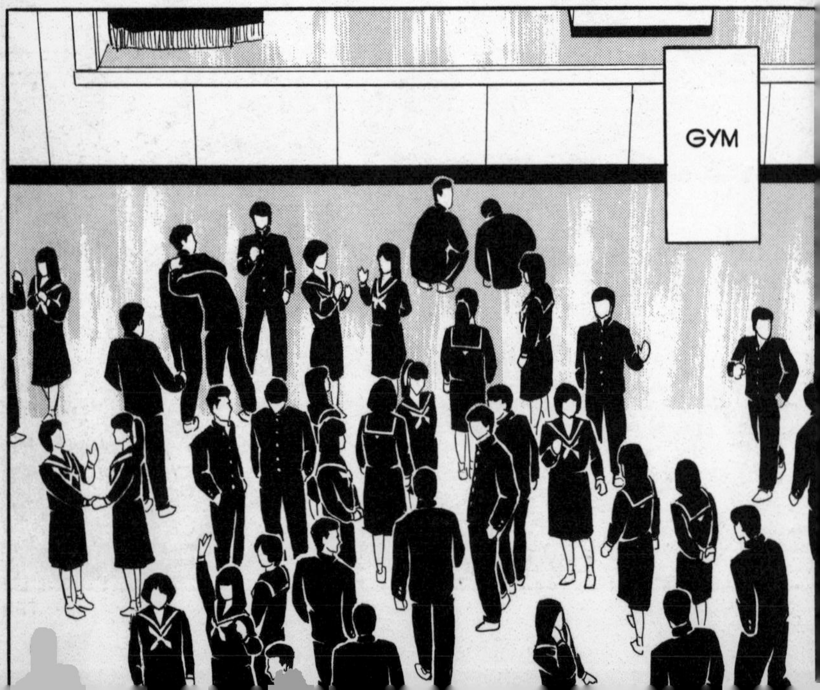
GYM

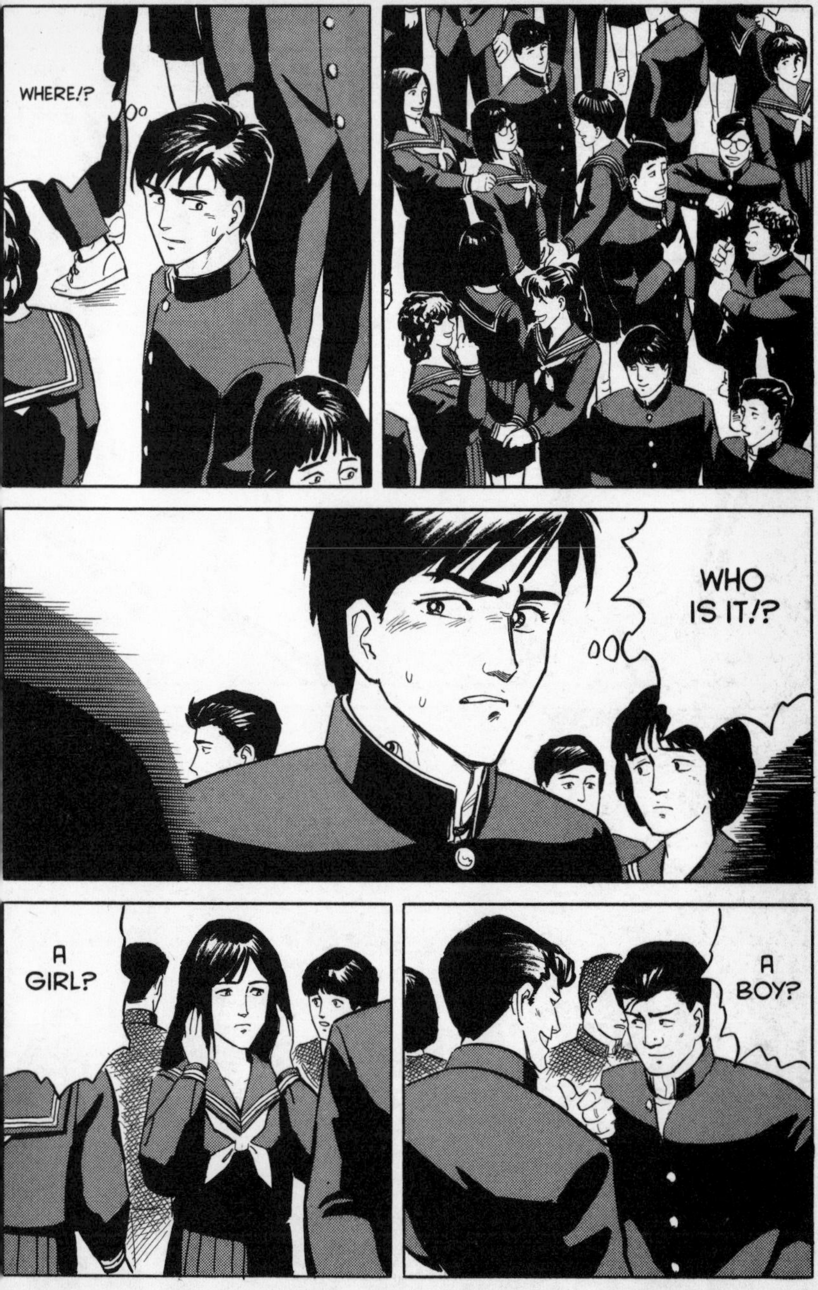
WHERE!?
WHO IS IT!?
A BOY?
A GIRL?

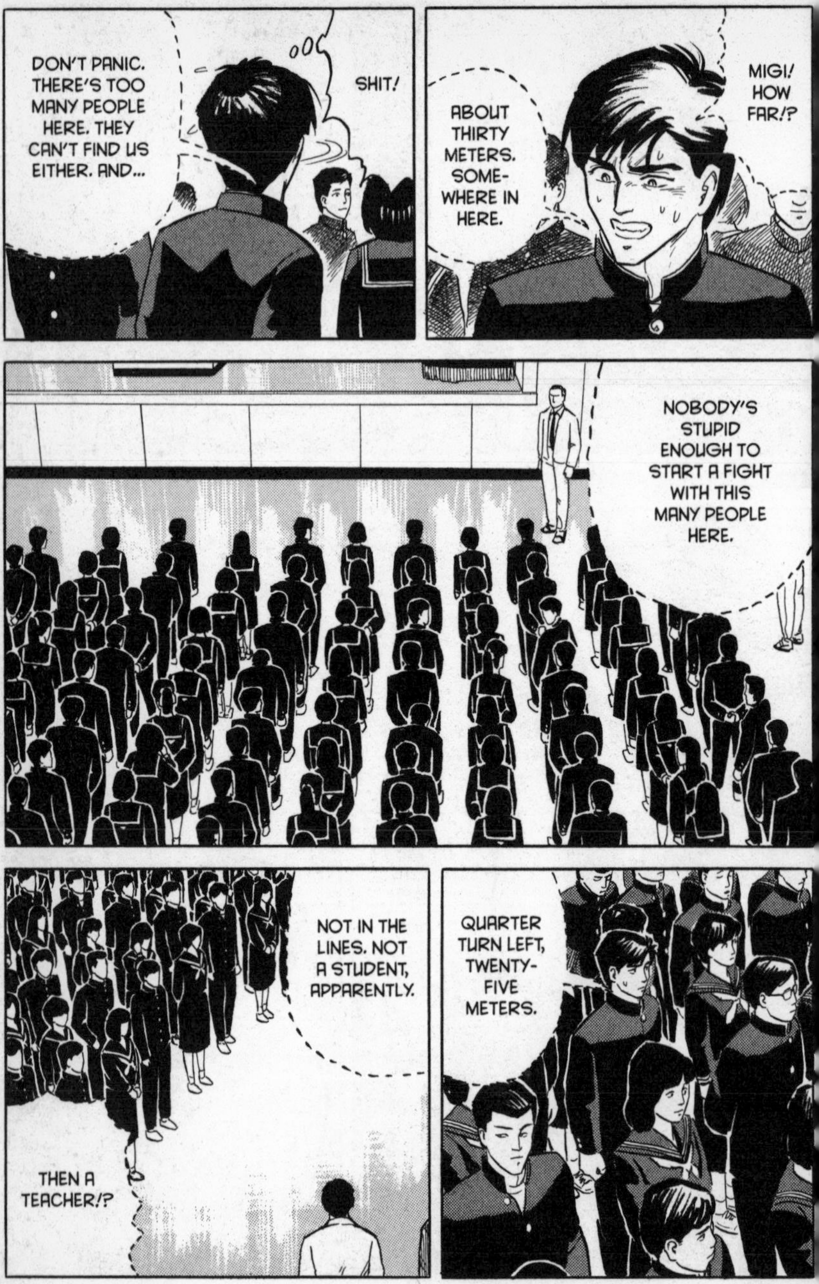
MIGI! HOW FAR!?
ABOUT THIRTY METERS. SOME-WHERE IN HERE.
SHIT!
DON'T PANIC. THERE'S TOO MANY PEOPLE HERE. THEY CAN'T FIND US EITHER. AND...
NOBODY'S STUPID ENOUGH TO START A FIGHT WITH THIS MANY PEOPLE HERE.
QUARTER TURN LEFT, TWENTY-FIVE METERS.
NOT IN THE LINES. NOT A STUDENT, APPARENTLY.
THEN A TEACHER!?

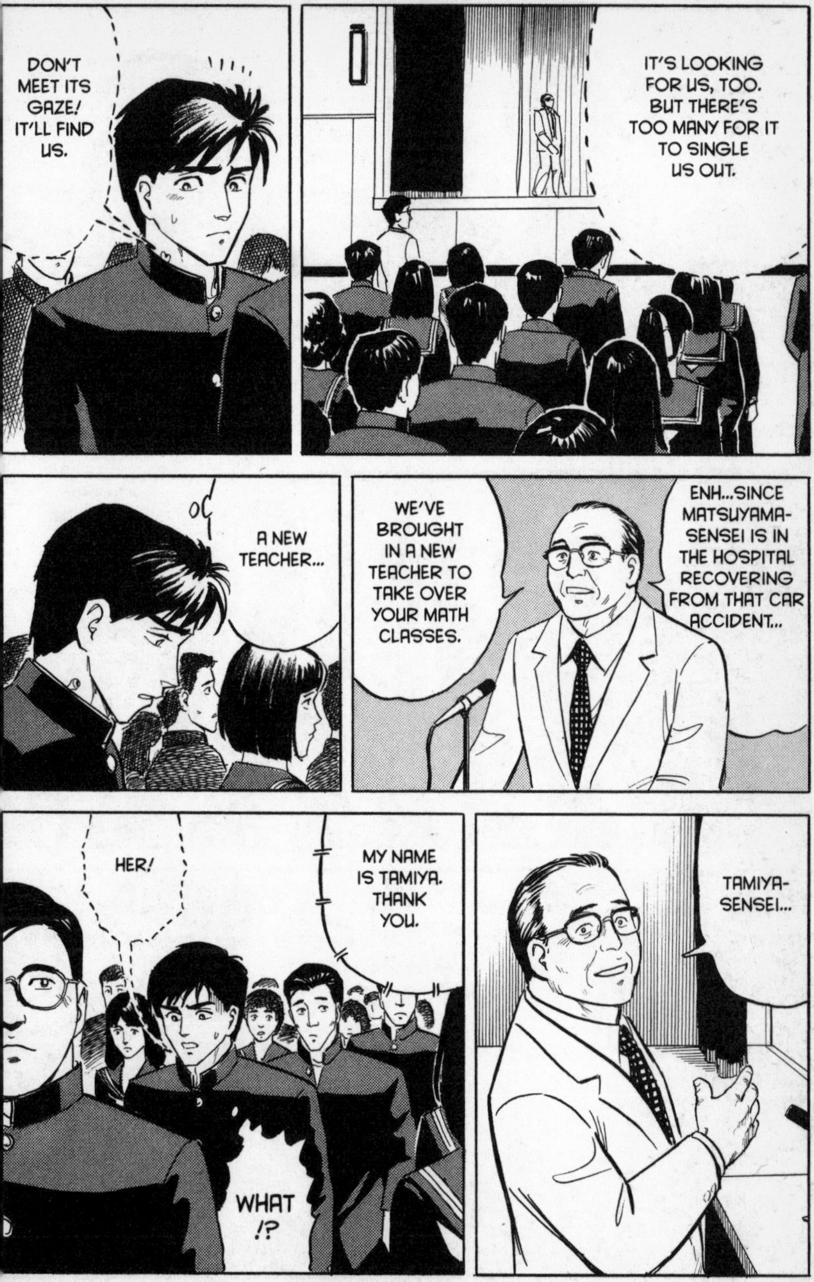
IT'S LOOKING FOR US, TOO. BUT THERE'S TOO MANY FOR IT TO SINGLE US OUT.
DON'T MEET ITS GAZE! IT'LL FIND US.
ENH...SINCE MATSUYAMA-SENSEI IS IN THE HOSPITAL RECOVERING FROM THAT CAR ACCIDENT...
WE'VE BROUGHT IN A NEW TEACHER TO TAKE OVER YOUR MATH CLASSES.
A NEW TEACHER...
TAMIYA-SENSEI...
MY NAME IS TAMIYA. THANK YOU.
HER!
WHAT !?

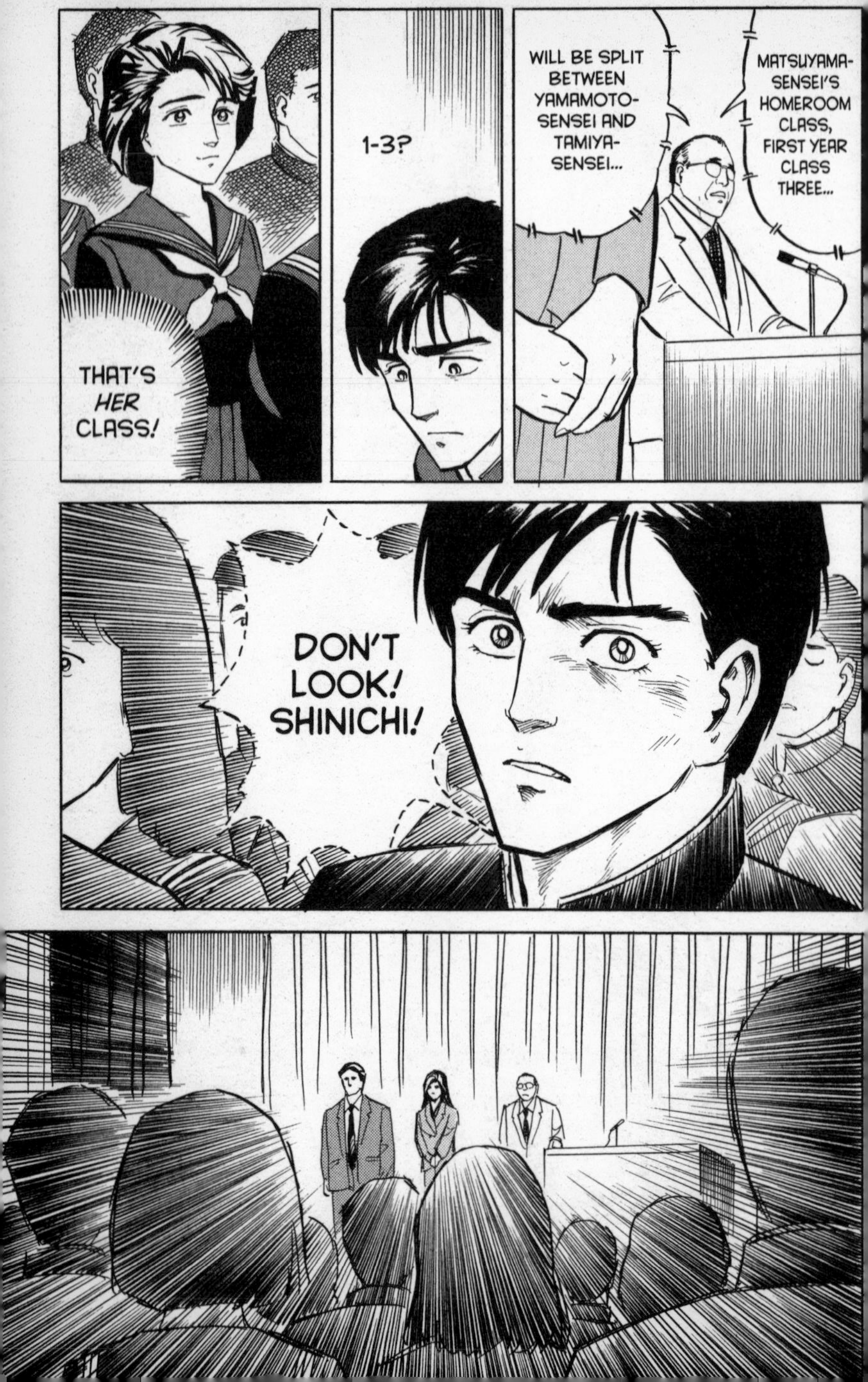
MATSUYAMA-SENSEI'S HOMEROOM CLASS, FIRST YEAR CLASS THREE...
WILL BE SPLIT BETWEEN YAMAMOTO-SENSEI AND TAMIYA-SENSEI...
1-3?
THAT'S *HER* CLASS!
DON'T LOOK! SHINICHI!

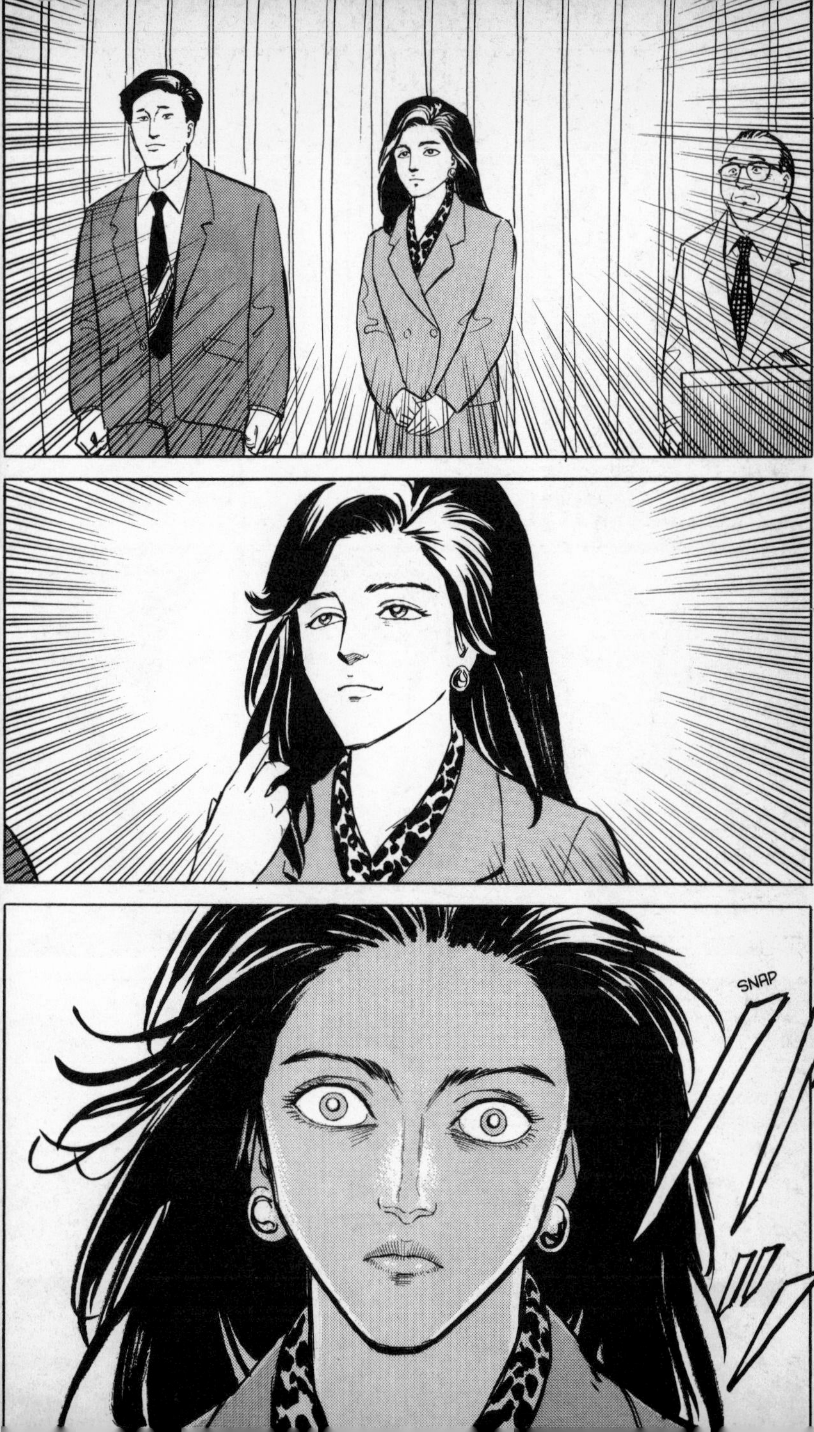
SNAP

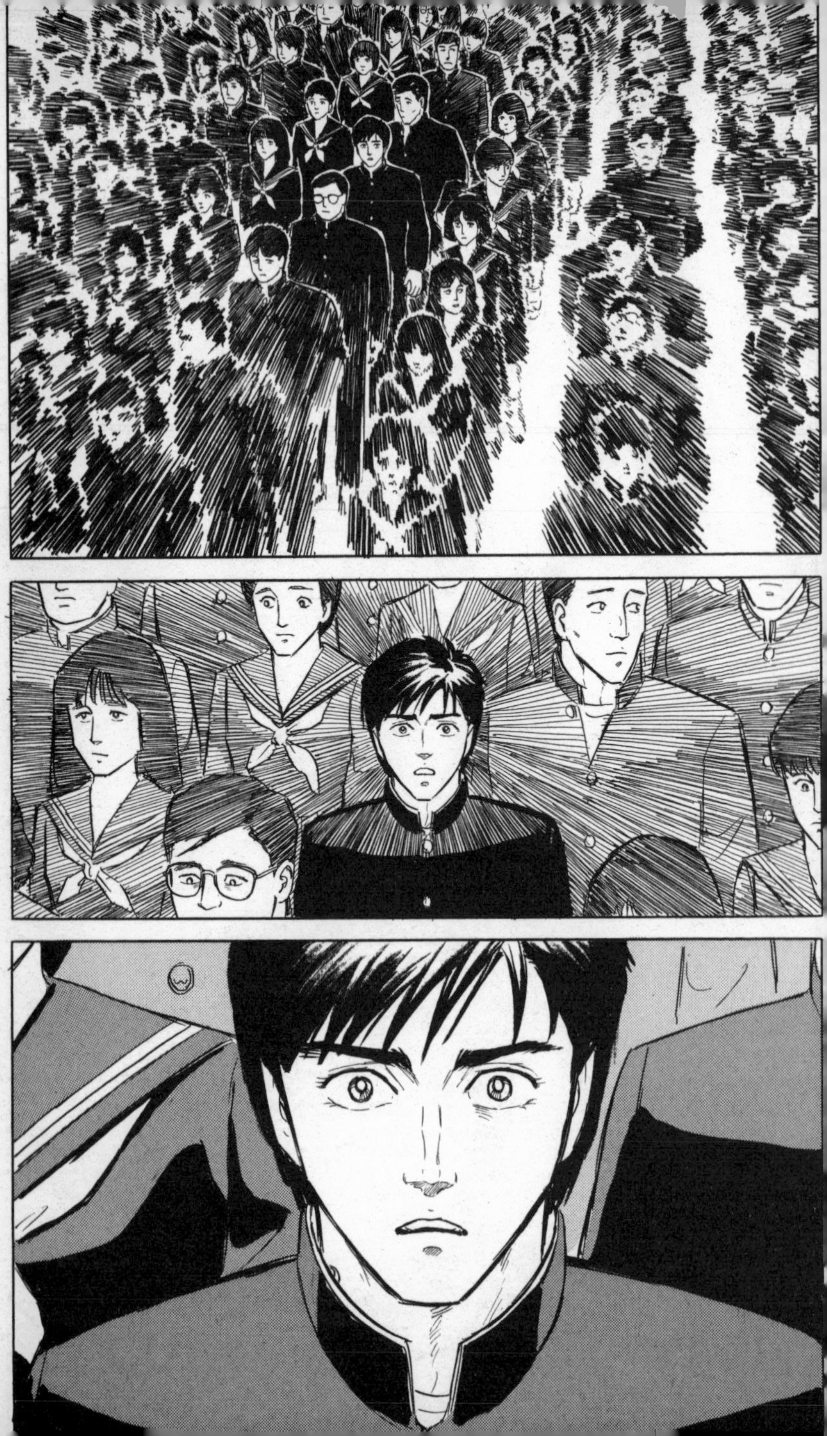

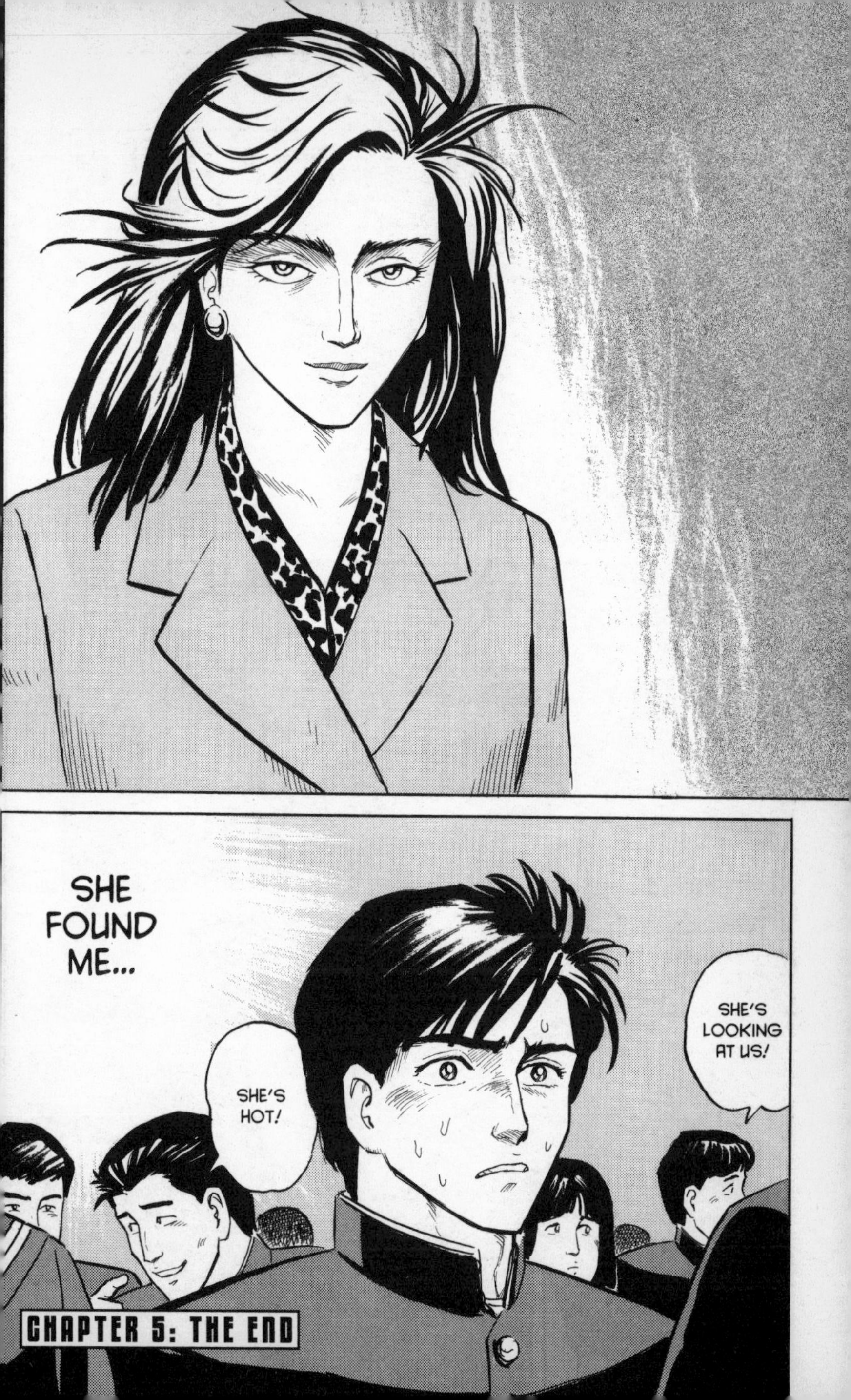
SHE FOUND ME...
SHE'S LOOKING AT US!
SHE'S HOT!
CHAPTER 5: THE END

CHAPTER 6: TAMIYA RYŌKO

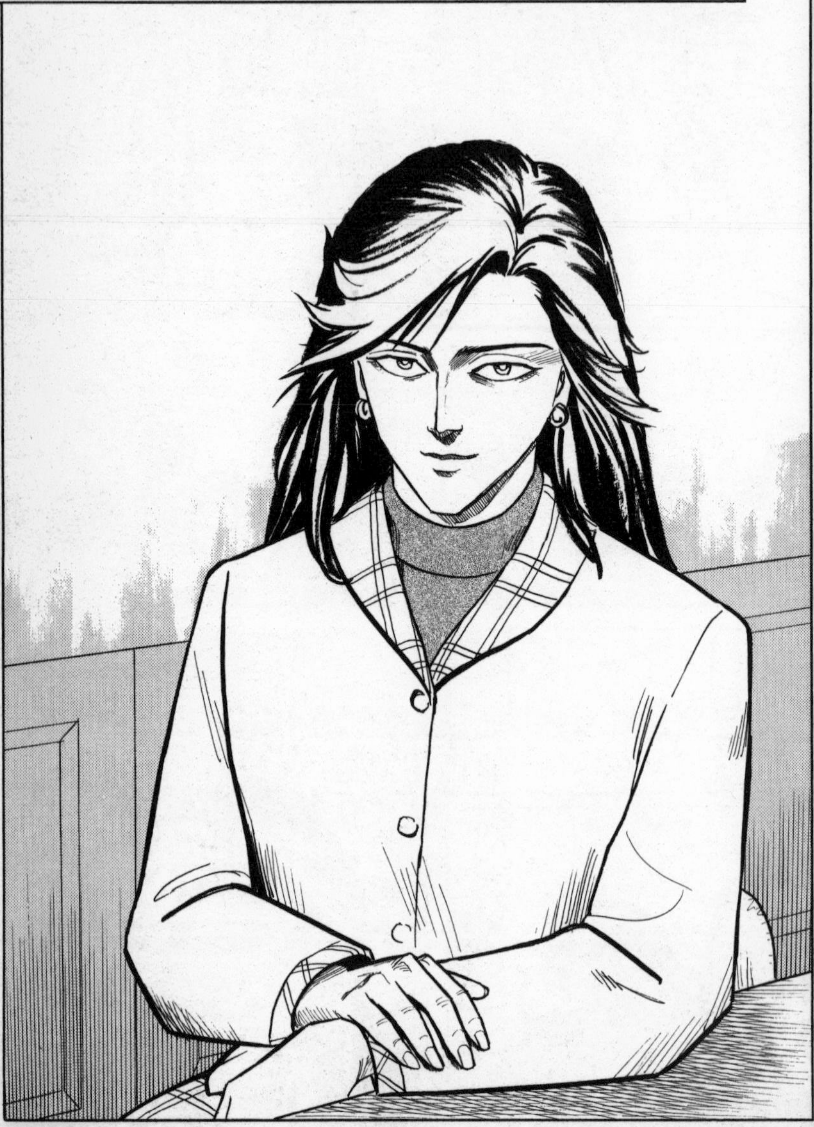

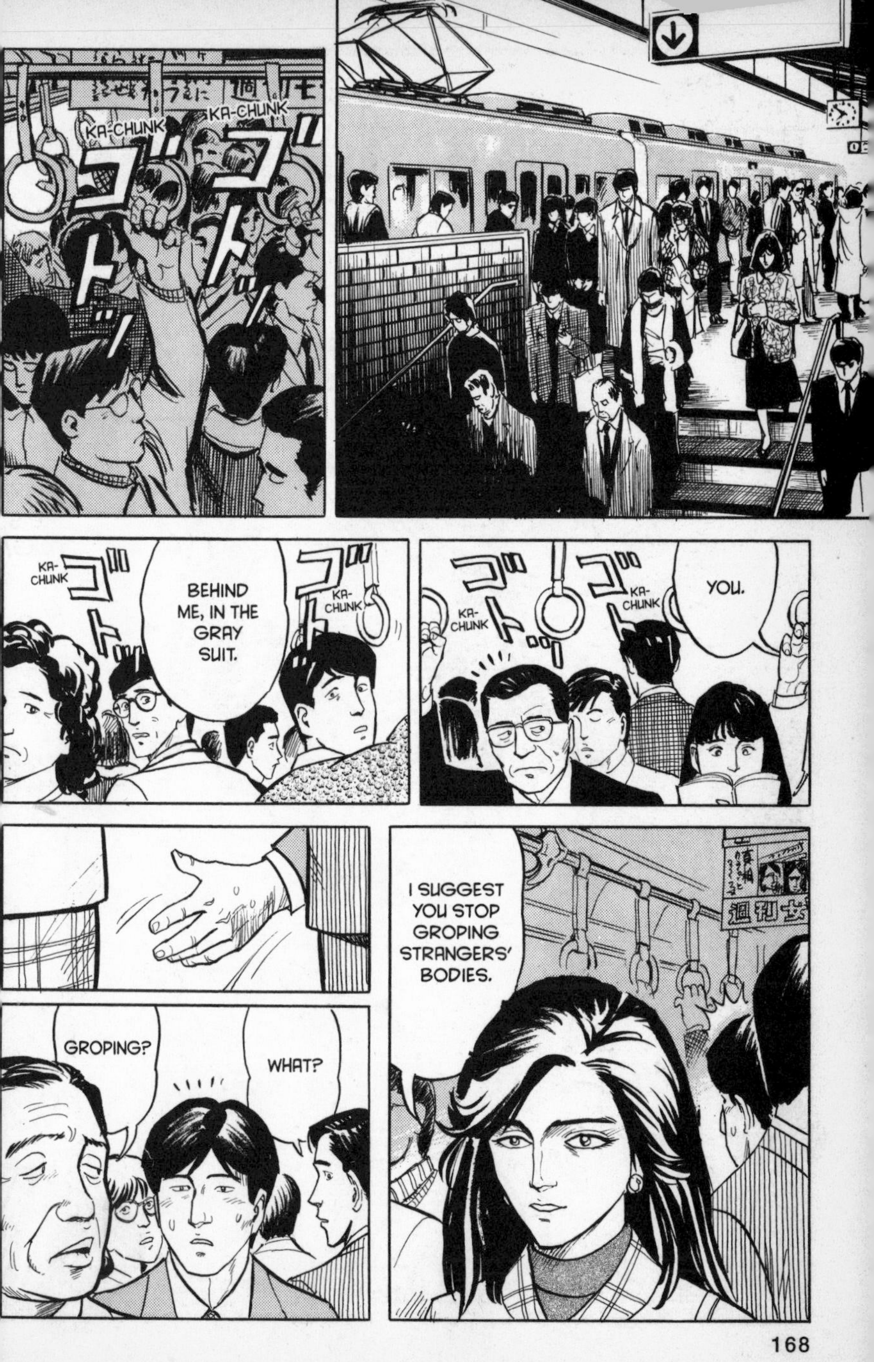
KA-CHUNK
KA-CHUNK
KA-CHUNK
KA-CHUNK
YOU.
KA-CHUNK
BEHIND ME, IN THE GRAY SUIT.
KA-CHUNK
I SUGGEST YOU STOP GROPING STRANGERS' BODIES.
WHAT?
GROPING?

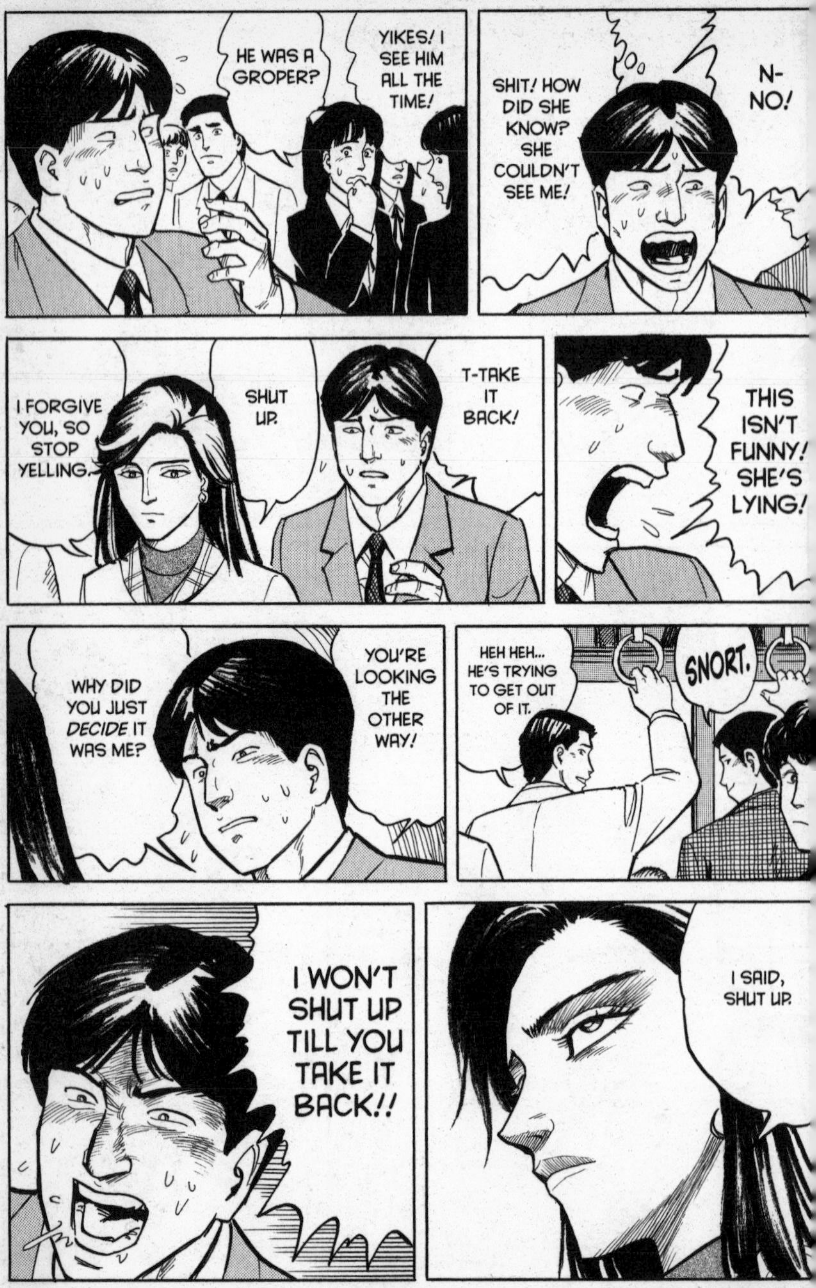
N-NO!
SHIT! HOW DID SHE KNOW? SHE COULDN'T SEE ME!
YIKES! I SEE HIM ALL THE TIME!
HE WAS A GROPER?
THIS ISN'T FUNNY! SHE'S LYING!
T-TAKE IT BACK!
SHUT UP.
I FORGIVE YOU, SO STOP YELLING.
SNORT.
HEH HEH... HE'S TRYING TO GET OUT OF IT.
YOU'RE LOOKING THE OTHER WAY!
WHY DID YOU JUST *DECIDE* IT WAS ME?
I SAID, SHUT UP.
I WON'T SHUT UP TILL YOU TAKE IT BACK!!

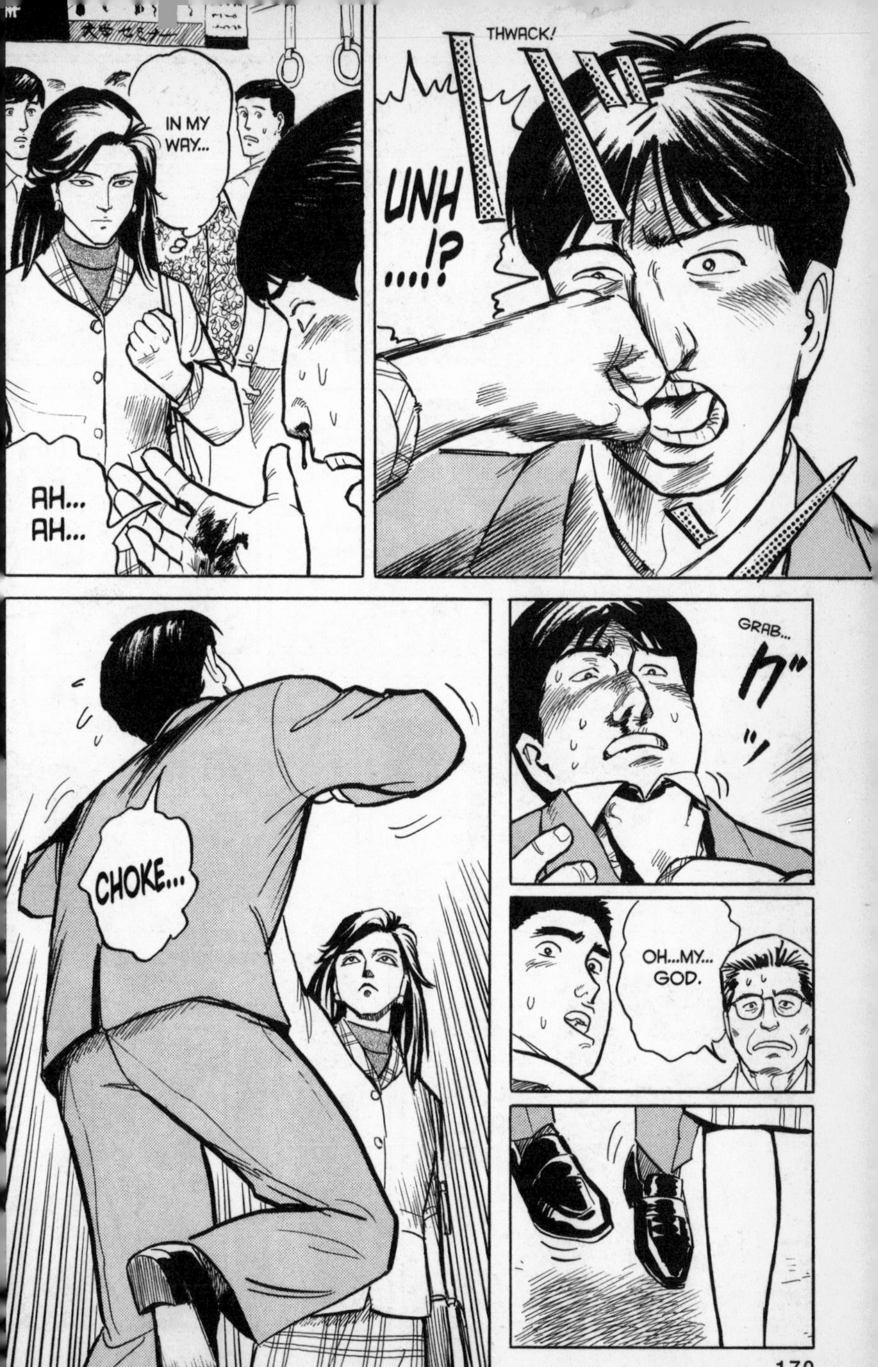
THWACK!
UNH !?
....!?
IN MY WAY...
AH... AH...
GRAB...
グッ
OH...MY... GOD.
CHOKE...

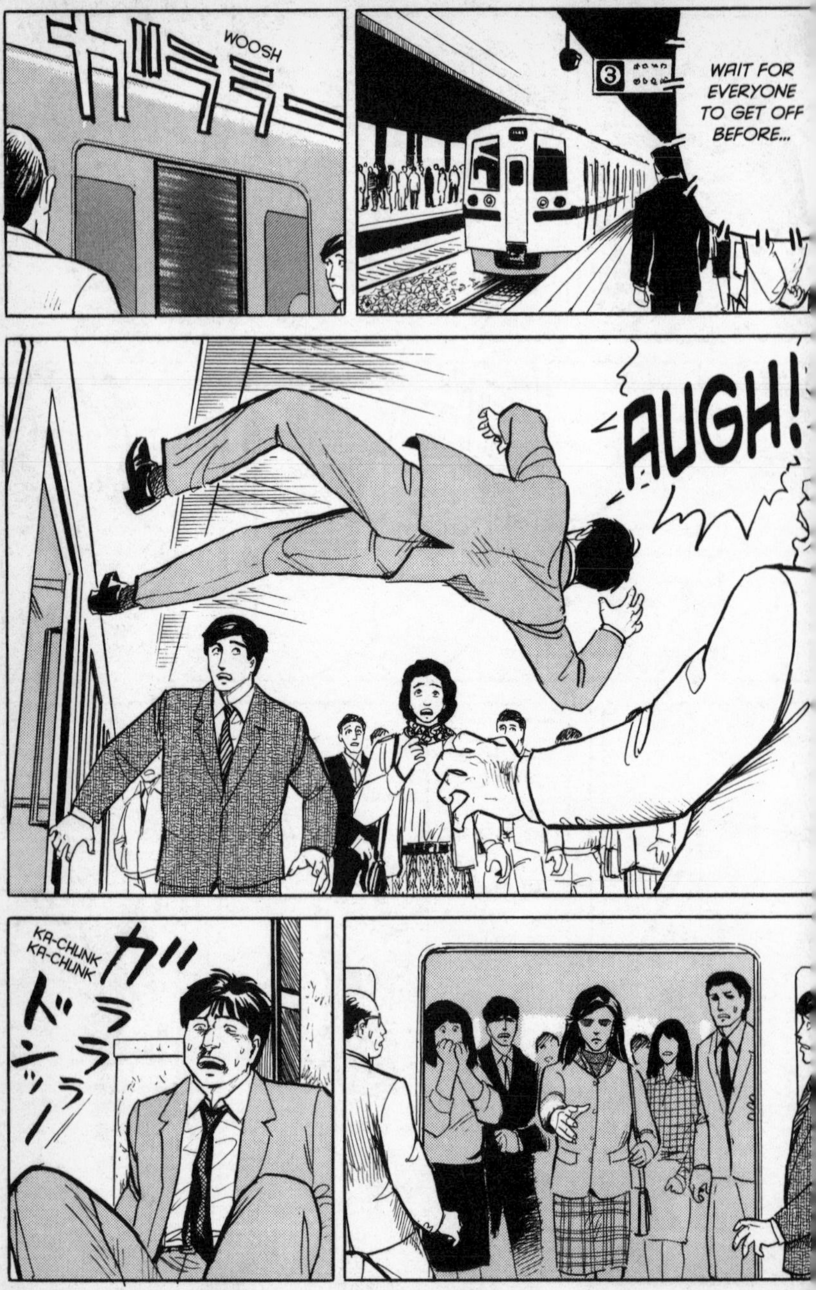
WAIT FOR EVERYONE TO GET OFF BEFORE...
ガラララー
WOOSH
AUGH!
ガラララッ
ドンッ
KA-CHUNK KA-CHUNK

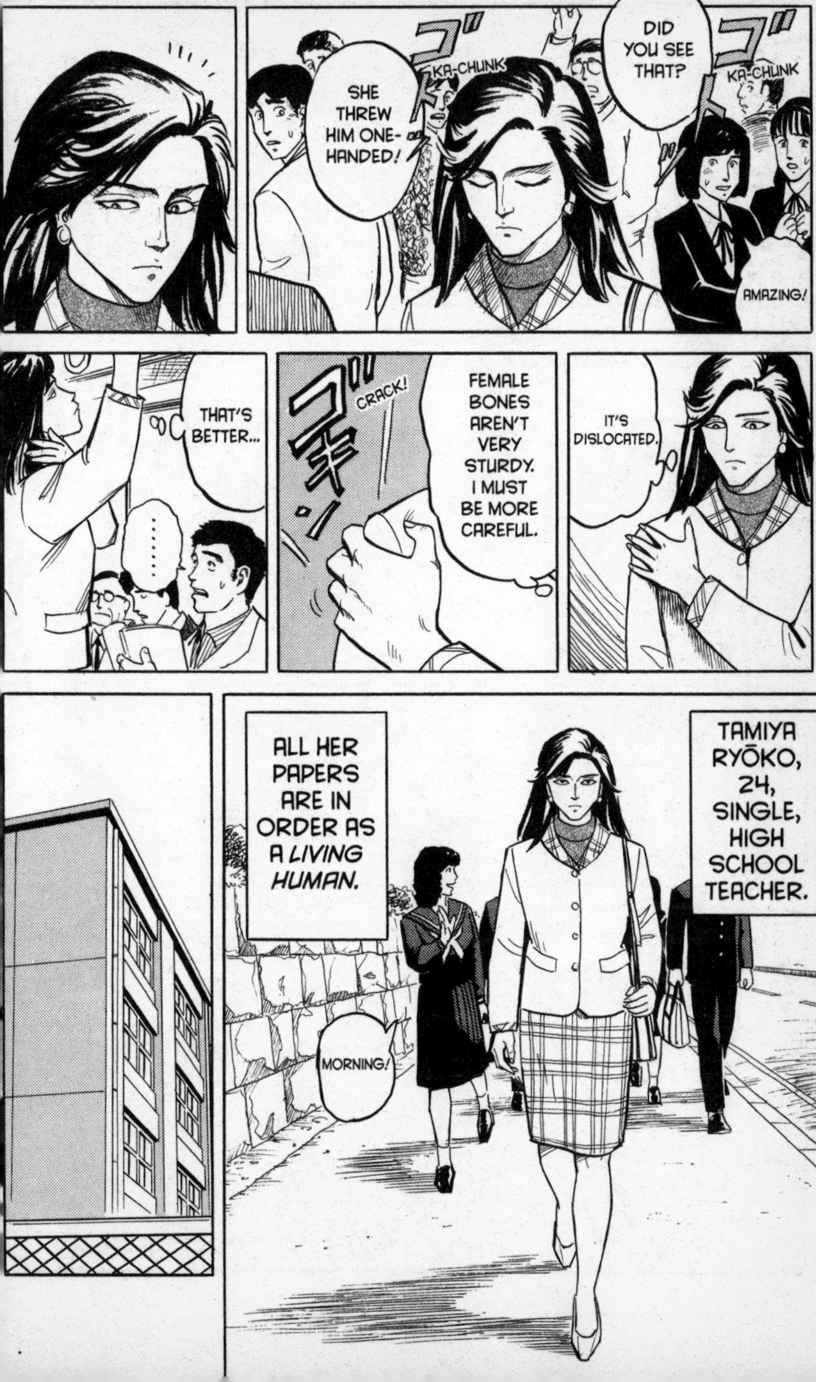
DID YOU SEE THAT?
KA-CHUNK
KA-CHUNK
SHE THREW HIM ONE-HANDED!
AMAZING!
IT'S DISLOCATED.
FEMALE BONES AREN'T VERY STURDY. I MUST BE MORE CAREFUL.
CRACK!
THAT'S BETTER...
......
TAMIYA RYŌKO, 24, SINGLE, HIGH SCHOOL TEACHER.
ALL HER PAPERS ARE IN ORDER AS A *LIVING HUMAN.*
MORNING!

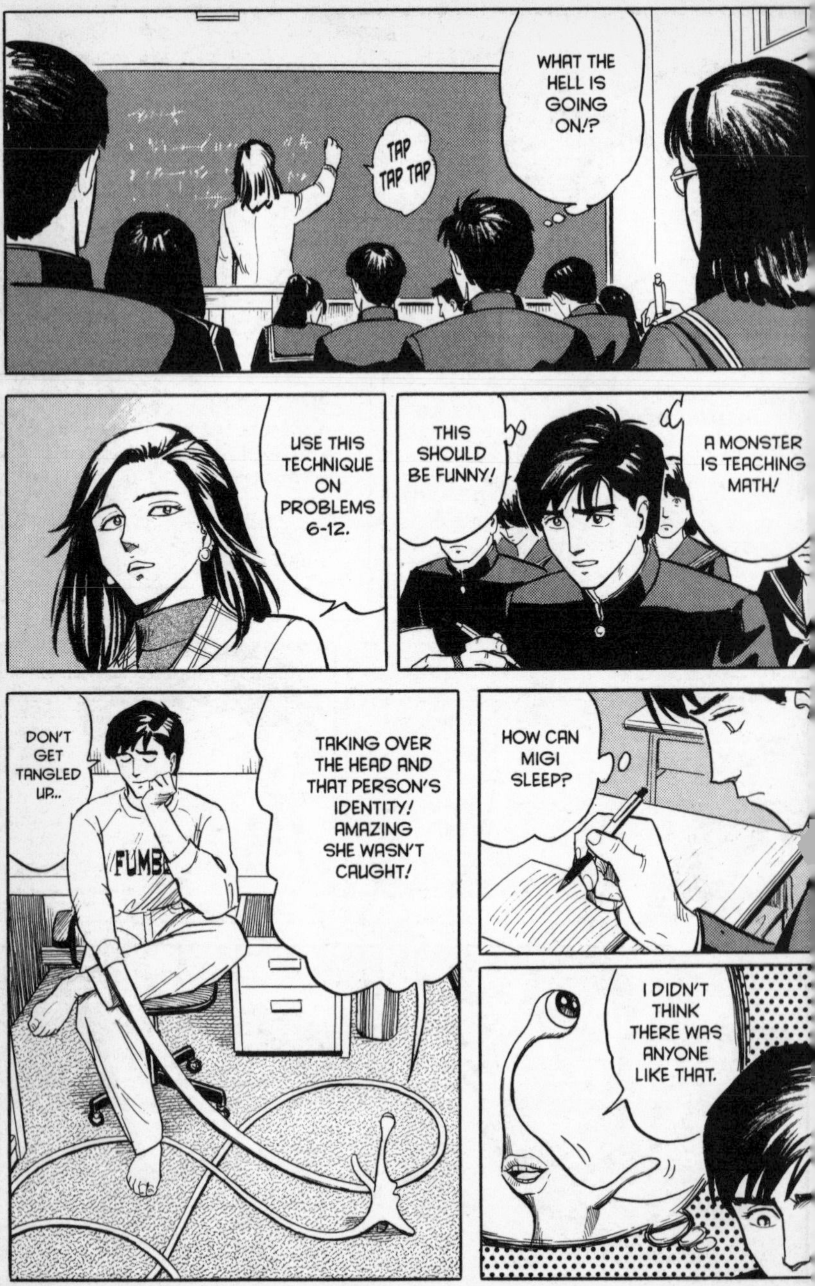

WHAT THE HELL IS GOING ON!?
TAP TAP TAP
A MONSTER IS TEACHING MATH!
THIS SHOULD BE FUNNY!
USE THIS TECHNIQUE ON PROBLEMS 6-12.
HOW CAN MIGI SLEEP?
I DIDN'T THINK THERE WAS ANYONE LIKE THAT.
TAKING OVER THE HEAD AND THAT PERSON'S IDENTITY! AMAZING SHE WASN'T CAUGHT!
DON'T GET TANGLED UP...

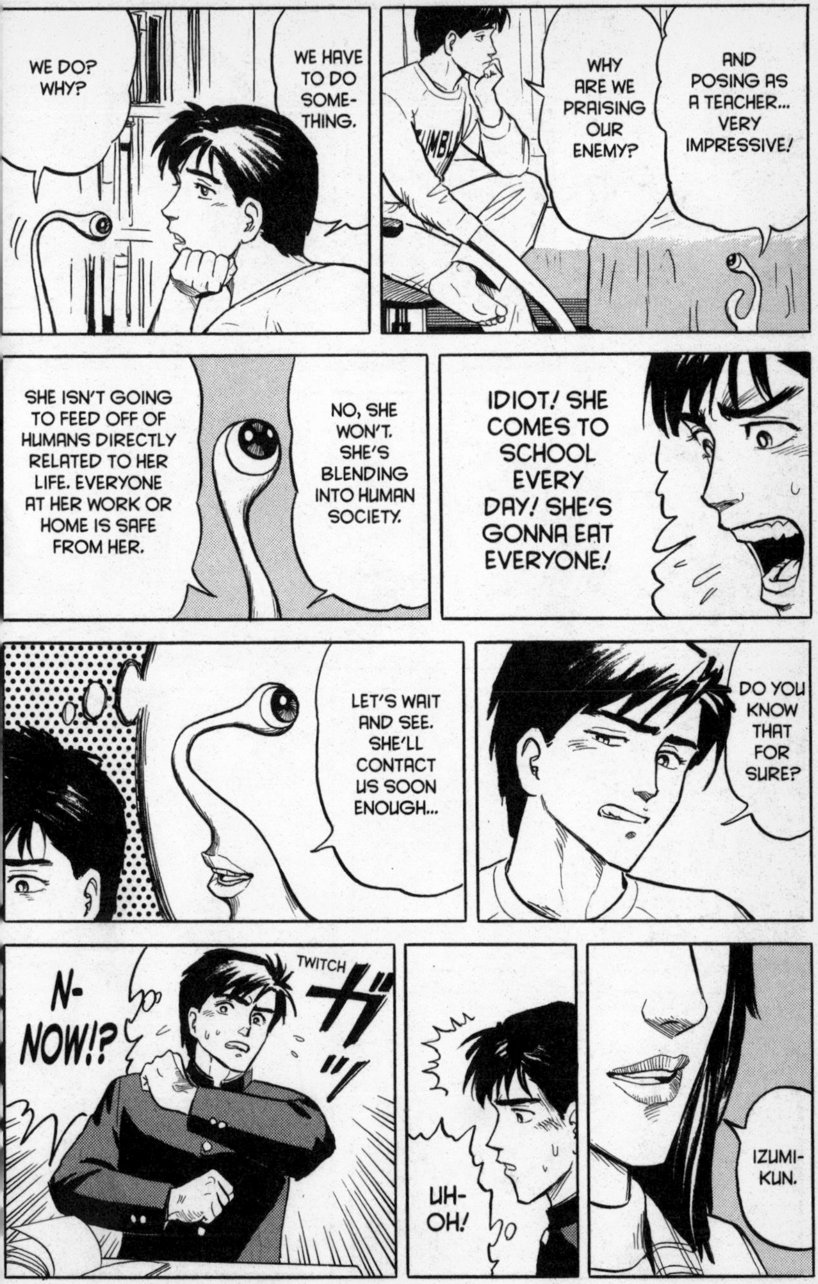
AND POSING AS A TEACHER... VERY IMPRESSIVE!
WHY ARE WE PRAISING OUR ENEMY?
WE HAVE TO DO SOME-THING.
WE DO? WHY?
IDIOT! SHE COMES TO SCHOOL EVERY DAY! SHE'S GONNA EAT EVERYONE!
NO, SHE WON'T. SHE'S BLENDING INTO HUMAN SOCIETY.
SHE ISN'T GOING TO FEED OFF OF HUMANS DIRECTLY RELATED TO HER LIFE. EVERYONE AT HER WORK OR HOME IS SAFE FROM HER.
DO YOU KNOW THAT FOR SURE?
LET'S WAIT AND SEE. SHE'LL CONTACT US SOON ENOUGH...
IZUMI-KUN.
UH-OH!
TWITCH
N-NOW!?

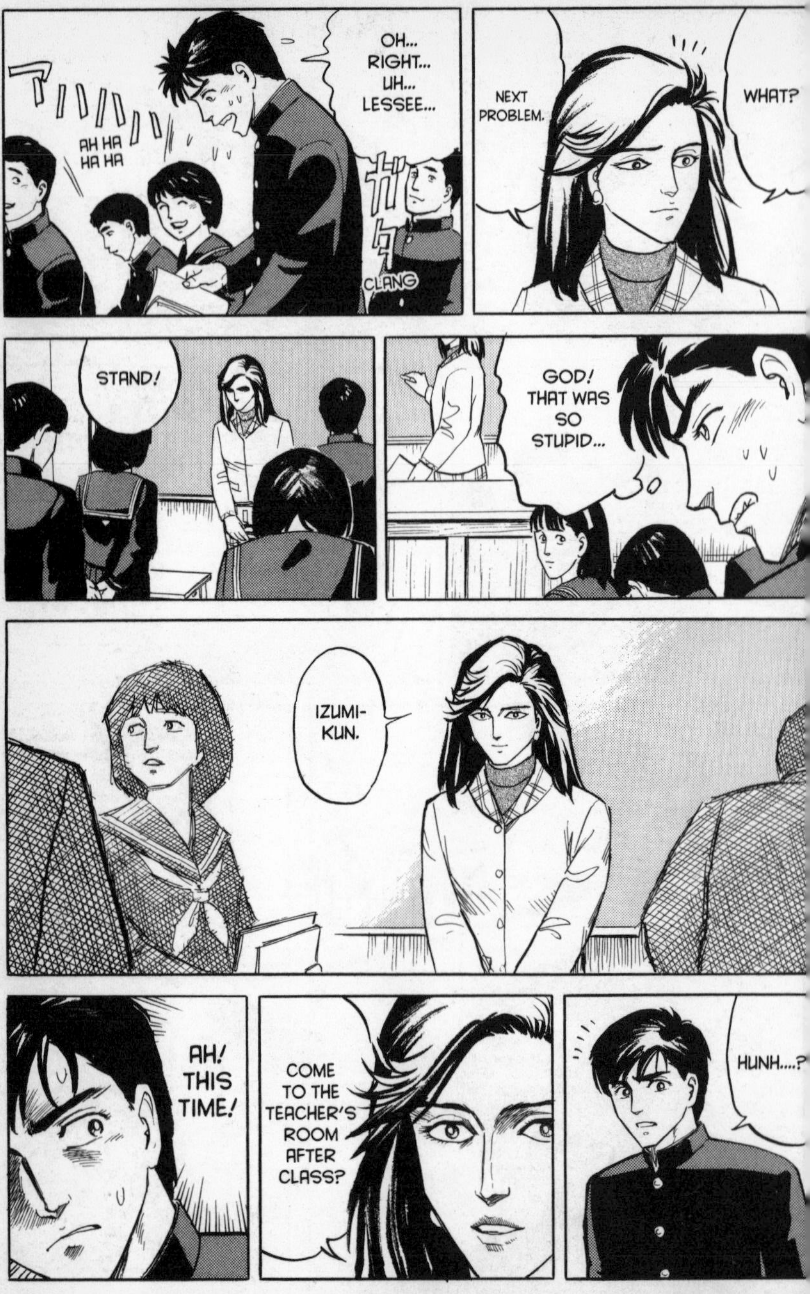
WHAT?
NEXT PROBLEM.
OH... RIGHT... UH... LESSEE...
AH HA HA HA
CLANG
GOD! THAT WAS SO STUPID...
STAND!
IZUMI-KUN.
HUNH....?
COME TO THE TEACHER'S ROOM AFTER CLASS?
AH! THIS TIME!

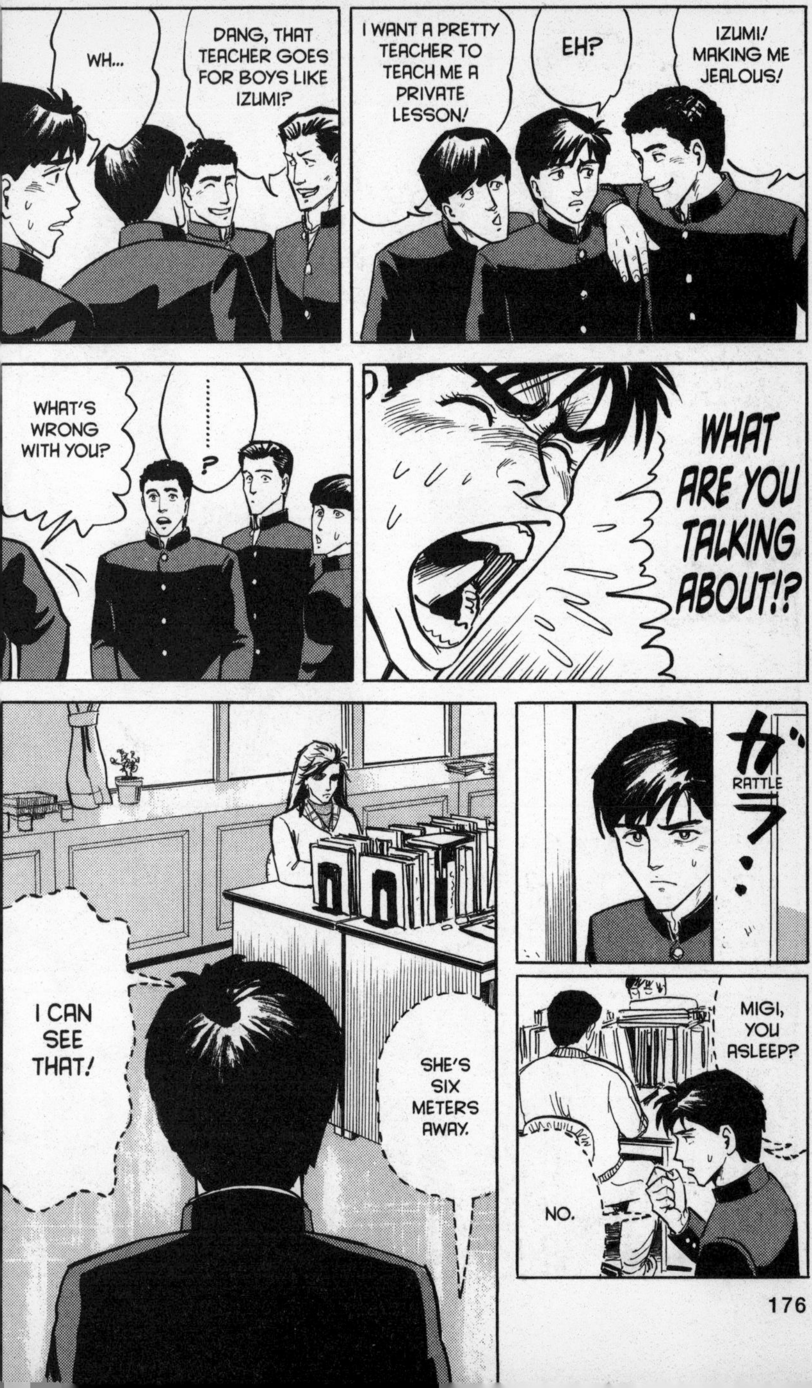
IZUMI! MAKING ME JEALOUS!
EH?
I WANT A PRETTY TEACHER TO TEACH ME A PRIVATE LESSON!
DANG, THAT TEACHER GOES FOR BOYS LIKE IZUMI?
WH...
WHAT ARE YOU TALKING ABOUT!?
......?
WHAT'S WRONG WITH YOU?
ガラ
RATTLE
MIGI, YOU ASLEEP?
NO.
SHE'S SIX METERS AWAY.
I CAN SEE THAT!

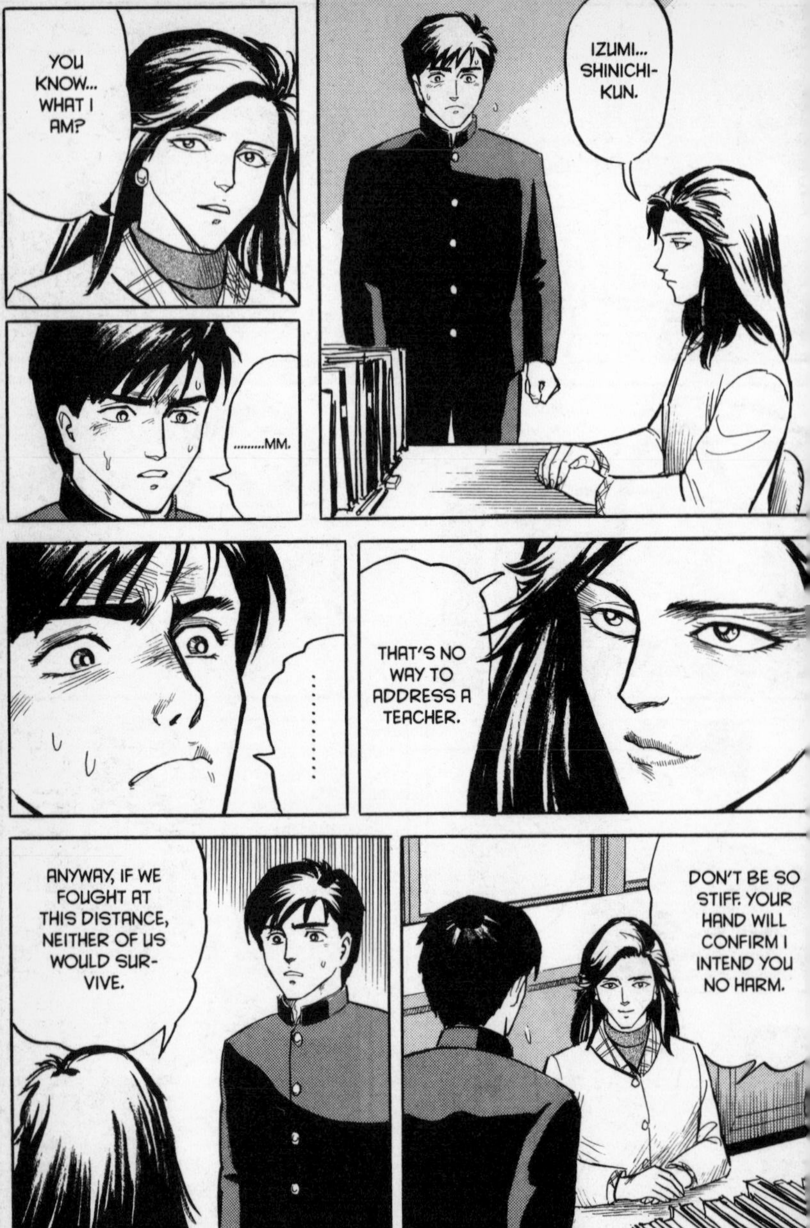
IZUMI... SHINICHI-KUN.
YOU KNOW... WHAT I AM?
.........MM.
THAT'S NO WAY TO ADDRESS A TEACHER.
....
DON'T BE SO STIFF. YOUR HAND WILL CONFIRM I INTEND YOU NO HARM.
ANYWAY, IF WE FOUGHT AT THIS DISTANCE, NEITHER OF US WOULD SUR-VIVE.

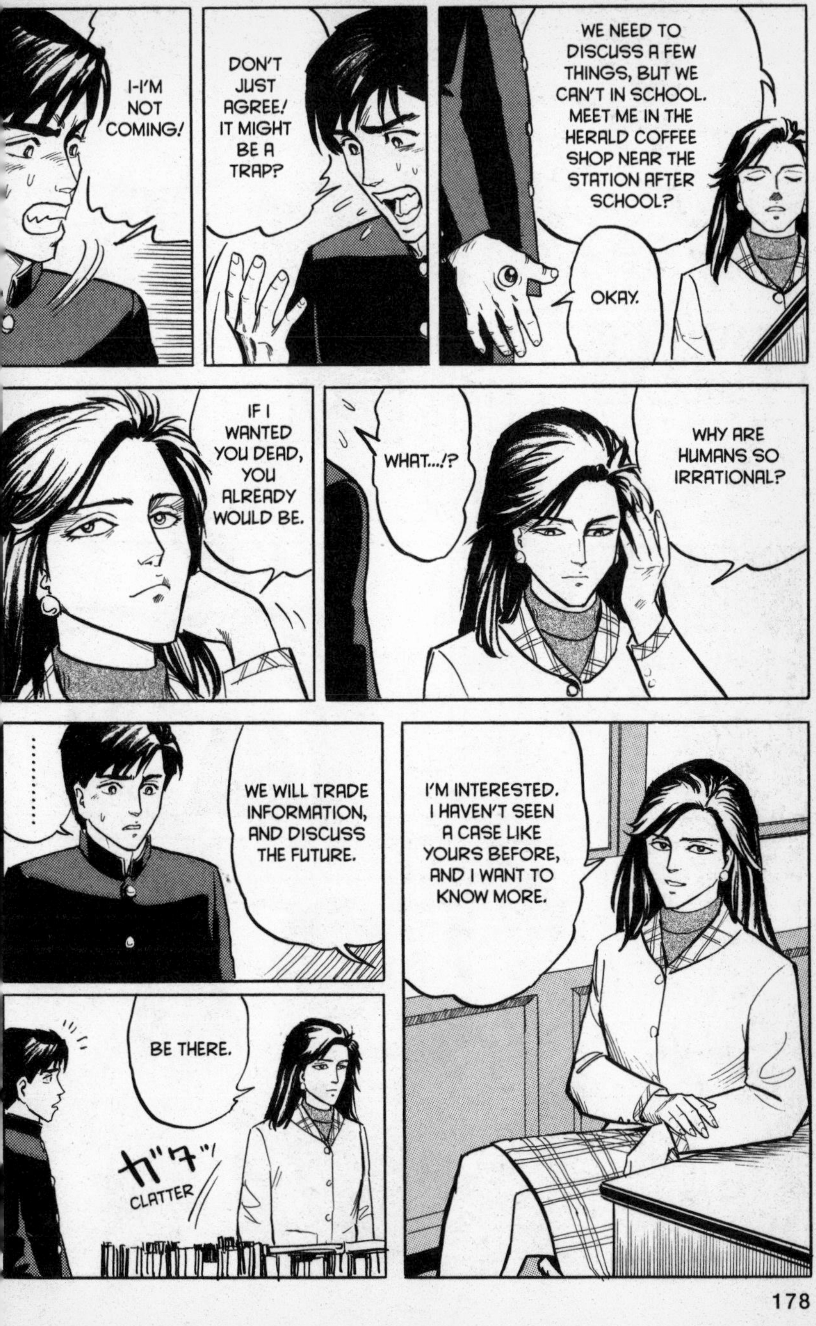
WE NEED TO DISCUSS A FEW THINGS, BUT WE CAN'T IN SCHOOL. MEET ME IN THE HERALD COFFEE SHOP NEAR THE STATION AFTER SCHOOL?
OKAY.
DON'T JUST AGREE! IT MIGHT BE A TRAP?
I-I'M NOT COMING!
WHY ARE HUMANS SO IRRATIONAL?
WHAT...!?
IF I WANTED YOU DEAD, YOU ALREADY WOULD BE.
I'M INTERESTED. I HAVEN'T SEEN A CASE LIKE YOURS BEFORE, AND I WANT TO KNOW MORE.
WE WILL TRADE INFORMATION, AND DISCUSS THE FUTURE.
......
BE THERE.
ガタッ
CLATTER

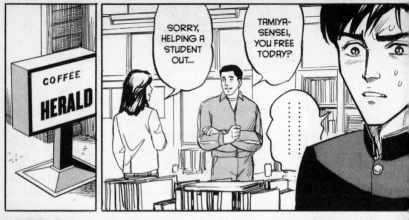

COFFEE **HERALD**

TAMIYA-SENSEI, YOU FREE TODAY?

SORRY, HELPING A STUDENT OUT...

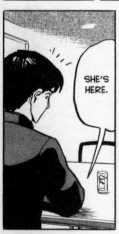

SHE'S HERE.

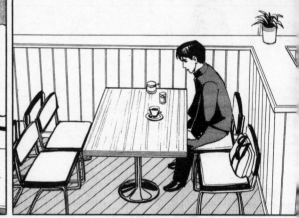

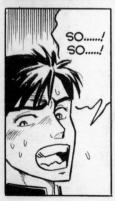

SO......! SO......!

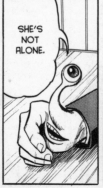

SHE'S NOT ALONE.

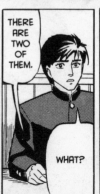

THERE ARE TWO OF THEM.

WHAT?

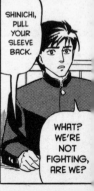

SHINICHI, PULL YOUR SLEEVE BACK.

WHAT? WE'RE NOT FIGHTING, ARE WE?

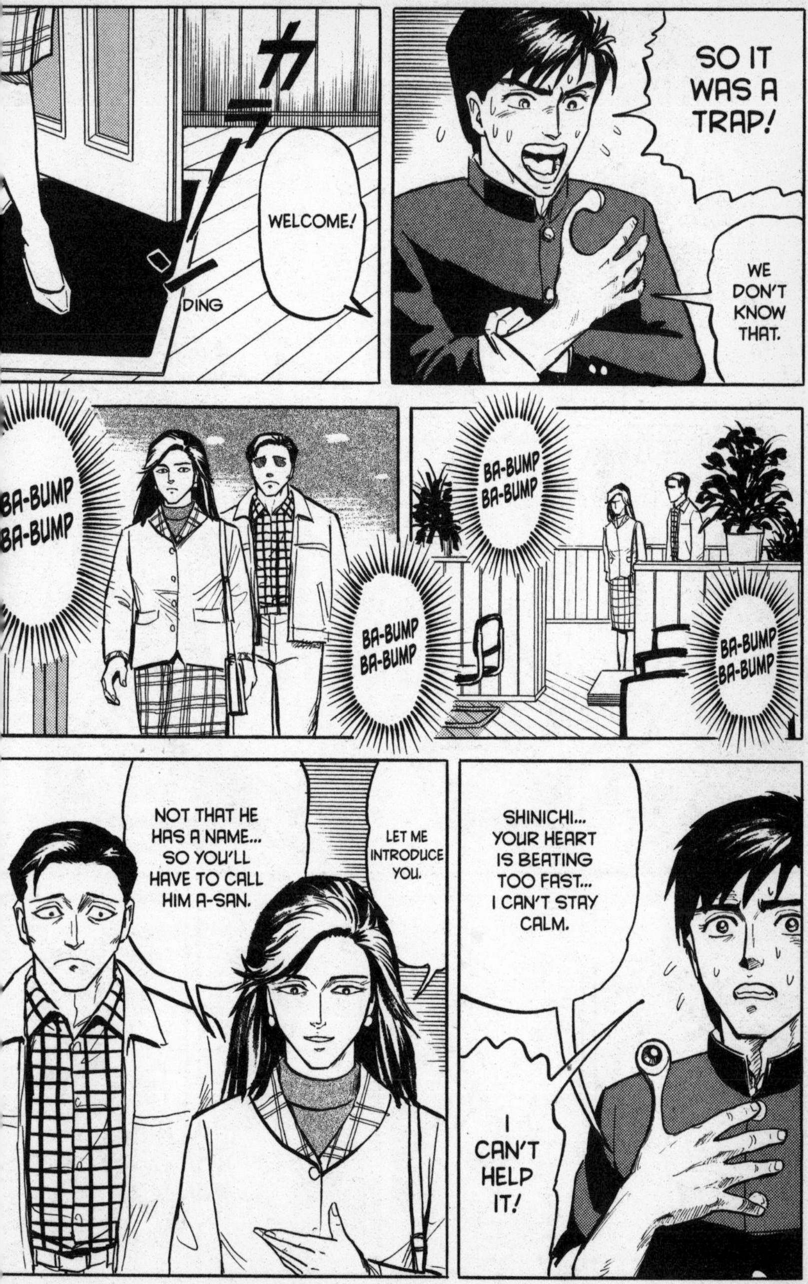
SO IT WAS A TRAP!
WE DON'T KNOW THAT.
カラ
DING
WELCOME!
BA-BUMP BA-BUMP
BA-BUMP BA-BUMP
BA-BUMP BA-BUMP
BA-BUMP BA-BUMP
SHINICHI... YOUR HEART IS BEATING TOO FAST... I CAN'T STAY CALM.
I CAN'T HELP IT!
LET ME INTRODUCE YOU.
NOT THAT HE HAS A NAME... SO YOU'LL HAVE TO CALL HIM A-SAN.

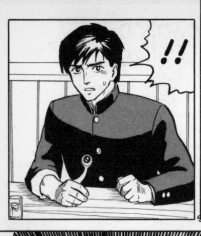

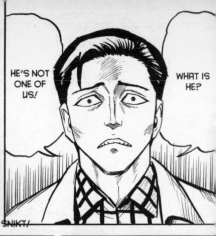

HE'S NOT ONE OF US!

WHAT IS HE?

SNIKT!

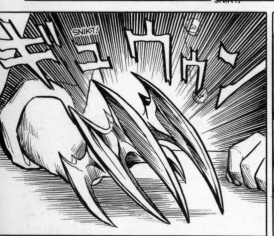

SNIKT!

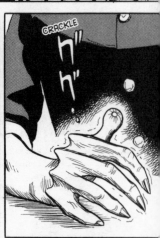

CRACKLE

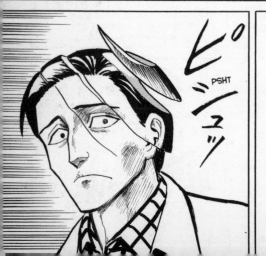

PSHT

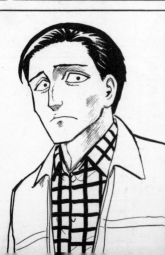

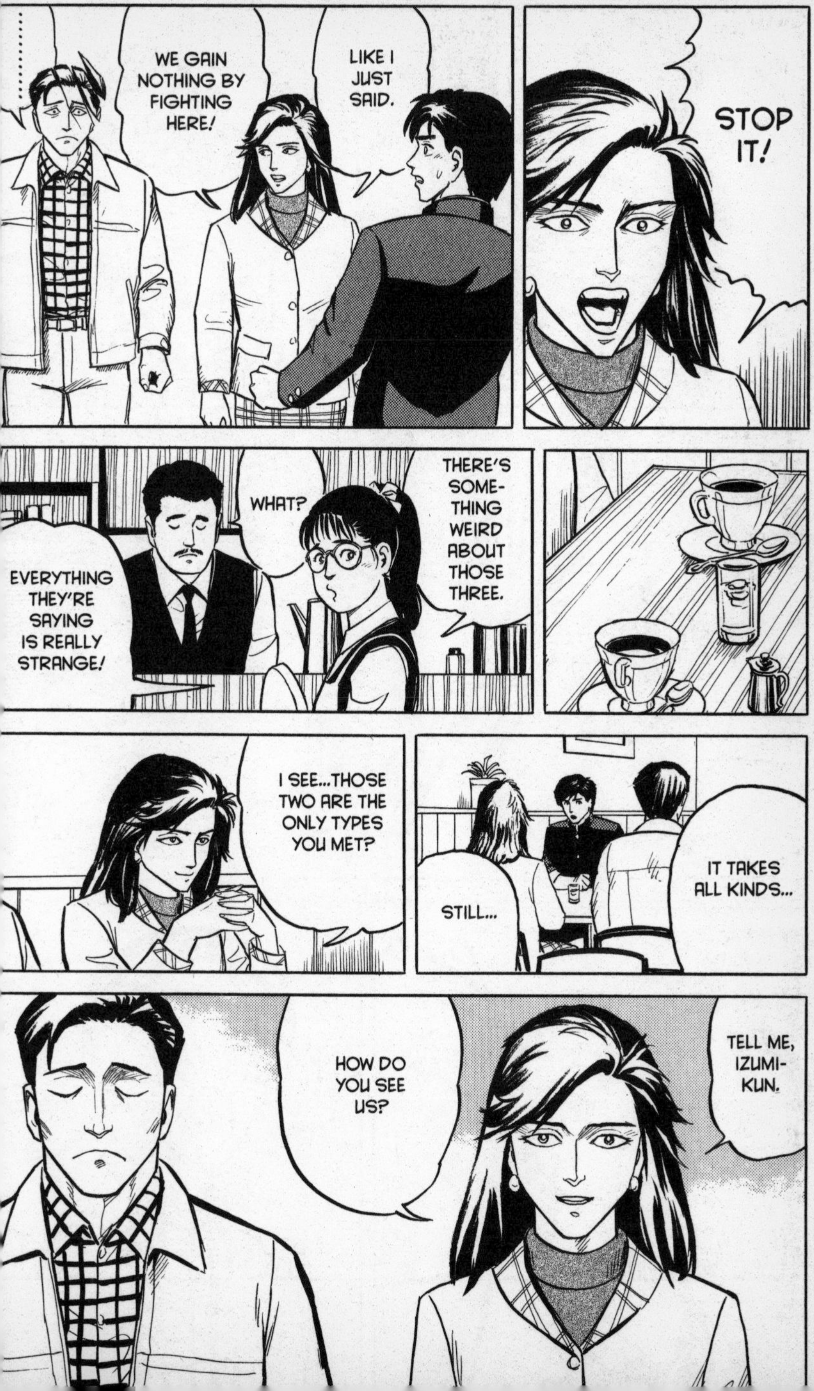
STOP IT!
LIKE I JUST SAID.
WE GAIN NOTHING BY FIGHTING HERE!
......
THERE'S SOME-THING WEIRD ABOUT THOSE THREE.
WHAT?
EVERYTHING THEY'RE SAYING IS REALLY STRANGE!
IT TAKES ALL KINDS...
STILL...
I SEE...THOSE TWO ARE THE ONLY TYPES YOU MET?
TELL ME, IZUMI-KUN.
HOW DO YOU SEE US?

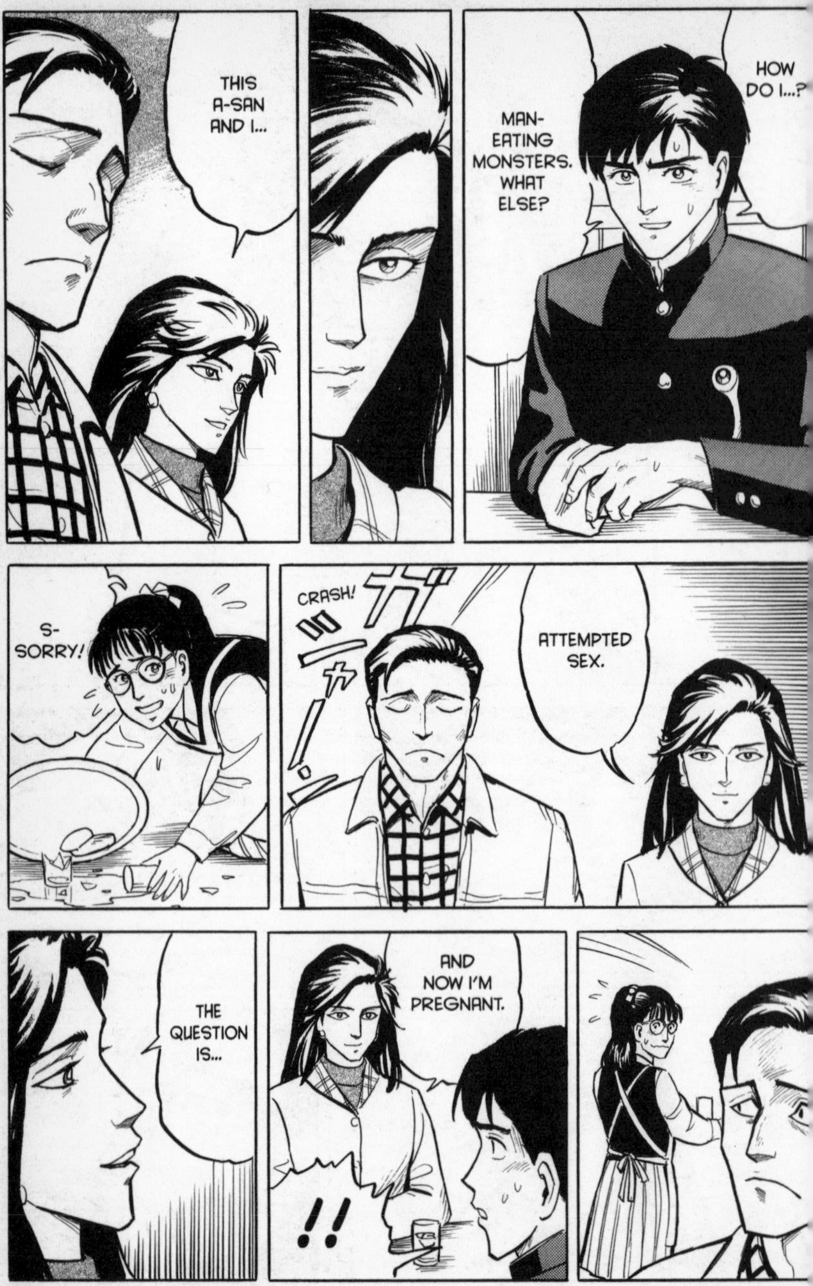
HOW DO I...?
MAN-EATING MONSTERS. WHAT ELSE?
THIS A-SAN AND I...
ATTEMPTED SEX.
CRASH!
S-SORRY!
AND NOW I'M PREGNANT.
!!
THE QUESTION IS...

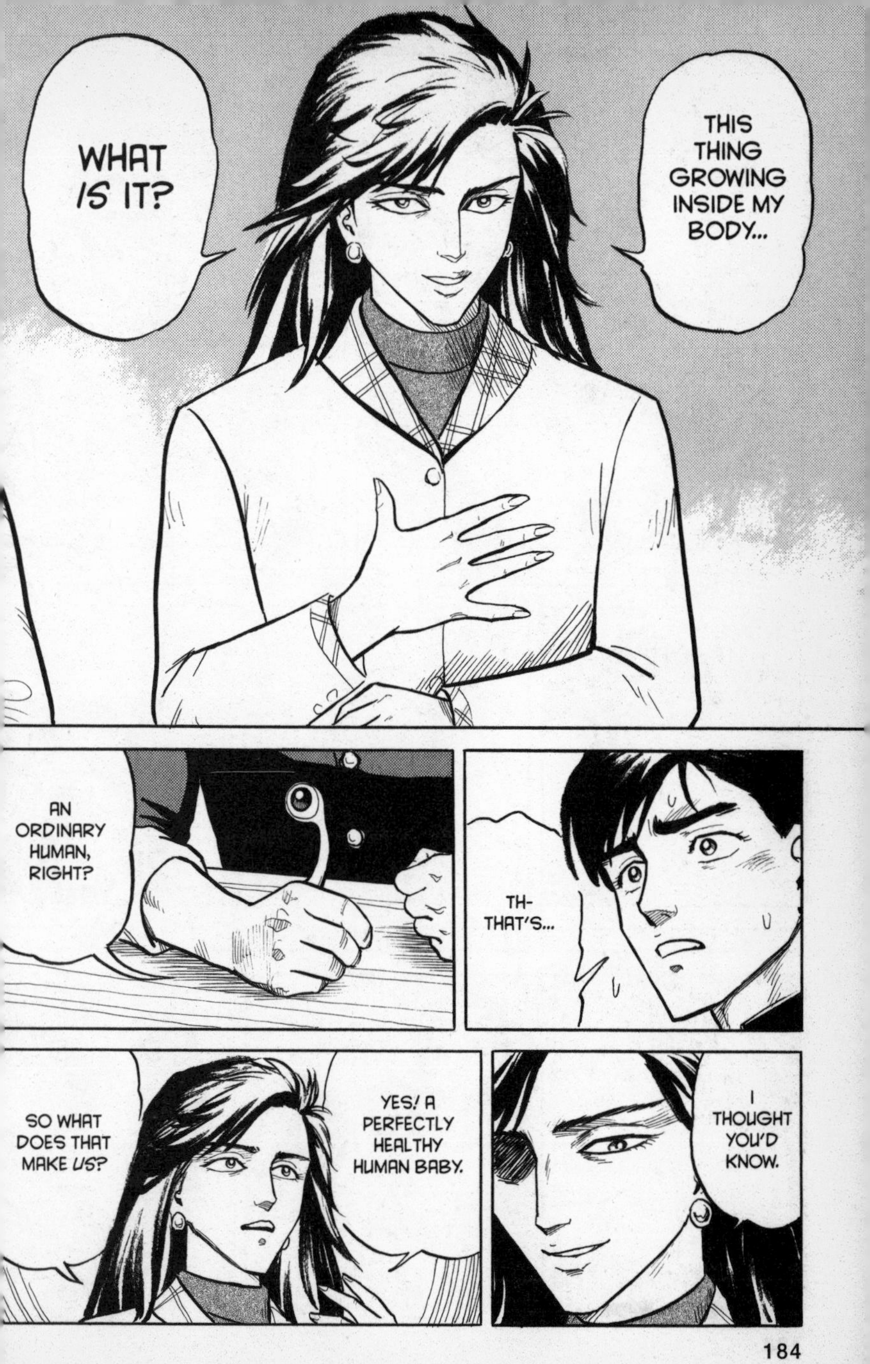
THIS THING GROWING INSIDE MY BODY...
WHAT *IS* IT?
TH- THAT'S...
AN ORDINARY HUMAN, RIGHT?
I THOUGHT YOU'D KNOW.
YES! A PERFECTLY HEALTHY HUMAN BABY.
SO WHAT DOES THAT MAKE *US*?

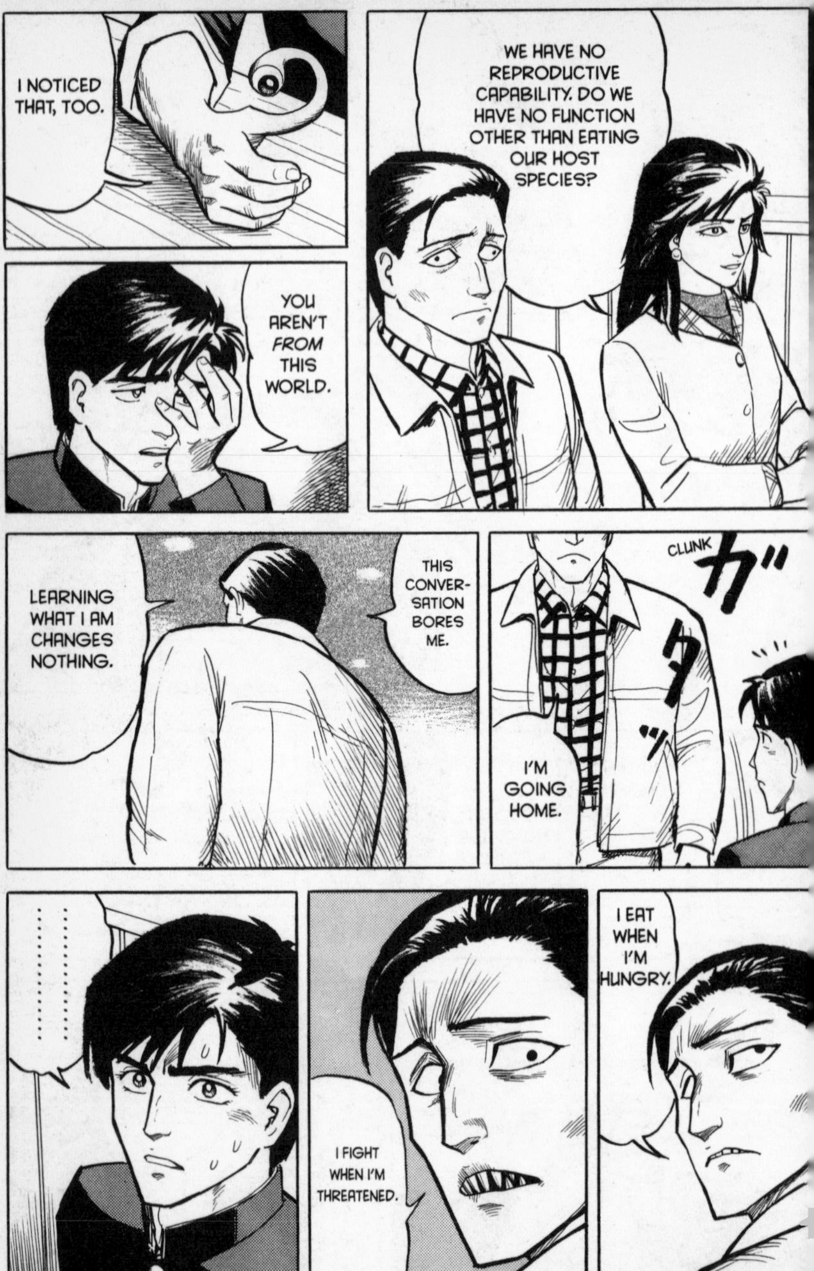
WE HAVE NO REPRODUCTIVE CAPABILITY. DO WE HAVE NO FUNCTION OTHER THAN EATING OUR HOST SPECIES?
I NOTICED THAT, TOO.
YOU AREN'T *FROM* THIS WORLD.
CLUNK
ガタッ
I'M GOING HOME.
THIS CONVERSATION BORES ME.
LEARNING WHAT I AM CHANGES NOTHING.
I EAT WHEN I'M HUNGRY.
I FIGHT WHEN I'M THREATENED.
......

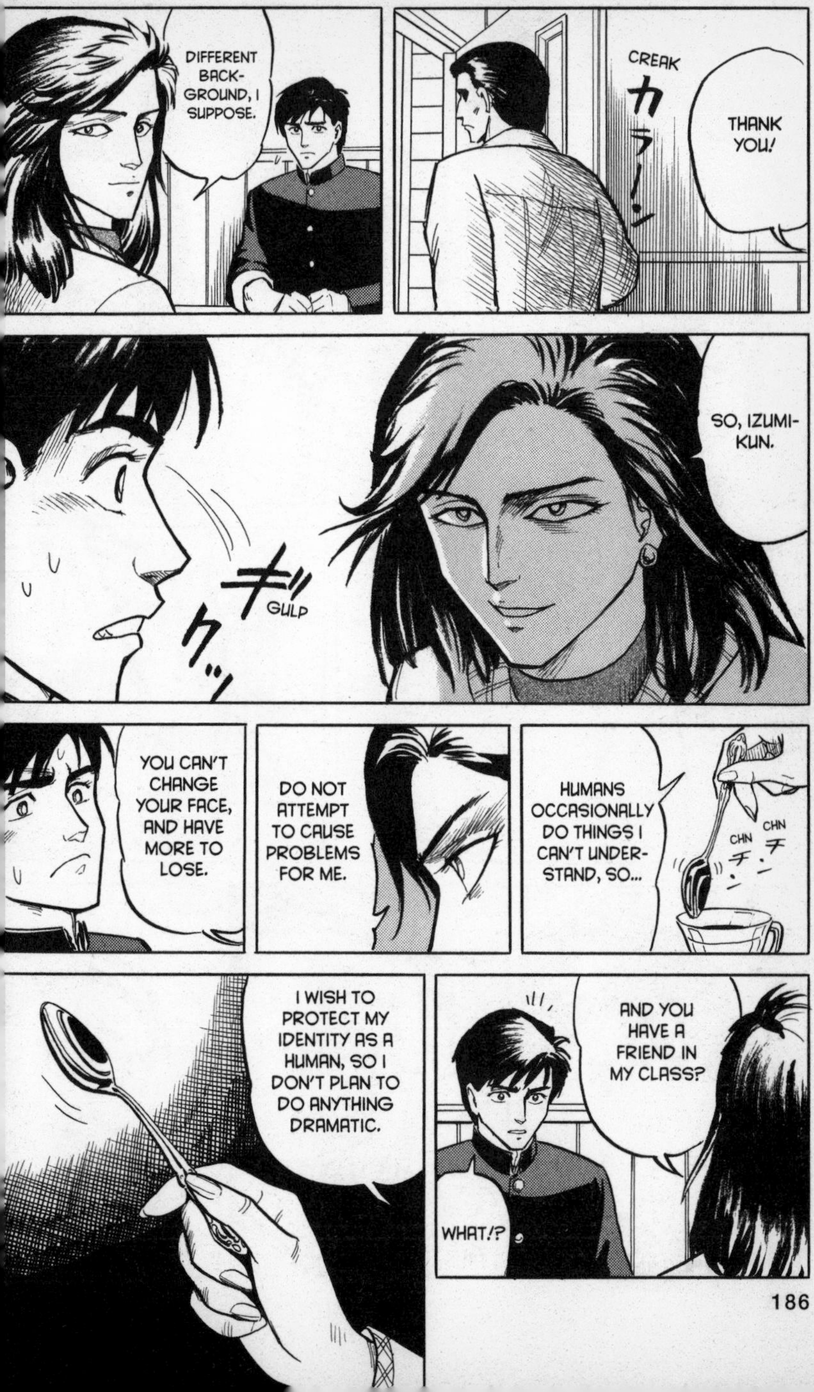
THANK YOU!
CREAK
カラーン
DIFFERENT BACK-GROUND, I SUPPOSE.
SO, IZUMI-KUN.
ギクッ
GULP
HUMANS OCCASIONALLY DO THINGS I CAN'T UNDER-STAND, SO...
CHN
チ
CHN
チ
DO NOT ATTEMPT TO CAUSE PROBLEMS FOR ME.
YOU CAN'T CHANGE YOUR FACE, AND HAVE MORE TO LOSE.
AND YOU HAVE A FRIEND IN MY CLASS?
WHAT!?
I WISH TO PROTECT MY IDENTITY AS A HUMAN, SO I DON'T PLAN TO DO ANYTHING DRAMATIC.

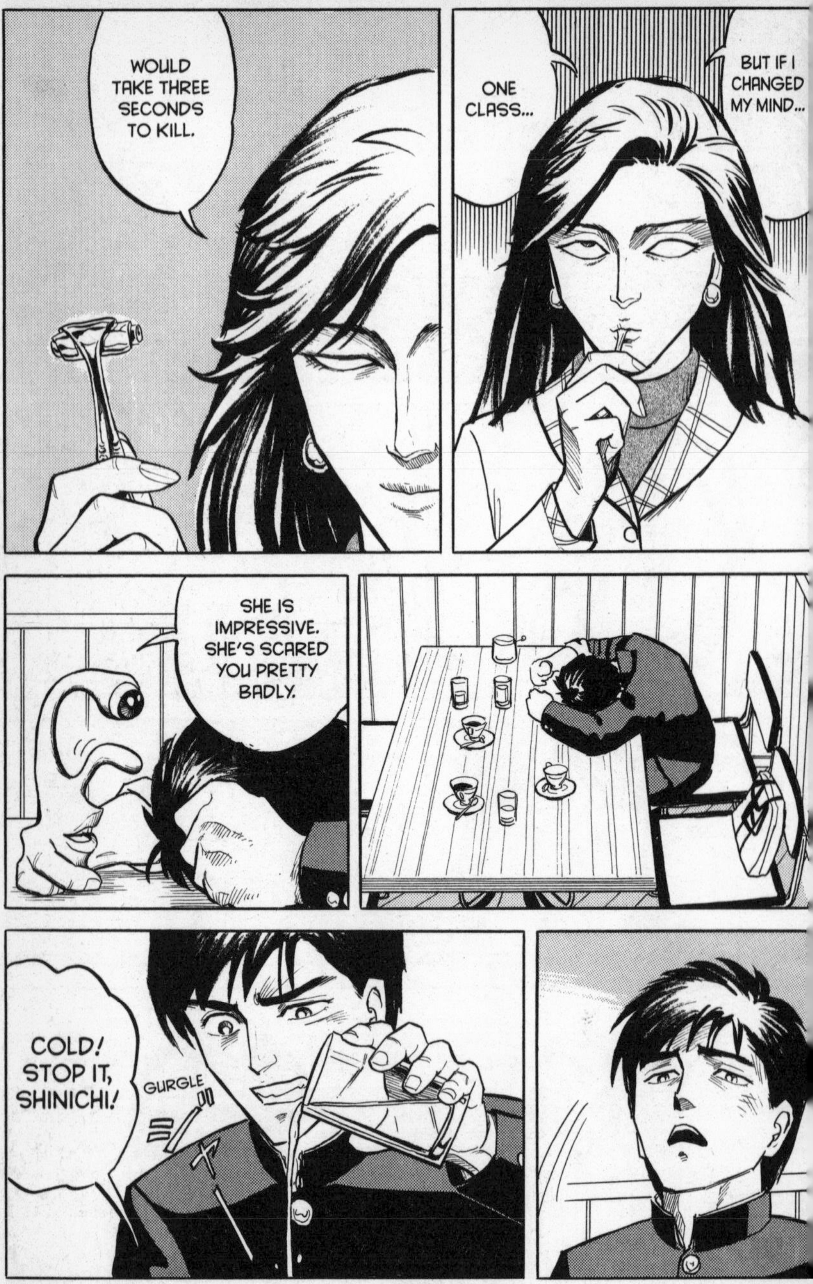
BUT IF I CHANGED MY MIND...
ONE CLASS...
WOULD TAKE THREE SECONDS TO KILL.
SHE IS IMPRESSIVE. SHE'S SCARED YOU PRETTY BADLY.
GURGLE
COLD! STOP IT, SHINICHI!

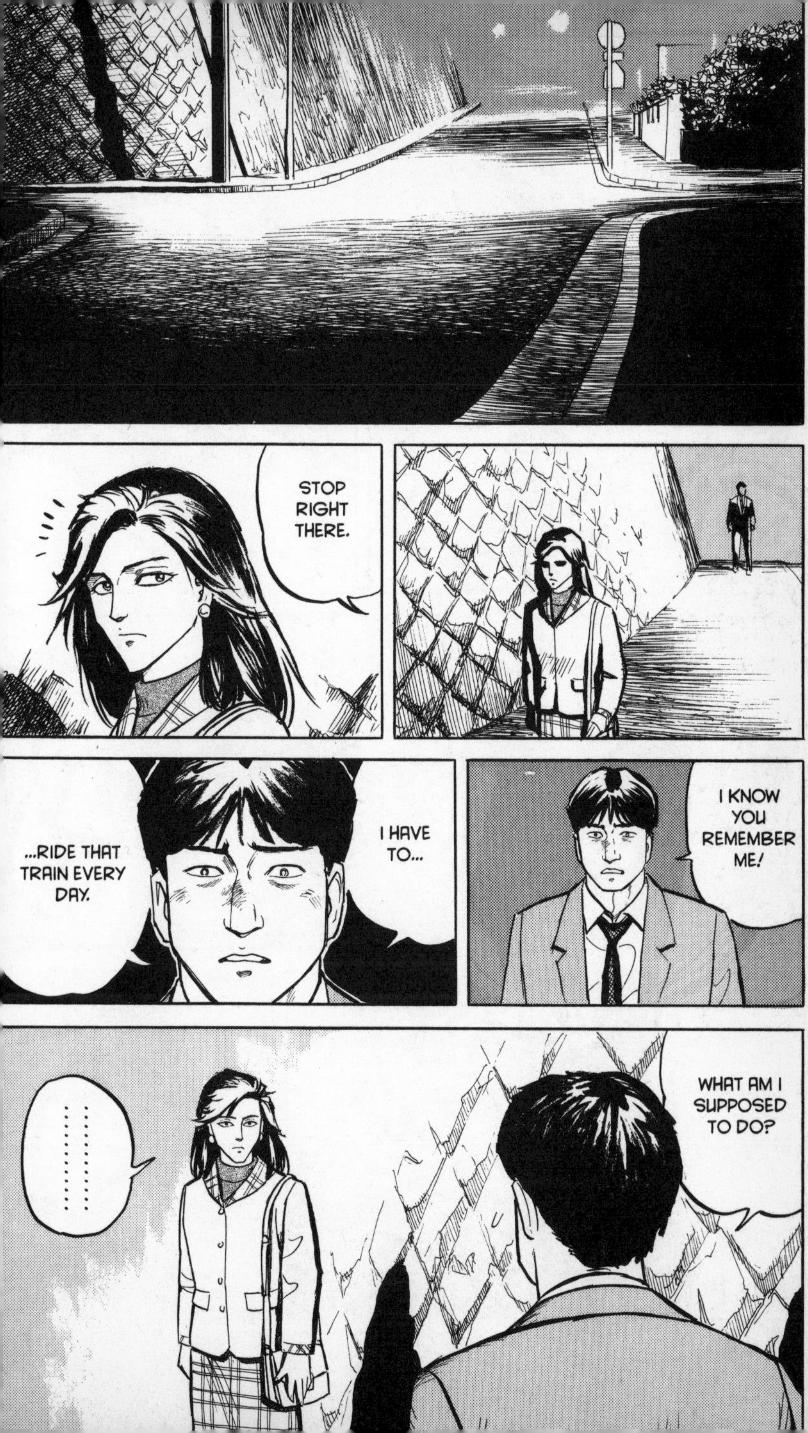
STOP RIGHT THERE.
I KNOW YOU REMEMBER ME!
I HAVE TO...
...RIDE THAT TRAIN EVERY DAY.
WHAT AM I SUPPOSED TO DO?
......

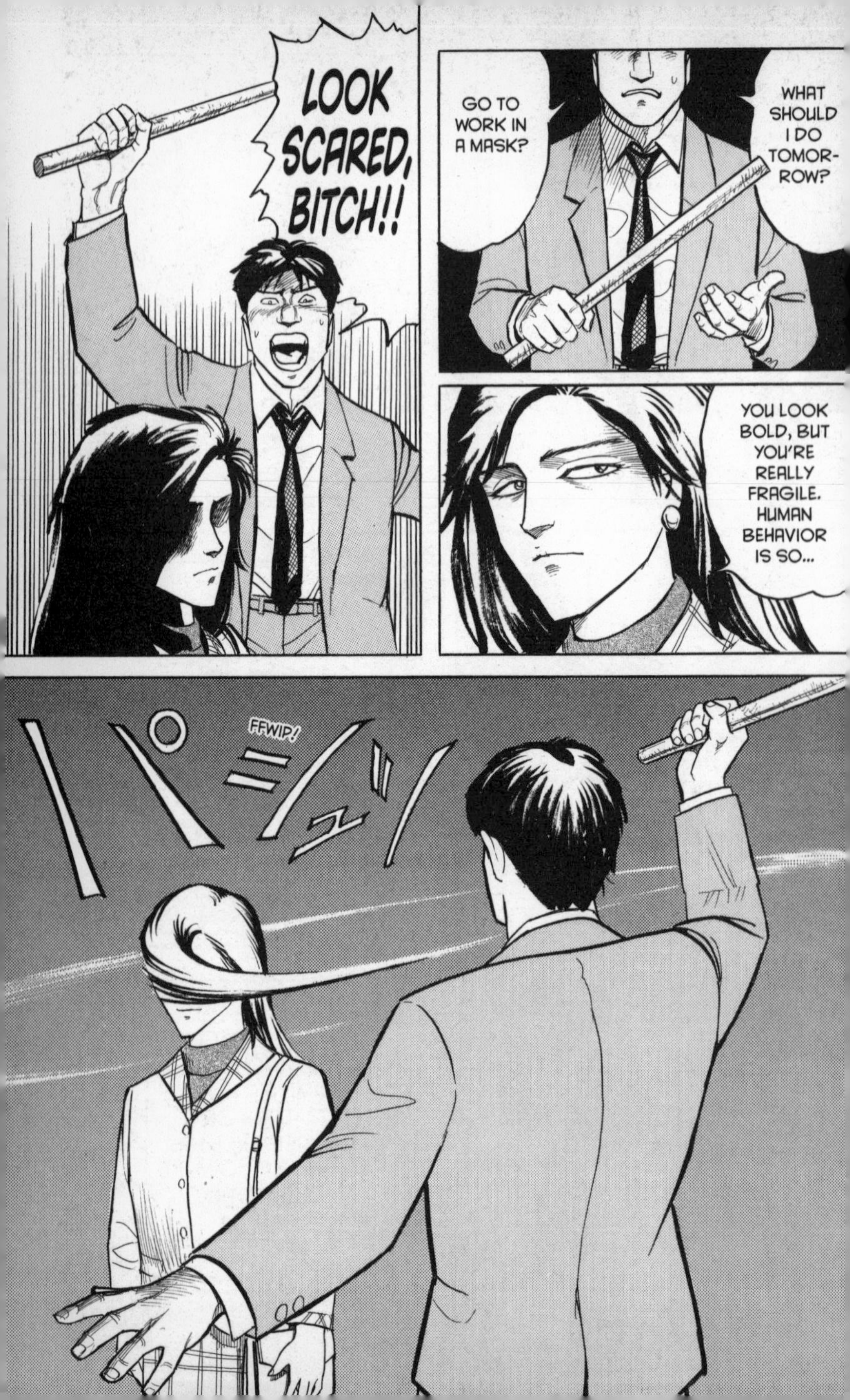
WHAT SHOULD I DO TOMORROW?
GO TO WORK IN A MASK?
YOU LOOK BOLD, BUT YOU'RE REALLY FRAGILE. HUMAN BEHAVIOR IS SO...
LOOK SCARED, BITCH!!
FFWIP!

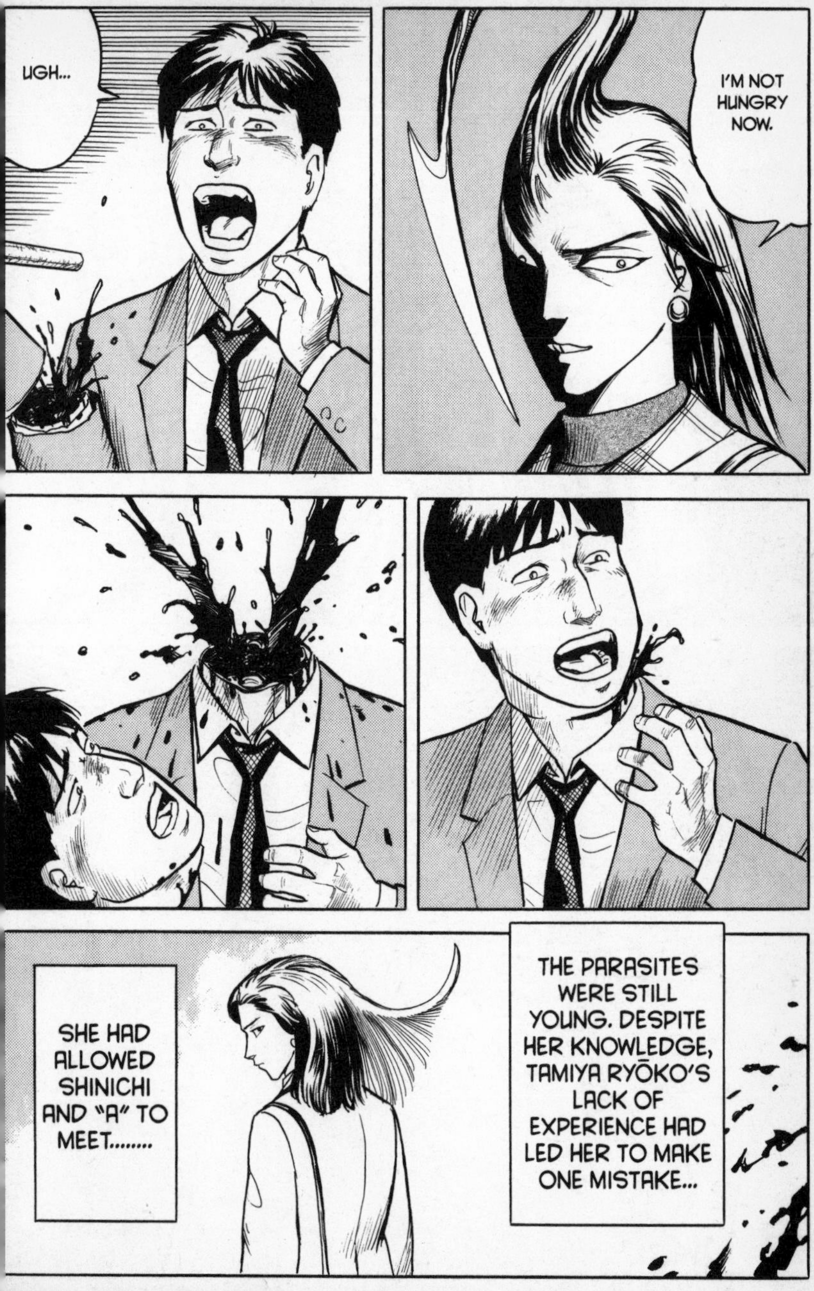
I'M NOT HUNGRY NOW.
UGH...
THE PARASITES WERE STILL YOUNG. DESPITE HER KNOWLEDGE, TAMIYA RYŌKO'S LACK OF EXPERIENCE HAD LED HER TO MAKE ONE MISTAKE...
SHE HAD ALLOWED SHINICHI AND "A" TO MEET........

CHAPTER 6: THE END

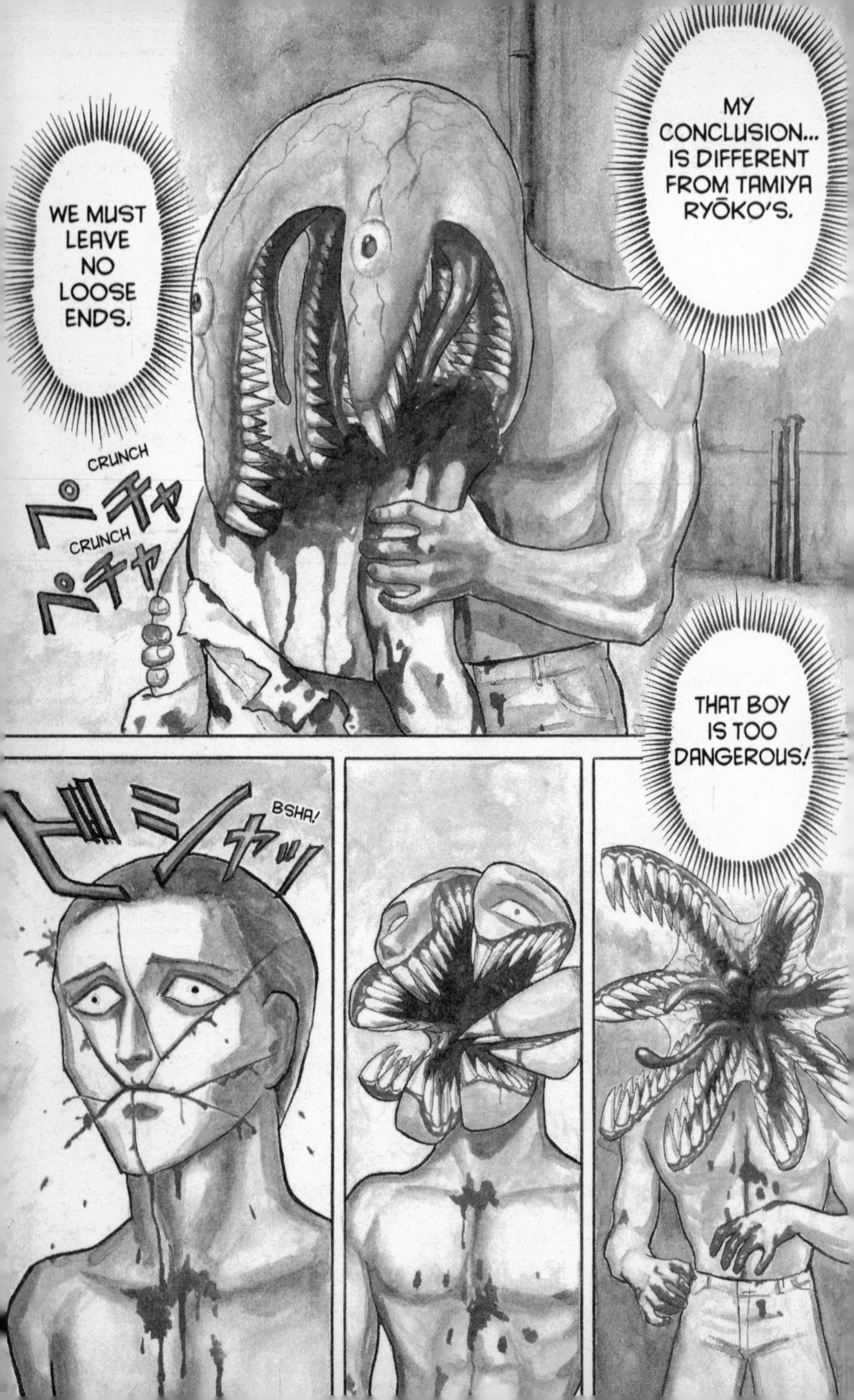
MY CONCLUSION... IS DIFFERENT FROM TAMIYA RYŌKO'S.
WE MUST LEAVE NO LOOSE ENDS.
CRUNCH
ペチャ
CRUNCH
ペチャ
THAT BOY IS TOO DANGEROUS!
BSHA!

CHAPTER 7: ATTACK

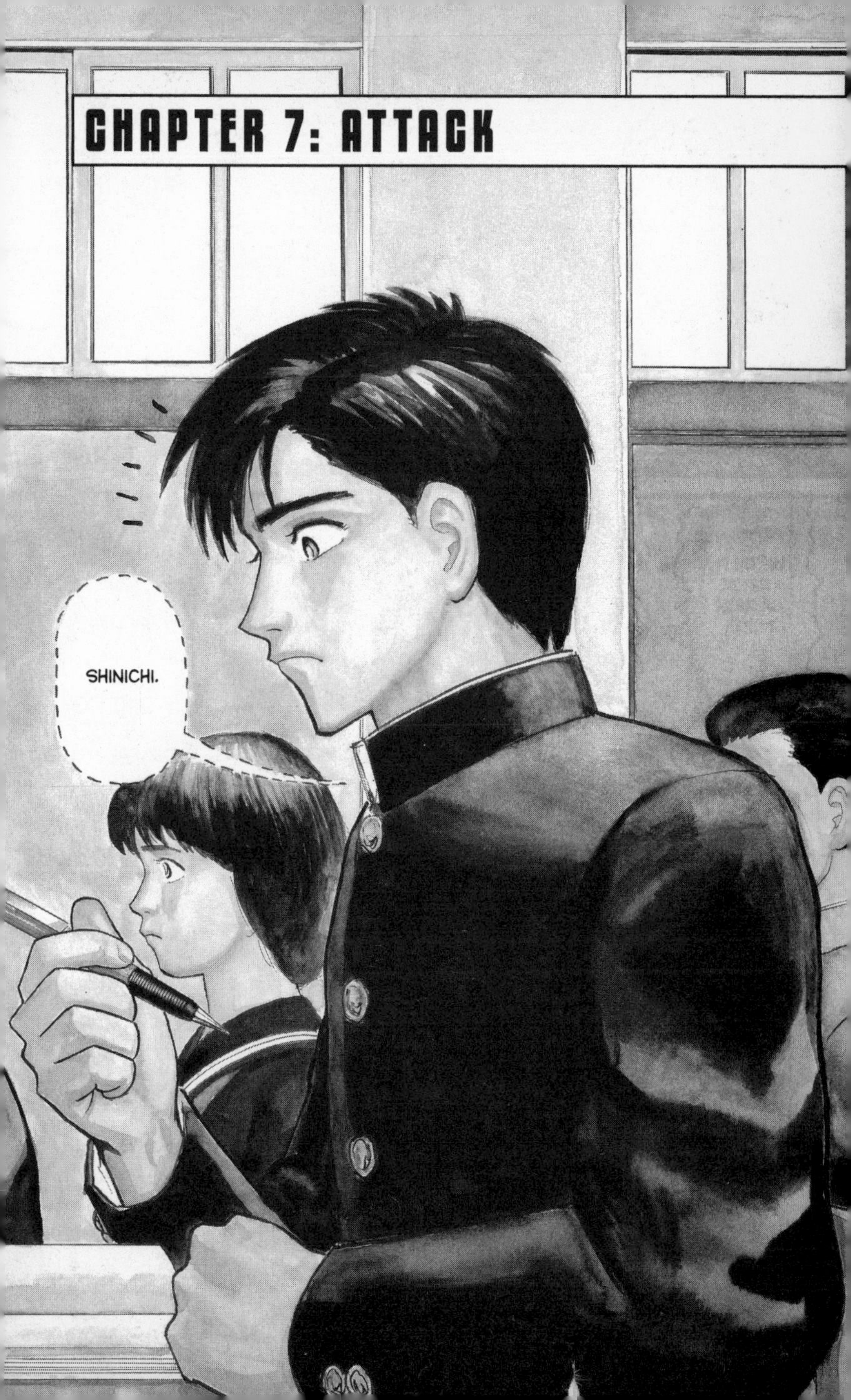
SHINICHI.

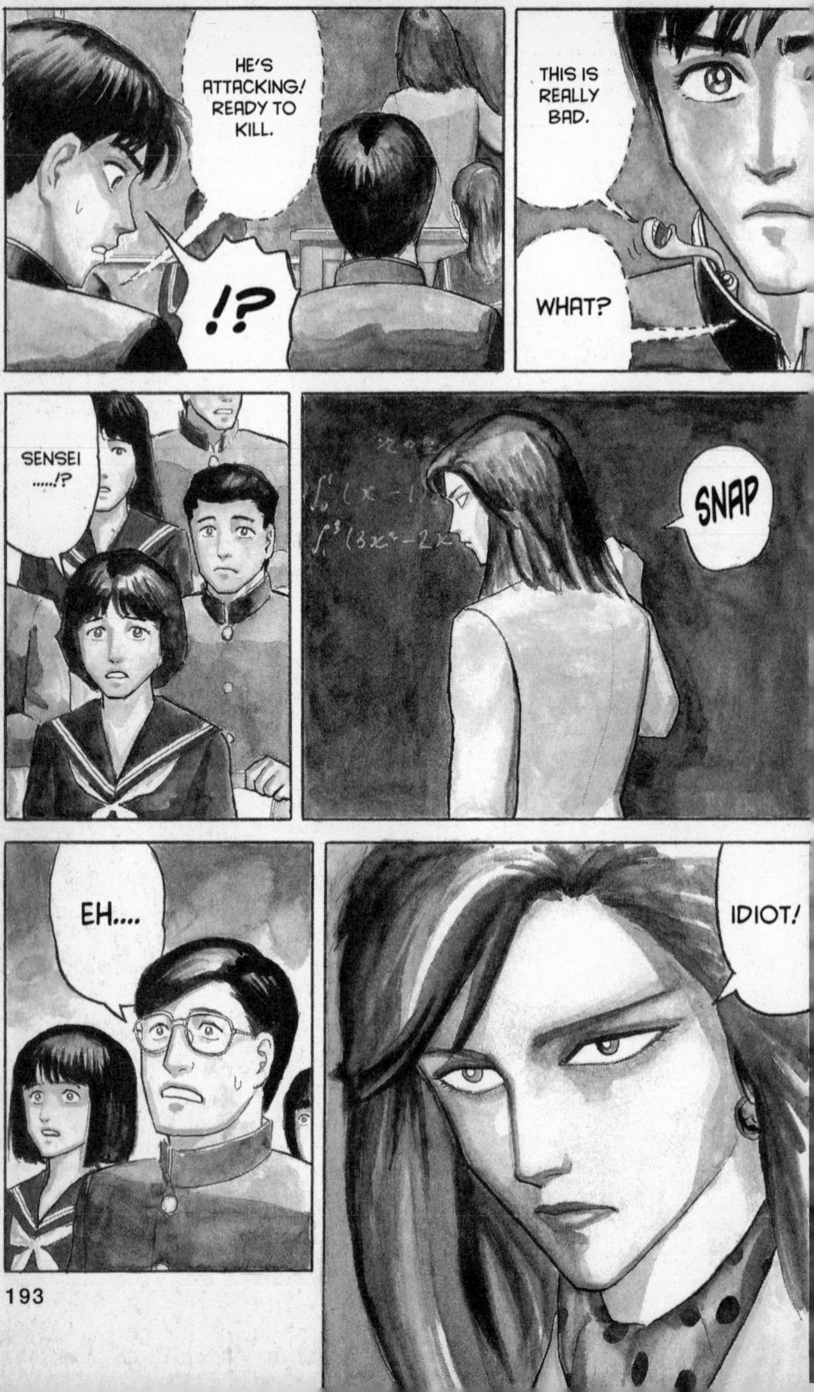
THIS IS REALLY BAD.
WHAT?
HE'S ATTACKING! READY TO KILL.
!?
SNAP
SENSEI .....!?
IDIOT!
EH....

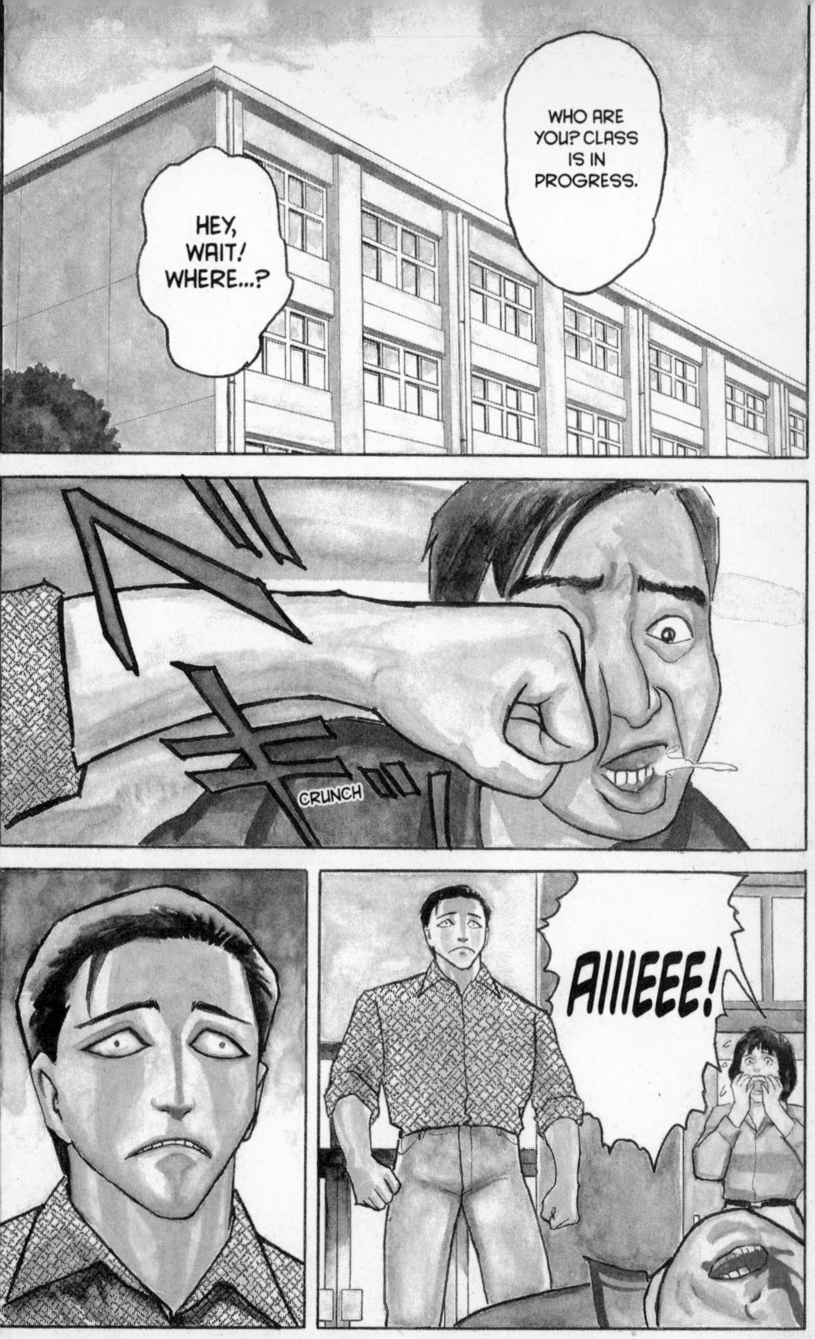
WHO ARE YOU? CLASS IS IN PROGRESS.
HEY, WAIT! WHERE...?
CRUNCH
AIIIEEE!

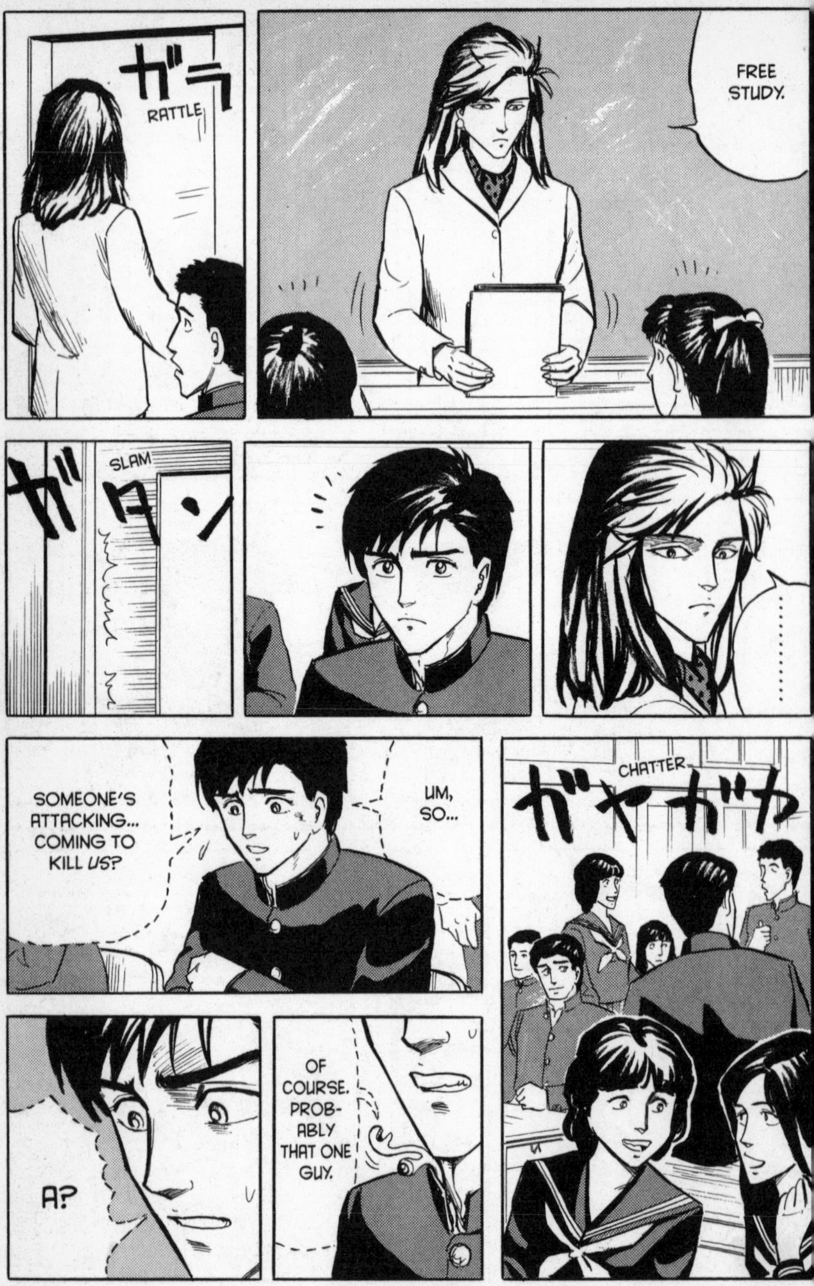
FREE STUDY.
ガラ
RATTLE
......
ガタン
SLAM
ガヤガヤ
CHATTER
UM, SO...
SOMEONE'S ATTACKING... COMING TO KILL *US*?
OF COURSE. PROB-ABLY THAT ONE GUY.
A?

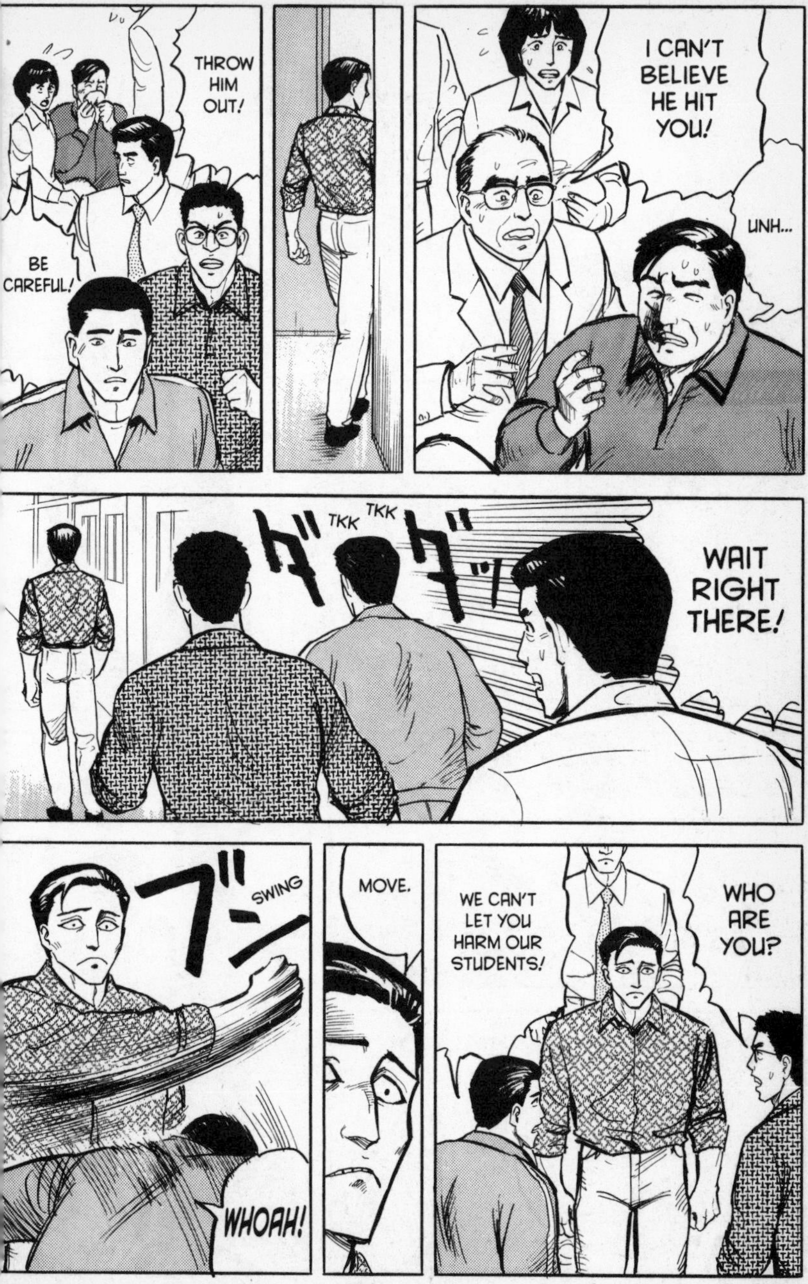
I CAN'T BELIEVE HE HIT YOU!
UNH...
THROW HIM OUT!
BE CAREFUL!
WAIT RIGHT THERE!
TKK
TKK
WHO ARE YOU?
WE CAN'T LET YOU HARM OUR STUDENTS!
MOVE.
SWING
WHOAH!

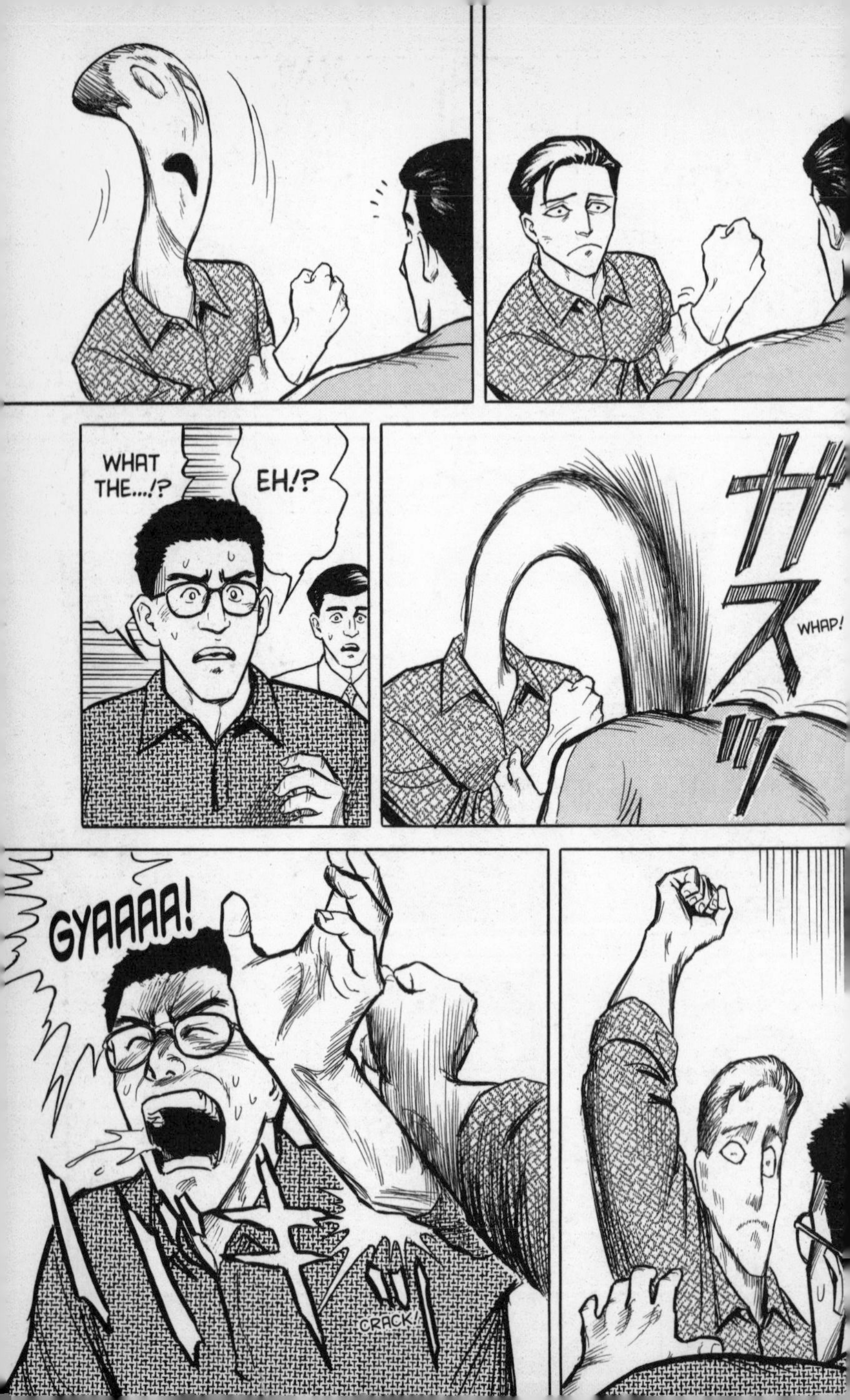
ザスッ
WHAP!
EH!?
WHAT THE...!?
GYAAAA!
CRACK!

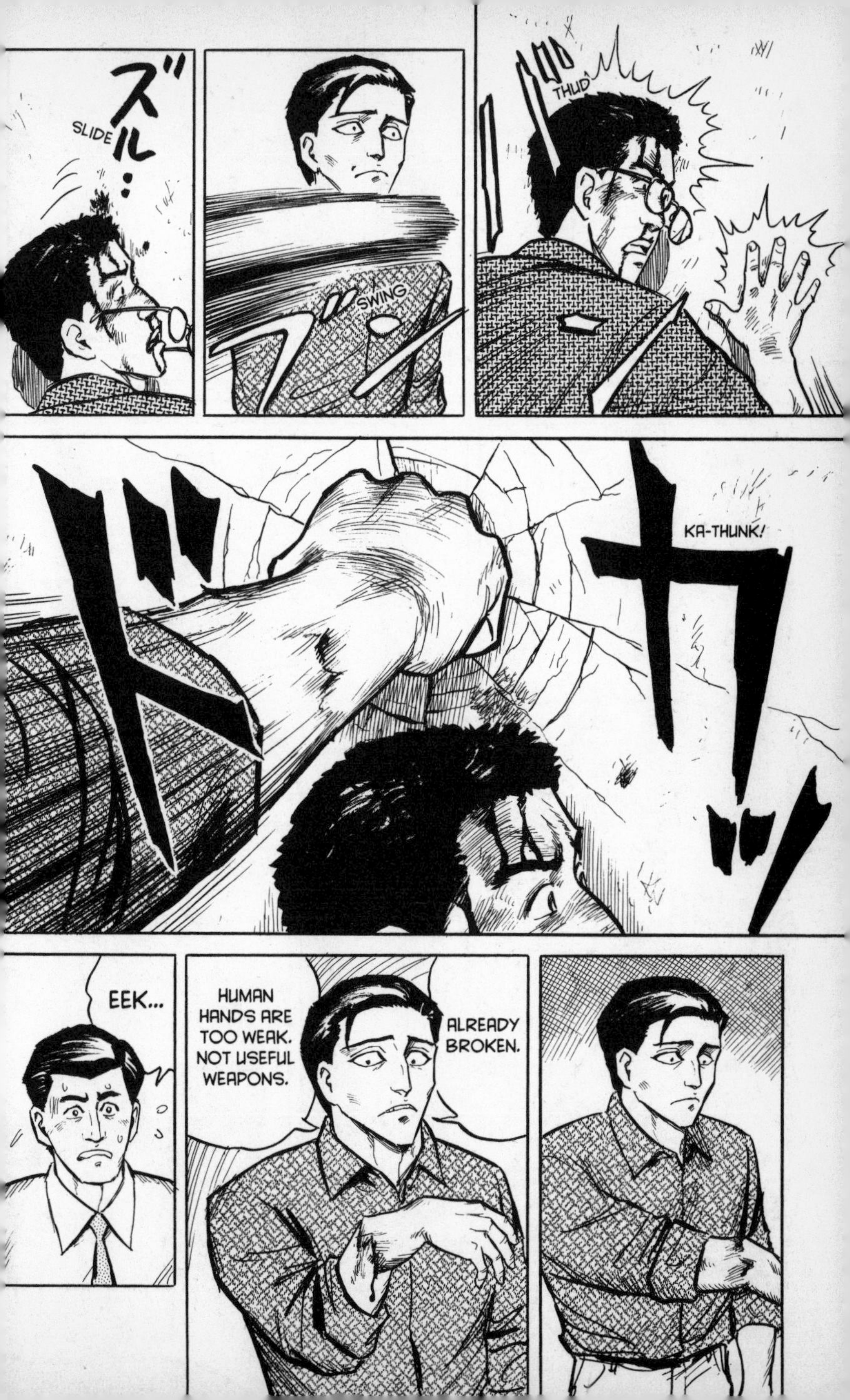
THUD
SWING
ズル…
SLIDE
ドカッ
KA-THUNK!
ALREADY BROKEN.
HUMAN HANDS ARE TOO WEAK. NOT USEFUL WEAPONS.
EEK...

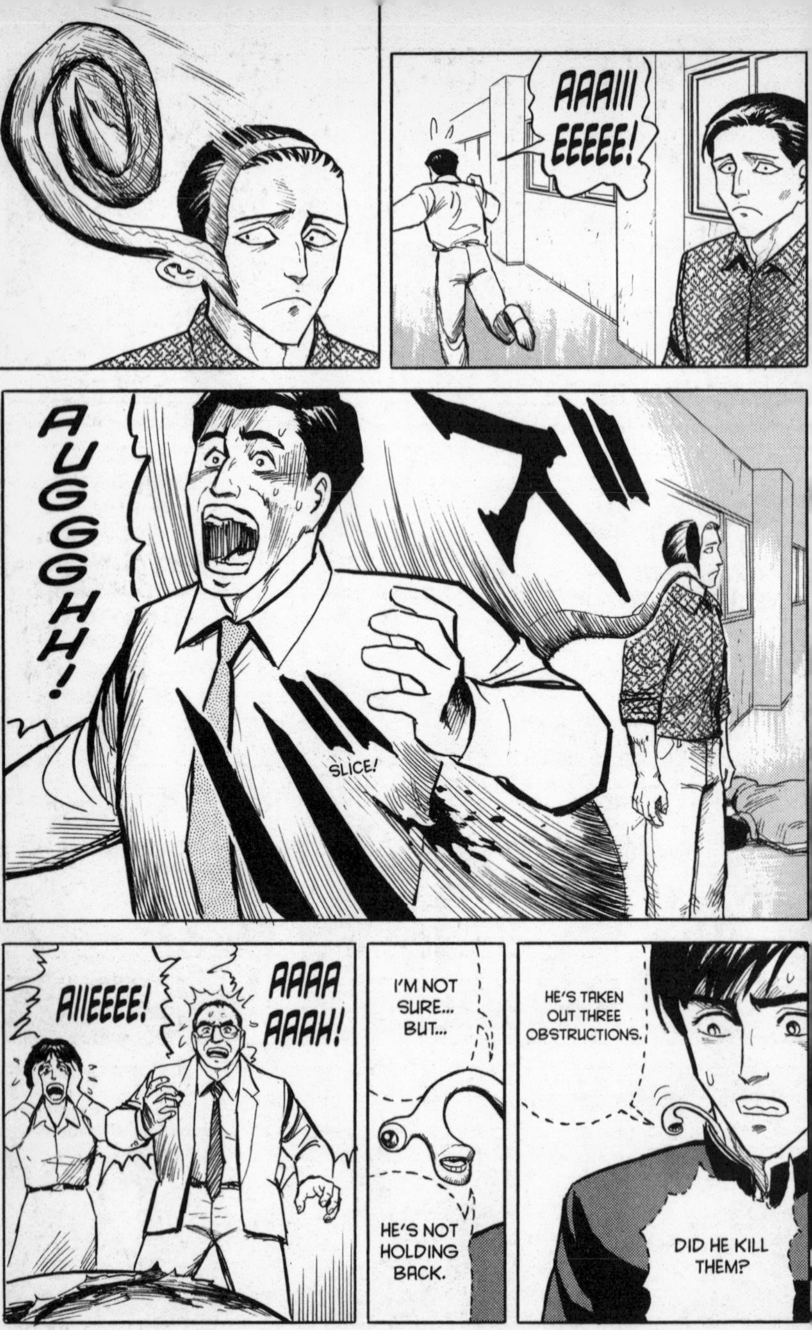
AAAIII EEEEE!
AUGGGGH!
SLICE!
HE'S TAKEN OUT THREE OBSTRUCTIONS.
DID HE KILL THEM?
I'M NOT SURE... BUT...
HE'S NOT HOLDING BACK.
AAAA AAAH!
AIIEEEE!

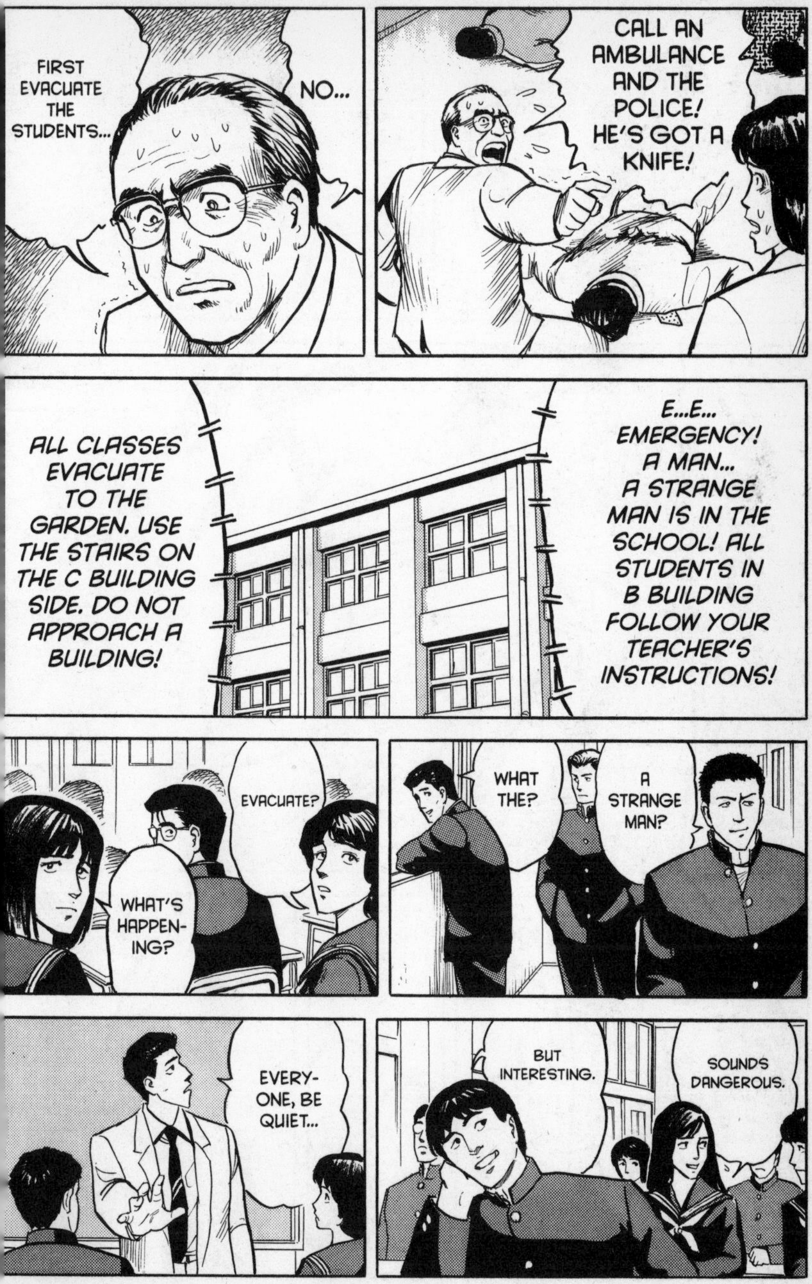
CALL AN AMBULANCE AND THE POLICE! HE'S GOT A KNIFE!
NO...
FIRST EVACUATE THE STUDENTS...
E...E... EMERGENCY! A MAN... A STRANGE MAN IS IN THE SCHOOL! ALL STUDENTS IN B BUILDING FOLLOW YOUR TEACHER'S INSTRUCTIONS!
ALL CLASSES EVACUATE TO THE GARDEN. USE THE STAIRS ON THE C BUILDING SIDE. DO NOT APPROACH A BUILDING!
A STRANGE MAN?
WHAT THE?
EVACUATE?
WHAT'S HAPPEN-ING?
SOUNDS DANGEROUS.
BUT INTERESTING.
EVERY-ONE, BE QUIET...

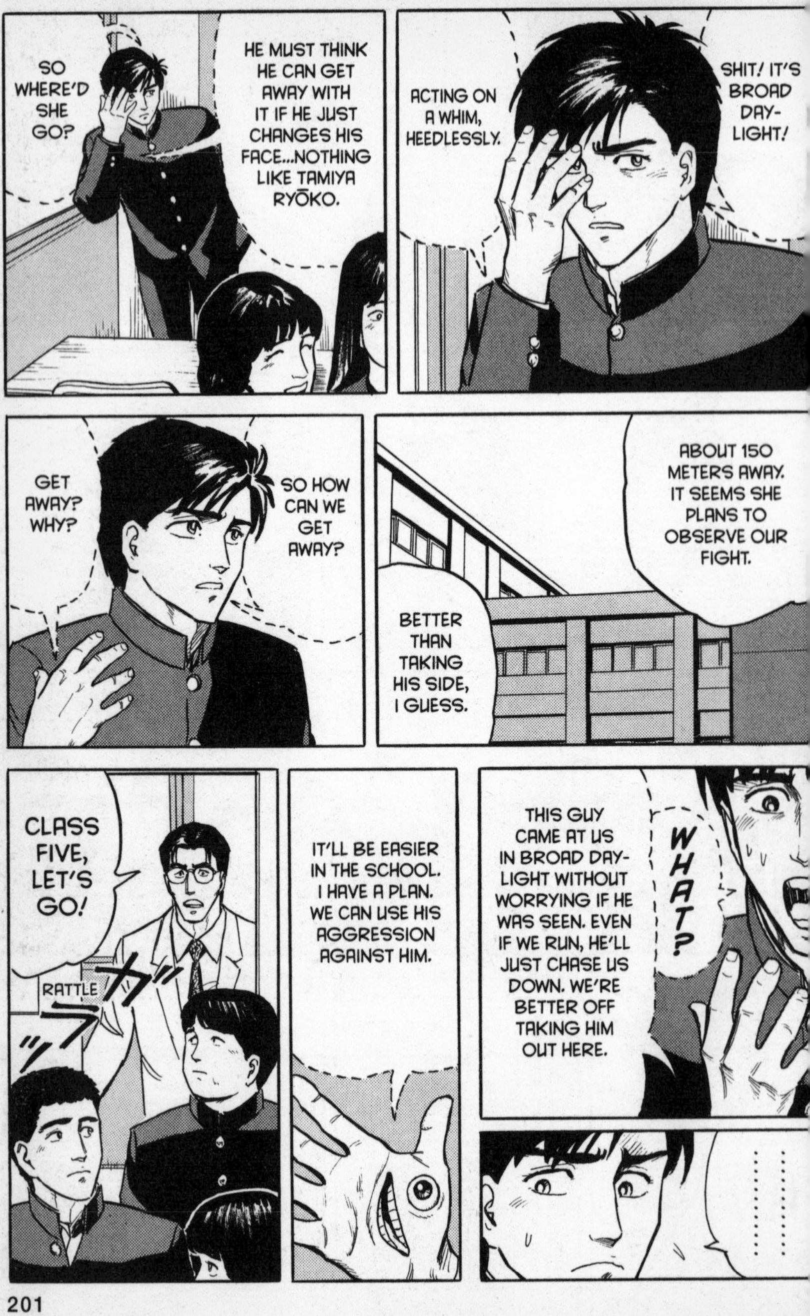
SHIT! IT'S BROAD DAY-LIGHT!
ACTING ON A WHIM, HEEDLESSLY.
HE MUST THINK HE CAN GET AWAY WITH IT IF HE JUST CHANGES HIS FACE...NOTHING LIKE TAMIYA RYŌKO.
SO WHERE'D SHE GO?
ABOUT 150 METERS AWAY. IT SEEMS SHE PLANS TO OBSERVE OUR FIGHT.
BETTER THAN TAKING HIS SIDE, I GUESS.
SO HOW CAN WE GET AWAY?
GET AWAY? WHY?
WHAT?
THIS GUY CAME AT US IN BROAD DAY-LIGHT WITHOUT WORRYING IF HE WAS SEEN. EVEN IF WE RUN, HE'LL JUST CHASE US DOWN. WE'RE BETTER OFF TAKING HIM OUT HERE.
......
IT'LL BE EASIER IN THE SCHOOL. I HAVE A PLAN. WE CAN USE HIS AGGRESSION AGAINST HIM.
CLASS FIVE, LET'S GO!
RATTLE

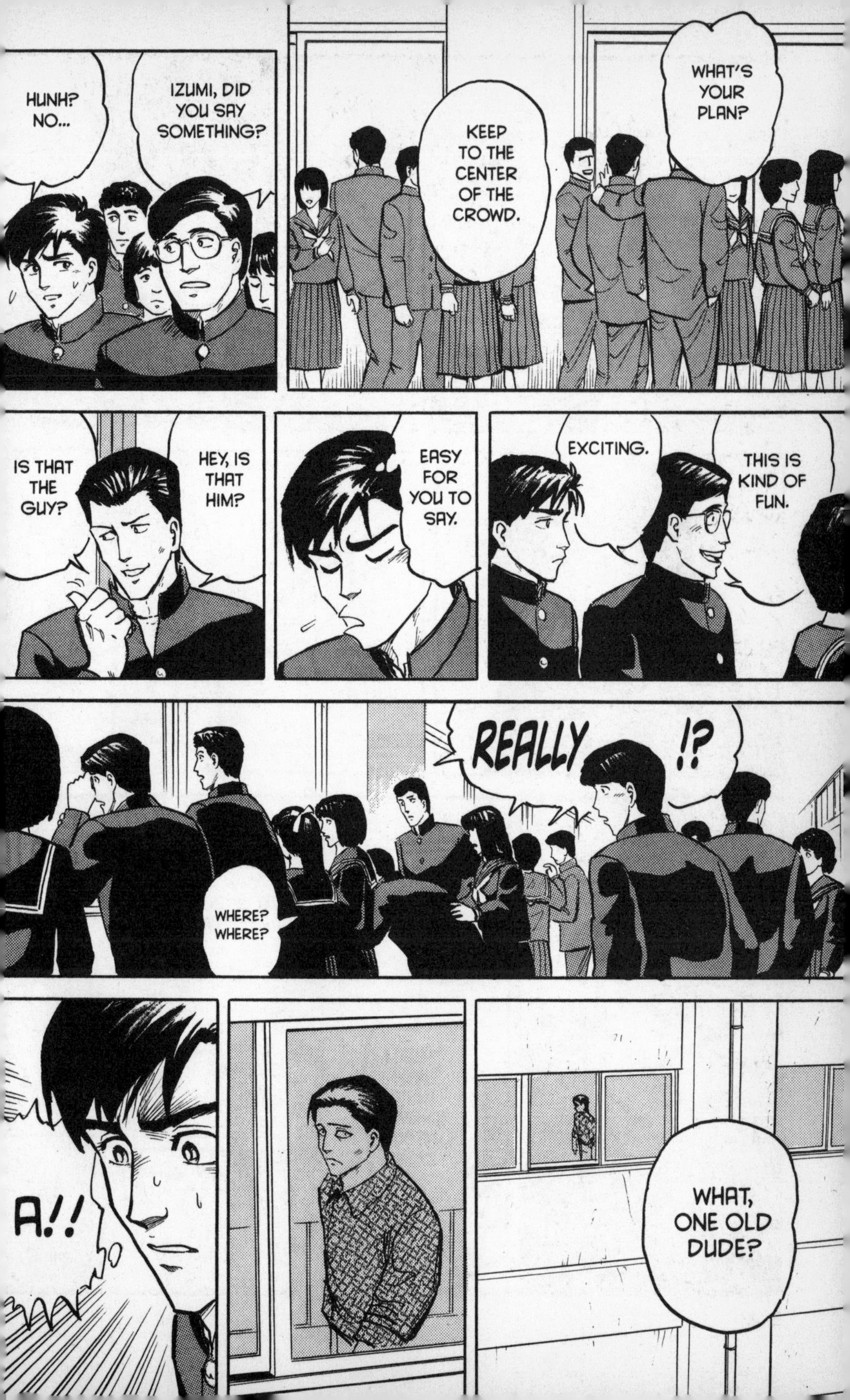
WHAT'S YOUR PLAN?
KEEP TO THE CENTER OF THE CROWD.
IZUMI, DID YOU SAY SOMETHING?
HUNH? NO...
THIS IS KIND OF FUN.
EXCITING.
EASY FOR YOU TO SAY.
HEY, IS THAT HIM?
IS THAT THE GUY?
REALLY !?
WHERE? WHERE?
WHAT, ONE OLD DUDE?
A!!

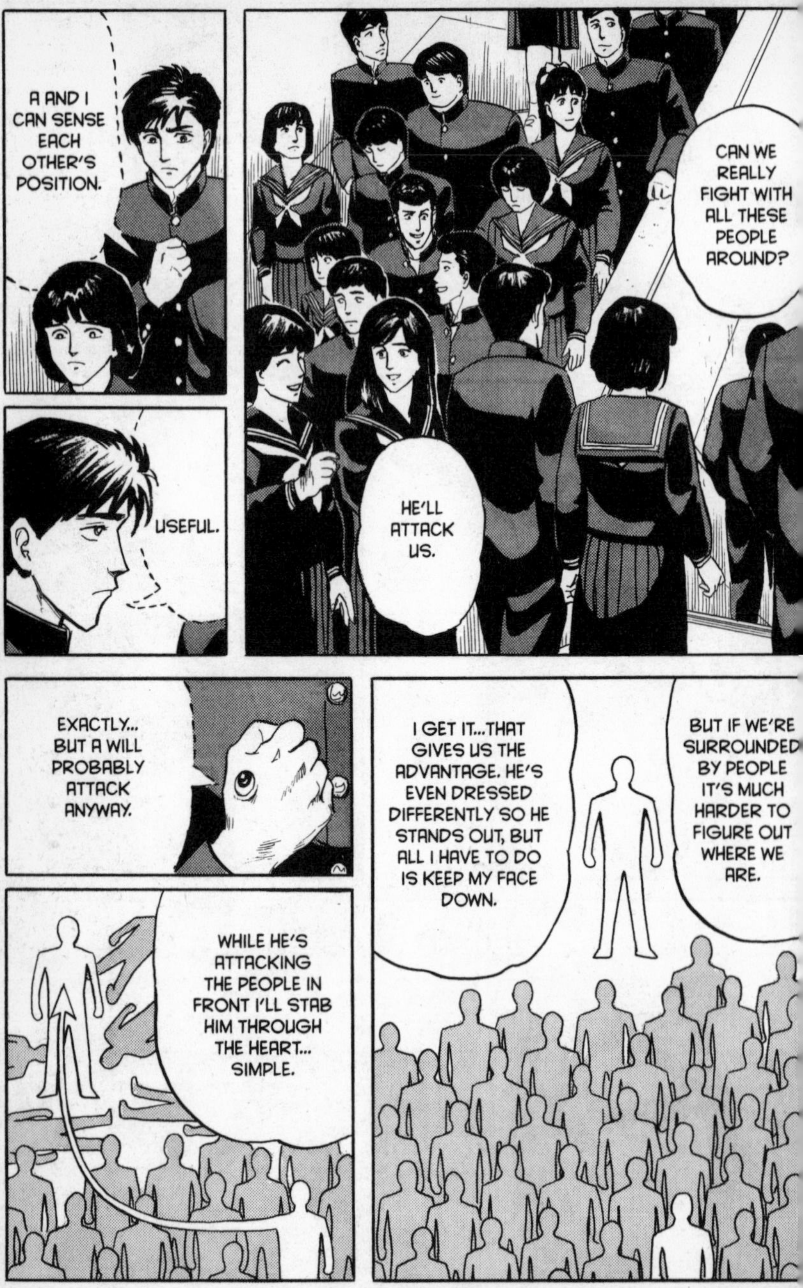
CAN WE REALLY FIGHT WITH ALL THESE PEOPLE AROUND?
HE'LL ATTACK US.
A AND I CAN SENSE EACH OTHER'S POSITION.
USEFUL.
BUT IF WE'RE SURROUNDED BY PEOPLE IT'S MUCH HARDER TO FIGURE OUT WHERE WE ARE.
I GET IT...THAT GIVES US THE ADVANTAGE. HE'S EVEN DRESSED DIFFERENTLY SO HE STANDS OUT, BUT ALL I HAVE TO DO IS KEEP MY FACE DOWN.
EXACTLY... BUT A WILL PROBABLY ATTACK ANYWAY.
WHILE HE'S ATTACKING THE PEOPLE IN FRONT I'LL STAB HIM THROUGH THE HEART... SIMPLE.

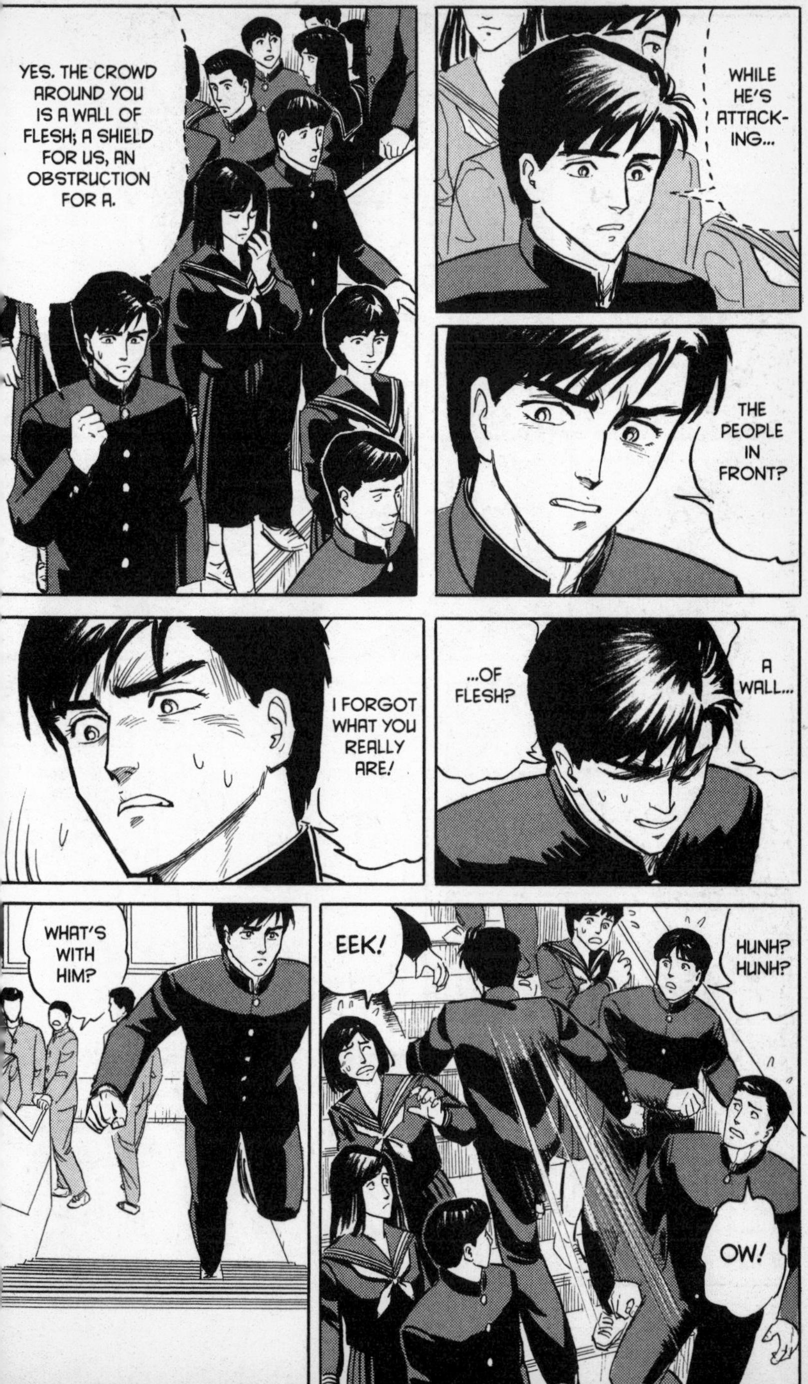
WHILE HE'S ATTACKING...
THE PEOPLE IN FRONT?
YES. THE CROWD AROUND YOU IS A WALL OF FLESH; A SHIELD FOR US, AN OBSTRUCTION FOR A.
A WALL...
...OF FLESH?
I FORGOT WHAT YOU REALLY ARE!
HUNH? HUNH?
EEK!
OW!
WHAT'S WITH HIM?

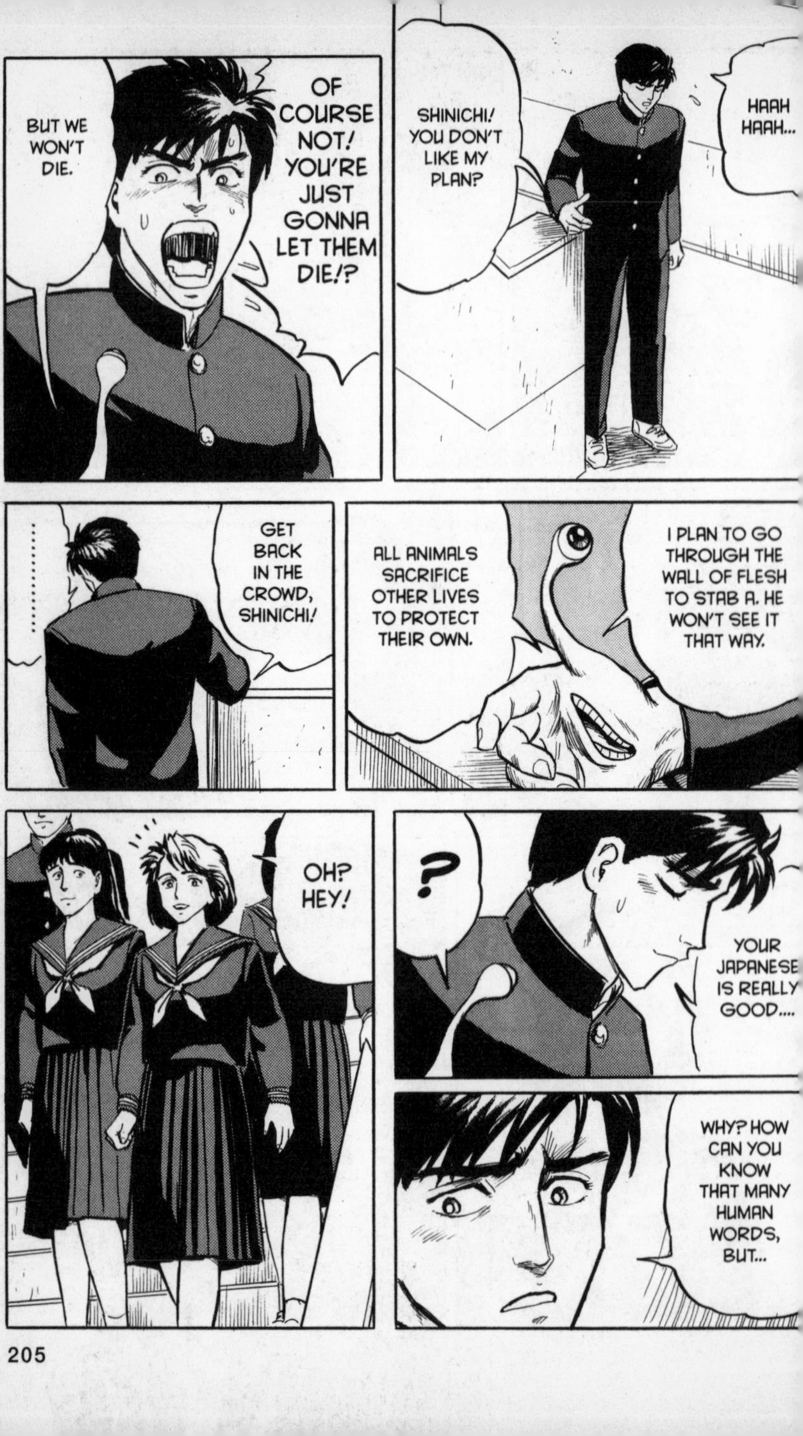
HAAH HAAH...
SHINICHI! YOU DON'T LIKE MY PLAN?
OF COURSE NOT! YOU'RE JUST GONNA LET THEM DIE!?
BUT WE WON'T DIE.
I PLAN TO GO THROUGH THE WALL OF FLESH TO STAB A. HE WON'T SEE IT THAT WAY.
ALL ANIMALS SACRIFICE OTHER LIVES TO PROTECT THEIR OWN.
GET BACK IN THE CROWD, SHINICHI!
....
YOUR JAPANESE IS REALLY GOOD....
?
WHY? HOW CAN YOU KNOW THAT MANY HUMAN WORDS, BUT...
OH? HEY!

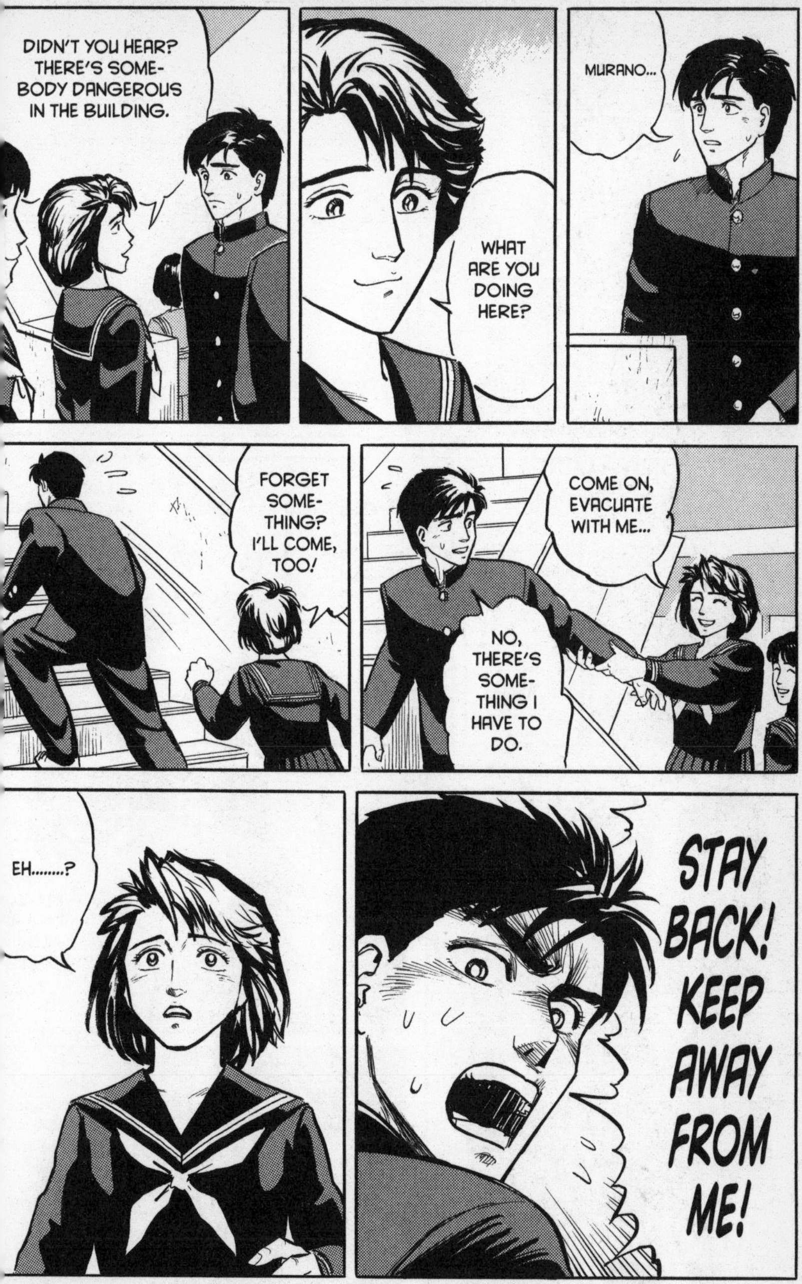
MURANO...
WHAT ARE YOU DOING HERE?
DIDN'T YOU HEAR? THERE'S SOME-BODY DANGEROUS IN THE BUILDING.
COME ON, EVACUATE WITH ME...
NO, THERE'S SOME-THING I HAVE TO DO.
FORGET SOME-THING? I'LL COME, TOO!
STAY BACK! KEEP AWAY FROM ME!
EH........?

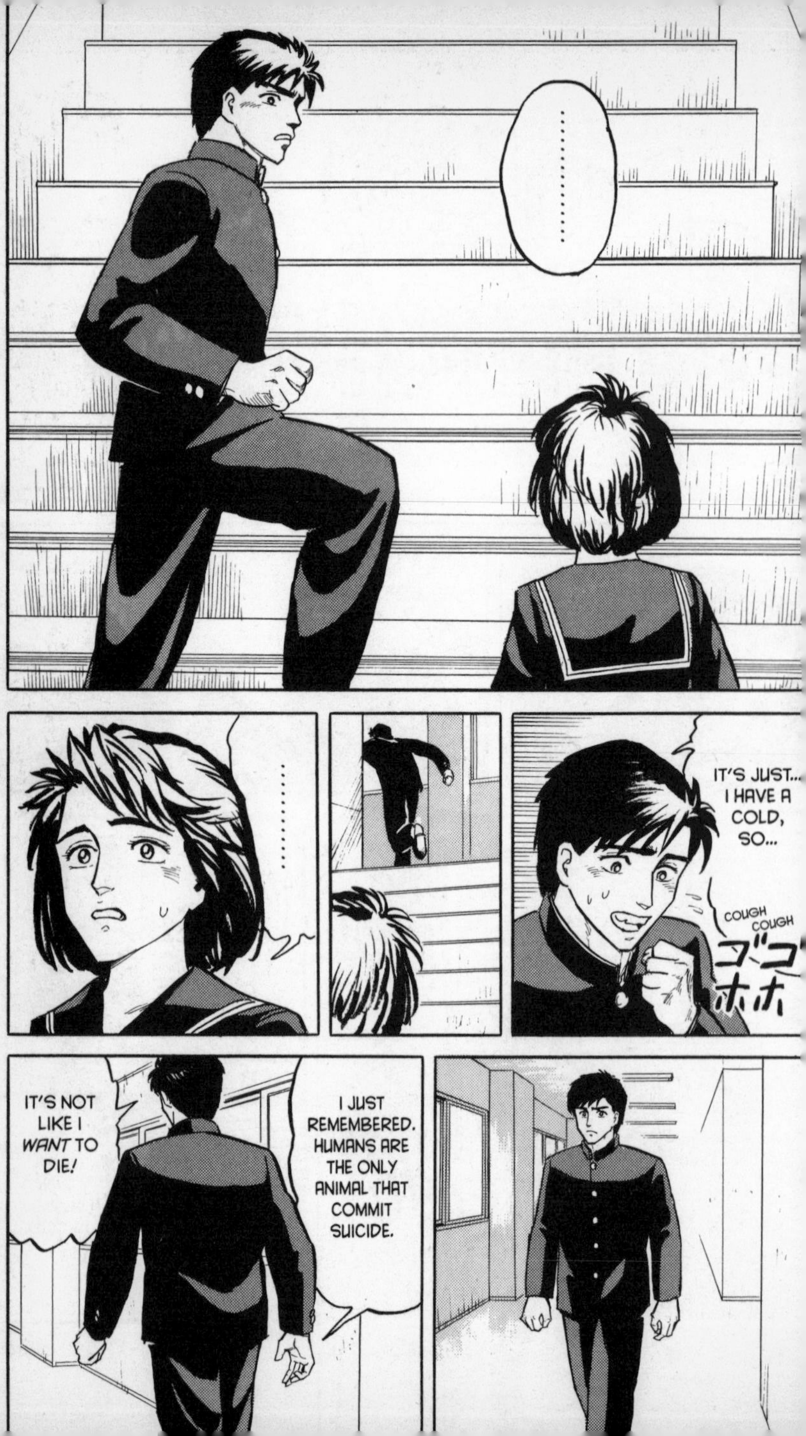
......
IT'S JUST... I HAVE A COLD, SO...
COUGH COUGH
ゴホゴホ
......
I JUST REMEMBERED. HUMANS ARE THE ONLY ANIMAL THAT COMMIT SUICIDE.
IT'S NOT LIKE I *WANT* TO DIE!

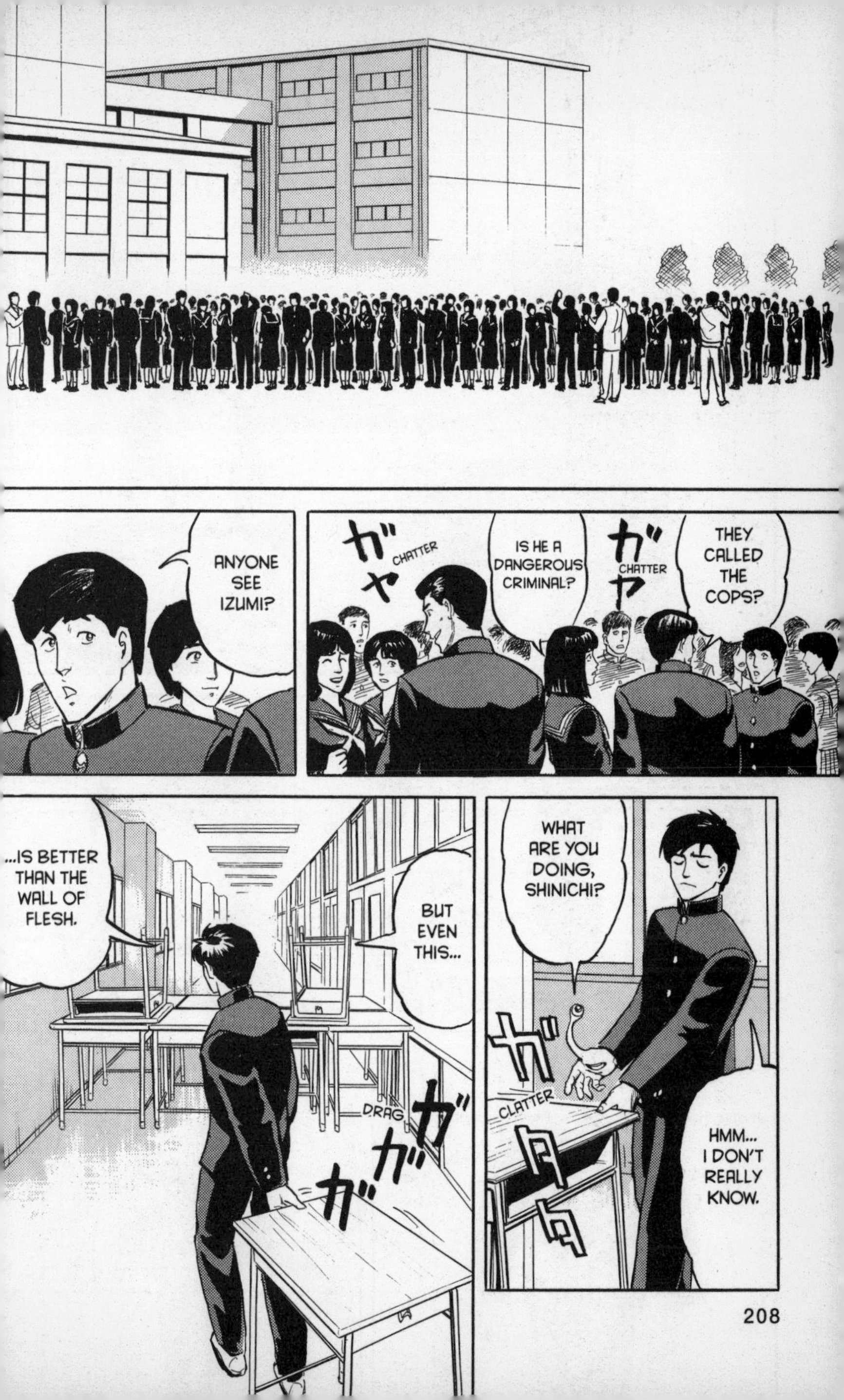
THEY CALLED THE COPS?
ガヤ
CHATTER
IS HE A DANGEROUS CRIMINAL?
ガヤ
CHATTER
ANYONE SEE IZUMI?
WHAT ARE YOU DOING, SHINICHI?
ガタ
CLATTER
HMM... I DON'T REALLY KNOW.
BUT EVEN THIS...
...IS BETTER THAN THE WALL OF FLESH.
ガガガ
DRAG

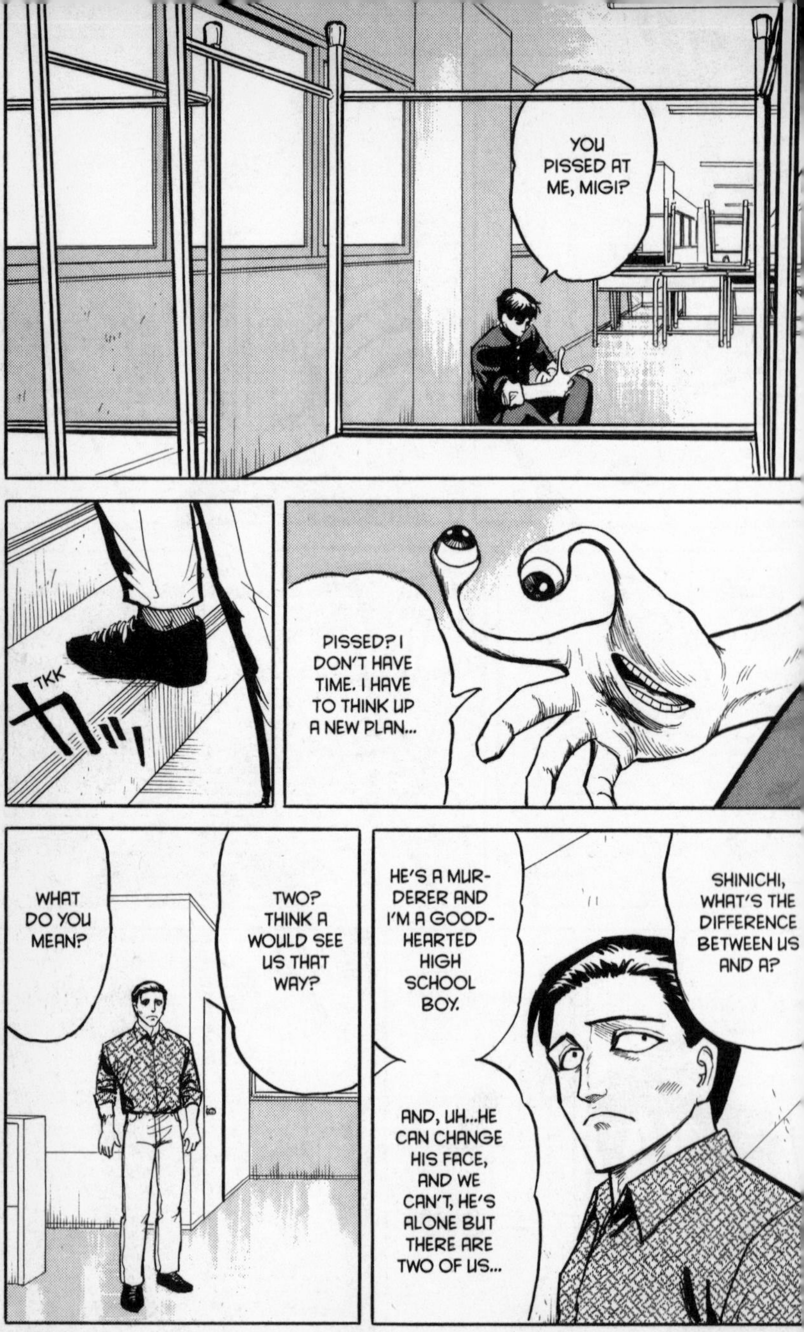
YOU PISSED AT ME, MIGI?
PISSED? I DON'T HAVE TIME. I HAVE TO THINK UP A NEW PLAN...
TKK
SHINICHI, WHAT'S THE DIFFERENCE BETWEEN US AND A?
HE'S A MUR-DERER AND I'M A GOOD-HEARTED HIGH SCHOOL BOY.
AND, UH...HE CAN CHANGE HIS FACE, AND WE CAN'T, HE'S ALONE BUT THERE ARE TWO OF US...
TWO? THINK A WOULD SEE US THAT WAY?
WHAT DO YOU MEAN?

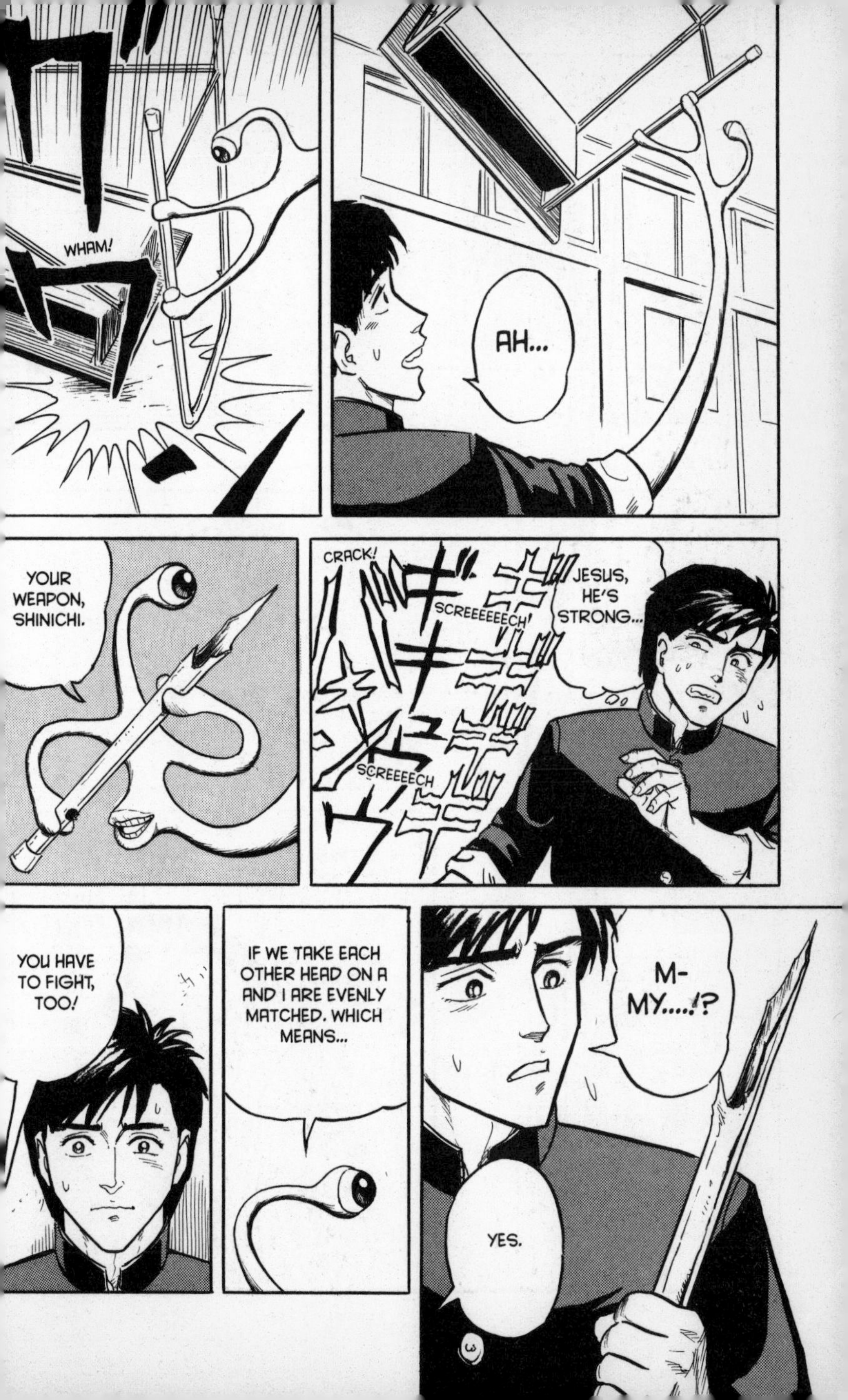
AH...
WHAM!
JESUS, HE'S STRONG...
CRACK!
SCREEEEEECH
SCREEEECH
YOUR WEAPON, SHINICHI.
M- MY.....!?
YES.
IF WE TAKE EACH OTHER HEAD ON A AND I ARE EVENLY MATCHED. WHICH MEANS...
YOU HAVE TO FIGHT, TOO!

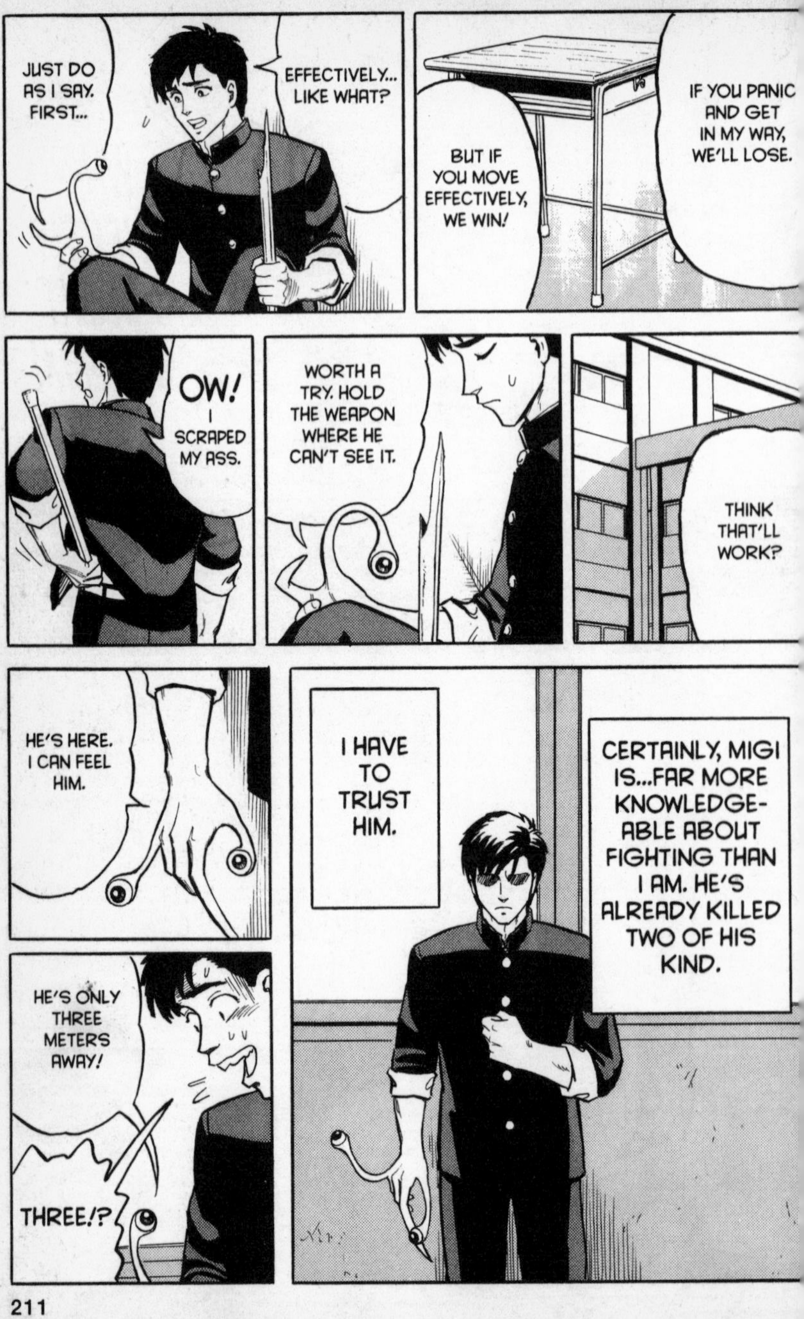
IF YOU PANIC AND GET IN MY WAY, WE'LL LOSE.
BUT IF YOU MOVE EFFECTIVELY, WE WIN!
EFFECTIVELY... LIKE WHAT?
JUST DO AS I SAY. FIRST...
THINK THAT'LL WORK?
WORTH A TRY. HOLD THE WEAPON WHERE HE CAN'T SEE IT.
OW! I SCRAPED MY ASS.
CERTAINLY, MIGI IS...FAR MORE KNOWLEDGE-ABLE ABOUT FIGHTING THAN I AM. HE'S ALREADY KILLED TWO OF HIS KIND.
I HAVE TO TRUST HIM.
HE'S HERE. I CAN FEEL HIM.
HE'S ONLY THREE METERS AWAY!
THREE!?

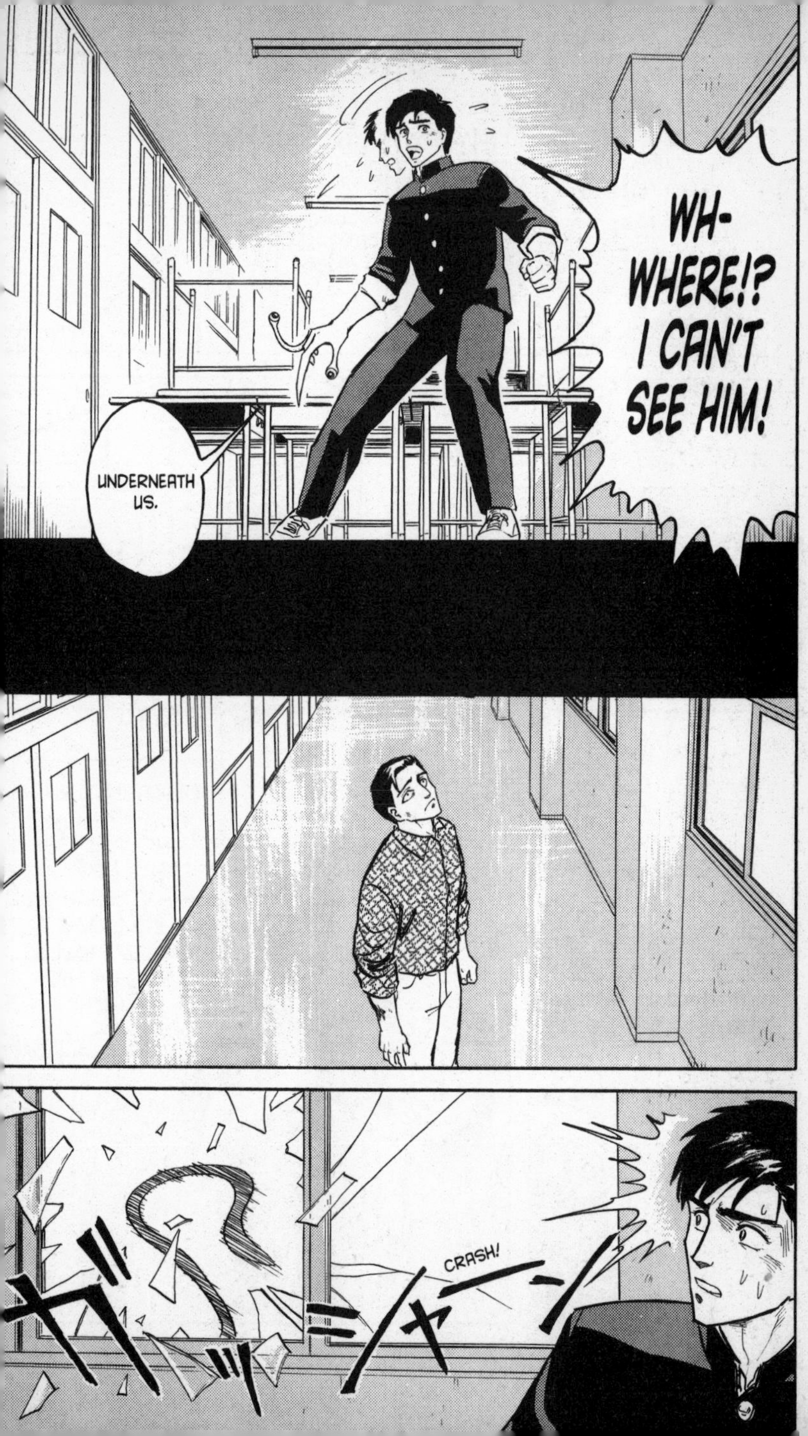
WH- WHERE!? I CAN'T SEE HIM!
UNDERNEATH US.
CRASH!

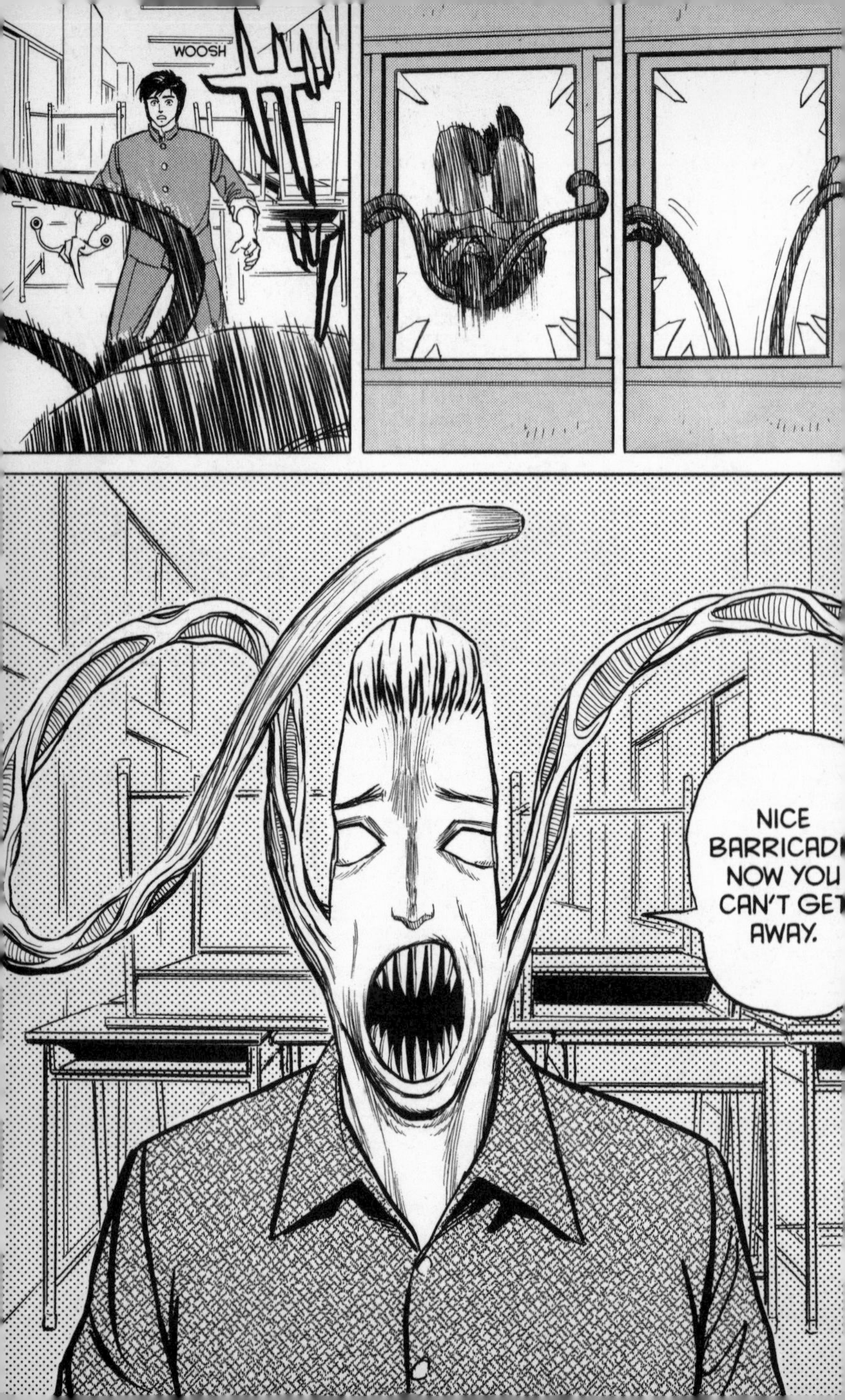
WOOSH
NICE BARRICAD NOW YOU CAN'T GET AWAY.

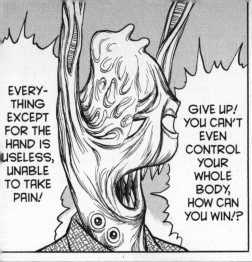

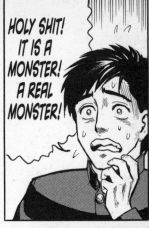

HOLY SHIT! IT IS A MONSTER! A REAL MONSTER!
GIVE UP! YOU CAN'T EVEN CONTROL YOUR WHOLE BODY, HOW CAN YOU WIN!?
EVERY-THING EXCEPT FOR THE HAND IS USELESS, UNABLE TO TAKE PAIN!
!
OH! HE'S TRYING TO MAKE ME PANIC, TRYING TO GAIN THE ADVANTAGE.
IT WON'T WORK!
SWISH
CLANG!

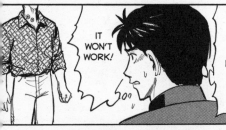

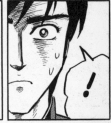

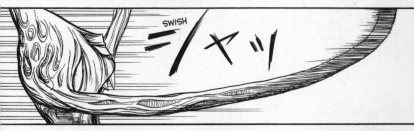

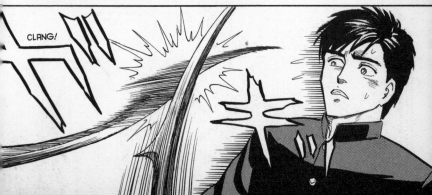

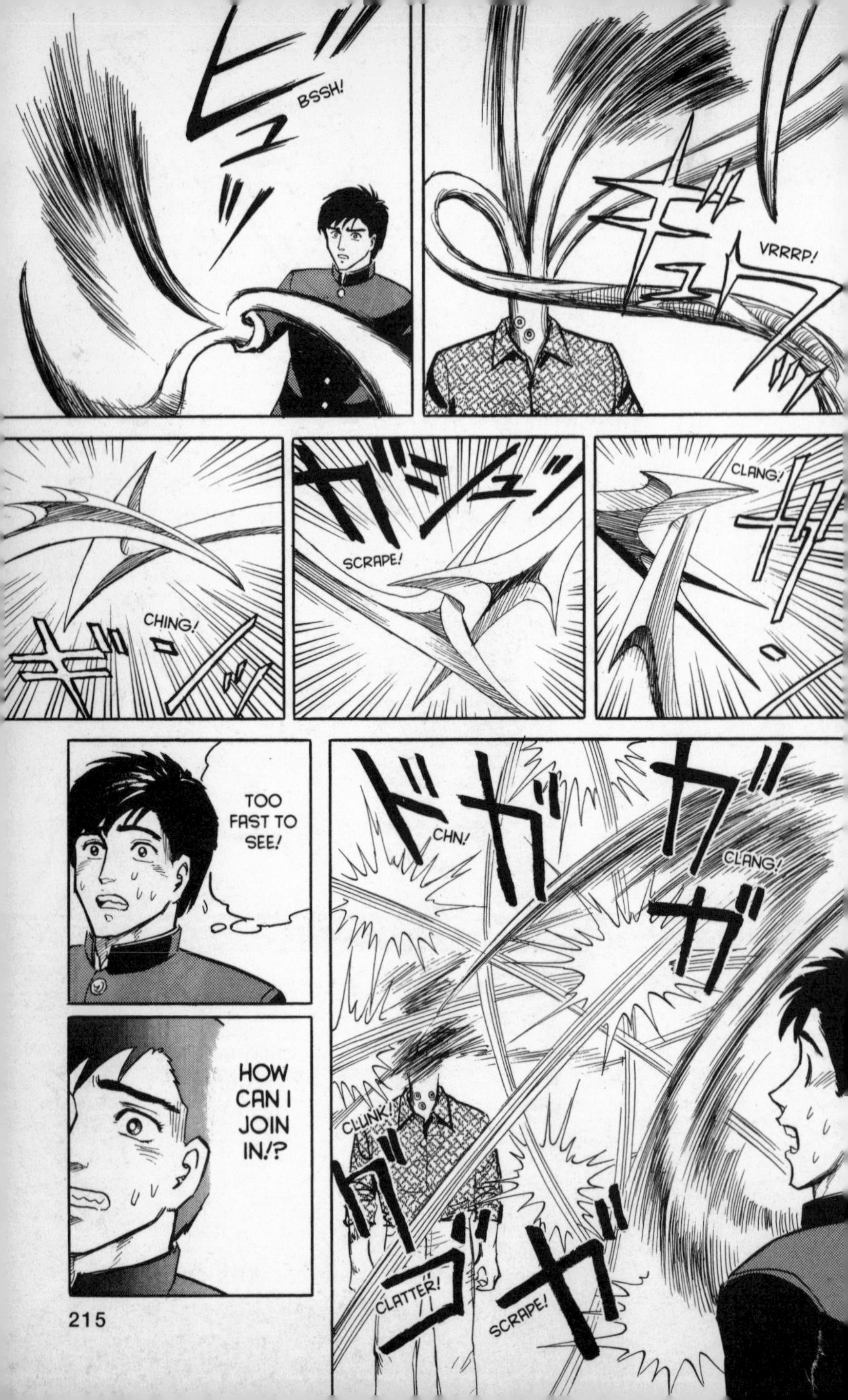
VRRRP!
BSSH!
CLANG!
SCRAPE!
CHING!
CHN!
CLANG!
CLUNK!
CLATTER!
SCRAPE!
TOO FAST TO SEE!
HOW CAN I JOIN IN!?

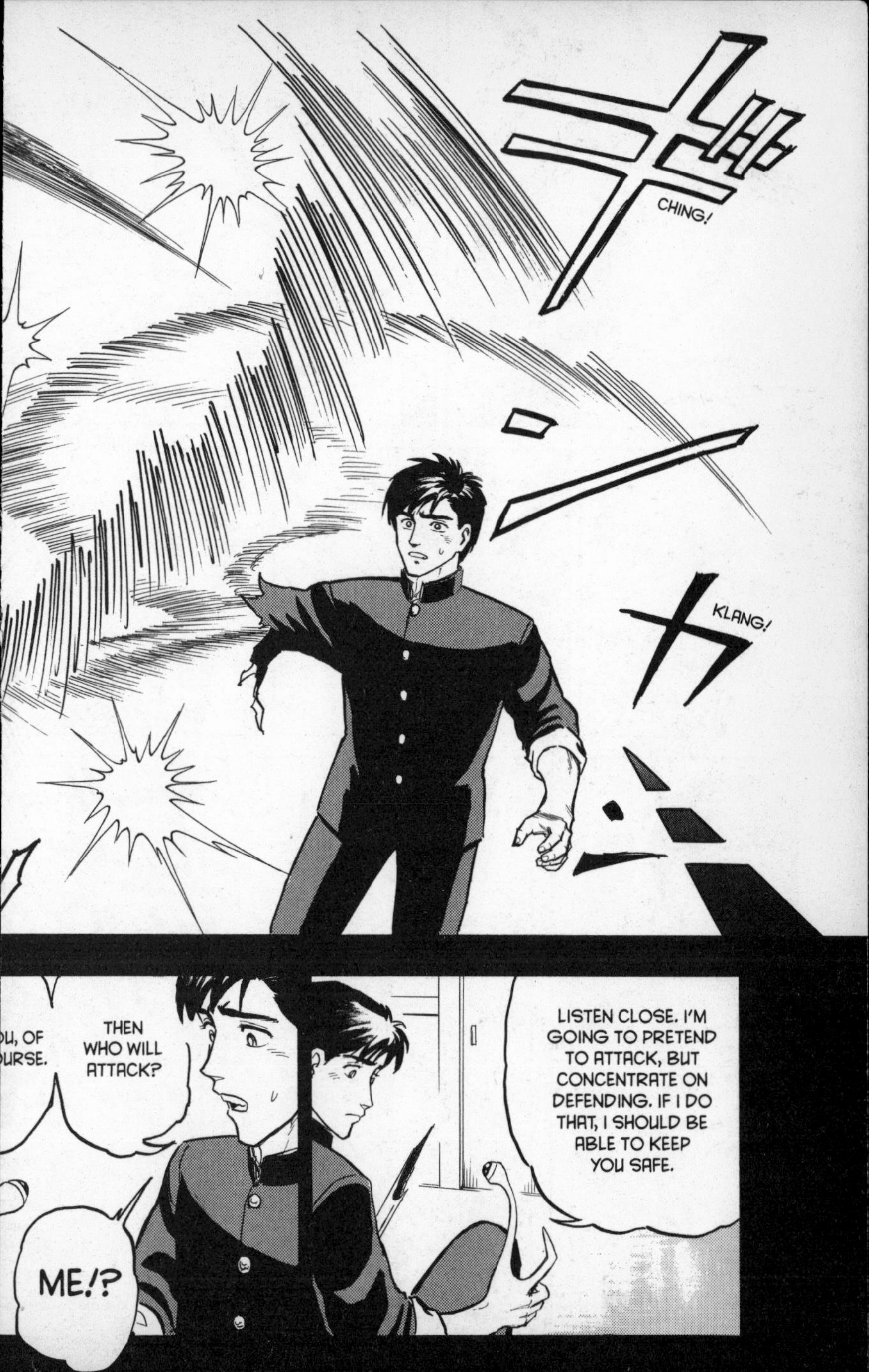
CHING!
KLANG!
LISTEN CLOSE. I'M GOING TO PRETEND TO ATTACK, BUT CONCENTRATE ON DEFENDING. IF I DO THAT, I SHOULD BE ABLE TO KEEP YOU SAFE.
THEN WHO WILL ATTACK?
U, OF URSE.
ME!?

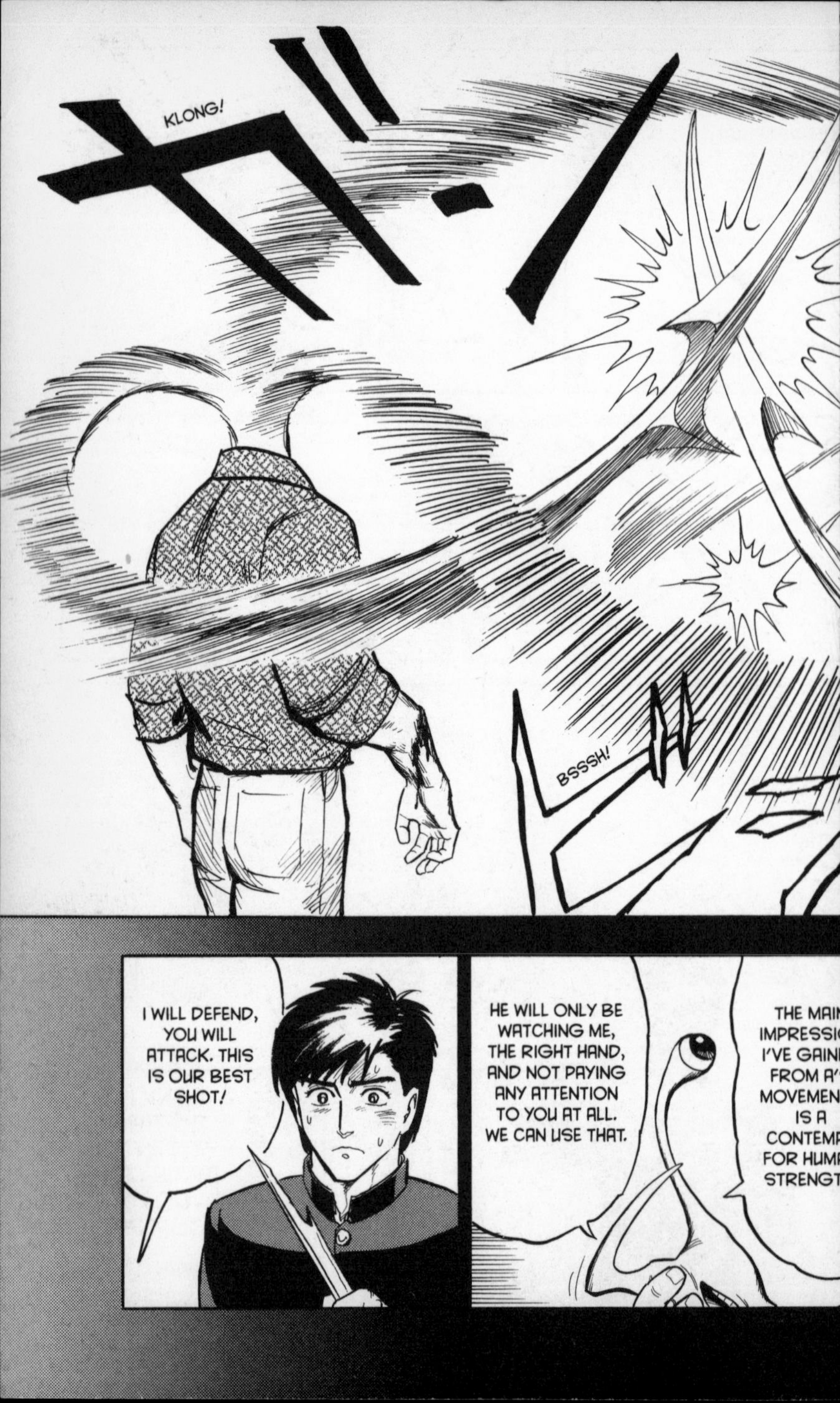
KLONG!
BSSSH!
THE MAIN IMPRESSIO I'VE GAINE FROM A' MOVEMEN IS A CONTEMP FOR HUMA STRENGT
HE WILL ONLY BE WATCHING ME, THE RIGHT HAND, AND NOT PAYING ANY ATTENTION TO YOU AT ALL. WE CAN USE THAT.
I WILL DEFEND, YOU WILL ATTACK. THIS IS OUR BEST SHOT!

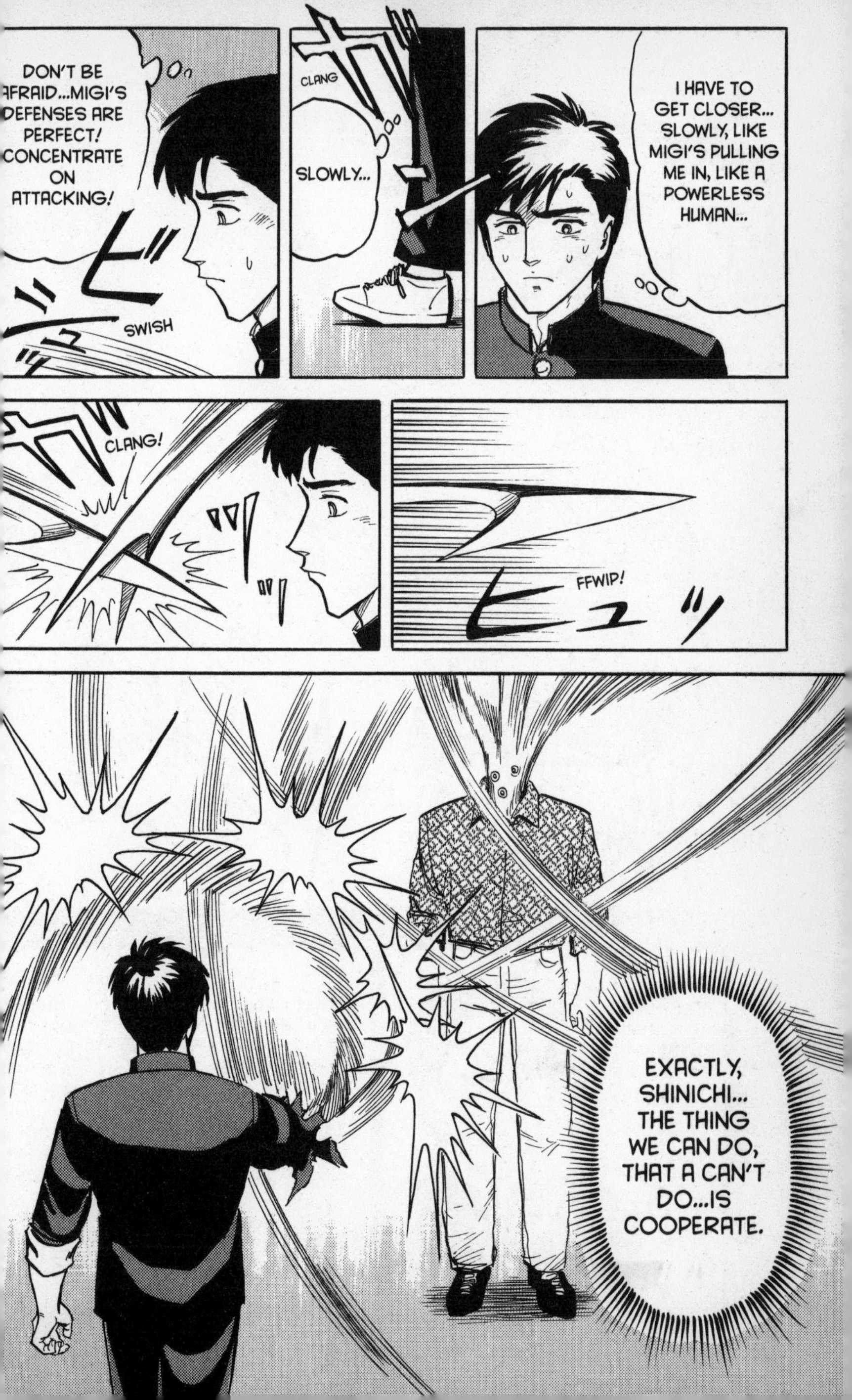
I HAVE TO GET CLOSER... SLOWLY, LIKE MIGI'S PULLING ME IN, LIKE A POWERLESS HUMAN...
CLANG
SLOWLY...
DON'T BE AFRAID...MIGI'S DEFENSES ARE PERFECT! CONCENTRATE ON ATTACKING!
SWISH
FFWIP!
CLANG!
EXACTLY, SHINICHI... THE THING WE CAN DO, THAT A CAN'T DO...IS COOPERATE.

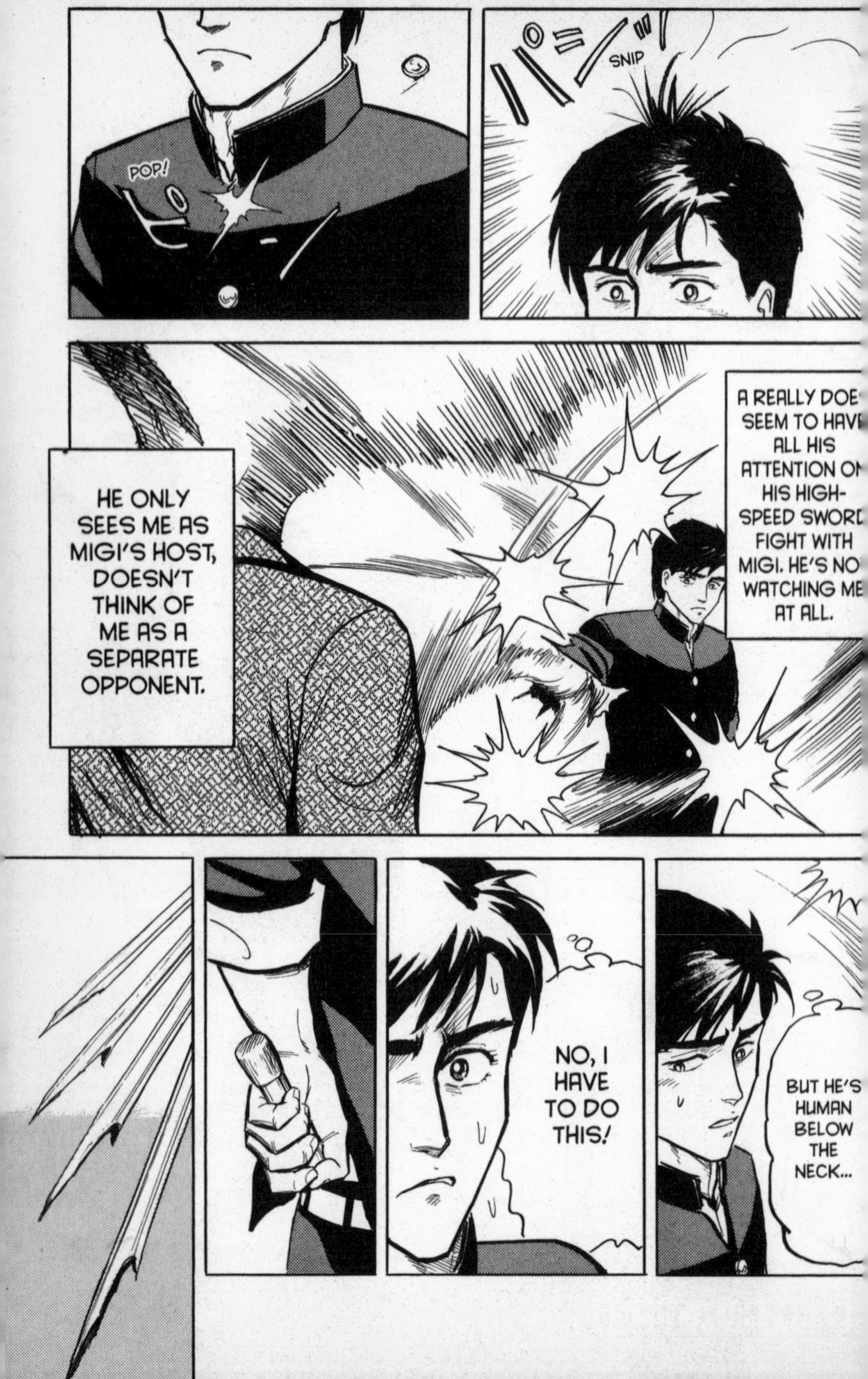
SNIP
POP!
A REALLY DOE
SEEM TO HAV
ALL HIS
ATTENTION O
HIS HIGH-
SPEED SWORD
FIGHT WITH
MIGI. HE'S NO
WATCHING ME
AT ALL.
HE ONLY SEES ME AS MIGI'S HOST, DOESN'T THINK OF ME AS A SEPARATE OPPONENT.
BUT HE'S HUMAN BELOW THE NECK...
NO, I HAVE TO DO THIS!

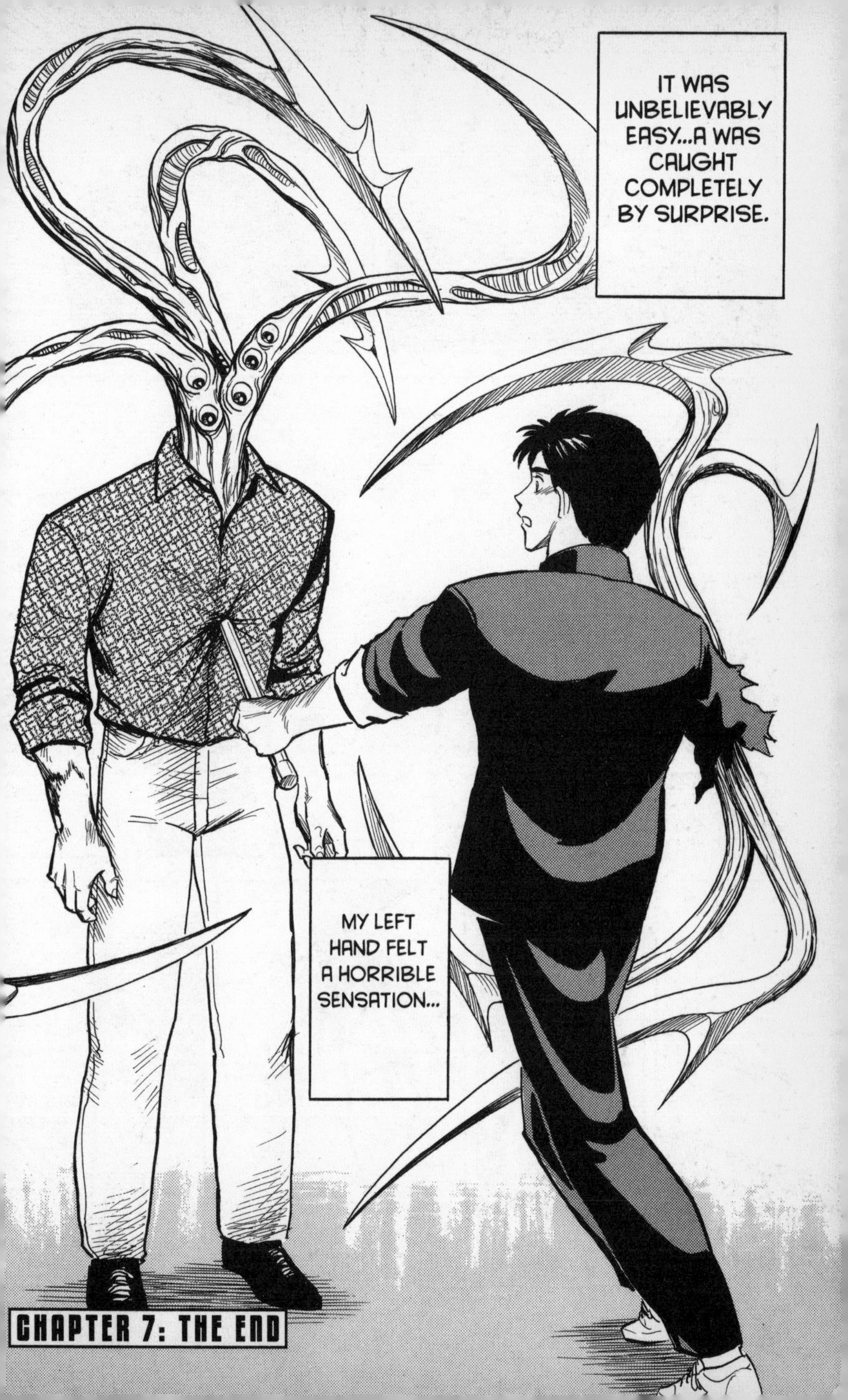
IT WAS UNBELIEVABLY EASY...A WAS CAUGHT COMPLETELY BY SURPRISE.
MY LEFT HAND FELT A HORRIBLE SENSATION...
CHAPTER 7: THE END

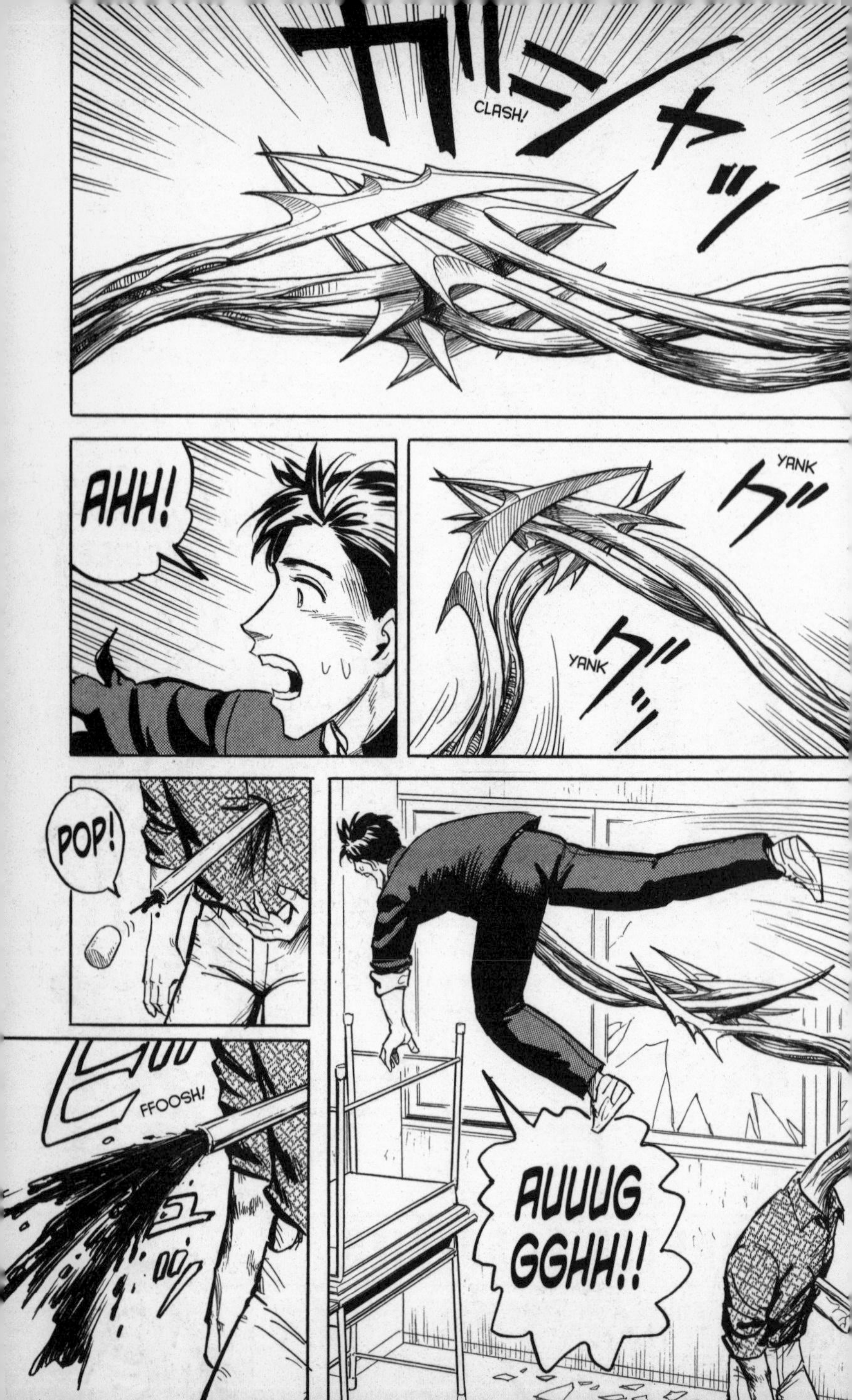
CLASH!
YANK
YANK
AHH!
AUUUG GGHH!!
POP!
FFOOSH!

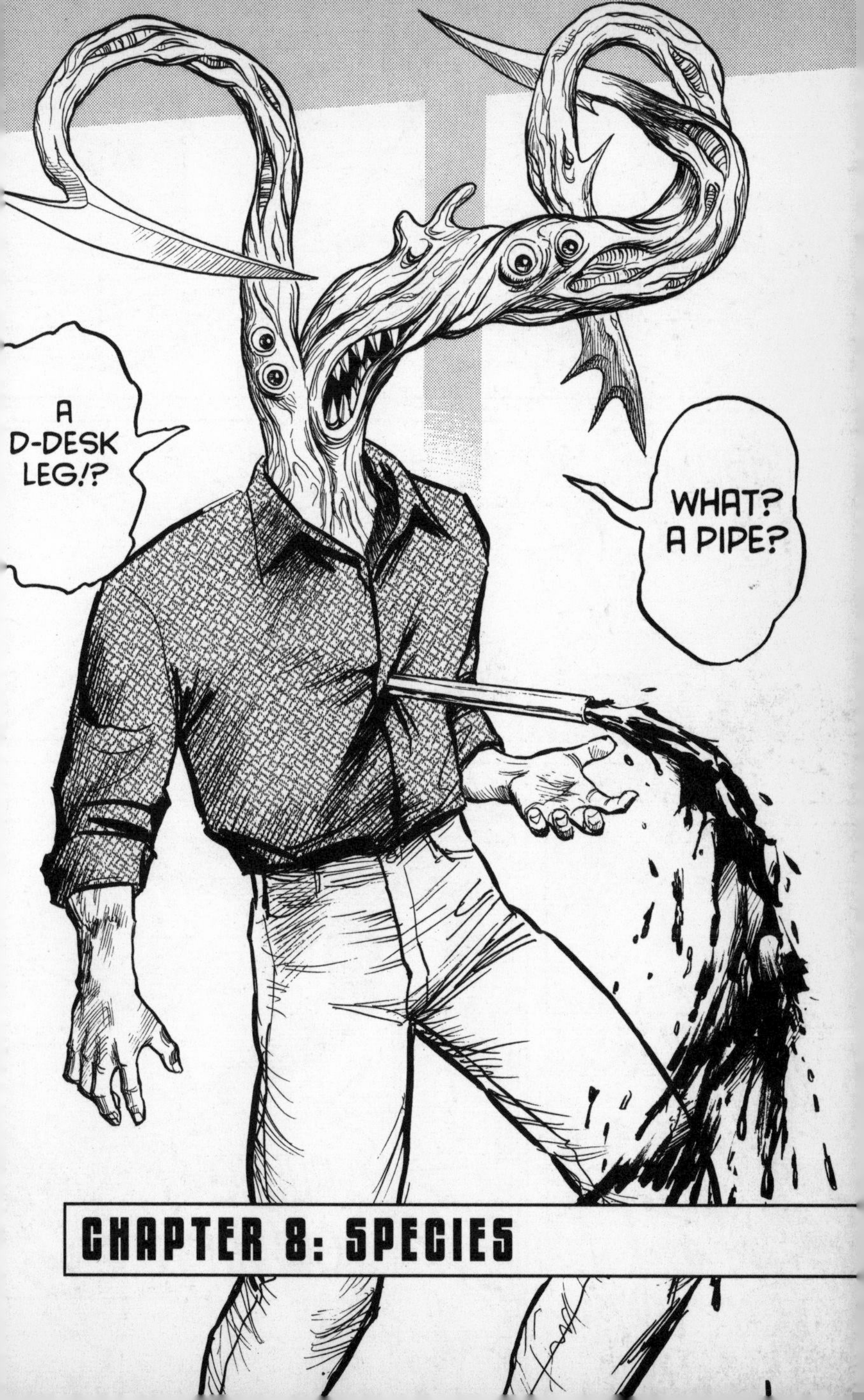
WHAT? A PIPE?
A D-DESK LEG!?

CHAPTER 8: SPECIES

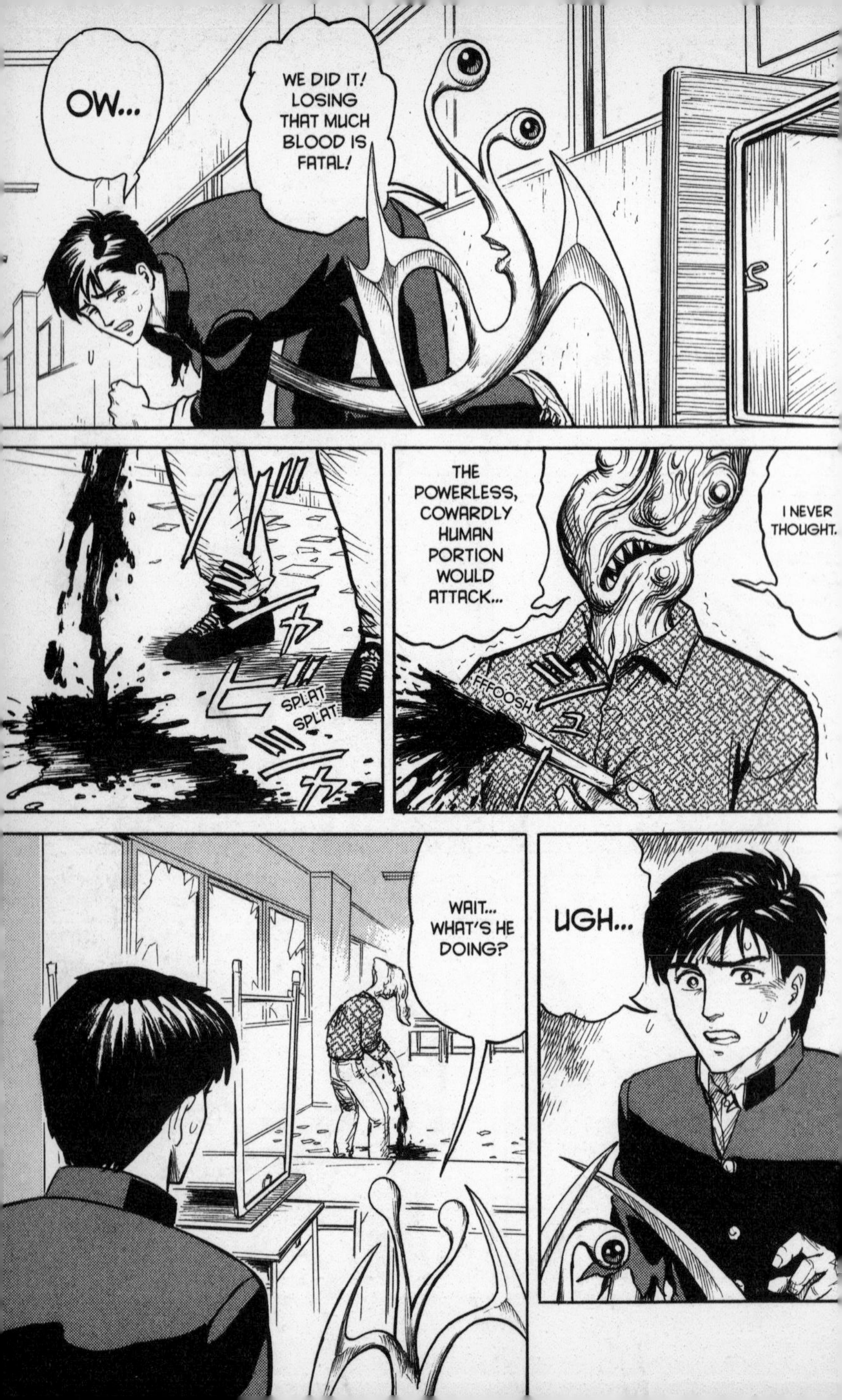
WE DID IT! LOSING THAT MUCH BLOOD IS FATAL!
OW...
I NEVER THOUGHT.
THE POWERLESS, COWARDLY HUMAN PORTION WOULD ATTACK...
FFFOOSH
SPLAT
SPLAT
UGH...
WAIT... WHAT'S HE DOING?

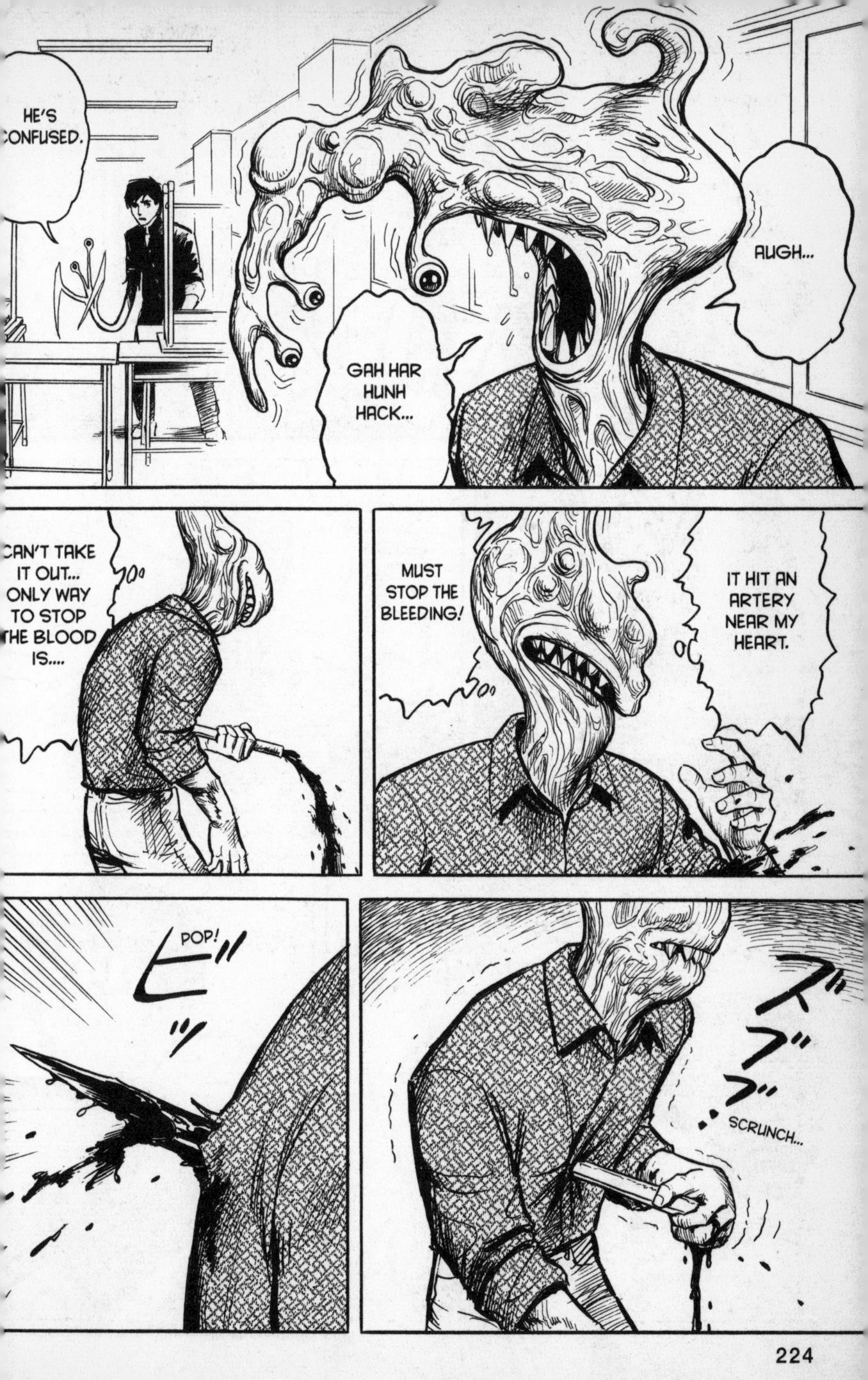
AUGH...
GAH HAR HUNH HACK...
HE'S CONFUSED.
IT HIT AN ARTERY NEAR MY HEART.
MUST STOP THE BLEEDING!
CAN'T TAKE IT OUT... ONLY WAY TO STOP THE BLOOD IS....
SCRUNCH...
POP!

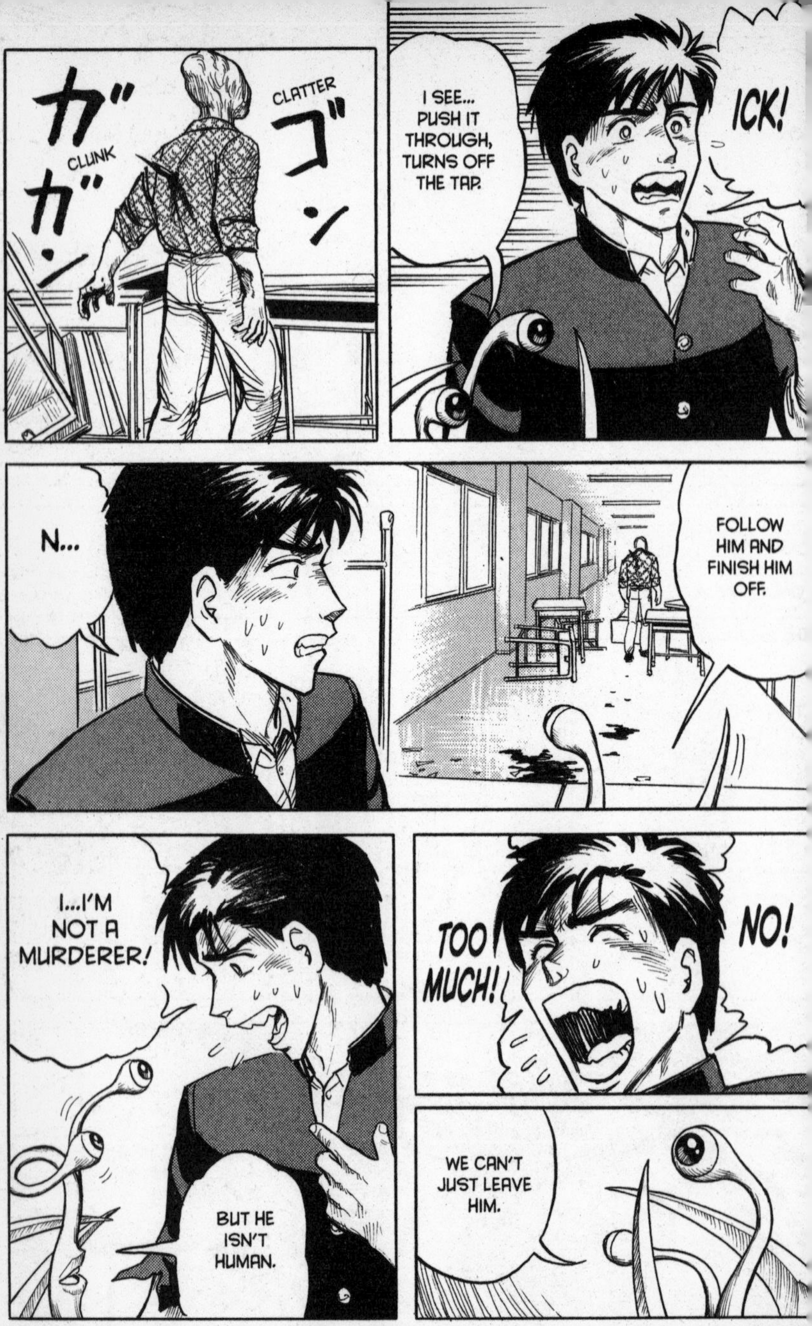
I SEE... PUSH IT THROUGH, TURNS OFF THE TAP.
ICK!
CLATTER
ゴン
CLUNK
ガガン
FOLLOW HIM AND FINISH HIM OFF.
N...
NO!
TOO MUCH!
WE CAN'T JUST LEAVE HIM.
I...I'M NOT A MURDERER!
BUT HE ISN'T HUMAN.

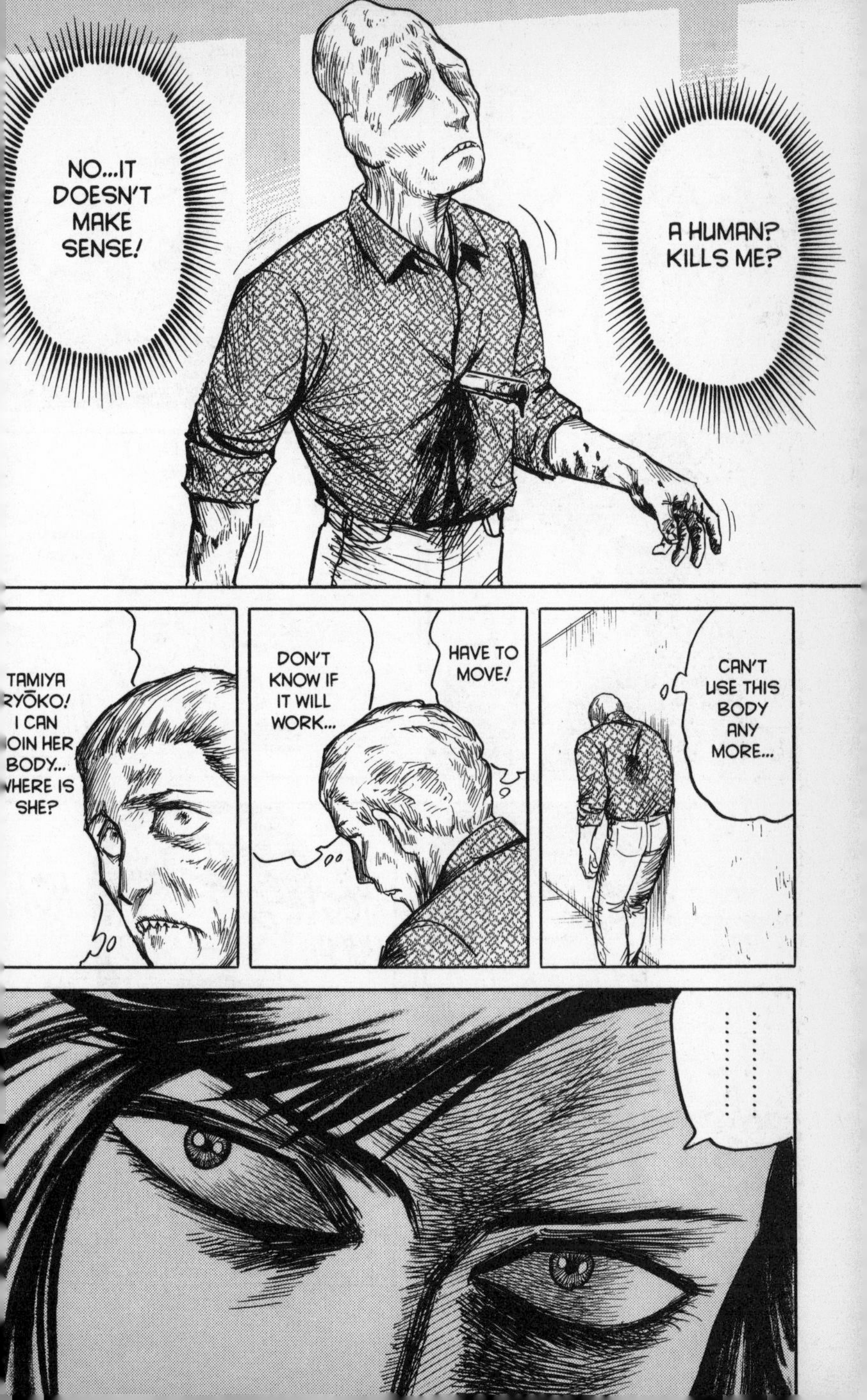
A HUMAN? KILLS ME?
NO...IT DOESN'T MAKE SENSE!
CAN'T USE THIS BODY ANY MORE...
HAVE TO MOVE!
DON'T KNOW IF IT WILL WORK...
TAMIYA RYŌKO! I CAN OIN HER BODY... HERE IS SHE?
....

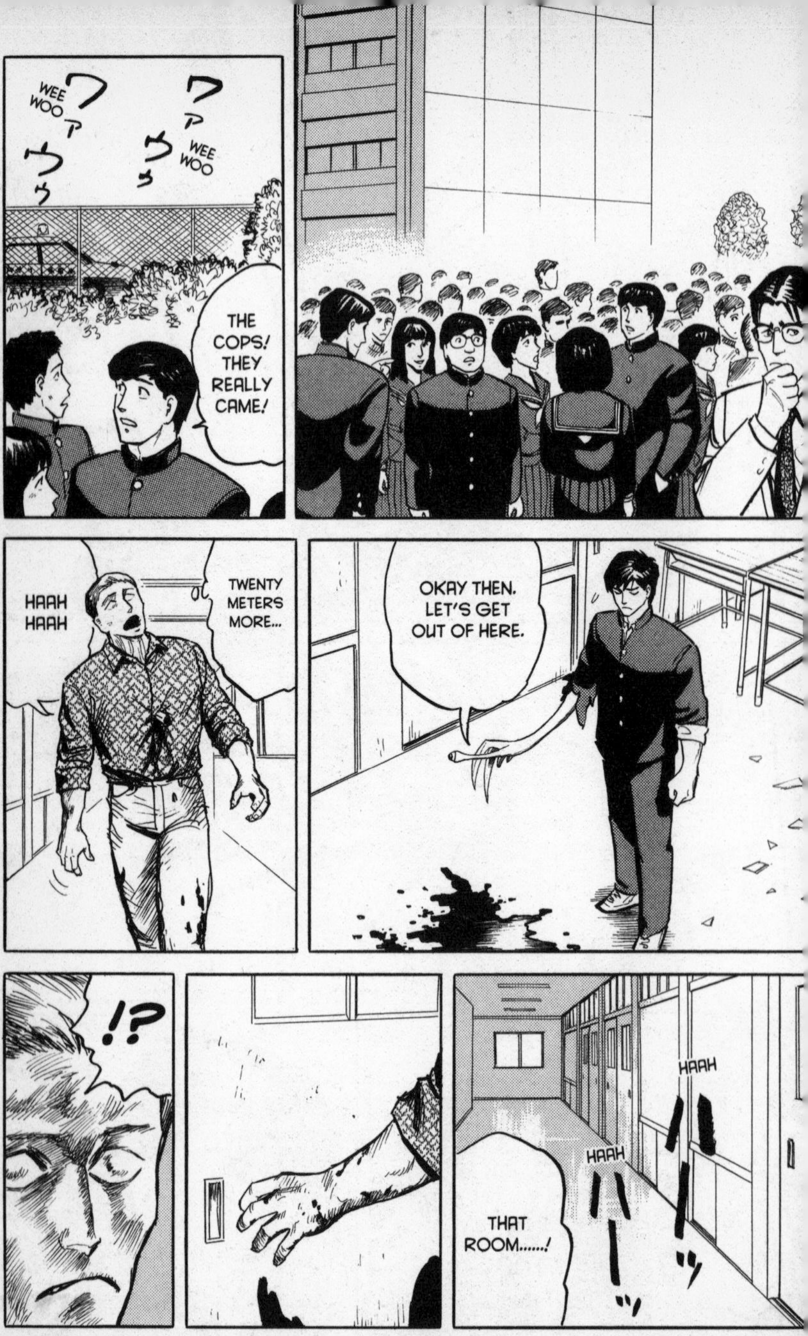
ワァウゥ
WEE WOO
ワァウゥ
WEE WOO
THE COPS! THEY REALLY CAME!
OKAY THEN. LET'S GET OUT OF HERE.
TWENTY METERS MORE...
HAAH HAAH
HAAH
HAAH
THAT ROOM......!
!?

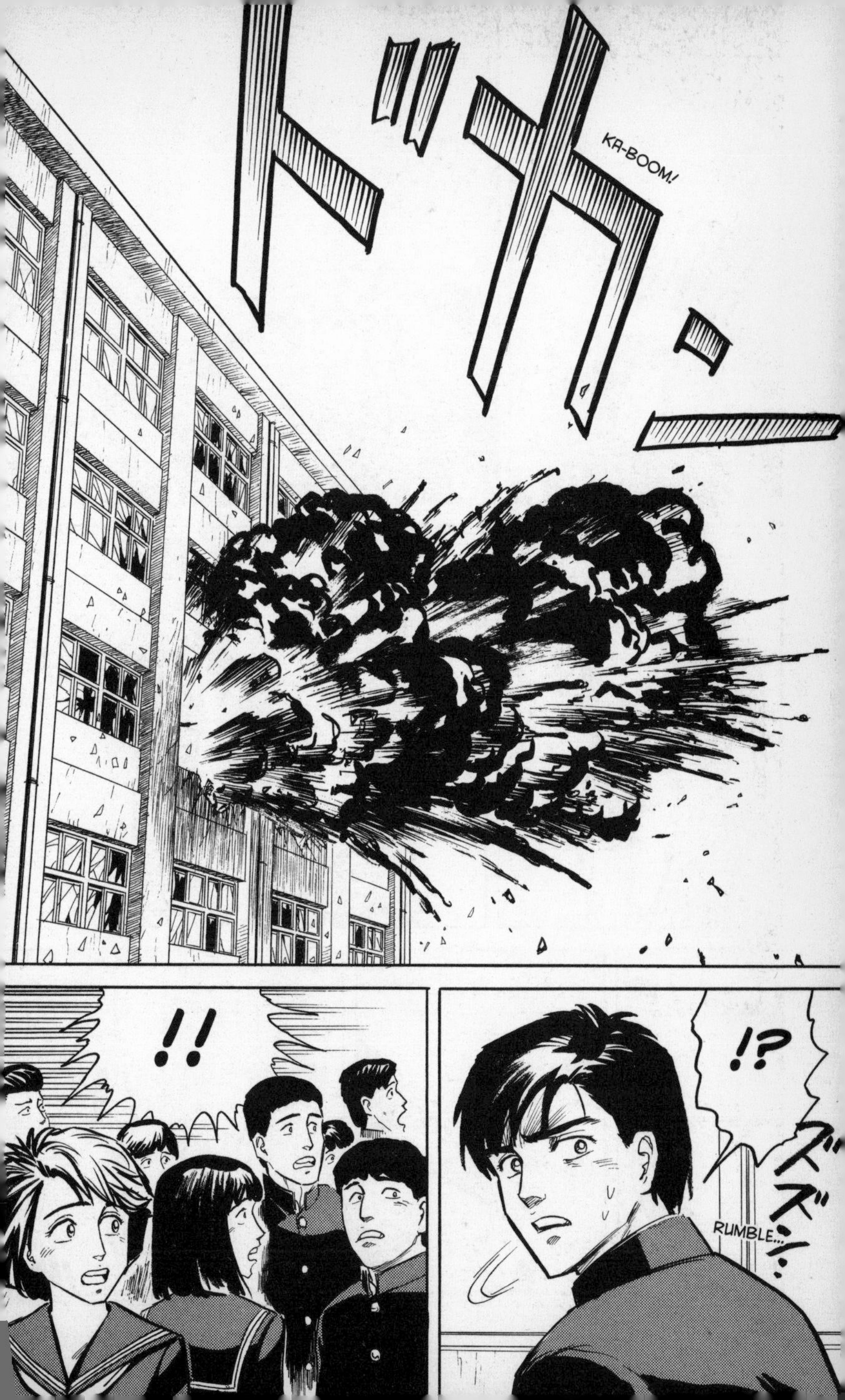
KA-BOOM!
!?
ズズ
RUMBLE...
!!

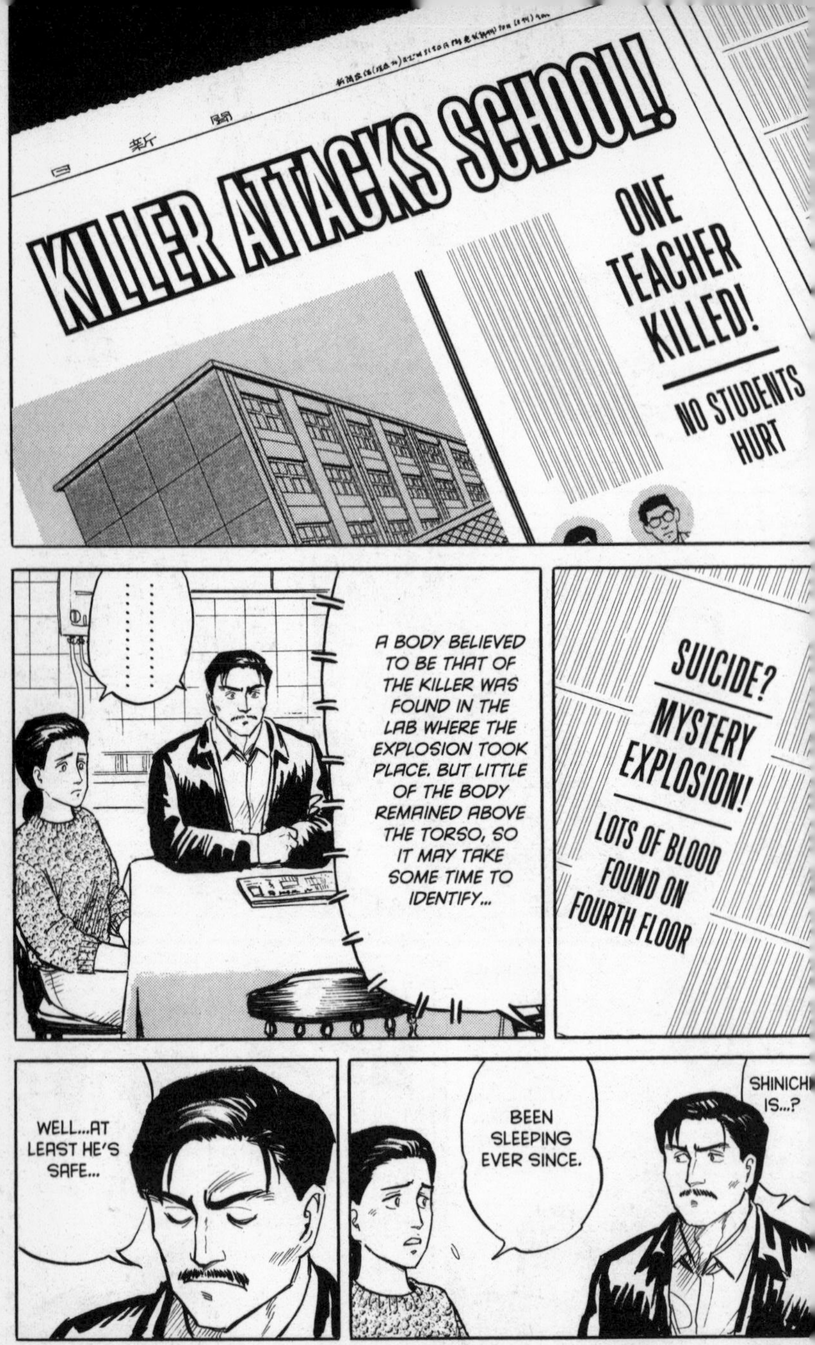
KILLER ATTACKS SCHOOL!
ONE TEACHER KILLED!
NO STUDENTS HURT
SUICIDE? MYSTERY EXPLOSION!
LOTS OF BLOOD FOUND ON FOURTH FLOOR
A BODY BELIEVED TO BE THAT OF THE KILLER WAS FOUND IN THE LAB WHERE THE EXPLOSION TOOK PLACE. BUT LITTLE OF THE BODY REMAINED ABOVE THE TORSO, SO IT MAY TAKE SOME TIME TO IDENTIFY...
......
SHINICHI IS...?
BEEN SLEEPING EVER SINCE.
WELL...AT LEAST HE'S SAFE...

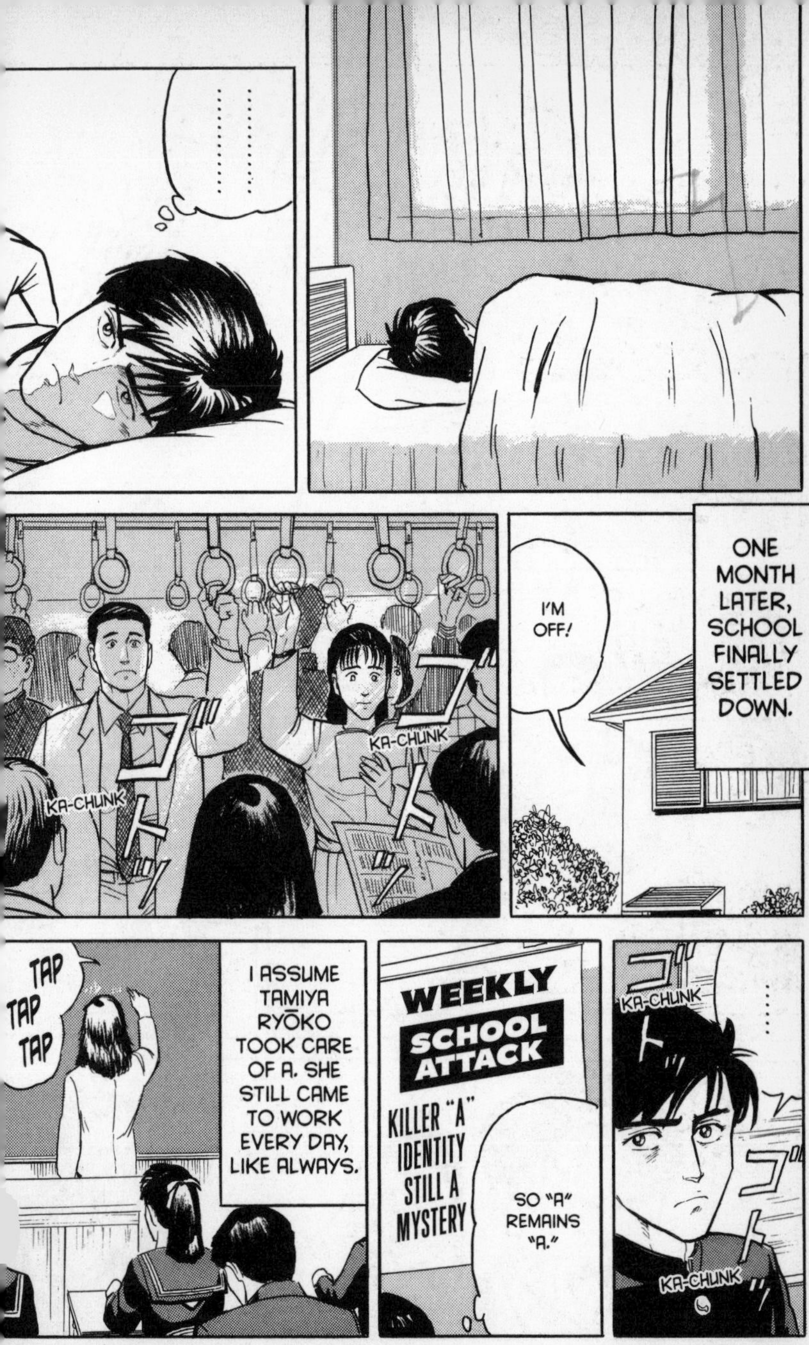
......
......
ONE MONTH LATER, SCHOOL FINALLY SETTLED DOWN.
I'M OFF!
KA-CHUNK
KA-CHUNK
......
KA-CHUNK
KA-CHUNK
WEEKLY SCHOOL ATTACK
KILLER "A" IDENTITY STILL A MYSTERY
SO "A" REMAINS "A."
I ASSUME TAMIYA RYŌKO TOOK CARE OF A. SHE STILL CAME TO WORK EVERY DAY, LIKE ALWAYS.
TAP TAP TAP

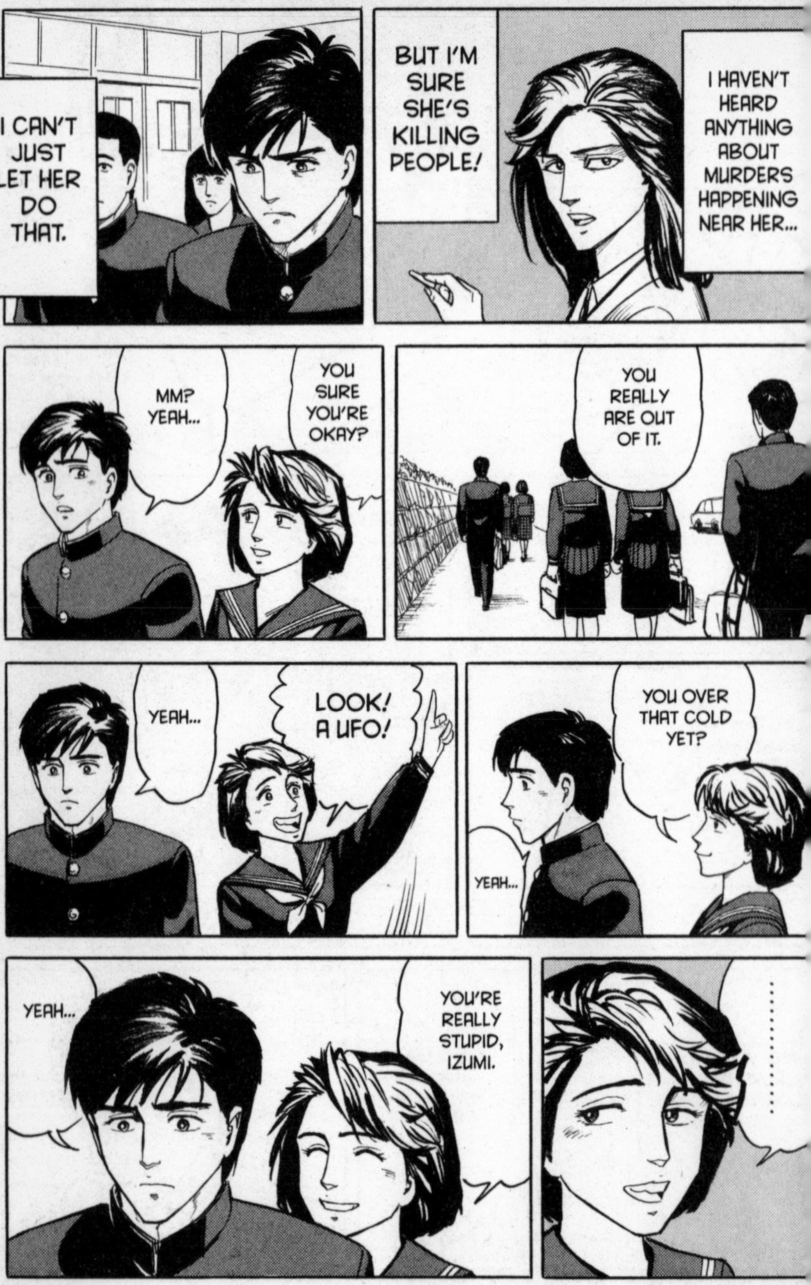
I HAVEN'T HEARD ANYTHING ABOUT MURDERS HAPPENING NEAR HER...
BUT I'M SURE SHE'S KILLING PEOPLE!
I CAN'T JUST LET HER DO THAT.
YOU REALLY ARE OUT OF IT.
YOU SURE YOU'RE OKAY?
MM? YEAH...
YOU OVER THAT COLD YET?
YEAH...
LOOK! A UFO!
YEAH...
....
YOU'RE REALLY STUPID, IZUMI.
YEAH...

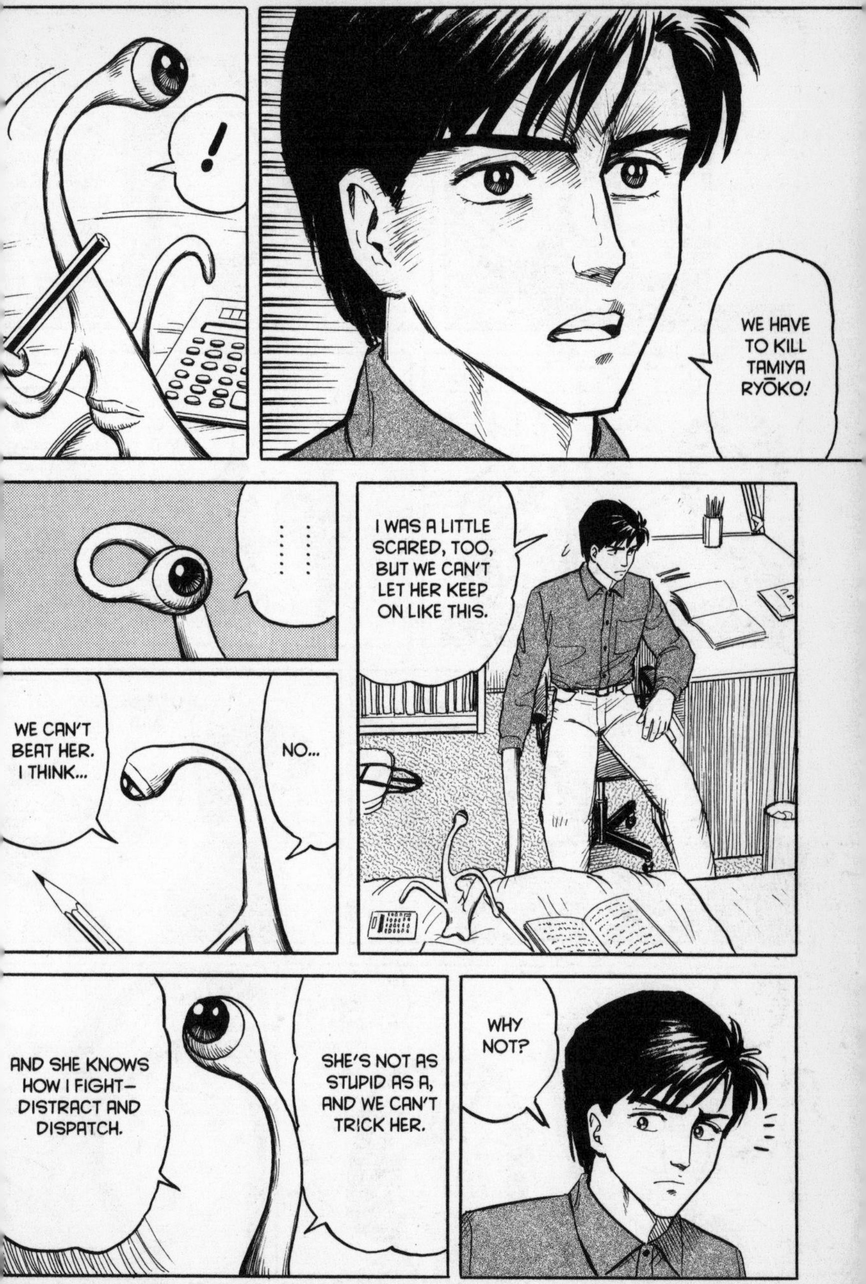
WE HAVE TO KILL TAMIYA RYŌKO!
!
I WAS A LITTLE SCARED, TOO, BUT WE CAN'T LET HER KEEP ON LIKE THIS.
......
NO...
WE CAN'T BEAT HER. I THINK...
WHY NOT?
SHE'S NOT AS STUPID AS A, AND WE CAN'T TRICK HER.
AND SHE KNOWS HOW I FIGHT— DISTRACT AND DISPATCH.

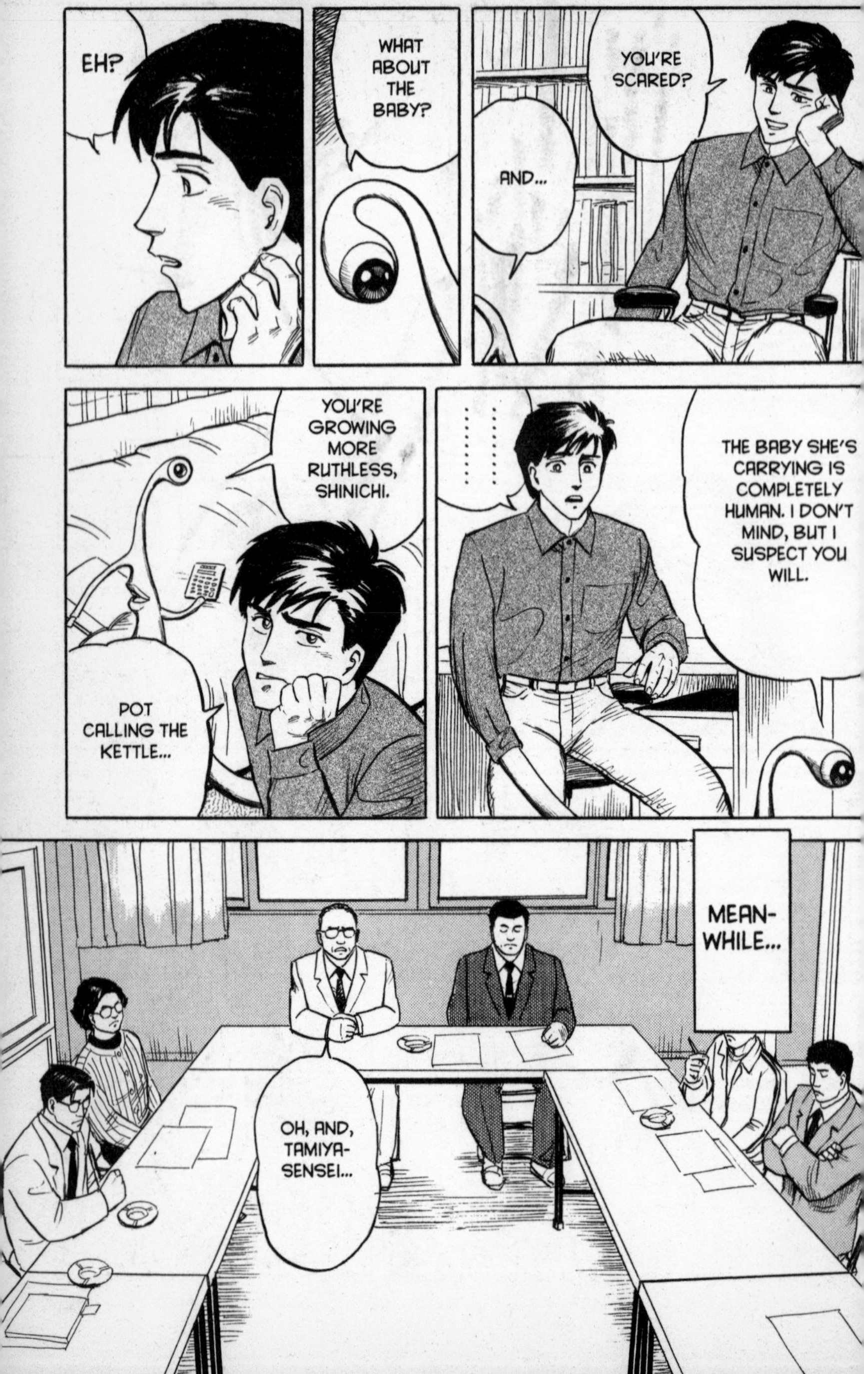
YOU'RE SCARED?
AND...
WHAT ABOUT THE BABY?
EH?
THE BABY SHE'S CARRYING IS COMPLETELY HUMAN. I DON'T MIND, BUT I SUSPECT YOU WILL.
......
YOU'RE GROWING MORE RUTHLESS, SHINICHI.
POT CALLING THE KETTLE...
MEAN-WHILE...
OH, AND, TAMIYA-SENSEI...

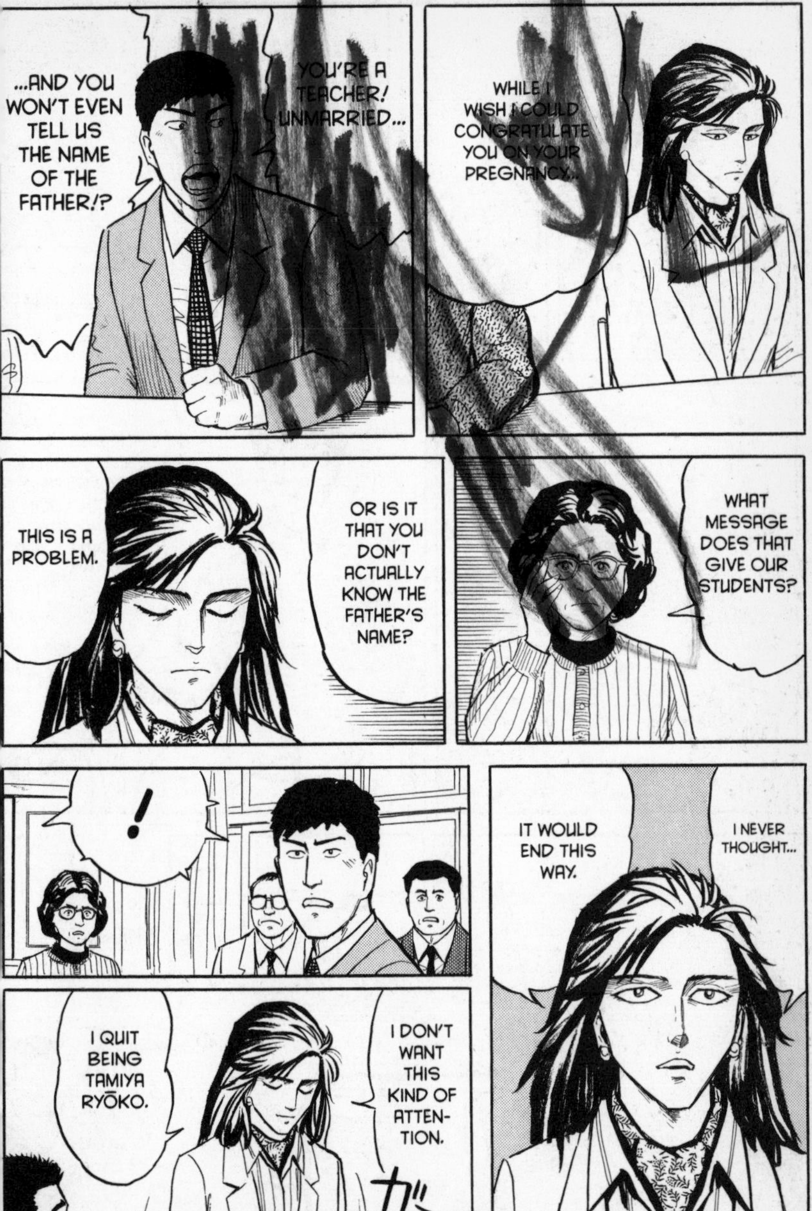
WHILE I WISH I COULD CONGRATULATE YOU ON YOUR PREGNANCY...
YOU'RE A TEACHER! UNMARRIED...
...AND YOU WON'T EVEN TELL US THE NAME OF THE FATHER!?
WHAT MESSAGE DOES THAT GIVE OUR STUDENTS?
OR IS IT THAT YOU DON'T ACTUALLY KNOW THE FATHER'S NAME?
THIS IS A PROBLEM.
I NEVER THOUGHT...
IT WOULD END THIS WAY.
!
I DON'T WANT THIS KIND OF ATTENTION.
I QUIT BEING TAMIYA RYŌKO.
ガ
SCRAPE
タッ

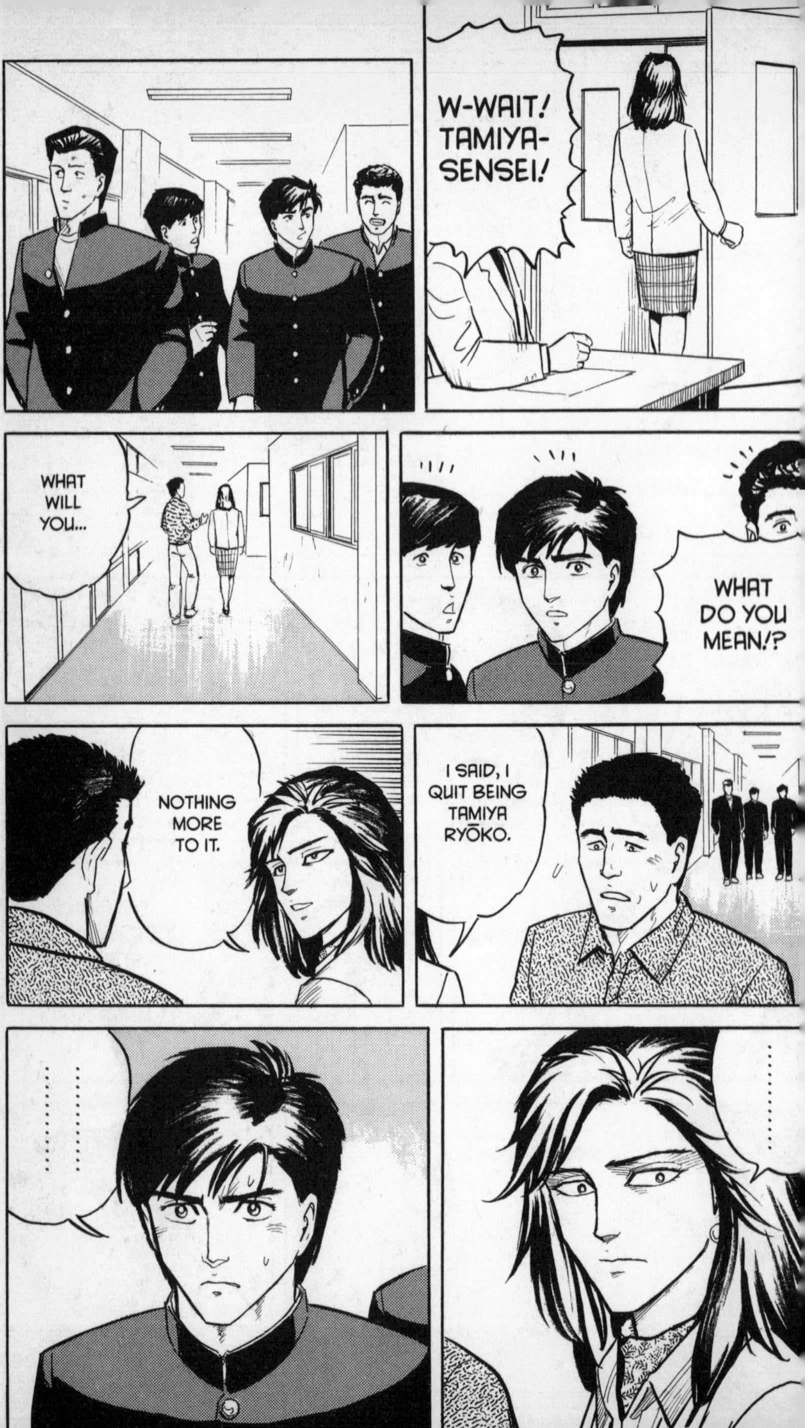
W-WAIT! TAMIYA-SENSEI!
WHAT DO YOU MEAN!?
WHAT WILL YOU...
I SAID, I QUIT BEING TAMIYA RYŌKO.
NOTHING MORE TO IT.
......
......

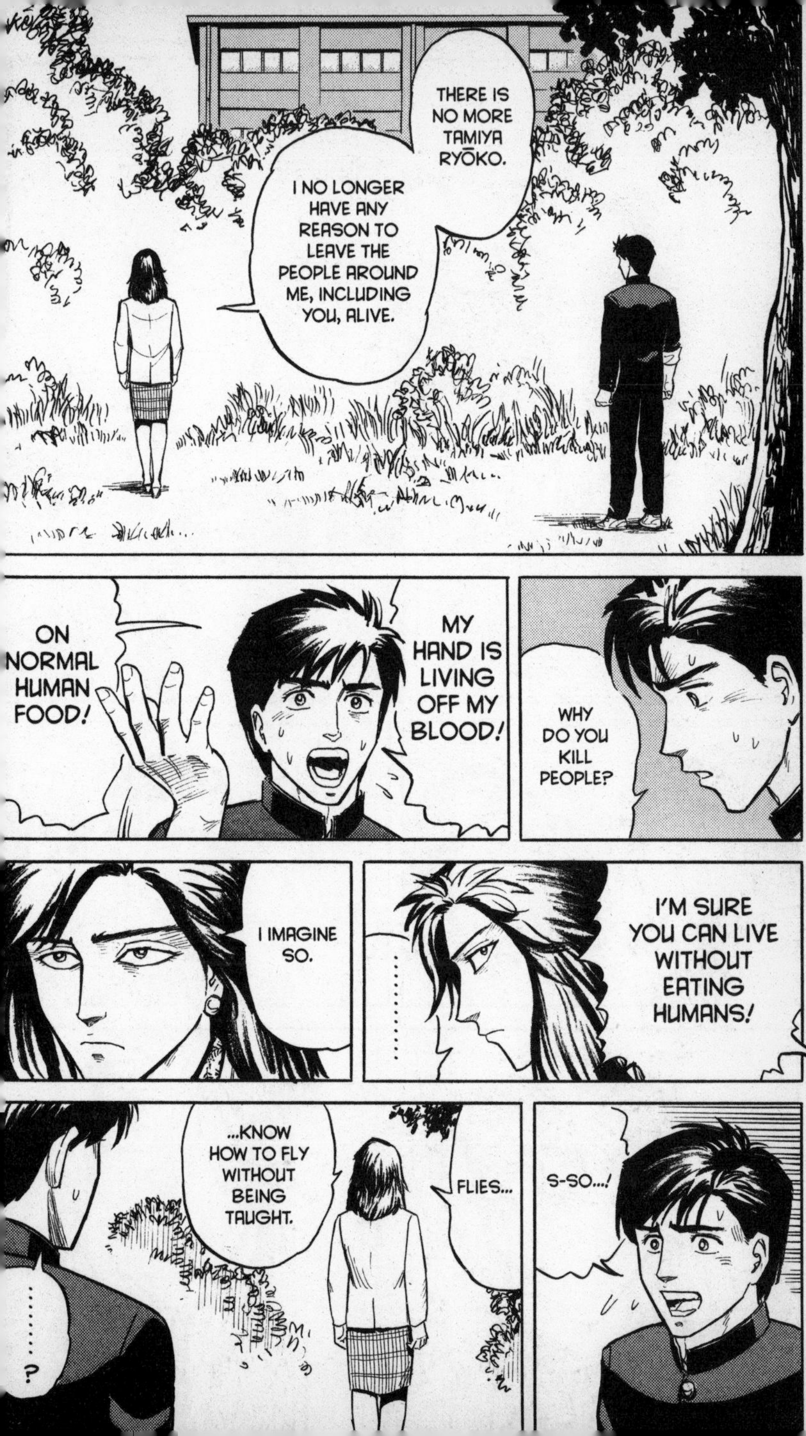
THERE IS NO MORE TAMIYA RYŌKO.
I NO LONGER HAVE ANY REASON TO LEAVE THE PEOPLE AROUND ME, INCLUDING YOU, ALIVE.
WHY DO YOU KILL PEOPLE?
MY HAND IS LIVING OFF MY BLOOD!
ON NORMAL HUMAN FOOD!
I'M SURE YOU CAN LIVE WITHOUT EATING HUMANS!
....
I IMAGINE SO.
S-SO...!
FLIES...
...KNOW HOW TO FLY WITHOUT BEING TAUGHT.
........?

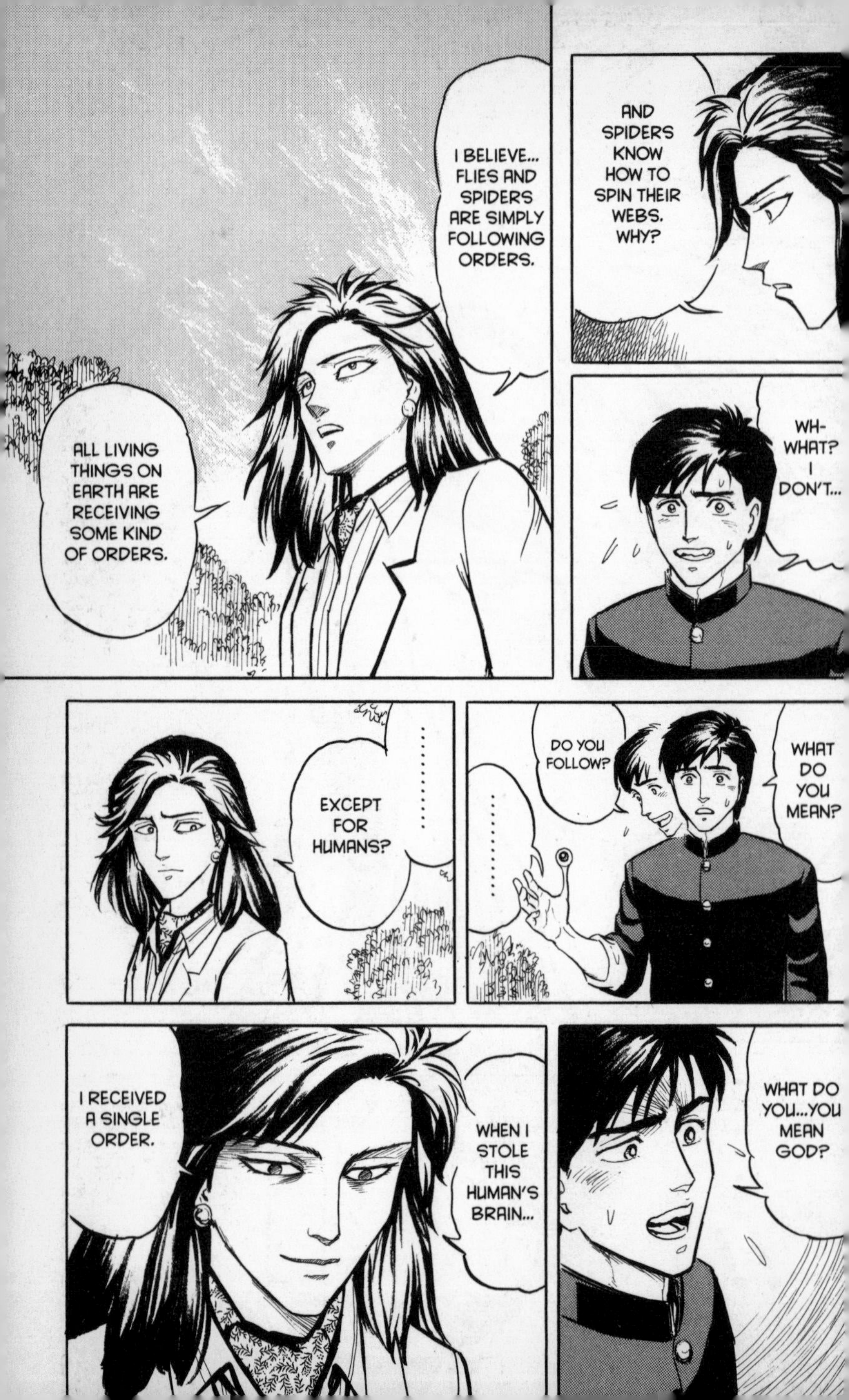
AND SPIDERS KNOW HOW TO SPIN THEIR WEBS. WHY?
WH-WHAT? I DON'T...
I BELIEVE... FLIES AND SPIDERS ARE SIMPLY FOLLOWING ORDERS.
ALL LIVING THINGS ON EARTH ARE RECEIVING SOME KIND OF ORDERS.
WHAT DO YOU MEAN?
DO YOU FOLLOW?
......
......
EXCEPT FOR HUMANS?
WHAT DO YOU...YOU MEAN GOD?
WHEN I STOLE THIS HUMAN'S BRAIN...
I RECEIVED A SINGLE ORDER.

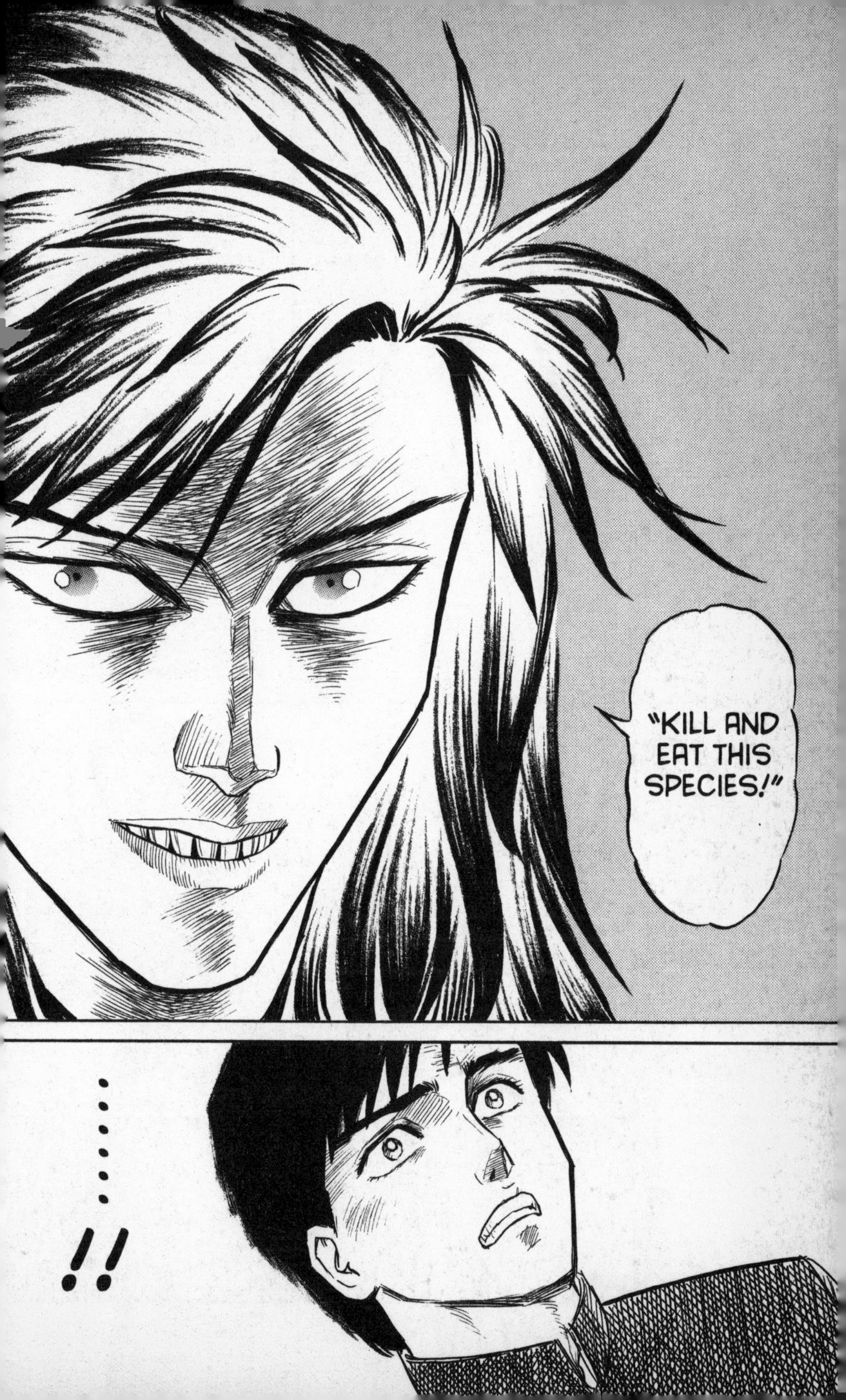
"KILL AND EAT THIS SPECIES!"
......
!!

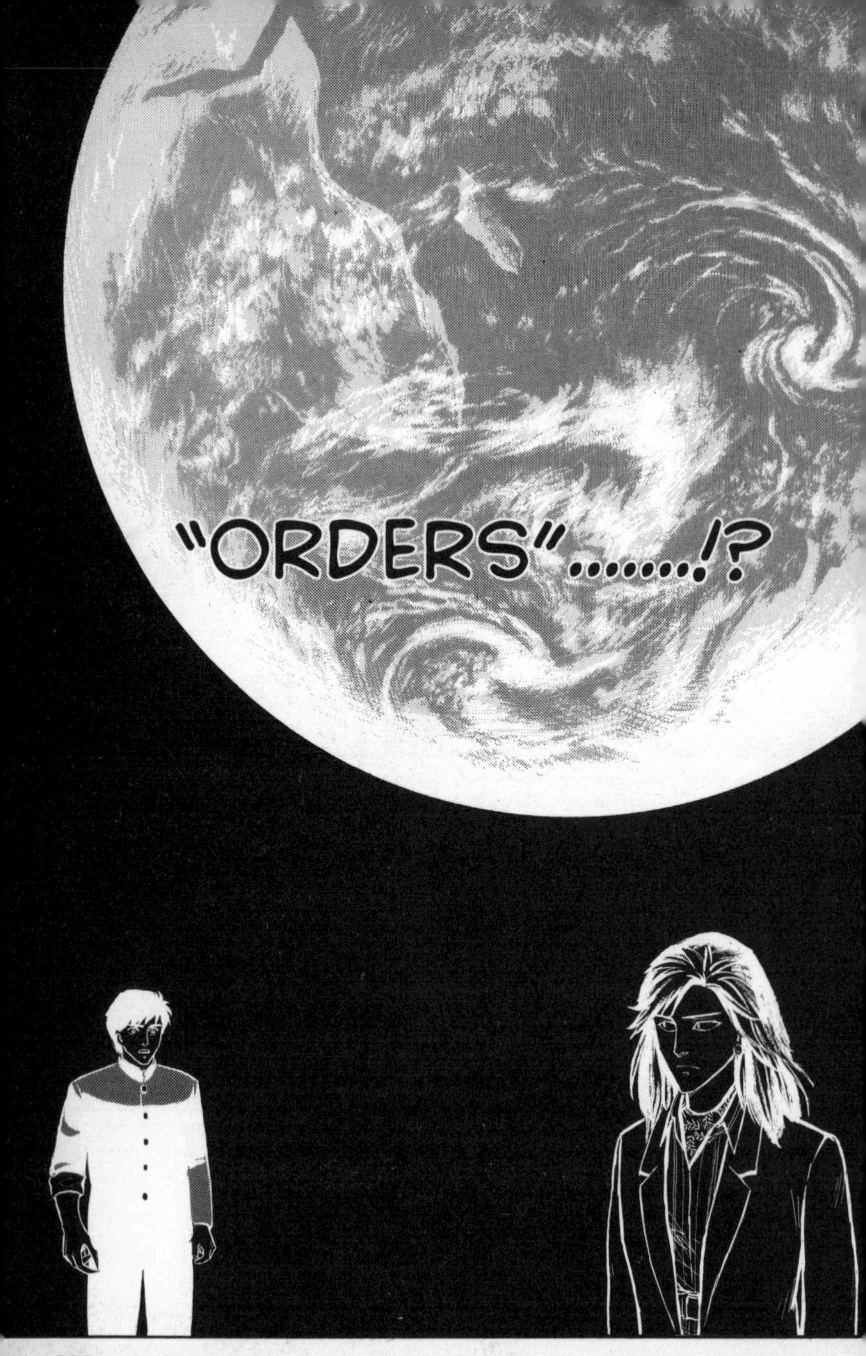
"ORDERS"........!?

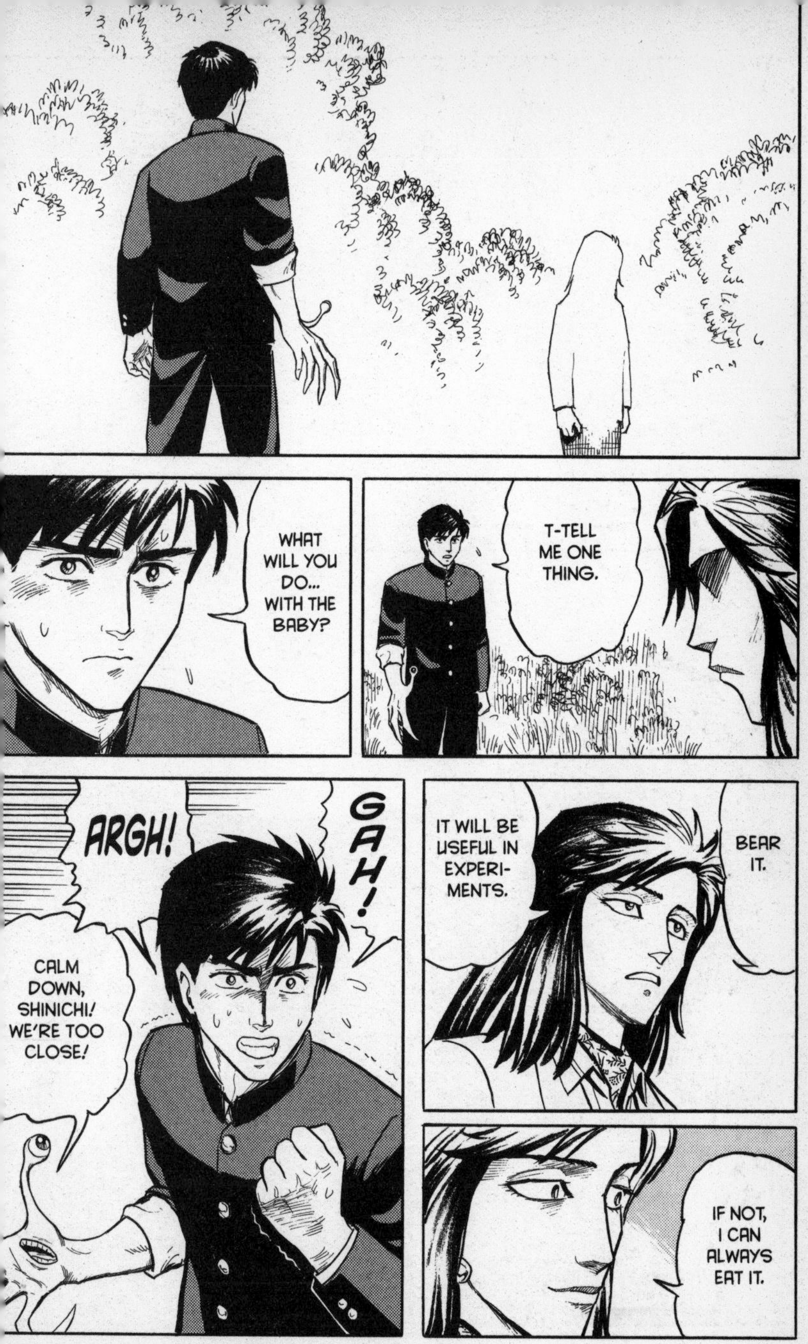

T-TELL ME ONE THING.
WHAT WILL YOU DO... WITH THE BABY?
BEAR IT.
IT WILL BE USEFUL IN EXPERI-MENTS.
IF NOT, I CAN ALWAYS EAT IT.
GAH!
ARGH!
CALM DOWN, SHINICHI! WE'RE TOO CLOSE!

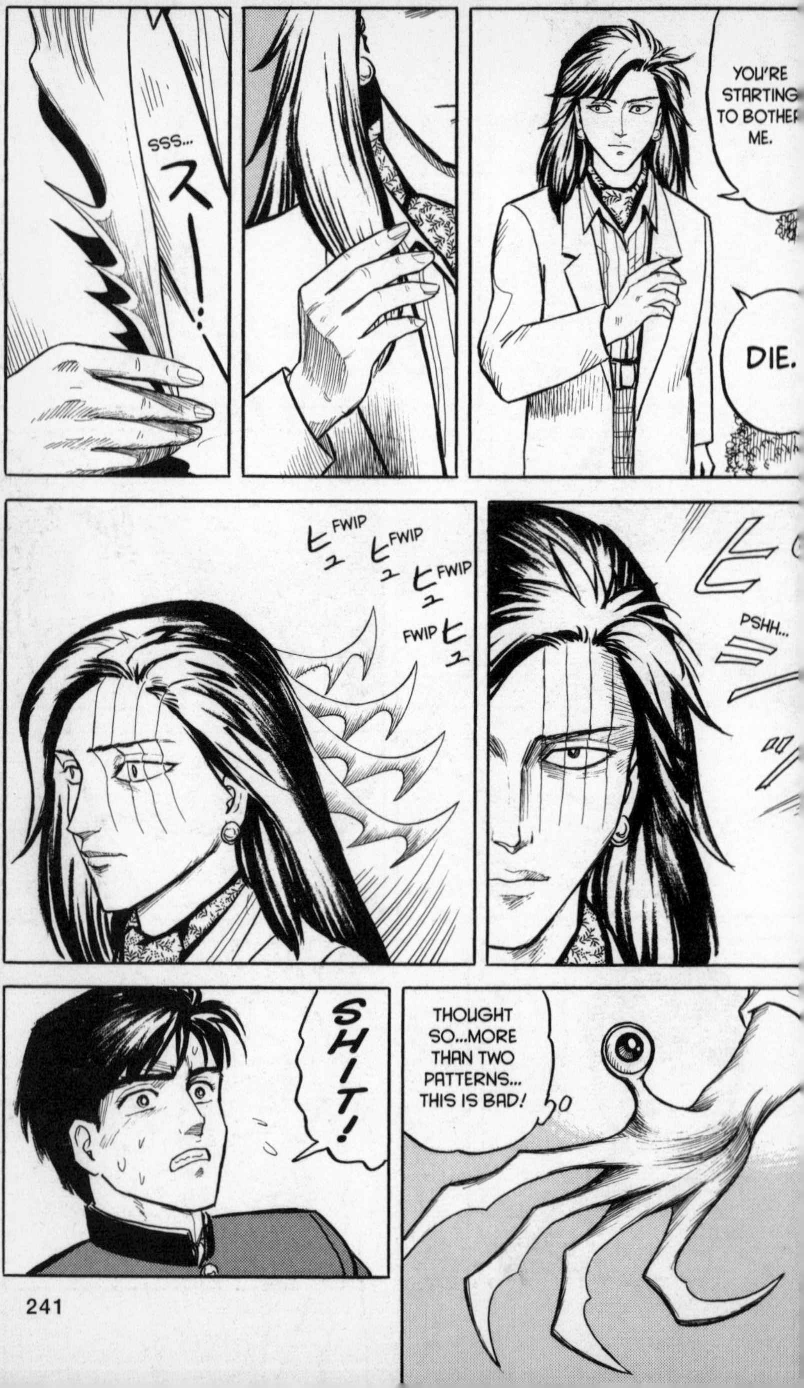
YOU'RE STARTING TO BOTHER ME.
DIE.
SSS...
スー
PSHH...
FWIP
FWIP
FWIP
FWIP
THOUGHT SO...MORE THAN TWO PATTERNS... THIS IS BAD!
SHIT!

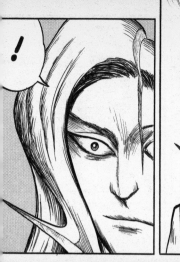

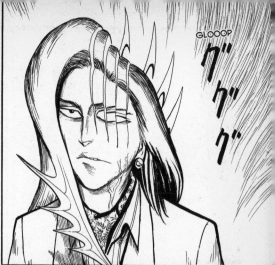

GLOOOP

 グ
グ
グ

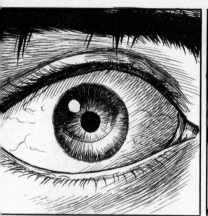

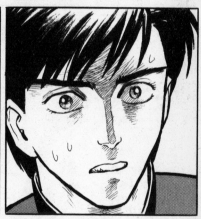

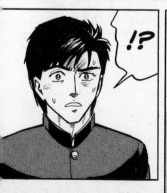

!?

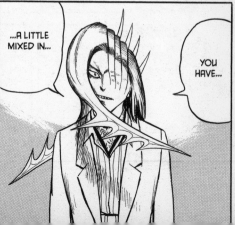

...A LITTLE
MIXED IN...

YOU
HAVE...

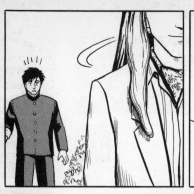

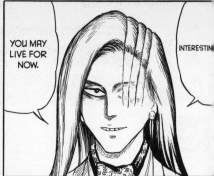

YOU MAY LIVE FOR NOW.

INTERESTING

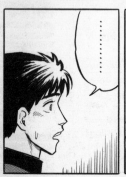

. . . .

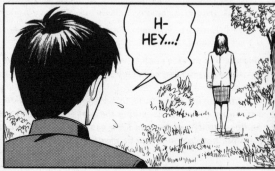

H- HEY...!

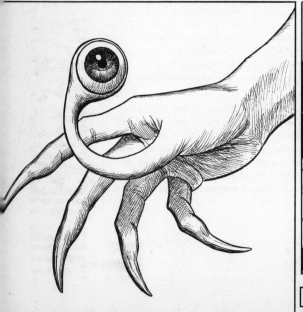

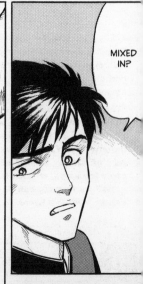

MIXED IN?

CHAPTER 8: THE EN

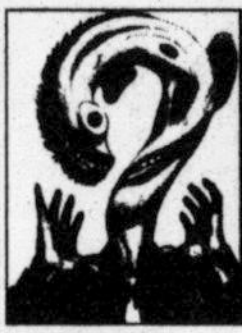

From the Monthly Afternoon Readers' page...

vol. 2

PARASYTE [PERFECT EDITION] 1

THE READERS ASK, THE AUTHOR ANSWERS

"This impressed me more than any novel or movie. Not just sci-fi horror—it made me think about the strengths and weaknesses of mankind." (Hyogo Prefecture, Ikeda Nobuo, 33, Office Worker)

"I hope they make a movie out of *Parasyte*. I think Cronenberg could do a great job with it." (Tokyo, Yuuji, 20, Student)

"Manga and movies each have their own essence and flexibility, so bad works can suddenly shine when filmed, or the other way around.

"The movies I like tend to be like a single life-form from beginning to end. Presumably the makers put their blood and bodies into it, and captured the essence of the work. Without passion, nothing good can be made." (Hitoshi Iwaaki)

(From *Afternoon*, August 1991)

"Reading *Parasyte* makes me think about human arrogance (toward nature), makes me wonder if humans are denying the fact that they are part of nature. Iwaaki-san, what do you think about artificial versus natural?"

"The word 'nature' can mean many things. In the narrowest sense of the word, then, artificial and natural are opposites. The nature we humans are trying to protect fits that narrow definition. But in the broader sense of the word, humans are part of nature. Even if we become arrogant, pollute and destroy the world, that is all part of nature.

"All we humans can do is protect nature as we would ourselves." (Hitoshi Iwaaki)

(From *Afternoon*, December 1991)

CHAPTER 9: MOTHER

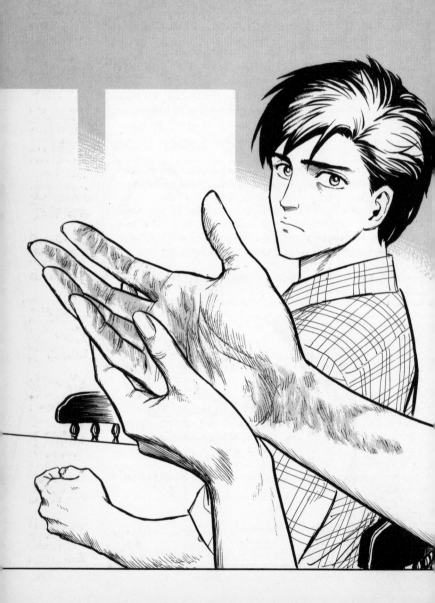

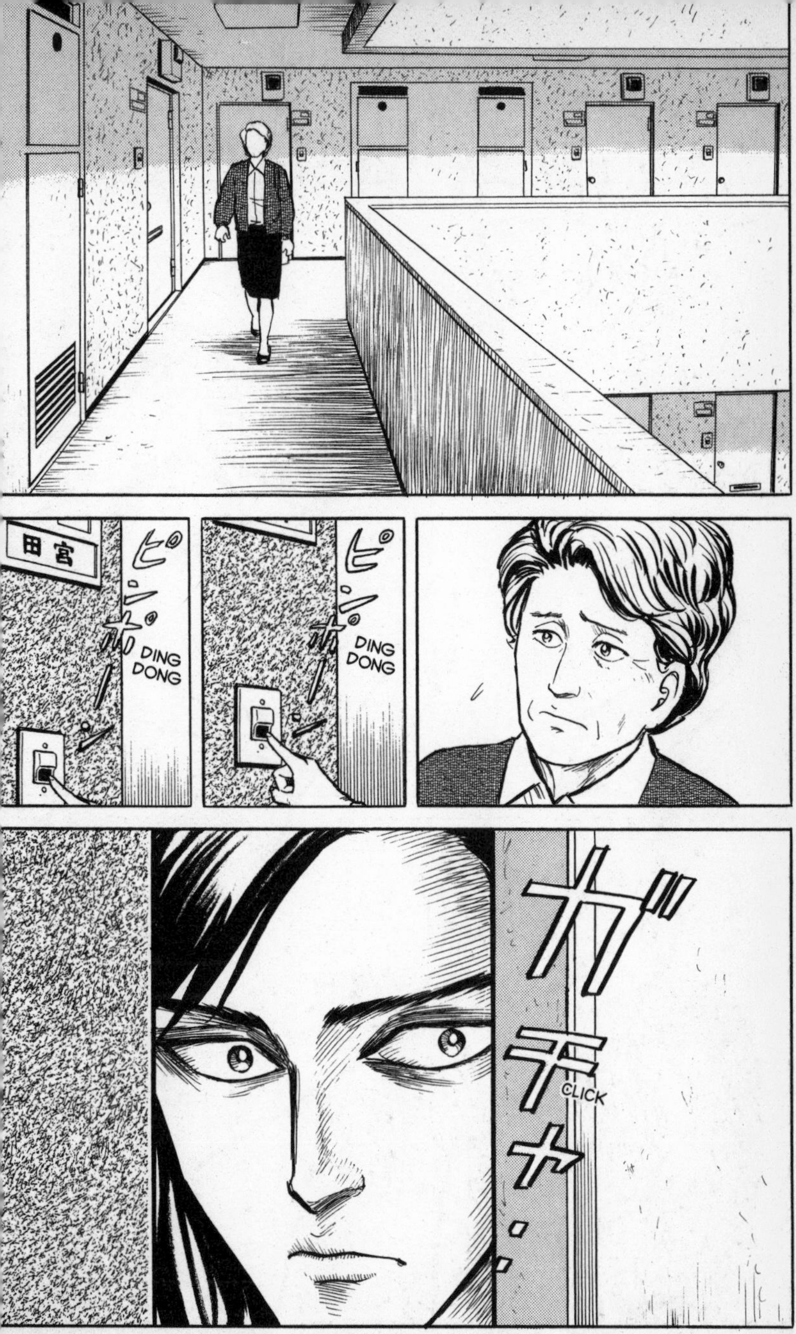
ピンポーン
DING DONG
田宮
ピンポーン
DING DONG
ガチャ
CLICK

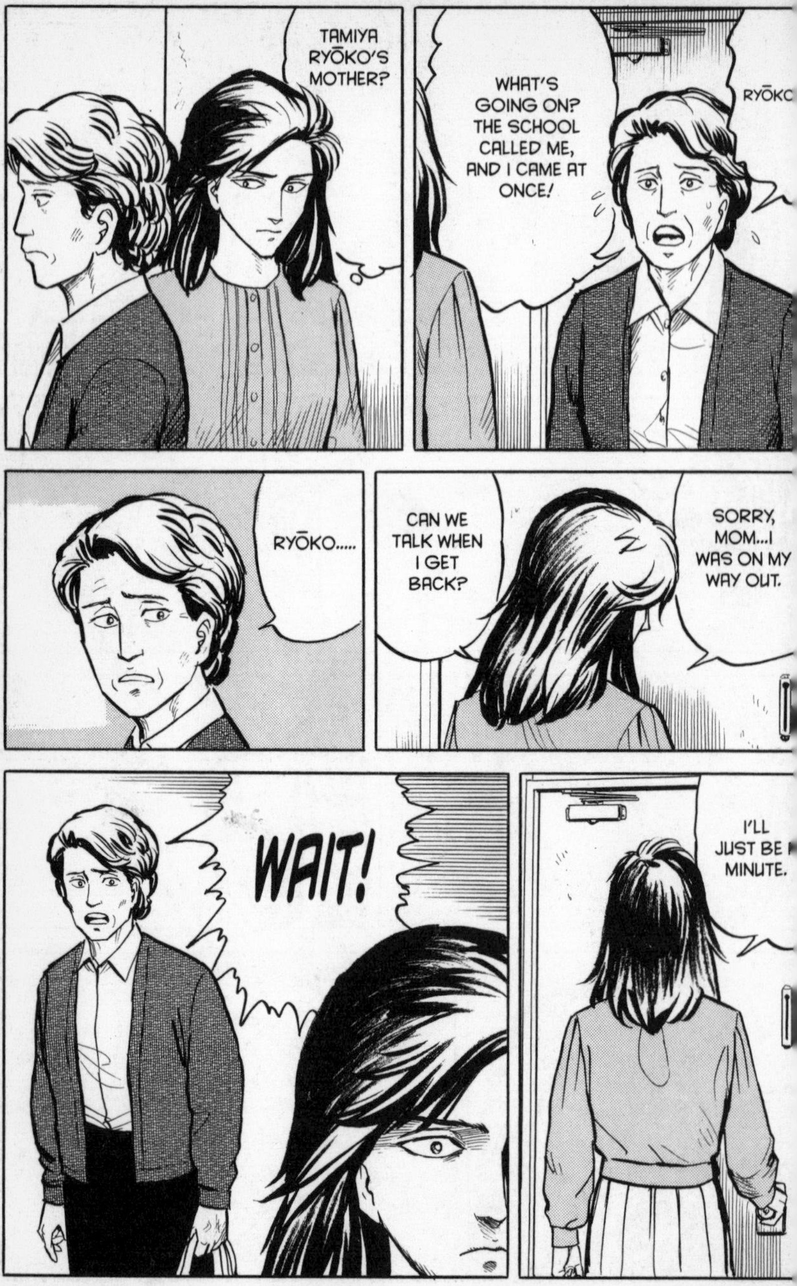
RYŌK
WHAT'S GOING ON? THE SCHOOL CALLED ME, AND I CAME AT ONCE!
TAMIYA RYŌKO'S MOTHER?
SORRY, MOM...I WAS ON MY WAY OUT.
CAN WE TALK WHEN I GET BACK?
RYŌKO.....
I'LL JUST BE MINUTE.
WAIT!

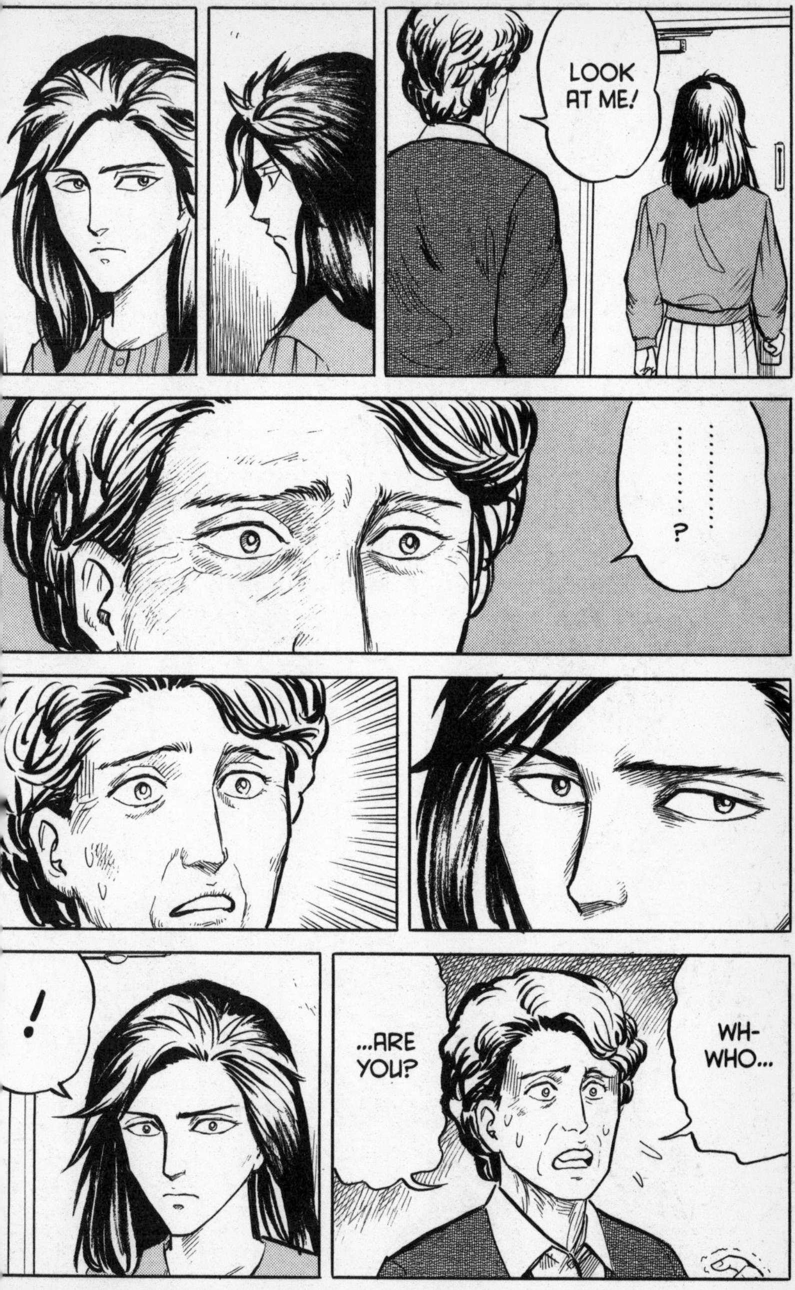
LOOK AT ME!
......?
WH- WHO...
...ARE YOU?
!

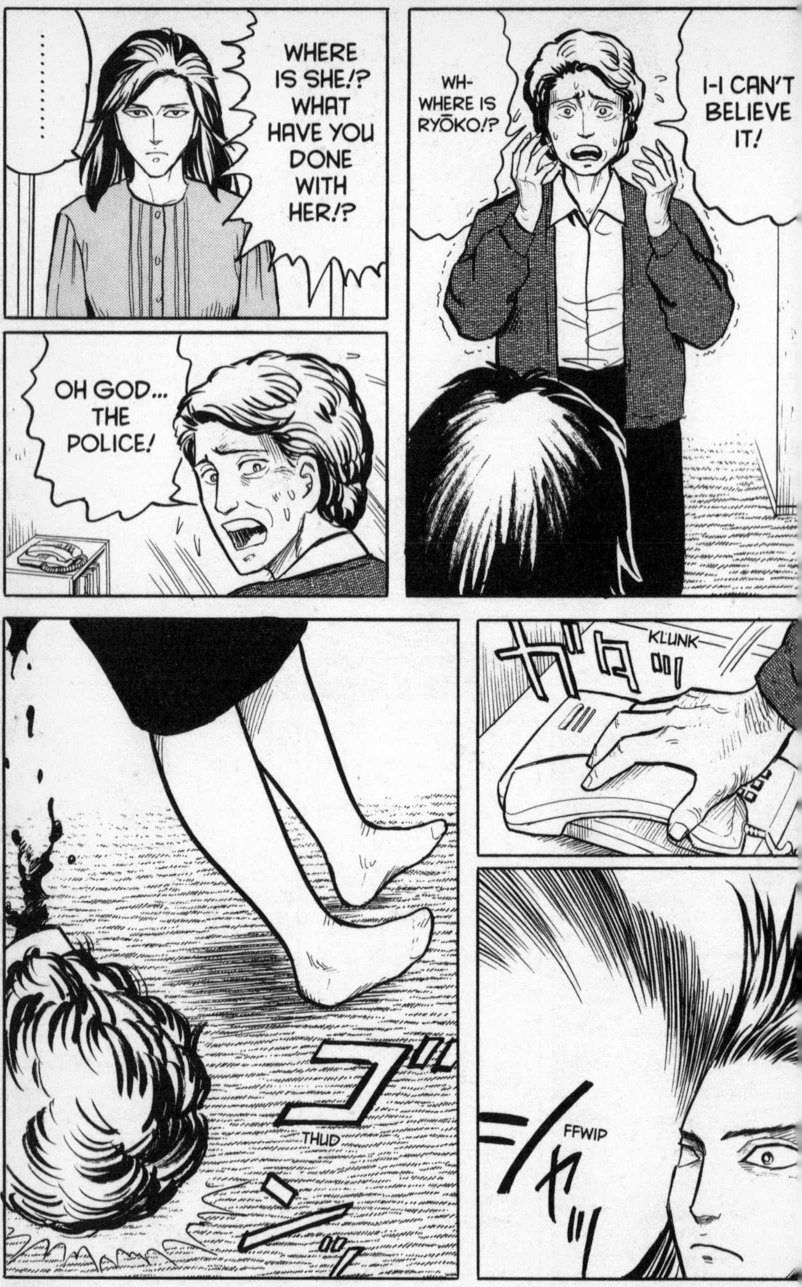
I-I CAN'T BELIEVE IT!
WH- WHERE IS RYŌKO!?
WHERE IS SHE!? WHAT HAVE YOU DONE WITH HER!?
......
OH GOD... THE POLICE!
KLUNK
FFWIP
THUD

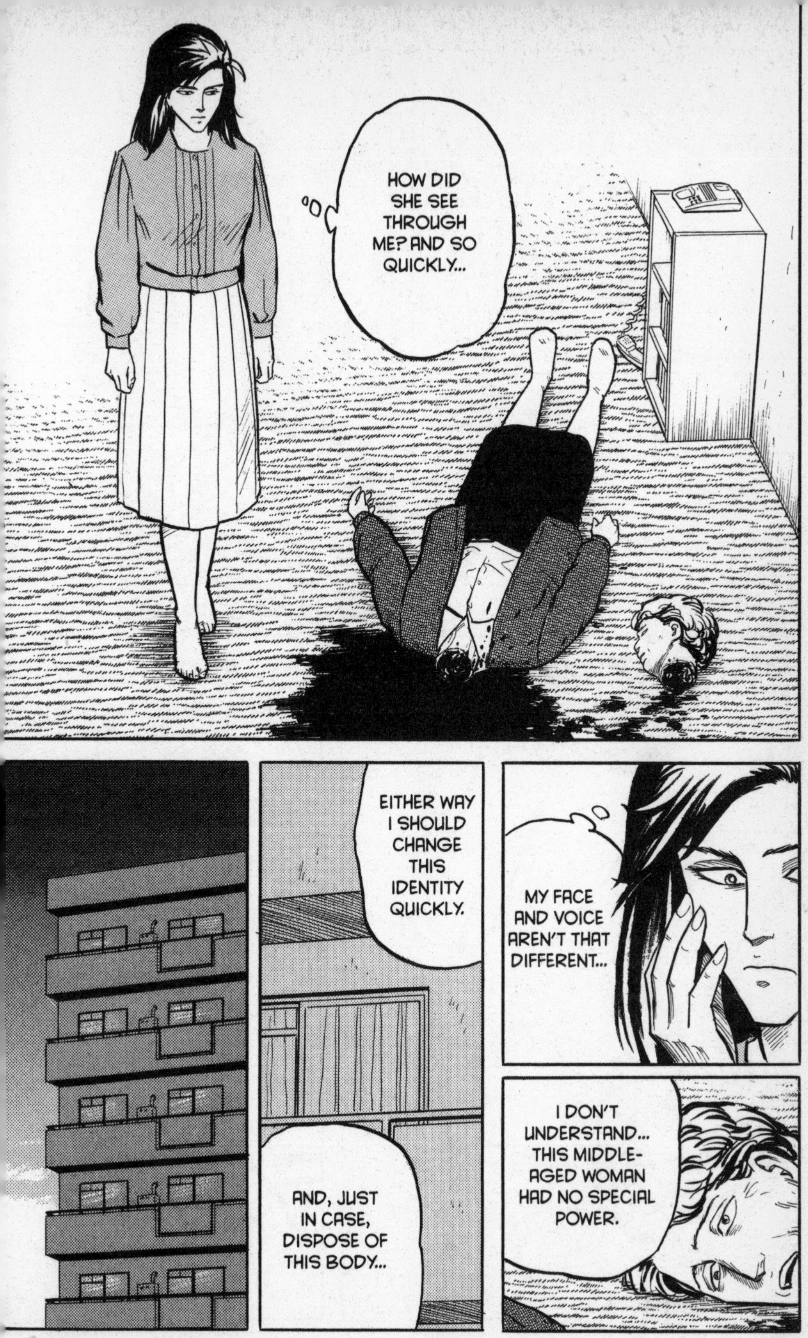
HOW DID SHE SEE THROUGH ME? AND SO QUICKLY...
MY FACE AND VOICE AREN'T THAT DIFFERENT...
I DON'T UNDERSTAND... THIS MIDDLE-AGED WOMAN HAD NO SPECIAL POWER.
EITHER WAY I SHOULD CHANGE THIS IDENTITY QUICKLY.
AND, JUST IN CASE, DISPOSE OF THIS BODY...

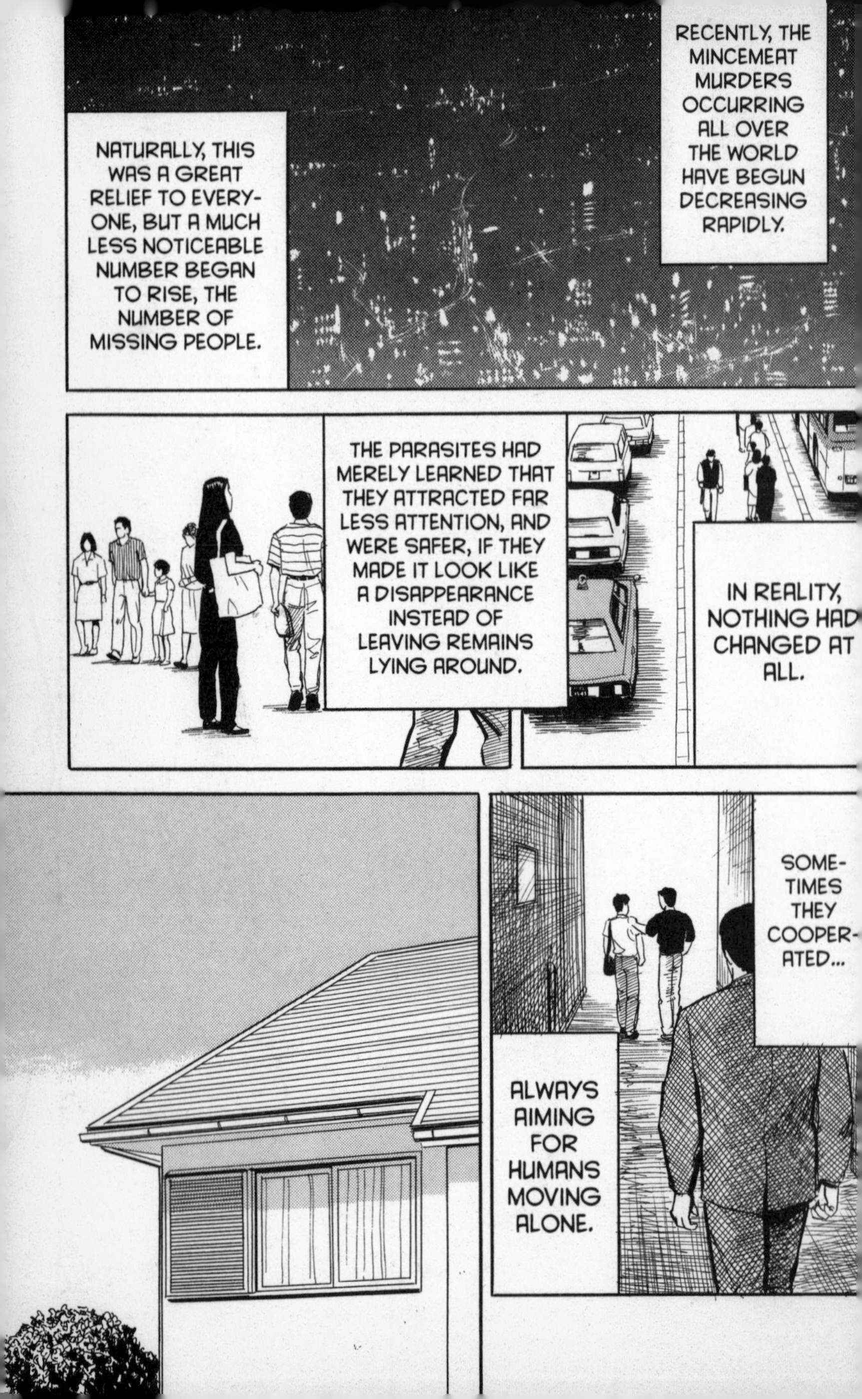
RECENTLY, THE MINCEMEAT MURDERS OCCURRING ALL OVER THE WORLD HAVE BEGUN DECREASING RAPIDLY.
NATURALLY, THIS WAS A GREAT RELIEF TO EVERY-ONE, BUT A MUCH LESS NOTICEABLE NUMBER BEGAN TO RISE, THE NUMBER OF MISSING PEOPLE.
IN REALITY, NOTHING HAD CHANGED AT ALL.
THE PARASITES HAD MERELY LEARNED THAT THEY ATTRACTED FAR LESS ATTENTION, AND WERE SAFER, IF THEY MADE IT LOOK LIKE A DISAPPEARANCE INSTEAD OF LEAVING REMAINS LYING AROUND.
SOME-TIMES THEY COOPER-ATED...
ALWAYS AIMING FOR HUMANS MOVING ALONE.

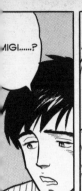

MIGI......?

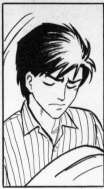

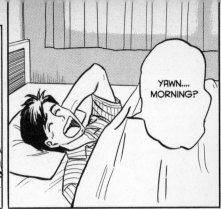

YAWN....
MORNING?

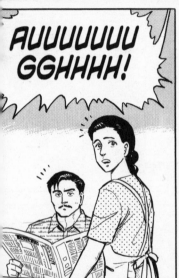

AUUUUUUU
GGHHHH!

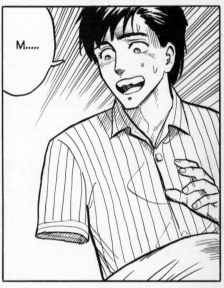

M......

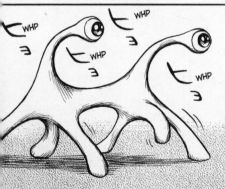

WHP
WHP
WHP
WHP

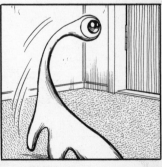

252

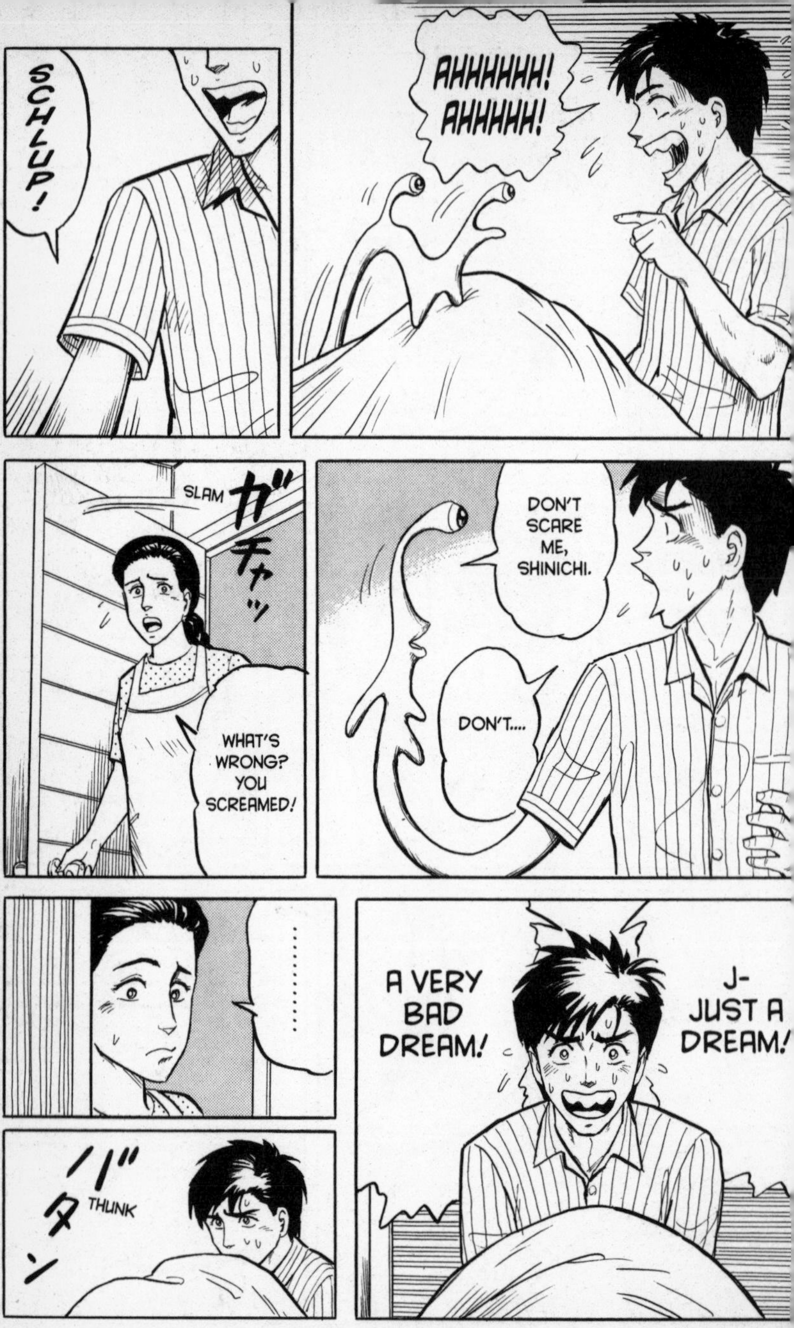
AHHHHHH! AHHHHH!
SCHLUP!
DON'T SCARE ME, SHINICHI.
DON'T....
SLAM
ガチャッ
WHAT'S WRONG? YOU SCREAMED!
J- JUST A DREAM!
A VERY BAD DREAM!
......
バタン
THUNK

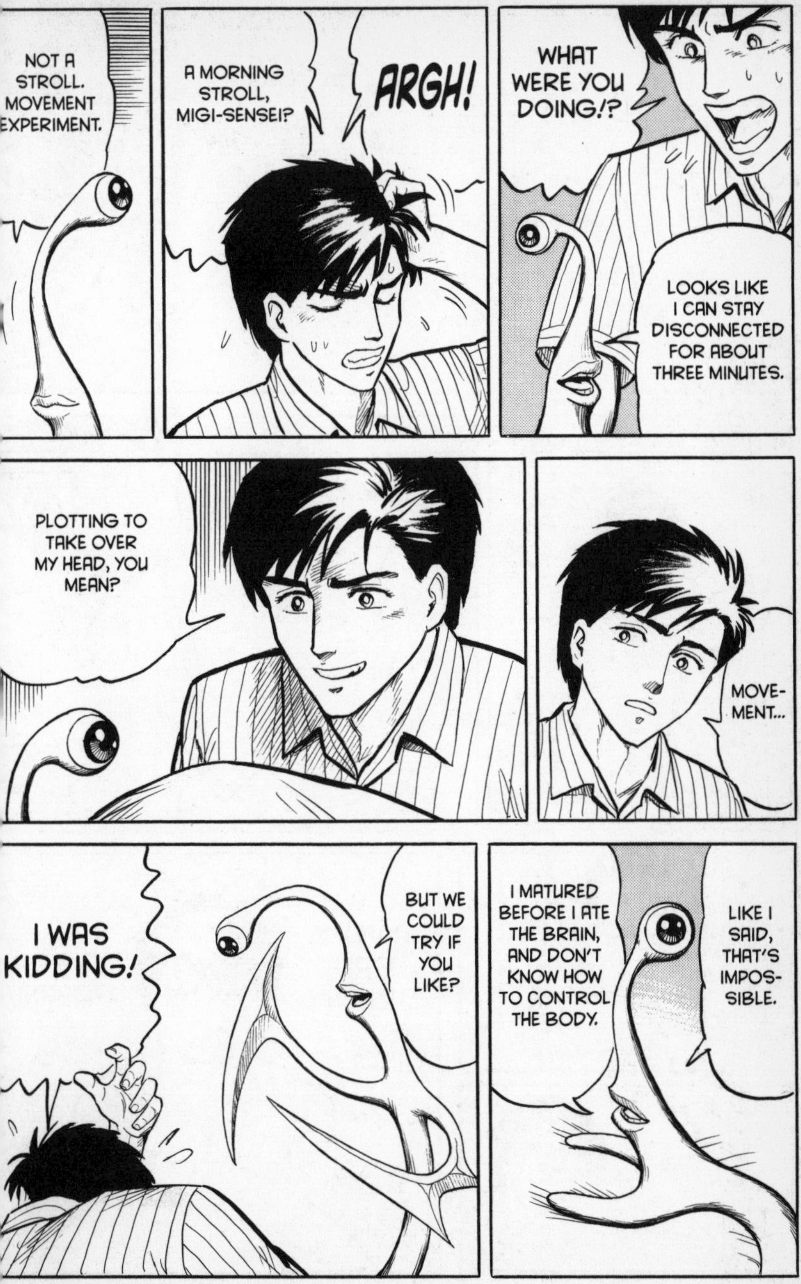
WHAT WERE YOU DOING!?
LOOKS LIKE I CAN STAY DISCONNECTED FOR ABOUT THREE MINUTES.
ARGH!
A MORNING STROLL, MIGI-SENSEI?
NOT A STROLL. MOVEMENT EXPERIMENT.
MOVE-MENT...
PLOTTING TO TAKE OVER MY HEAD, YOU MEAN?
LIKE I SAID, THAT'S IMPOS-SIBLE.
I MATURED BEFORE I ATE THE BRAIN, AND DON'T KNOW HOW TO CONTROL THE BODY.
BUT WE COULD TRY IF YOU LIKE?
I WAS KIDDING!

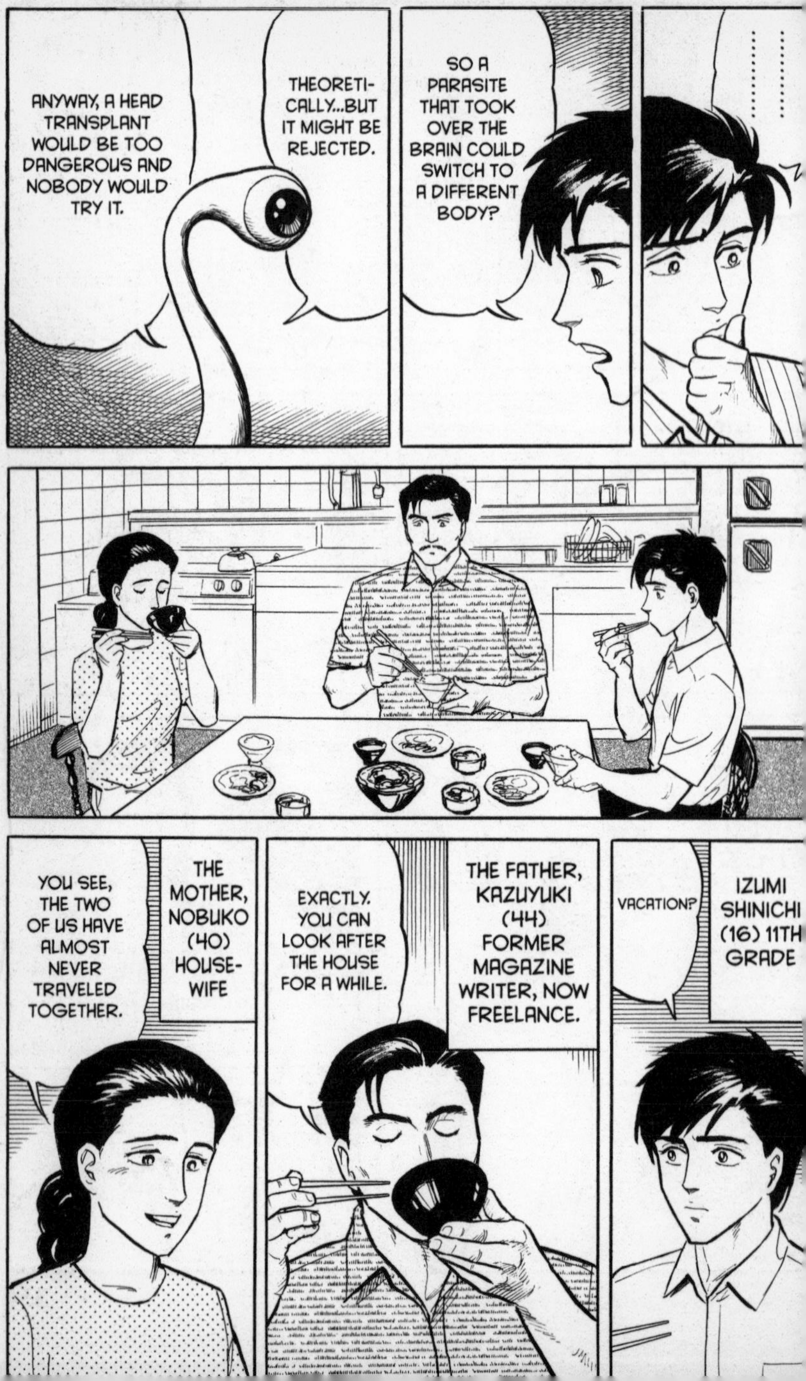
......
SO A PARASITE THAT TOOK OVER THE BRAIN COULD SWITCH TO A DIFFERENT BODY?
THEORETICALLY...BUT IT MIGHT BE REJECTED.
ANYWAY, A HEAD TRANSPLANT WOULD BE TOO DANGEROUS AND NOBODY WOULD TRY IT.
IZUMI SHINICHI (16) 11TH GRADE
VACATION?
THE FATHER, KAZUYUKI (44) FORMER MAGAZINE WRITER, NOW FREELANCE.
EXACTLY. YOU CAN LOOK AFTER THE HOUSE FOR A WHILE.
THE MOTHER, NOBUKO (40) HOUSEWIFE
YOU SEE, THE TWO OF US HAVE ALMOST NEVER TRAVELED TOGETHER.

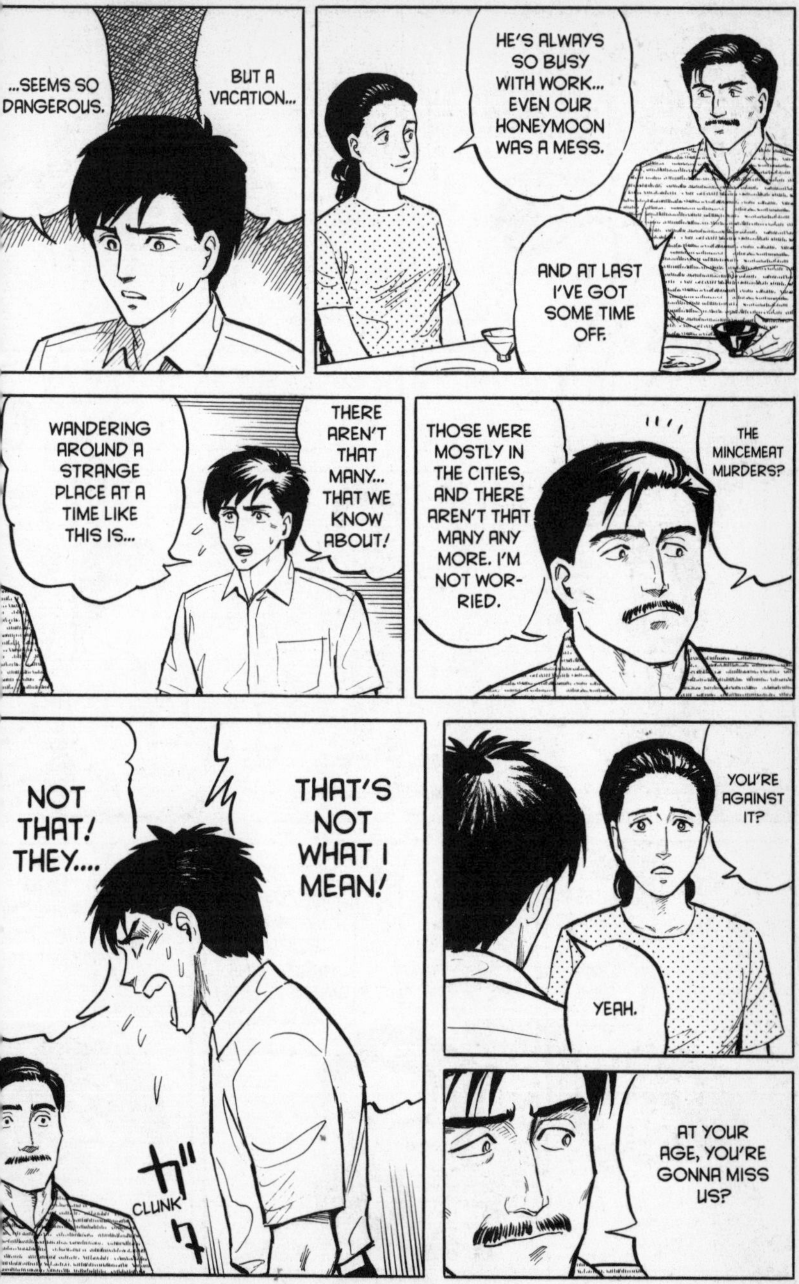
HE'S ALWAYS SO BUSY WITH WORK... EVEN OUR HONEYMOON WAS A MESS.
AND AT LAST I'VE GOT SOME TIME OFF.
BUT A VACATION...
...SEEMS SO DANGEROUS.
THE MINCEMEAT MURDERS?
THOSE WERE MOSTLY IN THE CITIES, AND THERE AREN'T THAT MANY ANY MORE. I'M NOT WOR-RIED.
THERE AREN'T THAT MANY... THAT WE KNOW ABOUT!
WANDERING AROUND A STRANGE PLACE AT A TIME LIKE THIS IS...
YOU'RE AGAINST IT?
YEAH.
AT YOUR AGE, YOU'RE GONNA MISS US?
THAT'S NOT WHAT I MEAN!
NOT THAT! THEY....
ガク
CLUNK

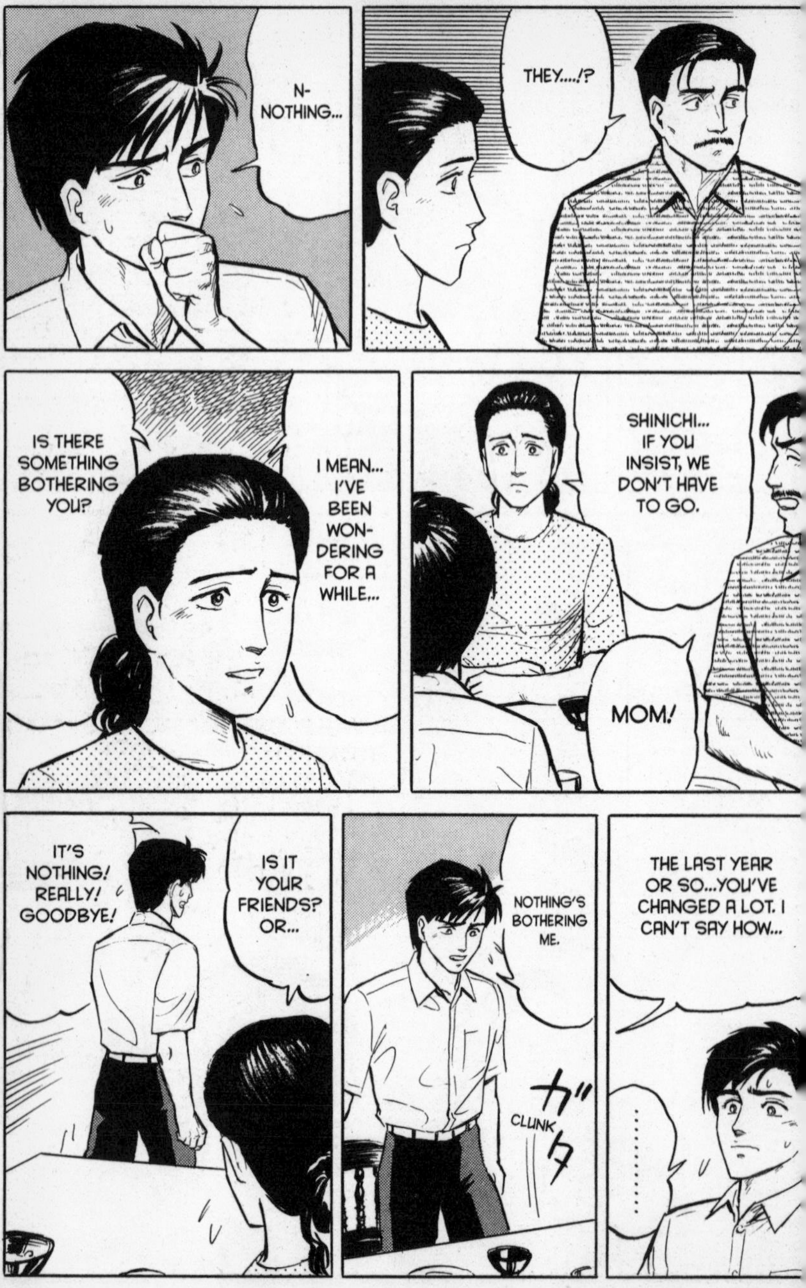
THEY....!?
N- NOTHING...
SHINICHI... IF YOU INSIST, WE DON'T HAVE TO GO.
MOM!
I MEAN... I'VE BEEN WONDERING FOR A WHILE...
IS THERE SOMETHING BOTHERING YOU?
THE LAST YEAR OR SO...YOU'VE CHANGED A LOT. I CAN'T SAY HOW...
......
NOTHING'S BOTHERING ME.
ガタ
CLUNK
IS IT YOUR FRIENDS? OR...
IT'S NOTHING! REALLY! GOODBYE!

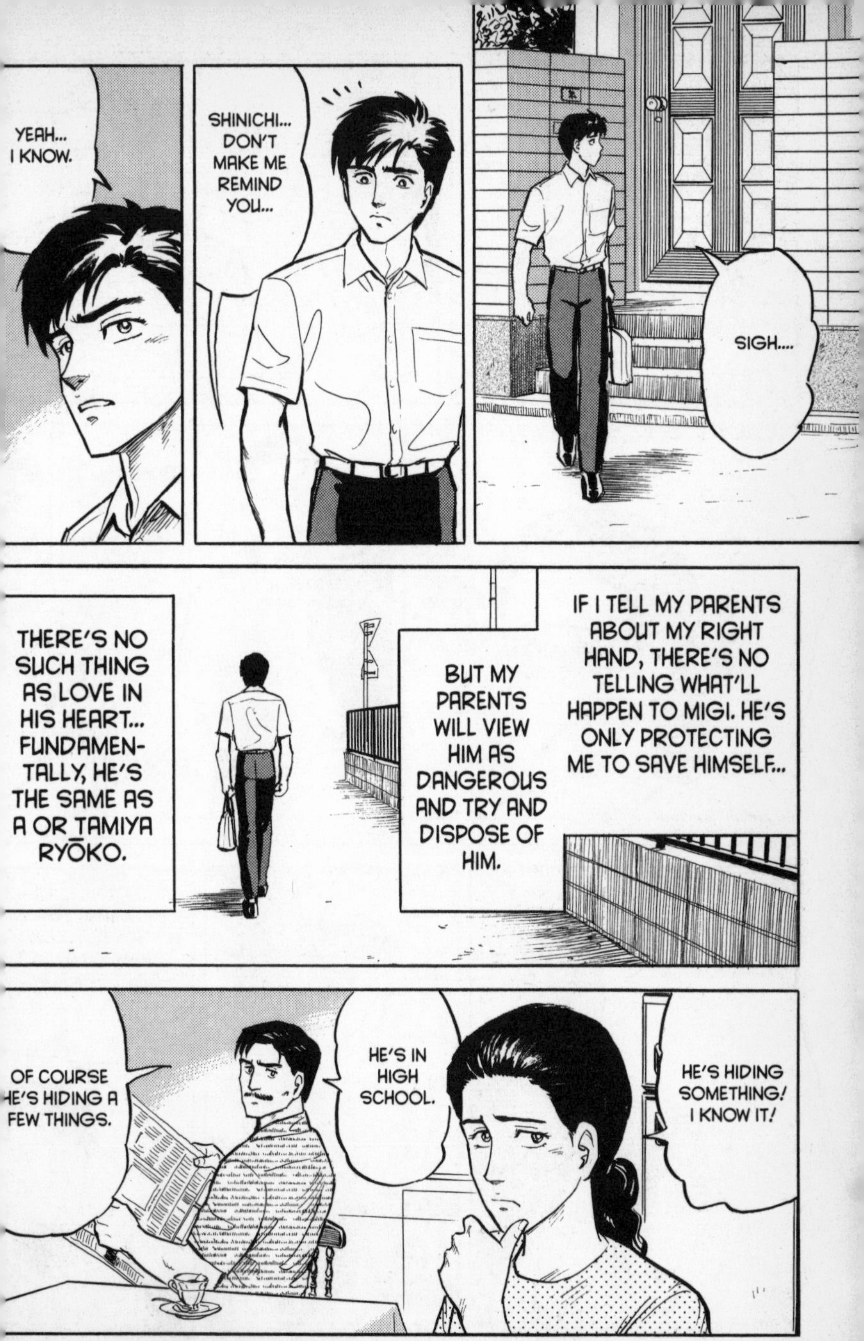
SIGH....
SHINICHI... DON'T MAKE ME REMIND YOU...
YEAH... I KNOW.
IF I TELL MY PARENTS ABOUT MY RIGHT HAND, THERE'S NO TELLING WHAT'LL HAPPEN TO MIGI. HE'S ONLY PROTECTING ME TO SAVE HIMSELF...
BUT MY PARENTS WILL VIEW HIM AS DANGEROUS AND TRY AND DISPOSE OF HIM.
THERE'S NO SUCH THING AS LOVE IN HIS HEART... FUNDAMENTALLY, HE'S THE SAME AS A OR TAMIYA RYŌKO.
HE'S HIDING SOMETHING! I KNOW IT!
HE'S IN HIGH SCHOOL.
OF COURSE HE'S HIDING A FEW THINGS.

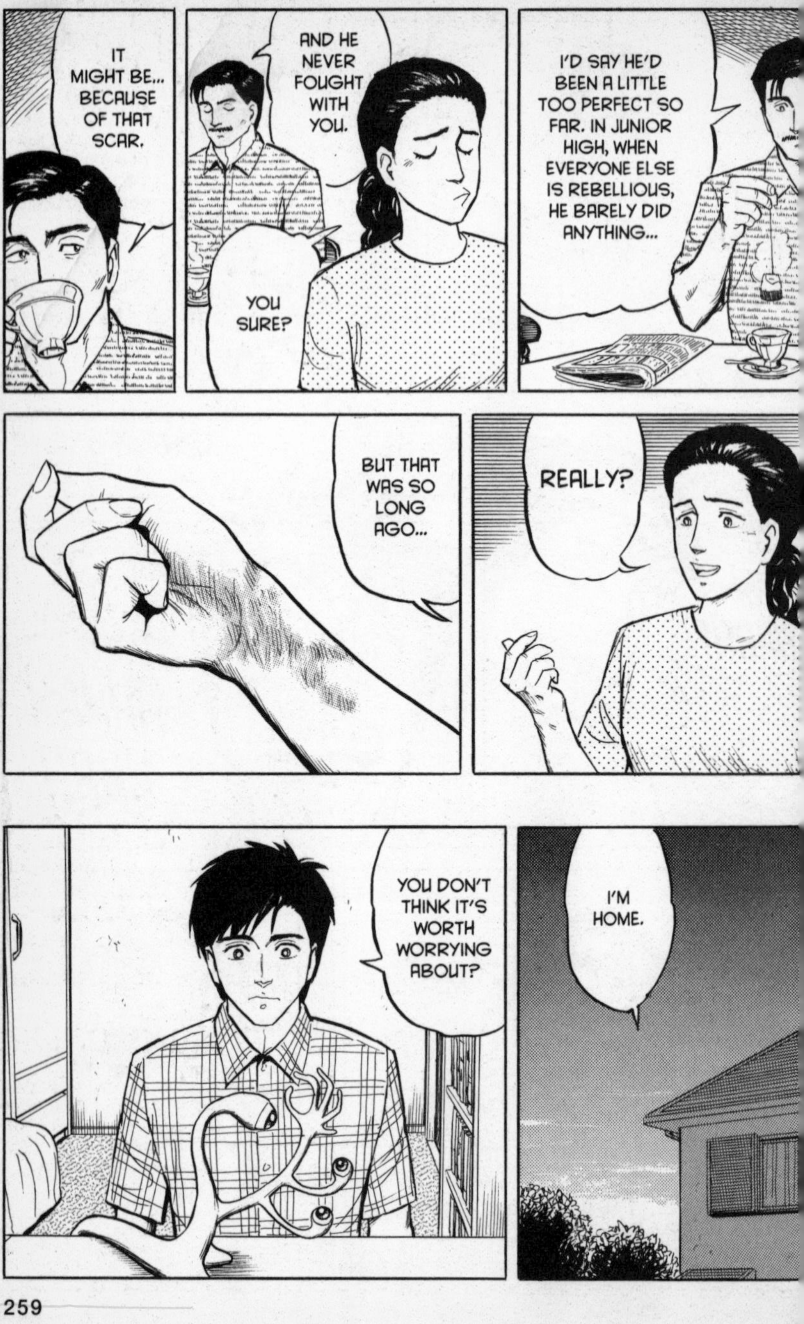
I'D SAY HE'D BEEN A LITTLE TOO PERFECT SO FAR. IN JUNIOR HIGH, WHEN EVERYONE ELSE IS REBELLIOUS, HE BARELY DID ANYTHING...
AND HE NEVER FOUGHT WITH YOU.
YOU SURE?
IT MIGHT BE... BECAUSE OF THAT SCAR.
REALLY?
BUT THAT WAS SO LONG AGO...
I'M HOME.
YOU DON'T THINK IT'S WORTH WORRYING ABOUT?

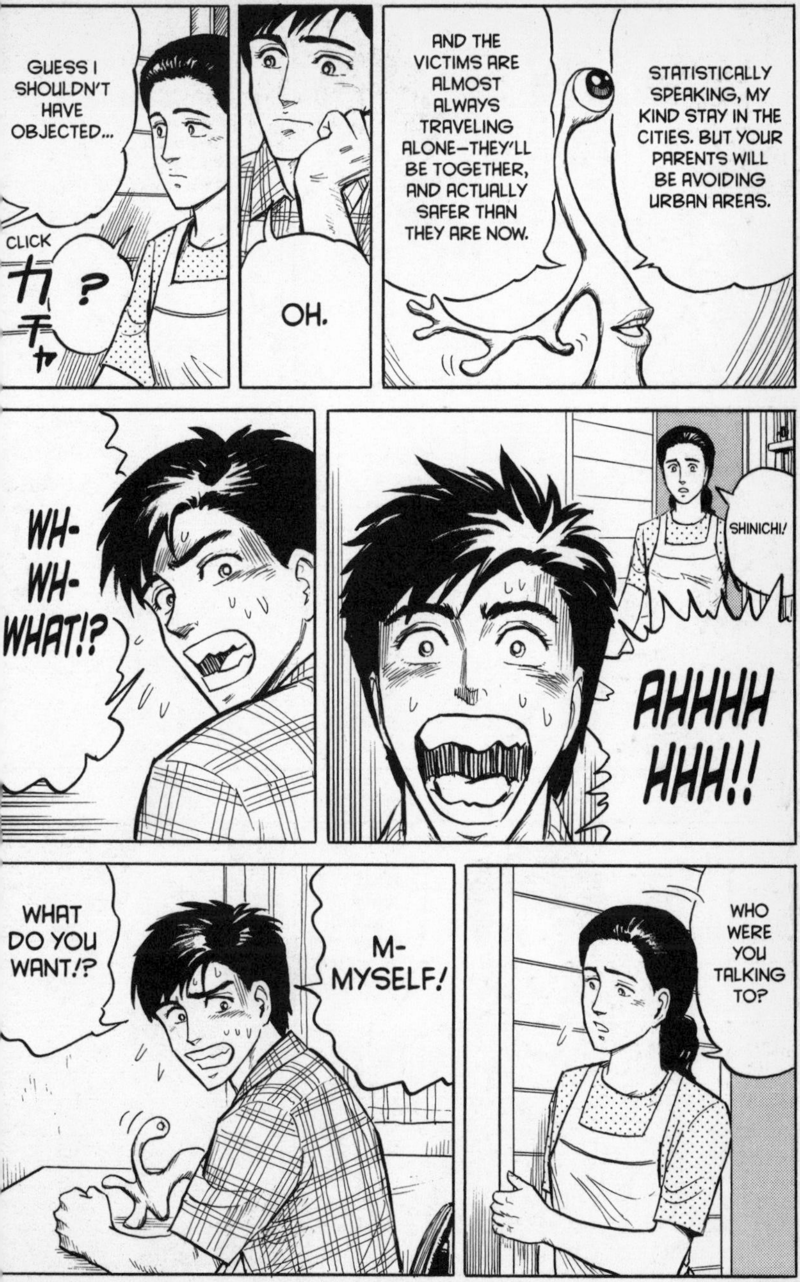

STATISTICALLY SPEAKING, MY KIND STAY IN THE CITIES. BUT YOUR PARENTS WILL BE AVOIDING URBAN AREAS.
AND THE VICTIMS ARE ALMOST ALWAYS TRAVELING ALONE—THEY'LL BE TOGETHER, AND ACTUALLY SAFER THAN THEY ARE NOW.
OH.
GUESS I SHOULDN'T HAVE OBJECTED...
?
CLICK
カチャ
SHINICHI!
AHHHHHHH!!
WH-WH-WHAT!?
WHO WERE YOU TALKING TO?
M-MYSELF!
WHAT DO YOU WANT!?

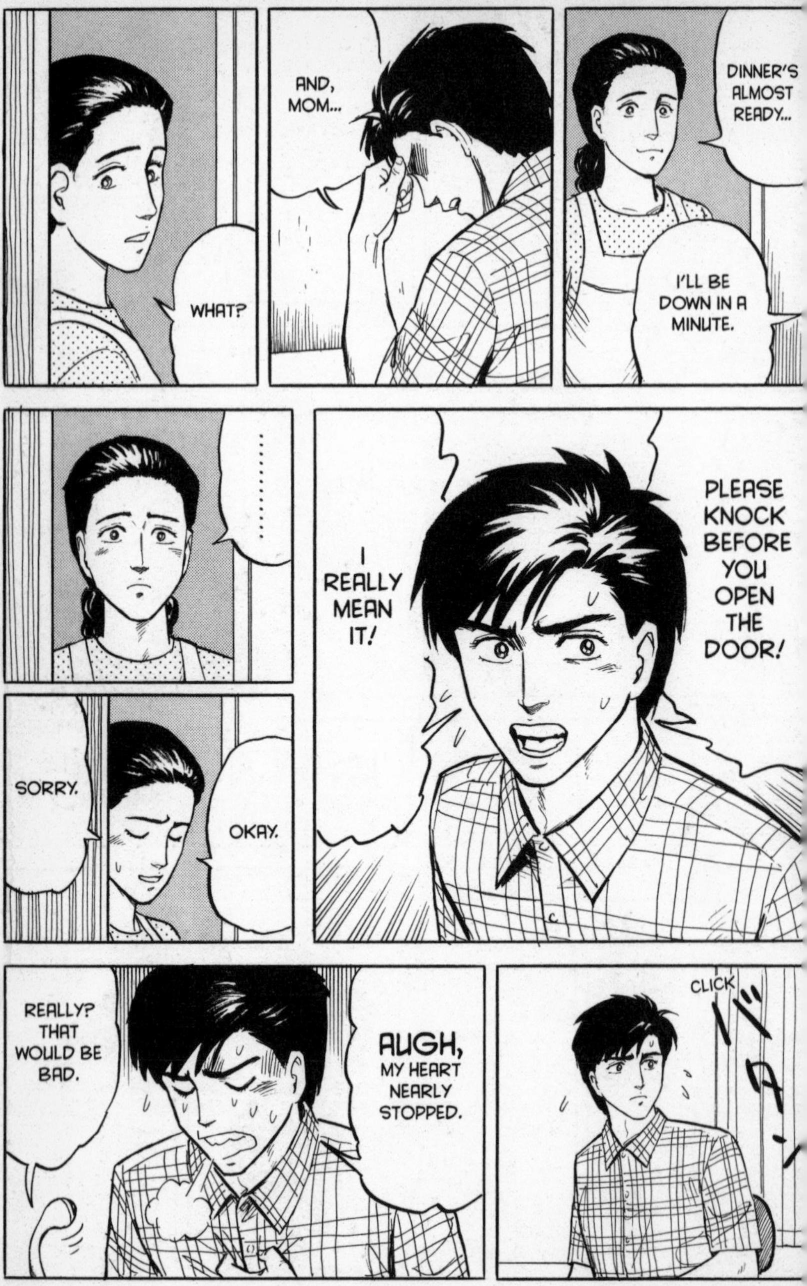
DINNER'S ALMOST READY...
I'LL BE DOWN IN A MINUTE.
AND, MOM...
WHAT?
PLEASE KNOCK BEFORE YOU OPEN THE DOOR!
I REALLY MEAN IT!
......
OKAY.
SORRY.
CLICK
AUGH, MY HEART NEARLY STOPPED.
REALLY? THAT WOULD BE BAD.

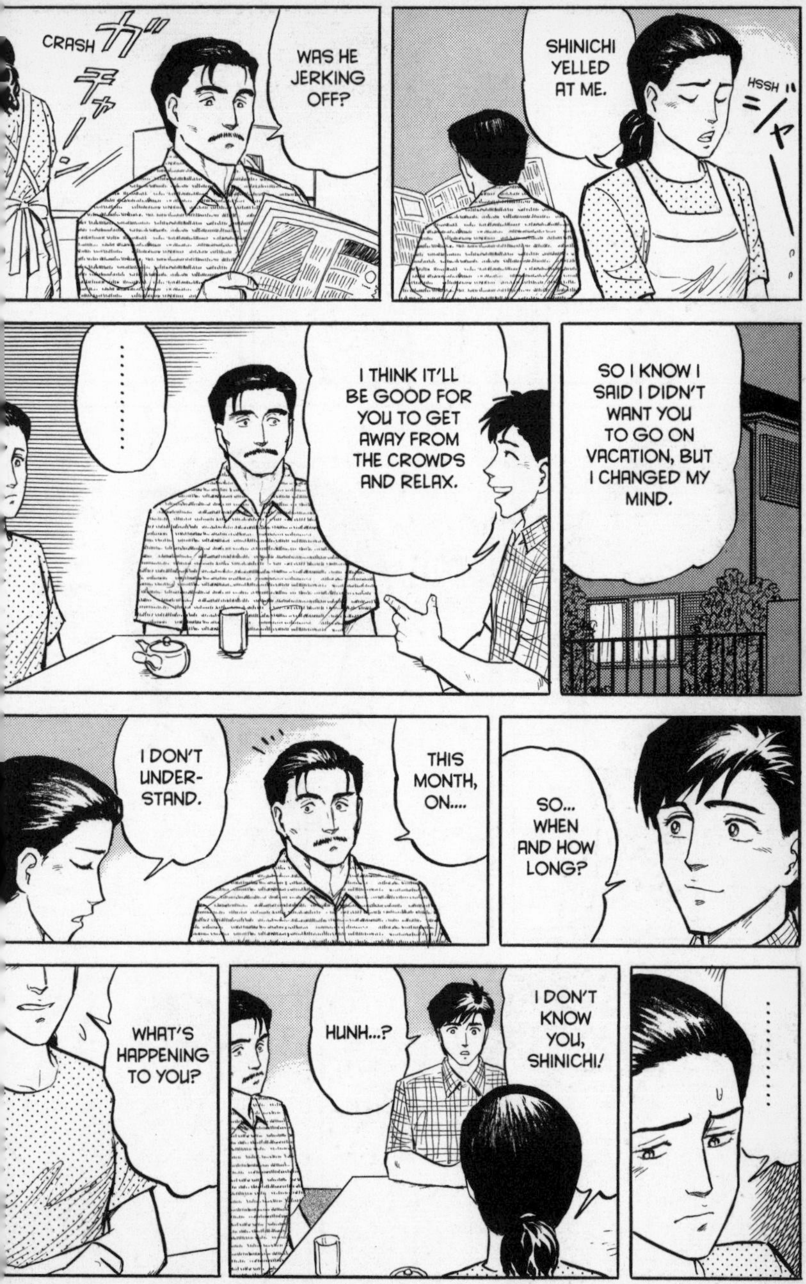
SHINICHI YELLED AT ME.
HSSH
CRASH
WAS HE JERKING OFF?
SO I KNOW I SAID I DIDN'T WANT YOU TO GO ON VACATION, BUT I CHANGED MY MIND.
I THINK IT'LL BE GOOD FOR YOU TO GET AWAY FROM THE CROWDS AND RELAX.
......
SO... WHEN AND HOW LONG?
THIS MONTH, ON....
I DON'T UNDER-STAND.
......
I DON'T KNOW YOU, SHINICHI!
HUNH...?
WHAT'S HAPPENING TO YOU?

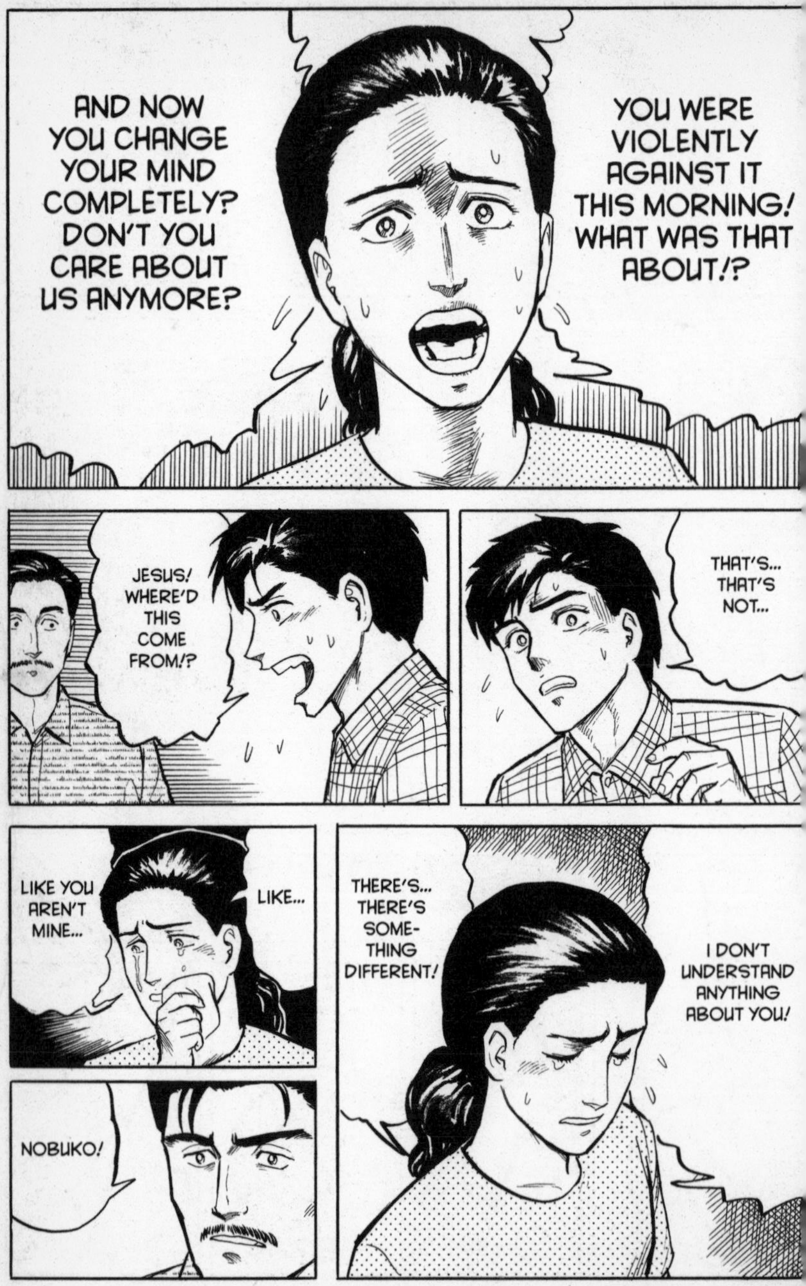
YOU WERE VIOLENTLY AGAINST IT THIS MORNING! WHAT WAS THAT ABOUT!?
AND NOW YOU CHANGE YOUR MIND COMPLETELY? DON'T YOU CARE ABOUT US ANYMORE?
THAT'S... THAT'S NOT...
JESUS! WHERE'D THIS COME FROM!?
I DON'T UNDERSTAND ANYTHING ABOUT YOU!
THERE'S... THERE'S SOME-THING DIFFERENT!
LIKE...
LIKE YOU AREN'T MINE...
NOBUKO!

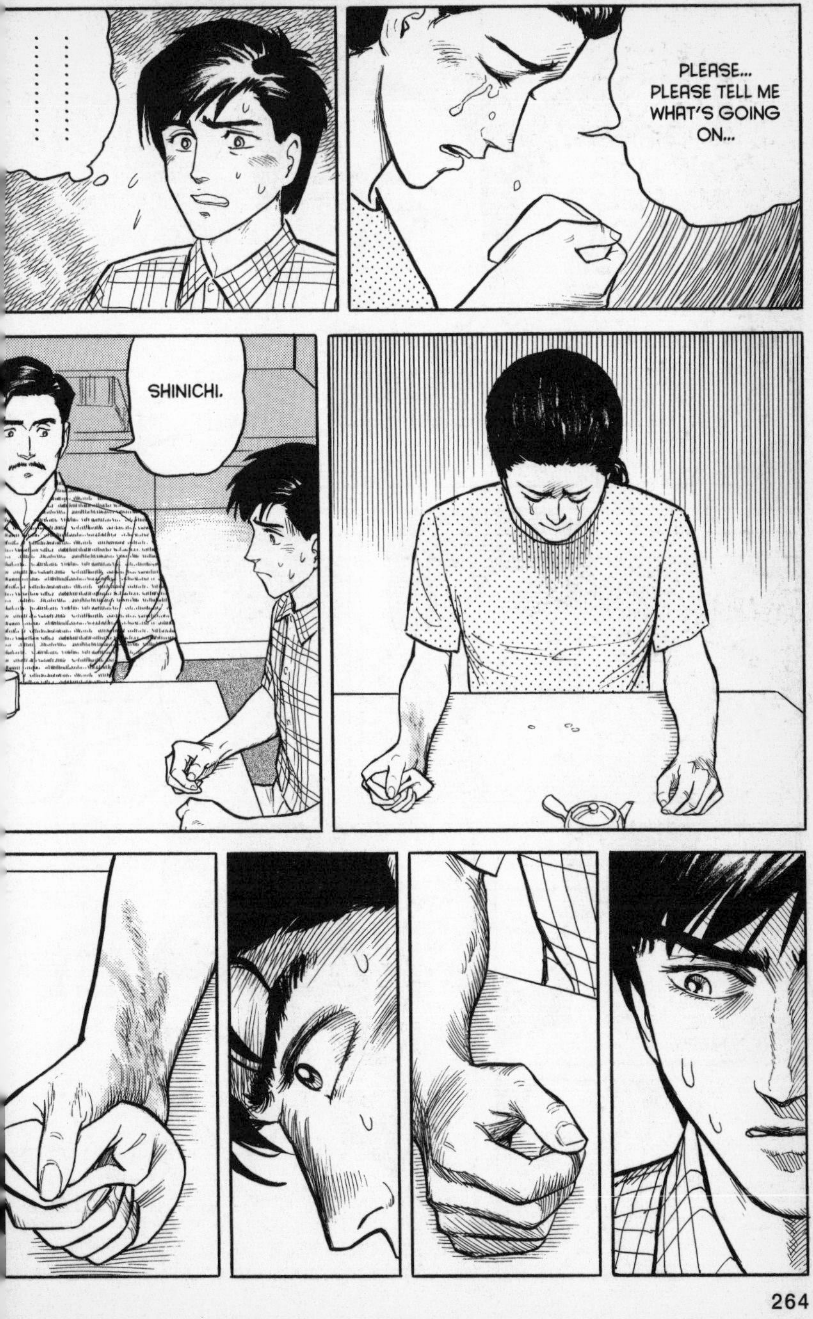
PLEASE... PLEASE TELL ME WHAT'S GOING ON...
......
SHINICHI.

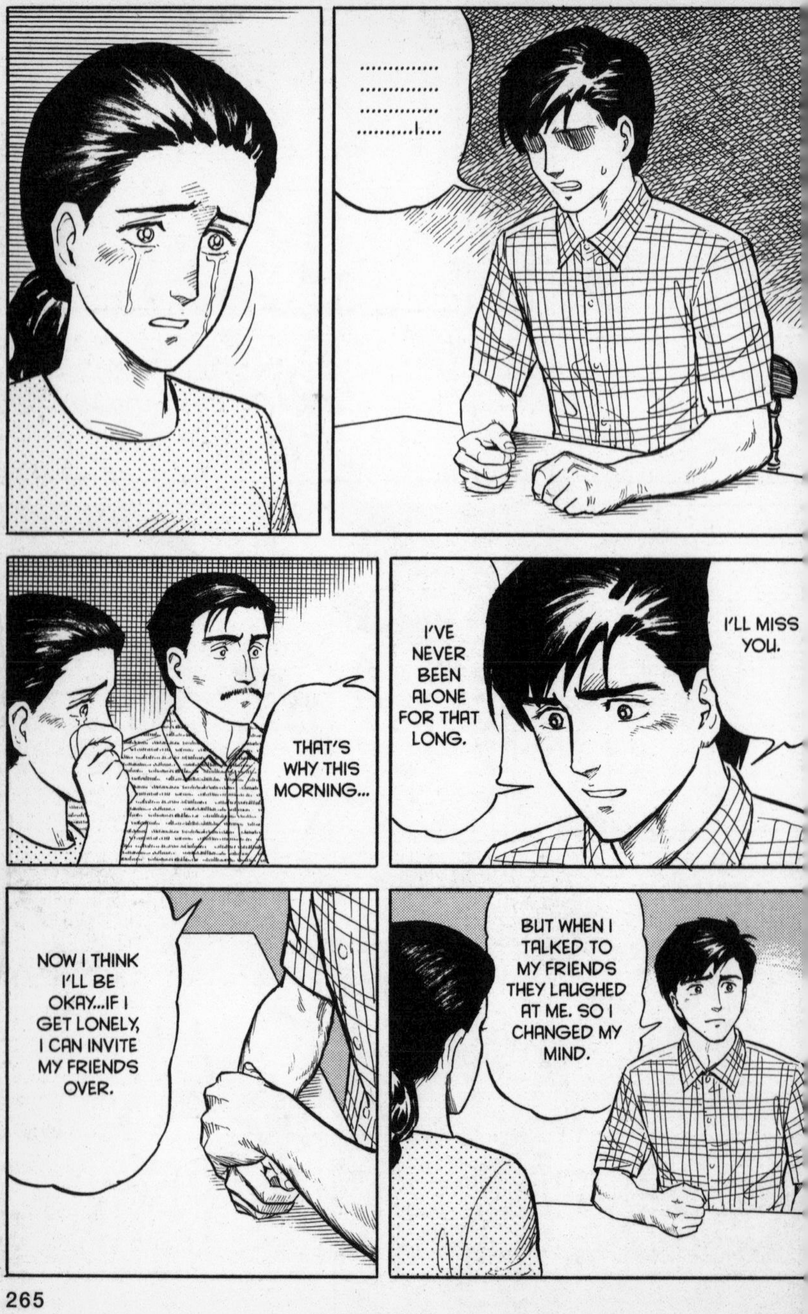
....I....
I'LL MISS YOU.
I'VE NEVER BEEN ALONE FOR THAT LONG.
THAT'S WHY THIS MORNING...
BUT WHEN I TALKED TO MY FRIENDS THEY LAUGHED AT ME. SO I CHANGED MY MIND.
NOW I THINK I'LL BE OKAY...IF I GET LONELY, I CAN INVITE MY FRIENDS OVER.

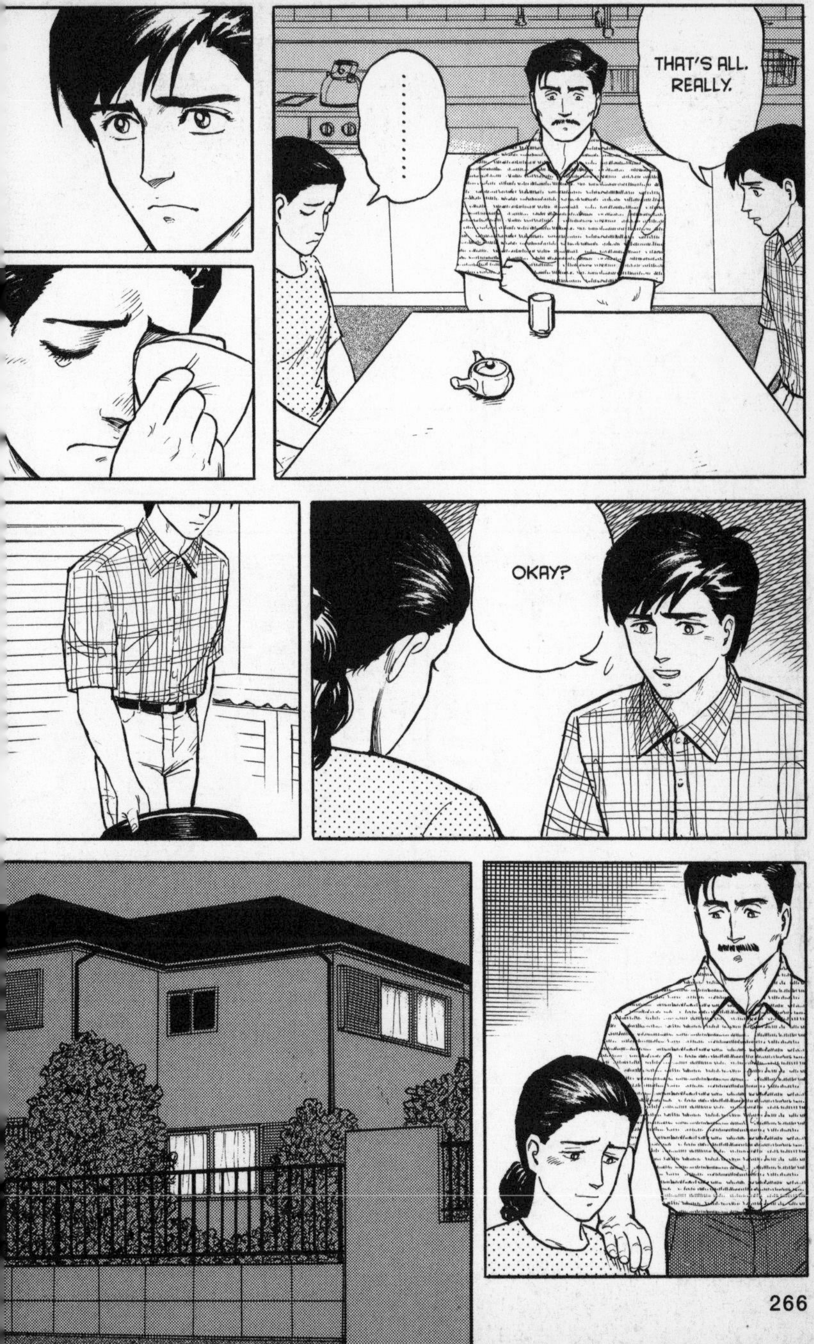
THAT'S ALL. REALLY.
......
OKAY?

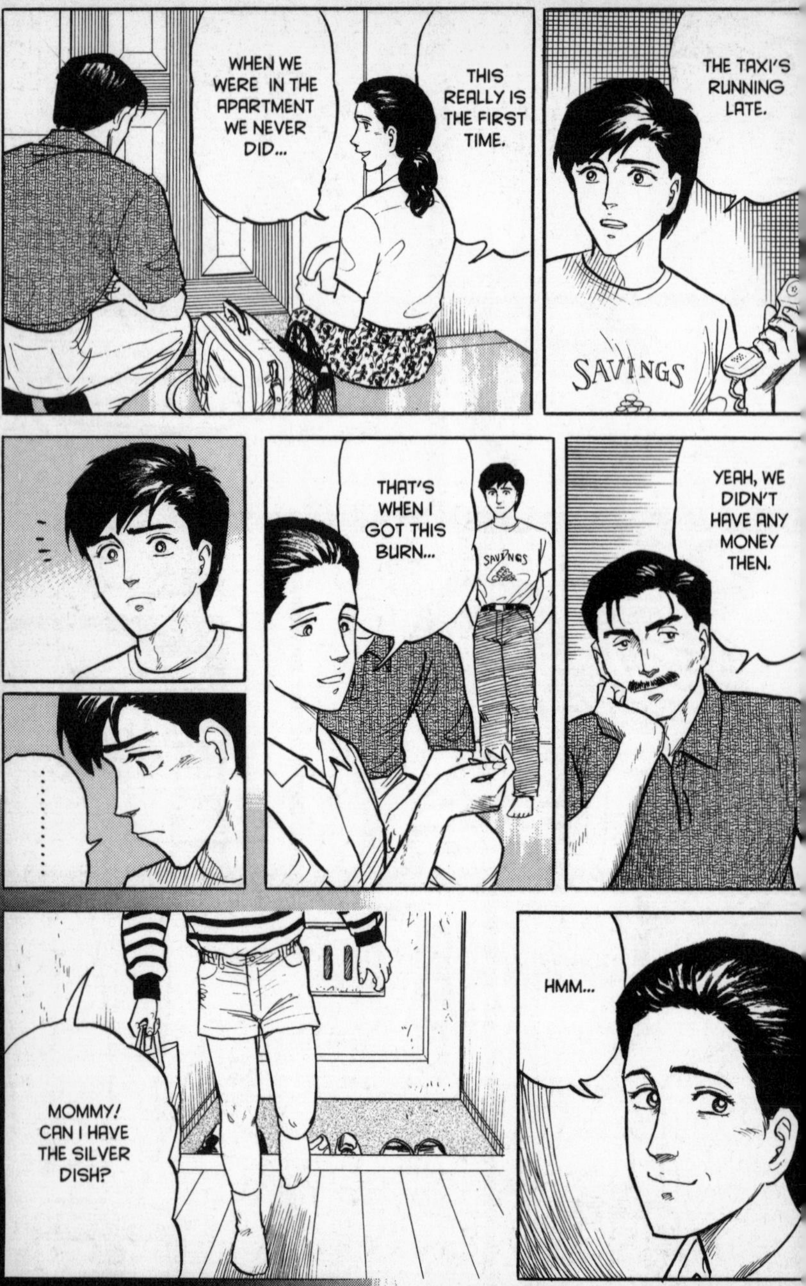
THE TAXI'S RUNNING LATE.
SAVINGS
THIS REALLY IS THE FIRST TIME.
WHEN WE WERE IN THE APARTMENT WE NEVER DID...
YEAH, WE DIDN'T HAVE ANY MONEY THEN.
THAT'S WHEN I GOT THIS BURN...
HMM...
MOMMY! CAN I HAVE THE SILVER DISH?

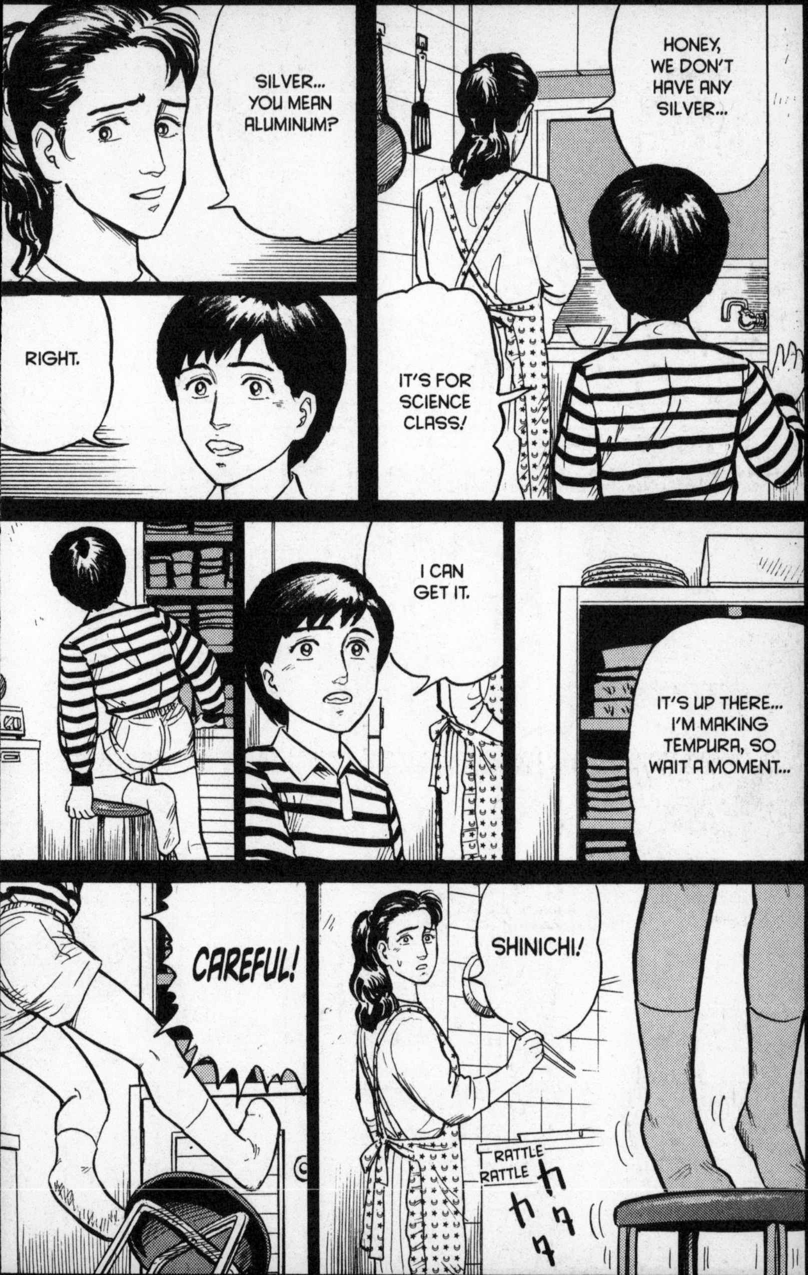
HONEY, WE DON'T HAVE ANY SILVER...
IT'S FOR SCIENCE CLASS!
SILVER... YOU MEAN ALUMINUM?
RIGHT.
IT'S UP THERE... I'M MAKING TEMPURA, SO WAIT A MOMENT...
I CAN GET IT.
SHINICHI!
RATTLE
RATTLE
CAREFUL!

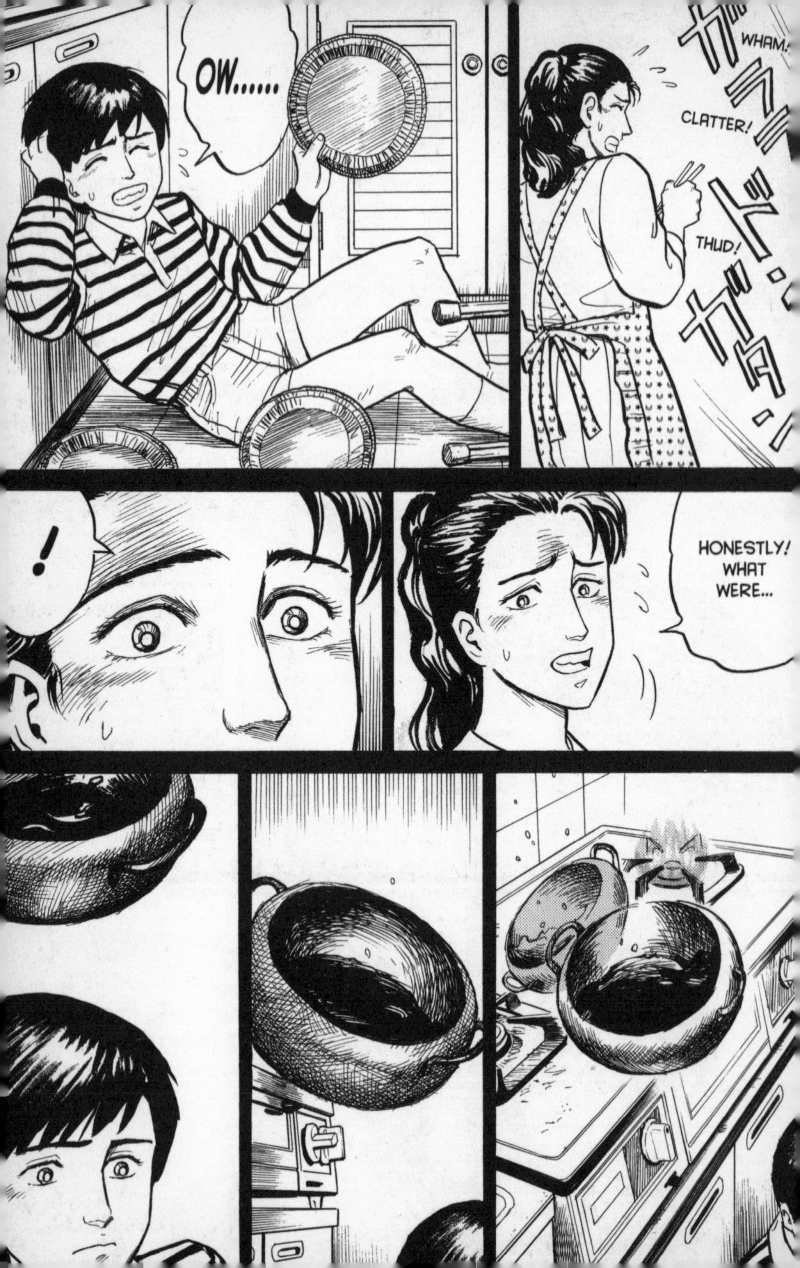
WHAM!
CLATTER!
THUD!
OW......
HONESTLY! WHAT WERE...
!

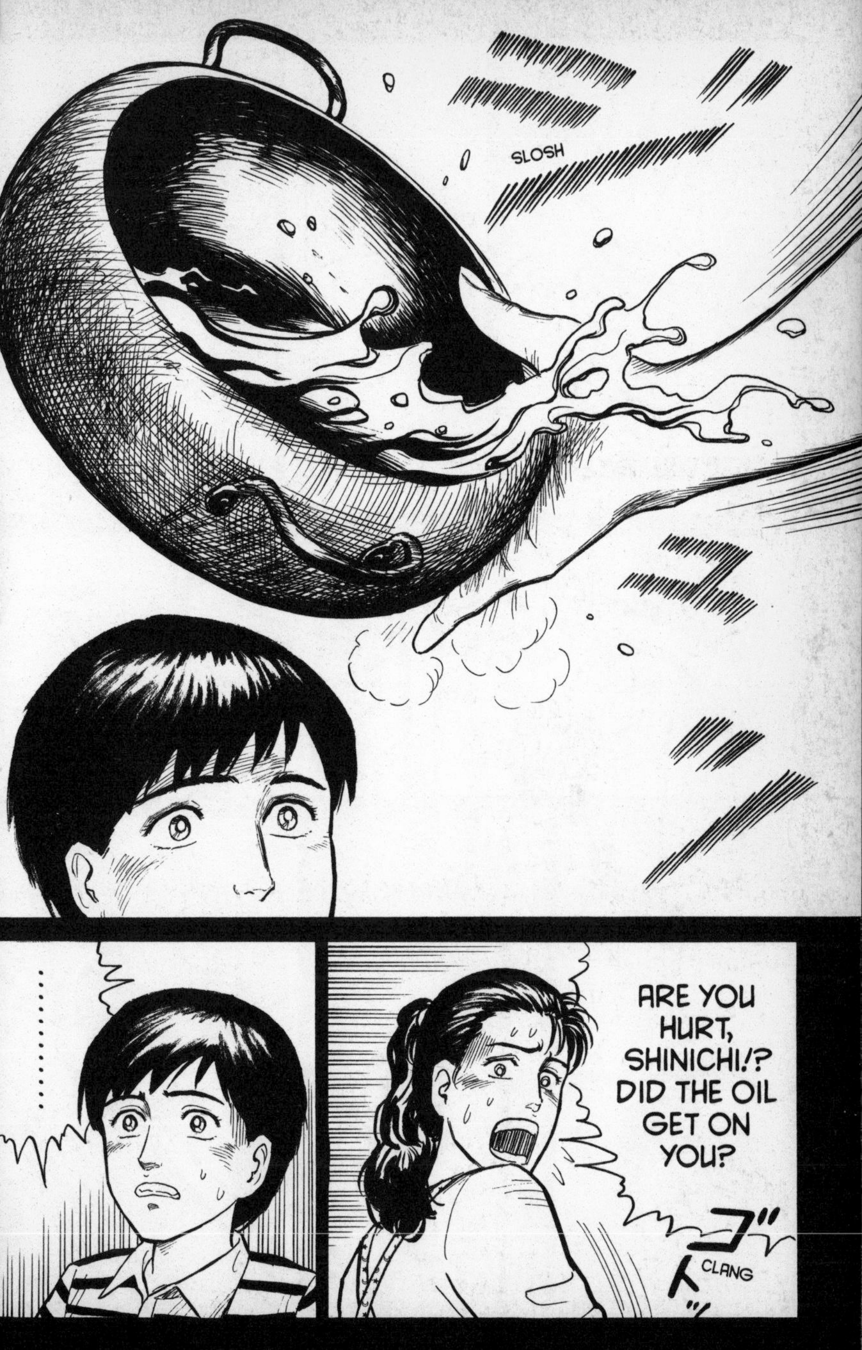
SLOSH
ARE YOU HURT, SHINICHI!? DID THE OIL GET ON YOU?
CLANG
....

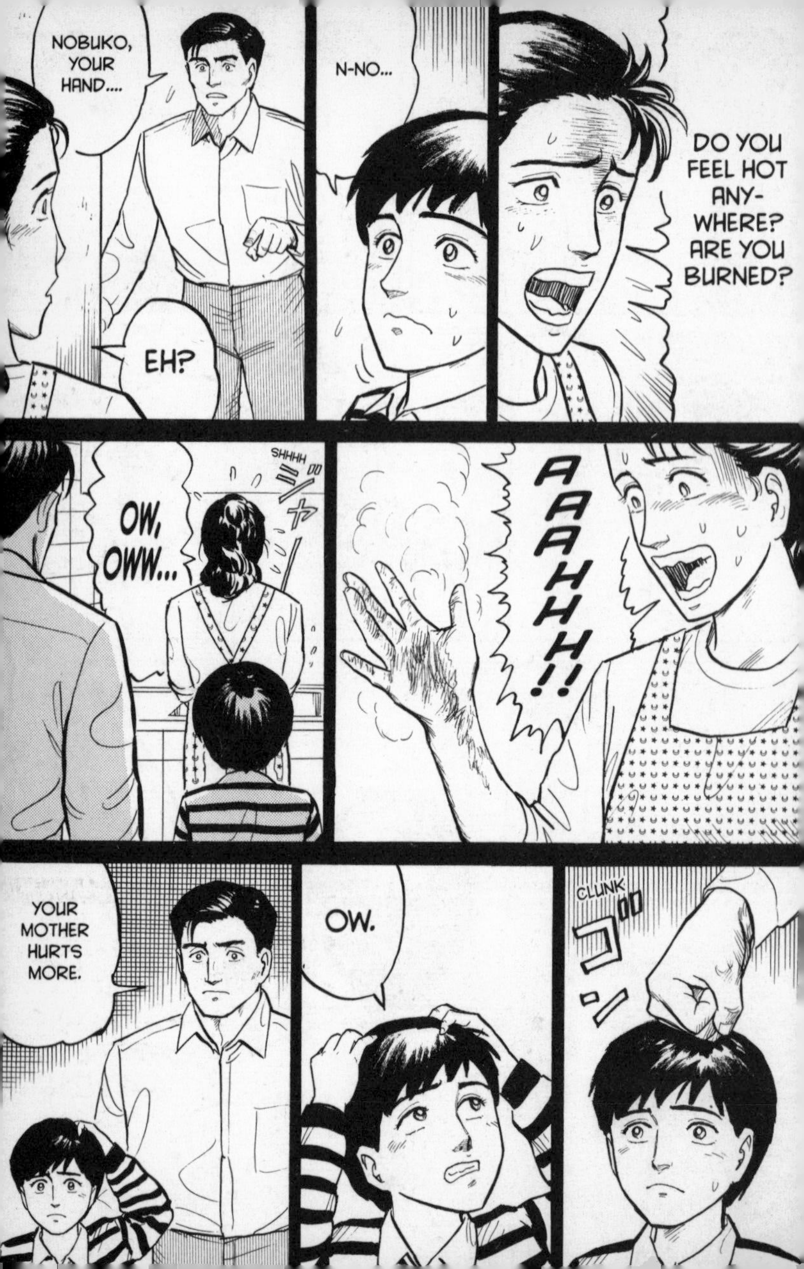
DO YOU FEEL HOT ANY-WHERE? ARE YOU BURNED?
N-NO...
NOBUKO, YOUR HAND....
EH?
AAAHHHH!!
SHHHH
OW, OWW...
CLUNK
OW.
YOUR MOTHER HURTS MORE.

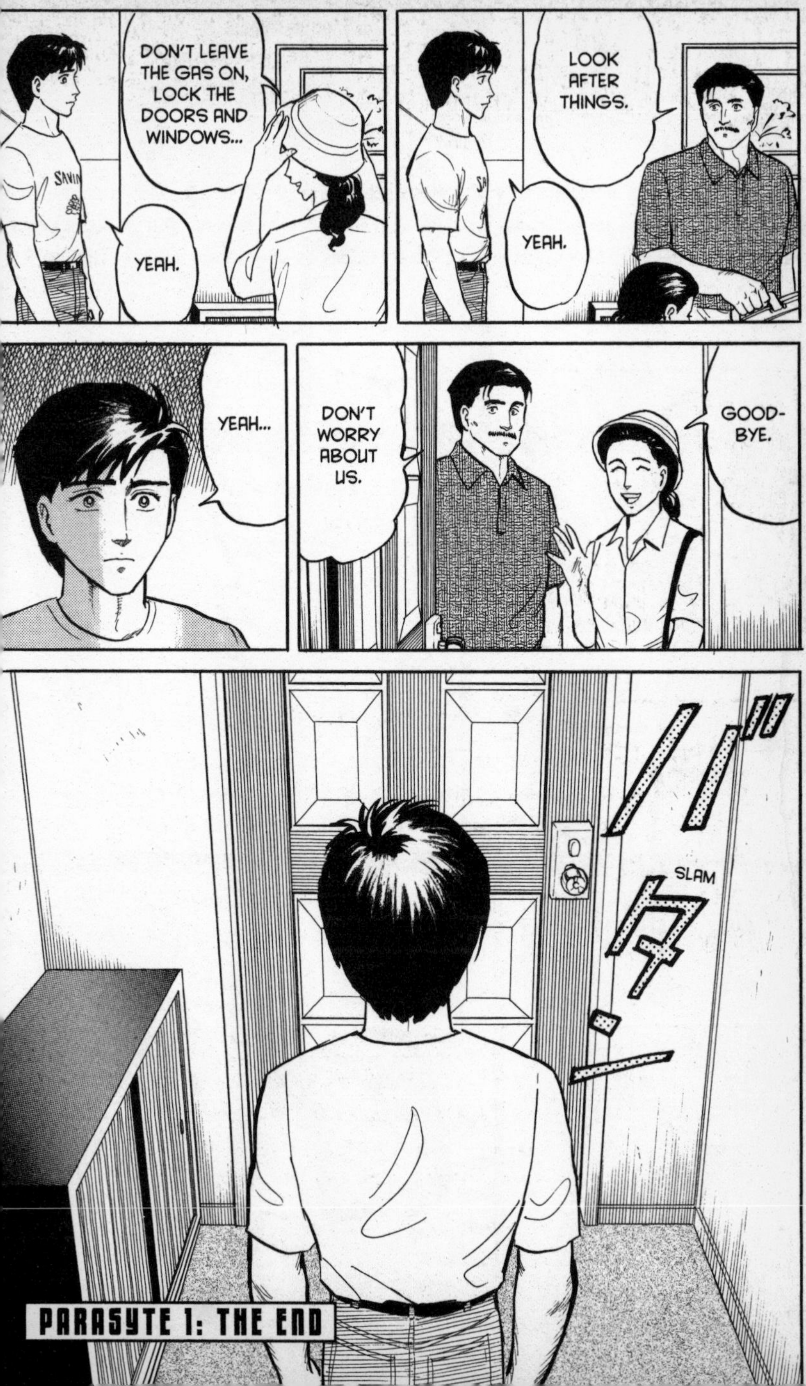
LOOK AFTER THINGS.
YEAH.
DON'T LEAVE THE GAS ON, LOCK THE DOORS AND WINDOWS...
YEAH.
GOOD-BYE.
DON'T WORRY ABOUT US.
YEAH...
SLAM
PARASYTE 1: THE END

TRANSLATION NOTES

Japanese is a tricky language for most Westerners, and translation is often more an art than a science. For your edification and reading pleasure, here are notes on some of the places where we could have gone in a different direction or where a Japanese cultural reference is used.

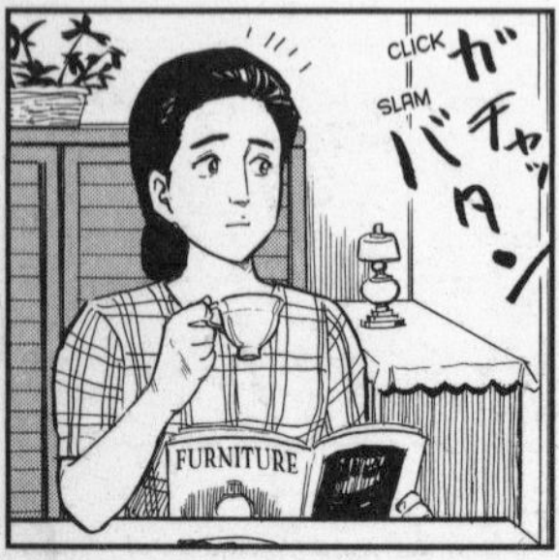
CLICK
SLAM
ガチャッ
バタン
FURNITURE

Catalog, page 38

Shinichi's mother is reading a furniture catalog here. Mail-order furniture is much more popular in Japan than in America, and most people order all their furniture from catalogs.

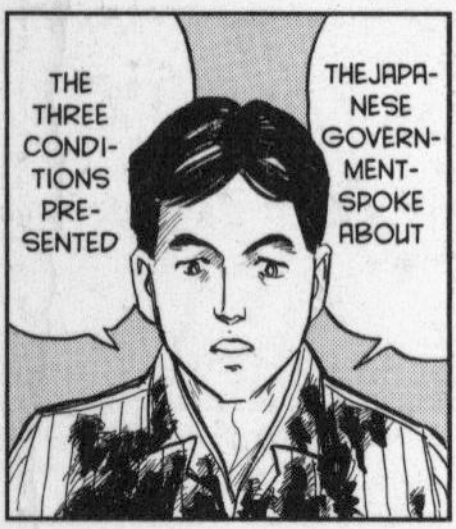
THEJAPANESE GOVERNMENT-SPOKE ABOUT
THE THREE CONDITIONS PRESENTED

Run-together text, page 42

When the parasite repeats the news in the original Japanese, he doesn't use any kanji characters. The implication is that he is mouthing the sounds of the language without registering their meaning.

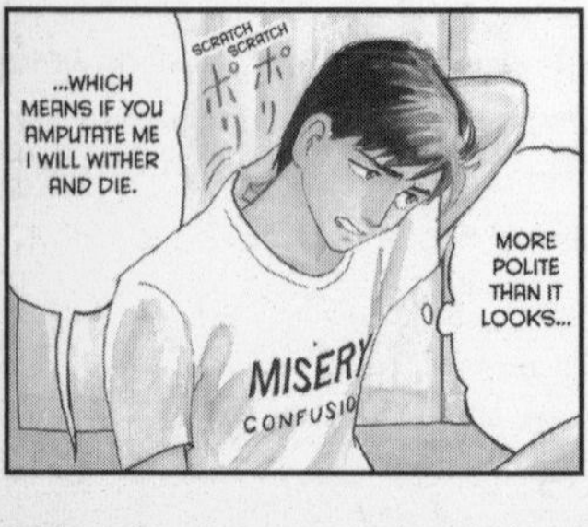
SCRATCH SCRATCH
ポリポリ
...WHICH MEANS IF YOU AMPUTATE ME I WILL WITHER AND DIE.
MORE POLITE THAN IT LOOKS...

More polite than it looks, page 46

I've replaced the original line here. Migi's choice of personal pronouns has shifted from the rough, common *ore* to the polite, formal *watashi*. In the original Japanese, Shinichi comments that the polite *watashi* doesn't match Migi's face.

Tsukahara Bokuden, page 56

Tsukahara Bokuden (name given in Japanese order, 1489–1571) was a famed swordsman of the Sengoku Warring States Period.

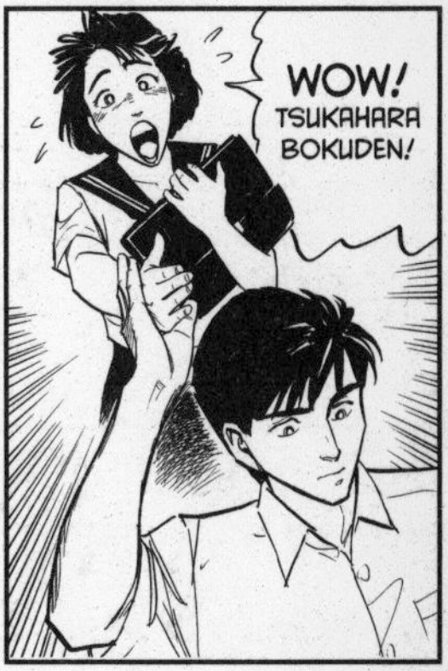
WOW! TSUKAHARA BOKUDEN!

Migi, page 66

The word *migi* means "right." *Parasyte* was first published in English by TokyoPop in a now-out-of-print edition that "flipped" the original Japanese artwork so that it would read left to right—which meant that the parasite had to be named "Lefty"! This Del Rey reissue restores the original orientation, but even now that Migi is again truly on the right side, "Righty" just doesn't sound right!

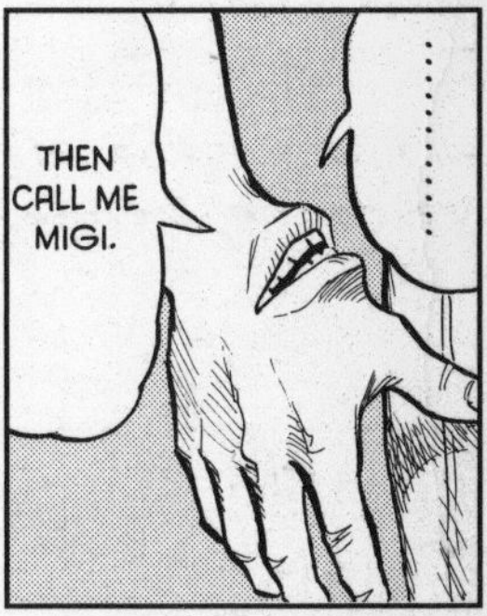
....
THEN CALL ME MIGI.

Killer's aura, page 117

The title of this chapter, "Satsuki," is a great word that we just don't have in English. Just before a human kills another, they emit *satsuki,* which skilled fighters can sense. Later in the chapter this is shown as an insect hovering behind them. I've translated this phrase as "killer's aura."

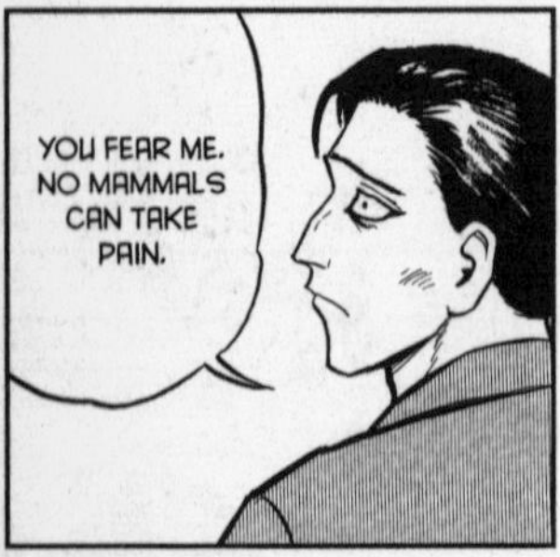
YOU FEAR ME. NO MAMMALS CAN TAKE PAIN.

Pain, pages 124, 141, 214

Both Migi and the lion killer use the same expression, *itagariya,* for someone who feels pain easily.

Recap, page 143

Parasyte began serialization in *Morning* (possibly *Morning Special*) magazine and changed to *Afternoon* magazine a few issues later, presumably with this issue. Hence the opening recap.

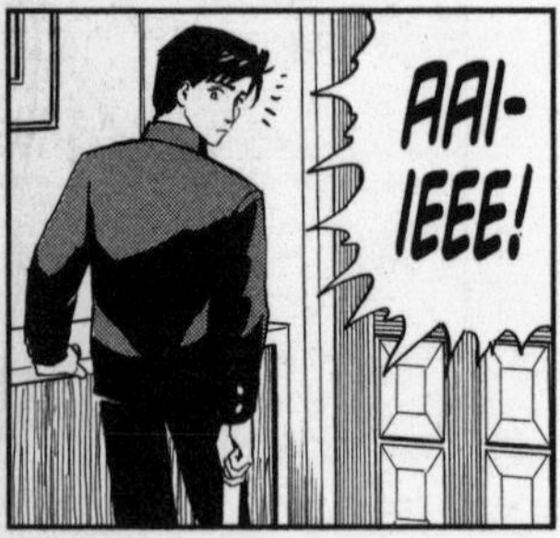
AAI-IEEE!

Roaches, page 152

Japanese roaches are really, really big. They also fly. When you try to kill them, they fly right into your face, so you scream and fall over and give them time to get away. Very effective technique.

Spoiled, page 153

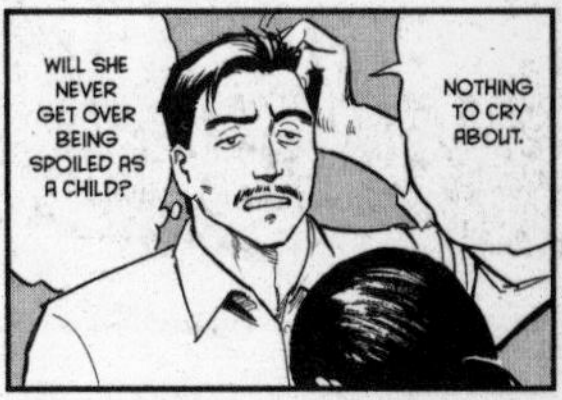
NOTHING TO CRY ABOUT.
WILL SHE NEVER GET OVER BEING SPOILED AS A CHILD?

The original Japanese line—*ojou-sama sodachi*—implies that Mom was raised by upper-class parents, hence her fear of roaches. It also implies that even though she's a mother now, she still hasn't fully adjusted to her new life.

Tempura oil, page 269

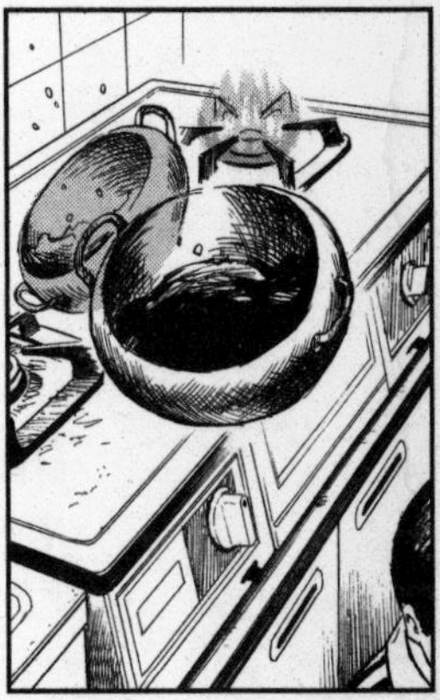

That isn't water, but boiling oil. Far more dangerous. Tempura is breaded and deep-fried vegetables and shrimp, usually more delicate than greasy. Try it sometime!

PREVIEW OF VOLUME 2

We're pleased to present you with a preview of Volume 2. This volume will be available in English on July 31, 2007, but for now you'll have to make do with the Japanese!

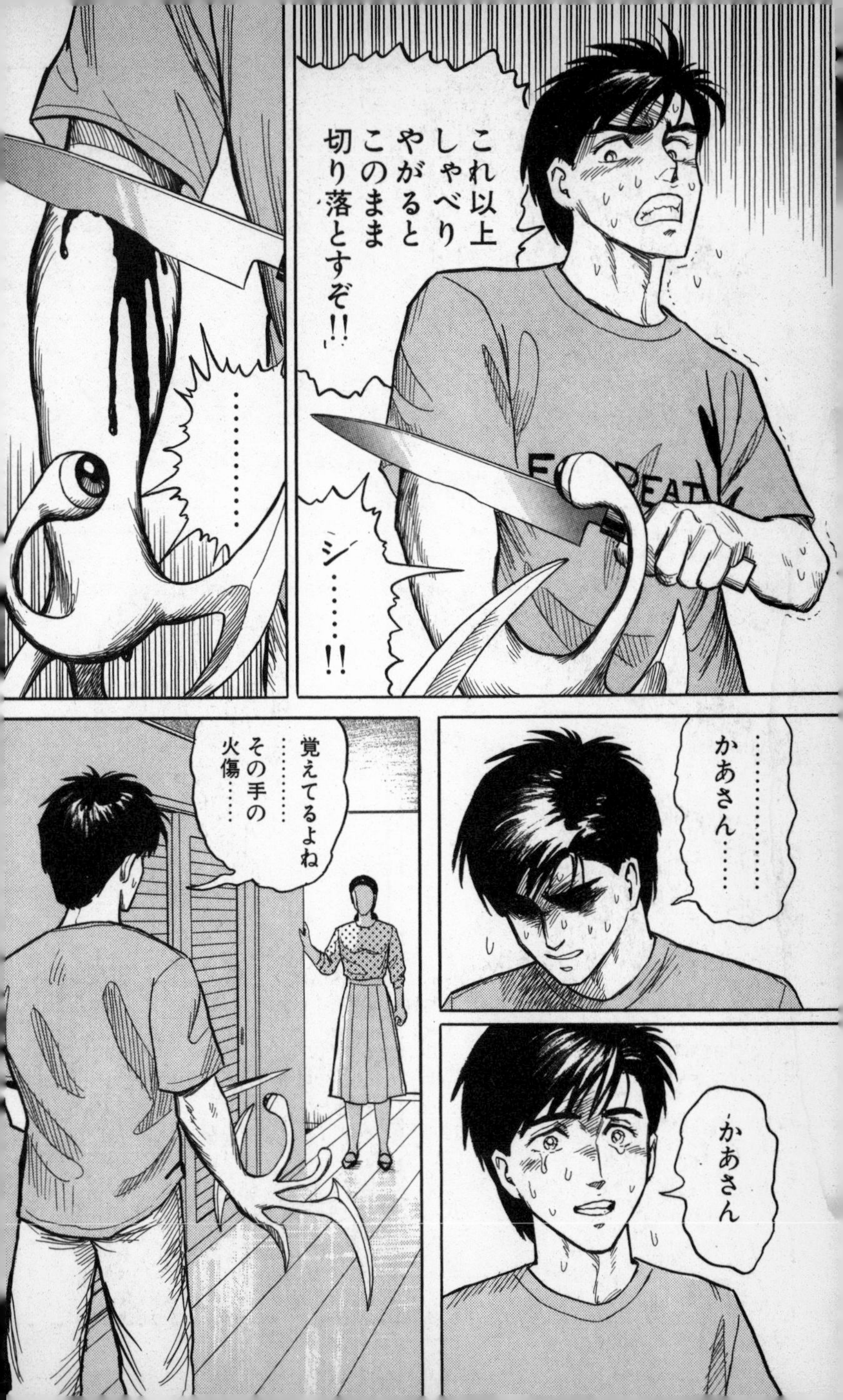
これ以上しゃべりやがるとこのまま切り落とすぞ!!
シ……!!
……
……かあさん……
かあさん
覚えてるよね……その手の火傷……

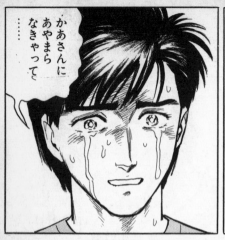
……かあさんにあやまらなきゃらって……

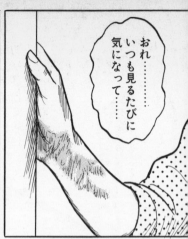
おれ……いつも見るたびに気になって……

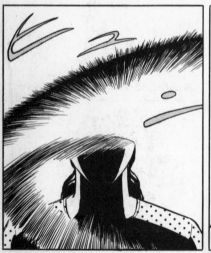

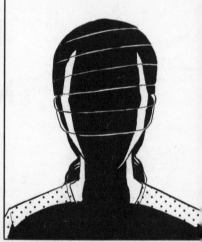

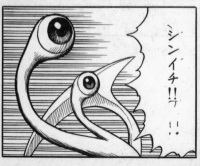
シンイチ!!テ!!

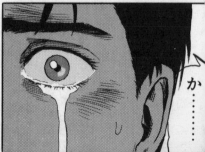
か……

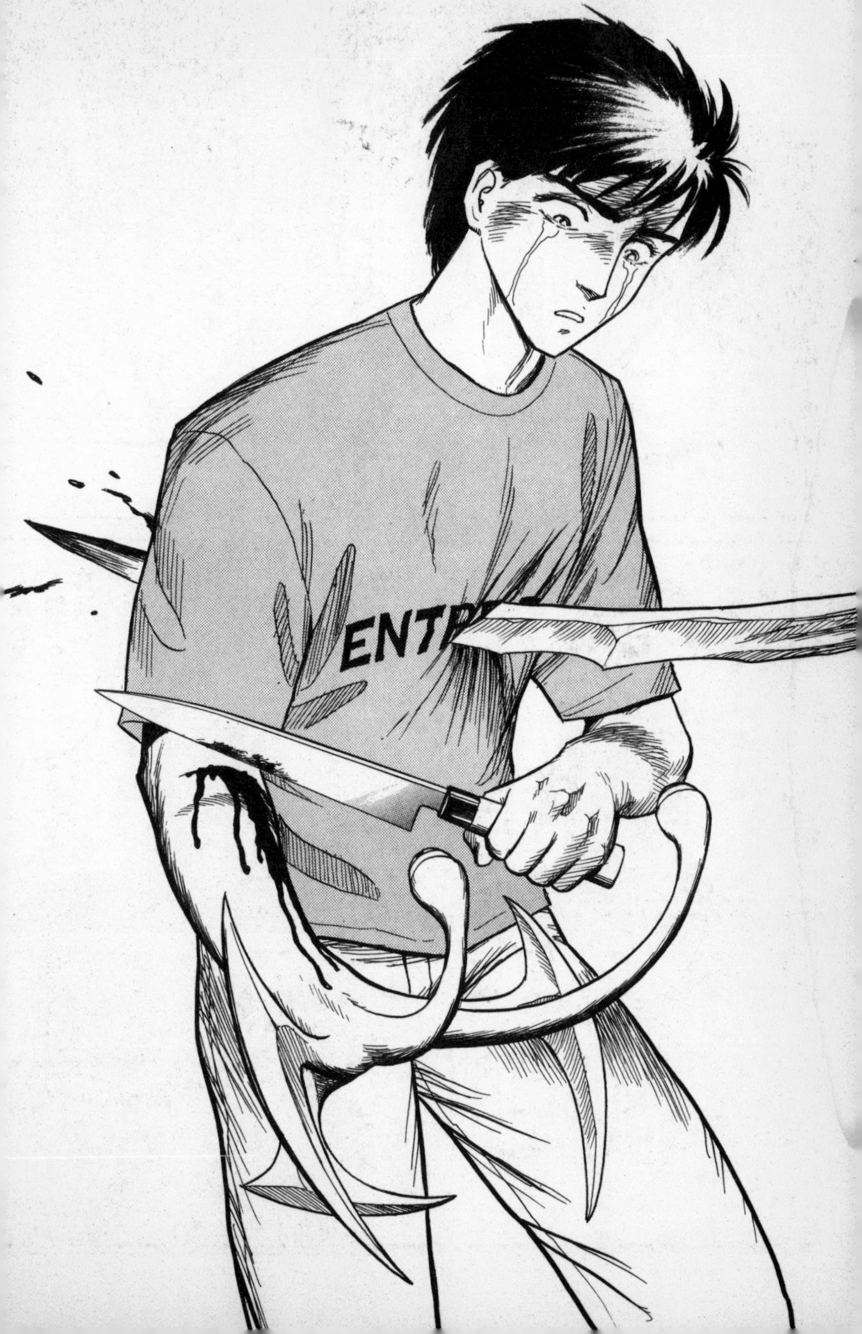
ENTR

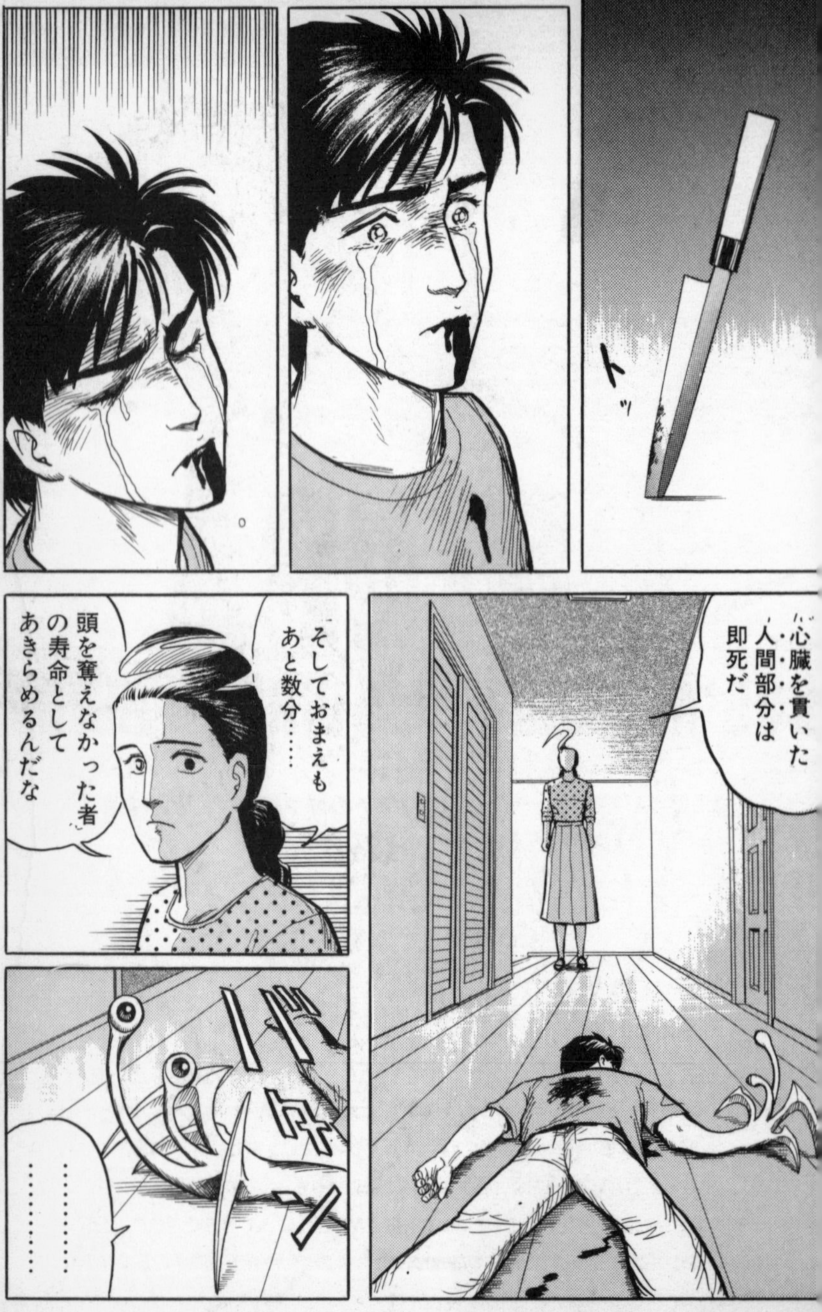
トッ
心臓を貫いた人間部分は即死だ
そしておまえもあと数分……
頭を奪えなかった者の寿命としてあきらめるんだな
…………

TOMARE!

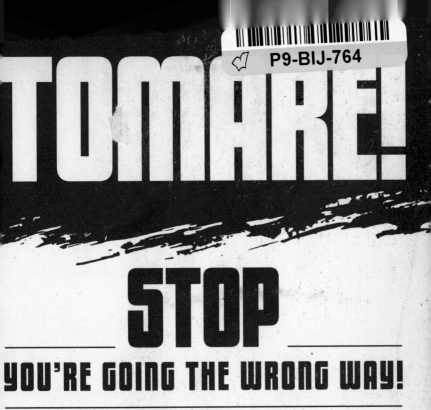

STOP

YOU'RE GOING THE WRONG WAY!

MANGA IS A COMPLETELY DIFFERENT TYPE OF READING EXPERIENCE.

TO START AT THE BEGINNING, GO TO THE END!

THAT'S RIGHT!

AUTHENTIC MANGA IS READ THE TRADITIONAL JAPANESE WAY—FROM RIGHT TO LEFT, EXACTLY THE OPPOSITE OF HOW AMERICAN BOOKS ARE READ. IT'S EASY TO FOLLOW: JUST GO TO THE OTHER END OF THE BOOK, AND READ EACH PAGE—AND EACH PANEL—FROM RIGHT SIDE TO LEFT SIDE, STARTING AT THE TOP RIGHT. NOW YOU'RE EXPERIENCING MANGA AS IT WAS MEANT TO BE.